ESSENTIAL WICCA

by Paul Tuitéan and Estelle Daniels

THE CROSSING PRESS

DEDICATION

To our parents, families, teachers, students, and friends.
They have helped us become who we are.
And to the greater Wiccan Community,
without which this book could not have been written.

The Crossing Press
www.crossingpress.com

A division of Ten Speed Press
P.O. Box 7123
Berkeley, California 94707
www.tenspeed.com

Library of Congress Cataloging-in-Publication Data
Tuitéan, Paul.
    Essential wicca / Paul Tuitéan and Estelle Daniels.
       p. cm.
    Includes bibliographical references.
    ISBN 1-58091-099-8 (pbk.)
    1.Witchcraft. I. Daniels, Estelle. II. Title.

BF1566.T85   2001
299--dc21   2001017460

Cover art by Lena Bartula
Cover design by Courtnay Perry
Text design by Courtnay Perry and Petra Serafim
Original interior illustrations by Anne Marie Garrison

2 3 4 5 6 7 8 9 10 — 05 04 03 02

CONTENTS

Author's Note

This book was a labor of love for both of us. Were dedicated to each other, to Wicca, to the Gods, and to the greater Wiccan Community. Wicca brought so much into our lives, including each other. We feel honored to be able to pass on what we have learned through our years in Wicca and our life experiences.

Sadly, Paul and Estelle experienced a life passage as this book was going to press. Reverend Paul Tuitéan passed away peacefully on April 26, 2001, due to a lifelong asthma condition. This book is a part of Paul's legacy of learning, studying, and teaching. The book was essentially finished when Paul died, so Paul was fully involved with this book in its entirety.

Paul was the first Wiccan to have a completely Wiccan funeral and burial in the Twin Cities. Paul's family who for the most part are not Wiccan, were lovingly cooperative and helped make everything work smoothly. The non-Wiccans who attended the funeral (nearly half of the attendees) said the service was beautiful, meaningful, and moving. Estelle's family was loving, and supportive, and they contributed greatly by allowing Paul to be buried in Estelle's family plot. Both families contributed a gift to Estelle, Paul, and the Wiccan Community which is priceless and will be remembered as long as there are those able to read these words.

Though Paul has passed on, he leaves behind many unpublished writings. Estelle will work on that material as well as her own and plans to keep writing until she rejoins Paul in the Summerlands.

And Thus the Wheel Doth Turn.   Blessed Be.

INTRODUCTION

WE ARE MINNESOTANS, ONE NATIVE AND ONE TRANSPLANTED. WHILE we have traveled extensively to Pagan festivals throughout the United States, we are most familiar with the middle of the country, between the mountains.

We chose to write about Wicca because it is an integral part of our lives. While we both teach and find that people appreciate what we have to say, we want to share our ideas and viewpoints with a wider audience.

Our books about Wicca focus on the religion, lifestyle, and philosophies of Wicca, which is somewhat different from some other authors who concentrate on the practices of Wicca, especially divination. We enjoy Wicca, it adds a great deal to our lives, and we hope that our love for and enthusiasm about Wicca comes across in these pages. We firmly believe that there is no one right, true, and only style of Wicca. One feature of Eclectic Wicca (our personal practice style) is that each practitioner can change, adapt, and add to it to suit their tastes and needs.

This book is actually three books in one, a general introduction to Wicca, a comprehensive guide to the religion and practice of Wicca, and a detailed reference to terms, ideas, and concepts encountered in Wicca. While this book is a good start to a substantial Book of Shadows, we do not intend it to be the only reference or last word on Wicca. There are many voices and viewpoints, and we encourage you to explore others.

With *Essential Wicca* we have made every effort to provide you with everything you need to know to start a coven and practice Wicca.

We begin with the basics in part 1. Next we delve into the principles and practices of Wicca, including detailed descriptions of celebrations and ceremonies, rituals, magick, covens, and Deities, to name a few.

The final section of the book is Wicca A to Z, a glossary (or brief encyclopedia) of all things Wiccan.

To create a book that contains everything you ever wanted to know about Wicca is a big order. Unfortunately nobody can do all of that in one book. But we did our best to provide a good solid framework and foundation for being a Wiccan, and practicing the religion of Wicca.

Wicca is a modern version of the original pre-Christian, European shamanic religious tradition. It is a Pagan religion, that is, a religion not Judeo-Christian in origin. The word Pagan comes from the Latin root, *paganus*, meaning "not of the city," or rural. Because Christianity spread most slowly in the outlying rural areas, it was the Pagans who were converted last—and sometimes incompletely—so their faith became a mixture of the old and new religions. Many local saints are Christianized versions of Pagan Deities (like Saint Brigit), adapted so that locals would more easily integrate Christianity into their beliefs.

Wicca is earth-, nature-, and fertility-oriented; its followers worship at the turn of the seasons and at New and Full Moons. They generally acknowledge both male and female Deities, and believe in reincarnation, magick, and divination. While Wicca is a spiritual and philosophical path, it is first and foremost a religion, termed "the Craft," meaning the craft of the wise.

The word Wicca has two possible sources. The first is the Anglo-Saxon "wic" or "wit," meaning wise or learned. A person "of the Wicca" was a person who had knowledge (usually of healing and herbs) which placed them apart from ordinary people. Another possible origin is the Celtic word "wick," which means to bend or be supple. Wiccans were people who bent as life and conditions warranted. In the story of the oak and the willow, the oak does not bend and is blown down in the storm, while the willow is supple, bends, and survives the storm with little damage. Another interpretation of wick, or bending, is "bending with your will" as in the process of magick.

While reading this book you will notice that certain words are capitalized because they have specific Wiccan connotations, for example, Pagan, First Degree (of Initiation), and Out (being open about one's Wiccan affiliations).

Wicca is unique as a religion in that it lacks a doctrine imposed by a hierarchical organization, does not provide a bible or holy book to which Wiccans can turn for spiritual guidance and instruction, includes a number of Traditions, allows individuals to worship and practice by themselves, and significantly assumes that each person will develop and continue to refine their own belief system and spiritual practices.

An individual's practice tends to draw from the practices of other Wiccans with whom they interact. If a person lives in an area where there are several Wiccan-type groups, they have the luxury of choice. More often, there is only one existing small group and that becomes their model. Some estimate that up to half of practicing Wiccans practice solo, or solitaire. Most Wiccans are ecologically minded in some way, are spiritual, seek knowledge and self-improvement, try to be tolerant and accepting of others, and are just "regular people."

The emphasis on individualism within Wicca is both a strength and a weakness. Wiccans are strongly encouraged to think for themselves, but they also sometimes suffer from numerous disagreements, which all that individualistic thinking can generate. Wiccans have a tendency to go off by themselves if they are not happy with the current state of things in the local coven, group, community, or whatever. Therefore Wicca is not a strongly cohesive religion. One can be in a coven or other small group and be very tightly knit, but there may not be a lot of intergroup loyalty or cohesiveness. Still most Wiccans have more in common than they do differences, so they gather at festivals or in larger groups for interaction, communication, and to share the benefits that larger communities offer. These gatherings tend to be more time-specific than permanent and ongoing. Here is a list of a number of beliefs that most Wiccans hold in common. With all the differences, it is good sometimes to remind ourselves just how much we do have in common.

1. Dual polarity of Deity
2. Belief in reincarnation
3. Respect for all—human, animal, plant, mineral, celestial, and spiritual kingdoms alike
4. Immanence of Deity
5. Respect for the Earth Mother
6. Turning the Wheel and changing seasons mark the Sabbats
7. Eight Solar Sabbats and 12 or 13 Lunar Esbats
8. Wicca is a free choice religion—no proselytizing
9. All Initiates are Priests and Priestesses
10. Equality of all sexes and races
11. Magickal Circle is used for worship and celebration
12. Education and learning are valued and continually pursued
13. Wicca is counterculture and somewhat underground

The main Tradition or style of Wicca we outline here has become known as Eclectic Wicca. Just as Christianity is not practiced the same way everywhere, neither is Wicca.

There will be many analogies made between Wicca and Christianity or other religions. This may offend some Wiccans, but it is necessary. We want to explain Wicca to people who have little knowledge of Wicca, as well as elucidate our ideas to those who are knowledgeable, and it is often helpful to make comparisons to what is familiar to most people. Once a person has been in the Wiccan culture and lifestyle for a while, the Christian analogies are no longer necessary, but to a person to whom Wicca is new, there are still many things which seem strange, different, or confusing.

To become Wiccan necessitates some changes in one's mind-set and lifestyle. We call this paradigm shifting. Wiccan values and priorities are not necessarily the same as those of the mainstream culture, which in the English-speaking world is predominantly Christian, but our values are quite compatible with most people's, mainly it's a question of emphasis. For instance, we believe in families and the sanctity of the home, although we may define who is included in that family differently. We believe in committed relationships, but how we celebrate and run these relationships may be different. And then again, they may not be that different. After all, the majority of Wiccan couples are still heterosexual, monogamous, and legally married.

The area of Wicca that requires the largest shift in thinking is the practice of magick. Wiccans tend to spell magick with a K to differentiate it from stage magic, prestidigitation, slight-of-hand, illusions, and other entertainments. Our magick is executed in a Sacred Circle, and accomplishes change through the controlled use of personal or group will. To say we believe in magick is not strong enough a statement to make it work. Belief implies a margin of error, a measure of doubt. We KNOW magick works. If you are a practicing Wiccan for any length of time, you have seen magick work enough times to realize how well it can work, but sometimes it works in ways different from your expectations. Some people consider prayer a form of magick, and it can be seen that way.

Eclectic Wicca descends from several sources, and is an amalgam of the best elements of each. One phrase we use is, "Take what works, change what you need to, discard what doesn't work. We only borrow from the very best." Eclectic Wicca tends to be less structured and hierarchical then Gardnerian Wicca or other similar Traditions, but usually more organized and defined than most Dianic feminist spirituality groups. In a way Eclectic Wicca is the end amalgam of all the various elements of Wicca and witchcraft spirituality that have manifested in North America since 1964.

Eclectics generally have three degrees of Initiation, and covens of various structures, depending on the group. We have basic Circles we use, though we can change and adapt them as needed. There are certain conventions of elements and tools and other things, which are fairly universal, though naturally variants do exist here and there. There are generally no defined chains of lineages—who initiated whom is not as important as it might be to a Gardnerian for example—although one's teachers and initiators are important to the individual, and perhaps their students.

The level of learning, teaching, and training varies widely throughout North America. Some groups train rigorously, while others require only passing knowledge on a few subjects. It is in this area that comparisons—especially degrees or levels of initiation—can break down, because between or even within some Traditions of Wicca, there are no set standards or curricula. But with the explosion of books and publicly available information on Wicca, possibly the most common style of Wicca practiced today may be described as Eclectic Wicca.

There is no unified structure of Eclectics. There are no specific gatherings for Eclectics. Nobody can say with any certainty how many Eclectics are practicing Wicca in North America today. We don't know how many Wiccans there are, although there is a general consensus that there are a lot of Wiccans out there; estimates range from twenty thousand to one hundred thousand plus. Wicca is a fast-growing religion and spiritual path. Its growth seems to have increased exponentially in the past few years, especially to those of us who have been Wiccans for a decade or two. But since not all Wiccans can necessarily agree on who is and is not a Wiccan, actual statistics are impossible to obtain. But interest is high, and books on Wicca sell quite well, so it is apparent that people are hungry for information about Wicca.

This book is slanted toward the religion, spiritual practices, and lifestyle of Wiccans. Though divination is a part of our spiritual practices, we do not teach how to do divination. There are many other good books available on those topics. We instead tell you how to use divination as a part of the religion of Wicca. We will show you Circles, rituals, and some spells, as they relate to being a Wiccan.

This book also contains substantial information about Wiccan philosophy. This wasn't necessarily intentional. It's just that when describing how to do things, and why we do and believe what we do and believe, a good deal of the philosophy inevitably becomes part of the explanations. As ecology is an important part of the Wiccan lifestyle, we discuss ecology and sharing the Earth and its resources, but that manifests in many interesting and subtle ways. Wiccans also value learning, study, and teaching. This is also reflected in what we do and how we live. And we believe we can make a positive difference in whatever we turn our minds and magicks to. We see this every day, and we know our magick works. We have used it for so many worthwhile things. We believe in self-determination and consciously choosing what to and not to participate in from the latest fads to political movements to how we choose to use the Earth and her resources.

Wicca is a bona fide religion. There are Wiccan churches that have been granted state and/or federal tax-exempt status, a status we share with other churches in the United States. We have credentialed clergy in the Wiccan faith, including the authors who are both registered clergy in their state of residence, Minnesota.

Wicca tends to be inclusive about what is considered religion and spirituality, a point of view that is different from Christianity, which has generally been exclusive and narrowly defines what is and is not acceptable dogma, beliefs, and practices. Wicca is certainly a different kettle of fish from modern Christianity, which may account for the appeal. But Wicca is definitely not for everyone.

Hopefully after you read this book, you will have a much more thorough understanding about the religion, spirituality, and lifestyle of Wicca. We are writing this book to disseminate information, not to gain converts. People should make up their own minds about whether or not Wicca is for them. If it is not, that's okay. If it is for them, then welcome. We hope we have provided a good basic guide and framework for your practices as you learn and grow.

This book cannot be the complete and last word on being Wiccan. Wicca is still growing, changing, and evolving. But it can be a guide to practicing Wicca as it manifests in you now and in the future, Goddess willing. Blessed be, and enjoy.

WHAT WICCA IS NOT

MANY PEOPLE HAVE HEARD AT LEAST A little about Wicca. However, some of the information about Wicca is inaccurate due to distortion or general misconceptions.

THE MOST COMMON MISCONCEPTIONS

To try and remedy this situation a little bit, we refute what we believe to be the most commonly held misconceptions about Wicca circulating in modern North America today.

There are no animal sacrifices. There are no blood sacrifices. Occasionally we sacrifice bread or a vegetable or two, but that's about it.

There are no orgies, although some Wiccans choose to worship skyclad (i.e., naked), nor are we pederasts or pedophiles. We are a fertility religion and consider procreation a sacred act, and we symbolically recreate the procreative act in the practice known as the Great Rite, but there are no orgies or child abuse.

The pentagram—the five-pointed star—is not a satanic symbol. It is an ancient symbol. The Pythagoreans used it as the symbol of their worship of the mathematical beauty of the universe. It has been used in many places and times as a sacred geometric symbol. Although both Wiccans and some Satanists use the same symbol, that does not make them analogous. Both the Nazis and ancient meso-Americans used the swastika as a sacred symbol. They aren't the same, either.

We do not wish to destroy Christianity, just to live and practice our religion. Wicca attempts to recreate the indigenous religious systems of pre-Christian Europe, in a modern context. Christianity did try to destroy those systems, but Wiccans do not wish to destroy Christianity.

The Wiccan religion does not proselytize. In general Wiccans do not train or teach anyone under eighteen years of age, for a number of reasons including legal considerations. One of the major controversies within Wicca in the past few years has been what to do about the children, with many feeling that there is no place for children at all in Wicca. We are Goddess worshippers, with a strong maternal bent to our beliefs, and Wiccans are vehemently opposed to any form of child abuse. Wicca is a religion of choice (few people have been born into a Wiccan household), and it behooves most teachers to be sure the choice to study Wicca is a mature and intelligent one and not just rebellion, fad, or whim. There are certainly many earnest mature young people out there, but because of the legal system and familial restraints being what they are, most Wiccan teachers will not risk teaching minors.

We don't condone ritual abuse or engage in it. The accusations that some Wiccans practice ritual abuse appear to stem from some who equate Wicca with satanic practices. One of the major credos of almost all Wiccans is "And it harm none, do what you will." This would seem to make it difficult for us to intentionally harm anyone, let alone our fellow worshippers. Wiccans cannot and do not generally condone any type of abuse whatsoever, especially in a ritual or religious setting. In fact many Wiccans try to teach abuse awareness and counsel what to do when confronted by abuse.

We are not involved with any illegal activities including selling drugs and/or gun-running, pornography, or white slavery to finance our organizations. This accusation originated from a pastor of a fundamentalist Christian organization around 1989/1990 as part of the then-popular satanic scare. He purported to have newspaper clippings and other proofs showing Wiccans making money illegally, but never managed to produce these proofs, even when the police requested them. Logic dictates that if Wiccans did have big money like the big drug dealers, there would be lots of big fancy Wiccan churches, comparable to some of the charismatic Christian churches dotting the landscape. We don't know of one. All the Wiccan groups the authors know of are chronically short of funds for the most basic needs, few own property, and most cannot even afford to rent building space.

We are not a cult. There is an evaluation tool, the Advanced Bonewits' Cult Danger Evaluation Frame (ABCDEF) (see appendix 1), used by many groups and organizations to assess groups for cult-like behavior. True cults score very high on the scale—the more dangerous or oppressive, the higher the score. Mainstream religious groups tend to score around the middle of the scale, while Wiccans are at the other end of the scale, extremely low, tending toward non-organization. You could accurately say that because of the non-organized state many Wiccans are so proud of, we are anti-cult in our practices.

For those who claim that any new religion is a cult until it has been around for three or more generations, Wicca passed that milestone in the last decade. Dating from the first written public accounts, Wicca began in 1951, and since a generation is approximately twenty years, Wicca was into its third generation in 1991. And if you date from Gardner's writings—he started in 1939—that milestone came even earlier.

We are not an anti-Christian (satanic) religion. Wicca tries to recreate the pre-Christian indigenous European religious systems. Satanism, in most of its forms, is a deliberate perversion or reversal of Christianity.

Some fundamentalist Christians assert that anyone not practicing their form of Christianity is by definition a Satanist, including Mormons, Quakers, Seventh-Day Adventists, Catholics, Jews, Muslims, Buddhists, Hindus, Methodists, and Presbyterians. If this is true, then Wiccans are part of a very a large group.

We are not a spiritual arm of the eco-terrorists. Yes, Wicca is a nature-based spirituality, and we revere ecology and the Earth, but we know that terrorism is not the way to bring people to your way of thinking.

We are not into BDSM (Bondage-Discipline

and Sado-Masochism). This misconception goes along with the practice of skyclad worship and certain practices during Initiations. Binding an Initiate is ancient (and by any BDSM standard, what certain Traditions who do bind their Initiates, is extremely tame), and BDSM is a relatively new fad and has been glamorized by popular culture.

We believe that what individual Wiccans do in the privacy of their own homes is their business, but we suspect it's pretty much the same as non-Wiccans. The religion of Wicca does not require or proscribe sex practices among consenting adults, but considering our "Harm None" provision, that would eliminate BDSM practices.

Wicca is not a tax-dodge, but a true religion. We do not have churches and don't maintain a clergy like mainstream (Christian) denominations, but we are people of deep spiritual convictions and a faith and world-view that answers life's questions for us. There are fewer Wiccan churches that have tax-exempt status than almost any Christian denomination. Those that do have full tax-exempt status usually have acquired the legal status of a church, to provide specific mundane services—like the right to marry and bury our own people—that only a legally recognized tax-exempt church can provide.

Most Wiccans would rather not bother with any federal bureaucracy, but because the only legal recognition available to a church in this country is the IRS's tax-exempt status, we have had little choice. But as of the writing of this book, the authors know of no Wiccan church in existence today with an organization large enough to make a tax-dodge possible.

There is no secret master (or masters) of Wicca who controls and guides all Wiccan activity for his (or their) nefarious ends. This is a variation of that propaganda promulgated by the document called the Priories of the Elders of Zion, created by the czar's secret police around 1900 to justify the pogroms against the Jews in czarist Russia. It is a hate propaganda document, created by anti-Wiccan weirdos.

Wiccans are universally anti-organization. Commonly the size of our groups is about thirteen people. We generally believe whatever works for you is right for you, so it is very hard for us to develop organizations larger than the thirteen member coven, let alone allow anyone else to dictate what we will do.

We are not out to take people's money.

There are no more than three degrees (or ranks) of Initiation in the Wiccan religion. According to Christian mythology, there are secret advanced Fourth and Fifth degrees of Initiation, which are really blood pledges to Satan. This is a complete fabrication. Some groups may have fewer or more than three degrees of Initiation. The few who may have more than three degrees usually use them to recognize some sort of mundane-oriented organizational post within the group, like secretary or treasurer. But no group requires any sort of pledge to Satan for anything.

Some have accused Wicca of practicing only black magick because in their estimation there is really no white, healing magick—only black, hurtful magick, and we hook people in by seeming innocuous at first, then bringing on the black magick practices. One of the main tenets of Wicca is known as the Law of Three: "Whatever you do will return to you threefold." If you send a curse, you are cursing yourself threefold. Would anyone be stupid enough to curse using those rules?

We do not cast spells and hurl curses and control demons to torment those who are in our way. See above about the Law of Three. Historically, the controlling of demons has been the province of certain types of Christian ceremonial magic. We do not waste energy cursing our enemies, especially since most people seem much more accomplished at cursing themselves.

All witches are neither psychic, read cards, nor have massive Extra Sensory Perception (ESP), etc. All witches are not Gypsies. Not all Wiccans are witches and not all witches are Wiccans. But some of both categories do read cards, and some are psychic or have more developed ESP; ESP is not a requirement for being Wiccan, nor do you have to be Rom or Roma (the ethnic group colloquially called Gypsies). Some are, most are not. For the most part, we are just plain people who also happen to be practitioners of the Wiccan religion.

The general misconceptions held about Wicca make us infinitely more important, powerful, rich, and influential (not to mention evil, crazy, and obsessed with other people's lives) than we could ever dream of. Mostly Wiccans are just people who happen to practice a nature- and seasonal-based spirituality. We have jobs and kids and lives within the American norm, and just want to practice those beliefs and spirituality and live our own lives.

OTHER MISUNDERSTANDINGS

Wicca is not a religion for everyone and anyone. Wicca is a religion of choice, self-determination, and self-responsibility, and it isn't easy being a Wiccan today. Many Wiccans have suffered discrimination, lost jobs, homes, spouses, and children because of their beliefs. At the very least, to be Wiccan is to be constantly reminded you are a minority, not a part of mainstream culture and mindsets, and you have to either adapt and be silent or fight hard for your rights to be recognized. For instance, few employers allow Wiccan workers to take Samhain (Halloween) off as a religious holiday, although most Wiccans are forced to take off

Christmas, even though it means nothing to them, and of course we are not alone in that; Jews, Muslims, Buddhists, and Hindus are in the same situation.

Wicca is not a religion for people who want a ready-made set of beliefs, Deities, practices, and rules. There is no Holy Bible in Wicca. There is no one God the Father who is above all others. There is no one right, true, and only way to practice Wicca. There is no forgiveness or absolution of sins, no automatic salvation. Wiccans are expected to face up to their mistakes and problems, try their best to fix and/or resolve them, and take responsibility for their actions and inactions. Wicca comes with no guarantees. Wiccans are expected to think for themselves, and make up their own minds about what their ethical codes will be or not be, and then stick to it.

Wicca does not advocate anarchy or "do what you want, so long as it feels good"; "An ye harm none, do what ye will" is the Wiccan Rede. That means you can do what you want, but only as long as you don't hurt anyone or anything, including yourself. You have to think about your actions before you take them, and take responsibility for things when they don't turn out as you wanted, even though circumstances were beyond your control. And debating what constitutes harm can take up many interesting hours within Wiccan groups. Tough love, for example, is a concept, which naturally goes with harm none. Sometimes you have to be tough, even if you don't want to, but in general all choose the options that do the least harm, that will cause the least anguish and upset in the long run.

Wicca is not a mainstream religion. There are not many Wiccans everywhere. You cannot go almost anywhere and find a group of Wiccans and be with them for Sabbats. For the most part, Wicca is a religion of small tightly knit groups of people, who are loosely connected and in communication with each other. Some Wiccans are not aware of any other Wiccans anywhere outside of books and the Internet.

Wicca is not a religion for people who want to go someplace for an hour or so a week, and have their religious needs cared for. Being Wiccan usually means you practice your religion every day, all the time. It is a lifestyle and world-view as much as anything else. Because there is no one holy book, Wiccans are constantly reading, studying, and learning about things that pertain to their religious life, and life in general.

And possibly most important, Wicca is not a religion where you can go and have someone perform the services for you. All Wiccan Initiates are Priestesses and Priests in their own right and we perform almost all of our own rituals and ceremonies ourselves. There are no intermediaries between Wiccans and their Gods.

WHAT WICCA *IS*

NOW THAT WE'VE DISPELLED SOME OF THE myths and misconceptions, just what is Wicca? In one way, this entire book is about what Wicca is, and it is not the last word nor by any means the only word on the topic.

The most basic definition is that Wicca is a modern attempt at the recreation of pre-Christian European religious beliefs. Yet this is really not sufficient. It is a nature-based spirituality, yet paradoxically most Wiccans live in urban areas. It celebrates the seasons as they occur throughout the cycle of the year, known to us as the Wheel of the Year, yet most Wiccans worship indoors. It is a fertility religion, yet most Wiccans are as sexually prudent (some might say prudish) as the majority of the rest of the people in our society are. And Wiccans use magickal Circles to worship, perform magick, and create spells to make life better for themselves, their families, and the world around them, yet most Wiccans still live in the everyday world of making a living.

Wicca is a relatively new religious path for people in the modern world. It is still evolving and growing. Wicca today is different from Wicca in 1975 or Wicca in 1951. Wicca is, for the most part, a religion of choice; few people were born into a Wiccan family, and even those who were are not guaranteed to be Wiccan like their parents. Wicca is a religion of small intimate groups, where people do for themselves what they feel necessary for worship and spiritual satisfaction.

Wiccans are ecologically minded. This ranges from reusing, renewing, and recycling to walking gently on the Earth and planning actions as if it affected the seventh generation. Practically it may mean Wiccans buy a used car instead of a new one, remodel an existing home instead of building a new one in a former wetland, choose environmentally safe products and investments. It may mean adopting a vegetarian diet, or choosing only to eat free-range meat. It may mean avoiding certain companies, products, and services, which depend upon non-ecological practices.

Being Wiccan means that we are not necessarily caught up in mainstream hype. Wiccans enjoy popular culture, but not mindlessly. They choose what they adopt, and do not waste time with fads just because everybody's doing it. Wiccans have chosen to stray off the beaten path, so keeping up with the Joneses is meaningless to them. Wiccans read a lot. (Ninety percent of Americans read less than one book a year.) The average Wiccan reads one book a month, usually lots more.

Wiccans are constantly learning, changing, and growing. Wiccans are expected to evolve and adapt to life and the world. Wiccans constantly ask why or why not? So, in many ways Wiccans are similar to many other people who think, act, and determine for themselves how they live.

A HISTORY OF WICCA

There are many myths and practices within Wicca related to the origins and lineage of various Wiccan Traditions and belief systems. Most of this knowledge we owe to Margaret Murray, Robert Graves, and other historians, scholars, and anthropologists. But the history of modern Wicca cannot be reliably documented before 1951 and the work of Gerald Gardner. The modern incarnation of Wicca is an amalgam of Ceremonial Magick, mysticism, theosophy and the spiritualist movement, Masonic practices, Eastern religions and thought, fairy tales, mythologies, folklore and legends, divination, and individual imagination and belief.

There are Traditions that claim to derive or descend from original hereditary sources (for example, the English Gardnerian and Alexandrian, and the Italian Strega Traditions or Lineages). There are Traditions that were created by authors and published in books (Seax Wicca, and Starhawkian, adapted from Starhawk's book *The Spiral Dance*). And there are Traditions that have evolved their own distinctive characteristics over time (Eclectic Wicca). Some Traditions are schismatic, having broken away from other older, established Traditions (Georgian, Blue Star, and Elite). Some Traditions are exclusive, providing

teaching and training only to their Initiates (Gardnerian and Alexandrian), and some Traditions will teach almost anyone (Eclectic). Some Traditions require only self-recognition and proclamation to become an adherent (Dianic). Some Traditions recognize degrees of Initiation and rank from other Traditions, some recognize degrees from non-Wiccan Traditions, and others only recognize their own.

Gerald Gardner was a British civil servant who spent most of his career in India. When Gardner retired to England, he was initiated into Wicca through a group, which called itself the New Forest Coven, headed by a woman called "Old Dorothy" Clutterbuck. This woman was a hereditary witch, and this coven had been in existence for decades. Gardner was a Mason who had also studied Oriental mysticism and related topics most of his life, and he had written several books on those subjects.

Gardner blended the hereditary Witchcraft of the New Forest Coven, called Wicca, with Masonic-like ceremonies and a handful of other practices popularized in the Golden Dawn shortly before W.W.I, creating the religion we know today as Gardnerian Wicca. Gardner's religion did not spring full-blown, but evolved over a number of years, benefiting from several other contributors, including Doreen Valiente.

Gerald Gardner, considered by most to be the founder of modern Wicca, started practicing Wicca around 1939, and he publicized it as a religion in 1951. Wicca was brought to North America around 1964 by Raymond and Rosemary Buckland who had been initiated by Gardner and one of his High Priestesses the year before. There are stories of other Wiccans who came to the United States and possibly Canada before 1965. However, the current explosion of American Wicca is reliably traceable to the Bucklands, and some of the earlier offshoot groups have been consciously reintegrated with the Bucklands' lines over the years. Alexandrian Wicca came to the United States in 1964, but it is generally considered to be an early offshoot of Gardnerian-style Wicca.

Sorting Gardner's contributions from those of Doreen Valiente is difficult. However in 1949 Gardner published a book of fiction, *High Magic's Aid*, which detailed the workings of an English Coven at Lammas in 1940 trying to repel Hitler's forces magically. In Britain in 1951, the last witchcraft laws were repealed which mandated all witches should be put to death for practicing witchcraft. Because of these laws, the witches in Britain have long been extremely secretive about their practices. In 1954 Gardner published a book, *Witchcraft Today*, about the practices of witches, which asserted that witchcraft was alive and well in Britain, and that he was a witch.

Gardner became an instant celebrity and for the rest of his life flirted with the press and became the "official Witch" of Britain. He eventually purchased a witchcraft museum on the Isle of Man, which he ran for some years. At his death, Gardnerian Wicca (the label Gardnerian was first used by a personal enemy of Gerald's) was well established, with a schismatic offshoot (Alexandrian Wicca) and a number of covens in Britain, Europe, and America.

Gardnerian Wicca is not the only type of Wicca said to have survived since the Burning Times, the days of the Inquisition and Witch Trials in Europe and America. But Gardnerian Wicca was the first to be widely publicized and published. Gardner's books and numerous interviews and articles about him served to bring the idea and the reality of practicing witches to the attention of the modern world. The publicity attracted many who wanted to join the movement and become Traditional witch-

es also. Though other Traditions co-existed, it was Gardner who brought Wicca into the public view and thus he is known as the founder of modern Wicca.

Whether Gardner ever met and talked with Aleister Crowley (one of the most prominent and infamous occultists of the first half of this century, the self-styled "wickedest man in the world") about Crowley's practices and research into magick and the like is unproven, but probable. Crowley's books were widely available, and as he wrote a great deal about the practices of magick, Gardner almost certainly borrowed from Crowley, perhaps with Crowley's knowledge and blessings.

Stories abound about Gardner's quirks of character, which became incorporated into his version of Wicca. Be that as it may, Gardnerian practices have validity and can be highly effective, with respect to the altering of consciousness and the raising of power.

Since 1951 many Wiccans have evolved and moved away from strict Gardnerianism. Eclectic Wicca is considered by some to be the most common form of Wicca in the United States today, although secrecy and confidentiality make any attempt to count how many Wiccans practice a given Tradition pure guesswork at best. But all Wiccans owe a debt of gratitude to Gerald Gardner for making the practice of our religion possible in the modern world.

At first most of the true Wiccan groups were Gardnerian or Alexandrian. Period. As the years passed, people started innovating and adding to the basic Gardnerian Book of Shadows. This original Book of Shadows is less than one hundred pages long, and some more recent ones are three or four times that size. The original Gardnerian Book of Shadows has also become the basis for many other Wiccan Traditions, some of which are using the material not knowing it is basically Gardnerian. Stewart Farrar was a prominent witch of recent years (now deceased). During several tours of Europe and the Americas he stated that he had been privileged to view scores of secret Books of Shadows from many Wiccan Traditions, and he asserted that almost all of them were pretty much the same as that one hundred pages of the original Gardnerian Book. Raymond Buckland has said that he has had a similar experience with many Wiccans of various Traditions. Some Traditions have dropped certain practices passed down to them from Gardnerian Wicca, while other Traditions have added various other things. Alexandrian Wicca, for instance, added much Ceremonial Magick to their version of the Gardnerian Book of Shadows.

Before Buckland and 1964, there was little written material available in North America on Wicca and/or Goddess worship. Gardner's books were not generally available in the United States and Margaret Murray's books were printed only in England. We will try to give you a thumbnail sketch of the history of the various books important to Wicca.

SIGNIFICANT BOOKS

In the beginning, a revised version of *The White Goddess* (1948) by Robert Graves (of *I, Claudius* and *Claudius the God* fame), was published in New York (the original version was published in England in 1946). This poetic book attempts to unify all Goddess worshipping cultures by claiming that they all worshipped the same archetypal "White Goddess" or Moon Goddess. The book is not perfect—it has been found to contain major mistakes, omissions, and historical errors—but it became the basis for much Goddess religion research and scholarship. It was the basis for at least one Wiccan

Tradition, and it was the only book readily available in the United States before the 1970s on historical Goddess worship. But while they may have much in common, and while there may be some controversy as to who invented who, Goddess worship and Wicca are not necessarily the same.

At first the religion of Wicca was passed from person to person, similar to the practices of the various "Fam-Trads" (i.e., Family Traditions, some of whom claim to have existed for centuries). Someone would be Initiated into a coven, rise through the degrees, and eventually hive off and start a coven of their own. Or someone would move away and start a new group in their new place of residence. But in 1971, Raymond Buckland's book *Witchcraft from the Inside* was published. This book describes some of his experiences in the Gardnerian Craft. Also in 1971, Janet and Stewart Farrar published their book *What Witches Do*, which was an Alexandrian Book of Shadows. And in 1972 the *Grimoire of Lady Sheba* (rev. 1974, reissued 2001) was published. Lady Sheba's was an adaptation of a Gardnerian Book of Shadows, with some Traditional Family practices of her own added. These books were groundbreaking in that they made accessible to the public in the United States the rites and practices of Wiccans. No longer did a person have to know someone to learn about Wicca. They could buy a book and read about it on their own. Alex Sanders himself commissioned and collaborated with the Farrars on their book. Lady Sheba wrote her book on her own (with the unacknowledged help of Gardner and his associates) and stirred up controversy. Some felt she was breaking her oaths to make that material public.

In 1973 Raymond Buckland created Seax Wicca—Saxon Witchcraft. It is an amalgam of Saxon and Norse mythology and basic Gardnerian Wicca, without violating any oaths or revealing any secrets. *The Tree* was published in 1974 in the United States, in which Buckland claims it is okay to initiate oneself as a witch and found a coven with no formal training. This was a new innovation from Gardnerian Tradition, and illustrates the trend in American Wicca today, amalgamating with the feminist witch movement.

After these books were published, more books came. The floodgates had been opened, and within five years there were a score or more of books, which detailed various Wiccan practices, rites, rituals, circles, and the rest. This started a new generation of Wiccans who could read a book and start practicing the religion, without first having to find another Wiccan to teach them.

MODERN GROUPS

Modern American Wicca derives mainly from two disparate lines: Gardnerians, and the Z Budapest "I am a Witch" (Dianic) school.

The Gardnerians, and through them, the Alexandrians and others are hierarchical, have Initiations, degrees, and an established set of rituals and practices. These Traditions could be called the high Ceremonial Magick (or high church) versions of Wicca. A person must go through training and demonstrate ability before receiving an Initiation. Most of these groups are considered closed, that is, they commonly require some sort of sponsorship, and you must make some sort of commitment before you can receive any training or membership. They are extremely secretive and will only share information with other properly credentialed Initiates. They are also secretive about membership (more so than other Wiccan Traditions) and when and where they meet, and they can be very difficult to find, even if you know what you are looking for.

The Dianic groups are feminist in origin evolving mainly from the women's movement of the '70s, open generally to women only. They have loosely evolved from the teachings of women such as Z Budapest, Starhawk, and many other not-quite-so-publicly-prominent feminists. They are Goddess-oriented, have few Initiations or rules, and are more free form in their beliefs and practices. With many of these groups, one need only to proclaim, "I am a Witch" three times (if only in front of one's own mirror) to be considered a member. They are often very much oriented toward public ritual, dance, and song, and can have large rituals with people from many smaller groups. These groups occasionally advertise widely, especially at feminist bookstores and other places where women gather. They range from simple women's spirituality groups, sometimes nominally Christian, all the way to stridently feminist or lesbian separatist groups. Exploring women's spirituality is the main focus of these groups, and little, if any, magick is consciously practiced.

There are other Wiccan Traditions and lines, which evolved over the years in response to the interests of others who wanted a religion that met their needs. Radical Faery Wicca is a gay men's Tradition. There are Wiccans who worship the Greek pantheon, and Wiccans who follow Celtic traditions and pantheons (separate from the Druids, which is a distinct Neo-Pagan religion by itself).

Then there are various Family Traditions or Fam-Trads, which are a set of beliefs and practices preserved by members of a family over the generations. What "Old Dorothy" Clutterbuck taught Gardner years ago in the New Forest Coven, was her Fam-Trad.

Strega (which is Italian for witch) is an Italian Tradition descended from ancient Roman beliefs. Diana is worshipped as the Goddess, and there is a mixture of herbal, healing, and folklore, which accompanies these beliefs. The book, *Aradia, or the Gospel of the Witches*, by Charles G. Leland, transcribed around 1900 is a main sourcebook for the Strega Tradition, though there are adherents who have had practices and lore passed down from their mothers and grandmothers.

There are also other Fam-Trads extant in the United States. Most true Fam-Trads are extremely secretive and totally closed to all but family members, and not all family members may receive training and knowledge. Some Fam-Trads only train one or two people in each generation. Some teach all their children, and offer more advanced training to those who express strong interest in continuing the training. Within mainstream Wicca there are individuals who may have been raised in a Fam-Trad and then also received training in another Wiccan Tradition and now practice both.

FESTIVALS

In the fall of 1973, Carl Llewellyn Weschcke, owner of Llewellyn Publications (the largest occult publishing house in the world), hosted a specialty convention in Minneapolis, Minnesota called Gnosticon, focused on magick, Wicca, and the occult. It was successful, and another was held in the spring of 1974. One product of this second gathering was *The Principles of Wiccan Belief* formulated by The Council of American Witches, namely those notables who had come to Gnosticon. *The Principles of Wiccan Belief* is dated April 14, 1974, and has become perhaps the single most important document to come out of the American Wiccan movement. It formed the foundation upon which almost all American Wiccans expressed their commonalities of beliefs. This document has been accepted as a working definition for Wicca by American Wiccans, the United States government (in the *Army Chaplain's Manual*), and other organizations. There were several more Gnosticons, but they ended by 1980. It is possible that Gnosticon was the first general Wiccan/Pagan gathering in North America.

The various Gardnerian Lines had been holding grand councils for many years, in various sites around the United States, but these were exclusive to Gardnerians. Gnosticon was open to anyone who was interested. Some people attending the Gnosticons were Traditional Gardnerians, but many were not. Gnosticon was held to be a vehicle for Weschcke to publicize his authors and Llewellyn's occult line, but it also provided a vehicle for Wiccans and Pagans to meet, interact, and exchange ideas, spells, recipes, and the like.

Selena Fox and Jim Allen, ex-hippies and radical activists, founded a Wiccan church organization, Circle Sanctuary, Inc. In 1975, they held the first outdoor camping event, Pagan Spirit Gathering (PSG), in Wisconsin. It has continued to the present day, moving to Ohio in 1997. They also began publishing *Circle Network News*, which became one of the largest Wiccan/Pagan contact vehicles in America. PSG has become one of the largest of the now numerous outdoor Pagan festivals, reportedly over 800 in attendance in 1996.

In 1977 the first Pan-Pagan festival was held in Illinois by the Midwest Pagan Council. These festivals have been successful, and this group started an additional indoor hotel festival, called InVocation, in 1997 in Illinois.

By the 1980s more outdoor Pagan festivals or gatherings were taking place. These were loosely patterned after scouting events or a church camp. People came, camped, and usually cooked their own food. There were workshops, rituals, seminars, and merchants. Many were able to meet Wiccans from other places for the first time. Large group rituals were conducted by people of various

Traditions, and for many this was the first time they had a chance to see how others worked.

This communication between groups of varying Traditions was revolutionary. Before this time, many groups had strict rules mandating secrecy about rituals, Books of Shadows, lore, words of power, and other information pertaining to Wicca and witchcraft. Just the first ritual held at Pan Pagan, which had people both robed and skyclad, elicited controversy, as people were very worried about what the energies would do in such a mixed group. There was a very real belief that energies flowed differently if participants were robed versus skyclad, and it was a concern that the clash of energies might cause something bad to happen. Nowadays we might find this idea alarmist, but it had never been done before, and the concerns at the time were real.

Everyone benefited from this sharing of rituals, recipes, lore, and ideas. Some groups had better information on some subjects, and little on others. Other groups had experimented in various areas and shared their findings. Resources were traded and recommended and, with this explosion of information, magick became more effective and rituals became better. Large group rituals (with over fifty participants) became possible, and almost common.

Simultaneously with the Pagan festivals, many books were published on magick and witchcraft. The occult revolution of the 1960s had resurrected many books on divination and similar topics, and by the mid-1970s the books were taking a more spiritual turn, and magick and witchcraft had become hot topics. Sybill Leek was the first major witch-author, as opposed to Wiccan, to be public about her beliefs and practices in the United States, and she published books about that as well as astrology and other forms of divination. She was also a perennial talk-show guest, and disseminated her message that way to many more people than just with her books.

THE MEDIA

Hollywood has also had a big role in expanding the Wiccan movement, though not always in beneficial or accurate ways. Witchcraft, ancient and modern, has been portrayed in movies. *I Married a Witch* (1942) was a light romantic movie that portrayed psychic abilities, but still made witchcraft out to be something not desirable for modern people, though not totally demonizing it. *Bell, Book and Candle* (1958), from the play of the same name, was more popular and more sympathetically portrayed witches, though the female witch ends up abandoning her powers for love of a mortal. *Rosemary's Baby* (1968) was a wildly popular movie based upon a best-selling book that used the terms witch and witches to portray what we would nowadays term Satanists. This together with the occult revolution in the mid-1960s fueled the popularity of witchcraft, but lasting damage was done also. The interchangeable use of the terms witch, witchcraft, and Satanism are still common in circles where people have only passing knowledge of those specific subjects. Since then witchcraft has been portrayed variously by Hollywood. The TV series *Bewitched* (1964–1972) was again about a witch marrying a mortal, but this time she did not lose her powers; she just voluntarily chose not to use them, until each week there was a situation where she was forced to twitch her nose and fix things. More recently the movies *The Craft* (1996) and *Practical Magic* (1998) have rekindled the popularity in witchcraft and Wicca. The TV series *Buffy the Vampire Slayer* (1997–) and *Charmed* (1998–) have characters that are Wiccan and are portrayed very sympathetically, and realistically, for fantasy series.

With the rise of Wicca as a living religion in the United States the portrayals are becoming more accurate and sympathetic.

By the mid-1970s there were many variants of Wicca. In meeting and trading ideas, a new type of Wicca started to emerge, Eclectic Wicca. This was to become for many the most familiar type of Wicca. Some people objected to certain conventions of Gardnerian Wicca. Some objected to the emphasis on ceremonial-type magick. In consciously abandoning these conventions, people began to formulate Eclectic Wicca for themselves.

WICCA TAKES OFF

The next momentous events took place in 1979, on October 31. That day two books were published that changed Wicca forever. The first one was *The Spiral Dance* by Starhawk (1979, 2nd revised edition 1989, 3rd revised edition 1999). This book recorded the practice of a feminist Dianic type of witchcraft, which later evolved into the Reclaiming Tradition. This was feminine empowerment in a religious and spiritual arena. The second book was *Drawing Down the Moon* by Margot Adler (1979, revised and expanded 1986, and also again 1999), which presents the practices and practitioners of Wicca, witchcraft, and Paganism in the modern United States. Adler, who was a Wiccan, interviewed many people across the United States over a period of years. This book officially brought Wicca out of the broom closet. Though some people might have heard of Wicca, there had been no book, that came out and said there are many people who are practicing Wicca, and they probably live in the same city as you! These two books brought Wicca to the forefront of the popular mind, and an explosion of new seekers came into Wicca and Paganism. The occult revolution and the Age of Aquarius are normally considered to have started in the mid-1960s. Because of these two books (among other reasons) the Pagan revolution started in the early 1980s. After those books, many others followed, and Wicca has never been the same.

MYTHOLOGICAL ORIGINS

Some feel that modern Wicca is just the latest in a long line of indigenous pre-Christian religions that have existed since before history. This is characterized by Goddess worship (with or without a God), fertility worship, Moon worship, celebration of the seasons and the cycles of life, and is primarily agricultural in origin. Since the beginning of Christianity these indigenous religions have been suppressed and the adherents either forcibly converted or put to death. Still, despite the persecution, this Goddess spirituality has existed secretly in parallel to Christianity, sometimes with the adherents of the Old Religions openly professing Christianity while practicing their Old Religion in secret with their covenmates. This has recently become public through the writings of various authors, Gerald Gardner, Sybill Leek, Rhiannon Ryall, and others.

TEN THOUSAND YEARS

Ten thousand years of the Goddess is a popular conception in certain Pagan circles that believe that Goddess worship emerged around 10,000 BCE or alternatively 10,000 years ago, roughly 8,000 BCE. It is generally accepted among Wiccans that the current era of patriarchal worship and societal dominance are just a phase in the Goddess' cycle that started approximately 5,000 years ago with the legendary peaceful matriarchal, agricultural, Goddess-worshipping cultures (like the Minoans), and was slowly replaced by the also legendary, warlike, pastoral, herding, patriarchal, God-worshipping cultures (like the desert-dwelling Semites).

Worshipping Around a Dolmen

And soon, because we are now at the start of another 5,000 year half-cycle (which varies widely among adherents and, according to some, has some sort of astrological basis), She will re-emerge to take again Her rightful place as Great Goddess. Because of this, Goddess worship, with its attendant values, will start replacing the currently dominant patriarchal culture, until a full cycle of 10,000 years is achieved when She will be again preeminent. At that time we assume the cycle will start again.

Supposedly it was the Goddess who led humankind into agriculture and civilization—certainly most ancient societies credited various Goddesses with the gifts of letters, writing, agriculture, and even beer. These beliefs also manifest themselves in the way some people date time with an extra digit (i.e., 1999 becoming 11999), reflecting that supposed extra 10,000 years that the Goddess has given her followers, as opposed to modern dating which is based upon Christianity and God worship. Also, the extra digit is supposed to remind people that civilization and religion have existed longer than the mere 2,000 years with which we number our calendars, and thereby not acknowledging the breadth of civilization and religion tacitly denigrating all times before that special 2,000 years.

RECENT HISTORICAL CONNECTIONS?

The historical facts of the witchcraft trials and persecutions in Europe and later America are seen by some Wiccans as part of the history of the religion and faith of Wicca. Others see them as a sociological phenomenon that repressed and discriminated against women and others, but which cannot be conclusively proven to have any religious link to Wicca. Certainly most modern Wiccans feel a tie of kinship with those people who were persecuted for their beliefs, and the cry "Never again the Burning" is used to affirm that modern Wiccans will not stand for that sort of treatment, or indeed any sort of persecution. The First Amendment of the United States Constitution is seen as a great boon to Wicca and other minority belief systems.

CONCLUSION

So Wicca is either the oldest existing religion or one of the newest, depending upon which history you believe. What should matter is not the history, but how effective Wicca is as a religion for the individual people practicing it. Does it work in the good times? Does it help you through the bad times? Does it help answer the big questions for you? Does it help you to be a better person? If your answer to any or all of these questions is yes, then Wicca is a positive and beneficial force in your life. That should be the test of a religion, not how old it is or who invented it and when.

PART I

WICCAN BASICS

RELIGIOUS BELIEFS

WICCA AS A RELIGION IS DIFFERENT FROM mainstream Judeo-Christian religion in that there are very few absolutes, little dogma or doctrine, but rather a more general guideline of beliefs that most Wiccans share in common. The Wiccan Rede and the Law of Three (similar to the Golden Rule) are the two main principles that guide a Wiccan's life. They may seem simplistic, but the simpler the tenet, the more it applies to in everyday life.

THE WICCAN REDE

"An ye harm none, do what ye will." The Wiccan Rede (pronounced *reed*) is generally considered the main guiding tenet of Wicca. It mandates that you can do whatever you want, but only if it harms no one including yourself. This implies a person should always be aware of the myriad consequences of each action, and how others might feel or respond. It definitely does not give a person free rein to act without regard to consequences. Most Wiccans consider an action before actually doing anything. If harm might result from the action, they assess the various levels of harm and then choose the action that will likely cause the least harm, or offer the most benefit while harming the least. The Rede also helps a person not to take anything for granted. Following the Rede readily leads one to live ecologically and to tread lightly upon the Earth. One may become a vegetarian, adopt a mindset of waste not want not, and develop a disdain for the rat race and keeping up with the Joneses. What constitutes harm is a popular topic for group discussion. Generally people agree that harm means negative actions—actions that affect others or oneself adversely. Sometimes *not* acting can cause the greatest harm.

THE LAW OF THREE

"Whatever you do will return to you threefold." The Law of Three is used as a way of monitoring day-to-day behavior. It means that if you send love, you will receive love threefold; if you send animosity or negativity, that too will return threefold. It is this main tenet that prevents Wiccans from cursing others. Because Wiccans do practice magick, there exists the possibility of putting that practice to unpleasant, restrictive, or retributive use. Wiccans are well schooled in what constitutes "black magick." When following the Law of Three, they will avoid it. Besides, most magick is used for personal self-development and is never as easy or instantaneous as that which Samantha—from the '60s TV show *Bewitched*—could call up with a twitch of her nose. Wiccans might occasionally wish for such powers, but none have gained them.

THE GOLDEN RULE

"Do unto others as you would have them do unto you." The Golden Rule is a corollary to the Law of Three and simply a good guideline to live by. Though people may want to be treated in widely differing ways, the Golden Rule mandates a person think about and take personal responsibility for their actions and the consequences of these actions. Wiccans don't have confession or absolution of sins; they are expected to face up to their actions and own up to their mistakes. If they do err, they examine what they did and why they did it, hopefully becoming more aware and avoiding such problems in the future. If possible, they set things right in the present.

THE NOTION OF DARKNESS

Most Wiccans acknowledge some sort of dark side to the Universe. This may or may not include evil. Generally, what is considered to be light or bright is what is beneficial; it builds and creates. What is termed dark is what is harmful, destroys, and tears down. One could also call these principles Creation and Entropy. Instead of equating all that is dark with bad and evil, Wiccans understand that the dark is an integral part of life and the Universe. For example, where would a garden be without compost? Yet compost is rot and decay, the process of breaking down to simpler chemical components. By the above definition, decay is dark. But it also

brings benefit. Death is a dark process, yet it is an integral part of life. Our present society is death denying. Wiccans honor death as a natural part of the Cycle of the Year. Therefore, Wiccans prefer to think of the dark as a natural part of life, not to be feared or battled, but understood and respected for its essential role.

Evil, as it refers to human actions, is something different. Death and destruction are natural processes, but when they become specific actions to serve a personal end, they may be called evil. So perhaps evil is a phenomenon of intent. When a river floods and destroys a building, that is certainly "of the dark," but it is a natural force, not from evil intent. But if someone dynamites a building, deliberately blowing it up to hurt or harm, then that is evil. If it was done to clear the property so a new building could be built, with the willing consent of the owners, then it could hardly be called evil. It's not merely the act, but the intent behind it, which matters.

If a person says, "God told me to sexually abuse and kill young people," that is evil, though the person may also be insane. That sort of action (or any blood sacrifices, be it animal or human) is not condoned by Wiccans. Wiccans also vehemently oppose any sort of physical or sexual abuse of children or adults. Wiccans are generally open about sexuality but still guard the innocence of children. Wiccans are commonly more accepting of alternative sexualities and lifestyles, but this absolutely does not include abuse. What happens between consenting adults is their private business. Children are to be properly educated and protected from those who would harm them.

Some might say that Wiccans have a specific Sabbat devoted to death and to understanding that the dark is a part of the whole cycle of life, death, and rebirth. Because of that, some might say that

Wiccans worship the Devil. This is absolutely not so. The Devil (Satan, Old Scratch, and the rest of the names this demon goes by) is a Christian fallen angel and the adversary of Jehovah and his son Jesus Christ. Wicca is not a Christian religion, so the notion that Wiccans would worship a Christian Deity (or fallen angel) is erroneous. Most of the traditional trappings of Devil worship were the result of the Inquisition, which created a kind of reverse Christianity. Wicca is trying to resurrect pre-Christian practices and beliefs. Wiccans are respectful of all religions and spiritual paths; this is an integral part of Wiccan training.

REINCARNATION

Some belief in reincarnation is practically universal throughout Wicca. What mechanism it takes or what criteria are used differs from individual to individual. Certainly a belief in some sort of soul or spiritual self that lives after the death of the body is universal. An understanding of karma and cosmic payback for one's actions is also strongly present. With the belief in reincarnation and karma, the need or existence of a specific heaven or hell is unnecessary. There is a place some believe in, called "the Summerlands," where people go after death to rest between lives but it is not a place where they will dwell permanently. The idea of karma eliminates the need for redemption, salvation, or purgatory. People, by their actions or lack thereof, make their own fate for future lives, and if they strive to be the best they can and help others, they will eventually not need to return to improve their souls. What happens after that is not really an issue. Most of us have far too much to deal with to realistically contemplate that part of existence.

But Wiccans take responsibility for their actions. They realize that usually what the Universe hands them is the result of their actions in the past, and what they may get in the future will be the result of their actions now. There is no shortcut for redemption. It takes hard work, personal responsibility, and a willingness to acknowledge faults to correct or overcome them. Self-examination with the end result of self-betterment is one way a person can clean up karma, so to speak. It isn't easy, sometimes is very painful, but is ultimately cleansing. This self-betterment is what is termed the Great Work.

WICCANS AND DEITY

How each individual Wiccan views the Universe and interacts with their Gods is a personal choice. There is no set doctrine that mandates certain beliefs or practices with regards to Deity. Apart from the general belief that Deity manifests in both male and female forms, what speculation there is about life, the Universe, and everything is considered to be just that—speculation, with no definitive pronouncements from on high.

Some Wiccans are Deistic, believing that a spiritual entity created the Universe but that now we are on our own. Some are monotheistic, believing there is only one Deity, but that it takes many forms and attributes. Some are polytheistic, believing there are many different Gods, each with their own characteristics and areas of influence. Some are Gnostic in outlook and belief, holding that each person is to seek Deity in their own way, and that each person's religious revelations and experiences are true and valid for them. There is no absolute right, true, and singular way to experience Deity or view the Universe. Some Wiccans are even agnostic or atheistic. This is very difficult for many non-Wiccans to comprehend. Two people can be Wiccan, they might even be members of the same coven, and yet the religious practices and beliefs of each may be very different. How one views their

Gods or the Universe and how each practices worship is a private matter. Occasionally people will inquire, "Which Gods do you worship?" But that is rare.

There are many books published which list Gods and Goddesses and their attributes and characteristics. Wiccans will usually choose a patron Deity, often two—one male and one female. But there are no rules or conventions for choosing, nor do the Deities chosen have to be from the same pantheon. Most Wiccans choose according to an affinity they have for certain Gods, or perhaps they feel they have been chosen by or spoken to by a God or Goddess. However a person feels called, they decide how they want to worship. And there is nothing that restricts a Wiccan to worshipping only two Deities. A person might choose primary Deities, but have affinity for others and include them whenever appropriate.

Wiccans do not worship Satan, nor do they engage in any sort of blood rituals or sacrifice. The fact that Wiccans worship non-Christian Deities may be interpreted by the misguided to mean they worship the Devil, but nothing is farther from the truth. Along with practicing Hindus and Buddhists, who far outnumber Christians in the world, Wiccans are certainly not alone or even in the minority in their worship of non-Christian Deities.

Understanding the variety of worship and the spectrum of Deities is confusing to those new to Wicca. A teacher once told Paul, "My religion is different from your religion. I wouldn't expect you to follow my path; you have to find your own." This confused Paul, until he realized the teacher was talking about which Gods he worshipped and how he worshipped them. Among Wiccans, the fact that each is Wiccan is more important than the fact that one might worship Apollo or another is a follower of Freya.

The immanence of Deity is generally understood by Wiccans. Our Gods are not just up in heaven watching down on us, but manifest in our daily lives. Many Wiccans have a personal relationship with the Gods; they talk to them and can get guidance and instruction. A Wiccan needs no intermediary to talk to the Gods. They are seen as manifest in many small ways, day in and day out, as well as in the grand scheme of things on a cosmic scale.

Most Wiccans believe that Deity manifests in both male and female guises. Some Dianic groups prefer to ignore the male aspect of Deity entirely. Some Wiccans are more Goddess-oriented, some are more God-oriented, and many are strongly dualistic, that is, they believe that one polarity cannot exist without the other. Which Deities any particular Wiccan chooses to worship is entirely up to that individual. Usually one particular patron or pantheon is chosen, though, again, it is up to the individual. The Gods worshipped by Wiccans are, for the most part, not jealous Gods. You can simultaneously worship several, or just one, or even generically (The Goddess and The God). Which Goddess and/or God you worship is your own private business.

Religious Practices

RELIGIOUS TRAINING

Wicca is often criticized for its lack of doctrine. Westerners have been brought up to believe that followers of a religion have uniform beliefs and practices mandated by the religion. If an adherent strays from the specific path, then they are no longer considered a member of the religion. Many Christian denominations started this way. But nowadays Christians are coming together in ecumenical congresses, celebrating shared elements. Wicca is based upon commonalities, and tends to acknowledge but not emphasize the differences between adherents.

Wicca is a free choice religion. There is no proselytizing for converts. In fact, many people who really want to join have a hard time finding a group to join! Wicca is for the most part a chosen religious path, the choice being made in adulthood. Few people have been born into the Craft or brought up Wiccan. Most Wiccans consider themselves reformed from whatever religion they were raised in, if any. Children are named and put under the protection of Deity, but are not automatically considered Wiccan or sealed into Wicca as with various Christian baptisms. Most Wiccan parents do not expect their children to follow their religious path, but encourage them to explore their own beliefs and make their own decisions. Most Wiccan parents just want their children to grow up to be healthy and well-adjusted and to make their own way without hurting others.

Wiccans have a strong ethic that prohibits taking money for teaching Wicca or for granting degrees of Initiation. A few Wiccans offer courses and charge for classes, but the majority of Wiccan training is done in small groups at home where no charge is made other than for services or supplies such as photocopying, candles, and consumables. In this way Wiccan training is very similar to any religious catechism or confirmation course. Learning Wicca is an ongoing process. The first classes may have one of three initiatory degrees as their end goal, but Wiccans are expected to learn, teach, and study all their lives. Once in Wicca for a few years, they start to develop expertise in various areas, and they continue to study, sometimes teaching others, sometimes being taught. Each individual is unique and has some expertise they can share with others. For example, one can

• become well-versed in some divinatory system;

• write and perform rituals;

• do research on a specific topic;

• work with herbs, oils, or incense;

• use food for healing and celebration;

• run a coven and teach Wicca;

• organize festivals;

• provide medical services at festivals or in a Wiccan Community.

There is no limitation to how a person can further the Craft.

PRIESTS AND PRIESTESSES

All Initiates are technically Priests and Priestesses. How this plays out in practice differs from group to group. Most Wiccans (with the exception of Dianics) acknowledge Initiations, ceremonies a person goes through to raise understanding and skill levels. Initiations can be done by others or by oneself or by the Gods. If a group does Initiations, there are usually three. These are commonly known as the First, Second, and Third Degrees. Because all Wiccan Initiates are considered to be Priests, the terms High Priest and High Priestess are used to designate the people in charge of any given ritual or coven, no matter what their degree level. What training and/or experience is required for each level of Initiation varies widely among the Traditions and paths of Wicca. With Wicca being a religion of Priests for the most part, the need for a Priest to intercede between a Wiccan and God is unnecessary.

BOOK OF SHADOWS

In Wicca there is no one sourcebook for the practice and faith. There is no Holy Bible from which all the Wiccan teachings, doctrine, and worship are derived. There is also no one right, true, and only way to be a Wiccan. Wicca is more a spiritual path and way of life than just a set of teachings and practices

One of the things almost all Wiccans have in common is something called a Book of Shadows. This is an individual's combination notebook, journal, memoir, spell book, cookbook, encyclopedia, and general catchall for information magickal and Wiccan. This term refers to the collection of writings, books, and other materials, written or on disk, which comprise the teachings and practices of that person's Wiccan path and/or Tradition. Rarely is a Book of Shadows limited to only one book. Some of us refer to an encyclopedia of shadows or a bookcase of shadows. This collection can start well before a person actually decides to become Wiccan, or even before they have ever heard of Wicca. Estelle's oldest entries in her Book of Shadows date from her high school days when she made a study of astronomy, and star names and their meanings.

The Book of Shadows most traditionally consists of notes and journals, kept by hand. These writings are in part frequently derived from the accumulated teachings of one's coven or Initiator, plus whatever notes an individual has from lectures and the like. They may also include a journal which details one's magickal Workings, listing day, date, and time, perhaps the phase and sign of the Moon, the Working attempted, how the Working went, and perhaps a listing of results. This is like a scientific notebook of magick. There are also rituals for Sabbats, Esbats, Initiations, and other lore which make up the particular Tradition of the person. This Book of Shadows, as it evolves, becomes the sourcebook for each Wiccan. Unless a person can afford to buy all the books they want, they usually borrow them and then take notes.

With the explosion of books about Wicca and magick, several Books of Shadows have been published and can be bought off the shelf. There are Wiccan Traditions which have been published and exist whole within the covers of books. Most Wiccans also keep a personal Book of Shadows. For one thing, no published book will have the personal notes and journal of each individual as they study and practice Wicca. And, unless the person is in a strictly Traditional group, the Wicca one practices is bound to vary even from the most thorough book. A person might go to a festival and discover a new ritual, that they just fall in love with and add to their Book of Shadows—it then becomes part of their personal Tradition. Some Traditions mandate that the Book of Shadows be kept secret and shown only to students and fellow Initiates, sometimes within just one coven. Some mandate the Book of Shadows must be destroyed upon the owner's death, while others require that the Book of Shadows be passed on to a person's successors in the coven.

So just how does a Book of Shadows come into being? The person may take a class. The notes taken in that class become the first entries for a Book of Shadows. If there are readings assigned, notes from the readings are added. If rituals are performed, those are added. If there are Sabbats and Esbats performed, those are also added. Perhaps the person starts a dream journal; that also becomes a part of the Book of Shadows. If one studies the tarot and keeps notes of teachings or specific readings, those are added. If one goes to a festival and receives handouts, those go into their Book. If one comes across a recipe for Mooncakes, that is added. A journal of books read, classes attended, festivals attended, workings done, Sabbats and Esbats attended, all this becomes a part of the Book of Shadows. Personal notes, poetry, writings, musings, and the like are also included.

Newspaper articles, magazine articles, downloaded information from the Internet, and chat room transcripts can also be added. In short, anything that relates to Wicca is included.

Even though a few Traditions still maintain all material must be copied by hand, in reality, the personal computer and photocopier have streamlined the process considerably. Before personal desktop publishing, all materials were either handwritten or typed. Because handwriting is so individual and personal, there was the very real threat during more repressive times that Wiccans could be traced through their shared materials. Therefore each Wiccan hand-copied the materials, so if caught, no one else would be implicated. Typewriters were never widely used, and carbon paper, mimeo, and ditto were not very permanent records.

Nowadays, all you need is access to a copy machine and a PC, and you can crank out volumes that can be easily duplicated and never really traced back to the source. Xerography provides cheap, clear, and permanent copies, and the three-hole punch, the three-ring notebook, and even plastic page protectors can make for a really first-class Book of Shadows.

All this instant copying does have drawbacks, however. If you hand copy material, you have to process it through your brain while you copy. This ensures that the material will be fully read at least once. And the process of copying the books of another usually ensures personal contact, as most Wiccans will never lend out their Book of Shadows. This can then lead to questions and discussion about the material being copied, and the student thereby gets more information and the training progresses. So the old ways had more reasons behind them than just keeping people safe. It was a way to pass along information and ensure comprehension. Just because a person receives a photocopied handout does not guarantee that they will either read it or understand it.

Incidental material that may find its way into a Book of Shadows includes: recipes, songs, newspaper or magazine articles, personal correspondence (including e-mail printouts), astrological charts, photocopies of rare old books, and price lists and addresses of places one can buy herbs, jewelry, books, and magickal paraphernalia. One thing it should *not* include are the names, addresses, and phone numbers of fellow Wiccans, especially not lists that correlate Craft names with mundane names or addresses or phone numbers. A mundane name is the regular everyday name a person uses in the non-Wiccan world, the one that would be in the phone book. It's usually the one given at birth by one's parents. They are usually included in one's personal address book, but not identified as Wiccan. Craft names are usually remembered. If the people you know are Out, this might not be a big issue, but not all Wiccans are Out, so they are very reluctant to have their names or telephone number and/or address given out with specifically Wiccan material.

"Being Out" is a term that refers to a Wiccan's openness to the rest of society about their religious beliefs. Many Wiccans are not Out, that is, when directly questioned about their religion they will answer with a portion of the truth but will not directly state "I am Wiccan." Other Wiccans are definitely Out and may even make a point of stating "I am Wiccan" to any and all who will listen. There are also many shades of being Out, from "in the broom closet" to totally open.

With respect to Craft names, most Wiccans do adopt a Craft name that is used with others and in coven or Wiccan settings. It is not at all uncommon to have very close friends whose real names you do not know, because you only relate to them in a Wiccan context. You may also not know their addresses or telephone numbers, let alone where they work. This can be a drawback, but it can also protect people if they are not Out or feel their Wiccan affiliations might cause them trouble at work or elsewhere. Craft names are usually used and memorized, and not written down, especially where they would be easily accessible to people who might use them in unfriendly ways. When such information has leaked out, some Wiccans have been barraged with phone calls and witnessing by well-meaning Christians who want to save them. People have also received hate mail and other more unsettling communications. Especially when communicating by e-mail, in a chat room, or on the Internet, it is vital that names or handles not be associated with telephone numbers or addresses or mundane names.

ETHICS

Ethics are very important in Wicca, because of the personal responsibility each Wiccan is expected to hold. Each person must form their own ethical belief system and do their best to adhere to it. The Wiccan Rede, Law of Three, and Golden Rule help set some guidelines, but as the modern world is full of compromises and contradictions, each person must think actively about which compromises and contradictions are acceptable and which are not. Ethics can change, evolve, and grow over time. Other religions have a ready-made ethical code and rules which adherents are expected to abide by, though the interpretations may differ from sect to sect. Wiccans, on the other hand, have few. Each Wiccan builds their own. In practice there are many areas where most Wiccans tend to agree. The active exploration of ethics and values is ongoing throughout a Wiccan's life. It is an integral part of the Great Work which results in self-betterment.

CONFIDENTIALITY

Confidentiality is a crucial ethical principle among Wiccans. Our religion stresses secrecy as a safety measure, for in the past witches were persecuted and occasionally put to death for their beliefs and practices. This happens even occasionally today, though to a much lesser degree. Confidentiality means never exposing another Wiccan's identity or affiliation to anyone.

Confidentiality also is important for keeping Craft secrets, to ensure that certain practices and techniques do not fall into untrained, unprepared hands.

Most Traditions have oaths of secrecy, which initiates must swear to: keep the secrets within the group; and not reveal the identities of one's coven-mates, where and when the coven meets, and the like. Most Wiccans are not Out, preferring to keep their religion a personal, private matter. There are real, frequently justified fears that a person's Wiccan affiliation could cost them their job, home, friendships, marriage, children, or other important real-world possessions or affiliations. Because of this, Wiccans tend to view themselves as a persecuted minority. Certainly some Christian sects would like to convert all witches to their brand of Christianity, and generally there is still a great deal of misunderstanding and many misconceptions about Wicca, Wiccans, and witches.

In an attempt to counteract some of this perceived persecution, some Wiccans readily adopt the term "witch" to describe themselves. Others take longer to adopt the "w" word. A few never adopt it. The word "witch" has certain connotations in this culture that Wiccans are trying to overcome and dispel. To this end, a few Wiccans have taken an "in-your-face" attitude with respect to being a witch and practicing Wicca. But most Wiccans are just plain people who have a home, job, spouse, and kids and also happen to be Wiccan.

With the persecuted minority issue comes the issue of teaching minors about the Craft. Most Wiccan training groups will not accept people under eighteen, because the teachers fear prosecution by an irate parent, grandparent, or school-teacher. Those who *will* teach minors usually require a parental consent form. Wiccans who have minor children may teach them about the Craft, but they are also careful to make sure that their children will not casually talk about what they are learning. Well-meaning schoolteachers have tried (and occasionally succeeded) to get children taken away from parents, believing the parent was teaching the children about demon worship. In some areas of the country, parents may choose to keep their religious interests secret even from their children until the children are old enough to understand and abide by the secrecy, which may be necessary. Each family makes these decisions for itself, and Wiccans respect the decisions each family makes.

The perception of being a persecuted minority, and the threat of exposure, can make some Wiccans paranoid. The average Wiccan is highly cautious about discussing with non-Pagans matters pertaining to the Craft and will think carefully before opening up to persons who might not be fully aware of what Wicca is. Some people carry this caution to extremes, never breathing a word about Wicca to anyone except within their own coven. When asked what they did the previous night, most practitioners will not answer, "We celebrated Samhain." They might say instead, "I was at a church function" or "I was at a party with a few close friends" or "I was at a family gathering." All of which is true, of course, depending upon your perspective. Being low-key about their beliefs is the way most Wiccans operate if they are not Out.

Wiccan Culture

THE IDEALS AND VALUES THAT WICCANS PURSUE at times run directly counter to the consumer-oriented, keeping-up-with-the-Joneses, more-is-good, progress-is-desirable, we-own-the-Earth mindsets of the mainstream culture. "Renew, reuse, recycle" is a mantra understood and practiced by most Wiccans. The pursuit of riches for its own sake is considered illogical, though most Wiccans have a regular nine-to-five real world job to pay the bills and provide the resources to practice their chosen lifestyle. Many Wiccans would happily do Wicca full-time if they could manage it, even if the money was less, for they would be doing what makes them happy. While there are a number of Wiccans who have managed to go back to the land and are working toward self-sufficiency, most Wiccans are suburban Pagans. They try to honor and work within the Cycle of the Seasons rather than try to dominate or conquer the natural cycles. Most of the average things which "push the buttons" of people today hold little fascination for Wiccans. Wiccans tend to socialize together and stay within their own groups simply because they all share similar values and mindsets. Mundane is the term used to describe things or people non-Wiccan or non-Pagan, and for those in the culture of Wicca the term is very specific. This gives the impression to outsiders that Wiccans are cliquish or elitist or even closed, but this isn't necessarily so. Rather, Wiccans have a specific culture they want to pursue without outside interference. Once a new person passes the initial screening to guarantee similar interests and mindset, they are usually welcomed with open arms into the fold.

COMMON VALUES

Respect for the Earth Mother

Ecology, recycling, walking gently on the Earth, and trying to reuse, renew, and recycle are all widely adopted practices. Self-sufficiency is an ideal, but few attain it. Generally, Wiccans do what they can in their own way to contribute to making the world a better place than before they came along. At festivals, Pagans and Wiccans regularly clean up and cheerfully remove whatever was left behind by the previous group. The site is usually in better shape afterward (although at home most Wiccans are notoriously sloppy housekeepers). Wiccans believe that we do not own the Earth, nor are we the masters of the Earth, nor was the Earth given us to use, exploit, or destroy as we want. This is our home, and we live here, but nobody can really own the Earth or any part of it. That notion of ownership of land is just a societal convention. Wiccans believe that we are stewards of the Earth and will work to keep it clean and well-managed and as unspoiled as possible. This can range from participating in a Save-the-Rainforests campaign; to choosing not to have a conventional yard, but rather to let natural animals and plants be in the space; to composting and not using chemical fertilizers or pesticides; to not building a new home but rather renovating an existing home; to refusing to use certain products or support certain industries which pollute or exploit the Earth and/or its peoples. There is a strong respect for life—all life, not just human life or the life of certain privileged humans. But quality of life is also honored. Most Wiccans are strongly pro-choice, and that includes the absolute right to choose to *not* have an abortion as well as have one, if that is the option that causes the least harm.

Wicca is a nature-oriented religion, so Wiccans are aware of the seasons and how the world changes as the years progress. There is a simultaneous understanding of the endless Cycle of the Seasons, and yet also the uniqueness of each day as it comes and goes. There is also some mindfulness of the longer cycles of time, and how what we do today has an impact upon what others may or may not be able to do tomorrow or decades or centuries from now.

Equality

Belief in the equality of the sexes and races is fairly universal among Wiccans. Some groups may choose to be open to only one sex or those practicing a certain lifestyle choice, but that does not mean others are denigrated. It just means that this group is working on that particular path. People are generally taken as they are and are not judged by their skin color, size, ability, background, or education. Sexual preference is a matter for personal choice, and as long as a person harms no one, s/he is free to practice with other consenting adults. Violence is not tolerated, and abuse is considered something to be eliminated from all families and other groups. Children are valued and encouraged to be as free as possible to learn and grow within the guidelines of a loving family structure, whatever that may be.

Education

Education, reading, and general intellectual pursuits are valued highly. Festivals and gatherings strongly emphasize teaching and workshops. Wiccan training includes reading, discussion, experiential learning, and research. The average Wiccan reads numerous books a month, usually several books at a time. Many Wiccans are either actively writing a book, or have ideas for several books they are planning to get to when they have the time. Authors are often featured guests at festivals and gatherings. As Wicca has been primarily spread through the printed word over the decades since its revival, this obsession with books, education, reading, and learning is understandable. Formal education is considered nice, but there is little intellectual snobbery. Being self-taught is as valid as a university degree, provided you know your stuff. With all this emphasis on reading, there is relatively little time for TV or other popular cultural pursuits. However, having a computer is becoming more and more important, as is being hooked up to the Internet. There has been no concrete survey, but some authors estimate that sixty to seventy percent of all Wiccans are currently on the Internet.

The proliferation of Web sites dedicated to Pagan and Wiccan topics attests to this. The drawback is that being on the Internet will take up as much time as you are willing to give it, and can become an empty pursuit, if not carefully monitored.

GROUP ORGANIZATION

Wiccans are usually proud and frequently vocal about being anarchistic and anti-hierarchical. While you can argue that the term "organized Wicca" may be somewhat of an oxymoron, Wiccans, like all human beings, have developed their own systems of organization, hierarchies, and pecking orders. Though most non-Wiccans may find our organizations unfamiliar and possibly confusing, the systems that we work with are pretty simple.

The Coven

The coven is the basic small-group structure of Wicca. As a religion, there are certainly larger, organized Wiccan "churches" with even hundreds of people in rare instances, but most Wiccans still meet and interact within their own covens at home. A coven is a group of Wiccan people who have come together to work magick and to study Wicca and other related things. In many ways a coven can be likened to a Bible study group. People meet, usually at a private home, to read materials and discuss and study Wicca as a religion and as a life path.

Traditionally, it is said, a coven always contained thirteen members, but modern covens can be as large or as small as the members want. The internal hierarchy, rules, and operations of a coven are strictly up to its members. Covens are formed for many reasons. Teaching or training covens train new people. Working covens are groups of Initiates who meet to work magick and study Wicca and related topics. Covens can also be subsets of various denominations of Wicca; a "Gardnerian Coven" would be a local branch of a larger lineage of Gardnerian Wicca.

The modern Wiccan coven usually consists of three to ten people who meet weekly, though this can vary widely. Traditionally, a High Priestess and a High Priest are the leaders of the coven, although this is not mandatory. If a person is lucky enough to be able to join a working coven as a student, they will probably receive training and get a wonderful Wiccan education. Many covens have been started by a few friends who have read about Wicca and, finding no one who could teach them, have decided to get together and do things on their own. Thirteen was traditionally the maximum membership of a coven, because thirteen people are few enough to interact easily on a personal level and yet factions remain a large enough percentage of the group to make secret activities very difficult. Also, getting many more people together requires renting a hall, as most living rooms are pretty crowded even with thirteen people.

A document detailing the rules and regulations of being a member and running the coven may be drawn up. This document is known as a covenant. A covenant can be as simple as one or two lines, or it can be as elaborate as the United States Constitution. Generally, only long-running, well-established covens require a written covenant; verbal discussions are the standard. The group does need to make a few joint decisions, though, such as:

- What are the purposes and goals of our meetings? (teaching, working, research, magickal, etc.)

- Are we going to be an Eclectic group, or tied to a certain Tradition?

- Is our membership closed or open?

There are also decisions to be made regarding internal organization:

- Will there be a specific High Priestess (HPS) and High Priest (HP) in charge?

- Will new members be admitted by majority vote? (Is blackballing allowed?)

- Is the coven to be secret or open?

- When and how often will the group meet?

- Will the coven have a group altar, Sacred Space, temple, tools, books, and the like?

- Where will the group meet?

The place that the coven most commonly meets is traditionally called the covenstead, usually a private home (but not necessarily that of the HPS or HP). Frequently it is the place with the most room, or where the group can keep their stuff.

Sometimes Wiccans start meeting, and only after a time realize they are actually a coven. Sometimes the organizational discussions come only after problems develop within the group.

Creating New Covens

Interpersonal conflicts occur among Wiccans just as they do with everyone else. Conflict is a part of human interaction. A Wiccan tradition called hiving off allows for disaffected people in a coven to leave and start their own new independent coven. There are many reasons for a new coven to hive off:

- The original coven gets too big.

- People move away and are unable to continue meeting with the original coven.

- People become dissatisfied and leave.

- People are asked to leave a coven and go off and start their own.

- People may want to try something new and different, and the old coven is just not interested in changing.

As you can see, hiving off is a mechanism for allowing disagreement without having it turn into acrimony or hard feelings. But the tradition is that once a coven had hived off of a parent coven, the daughter coven is independent and there is usually no mixing of memberships. Generally, you must choose one coven over the other. This also varies from Tradition to Tradition. There is, for instance, in some Traditions the custom of the "Witch Queen," in which the High Priestess of the parent coven is recognized as sort of a "senior" High Priestess by the High Priestesses of any daughter covens. This custom sometimes helps when there are intercoven disputes.

Wiccan tradition states that a person can only belong to one coven at a time. This is to prevent divided loyalties, but also to prevent group hopping. This may seem restrictive, and some Wiccans have modified the rule to mean one coven of a type. In other words, a person may head up a teaching coven, and be a member of a separate working coven as well. Or one might be a member of a coven that puts on regular large-group rituals and a more secretive Ceremonial Magick coven as well. In this case, covens become more like small organizations than tightly knit groups of compatriots. Most of the long-established Wiccan Traditions have their own specific rules regarding coven membership.

Like Wicca itself, your coven becomes what you make of it. As an example, the authors are members of a small, highly eclectic, and anti-hierarchical working coven. Who is in charge depends upon who is leading the unit at the time. Whoever is doing the Sabbat is in charge for that Sabbat. Additionally, Estelle is co-head of a separate teaching coven, which meets for a year-and-a-day, providing a Wiccan First Degree Initiation. Paul participates as a guest speaker on occasion.

Paul is a member of a national-level Wiccan coven that helps provide security at festivals and gatherings throughout the United States. Estelle is not a member of this group, though she has helped out on occasion. Both Estelle and Paul are members of a local Wiccan church with tax-exempt status, and both hold ministerial credentials through that church. Estelle considers herself a member of two covens (the working group and the teaching group), but as each has different purposes, she sees no conflict between the two. Paul is officially a member of only one coven (the security group), though he is active in several other Wiccan groups. The Wiccan church they belong to is not a coven (it says so in its bylaws), though it provides an umbrella structure for members to receive federal recognition and protection for their separate covens if they wish.

There are very few hard-and-fast rules. A coven is what you make of it, and it grows and evolves and changes over time. Some covens are reputed to have been in existence for centuries. Some can be documented for several decades. Some, like Estelle's teaching coven, are meant to exist for only a specific period.

Traditions or Lineages

A "Tradition" or "lineage" is a group of covens in which all trace their descent from a single group or person, and follow basically the same tenets and teachings and practices. How large any specific Tradition might be varies widely. There are estimates of about 20,000 Gardnerians throughout the world. Other Traditions may be no larger than a single coven.

Traditions spread in various ways. They can grow through the hiving off process. Or people might come to a certain place, or covenstead, to get the training and carry the teaching back to their homes. Some Traditions derive from other Traditions (Seax Wicca, for example, is an offshoot of Gardnerian Wicca). Some derive from older Fam-Trads and have been modified and changed so outsiders may enter. The original Fam-Trad may still exist, but the derivation has grown well beyond the original. A Tradition may be created by a person publishing a book (like Starhawkian Wicca) and grow as more people read the book and adopt that way of doing things.

Churches and Clergy

Actual Wiccan churches do exist. There are a number, in several states, which have organized and gone to the trouble of gaining state and/or federal recognition and tax-exempt status. These groups are usually small (under fifty people) and rarely own land or buildings. Even tax-exempt groups for the most part meet in people's homes. Some groups rent space for Sabbats and other large celebrations, but the bulk of group business is conducted in homes. These churches are usually loose groups of people and may or may not be of one single Tradition. Others are umbrella organizations, which allow members to practice as they choose yet gain state and federal recognition and status. Most Wiccan churches hold Sabbats in a regular place. Individual members are encouraged to hold Sabbats in their own covens as well.

Once registered, these groups can ordain ministers who are empowered to perform weddings and generally enjoy the rights and privileges of any other recognized clergy. It is becoming increasingly important to Wiccans to have their own clergy legally perform weddings, officiate at the namings of children (similar to a Christian christening), minister to Wiccans in prison and in hospitals, conduct memorial services, and provide all the other services and support that clergy offer.

Though many people hold ministerial credentials through a Wiccan church or other organization—the Universal Life Church and the Unitarians are also popular—there are few if any paid clergy within Wicca in the United States today. Due to the nature of the religion and the structure of Wicca, it is rare for a congregation of Wiccans to be sizable enough to support full-time professional clergy. Wicca resembles the Quakers, the Jehovah's Witnesses, the Mormons, and many other Christian denominations, all of which survive well without a professional clerical body.

Ordained Wiccan ministers usually offer their services in the context of their everyday lives, which generally includes a regular job. The ratio of registered ministers to parishioners in Wicca may be higher than in the mainstream Christian population. Each coven may not have a minister, but generally there is at least one Wiccan clergy person in any sizable city throughout most of the United States.

Wiccan ministers are popular among people who are spiritual, but do not belong to a specific church or ascribe to a specific faith or creed. Paul has conducted more weddings for non-Wiccans than for Wiccans. The clergy of most mainstream faiths require people to be members of their church, or at least to be of a compatible faith, to marry them. Wicca, on the other hand, is a religion that has little set faith or dogma, so there is less conflict with differing beliefs. And because of the diversity of beliefs within Wicca, most Wiccan clergy are able to operate in many different creeds and work with differing ceremonial structures and formats, according to who is being served. This is not a special part of Wiccan clerical training, it is just a natural expression of the way Wicca is.

Other Organizations

Because of the structure of Wicca—based on small groups, generally the size of an extended family, possibly linked by ties and/or Tradition—Wicca is more like a network or a web than a congregation or a community. Wiccans have friends who are Wiccan, and they might socialize together and even possibly meet at open Sabbats in a particular area, but there are few, if any, larger organizations of Wiccans anywhere. Groups that have members nationwide are still usually based on the coven model and operate as a loose confederation of local covens. There may or may not be an annual meeting of members or representatives. It is quite common to have Wiccan friends you see regularly at festivals and yet not know their mailing address, full legal name, where they live, what they do for a living, or even their phone number. Most Wiccans use Craft names within Wicca; that is, they choose a name for themselves. It is quite common to have Wiccan friends whom you know well, but only by their Craft names, and whom you have no idea how to contact outside a festival.

FESTIVALS (GATHERINGS)

At festivals and gatherings, Wiccans from all over meet, share teaching and ideas, and celebrate being Wiccan. Festivals started out as a sort of Wiccan version of church camp. People would gather at an outdoor site, camp, and hang out together for a weekend or a week. As the years have gone by, outdoor festivals still thrive, but nowadays there are almost as many indoor festivals. These resemble conventions or trade shows.

Festivals have become the Pagan melting pot in the United States. At a festival you can meet Gardnerians, Dianics, and all sorts of Wiccans in between, as well as people of many other Pagan paths. This was the first venue at which people of different Wiccan Traditions could meet and talk and get a chance to see how the others did it. Many Pagans plan their vacations around these festivals, which now take place year-round.

All festivals are heavily education-oriented. The standard festival, whether it is a weekend or week-long (or longer), starts with some sort of opening ritual followed by many workshops, lectures, and demonstrations. Authors come to talk about and sell their books. People vie for the privilege of hosting an evening group ritual and help with the staffing duties that allow the festival to run smoothly. People specialize in safety, gatekeeping, cooking, administration, first aid, psychological centering, childcare, or other necessary duties. Typically, there are three to five or more workshop periods in a festival day with a break for lunch, and then some sort of communal supper followed by an evening ritual or entertainment. Drumming and dancing carry well into the night, and the whole process starts again the next morning.

Most festivals are family-oriented, and children are welcome. The festival is the time to catch up with friends, meet new people, trade stories and tips, and generally relax in a very Pagan-friendly atmosphere. And because some of the same people return year after year, most festivals have evolved their own individualistic styles, with almost a life and identity of their own. One might be mainly focused on partying, while another is more concerned with exploring certain specific issues.

At most typical festivals something known as "Pagan Space" is created. This is a community gestalt which arises out of many Pagans living together and interacting without outsiders present. Most Pagans never experience such a feeling except at a festival. For once, we are not a minority. The atmosphere is relaxed and people can speak freely about almost any topic of interest and find willing participants to converse with.

Many outdoor festivals are clothing optional, or at least have an area where one can go without clothing if desired. For Pagans, nudity is just another clothing option, not exhibitionistic or prurient in nature.

Nudity is an issue for Wiccans because it touches upon so many cultural paradigms that Wiccans want to change. The issue of the best, proper, or correct body shape, size, color, or type is laid to rest when all are nude and it can be observed there is nobody with a perfect body. Clothing as a mark of status and wealth is eliminated when all are nude. Nudity can also be a way of breaking down personal inhibitions, not as a prelude to sex, but as a lowering of defensive barriers in a creation of a group mind, preparatory to doing magick. Clothing can interfere with magickal energy, and almost all Wiccan Initiations are performed with the Initiate nude. Partial or nearly total nudity has been a clothing norm in many societies, past and present, and most of those societies were Pagan. One of the first things the Christian missionaries did to the "primitive" tribespeople they converted was to make them wear clothing. So having nudity as another clothing option can be another way Wiccans have of consciously changing the Christian mind-sets they may have been raised with. How one reacts to nudity can also be a way in which Wiccans tell who is "one of us" and who is not.

Festivals also usually include a "Merchant's Row," an area where people set up their wares for sale to the participants. Most Wiccans do their holiday and ritual tool shopping here, no matter what time of the year the festival takes place. The merchants display a great assortment of wares, from handmade to commercial, but all of interest to the average Wiccan.

The festivals and gatherings are the closest you can get to an actual Wiccan Community.

THE INTERNET

Internet communication is fast becoming popular within Wicca. The Internet lends itself readily to Wiccan communication, and many Wiccans are comfortable working in "virtual reality." If a person is a solitaire (that is, practicing Wicca by themselves or with only a couple of close friends), the Internet can be their only contact with the wider Wiccan Community outside of books. And virtual reality is the only real-world construct where mundanes (non-Wiccans) can experience the "time without a time and a place without a place" phenomenon, which is created while in a Circle. All you need to know is an e-mail address and you are in touch with whomever. You can hold conversations in real time in chat rooms. There are many Wiccan/Pagan chat rooms, usually under the larger category of alt.religion, either Wiccan or Pagan. More commonly, people just leave messages and have a conversation over days and weeks, each person reading and replying at leisure. People can easily retain their anonymity and speak as freely as they want, but it is wise to follow the conventions of polite communication.

Also remember that Internet communication, though it feels like conversation, is still written and therefore possibly permanent. People have gone off on certain topics without either reviewing or thinking twice about what they are saying, or the way they are saying it, and these ideas and expressions have returned at a later date to haunt them. It is wise to err on the side of being polite and circumspect.

Privacy on the Internet is an important issue. Internet communication uses handles, and one should be careful not to have names or addresses or phone numbers associated with handles. People unfriendly to Wicca have been known to intercept such information and use it to either proselytize or intimidate. Keep in mind most Internet communications are not confidential; you should be able to anticipate problems before they happen.

The Wheel of the Year

There are eight major Wiccan holidays that make up the Wheel of the Year. These eight Sabbats or Solar holy days occur at roughly six-and-a-half-week intervals throughout the calendar year. They have evolved from several Traditions. They are seasonal, and reflect the growing cycle in both agrarian and hunting societies. Mythologically, they represent the yearly cycle of the Maiden, Mother, and Crone of the Goddess, and the birth, marriage, maturation, and death of the God.

The New and Full Moons—twelve or thirteen of each during the year—are the Esbats or Lunar holy days. A Wiccan can also worship every week, though there is no standard day of the week set aside for worship.

THE SABBATS

Samhain, October 31 or November 1 (also called Halloween, All Hallows Eve, Hallowmass, Day of the Dead). Samhain (pronounced *sow-enn*) has come to be known as the "Witches' New Year," so we will start with Samhain, though the wheel is cyclical and ever turning, without a definitive start-ing point. This holiday is one of the most impor-tant and revered in the Wiccan calendar. In an agrarian society, this is the time of year (depending on the local climate) when farmers culled the herds, slaughtering the excess livestock and saving the best breeding stock. It is therefore occasionally also called the Blood Harvest. The grain harvest was in, and farmers were able to accurately assess how many animals they could reasonably feed through the winter. They also knew how many people they could feed. The frost had come and winter was coming, so the meat would stay fresh longer in nature's "refrigerator." In hunting societies, the "Wild Hunt" was abroad, and the tribe was more dependent upon their hunters for food, as the plants were becoming dormant for the winter.

This holiday marks the time when the souls of all who have died throughout the year pass over to the other side, and all the souls of those who will be born in the next year come into our world. Celebrations are oriented toward mourning and letting go of those who have died, especially those who have died in the past year. There is also a gen-eral remembrance of one's ancestors, with the telling of the family stories, personal histories, and coven lore. This is the time of the year when "the veil between the worlds is thinnest." Magick can be very strong and extremely effective.

A common practice at Samhain is the "dumb supper." This is a meal that is shared with those who have gone before. An extra plate is set and filled with food for those who are no longer with us. After the meal, this food is usually set outside for whatever creatures happen along; Wiccans try not to waste. This dumb supper is a meal when nobody speaks; the time instead is used to reflect upon those who have gone before. Traditionally, "dumb" referred to those who could not speak (i.e., your ancestors), not the silent diners at the meal. But as Wicca is an evolving religion, this silent meal has come to have modern interpretation of this tradition. The Samhain feast may frequently consist of the root crops, also the last fruits of the harvest, as well as many meat and game dishes. Some Wiccans eat meat only at Samhain.

Mythologically, this holiday is when the Goddess mourns her slain consort, the God, and she contemplates the coming birth of her child by him. The Goddess is also honored in her Crone aspect. This holiday also mythically celebrates the death of the God, as he lays down his life for the community, or as the God of the Wild Hunt, symbolizing the animals hunted for food.

Yule, December 21st (also called Winter Solstice). Yule is the holiday which was transmuted into Christmas (Christ's actual birth has variously been calculated to have been in the springtime, nearer the Spring Equinox or in March). This is the time of the year when winter is full upon the land. It is a time of leisure, storytelling, and sharing skills and traditions. It is the longest night, and Wiccan traditions include burning the Yule log, which is lit before the Sun goes down and tended all night until the Sun comes up the next morning. Many Wiccan groups meet and greet the Sunrise after this longest night. Yule trees are a Pagan tradition and are decorated each year. The Yule feast includes many of the traditional "Christmas foods," including cookies and candy and hearty roasts or stews. Presents are exchanged over the days starting at Yule and continuing through Twelfth Night (January 6th). Twelfth Night is also an official Christian Holiday, also known as "Little Christmas," which started in the Middle Ages and falls on the twelfth day after Christmas. Some Wiccans celebrate Twelfth Night, and keep the traditional Christian date of January 6th. It gives us a few more days to catch up on the sales.

Mythologically, the Goddess gives birth to the Sun God on the longest night, and Wiccans celebrate the birth (or rebirth) of the Sun God. Some Wiccan groups have Mother Bertha come and pass out presents. Mother Bertha is a Crone who gives presents, and sometimes steals children, if they are bad. Some Traditions see this as a God day in the middle of the Goddess (dark) time of the year.

Candlemas, February 1st or 2nd [also called Imbolc, Immilch, Brigid's Day or Bride (pronounced *breed*)]. Candlemas is the time when winter is still on the land, but spring is coming. In earlier agricultural societies, this was the break point; you either had enough food to last until the first spring plants came up, or you didn't. If you did, it was a time to celebrate. If you didn't, it was still a time to have a party with what was left, so not to prolong the starvation. It is also the time when it is readily apparent that the days are lengthening, and the time of the long, dark nights is ending. It is also usually the coldest time of the year, so survival is a big issue, even with the coming of spring. Wiccans celebrate with a bonfire and a blessing of the tools. In some agrarian societies, it was the time when the planting and plowing tools were brought out and readied for the planting in the spring. It was called Brigid's Day, because Brigid is a Goddess of the forge, and she would bless their tools. Nowadays, Wiccans use a number of tools, and the blessing of the tools brings a fertility of ideas as well as fertility of the soil. In other societies (depending on location), this was the time of the birth of the new lambs, thus it is called Immilch or the time of new milk.

Mythologically, the Goddess has recovered from the birth of her child, and the child has lived and gotten strong so he will survive. Imbolc can also be a time of Dedication and Initiation. Some see this as the time when the Goddess is renewed as Maiden after the birth of her child.

Oestarra, March 21st (also known as Spring Equinox, Eostre). Oestarra is one of the two holidays that may or may not be celebrated by Wiccans. Some Traditions do not celebrate Oestarra or Mabon. This holiday may or may not correspond with spring, depending upon where you live. It is a time to celebrate spring (or the coming of spring) and fertility and get things ready for the coming growing season. In most places there has been a significant thaw, and even if there is still snow, it is becoming obvious that winter will end soon. Wiccans celebrate with painting eggs and celebrating fertility. It is a day of balance, when day and night are of equal length.

Mythologically, some Traditions celebrate the change from the Goddess half or dark half of the year to the God half or light half. If it is spring, a feast of asparagus, new greens, and other spring plants is appropriate. The Goddess has changed from Crone to Maiden, and she is a young girl ready to grow with her son/consort as the year grows. The Sun God is growing fast and is a vital and healthy child.

Beltane, April 30 or May 1 (also known as May Eve, Walpurgisnacht, Bealtain.) Beltane is the second biggest holiday in the Wiccan calendar. It is a fertility festival.

Mythologically, the Goddess and God achieve puberty and become sexually aware. Beltane celebrates their wedding, and the Goddess—in mating with the God—changes from Maiden to Mother. It is also the time of spring and the planting of the crops. Animals come into season and mate. In agricultural societies, the fields were blessed and occasionally couples went out into the fields and made love to help renew the fertility of the soil. In hunting societies the emphasis changed from hunting to gathering as the main source of food for the group.

Wiccans frequently celebrate with a feast of spring plants, asparagus, new greens, and other early plants. Usually fresh flowers are brought to celebrate the new growing season. There can be a Beltane Lottery, by which a "May Queen" and "Green Man" are chosen, and they become the living representatives of the Goddess and God for the community. People serve as May Queen and Green Man sometimes for the day, sometimes for longer, depending upon the group's traditions and customs. In some groups these people act as spiritual advisors for the time they serve. They may prophesy for group members. They might give guidance to the group as a whole or to individuals. This office is considered sacred and usually is open to Initiates only. May baskets may be exchanged with wishes for fertility and a prosperous summer. Beltane is a happy time; spring is here, summer is coming, and we all can see the abundance and gifts of the Goddess and God. The outdoor festival season unofficially starts.

Midsummer, June 21st (also known as Litha or Summer Solstice) is the longest day of the year. The crops and gardens are planted. We are starting to get the first fruits of our plantings. Life is easy and good. Days are warm and long, and winter is only a memory.

Mythologically, the Goddess is pregnant by the God, and her belly swells with new life. In farming societies this was the time for celebration between planting and harvest. In hunting societies, the hunters made new weapons and traveled to get the supplies they needed for successful hunting in the winter.

This is the prime time for vacations and festivals. Wiccans celebrate with a feast of strawberries and other fruits and greens. It is a time to get together, visit, and relax. It is the longest day, but we are also aware that now the nights get longer, and that winter will come again. Some Traditions consider this to be a Goddess day in the middle of the God time of the year. The Goddess as Mother is in her glory.

Lughnasadh, August 1st (also known as Lammas). Lughnasadh is the celebration of the first harvest and the first fruits of the harvest. A big feast is part of the sacred rites, often with a corn dolly or other homemade breads. The summer fruits are ripening and our gardens are yielding many wonderful things. The days are getting shorter, and we are very aware that winter will come.

Mythologically, some Traditions see this as the time of the death of the God, a willing sacrifice to allow the community to continue. Though the God may die, the Goddess is with child and the family will continue. A feast of grains, fruits, and vegetables is celebrated. In locations where this is the time of the main grain harvest, the God is in his guise as John Barleycorn, the Grain God. In hunting societies, the boys were initiated into the mysteries of hunting at this time of the year, and they prepared to take part in the hunting over the winter to come. There were contests and games designed to test and improve hunting skills. Therefore, some groups also hold Lughnasadh games, contests of athletics for the young to show their prowess and for the old to enjoy their skill and cunning. Other Traditions see this time as the God's time when he can display his prowess and strength for all to admire.

Mabon, September 21st (also known as Autumnal Equinox). Mabon is the other day of balance, of equal length of day and night. It can symbolize the change from the God or light time of the year to the Goddess or dark time of the year. This is the time of the grain harvest in some areas, and so the death of the God can be celebrated at this Sabbat as well. This is also the period of highest energy within the animal kingdom, as many wild species come into rut, while others are busy preparing for their winter hibernations.

Mythologically, the death of the God is a willing sacrifice, the God in his prime who willingly lays down his life so his people may live and grow. In hunting societies, with plants dying and gathering ending, hunting began in earnest.

Wiccans celebrate with a feast of grains, fruits, and vegetables, especially the first apples. This is also the time of the main harvest, and Wiccans will offer the first and best fruits to the Gods as thanks for the fertility that they have granted to their people. The harvest is celebrated and the abundance is stored for the coming winter. The Goddess is pregnant, yet also a widow.

The next Sabbat is Samhain, and so the wheel has turned yet again. Wiccans see the year as a cycle, ever-changing and never-ending. Sometimes celebrating the Sabbats is referred to as "Turning the Wheel," implying the seasons will only progress if we help the cycle along. There are several cycles represented in the year:

• the Goddess/God cycle (light and dark times);
• the cycle of Goddess as she progresses from

Maiden to Mother to Crone and through renewal/rebirth bath to Maiden;

- the cycle of the life of the God from birth through marriage and maturity to death and rebirth;
- the cycle of the growing year;
- the cycle of the hunting/gathering year.

Different Traditions honor different cycles. And the seasons are different in various parts of the country. So Wiccans change and adapt the Sabbats to their needs as they see fit in their lives and localities.

THE ESBATS

The Lunar cycle gives rise to the Esbats, celebrations that are based on the Lunar month. Esbats are seen as mainly Goddess-oriented. The New Moon symbolizes the Maiden, and as she waxes, she changes from Maiden to Mother. At Full Moon the Goddess is at her greatest power and fertility. Sometimes the Full Moon symbolizes the pregnant Goddess. As the Moon wanes, the Goddess changes from Mother to Crone until she "dies" (or goes into seclusion) each month at the Dark of the Moon (the Moon's Fourth Face) and is reborn as Maiden when the Moon is New again. This Lunar cycle is also seen as a celebration of a woman's menstrual cycle, with the time of actual menstruation the time of the Dark of the Moon when she goes into seclusion. Wiccans may celebrate Esbats at Full Moons only, at both New and Full Moons, or at each quarter, roughly every seven days. In feminist Dianic Wiccan groups, Esbats are more important than the Sabbats.

The Full Moon is the time for the ceremony known as "Drawing Down the Moon" into the High Priestess. This is a rite in which the Goddess is made manifest in her Priestess, and the Priestess may prophesy, offer advice, and/or give counsel to her coven members. "The Charge of the Goddess" (see below) refers to the Full Moon ceremony and is possibly the one document that is common to most Wiccan groups. The original version and inspiration comes from the book *The Golden Ass* by Apuliaus and also *Aradia*. Doreen Valiente rewrote and expanded it. Gardner claimed to have discovered it. Whatever the history of the Charge, it is a beautiful expression of the faith and practice of Wicca.

The Charge of the Goddess

Listen to the words of the Great Mother, who of old was also called Artemis, Astarte, Athena, Diana, Melusine, Aphrodite, Cerridwen, Dana, Arianrhod, Isis, Brid, and many other names:

Whenever ye have need of any thing, once in the month, and better it be when the Moon is full, then shall ye assemble in some secret place and adore the spirit of Me Who am Queen of all Witches. There shall ye assemble, ye who are fain to learn all sorcery, yet have not won its deepest secrets; to these I will teach things that are yet unknown.

And ye shall be free from slavery, and as a sign that ye be really free, ye shall be naked in your rites; and ye shall dance, sing, feast, make music and love, all in My praise. For Mine is the ecstasy of the spirit and Mine also is joy on earth. For My Law is Love unto all beings. Keep pure your highest ideal; strive ever towards it; let naught stop you or turn you aside. For Mine is the secret door that opens upon the land of youth, and Mine is the cup of the wine of Life, and the cauldron of Cerridwen that is the holy grail of immortality. I am the gracious Goddess, who gives the gift of joy unto all hearts.

Upon Earth, I give the knowledge of the spirit eternal; and beyond death I give peace and freedom and reunion with those who have gone before. Nor do I demand aught of sacrifice, for behold, I am the Mother of all things and My Love is poured out upon the Earth.

Hear ye the words of the Star Goddess, she in the dust of Whose Feet are the Hosts of Heaven, and whose body encircles the Universe:

I Who am the beauty of the green Earth and the white Moon among the stars and the Mysteries of the waters, and the desire of all hearts, call unto thy soul. Arise and come unto Me. For I am the soul of nature who gives life to the Universe. From Me all things proceed, and unto Me all things must return; and before my face, beloved of Gods and of men, let thine innermost divine self be enfolded in the rapture of the infinite.

Let My worship be within the heart that rejoices, for behold, all acts of Love and pleasure are My rituals. And therefore let there be beauty and strength, power and compassion, honor and humility, mirth and reverence within you.

And thou who thinkest to seek for Me, know thy seeking and yearning shall avail thee not, unless thou knowest the Mystery: for if that which thou seekest, thou findest not within, then thou shall never find it without. For behold, I have been with thee from the beginning, and I am that which is attained at the end of desire.

How each group or Tradition celebrates the Sabbats and Esbats is a matter of the consensus and interest of its members. In general, Wiccans seem to be celebrating the Sabbats more regularly than the Esbats.

RITES OF PASSAGE

*I*N CREATING A RELIGION, WICCANS HAVE ADDRESSED the various "rites of passage" experienced by all people throughout their lives. This is an area where Wicca is still evolving, and practices vary widely from group to group and Tradition to Tradition.

WICCANINGS (NAMINGS)

"Wiccaning" or "Naming" is the term used to describe the celebration which accompanies the birth of a child. As Wicca is nominally a fertility religion, the birth of a child is seen as a gift from the Gods and a sacred rite in itself. Once the child is born, and the life of the family has settled down a bit, the parents and community celebrate the Wiccaning of the child, the act of introducing the child to the Gods and to the community, and asking the Goddess and God and community for their protection of the child as they grow. It is not a sealing of the child into Wicca. Wicca is a religion of choice, and where children may be placed under the protection of the Gods, the child is allowed to choose their religious path when old enough to make that decision. Wiccanings can take place immediately after birth or up to a year or more later. There is no set time frame.

COMING-OF-AGE

Celebrations of puberty are also Wiccan rites of passage. Especially in the feminist groups, when a girl has her first menstrual period, she is considered a woman. Many groups have the women gather for a party or celebration to honor the girl and also let her know the responsibilities of sexual maturity. Wiccans are very much choice-oriented. This includes the choice to not be sexually active, the choice not to have an abortion, to responsibly use contraceptives, and to understand the implications of being a sexual person. Just because Wicca is a fertility religion, it does not mean Wiccans engage in free sex. Quite the opposite. Personal responsibility and informed choice extends into the area of sexual activity just as much as any other area of life.

With boys, the timing of celebrating sexual maturity is less defined. It can be at the time of a boy's first wet dream, of the appearance of secondary sexual characteristics like beard and pubic hair, of his conscious assuming the responsibilities of a man. The tradition of celebrating a boy's sexual maturity is less universal and not as formalized. The gay men's movement currently seems to be doing the most with writing and holding rituals and celebrations in this area. Generally in the rituals, the boy will learn about sexual responsibility, as well as celebrate his new manhood.

Wiccans view sexuality as a normal, natural part of human life. How that sexuality manifests, whether homosexual, heterosexual, bi-sexual, or celibate, is a private matter as long as an individual practices their sexuality within the ideals of the Wiccan Rede, "An ye harm none, do what ye will." Pederasty and child pornography are not tolerated at all, anywhere within Wicca.

To Wiccans the family is sacred, but Wiccans are inclusive about what they view as family. A family can be a nuclear family of parents and children, but a family might extend to grandparents, aunts, uncles, and cousins. And it can include coven siblings, friends, High Priest and/or High Priestess, and co-religionists. "We are a family" is a phrase that Wiccans have readily adopted. And many Wiccans behave as if all other Wiccans are family; you may not love them, you may not get along with them, but you will come to their aid and defense if necessary.

Rites of passage help define Wiccan families and the greater Wiccan Community, which is much bigger and more diverse than most non-Wiccans would ever imagine.

THE INITIATION

Initiation is also seen as an important rite of passage. Ideally, an Initiation not only marks a stage of learning and/or achievement, it also acknowledges, or triggers, a change within. There is a definite mystical element to a good Initiation, and a person's Initiation has "taken" when they show evi-dence in their life of some deep inner revelation and/or change. Initiation rituals may differ little from Tradition to Tradition, but the words and ceremony are only the surface of an Initiation. The personal experience is what is important, and this cannot be understood through reading, but must be lived through and assimilated.

As Wiccaning does not guarantee a person will become Wiccan, the *choice* to take training and get an Initiation is an important rite of passage. The first step is Dedication. This is the commitment a person makes to himself or herself, to the Wiccan Community, and to the Goddess and God, to learn about Wicca and study the religion and Craft. Being a Dedicant shows a certain level of commitment, yet does not confirm the full membership that Initiation does. Each Tradition and group has its own rules, but a somewhat recognized standard in Wicca is that at least a year-and-a-day must pass to progress from Dedicant to Initiate. Since Wiccan training covers the religion and practice of Wicca, including possibly the practice of magick, ethics, and divination, a year-and-a-day may sometimes seem short. But many Dedicants may have already studied on their own and have a head start. An important part of Initiation is learning a group's technical language, the "buzz words," so the person can communicate effectively with others of the Tradition.

There is no specified age at which Initiation becomes an option, though many groups will not allow minors into their groups, for considerations of alcohol use and also legal protection. A fifteen-year-old may be fully informed and mature enough to make a choice of religious path, but the parents may not allow the person to actively pursue that interest. All these restrictions can cut off most young people from the possibility of Wiccan training, but until society takes a more benign view of

Wicca, the restrictions will probably continue to exist.

As a person learns and progresses within Wicca, there are three Initiations or degrees available. A somewhat common phrase states, "A First Degree is responsible for themselves, a Second Degree is responsible for others in their immediate coven or group, and a Third Degree is responsible for the community as a whole." Each group and Tradition has its own definitions and levels of learning and expertise for each level. The minimum time period for progression from First to Second, and Second to Third, is again the usual "year-and-a-day."

Not all Wiccans will get all three degrees, but ideally each Wiccan will train and study at least enough to get a First Degree. Wicca, as it is currently practiced, is a religion of "Priests," that is, Initiates are considered to be a Priestess or Priest in their own right and fully capable of communicating with their Gods directly.

Some Wiccan Traditions reserve the title "High Priestess" or "High Priest" for people who have been initiated to the Third Degree. Some use that title for the leaders of a coven.

HANDFASTINGS (MARRIAGES)

Handfasting is the life passage which comes when a Wiccan wishes to be bonded to a partner in the eyes of the Gods. This may or may not also be a legal marriage. Wiccans are broader in how they view committed partnerships. Same-sex partnerships may be celebrated just as heterosexual ones are. And a few Wiccans participate in multiple partnerships, though this is much less common. A Handfasting can be for a defined period, usually not shorter than a year-and-a-day. Or a Handfasting can be "until death do we part." It is up to the participants. Handfastings are celebrated much the same way as weddings, with all the variations

and styles seen in modern weddings. Wiccans usually hold the rite in a Circle of some sort. The couple shares their vows, and then their hands may be bound together as a symbol of their partnership. They then may "jump the broom" together, symbolizing the household they will share. Otherwise there are few set rules. Of course, some sort of party and feast follows.

HANDPARTINGS (DIVORCE)

Handparting is the ceremony Wiccans use to mark the life passage of divorce (or the ending of a committed relationship). As Handfasting is a magickal rite, so should be the ceremony of ending a relationship, which was solemnized before the Gods and community. Oftentimes, it is not possible to get both partners together for a Handparting ceremony. But when possible, the ceremony can bring closure, a concrete ending to a marriage or committed partnership. A Handparting is done in a Circle, and the hands which were bound are unbound. It can also serve to sever the emotional and magickal ties between partners, so each can go on with life free of the other's influence. This does not mean the relationship is denied, ignored, or forgotten, just that each person is free to go his or her own way. Sometimes there is a party and feast, sometimes not. It is usually most desirable to have the person who officiated at the Handfasting officiate at the Handparting also.

ELDERINGS

Eldering is a relatively new tradition and rite of passage in Wicca. Modern Western society has relegated older people to positions of obscurity. Wicca openly and consciously honors and values those who have lived and learned and are now valuable resources for the greater Wiccan Community. Perhaps because Wicca is for the most part a chosen religion, there are currently few Elders who have gone before and had the same experiences the younger Wiccans have. Those who do exist and who have been in the Craft for twenty years or more are valued. They become the wise counselors to the active leadership. They tell the stories of the times before and what it was like for them when they were younger. They share their knowledge and insight. They are honored for their achievements and accomplishments.

A ceremony of Eldering is sometimes held for those who have been around for a long time and who have gravitated to the role of Elder. Sometimes the Eldering ceremony happens at menopause for women, and a similar age for men. Retirement used to be a good societal marker, but with the changing society, few can actually count on a full retirement at a set age anymore. An Eldering ceremony is similar to a Wiccaning, a party celebrating the individual and the individual's place in the family and community of Wicca. Eldering is also seen as an Initiation of sorts, though not a degreed Initiation. Eldering can mark the time when a person gives up active leadership and gains a seat around the council fires.

PASSING OVER

Death is the last life passage each of us will experience. Wiccans view death as a natural part of life. Often some sort of reincarnation is a part of each individual's beliefs. Many Wiccans choose to start working on the death passage before actual death. If a person is known to be dying, Wiccans will often make an effort to visit the person, talk and make their peace with him or her, or at least visit one last time. Hopefully, the person who is dying will not be fearful or anxious about the coming final Initiation. Wiccans will be sad at the coming loss, but also hopeful of a rest in the Summerlands, a place where

Wiccans go between lives. It is said to be a place of eternal summer, warm, green, and pleasant. The spirits of those who have gone before are there and will greet the person upon arrival. Those who have passed away are still among us in spirit, and they can manifest themselves to the living in various ways. Many Wiccans have had what they consider to be concrete proof that there is a life after death. The dying person will try to make peace with the world, and prepare for the transition ahead. In any case, the Wiccan death passage hopefully starts before the actual death, so the person who is dying can take part and express his or her wishes.

BURIAL OF THE DEAD

The Wiccan memorial celebration is not as codified as the other life passages are. Death is a natural part of life. Wiccans honor the mystery of death each year at Samhain, so we already have a yearly mourning period set aside in one of our eight Sabbats. A Wiccan memorial can consist of a Circle and a group singing of the "Lyke Wake Dirge," which although a song, is a magickal Circle and rite in and of itself, and celebrates the cyclic nature of life and death. Some groups will have a Circle in which each person offers a short memorial about the deceased. There may be prayers for an easy passage or a pleasant sojourn in the Summerlands. In the case of a sudden unexpected death, there may have been psychic trauma for the soul of the deceased (which is one theory for the existence of "ghosts"). Then the person may need help to spiritually pass beyond. The group will try to aid in this with prayer and loving energy, which can help the spirit on its journey to the Summerlands.

Modern Wicca has had relatively few older people, so natural death isn't a thing that has become routine. On the other hand death through AIDS and other diseases or by accident are common.

Because Wicca is a less mainstream religion, often the Wiccan "Crossing Over," or funeral ceremony is held without the deceased or the family or most friends present. It is rare that a Wiccan can be openly mourned and buried as Wiccan. Usually the Wiccan ceremony is held after the "mundane" services and burial, often in the covenstead. For this reason, Wiccans seem ambivalent about memorials and burial rites. Often they have little or no say in these, the wishes of their surviving, often non-Wiccan, families being paramount. The secrecy of being Wiccan often extends even into one's birth family.

Wiccans have few preferences in regard to body disposal. Some prefer cremation (it's more ecologically sound), some want burial, and some express no preference, knowing their families will do what they will. The idea of special reverence for the dead body is illogical to most Wiccans, as the true self is the soul or spirit, and body is merely the fleshly vehicle. Once dead, the essence lives on, and the body is no longer needed. No matter what time of year a Wiccan dies, they will be remembered at the next Samhain, for that is what Samhain is for, remembrance of those who have passed on before.

Working the Sacred

SACRED SPACE AND CIRCLE STRUCTURE

Sacred Space is a term Wiccans use to define the area within a magickal Circle which has been defined, cleansed, and consecrated for ritual use, whether for a celebration or a Working. Within a magickal Circle, Holy Ground is created, even if only for a short time. Sacred Space is deemed as holy as a Christian altar or the ark in a temple. However, Sacred Space is usually temporary, as Wiccans have few permanent church buildings. Wiccans also believe that the Goddess and God are everywhere, so there is no urgent need for special buildings set apart from the rest of the world. Many Wiccans prefer to worship in nature when weather permits. Some groups meet in private homes or rented space for the Sabbats.

The magickal Circle is created anew each time. There is no one set formula for creating a Circle, but there are some guidelines of what elements need to be present for a Circle to be a Circle. Different Traditions may mandate different Circles for different occasions. However, there are ten basic steps for creating, using, and taking down the magickal Circle.

Scribing the Circle means outlining the area to be cleansed and consecrated and defining the boundaries the energy will be contained within.

Cleansing the Circle involves making the Circle free of stray or unwanted energies and/or beings—making a clean slate to work upon, so to speak.

Calling the quarters (or Watchtowers) invites guardian entities in to watch over and protect the Circle, entities that are allied to the participants (e.g., the Gods) to aid in the Working.

The binding is the act of declaring that the Circle is cast and ready for whatever the Wiccan is doing.

Calling in the Goddess and God may entail evoking the Goddess and God into the Circle, that is, inviting them to come and watch as guests or observers. Or it may entail invoking them into the Priestess and Priest presiding over the Circle, which means bringing them into the Working as principals along with the Priestess and Priest. When invoking, the Priestess and Priest do not give up their bodies to the Gods, but rather share their bodies with the Gods and act in partnership. This is usually done only within a properly consecrated Circle, under controlled conditions, and only for a specific length of time. When calling in the Goddess and God, there are usually candles, sometimes one black and one white, symbolizing the Goddess and God and their presence within the Circle and everywhere.

The Working can range from a celebration of a Sabbat or Esbat to a full magickal ritual to effect change in an individual or the world. Generally it is commonly considered proper to put up a Circle only for a specific purpose. Some Traditions mandate that there must be some sort of magick performed within a Circle each time one is erected. Some Traditions consider celebration or teaching to be purpose enough for a Circle.

Once the Working is finished and the energy of it is properly grounded, the Wiccan takes down the Circle in reverse order of how it was erected.

Dismissing the Gods closes the evoking or invoking with thanks and love.

Dismissing the quarters or watchtowers sends the guardian entities back to their ethereal realms.

Taking up the Circle is where all the remaining energy that was invoked or used during the Working is returned to where it came from.

Opening the Circle means you are done when you declare the Circle is open.

Ideally, there should be no evidence of a Circle left in the area. If outdoors, Wiccans are very careful to clean up anything they've brought and whatever others brought earlier that does not belong in the area. Most parks and campgrounds are very happy to host Wiccan and Pagan events, as the area usually ends up cleaner at the end than when the event started. This is one way Wiccans manifest their belief that all nature is sacred. Indoors at a temporary site, Wiccans sweep and clean up. In a home there may be more-or-less permanent altar furnishings that are left up, but the candles and other physical trappings, as well as whatever ener-

gies were raised in the Circle, are cleaned up so the room returns to normal.

When a Circle is up, Wiccans are very careful not to cross the Circle boundary without acknowledgment and precautions. This is because a Circle is Sacred Space and to violate it carelessly shows a lack of respect and can also disrupt the energies and spoil the Working. The Circle may be intangible to the naked eye, but for someone who is sensitive to such things, it is very real. Most dogs will not cross a Circle boundary. And although most cats will show by their behavior that they are aware a Circle is up, being cats, they will generally move in and out of a Circle at their whim. Small children, too, may move in and out of a properly constructed Circle without harm, but they can be distracting. Whether or not children are to be involved is best determined beforehand. It's good to remember that little children and cats are generally much more sensitive to the psychic/spiritual world than most adults, so they may be a rough gauge of how things are going. If, for instance, your previously content sleeping pussycat takes off at a dead run for parts unknown, or every baby within earshot starts screaming, you might want to check what's going on.

When a Circle is violated, either by accident or on purpose, the ritual is disrupted, and additional cleansing may be needed. Some groups might actually start over, while other groups might just close down the Circle and abandon the attempt. When Wiccans are disturbed during a ritual held outdoors, either by passersby or occasionally by police or other summoned officials, they can get quite upset if those who come in are not understanding or respectful of the Sacred Space that is created. This is not to say that Wiccans expect just anyone to be aware of a Circle, but they do hope that after an explanation the intruders will be respectful and moderate in their actions, giving the people time to close down the Circle before barging in with intrusions. Wiccans see the disruption of a Circle in the same way a Christian might view disrespectful intrusion on a church service or invasion of Hallowed Ground. Because many law enforcement departments are not aware of the religious implications of the disruption of a Wiccan Circle, they can cause animosity. Many Wiccan groups will not hold Circles outdoors without assurances they will not be disturbed (usually getting the appropriate permits is enough). Some municipalities are much more Wiccan friendly than others. Some Wiccan groups have engaged in educational activities for their local law enforcement communities, so such misunderstandings will not take place. Unfortunately there is still much misunderstanding of Wiccans and prejudice against them, even though there is the constitutional right to freedom of religion in the United States. Wiccans are becoming more active and aggressive in asserting their right to be treated as any other religious group.

PENTAGRAMS

Two separate pentagrams are used in Wiccan Circles. These are the invoking pentagram and the banishing pentagram. The invoking pentagram is drawn with a clockwise, deosil, or sunwise motion. The banishing pentagram is drawn with a counterclockwise, widdershins, or moonwise motion. Which point you start the pentagram at is a topic of contention among several Traditions. There are books that illustrate numerous pentagrams both from Wicca and High Magick, describing which point symbolizes which element and many other details. For this Circle we don't need to go into all of that. Illustrated here are the invoking and banishing pentagrams used by Estelle and Paul. They are more simplistic and generic than most, but they work. The invoking

pentagram is used when calling in the elements (or Watchtowers or quarters, whatever you might want to call them), and the banishing pentagram is used when dismissing them.

Elemental Pentagram

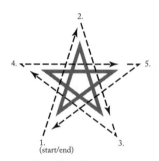

Invoking Pentagram

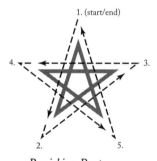

Banishing Pentagram

ELEMENTAL CROSS

The elemental cross is an equal-armed cross. There is also a three-dimensional form that is six-armed: up, down, left, right, in, and out. This is a variation of an ancient symbol known as the "Sun Wheel," and it can function like a pentagram. In this Circle, it is used for cleansing. If you want to create a Circle but not use a pentagram, the elemental cross is an acceptable and effective substitute. You might not want to use a pentagram, because a pentagram can create a strong resonating signal on the astral plane. It calls attention to you for anything or anyone who cares to come and investigate. There are times when a person might not want to attract attention on that level, and at those times an elemental cross is desirable.

Below is a diagram of the elemental cross. To aid in remembering which direction goes with which arm, Estelle visualizes a map of the United States, and then does the cross for each quarter over the map. It's simple but effective. When doing the elemental cross, start with the arm of the direction (East for East, South for South and so on), and then go around clockwise. For the three-dimensional cross, start with the quarter you are facing, go clockwise, and end with an "in" and an "out" for the third dimension.

Elemental Cross

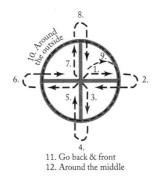

11. Go back & front
12. Around the middle

Elemental Cross in Two Dimensions

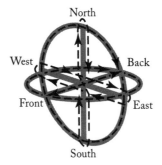

Elemental Cross in Three Dimensions

SACRED TOOLS

Wicca has occasionally been described as "a religion of stuff," with a tremendous variety of tools and other items used in a myriad of ways. Some of the most common sacred tools are the athame, the cup, the pentacle, and the wand.

The Athame

The first and most visibly obvious Wiccan ritual tool is the athame—the sacred knife used to "divide this from that" and direct magickal energies. The kind of knife used varies from Tradition to Tradition and from individual to individual. It is suggested in Craft lore that an athame is a black-handled, double-edged knife with a six-inch blade, about ten to twelve inches in total length. Most prefer a knife with a handle of some natural material, such as wood, leather, or bone. Knives can also come with handles of rubber, micarta, or metal, but these are considered by some to be less desirable as these materials are less natural. They all have been refined, processed, or altered substantially in some way from their original state. Plastic is also used as a knife handle material, and it is considered totally artificial. Personal preference can vary widely. Generally you get the best that's available within the constraints of your budget. You can always trade up later.

To Wiccans this knife is a sacred tool and would never be used as a weapon. It is also very personal. For one to touch another's athame without permission is considered a gross violation of personal space. The athame is used to direct magickal energies and to cast the Circle, drawing out and defining the area that is to make up the Circle. It is also used when calling and dismissing the quarters and doing other types of Workings. To an outsider it might look as if a Wiccan in a Circle is just waving a knife around, but the use of the athame is specific and controlled. The athame symbolizes either the element of Fire or Air depending on the Tradition.

An issue of contention between Wiccans and law enforcement is the use of the athame. Police generally only see the knives, and often react to what they justifiably perceive to be a threat. Wiccans, on the other hand, see their athames as sacred tools and can be offended if asked to put them away or angered if asked to hand them over. Education on both sides, before problems develop, is the best way to avoid these conflicts. If you travel to rituals and want to bring your athame, it should be sheathed and placed in some bag or case, so it is not visible nor readily at hand. Keeping it suitably stored in your car trunk while in transit is a good idea. Remember, most states and cities have blade laws, and the average legal knife is single-edged with a blade of no more than three inches in length. Check your local state and city ordinances for the specifics where you live. Your athame is a sacred tool to you, but most law enforcement personnel will not view it as such, and will err on the side of caution—their caution.

Wiccans usually choose to avoid public areas to avoid having to deal with possible misunderstandings. As Wicca becomes more widely recognized and better understood, these clashes will hopefully become less and less frequent.

The simplest substitute for an actual metal athame is the first two fingers of the right hand, raised and used to direct the energies as if you were pointing with two fingers. This "athame" has the advantage of not being threatening or easily confiscated, and is legal everywhere you want to go. It may take a bit of practice, but it can be just as effective as a metal athame when used correctly.

The Cup

The cup is used to hold wine (or a non-alcoholic substitute), and it symbolizes the womb, among other things. The act of blessing the wine symbolizes the procreative act and is called the Great Rite. Wicca celebrates nature and fertility and this is the most visible manifestation of that. Most Traditions feel that the cup symbolizes the element of Water. Our blessing of the wine and ritual cakes is similar to Christian Communion.

The Pentacle

The pentacle is generally considered a symbol of the element of Earth. It is usually a disk or plate with a pentagram (five-pointed star) on it. Traditionally, the pentacle was made of wax so it could be easily destroyed in emergencies. Nowadays, with the "Burning Times" over, pentacles can be made of wood, metal, stone, or other more permanent materials. The pentacle rests on the altar and is used for grounding the energies of a ritual, as well as possibly holding the cakes and wine before they are blessed and shared.

The Wand

The wand is most simply a stick, usually about eighteen inches in length, and it is used to direct magickal energies, though in a different way than the athame. Some Traditions use wands to hold energies or spells, others use them in casting the Circle. Wands can be just plain wooden sticks, or very elaborate creations of various materials with crystals and designs and the rest. The wand can most commonly be used to symbolize either the element of Air or Fire (whichever one of these two elements is *not* represented by the athame), depending upon the Tradition.

Other Tools

While the athame, cup, pentacle, and wand are the four main sacred tools of Wicca, there are many other items used by various people in various ritual ways. Some of the other common tools are

- the sword, sort of an overgrown athame;
- the staff, like a big wand, but also with other uses;
- an incense holder and incense;
- candles and candle holders;
- a bowl for water and a holder for salt, both used in cleansing;
- statues or pictures of the Goddess and God;
- sacred garb or ritual clothing;
- cords or braided belts, used as symbols of degree recognition as well as measuring devices for scribing the Circle;
- the altar itself, that can be as simple as a cloth on the ground, more substantial, like a card table, or permanent, made of wood or stone;
- the broom or besom, used by Wiccans today more for cleansing and not for flying. In cleansing, an area is swept clean of unwanted energies as well as dirt. (The broom is also used in Handfastings or weddings, during which the newly joined couple "jumps the broom," symbolizing their setting up housekeeping together.)

Wiccans have a penchant for collecting tools and ritual items. Craft lore states that you must never bargain when buying a ritual item. In other words, you don't haggle over the price. Some people, however, like getting goodies at garage sales and feel that bargaining is a sacred act in itself. How someone views this matter is individual or a matter of Traditional belief.

Craft tools should always be cleansed and consecrated before use. They are considered sacred objects and it is impolite and disrespectful to touch or use another person's tools without their permission. Some tools are highly personal (most prominently the athame), while other tools are for general use, like candles or incense. A good rule to use when attending a Wiccan function: "Don't touch anyone's anything without permission, ever."

CASTING A
BASIC WICCAN CIRCLE

DESCRIBED BELOW IS A BASIC WICCAN CIRCLE, which can be modified to suit individual purposes. Most Circles are similar, and the Circle outlined in the following pages has all the requisite elements of a good solid Circle. We encourage you to look further and see what other Circles are out there—there are endless possible variations. Some groups use the same Circle every time, while other Traditions mandate a different Circle be cast for each specific type of Working. Other groups use a slightly different Circle each time. What's important is that all the basic elements be present, so that the energies are built and contained properly.

The act of creating a Circle is known as "casting a Circle." A Circle, when fully formed, is a thing which is solid and tangible to those who are able to sense it. However, it is meant to be transitory. It is cast or put up or created for a specific time, and when that time is up, it is then taken down, banished, or sent away. Some groups use "circle" as a verb, as in "Will you be circling with us tonight?" (meaning "Will you join us in our Circle?" or "Will you help us create a Circle?") The act of casting a Circle is a process with specific steps and rules, which creates a thing that is then later destroyed. Perhaps "used up" is a better phrase. Casting a Circle can be likened to preparing a meal. You have to buy the food, get out the utensils, prepare and cook the food, and set the table. This is analogous to the casting of the Circle. When the cooking and other preparations are finished, the meal is served and you eat. This is analogous to the Working. After the meal is finished and the food has been consumed, you have to clean the utensils, wash the dishes, and tidy up. This is analogous to banishing the Circle.

There are endless debates among the various Traditions about altar placement and the quarter you begin from. North and East are the most commonly favored directions. In actuality, the energies will usually work no matter where your altar is placed or which quarter you start in. All that really matters is that you are consistent within each Circle, and you concentrate and correctly visualize the energies as you build it.

This Circle can be cast with a High Priestess (HPS), a High Priest (HP), and a group, with just an HPS and a HP, or with one individual taking both parts. The Circle can be done all male or all female with one person doing both parts, or better, two people, each one taking a part. In the latter case the terms HPS and HP refer to the "receptive" and "active" principles respectively. The roles are not necessarily gender specific. You can also call on just the Goddess (as Dianic groups do) or just the God, but the energies may not be as balanced as they are when calling on both.

RITUAL TOOLS

The Circle uses fairly standard ritual tools. The items and equipment listed here are pretty basic, and maybe ninety percent of all Wiccans use similar tools in their Circles. There are many others that can be used, with specific properties and meanings. Substitutions can be made (such as pictures or objects for the quarters). There is no one right, true, and only way to build a Circle, nor is there even *the* set of required ritual implements or equipment. Just use whatever works best for you and is available.

There are items and actions that are optional and are marked as such. The Circle will still be up and effective without them, but some people like the little extra touches the options provide. It's a matter of preference. The altar itself can be a permanent stone altar, a wooden altar, or a portable altar (like a card table), or maybe just a cloth on the ground. Whatever adapts itself to the place you are in and the materials and resources available is fine.

Immediately following you will find a description of casting a fairly standard Wiccan Circle. Note—for simplicity, brevity, and ease of reading the text uses HPS (High Priestess) with she and her and HP (High Priest) with he and his. This is because standard Wiccan convention has a female HPS and a male HP. However, any person may take the part of the HPS and/or HP, and as long as they realize that the HPS is the receptive principle and the HP is the active principle, the energies will work.

A CIRCLE RITUAL

STEP 1 **Assemble the following items for the altar:**
- reading candle and holder
- 2 "presence" candles
- lighter or matches
- candlesnuffer (optional, but an elegant touch)
- athame
- chalice and libation (typically wine, cider, some other juice, or water)
- plate of cakes
- pentacle
- incense holder with your favorite incense
- salt holder and salt
- water holder and water
- wand

A CIRCLE RITUAL continued...

- bell and striker (optional)
- 4 quarter candles, 1 for each quarter, and candle holders (optional)

STEP 2   **Pre-ritual preparations:**

Perform whatever personal "cleansing" you feel is needed to be done by yourself and the other participants. Dress in a manner that makes you feel "special" and "magickal," for example, special robes or jewelry.

Assemble your altar and set up your quarter candles (please refer to the diagram below).

Close the drapes, unplug the phone, lock the door (all to reduce possible interruptions).

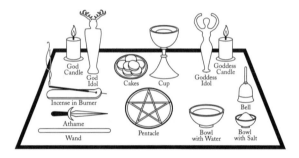

Altar Setup

STEP 3   **Begin the Circle:**

Light your (a) reading, (b) quarter, and (c) presence candles.

OPTIONAL: The HP goes to the altar and rings the bell three times to cleanse the area and to focus the attention of the participants, preparatory to "scribing" the Circle.

STEP 4   **The HP scribes the Circle:**

Using his athame, the HP "scribes," or draws a Circle in the air around the assembled gathering, beginning either at the East or the North quarter. Whichever point you choose, start in that same quarter for everything that is done in the Circle, and move deosil, or clockwise.

NOTE: Most Traditions feel that all movement within a Circle by all participants should be in a deosil direction. This is so the energies are not accidentally banished by moving widdershins, or counterclockwise. If you need to turn to the left, make a three-quarter (or whatever) deosil turn around to where you need to face. It will feel strange at first, but eventually it will be natural to move only deosil in a Circle. This is important.

STEP 5   **The HPS consecrates the water and salt:**

The HPS first goes to the container of water on the altar, takes her athame and places its point in the water, then visualizes all negative energies being driven out of the water. She says aloud:

> *I Exorcise thee, O creature of Water,*
> *That thou cast out from thee*
> *All Impurities and Uncleanliness*
> *Of the spirits of Phantasm*
> *In the names of the Lady and the Lord.*

Here and throughout, you may substitute the names of any particular Goddess and/or God you choose.

The HPS then takes the tip of her athame and, putting it into the salt, visualizes all negative energies being driven out of the salt and says:

> *Blessings upon thee, O creature of Earth.*
> *Let all malignancies and hindrances*
> *Pass forth and let all goodness enter in.*

The HPS then takes three tips of salt on her athame and puts them in the water. She says:

> *As we are ever mindful*
> *That as water purifies the body,*
> *So salt purifies the soul.*

The HPS then stirs the salt into the water. When finished she wipes her blade dry. She says:

> *Wherefore I do bless thee*
> *In the names of the Lady and the Lord,*
> *That thou mayest aid me.*

STEP 6   **The HPS then aspurges, or cleanses, the Circle with Earth and Water:**

Taking the water container, and starting in the quarter of choice, moving deosil, the HPS sprinkles the consecrated water three times at each quarter, also above and below. The altar may also

A CIRCLE RITUAL continued...

be sprinkled, to cleanse it, as well. This sprinkling should be light, a couple of drops on the end of the fingers.

STEP 7   **The HP then consecrates the Fire and Air:**

The HP takes the incense and lights it in one of the candles. He says:

> *I charge thee, O Creature of Fire,*
> *That thou allow no evil to defile this Circle.*

The HP then extinguishes the flame and watching the incense curl up, he says:

> *I invoke thee, O creature of Air,*
> *That thou may protect this our Circle with love.*

STEP 8   **The HP then censes, or cleanses, the Circle with Fire and Air:**

Beginning in the chosen quarter, the HP then censes the Circle using the burning incense by drawing, in the air, the appropriate elemental cross in each quarter, then, moving deosil, finishes in the center of the Circle using a full three-dimensional elemental cross.

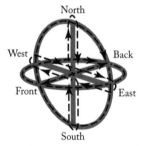

Three-Dimensional Elemental Cross

STEP 9   **The HPS then invokes the quarter guardians:**

The HPS now takes her athame, and starting at the quarter of choice, draws an invoking pentagram in each quarter, moving deosil around the Circle.

A CIRCLE RITUAL continued...

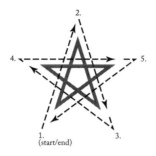

Invoking Pentagram

After each pentagram has been drawn, she says:

> *Guardians of the Watchtowers of the* _____,
> *Creatures of* _____, *(East/Air, South/Fire, West/Water,*
> *North/Earth)*
> *I welcome thee and ask that you witness this rite*
> *and guard this Circle and all within.*
> *Hail and Welcome!*

All those present now respond with:

> *Hail and Welcome!*

NOTE: You should fill in the appropriate name and direction of each of the above quarters, starting with the quarter of choice.

The HPS finally moves to the center of the Circle, makes an invoking pentagram while pointing first above and then below.

OPTIONAL: After drawing each of these pentagrams, the HPS says:

> *Hail and Welcome!*

OPTIONAL: All those present now response with:

> *Hail and Welcome!*

STEP 10   The HP now binds or closes the Circle:

The HP moves to the center of the Circle, and taking the wand he moves deosil, retracing the Circle he previously drew with his athame, to bind the energies, saying:

A CIRCLE RITUAL continued...

> *Thus we are met, at a time that is no longer a time,*
> *in a place that is no longer a place,*
> *for we are between the worlds and beyond.*
> *May the Goddess and God*
> *help and protect us on our Magickal journey.*
> *So Mote It Be!*

All those present now respond with:

> *So Mote It Be!*

STEP 11   **The Goddess and God are called:**

The HPS and HP stand together at the altar facing each other, holding hands: one hand up, one down.

If your Circle is to be an evocation—inviting the Goddess and God to the party—you might say:

> *Lady and Lord,*
> *we ask for your presence at this, our Circle.*
> *May you guard and watch over our Circle,*
> *and guide us with your loving presences.*
> *So Mote It Be!*

All those present now respond with:

> *So Mote It Be!*

If the Circle is to be an invocation—inviting the presences of the Goddess and God into the High Priestess and High Priest—you might say:

> *Lady and Lord,*
> *we invite you to be present within our Circle.*
> *Be present within our High Priestess and High Priest*
> *that you might participate fully in our rites.*
> *Share their bodies and senses*
> *and open their hearts to your Love.*
> *Be here with us in our Circle now.*
> *So Mote It Be!*

A CIRCLE RITUAL continued...

All those present should respond with:

> *So Mote It Be!*

STEP 12   **Insert Working here:**

Here is the heart of the ritual, be it a celebration or magickal Working or both. The Working can be a celebration of a Sabbat or Esbat, it can be an Initiation, or a cleansing, consecration, banishing, healing, or divination, it can be a spell designed to change yourself or the world around you. It can also be a combination of several of these elements. Within the bounds of the magickal Circle you have a safe space to raise energy and perform magick. This is the part which takes the most time and utilizes the energy which has been contained and brought forth. Once the energy has been raised and used, then sent on its way to accomplish what you want at the end of your Working, the rest of the ritual is to "seal" the Working, banish any excess energies, and take down the Circle.

STEP 13   **Perform the Great Rite:**

The Great Rite is the Wiccan form of Communion. To perform it, the High Priestess holds the cup in front of the High Priest, who is holding his athame, blade down, over the cup.
First the HPS says:

> *As the Cup is the Female;*

Then the HP:

> *And the Athame is the Male;*

As they each say their words, they are slowly bringing the cup and athame together, so the blade of the athame is dipped into the libation. The High Priestess and High Priest should feel the power of the Goddess and God enter the libation. And they both say:

> *Together they are One!*

After the blade is removed it is wiped clean. The High Priestess raises the cup in salute to the Gods and drinks. She then hands the cup to the High Priest saying:

> *Blessed Be.*

A CIRCLE RITUAL continued...

The High Priest then raises the cup in salute and also drinks, saying:

>*Blessed Be.*

Then the HPS takes the plate of cakes, and the HP holds his hands over them, and they bless them, both saying:

>*Lady and Lord,*
>*bless these cakes*
>*that we may partake of your bounty.*

The HPS takes a cake and eats it, and the HP does the same. The cup and cakes are then passed around the Circle so that all may share.

Once the cup has passed all around the Circle, it is handed back to the HPS who then drinks any remaining libation. (If there is too much for her to drink alone, she may pass it to others who help drain the liquid to a manageable level.) The HPS drains the cup, places it upside down on the pentacle (along with the last few drops of libation, for the Gods), and grounds the energy of the ritual through the pentacle. If there are cakes left they are also placed on the altar.

NOTE: You can pass the cup and cakes around the Circle either male to female and vice versa or just person to person. If it is male to female and there are more of one gender than the other, the HPS or HP interposes, to maintain the alternating pattern.

If a person has a cold or does not want to drink the libation (for instance if it is alcohol and the person does not drink alcohol) they can either raise the cup in salute or dip a finger in the cup and bring it to the lips. That is sufficient. If there is a problem with alcohol, you might substitute apple cider, non-alcoholic wine, or grape juice.

If there are too many people in the Circle for each to get a sip from the cup, it is permissible to refill the cup at appropriate intervals, but it should be refilled from a partially full state, not totally drained. The original container should sit beside the altar, waiting for refill if needed. There should be enough cakes for all, or each person should only take part of a cake to ensure each gets some. If a person cannot eat the cakes, they may just raise the plate in salute to honor the Gods.

It is considerate to announce beforehand the ingredients of the cakes and the cup so that people can ascertain if they can or wish to partake.

A CIRCLE RITUAL continued...

STEP 14   **Dismiss the Goddess and God:**

The HPS and HP face each other and join hands as above in Step 11.

If the Goddess and God were "evoked," they say:

> *Lady and Lord,*
> *we thank you for joining us in our Circle.*
> *We ask for your Blessings and Love*
> *as you depart to your chosen realms.*
> *Hail and Farewell!*

All those present now respond with:

> *Hail and Farewell!*

If the Goddess and God were invoked, they say:

> *Lady and Lord,*
> *we thank you for your presence in our Circle.*
> *We ask for your Blessings and Love,*
> *and as you depart to your chosen realms we bid you*
> *Hail and Farewell!*

All those present again respond with:

> *Hail and Farewell!*

STEP 15   **Dismiss the quarters:**

The HPS takes her athame and moving deosil around the Circle she makes a banishing pentagram at each quarter, and says:

> *Guardians of the Watchtowers of the _____,*
> *Creatures of _____, (East/Air, South/Fire, West/Water,*
> *North/Earth)*
> *we thank you for your presence at this our Circle.*
> *May there be peace between us, now and always,*
> *and as you depart, we bid you*
> *Hail and Farewell.*

A CIRCLE RITUAL continued...

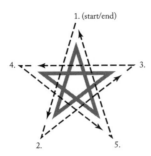

Banishing Pentagram

OPTIONAL: All those present respond with:

Hail and Farewell!

STEP 16   **Ground and cut the Circle:**

The HP finally takes his athame and erases the Circle he drew in Step 4.

When he has done that, he then makes a cut with his athame across where the boundary of the Circle had been, and says:

The Circle is open, but unbroken.

Then at last, all those present respond with:

Merry meet, merry part,
and merry meet again!

STEP 17   **Clean up:**

Clean up any food and liquid left, and put the dishes in the sink.

Put away all the candles and disassemble your altar.

Change back into your mundane clothes. Reconnect the phone, open the drapes, and unlock the door.

It is done.

Medieval Alchemical Illustration

The Characteristics of Magick

THE MOST BASIC DEFINITION OF MAGICK IS "a controlled use of will to effect a change in one's self or surroundings." The popular use of the term magic, without the "k," refers to stage magic, prestidigitation, and other flashy entertainments, which use misdirection and other theatrical tricks to appear to effect change through supernatural means. The "k" was added to magick to distinguish psychic-based work from stage magic. Wiccans employ magick like Ceremonial Magicians and other mystical/ fraternal/spiritual groups, as a tool for contact with Deity and for self-development. Wiccans will use magick to effect change in themselves and the world around them, often simultaneously. Sometimes a change in the world can be made by a simple change in the basic mental outlook or perspective of an individual. In the "magickal realms," one can also be closer to Deity, and use its help and guidance to make oneself a better person. One may use a specific technique such as Ceremonial Magick, meditation, divination, sacred song, and ecstatic dance to effect a change in mind and outlook, which takes the person out of the ordinary everyday world into the "higher realms." Wiccans use magick in controlled settings with controlled techniques to prevent unwanted results. Although Wiccans acknowledge no Devil, they do recognize the phenomenon of possession and work to avoid it.

Wiccans practice magick in Circles, an area of Sacred Space, which is cleansed and secured from unwanted outside influences. This is very important, as doing magick outside of a Circle is more difficult and subject to unwanted and unexpected influences and changes. The Circle Wiccans put up for magick is the same as a Circle for worship. Worship and magick may be combined in one Working. Some Wiccans consider magick to be a form of worship, or focused and directed prayer. Deity is always invited to participate, as Wiccans believe we are friends and co-workers with the Gods and they help us in all we do.

Wiccans practice what is termed "white magick," magick done for the benefit of all the people involved. They do not send energy to anyone who is not aware of it, or does not want it, as this is considered to be one type of "black magick," which is magick that either harms someone or imposes your will over someone. Even healing without permission is considered a form of black magick because it imposes your will. The Law of Three and the Wiccan Rede are very broad rules which apply in many more cases than are first apparent.

When a person is hurt and in need of healing energies, and their direct permission cannot be obtained, most Wiccans will send the energy to the cosmos, to be used however the person needs it. If they do not want to take the energy, that is their choice, conscious or unconscious.

When practiced properly and ethically, magick is a powerful tool for effecting change in oneself and one's environment. Generally, most Wiccans do spells for themselves or for their friends or fellow Wiccans. It is easier to effect change within oneself than in the entire world around you.

GROUNDING AND CENTERING

The first magickal technique most Wiccans learn is grounding and centering. This gets you into a relaxed mental state, clears your mind of distractions, and focuses and contains energy. It can be like a meditative state, but it gets you ready to act and move, as well as to sit and use your mind.

This feeling of being calm, relaxed, and firmly where you are is what Wiccans describe as being grounded and centered. The act of grounding and centering is the first step for any Working, be it magick or celebration. You should ground and center before starting any Circle.

A GROUNDING AND *C*ENTERING *R*ITUAL

STEP 1   Sit in a chair with your feet flat on the floor, your hands resting in your lap, and your spine straight.

STEP 2   Take three deep breaths and let them out slowly. As you let them out, relax your body, and let your tensions flow out. This is called taking three cleansing breaths.

STEP 3   Once you are relaxed, imagine roots extending from your feet and the base of your spine, growing deep into the earth.

STEP 4   Feel yourself in your body, in your skin. Feel the gravity holding you in your chair. As the roots grow, feel yourself rooted where you are, in the here and now, in the space you are occupying.

STEP 5   As you concentrate on being in the here and now, your mind should become free of extraneous thought and distractions. You should become more calm and relaxed.

Minerva

There are many other techniques for grounding and centering. Some are more elaborate, and some work instantaneously. Repeating to yourself a "mantra" or catch phrase is a good technique. Just using the three cleansing breaths can be enough for someone who is well practiced. As you practice, it becomes easier. All the techniques involve deliberately relaxing the body, becoming mentally aware of being in the here and now, clearing the mind of distractions, and focusing your thoughts for whatever is to come. Grounding and centering becomes useful for many everyday life activities. If you become upset or agitated, it can help calm the emotions and get the mind clear so action can be taken. If you have a health condition, grounding and centering can sometimes help lessen physical symptoms. You can ground and center before that big meeting or job interview, and you will find your mind is more organized.

These techniques are not at all exclusive to Wicca. Many self-help disciplines use these same techniques. Most schools of meditation use some forms of grounding and centering, though they are frequently less active. If you have a technique you already use, and it works for you, then stick with it. But it is recommended you try the technique described above just to see how it might differ. There is also no psychic danger in grounding and centering. This will not psychically or spiritually open you up to anything. It does not make you susceptible to possession, and, in fact, centering yourself is your first defense against any type of psychic attack. It does not put you in touch with anything. It just allows you to relax, clear your mind, and focus your thoughts. That's all. Period.

SHIELDING

Shielding is a technique in which you form a focused energy barrier around yourself to protect yourself from outside influences.

This bubble you have created is elastic and personalized. It expands as you stand or move, and it contracts if you sit. This golden bubble of energy is your shield. It is translucent, you can see through it, but stray energies and influences cannot penetrate it. It may be invisible to you until you come up against energies from outside. And because you have created this shielding bubble of energy largely within your own mind, it should be invisible to most everyone else. The bubble can also be contracted to fit around your skin, like an outer suit of "energy wear." If you think of the "energy shields" around the spaceships in TV shows like *Star Trek*, you have a good idea of what shields are and what they do.

As you become more adept at shielding, you can create bubbles of energy around your living space, your car, or other possessions. Just project the energy ball to rotate around whatever you want to shield. Shields are not permanent. They last for a time, depending on how strongly you made the shield and how much extraneous psychic energy is around. You have to renew your shields every so often. The more you do these techniques, the better you get and the more quickly you can erect or reinforce a shield. Start small with shielding yourself. Once you get comfortable with that, then try shielding your living environment. From that, you should be ready to shield other items.

Grounding, centering, and shielding are valuable techniques for living in today's hectic world. shielding yourself while you sleep can make for a more restful night.

A Shield Ritual

Step 1   First ground and center, as described above.

Step 2   Now relaxed and free of distractions, gather your internal energy. To do this, visualize a golden sphere of light about the size of a golf ball, either in your chest area or in your forehead, depending upon which feels better to you.

Step 3   Once you have that ball of light, project it outward until it floats in front of you, about two feet from your body.

Step 4   Now, slowly take that energy ball and move it around your body in a circle. Get it moving faster and faster until it becomes a golden hoop of energy encircling your body.

Step 5   Then, when you have the hoop, rotate the hoop so it turns into a sphere. This becomes a golden sphere of light, which totally encircles you.

Step 6   Now you anchor this golden energy sphere with a beam of light reaching straight up to the cosmos. You can also anchor the sphere of light with another beam of light to the eastern horizon, where the first light of the sun appears. This connects you to the Gods and their energies.

TOOL CLEANSINGS

The Working of cleansing and consecration is a ritual that almost every Wiccan performs. Below is a
condensed version of a simple cleansing and consecration ritual.

A Tool Consecration Ritual

STEP 1   **In addition to your typical set of ritual equipment, for the magickal Working of a
cleansing, you will need**

- water and salt
- incense
- sacred oil (scented or unscented)

STEP 2   **Pre-ritual preparations:**

First, physically clean the tool by washing, polishing, or whatever.

Before the Working, a person might want to inscribe the item to be consecrated with a magickal sigil or personal Craft name or motto. This can be done permanently, as in carving into
the wood handle of a knife, or just for the consecration, for example, with pen and ink on a
blade, to be washed off during the consecration or afterward.

NOTE: Whatever you put on the tool should be well-researched and personal to you. Don't just
pick some symbol as a sigil because you like it. Know what that symbol means and what energies you are permanently putting into your tool by using that symbol. A sigil is a drawn symbol
which has meaning for the person using it and possibly also for the world at large. It can be similar to a magickal trademark, or it can be used to show affinities and alliances, such as using an
owl as a sigil symbolizing wisdom or the Goddess Athena. Some people use a rune or letter of
some other magickal alphabet as their sigil. Some Traditions have their own sigil which is used
by all members. Also any magickal name or motto you choose should be well-researched and
one you can live with as the years go by. You can also consecrate an item without using any sort
of sigil, name, or motto. The very act of consecration puts your personal energy into the item
and magickally marks it as yours.

A TOOL CONSECRATION RITUAL continued...

STEP 3   Cast a Circle:

Cast in the manner you are accustomed to, or use the generic Wiccan Circle, as described earlier.

STEP 4   The Goddess and God are called into the Circle:

Call in the manner you are accustomed to, or again, you can use the generic Wiccan Circle, as described above.

STEP 5   Cleanse the tool with Earth and Water:

Once you have the Circle up and the Gods called, you take the item and psychically cleanse it by taking the salted water and running it over the item with your fingers, to remove unwanted or stray influences.

NOTE: You can wipe the salt water off afterward if it might damage the item.

STEP 6   Cleanse the tool with Fire and Air:

Psychically cleanse the item again with the lit incense, running it through the smoke.

NOTE: By doing these two actions, the item is cleansed with all four elements.

STEP 7   Affirm why you are doing this Working:

Now say a short affirmation and statement of purpose, such as:

> *This is my sacred Athame.*
> *May it serve me well in my magickal Workings,*
> *and may the Goddess and God aid me in my Workings.*

STEP 8   Anoint your tool:

Now take the oil and anoint the item while putting your energy into it, concentrating on the uses you will have for the tool and how it will aid you and be attuned to your personal energies.

NOTE: You can wipe the oil off afterward. You don't need large amounts of salt water or oil, just enough to place some of each on the item and let the energies of the liquids be absorbed into the item.

A TOOL CONSECRATION RITUAL continued...

STEP 9 **Seal your work:**

Once all the cleansing has been done, you should lay the tool on your pentacle so it can be grounded, or "sealed" for your purposes.

NOTE: You can consecrate more than one tool at a time, one after the other, but it is not recommended to do too many at any one time, because you can get burned out, and the last consecrations might not be as effective as the earlier ones in the same Working. In our classes we have students consecrate their four main tools in one Working, and perhaps one or two more, but no more than that.

STEP 10 **Finish the ritual and open the Circle:**

Once you are finished with the consecration you then ground any excess energy through the pentacle and close down the Circle as usual. You are done.

Once your tools are consecrated, they should be stored where they will be protected and out of the way, so they will not be handled by just anyone. Most people have some sort of sheath for their athame (which also makes it easier to wear and carry), and at the minimum wrap their other tools in silk. If you have a permanent altar, placing your tools there is a good thing. Some people have a ritual bag or small suitcase in which they store their tools and garb and the other items they bring to rituals. A special storage drawer or box might be better for you. Whatever suits you and your living space is fine, just so the tools are safely stored and out of the way.

PROBLEM SOLVING USING MAGICK

Defining the problem is the first step in doing any spell or Working. Once you have precisely defined a problem, you are usually halfway toward solving it. Focusing the mind and will are necessary for the successful practice of magick. This is one way of doing it.

Wiccans are very careful when performing magick. They strive to effect an outcome, yet not dictate exactly how it is to be done. This attitude leaves openings for possibilities which they might not have considered, but which might be better for all concerned. Sometimes a Wiccan has to do less of a spell than they might wish.

There was a Wiccan whose daughter was dating an extremely unsavory character, a criminal who was very unpleasant to be around. He would sponge off of the daughter, taking advantage of her good nature, and visit the Wiccan's house at all hours. The Wiccan wanted the daughter to stop seeing this man. But to do a Working to that effect would have been black magick, forcing the daughter to stop seeing this man against her will, or forcing the man to stop seeing the daughter. We were called in to help. Sometimes it helps to have an outside party to give perspective. After talking to the Wiccan the following was determined: The Wiccan didn't want this person around and wished the daughter would see for herself just what kind of a man he was.

To address these issues we performed a twofold Working. The first part was shielding the Wiccan's home and property against the boyfriend. So the boyfriend would feel extremely unpleasant if he came on the property or into the house, we created a shield like a psychic "unwelcome" mat. This is perfectly acceptable, as people certainly have the right to protect their property and decide which people to allow in their home. This shield was especially extended to the telephone line, so the boyfriend would be reluctant to call.

The second part of the Working was done to send energy to the cosmos to allow the daughter to see this man as he was, get a good look at his real character. If the daughter was, even unconsciously, discontented with her relationship, this could give her the energy to see him as he truly was and start to break his hold over her.

The first part of the spell worked very well. The daughter had been sneaking the boyfriend into the house while the Wiccan was away, or at night when everyone else was sleeping. He also called at all hours. These activities stopped almost immediately. He just didn't feel like coming around or calling anymore.

The second part took longer. After about six months, the daughter announced she was not seeing the boyfriend anymore, and had not for several months. When questioned why, she said she had observed him cheat a friend out of some money, and had seen other ways in which the boyfriend was dishonest and cruel to others. Eventually she realized he was pulling these things on her also. She

was about to drop him when he up and left her, because he just didn't want to see her anymore.

Now, whether all this was the direct result of the spells cannot be said for sure. But the daughter did stop seeing this boyfriend, and he did stop coming to the house and phoning.

THE BELIEF FACTOR

Magick works only when the practitioner believes in it. You have to believe what you are doing. If you scoff or doubt, the energy will not do what you want. Coincidences may happen, but to some Wiccans, there are no coincidences. Everything happens for a purpose. Sometimes you never find out what the purpose is, and sometimes you do. "Sometimes the magick works, and sometimes it doesn't." There are always larger forces working of which you might not be aware.

In the end, the way to judge the effectiveness of magick is, did the job get done? Whether the agent of accomplishment is yourself, the person you did the Working for, or a totally random factor, if the job gets done, the magick was successful.

Another factor is expressed in the saying, "The Gods help those who help themselves." You can do all the job-finding spells in the world, but to be effective you also have to pick up the paper, make some calls, get dressed up, go to the interviews, and present yourself in a favorable light. The Gods will not rain dollar bills on you from the blue. But if you do the magick and then go out and apply yourself, you can increase your effectiveness much more than if you did not do the magick. Maybe it is because the magick helps concentrate your intent and goals. Maybe it is because the magick works to make you irresistible to prospective employers. Maybe the magick helps put you in the right place at the right time and allows you to maximize your chances. In the end, it really doesn't matter as long as you got the job you wanted.

WORKING A SPELL

There are four elements to working a spell: to Will, to Know, to Do, and to Keep Silent.

"To Will" comes from having a firm resolve and a clear idea of what is to be accomplished, and the belief that what you are doing will work.

"To Know" has a twofold meaning: to know what is to be accomplished, or have a clear idea of just what is needed, and to know how to do the spell itself.

"To Do" is just that, doing the spell. Spells are not mere wishes. You have to put energy into the system to effect change. How much you *do* may have a direct correlation to how quickly and thoroughly you get results.

"To Keep Silent" means not to talk or brag about what you did. Just quietly go about your normal business and be pleasantly surprised when you discover that what you Willed has come to pass, though not always in the form you imagined. Keeping silent can be the most important, for once you do the spell and release the energy, your constant talking about and dwelling upon the subject can cause the spell to fizzle or backfire. If you are thinking about it, your thoughts haven't let go, so the spell has never been properly sent on its way. If you talk about it, you might let it slip to the wrong ears, and energy might be put into fighting the spell, whether the person who heard is affected or just a concerned well-wisher. Usually, after a magickal Working, most Wiccans will engage in the most mundane of tasks, like cleaning or other routine chores that occupy the mind and get their thoughts off the magick just performed. This creates a mental break between the practitioner and the energy sent, so that the thoughts of the sender do not inhibit the actions desired. It also can make for a cleaner house and more orderly living environment! Being active is an important key here. Just sitting and watching TV will not do it, for you are not mentally and physically engaged.

COMMON WORKINGS

CLEANSINGS, BLESSINGS, AND HEALINGS ARE BY far the most common magickal Workings, or spells, performed by most Wiccans. This chapter also reviews prayer, divination, and other forms of magick for specific purposes.

CLEANSINGS

Cleansings are used when a place, person, or item has negative or unwanted stray energies and a "clean slate" is needed. Cleansings are usually done with the four elements, using Water, and salt (for Earth), and incense (for Air and Fire). After a Circle is put up, the thing to be cleansed is first aspurged with the water and salt, and then purified with the incense smoke. As this is going on, the person performing the cleansing should visualize the negative energies being washed away. This should continue until it feels "clean." Sometimes, more than one cleansing is necessary. A cleansing is not a substitute for an exorcism, which is performed if a person or place is inhabited by unwanted entities. Exorcisms are advanced and occasionally dangerous activities, best left to those who are experienced in such matters.

Sage is an herb that is commonly used for cleansing. Smudging with sage is highly effective at chasing away unwanted energies, smells, spirits, and other entities.

BLESSINGS

A blessing is usually done after a cleansing, especially on a new home or living space. After the space is cleansed, take wine and cakes, and perform the Great Rite and blessing allowing the presence of the Goddess and God to fill the area. Ask for their protection of the space and their blessings upon all who enter and all who live there. Consecrating tokens that represent the Goddess and God is one way of maintaining their presence. These can be actual statues, pictures, or just a crystal, rock, or other item that symbolizes the Deities for you. Once the place is cleansed and blessed and the Circle is down, these items should be placed in a safe place, to aid in protecting and blessing the space. The cleansing and blessing can be renewed whenever it seems appropriate. Most do it at least once a year.

HEALINGS

Healings are a special form of blessing and cleansing. The recipient of the energy should *always* be aware and willing for the healing to be done. If the person is not present, or has not actively allowed a healing to take place, the energy can be "sent to the cosmos," for the person to use as they will (not using the energy always being an option). Additionally, an active healing should *never* be done on a person with a cardiovascular condition. The change in energies could trigger a heart attack, stroke, ruptured aneurysm, or similar problem. Usually the best way is to send the energies to the cosmos, allowing the person to tap into the energies as they need. This tapping into the energies can be done consciously or unconsciously.

PRAYER AND OTHER MAGICKS

Prayer is a type of spell, because it is sending focused energy for a specific purpose. Prayer is certainly encouraged, but be careful you are not trying to shape events to your personal purposes without the willing consent of the recipient. In this way, some types of prayers can be viewed as a form of black magick. If you pray for the salvation of others without their consent, you are trying to force your will on them. The best method is to pray to the Gods or the cosmos for things to turn out as they should, or to go well, and let the individuals make their own choices of how that will be for them. Just sending energy for the use of whomever is another generic type of prayer which does not involve unwanted coercion. Otherwise, just asking, "May I pray for you?" is acceptable.

Magick is the controlled use of will to effect change in a person or the world. It can be a powerful tool and should be used with caution and respect for what it can accomplish. As the saying goes, "Be careful what you wish for, for you just might get it." And just because you have an immediate need or want, the future may bring different circumstances that change your wishes and needs considerably. The best thing is to work for change within yourself, working toward self-betterment and refinement of the soul. Remember the political slogan "Think globally, act locally"? If you effect change within yourself, you change a little bit of your local part of the world. And when you change the world locally, you change the world!

DIVINATION

Another form of magick and spellwork which Wiccans use is "divination." Divination helps find answers, predict the future, find out what other people are thinking or doing, and get advice about things. Wiccans are not specifically required to do divination, but most do. You do not have to put up a Circle for divination, but if you do, you will find that outside distractions are greatly minimized, you can concentrate better, and you will probably get better results. Divinatory systems are not worshipped in themselves, but are tools for self-improvement, and for gaining insight into one's self, motivations, and possible strengths and weaknesses.

Wiccans use almost every divinatory method known to the modern world. Most will preferably use a tool (like the tarot cards or astrological charts) or device (like a magick mirror or pendulum) to focus upon for divination.

The most common divinatory system used by Wiccans is the tarot, which is a set of cards with symbols and pictures. When properly used, it can help the unconscious mind work out problems, help others, and discover information about the past, present, and future. Some Wiccans make money "telling fortunes" with the tarot. Most, however, use the tarot only as a self-guidance tool and will not take money if they do readings for others.

Other divinatory systems used by Wiccans include astrology, the Norse runes, and scrying, which uses something like a crystal ball to focus upon for symbol-impressions.

There are "natural psychics" in Wicca, but they are few and far between. (If you use something outside yourself, it becomes easier to control the experience.) One note: Most Wiccans do not use or recommend using Ouija™ boards, or practicing the spiritualist's techniques known as "table tapping" or "spirit spelling." These can be effective, and they require little or no skill, but unless used in a controlled environment (like a protected circle), they can allow discarnate entities to come through and possibly cause trouble, including even "possession," on rare occasions. For these and other reasons, we consider these practices potentially dangerous.

What form of divination a Wiccan might practice is entirely up to the individual. Many different methods are available, and it is best to experiment with a practice to test its effectiveness. There are many books available which detail the "how to" of all sorts of methods. Try to avoid spending lots of money on something, however, until you are sure you'll like it. Using a pendulum is one method that requires little cost or training. Paul always carries a pendant on a cord with him, which he uses as a pendulum for divination. He holds the cord and asks, "What is your yes? What is your no?" and observes how the pendulum moves in response for each question. Then come the questions.

It is perfectly acceptable to test a divinatory system, especially the pendulum. Asking two mutually exclusive questions like "Will I go to New York next week?" and then, "Will I stay in town all next week?" can help test if you are getting a true reading. Writing down the questions beforehand can help organize your thoughts. And writing down the answers and keeping track of their accuracy can also show if this is the system for you. This then becomes a part of your Book of Shadows.

Both Paul and Estelle practice several different forms of divination depending on the type of information desired and the time and materials available. But divination can become a crutch, and you should save it for the big stuff, or when you are truly stuck with a choice and do not know which option might be better. If you end up doing a divination every morning before you get dressed or go out, you are doing it too much. If you cannot simply get through life without divination to help you make decisions, then it is becoming more of a handicap than help, and you should stop. But divination is a very ancient tool and, if used carefully, it can be an effective aid in helping you make some of your life choices.

How divination works is debated. Some say when you use any form of divination you are really just tapping into your own subconscious intuition and actually guiding yourself. Some feel they are receiving advice directly from the Gods, or a guardian angel, or even perhaps dead Aunt Minnie. Paul and Estelle, however, think that it is better to leave dead Aunt Minnie out of it. She probably has other things to do.

Occasionally, it can help to get perspective by having someone else read for you, but it is not wise to make it a habit. If you do it for yourself, you are learning a skill and getting more in touch with your inner self, which aids in the self-betterment Great Work process. It is better if you put in the energy yourself, because it will probably be a better reading. Remember, "The Gods help those who help themselves."

PART II

EVERYTHING YOU NEED TO KNOW TO BE A WICCAN

COVENS

A GROUP OF PEOPLE WITHIN WICCA IS CALLED a coven. Traditionally, covens have thirteen members of varying degrees, a High Priestess, and six other couples. They meet regularly and celebrate Sabbats and Esbats, and they teach and learn together, although it is possible for a coven to be much more. The people who make up a coven can become as close and tightly knit as a family, a support group, a group of intimate friends, soul mates, magickal partners, or it can be just a group of like-minded people, who have agreed to hold some sort of regularly scheduled discussion or study meetings, and never see each other otherwise. It all depends what you can find, or organize, or what the personal needs of the individual members are.

WHAT IS A COVEN?

To outsiders a coven may seem like a group of friends who meet regularly and do a variety of activities together. Sometimes that is all a coven is. But most covens are tightly knit groups of deeply committed people who have agreed to bond and worship together, as well as practice magick.

A tightly knit coven of people creates a magickal gestalt, an entity that is made up of all the members and their energies. This gestalt is greater than the individuals and can operate more powerfully than the individuals could separately. The gestalt demands each member be totally committed to the gestalt, the group, and the coven, with no room for dissension or conflicting interests. For this reason, people in a coven who have created such a gestalt (though they may not realize or name it as such) are extremely careful when admitting new members.

Covens can form in several ways. Most commonly, a group of people decide to get together on a regular basis to pursue common interests. This can range from quite casual discussion and socializing to more serious study and teaching. These groups usually do not practice magick or form a gestalt. They may never go beyond a group of friends meeting and sharing interests. They may be more social and celebratory. These covens are good and are no less valid than the more serious magickal ones.

Sometimes a group of people want to start a serious coven, working magick and pursuing serious magickal researches. In this situation, each person should be fully aware of just what level of commitment this coven will demand. Some covens, especially in certain Traditions, demand a great deal of time and attention of their members, including socializing. These groups may meet three or more nights a week for study and teaching, and again on Friday or Saturday evening for socializing and serious magickal ritual, celebration of the Sabbats and Esbats, and more. If you join one of these covens, you are making a serious time and lifestyle commitment.

Most covens are somewhere between these two extremes, with the time commitment for members usually one evening a week, together with some socializing, possibly an informal support group, celebration of Sabbats and Esbats, and some teaching, study, and magick as well. Committing to more than one evening a week is difficult for most people. Often the people in a coven are also friends and may socialize outside the coven setting. The coven or its members may or may not be associated with a larger Wiccan or Pagan organization like a local Wiccan church or Covenant of the Goddess (COG) or Congregation of Unitarian Universalist Pagans (CUUPS).

Belonging to a coven is a serious religious commitment. It is more of a commitment than belonging to a fraternity or sorority, a business organization, a political organization, a charitable organization, or a social club. It is also more of a commitment than most people put into being a member of a Christian church. Each coven is autonomous and makes its own rules and decides what it will do. There is no framework (unless you are part of an established Tradition) for how to be in a coven, what the coven members should do, or what the rules are. All of this has to be established by the members of each coven individually. That is part of what makes it such a large commitment.

There is no hierarchy to oversee what each coven is doing or to help keep members' interests high. It is up to each individual.

The religious component also adds a layer of intensity and commitment to coven membership. It is in the coven that Wiccans practice their religion, unless they are solitary. Wicca is a religion with few set rules or guidelines, and again it is up to the coven members to decide on these matters for themselves, individually and as a group.

There is no non-Wiccan or Pagan entity that is quite like a coven.

SIZE OF A COVEN

While tradition dictates that the number of members of a coven is thirteen, in reality the number of people who will actually be involved in any given coven will normally be decided for various practical reasons. A group with thirteen members is considered desirable by many Traditions and is generally a good upper limit for groups who want to maintain close internal ties between members. Most Wiccans meet and celebrate in one of their member's private homes, usually the living room, and few modern living rooms can comfortably hold more than thirteen people. Although thirteen is in general the upper size limit, there is no lower limit. You can be successful with as few as two participating members, though three is usually a good minimum for a working group.

With more than thirteen members factions can develop and cliques can become isolated from the rest of the group. With fewer people, everybody has a chance to participate, be noticed, and it is easier to maintain a consensus of what the group wants to do. Factionalism may be kept to a minimum and a smaller group can become more cohesive more quickly.

HOW COVENS FORM

How covens form is as varied as the people who are in them. Occasionally, someone is invited to join a coven that has existed for years, but with the recent increase in interest in Wicca, it seems that it is more common for a group of people to meet, decide they are interested in Wicca, and want to start a group. Sometimes it takes a while before they realize they are a coven. Sometimes they begin with the intention of forming a coven.

Occasionally a coven forms by default. A group of people meets for some specific purpose, perhaps performing a Sabbat. They meet to organize what they had planned, and then meet the next week and do the Sabbat. Then they meet the week after to discuss what they did. And they meet the next week because they like meeting. And pretty soon meeting and working together becomes a habit and suddenly the people realize they have formed a coven.

People can also get together as a support group. They meet and share their issues and problems, and work together to solve them. They may read a self-help book and discuss it. They may decide one member needs a Working to help them overcome a problem or to attract something new into their life. They may decide to do a group project like cleaning up trash near a body of water. Pretty soon they realize their meetings have evolved into a coven.

The process can also be more deliberate. A group of like-minded friends, no more than ten, who express interest in becoming a coven meet to have a brainstorming session. This should not be too large a group, no more than ten at the outset. Each person in the group describes their interests and needs. A moderator limits each person to a set amount of time. Someone should take notes on the pertinent points.

At a second meeting, the group discusses what was decided at the first meeting. This second discussion can be more challenging. The person with the notes can see if any common threads or themes appeared. The group should discuss these and gradually come to some consensus. Maybe some people will decide their needs will not be met. They may drop out or want to form a separate group. Maybe there will be two factions with different needs and interests. This could be the basis for two separate covens.

At this point, there is little commitment or emotional investment. There are no rules or guidelines. These are just idea sessions.

There may be a third meeting, but by now some consensus should have been reached. People should have some idea about the type of group (or groups) they want, and what activities the group will participate in. Group members should be prepared to make a commitment to the group by this time. Dragging the process out any longer can be counterproductive. Each individual should also have some idea of what the other people are like, and whether or not they will be able to tolerate them in a close group. All these factors should be taken into account when making the commitment. The group should dictate what level of involvement is required—casual, moderate, or serious—and each person should carefully weigh all the factors and make a mature and informed decision. This is not a popularity contest or status symbol. A coven is a religious commitment and should be approached with the gravity and reverence serious religious study requires.

At this stage, the commitment should be a commitment to try this arrangement. It does not require any binding oaths or serious life changes. There is still a lot of work to do, but by the third meeting, a good start will have been made.

In exploring their common interests, the group members should explore whether or not these can sustain a group over months and years.

Celebrating Sabbats and Esbats will sustain a group. The weeks between the Sabbats and Esbats can be devoted to ritual planning, craft projects for the Sabbats, or just general socializing and support. One coven in Minnesota has lasted for over twenty years with this aim.

Study can sustain a group. For example, working with the tarot can last a lifetime. Devoting a week to each card would take seventy-eight weeks (one and one-half years). Then the group can start comparing decks or interpretations. They can explore different spreads, tarot symbolism, numerology and tarot, develop a deck of their own, etc. Astrology, Runes, and various other divinatory systems are also topics that can sustain a group over time.

Reading and discussing books—both fiction and non-fiction—can be a worthy goal. Scientific exploration of the properties of magickal tools and techniques can last a lifetime. Kabbalah ties in with many other pursuits, or can be studied alone. Working magick can also be worthwhile, but beware the spell-of-the-week syndrome. In spell-working there should be as much or more time devoted to study and planning as to the actual Working itself.

A group can decide to study various topics in units; for example, spending eight weeks on tarot, six weeks on the Runes, two weeks on pendulums, a few weeks reading a book and discussing it, three weeks planning and holding a Sabbat celebration, a week just socializing and having a barbecue, three weeks exploring death and dying, etc. The leader of each group can rotate among coven members, taking advantage of expertise or to research a topic and then disseminate their new

knowledge to the group. This model requires at least quarterly meetings to plan so all know what is expected and where they are in the schedule.

A group can decide they want to devote themselves to teaching Wicca and possibly granting degrees. This can also sustain a group, but beware the teachers do not burn themselves out. The members should have a plan or syllabus of what they will teach, a timetable to teach it, and share teaching duties evenly. Some thought should be given to what the students will do when they have "graduated." Will the class start over with a new crop of people? Will the students go on to earn higher degrees? Will a coven form with the former students and teachers devoting their energies to other pursuits?

When Estelle teaches her basic First Degree Wicca classes, she plans at least eighteen to twenty-four months per class. Three to four months are required to organize the group through interviews and discussion of curriculum and books with co-teachers before the class actually begins. Then at least a year-and-a-day is necessary for the class itself, then another month or two to do the Initiations, if any qualify. Then Estelle plans a few months off for rest and recharging before starting another class.

Some people teach ten or more students at once, most teach two to five at a time. Some teach one on one. For a beginning Wicca class with a First Degree as its goal, a small group with two or three teachers works well. The larger classes can work, but people come and go more often in a larger class, and it can be difficult to get to know each student individually. Some have "seekers" classes, a series of general information classes which last four to twelve weeks, in which there is no degree offered. However, students who are interested may then join other teaching covens for degrees. General information classes are a good introduction to Wicca without the commitment a First Degree class requires.

If you do choose to teach Wicca, you should have a Degree and some knowledge and education in Wicca before you pass it on to others. Alternatively, people can agree to learn together, and possibly work toward self-Initiation, if there is no teacher available.

With any type of coven, allow for unexpected meetings when someone has a problem or need that the coven can help solve. Beware the coven becoming devoted to the crisis of the week; that indicates a coven has lost focus. The coven should also be flexible enough to take advantage of unexpected happenings. Maybe the group will go to a lecture together, or plan to take a day trip to a local power spot. Getting out and doing different things can keep interest alive.

Once the coven is formed, time should be devoted to the various rules under which the coven will operate. At least twice a year, each coven should devote a meeting to reviewing their mission, goals, accomplishments, rules, and bylaws. This would be the time to enact new rules or change existing ones. If members wanted to change the mission or focus of a group, this would be the time to discuss that also.

AN AVERAGE COVEN MEETING

Generally a coven meets weekly. Since people will naturally socialize, time should be allowed for socializing and interaction among the members before and after the "heart" of the meeting. Coven members will be more comfortable with a group that includes pleasant conversation and congenial people. Below is a sample schedule of a coven meeting:

7–7:30 PM: Meet and socialize.

7:30–9:30 PM: Coven meeting. This is when the coven does what it was established to do.

9:30–10 PM: Cleanup, some casual support group discussions, general chatting, maybe some snacks.

You can change the amount of time spent for each section. Four hours is the maximum amount of time you can reasonably expect people to devote to an evening. You can plan a communal meal at the start, with each person bringing something, and then the meeting can be longer with food preparation and dining as part of the meeting. Eating together can help form bonds between people.

Two hours is a good amount of time for the heart of the meeting. Longer, and there will probably need to be a break because people usually don't want to sit for much longer than two hours; shorter, and people can't get much accomplished. Occasionally a Working or Sabbat may take longer. Have contingencies for the occasion when the meeting runs over. That's why it's also good to build in extra time, for if it runs long, the socializing and cleanup at the end can be abbreviated if necessary.

WHY FORM A COVEN?

When people work together in a coven rather than alone, people can pool their resources. Usually a group will amass a collection of tools and implements to practice Wicca with. A group athame or wand, some sort of altar, candles and incense, a nice pentacle, and a chalice can be more easily obtained if people pool their finances. Books and maybe subscriptions (*Green Egg, Circle*, etc.) can be bought and shared and in that way the coven can amass a library of materials for general resource and reference far greater than any one person could accumulate on their own.

More important than sharing resources is that in a coven you are not alone in your Workings.

With a group, you can get immediate feedback and encouragement on your performance of the Wiccan rites. Are you intoning the chants correctly? How *do* you pronounce all those funny words? The other members of your coven can help. Some people prefer to work solitary because they don't want anyone to see them doing things that seem as silly as some of our rituals sometimes seem to beginners. But if you share something—if you are all doing the same thing—it removes some of the strangeness from wearing unusual robes and chanting funny words.

TO JOIN A COVEN OR NOT?

Sometimes another group structure is more appropriate than a full coven. If you are in a group of college students, and you all know you will be moving on in a few years, another type of group might be more appropriate. Maybe you just want to hang out with a group of friends. Maybe you like the idea of being in a club, but aren't willing to devote a great deal of time and energy into keeping the club going. Some people are not comfortable with the intimacy and emotional bonding which frequently can form within a coven. Some people aren't comfortable with the connotations that word has garnered over the centuries. A study group, a student club or organization, a coffee klatch are all acceptable substitutes for the more traditional coven. They are more casual, have less emotional investment, and cause less controversy than a coven might. The bonds between group members may not be as strong in a more casual group, since there is less commitment and less opportunity to develop a group mind; hence you might accomplish less, but so are time and energy commitments.

Each person has to decide whether or not to be a member of a coven or a member of a more casual group. More casual groups can meet at more casual places. Coffee houses are great meeting places for casual groups, but are usually not good places to hold a Sabbat or for serious magickal study. Find out what type of organizations are available for you to join; discover what you can about how they work, who the movers and shakers of the group are; then weigh and balance that with your interests, needs, and resources, and decide for yourself how well any of the available groups might fill your needs. Make an informed decision. It's easier to start casually and become more serious about a group, than it is to be very serious initially and either have a bad experience or find your interest waning. This is a serious religious decision. Make it responsibly.

TO BEGIN A COVEN

When a group decides to become a coven, the first step is to decide on the ground rules. If these rules are written down they become a covenant. This can appear more formal and organized than some people will be comfortable with, but making a few rules at the beginning can reduce problems later on. We do recommend that you try to keep any rules you make as simple as you can. The less involved they are, the easier it is to change them later if the need arises.

Here is a list of ideas a group of people might want to consider when drafting their covenant, whether it is for a formal coven or a simple coffee klatch.

How often will the group meet? In general weekly meetings are best. More often, and people begin to miss meetings; less often, and some people don't get into the habit of meeting regularly.

Will there be attendance requirements? If someone misses three meetings in a row, will they be considered inactive? For smaller groups, it is very important for everyone to attend, and if one member is consistently late and/or absent, it might be best for them to find another group that is more in line with their needs.

How are members of the group chosen? How are new members to be admitted? What is the procedure for members leaving? Over time people will come and go, and original members may want a greater say about new members. Can people just leave the coven, do they have to ask to leave, or do they have to be voted out? Are leaves of absence allowed for members, and what reasons are valid and which are not? The issues about potential new members are covered later in this chapter.

Other questions may arise as the group decides on its structure. Once decisions have been reached, a record should be kept to refer to at appropriate times.

Who will fill what role? Will this be a hierarchical coven with a High Priestess and High Priest and other members? Who is in charge? Will there be a secretary who takes notes and keeps a coven journal or Book of Shadows? (This is highly recommended.) Are decisions reached by democratic vote, or are decisions made by a consensus—everyone must be in agreement—or will decisions be made by the leader after input from the members? Will there be elected officers who serve for a specific time period?

All these practical questions should be addressed. There is no universal "correct" group organization. The way your group will work best will depend on what your group wants to do. If you want to read and discuss the many books that are available, a consensus organization will work well. On the other hand, if you decide to delve deeply into the mysteries and the magick of Wicca, and your own souls, you may want a more rigid hierarchical structure, centered around your most competent people.

What will the coven be named? Naming a coven can be as significant or casual as the group decides. Some groups are named by default, for example, the Wednesday Night Gather (shortened to WNG). Some groups put time and energy into naming the group, because the name can also help create the gestalt which is (or will be) formed by the group. Naming the group is almost like naming a child. That gestalt can also be called a Magickal Childe, which is a magickal construct created for specific magickal purposes. Choose a name for a coven in the same way you would choose a magickal name.

What is the coven confidentiality policy? Will it be open (anyone can join) or closed (membership by invitation only)? Will the membership be Out (openly and publicly Wiccan) or not Out (not revealing their religious affiliation) or mixed (some of each)? Will the names of the members be divulged to others? Will the members be allowed to talk about what they do at their meetings? Can members even admit to membership in the coven?

What is the purpose of the coven? Worship and celebration? Teaching and/or training? Research and study? Socialization? Working magick? Or will it be task-oriented? Will you be

- keeping a garden?
- maintaining a Web site?
- experimenting with crafts and other activities?
- writing and creating?
- planning a festival or gathering?
- putting out a newsletter or journal?
- doing volunteer work in the community, etc.?

How will activities and roles be assigned? How does the group change its focus?

How is the covenant to be maintained? How can it be changed? Will all members get a copy, or will there be one master copy at the covenstead?

Can the lessons, materials, and researches of the

coven be shared? Will they be compiled in a master Book of Shadows? Will each member receive copies? Will the Book of Shadows be available for those outside the coven?

If you are starting a coven in a specific Wiccan Tradition, these questions are already addressed in the principles of that Tradition. If you aren't associated with a specific Tradition, then starting your coven with the activities of teaching, research, and study might be best. Then you can plan the Sabbats, and possibly the Esbats, and continue your reading and sharing of books and knowledge.

BOOK LEARNING

Without an experienced teacher (which most Traditions provide) most of your study of the Craft and Wicca will come from books. Luckily, there are many good written resources currently available. How your group explores this resource is up to you. Either one person can read a book and give a report on the pertinent data (the fastest way to get through the most material in the shortest time), or all can read the same book and have a discussion about it (the best way to absorb one book most completely). You can watch movies or videos and discuss them. Even not so positive examples can be instructive because seeing how people create a bad example may prevent you from repeating it in the future. Science fantasy offers many good books, movies, and concepts about magick and alternate worlds and/or realities. Exploring those can help a group achieve a more magickal mindset, and opens peoples' minds up to a multitude of options that are possible. Working as a group to learn tarot or astrology, for example, is a good coven endeavor. If one member has a special expertise, why not have them teach a unit about their specialty?

INTERVIEWING NEW MEMBERS

In the beginning a coven is usually made up of a group of friends. Frequently people know each other and there are no requirements for joining other than interest and being there at the appropriate time. However, as the group grows and matures, people will come and go and you might end up with a group of just two or three people. So it is important to decide how to recruit new members.

The group should have decided on certain criteria before any new members are interviewed. Some considerations are

- Do new members need a sponsor?

- Will new members be voted in?

- Can one "no" vote eliminate a person from consideration?

- Will there be a probationary period for new members?

- Do all members have to be a certain age? Sex? Degree? A certain Tradition? Follow a certain path? Be single or childless?

- Should new members swear an oath of secrecy? Be formally initiated into the coven? Undergo a hot seat?

- Will one person be in charge of interviewing candidates?

Once these questions have been answered, the group is ready to begin the process of choosing new members.

New members are usually chosen through an interview process. Often the procedure is as follows: **A potential member expresses interest in joining the group.** An interested person will approach a member and ask general information about the group and whether the group is open (admitting new members). This is a preliminary interview and can be invaluable to assuring the group and person are a good fit, with the group member and potential member casually questioning each other. The person is seeking information about the group, and usually what they want to know is

• When does your group meet?

• Where are you based (in general, we feel that it is best not to reveal the location of any covenstead)?

• What is the group about (ritual, study, social, etc.)?

• How is it structured (consensus, hierarchical, elected officers, etc.)?

And some of the information that your group wants to find out about the person is

• What is this person looking for?

• What is their previous training (both mundane and magickal)? Degrees? Interests? Skills and specialties?

• What other magickal or religious groups have they been members of in the past? Who did they train with? Do they have good relationships with their former teachers, friends, lovers, etc.?

Generally, the group has already discussed how these questions are addressed. If you have agreed that group members must not acknowledge their membership to an outsider, the process will end right there. How much is to be revealed to outsiders should be understood and enforced by all.

A preliminary interview determines the eligibility of a person for inclusion in the group and people who pass this casual interview are strong candidates for the group. If a few members of the group are Out, they should be the ones communicating with prospective members. Those who are not Out usually won't reveal their affiliation until the group is sure of a new person. These issues should be worked out in advance.

The group meets privately and discusses the need for new members in general and the person in question specifically. All members should discuss their opinions and share information, including whether you need this person in your group or not. If, according to your group's guidelines, a prospective member needs to be sponsored by some current member, then the sponsor is given the opportunity to give their reasons for selecting this new member. **Once the group has reached a decision about admitting the new person, a more formal interview with the new person by two or more of your group members is arranged.** During the interview, people in the group can question the new person, and the new person should be ready to answer questions about their interests, studies, background, and other questions necessary to determine if they are suited for the group. Try to keep the tone of this meeting somewhat relaxed—this is NOT a hot seat, but merely an interview. Sometimes the interview is conducted by two members at a neutral place, and a report is brought back to the group. Sometimes the interview is in the covenstead with the whole group. These arrangements depend on the group's needs, size, and style. The interview can be preliminary to setting up a hot seat, or it can stand alone.

After this interview (and the hot seat if held) the group should meet privately and discuss the candidate again. This should NOT be done while the candidate is present, nor should you keep them waiting around. These discussions can take weeks or less and include evaluating the information presented to the group by the candidate.

If there are people with whom the candidate has studied, then a group member should talk to them. But, if a candidate will not give names or phone numbers, that shouldn't rule them out as a potential member. After all, confidentiality is important in some circumstances. But do make every effort to assess the character and past of the prospective member before letting them into your group. Remember, a coven is not just a social clique, it is a religious unit, and you want maximum compatibility and understanding for all members. This is your spiritual life, and you want that to be as good as possible. Be cautious and move slowly.

THE HOT SEAT

A hot seat is a process that some covens use to assess potential new members. This is not a process for a casual or celebratory coven. It is meant to be used by those covens that work magick and have created a gestalt. Occasionally a teaching coven will require potential students to undergo a hot seat as a part of their training.

There are many reasons for covens, and many different activities they engage in. When interviewing a candidate, members of the coven do not usually disclose every detail and practice of their coven to an outsider. That knowledge is reserved for coven members only. A hot seat can be one way of exploring a candidate's feelings on matters, which may or may not have relevance to the coven.

A magickal coven is an intimate social group with a strong psychic and magickal agenda. New members must be fully compatible or the gestalt will not function properly. Candidates will probably not know the full extent of the coven's activities and interests, so the hot seat is performed as a final test to ascertain the new member's potential fit with the coven on a magickal, psychic, and interpersonal level. Sometimes a person is rejected for coven membership not because of any personal problem they have, but because of a potential incompatibility with a current coven member. Or perhaps the candidate holds viewpoints that makes them incompatible with the coven's magickal aims.

Because the candidate does not know the coven's full agenda, they probably will never know why they were rejected. And the coven members may be oathbound to keep certain activities of the coven secret. Rejection does not imply fault or defect, but rather differences that might interfere with the effectiveness of the group's gestalt.

The hot seat is also a traditional holdover from the Inquisition. A hot seat can evaluate a candidate's ability to operate under stress. It can also prepare a person for potentially difficult situations by allowing them to experience the stress first within a reasonably friendly forum. Some Wiccans feel that the hot seat is a necessary "evil" that all Wiccans must undergo to be able to have the full Wiccan experience. Eclectics have rejected some of these ideas, and many Eclectic Wiccans have never undergone a hot seat. We explain the process fully here so if people have an intimate magickal coven, they can use it as a tool to help screen new members.

Joining a magickal coven is a serious life commitment and demands a level of trust and emotional intimacy that is not commonly found outside of marriage in modern society. Sometimes a hot seat is necessary to test a person's level of commitment as well as probe their inner feelings. This is a serious psychological process and should not be undertaken or performed lightly. If you have doubts or misgivings, don't do it.

Arrange a formal hot seat. In some groups, especially very serious working covens, a hot seat interview is used to evaluate a candidate's ability to handle stressful situations. The procedure may seem a bit dramatic, but in groups that conduct serious rituals, this procedure helps determine whether a candidate is suitable.

Arrange for a member of the group (frequently someone who the candidate has not already met), to meet the candidate at some prearranged public place.

The candidate is driven by a circuitous route to their destination (usually the candidate doesn't recognize the route). The driver is as non-communicative as possible, not hostile, but with no unnecessary talking, smiling, etc. This is the start of the candidate's "ordeal," and it is intended that they be a bit uncomfortable. You may want to blindfold the candidate, make them keep their eyes closed, or pick them up after dark at a place they are unfamiliar with.

The candidate is then dropped off outside their destination, told to knock on a certain door, and then left alone. They are met at the door by someone they don't know (if possible) and, with little conversation, led to a prepared seat in the interview room, where their "inquisitors" are already waiting. This room is dark. The inquisitors are silent when not asking questions. They may be in hooded robes, or otherwise masked, and a bright light shines in the candidate's eyes. All of these procedures are designed to create an aura of discomfort and mystery.

The inquisitors ask questions tersely and directly. These questions can be on any subject considered relevant by the individual inquisitor, and often questions are repeated in different ways by different people.

After all the questions have been asked, the candidate is told that the group will be in touch with them, they are escorted to the door and the driver drops them off where they were picked up.

The group then meets to decide whether to admit the candidate. They will inform potential candidates of the group's decision after one week. No member of the group should talk to the candidate about group business before the full week is up.

The hot seat interview is the final interview prior to reaching a decision on membership. A hot seat is a very useful tool because it can tell you a lot about a person, but not everybody is willing to go through one. A hot seat should *never* be conducted with an unsuspecting person who has casually inquired about joining the group. There should always be a preliminary interview. The person should be informed that a hot seat interview is required for membership, and they should be told what it will consist of (i.e., the close questioning, possibly challenging their personality and integrity, and frequently emotionally charged). In general, if a person is successful in the hot seat, they will probably be admitted into the group. Only if some real character flaw or massive incompatibility is uncovered should they be rejected.

Hot seats are not for recreation but are a psychological tool, the purpose of which is not to see if you can get the person to break down, but rather to challenge them and move beyond emotional and personal barriers to see what they are really like. You want to see how they people react under pressure and stress, but not to threaten or frighten them.

WHY ALL THE BOTHER?

A coven interviews or "hot seats" a person to weed out potential problems with personality and to determine if someone is compatible with the rest of the group. If your group is primarily light-hearted and fun-oriented, and the prospective candidate is a scholar who wants a forum for their theories and concepts, they could be incompatible with your group. If a person has been kicked out of three other groups for sexual harassment and doesn't respect boundaries, then they probably wouldn't be acceptable for yours. If you have a gay group and the candidate is homophobic, forget it. If the person is shy and lonely, and doesn't seem to have activities outside their job and the group, it could mean the person will become very devoted to the group; caution is advised. If a person tells you your group needs massive reform and restructuring, watch out.

Even after the interview process sometimes a probationary period is called for in which the new person may participate in your group's activities, but only on a limited basis for a set amount of time. The rest of the group meets privately and assesses the new person's qualities to determine whether they are right for the group.

Some groups have inner and outer courts. The outer court is a group that is less formal and structured and has fewer restrictions and requirements for joining. Usually there is some course of study and after completion the person is considered for membership in the inner court, where the mysteries and more intense studies are practiced. The outer court and study time give all involved the chance to really get to know each other and fully assess whether or not full membership in the inner circle is right for all. Some people may only stay for the study, after which they might leave the group. You can evaluate a group by observing the ratio of people who stay, versus those who come for the training and then leave.

The criteria for admitting new people—by majority vote, by unanimous vote, by sole decision of the leaders with consultation with the rest of the group, or by consensus—should be decided before the process of admitting new people begins. Develop the procedures first then start working with the new potential members. Changing the rules in the middle of the process is unfair to the person and the group. Be consistent and fair.

PROBLEM SOLVING

In any tightly knit group, people can irritate each other. This can range from petty annoyance to major battles. The group should determine before-hand how interpersonal conflicts will be handled. This is a major issue for many Wiccans. Once you are a member of a tightly knit coven, you have invested much time and energy associating with the people in the group, and have attained some spiritual satisfaction and growth. If tensions arise, they can be magnified because of the close relationships within the coven.

There are several practical guidelines for living comfortably in a coven:

Practice good manners. This may seem elementary, but it is often neglected. Saying please and thank you are invaluable magick words. Being courteous, on time, remembering your responsibilities, coming through on your obligations, all are marks of good manners.

Don't overextend yourself, either in terms of time and/or money. If you cannot reasonably make it every Thursday and also pitch in five dollars every week, maybe you should reconsider your commitment to the group. Carry your own weight. Do your share of the work. Take turns being in charge, participating, and observing, and don't push yourself until you become resentful.

Know what you are getting into. If you want a group that is dedicated to celebrating all the Sabbats, and the group you join is dedicated to practicing spellwork, then there may be incompatibilities that arise. Sometimes you have no choice about the group you join. It may be the only one you know of. You can either go with what the group does, or possibly strike out on your own and start your own group.

Always trust your instincts. There are dysfunctional groups of people, and Wicca is no exception. Some may be run by people whose social skills are lacking, others may be exploitative in nature. If you find that your group isn't to your liking, then leave it. If you are threatened or coerced into doing things you don't want to, then definitely leave. If you are threatened with curses to yourself or your family if you do leave, leave immediately. But do take precautions to protect yourself, like strengthening your personal shields or the magickal shields around your home. And remember the Law of Three. If people are cursing you, they are cursing themselves threefold. The more effective they are at cursing, the worse it will be for them. Ethical Wiccans don't curse each other, or anyone for that matter.

What you get out of a group will be directly proportional to what you put into it. Do your share of work and participate to your best ability. We all have off nights. But if you find that you have more off than on nights at the group, it is usually best to reevaluate your attitudes about the group. Your attitude is something you can control. Be open and willing to try new and different things. A coven is a safe place, where you should always feel you are among friends who have your best interests at heart. Don't be afraid to try new stuff, experiment, take chances. If you fail, oh well, at least you tried. If you look silly, so what, we all look silly from time to time. If you succeed, then you not only benefit yourself, you are of benefit to the coven. Your coven can be like your magickal workshop. It can also be a fantastic resource, for you have the combined knowledge, learning, and wisdom of the group. You have a ready-made sounding board for whatever you want to do. You can benefit from the accumulated experiences and knowledge of the others. And you have the safety net of the others with you, so if you fall, they can help pick you up.

GROUP CONFLICTS

In any group there are conflicts. How these are dealt with can make the difference between a successful coven and one that disintegrates quickly. There are a number of ways conflicts can start and a number of ways to resolve them. While most covens operate smoothly, there are times when they do not, and because of all the emotional investment and religious ties this acrimony can be extremely traumatic if not dealt with carefully and swiftly. People have been emotionally damaged by a bad coven breakup, and we hope to give some tools to avoid the worst of the trauma. For the most part, common courtesy and polite manners will serve well, and your coven will be harmonious. But bad things do happen.

Irreconcilable Differences

There are people who just cannot fit comfortably into any group. Estelle calls them problem personalities, and they are many and varied. If you are in a group, and certain people seem to drag the group down, monopolize the group's time and resources, or just plain cause problems, you and the rest of the group should be prepared to deal with these people. Sometimes the best for all is to kindly ask the person to leave the group. Problem personalities cannot and will not be reformed by the average group of Wiccans. They enjoy group wrecking, personal attack, and/or social vampirism of various types. The average Wiccan coven is *not* set up to reform problem personalities.

One way to determine if a group is plagued by a problem personality is to monitor the group's activities:

- Is the purpose of the group being sidetracked in favor of one person to the exclusion of others?
- Is it a chore to attend group meetings?
- Do you often leave the meetings frustrated, angry, or discontented?
- Does conversation among group members center on the problem person and what to do or not

do, and how they or the group should change to accommodate them?

- Does one member repeatedly make everyone else uncomfortable?

An effective group will act together to determine who the problem person is and then work together to remove them from the group. If the problem person is in charge of the group, your only choice may be to leave. In some cases, if you are the only person having a problem, maybe the problem is with you, not the other person. Be cautious, because if this is a problem that is exclusively between you and another person, it is more than likely that the irritating member is not a group wrecker, not a problem personality. If there is no other choice, then you just might want to quietly leave, burning as few bridges as possible. After all, you don't want to alienate yourself from the rest of the people in the group.

There is another solution for personality problems that arise. If you are one of a faction who feels there is a problem, and others do not, you should consider hiving off and starting your own group. Hiving off is a tool to allow a large group to split into two or more smaller, more manageable ones. But it is also a tool to allow a portion of a group to leave with as little acrimony as possible, by providing an established mechanism for doing so.

The Root of All Evil

Money and expenses can cause conflict. Not everyone has the same means or resources. If one coven member is a systems analyst and makes a lot of money, and others are poor college students, it is not fair to expect one person to pay all the expenses. Ideally expenses should be shared. If one person is not satisfied and wants to contribute more, that should be their choice. But they should also realize they are not obligating others to their level of contribution. Expenditures should be discussed and agreed to before any purchases are made. Will there be a treasury or dues? If there are large amounts of money involved, some sort of treasurer and bank account might be in order. But be careful, because these can generate more expenses and work in themselves. The more things you have, the more time and money they take to keep up. Maybe passing the hat or taking contributions for each expense will be what your coven will find effective.

Who's the Boss?

Work roles can be another source of conflict. Who is to play which role? Will there be a coven secretary who maintains the Book of Shadows? Will they do it all themselves? Will the duties rotate through the group? Who will be in charge? If one or two people end up doing most of the work, there is something not right. If there is a High Priestess and High Priest they might do a lot of the work, but they should not do it all. Duties and responsibilities should be shared and the group must decide how this will be done.

Activities

It is important for the group to decide what activities they will perform. If someone joined to do Sabbats, and the group only puts on one Sabbat a year, is that member getting what they want?

Participation is related to activities and roles. Ideally each member should have a chance to participate as much as they like. Some people don't want to participate very much, preferring to be a member of the audience or a congregant. That doesn't work well in a small coven. Everybody should be willing to put in a certain amount of time and energy to make the group work. Being in a coven is not a spectator sport. It requires work,

Witches Brewing

energy, and commitment. Consciously rotating duties and responsibilities ensures all have a chance to do something, and a chance to try new and different roles.

Naturally skill levels vary among members. Designing activities and/or roles to take advantage of members' skills makes for a more effective group. But people with lesser skills or training should be allowed to try also. Impatience should be curbed, and people should allow others to try and even fail, for sometimes we learn more from failures than successes. Everybody is good at something, just as everybody is really bad at other things. Let people work on their skills as well as non-skills. Ideally the goal is for each coven member to be minimally skilled in every important area. Minimally skilled does not mean expertise, nor even necessarily comfortably competent, but each member should be capable of performing different tasks adequately, especially in a pinch.

The Generation Gap

Differing levels of maturity can cause friction and sometimes conflicts. Hopefully a coven will be a nurturing, safe, and encouraging place for all to learn and grow. Ridicule has no place there. Humor is valuable, but not when directed pointedly or cruelly at people. Having a good balance between humor, fun, and serious work and study is best, but maintaining that balance can be quite difficult. Remember, a coven is where people can trust, and so even small hurts and slights can easily be magnified. Be prepared to apologize if you inadvertently hurt someone. Be sensitive to the feelings, values, and comfort levels of others. Conversely, if one person has sensitivities and problems which continually cause friction, maybe that person should reevaluate their attitudes and sensitivities, and if that doesn't relieve the friction, perhaps they should consider finding a group that suits their needs better.

Ethics

We define "morals" as a code of right and wrong thoughts and behavior imposed from without by a society. "Ethics" is a personal code of right and wrong chosen by an individual after careful thought and study.

Wiccans talk a lot about ethics among themselves, because Wiccans don't usually adopt others' morals. Wiccans, in general, decide for themselves what their individual ethics will be. What happens when ethics collide? This can be a major crisis for a group. One member may be adamantly ethically opposed to eating meat, while another isn't. How do you reconcile opposing viewpoints based on ethics? Sometimes you don't. That's the time when people have to agree to disagree, without trying to convert each other. Sometimes clever solutions can be worked out. If the coven eats a communal meal, perhaps cook a main dish as vegetarian with a meat side dish. Or have two choices, one vegetarian and one not. Sometimes one member may choose to not participate in something they feel violates their ethics. As long as the differences are discussed, and each person is allowed to state their case without judgment or criticism, it should be possible to work out almost any differences. Forcing someone to choose between their ethics and participation in the group's activities is a good way to break up a coven.

Balancing individual needs and the needs of the group is a dynamic challenge. There are benefits to working in a group, but members do give up a certain amount of autonomy and freedom. Hopefully the benefits outweigh the sacrifices.

Power Net

Power is always an important issue in any group and can cause enormous conflict. Who has the power to make decisions and who doesn't is not always clearly defined. Sometimes this is determined by the way the group is structured. If there is a hierarchy and one High Priestess and High Priest are in charge, the rest of the group accepts that they have more power than other members. But the other members also have some power because, without these other members, the High Priestess and High Priest have no group to lead. The personal power of every individual member must be recognized, and awakening and increasing each individual's personal power is something most Wiccan groups and Traditions try very hard to improve.

Each person will have some voice in the group. Balance and awareness is the key. Leaders who dominate others, who ignore the interests and sensibilities of others, soon find themselves a leader with no followers and, conversely, members who allow leaders to dominate and won't speak out when they are dissatisfied are granting dominance to their leaders. Personal responsibility is the key. Each person has a choice about their participation.

Relationships

Trust arises from a close-knit group working together smoothly for a long time. People get to know each other, understand each other, and grow to like each other. How much more traumatic then, when one person feels another has betrayed that trust? What is truly unforgivable and what is merely thoughtless? When should you say I'm sorry? Accidents do happen. And how much actual damage was done? "Perfect Love and Perfect Trust" are good ideals, but we are not perfect, and sometimes forgiveness is the only viable choice.

Relationships and sex can wreck a group faster than anything else. If one member is preying sexually on others, they should be removed from the group immediately. Still, there are other situations that arise in which the group is affected. For exam-

ple, two people in a group decide to have a relationship, and it just doesn't work out. Some people can still co-exist in a small group under those circumstances, but most cannot. Who stays and who goes? Will there be a rule about dating within the coven? And what do you do when a couple divorces: Who stays and who goes? For most of these types of questions, there are no right answers. But these matters should be discussed and acknowledged.

Outside relationships and/or commitments can also be problematic. What do you do when a close friend finds a partner you cannot stand? If the partner isn't in the coven, usually you can ignore them, and still enjoy your friend within the coven. But what if they want their new partner in the group? In these kinds of circumstances the mechanism for selecting new members can be helpful. In social events, in which your coven shares activities with people outside the coven, for example, family members, sometimes you just have to grin and be polite.

If one member has a big project at their job, or they travel a lot and cannot attend meetings regularly, what then? It is best to see if the situation is temporary or permanent. If it is temporary, usually allowances can be made. If permanent, can or should the group change to accommodate one person's time schedule?

Non-coven family can also become a problem. Does the family support the coven member's participation in the group? Or are they hostile? Or do they even know about the coven? Many Wiccans are not Out, even to their families. Usually this means parents and siblings; rarely, it can also include a spouse. Some Wiccans hide their religion from their children. How this impacts the coven, the individual, and other members should be examined. How comfortable will other members feel about hiding their own beliefs in front of another member's family? Advance discussion is vital for the group to be able to deal with these touchy situations.

WHEN THE COVEN SPLITS UP

What do you do when a group does disintegrate due to conflict or choice? Usually there are two sides, with some people on the sidelines. In the ideal situation, mediation works best. Try to get the principals to sit down and rationally discuss their differences, perhaps with a neutral party overseeing the face-to-face discussion. We do *not* recommend an intermediary trying to mediate between the factions, if the factions refuse to meet face to face. This can lead to more problems than it solves.

Certainly the disagreement should not spread beyond the coven. It should not be aired or discussed in public. Dragging outsiders into a personal dispute is called a Witch War (in Wiccan terms), and is highly undesirable. Allowing others not intimately involved to intervene usually only escalates the conflict. If people disagree irreconcilably, then someone must go. That's it. Don't try to salvage a group that has been split in an acrimonious dispute. People disagree, usually no one is at fault, and sometimes each party just has to go their own way. Nothing lasts forever, not even a coven.

Most covens die through *ennui*. People drift away, develop other interests, or stop coming to meetings. Having a solid effective coven takes work, lots of work. And few people have the energy to maintain that level of commitment over the years. If a coven lasts longer than a year, it probably will last a few years or more. A few covens last five or ten years or even longer. But rarely does a coven last year in and year out with the same people, even among the established Traditions. Gerald Gardner, the founder of modern Wicca, had changes of personnel and at least three different major High Priestesses over the years. A good solid coven is built to be adaptable, and change and grow with the people in it. If you are lucky enough to be in a good coven for even a few years, those can be immensely productive years for you as a Wiccan. Realize that nothing is forever, and enjoy what you have while you have it, and give thanks to the Goddess.

MUSICAL CHAIRS

There is an unwritten rule that you cannot belong to more than one coven at a time. How that plays out in reality can vary. If you are a member of one coven and you find you want to join another, decide what will be best for you and the covens. Full disclosure to both groups is *vital*. If one or the other objects, be prepared to deal with it. Sometimes we have to make choices.

Why do you want to join another group? Is it because you have a new love interest and this is their group? This is usually not a good reason to join another coven, especially if the relationship is new. People break up and then that adds a layer of conflict to the coven it didn't have before. Some groups specifically forbid both members of a committed pair to be full members, while conversely, there are other Traditions that will only allow committed couples to join. With the first type of group, only one of the couple is considered a permanent member, while the other is considered a permanent guest. In either case, if the couple splits, the guest has to go.

Is your original group not meeting your needs? Just what your true needs are, and how well the original coven does meet these and other needs should be examined. Maybe you just want a group to practice spells with, and your original group is Sabbat-oriented.

Sometimes it can be a case of the grass being greener elsewhere. Or maybe you are just in a rut.

But understand, leaving one coven or joining another is a serious religious event. It requires thought and examination of your interests, needs, and motives. Be starkly honest with yourself about the issues. Don't make the move on a whim or because you want to shake up your life a bit. If those are your motives, a makeover would be more suitable.

LAST WORDS

If you commit fully, a coven can become like a chosen family. If you want that kind of entity in your life, embrace it. If not, you should reconsider your commitment. Your coven is what you make of it. Your commitment and participation are vital for the smooth running of the group, no matter what kind of a group it is. For most Wiccans, their coven IS Wicca to them. If you are aware and act responsibly and with forethought, a coven can last generations.

CIRCLES

Thus we are met in a Time without a time, and at a Place without a place. For we are between the worlds and beyond!

This statement, or one like it, is spoken by most High Priests/Priestesses (HP/HPS) at the end of the establishment of every formal Wiccan magickal Working or worship, before the actual worship or Working can commence. It is known either as the "binding," "closing," or "casting of the Circle." It usually signifies that an area, or Sacred Space, has been properly prepared for the coming worship/Working by describing the boundaries of the Sacred Space, warding or psychically separating the Sacred Space from the mundane world, and cleansing or banishing negative or disruptive influences from the working area.

Depending on both the Tradition and the purpose and design of a specific ritual, the HP/HPS may or may not say anything like the above quote. Setting up a Circle might take over an hour to perform, with much noise, a great deal of fancy equipment, language, and props. Or at another ritual, it could be cast in an instant, with little or no overt indications that anything has happened. But, if there are Wiccans performing any type of ritual, there has been some kind of Sacred Circle set up. One of the defining characteristics of Wicca, is that we worship and work magick in Circles.

WHY WICCANS WORK IN CIRCLES

There are several reasons Wiccans work in Circles. One of the main reasons is that, like other people, we prefer to meet Deity in a physical place that is symbolically and/or psychically removed from the mundane world. Some place where we can leave the cares of everyday life at the door, so to speak, and clear our minds for the simple pleasures of a focused spiritual experience. Most modern religions provide their congregations with their form of Sacred Space within a building dedicated to worship, whether it is called a church, a mosque, or a temple. With few exceptions, Wiccans do not have dedicated physical buildings suitable for creating a permanent Sacred Space. And because most Wiccans above First Degree Initiation are considered to be clergy (at least for themselves), we do not need a separate clerical organization, dedicated to provide and keep a separate physical space sacred for the untutored masses, as the mainstream churches do. Every Wiccan home may contain Sacred Space.

Another reason stems from the fact that we are a nature-worshipping religion, and many of us prefer to work outdoors, in nature, whenever possible. Because our Circles can be set up without changing the physical state of an area, and can be taken down leaving no discernible traces, we can worship literally anywhere. Anywhere there is nature can be a temple.

A third reason for Circles is a result of our perception that we are an oppressed religion. Many of us prefer to have no obvious indication that there is a Wiccan group present in a neighborhood. Some people consider this attitude excessively paranoid in today's world. But every year we hear of cases of Wiccans having their jobs or families placed in jeopardy because of their religious beliefs, so many still cleave to the traditional practices of the "Secret Children of the Goddess." Additionally, being a part of a secret group that performs secret rituals is just plain fun, and it is important for our rituals to be enjoyable if we want to enlist the cooperation of our subconscious mind. Because certain types of Wiccan Circles and the tools needed for them are completely unremarkable, it is usually impossible to find where Wiccans worship, unless they let you.

And finally, and perhaps most important, we work in a Circle because of our desire to worship and work "in a Time without a time, and a Place without a place." We try not to be attached or locked into any one time or place on the astral realms when we worship or work magick. If where we are is psychically no one time nor any one place, we can be any time and every place. Not being time or location bound is the realm of the Gods, it makes it easier to communicate with them, and helps our magick to be more effective. But to be in "a Time without a time,

and a Place without a place," we must somehow psychically separate ourselves from where and when we are. This is really the most important thing that a warded Circle does; it doesn't just keep out bad influences as some magicians believe, but also psychically removes us from the mundane world of time and place, so that we can be "between the worlds and beyond!"

WHAT IS A CIRCLE?

The standard Wiccan warded Circle dates at least to the Gardnerian Circles of 1950s, and probably much earlier because there are elements clearly taken from the Ceremonial Magick lodges of the previous century. There is no one right or true way to create the Circle. What we describe is a good, general way to create one. In fact, since the late 1970s there have been many, many experiments in different ways of making Circles, tried by many people across the country. Once you have adequately practiced the various Circles given in this book (including the two at the end of this chapter), you will probably experiment with your own creations.

Plan your Circle and assemble your equipment and paraphernalia. Decide before you start what you will be doing, why you will be doing it, how you will be doing it, and what you need to do it with.

First figure out what you will be doing, i.e., what type of ritual, whether it will be celebratory, healing, etc. This will help you define what the components of the ritual should be.

Next reaffirm (at the very least for yourself) why you are doing the ritual. Things tend to work better if you know why you are bothering the Gods. If you don't know why you are doing something, why should anyone (including the Gods and/or your subconscious mind) help you?

Then using the answers you receive from the "what" and "why" questions, mix your knowledge of how rituals should be done and how magick works, with your understanding of the Gods and beliefs in the spiritual worlds, and you should come up with the "how" of the ritual, if not the full script. And once you know how the Circle will be, the tools you will need should be self-evident.

Then assemble all the equipment and tools you will need in the area you will be working. Make every and all pre-ritual preparations; for example, take your ritual bath, get your cakes and wine together, make sure the candles are in working order and that you have some source of fire available for them. This phase should be a joint effort of all those participating in at least the running of a given ritual. And this procedure works pretty well for designing any type of ritual.

Physically set up your Circle. Clear all unnecessary physical items from your working area. Physically set up your altar, open your bottle of wine and arrange the tools, cakes, etc., that you will be using on it. Place and set up your elemental shrines. Arrange the candles around the Circle area and have a source of fire (matches, lighter) near the first candle you will light.

This step is commonly performed by the High Priestess and her helpers, but can be done by any one person (if working solo or in a small group) or more people (if it is a large group ritual and you want to involve more people in the ritual).

Visibly announce that you are starting the Working. Some Traditions ring a bell or light a candle to announce to the rest of the participants that mundane time is over and now we are starting. Others verbally declare the start of a ritual or use some other kind of consistent gesture or practice. This is normally the prerogative of the High Priestess.

Define the boundaries of your Sacred Space. Physically define the perimeter of your Circle by walking the perimeter. Frequently, walking the Circle is performed by the High Priest or Summoner, whoever is holding the wards of the Circle.

Cast the wards. This ritual removes the Circle from the mundane world. Frequently it is performed by walking around the Circle twice more raising your outer and inner wards. These two wards metaphorically form astral walls that separate you from time and space. Again, this part is commonly performed by the person who defines the Circle.

Cleanse the Sacred Space. The interior of your Circle is psychically cleansed or purified, banishing any unwanted astral influences. The High Priestess, using the elements of Earth and Water, sprinkles or aspurges the Circle with salt water, and the High Priest, using the elements of Fire and Air, censes the Circle with lighted incense.

Invoke the spirits of the elements. At each quarter shrine, the guardian/king/spirit of that particular direction/element (commonly East-Air, South-Fire, West-Water, and North-Earth) is called to enter and guard the Circle from anything attached to their realm and witness the rite so that things will go well. Frequently, the directions of up and down, which represent the higher and lower realms of spirit, are also added. This is the last step in creating your Sacred Space and is frequently performed by the High Priestess.

"The Circle is cast." The High Priestess binds all the elements of the Circle together into a cohesive whole, declares that the Circle is closed, and that the Working can begin. The High Priestess recites the invocation "Thus we are met in a Time without a time, and at a Place without a place. For we are between the worlds and beyond."

If the ritual is long or difficult, the High Priestess will describe the purpose of this ritual and what is going to happen next. This will help re-focus the attention of the participants on the Working, and give the officiants (i.e., the High Priestess, High Priest, Summoner, and/or Handmaiden—the people who set up the Circle) a small break before they have to concentrate again.

Invoking Deity. Now that you have a suitable place for them, invite whichever Gods you wish to be in attendance at your Working. We feel the best metaphor for this is that you should be inviting the Gods to a party. After all, that is what they consider a ritual to be, a chance to experience the physical world through the senses of their worshippers. So be polite, and treat it like a party, with you as the gracious host and the Gods as honored guests. This is commonly called "Drawing Down," or "Calling Down the Moon," and is usually performed by the High Priest and High Priestess on one another.

Insert Working here. Now you will do what it is that you have assembled for, be it worship, healing, spellwork, etc.

Great Rite. This ceremony is the symbolic sex act between the High Priestess and the High Priest, in which the athame and chalice are conjoined. After the Working is finished, all excess energy left over from the Working is used to charge the liquid in the chalice. This charged liquid is shared by the ritual participants in order to allow each participant to partake of the energy, and to diffuse and ground out any excess energy.

This step is normally performed by the High Priestess and High Priest, and may or may not include the Great Rite (sex act) symbolically or in actuality (a few Traditions still perform the actual sex act between the High Priestess and High Priest, and because we are a fertility/nature religion, consider this the right and duty of every Third Degree). Because of this these groups generally prefer that their Thirds be committed, prefer-

ably married couples. What is important is that all excessive or stray energy left over from the Working is grounded out. You do not want stray energy floating around after you open your Circle, it's likely to go somewhere, or get used by something you don't want. This rite is also known in certain Traditions as the Rite of Cakes and Wine. It is illustrated more fully later in this text.

Invite the Gods to leave. Inform the Gods that the ritual/party is over, and that it would be a good idea if they went home now. And while it is probably arrogant to really think that a human can command the comings and goings of the Gods, they really don't enjoy hanging around with nothing to do after a party is finished any more than you do. So while it always pays to be polite, let them know that the party is over. This is normally performed by the High Priestess and High Priest together and mirrors the process in which you called the Gods into the Circle.

Dismiss the elements. While it is a good idea to invite the Gods to leave, *tell* the elemental guardians/kings/spirits to go home. Be firm. You do not want any stray energy hanging around when you open the Circle. The common farewell salutation in some Traditions of "Go if you must, stay if you will" is for the Gods only. With the elementals, it's best if you tell them politely but unequivocally to "go home!" This step is normally performed by whoever called the elementals, in reverse order from how they were called, and also mirrors how they were called, at each respective quarter.

Open the wards. The inner and outer wards are cut or taken down, usually by the person who erected them.

"The Circle is open." These are the ritual words frequently spoken by the High Priestess at the very end of the Circle. During this part, she grounds any leftover energy, and then declares that the ritual is finished so everyone knows that the Circle is open to the mundane world of place and time. Traditionally the words spoken are as follows: "The Circle is open, but never broken. Merry meet, merry part, and merry meet again!"

"Clean up your room!" How many of us had mothers who kept telling us that? Well, the Goddess also expects us to make sure our rooms are clean. So when you are done, put away all your ritual tools, robes, and equipment, and return the ritual area to the state it was before you started. When outside, you should leave the area in a better state than it was when you found it.

BASIC CIRCLE JOBS

Before we discuss the basic jobs performed by the officiants of a ritual, it is important to understand that any First Degree Initiate of Wicca is expected to be capable of representing themselves to the Gods. We are all Priests in our own right, and need no one else to intercede with the Gods on our behalf, as is done by the clergy in most of the mainstream religions. So why do we need ritual officiants? Because, while a person's spirituality is an individual affair, religion is an attempt at a group experience. To have a focused group experience, there must be someone orchestrating what is going on, or you get chaos. That is what these officiants are, the people who are orchestrating or conducting a group ritual. For an individual Working, each participant is their own officiant.

There is another thing that we want you to remember: the jobs we describe are just that, job descriptions. We are not using these terms as positions of rank. What a High Priestess, High Priest, Summoner, or Handmaiden is, as far as the hierarchies of the various Traditions go, is up to the exclusive practices of each Tradition, and we don't address that here. Not only that, but because these are job descriptions, and because we are a religion of equality, it doesn't really matter what gender a person is when performing these jobs. It is just as possible for a male to perform the job of Handmaiden, as it is for a female to do the job of High Priest, or any other combination. The gender-based names have been retained to maintain some semblance of continuity with everyone's teachings, not because we feel that a person's sex has any bearing on their ability to perform any given job.

And finally, these job descriptions are operative only for the length of a ritual. We are not suggesting that these jobs carry over into the rest of the time the group is together. An absolute hierarchy, as we illustrate below with the High Priestess as absolute ruler and with the High Priest as her second in command, is not necessarily the best way to run a group. We feel the best way to run a group is by the cooperative effort of as many people as are willing to be involved. Absolute dictatorship, even if it is benevolent, does not necessarily work well if the aim of a group is the spiritual advancement of all its members. On the other hand, during a ritual, it is best that there is no question in anyone's mind who is in charge of what.

The High Priestess. The High Priestess is the interface between the magickal Working and the Gods, especially if she will be "aspecting" or invoking one or more Deities. She can be called the final transmitter, tuner, or focuser of the energy of a ritual. She gives the energy that is produced by the congregation its final form and direction. No matter the size of a Working, there should only be one High Priestess. Frequently she is the main architect of the Working and final decision maker, although any High Priestess may find that the more voices she heeds from the rest of the group, the better and more cohesive her group may become. Nevertheless, during a Working, the buck stops here. The High Priestess usually has the final responsibility for the ritual and the welfare of the participants, and therefore should have the final say.

The High Priest. The High Priest is the interface between the participants and the Working. In a large ritual, the High Priest might be called a collector, receiver, and/or amplifier of the energy generated from the congregation or granted from the Gods. In an effective working pair, he is the one who collects or assembles the energy generated for the Working, and transmutes that energy into a form that can be most easily assimilated by the High Priestess. This job involves gathering, integrating, and focusing the group's energy, then transferring it to the High Priestess. And if the High Priestess is not consciously available to make decisions (because she may be engrossed in her communication with the Gods) the High Priest is the decision maker.

There can be more than one Priest in a Working; the name High Priest is reserved for the most senior one (however a Tradition determines seniority). And if it is a really large ritual (one hundred or more participants) there should be several.

The Handmaiden. The Handmaiden is the interface between the participants, the officiants, and the physical aspects of the Working. The job of Handmaiden might be called that of a "Harmonious Chi Weaver." She tries to help everyone be of the right mind-set, maintain the integrity of the Sacred Space within the Circle, and ensures that everything runs smoothly during the Working. She can also act similarly to the "Circle Monitor" as described in Marion Zimmer-Bradley's *Darkover* science fantasy novels. Her job is to maintain the well-being of both the individual participants and the physical "dance of the officiants" during the Working, making sure all are doing well.

It has been said that the Handmaiden's tool is the altar, because not only does she traditionally set up the altar, she makes sure that whatever the other officiants might need is within easy reach. The larger the ritual the more Handmaidens are needed.

In some Traditions, the Handmaiden is in training to become a High Priestess. We have found that to help facilitate this, and effectively run a ritual, the Handmaiden should generally be considered the apprentice of the High Priestess, but during the ritual should be acting as the assistant of the High Priest.

The Summoner. In a large ritual or gathering, a Summoner is the "Definer of the Wards," also called a Warder or Tyler. In some cases the Summoner actually creates and (usually) maintains the wards the High Priestess and High Priest create for a specific Working, and the Handmaiden maintains the Sacred Space inside the Circle. Summoners are the Working's and/or gathering's interface with the mundane world and, frequently, in large rituals or gatherings, work from outside the Circle. The larger the ritual, the more Summoners may be needed.

In some Traditions, the Summoner is in training to become a High Priest. We have found that to help facilitate this, and effectively run a ritual, the Summoner should normally be considered the apprentice of the High Priest, but during a ritual should act as the assistant to the High Priestess.

The congregation. These are the participants of a Working. They are the people who produce the majority of the energy that the High Priest and High Priestess focus to do the Working. They are also the people for whom the Working should be designed. The Working's creators should make their plans to satisfy some need of the congregation, not to satisfy their own egos.

We hear some people ask, if this kind of top-down hierarchy (as we have described above) is not necessarily a good way to run a group, why should we do this for a ritual? The best reason is so that your group develops good ritual habits, and if and when something goes wrong, you know what to do. Frankly, the only time we feel that it is worthwhile to have a dictatorial hierarchy is during a disaster. If your group knows who is responsible for what in a ritual, it is possible to keep a problem from becoming a disaster. Problems happen during rituals—people get over them pretty fast. A disaster during a ritual, though, can wreck a group.

To illustrate, two separate rituals that Paul witnessed are presented as examples of what constitutes the difference between a problem and disaster.

Because of internal spiritual work a participant had been doing for a while—opening up to their "Inner Child"—a certain phrase spoken during a ritual caused a flashback to an early childhood trauma. This participant naturally proceeded to freak out. Everybody immediately wanted to help. Because no one was in charge of this ritual (everyone had met together as equals, the ritual had been planned and run by consensus), no one was listening to anybody else. Everyone was talking and trying to help at the same time and the ritual degenerated into confusion, panic, and despair. The ritual collapsed, which contributed to a later split in that community. Paul doesn't know if the participant who had the original problem ever got over the trauma.

During another ritual, when the Goddess was invoked, she (for some unknown reason) chose to manifest not in the High Priestess, but in the body of one of the newest neophytes. This participant didn't have any idea what was happening and became quite agitated. But in this case, the ritual's Handmaiden and Summoner responded immediately to help the participant. After all, that is their job, and they didn't have to decide if they should or should not interfere. Meanwhile the High Priest kept the congregation's attention in case their energy was needed. The High Priestess realized what had happened and was able to talk the participant through the experience of being the Goddess. The ritual went on, and that neophyte received advanced training very quickly.

In one situation a problem developed, but the problem was overcome. In the other, the problem developed into a full-blown disaster.

Developing good ritual habits (which include being polite to everyone and everything, totally dismissing everything you call up, etc.) is like locking your door at night if you live in a city. It is a habit worth cultivating, even if it might really be needed only one out of one thousand, or ten thousand nights. And besides, you can't anticipate every problem.

Admittedly, serious situations like the ones described above are extremely rare. But if your group becomes familiar with the little problems that do happen (for example, some of the candles blow over or someone spills the chalice or tears their robe, etc.), then any big ones (like the police knocking on your door, or someone igniting their hair in the candle flames) can also be handled with relatively little disruption.

CIRCLE PROTOCOLS

There are certain fairly standard protocols, or commonly recognized manners of behavior, within the Circle. And while some things differ from Tradition to Tradition (for instance while in one Tradition all use their athames at the same time, another only allows the High Priestess to use her athame. Everyone else must surrender their athame to the High Priestess, who places them on the altar when they enter the Circle), other behaviors are pretty much standard from group to group. For example, everyone customarily moves deosil or sun-wise within the Circle.

So you will have to learn any idiosyncratic protocols of the group you join or you can create your own. Below we have listed a few short rules that are pretty much universally accepted. If any group you join does not abide by a least a majority of these rules, you may want to reevaluate your association with them.

It is the responsibility of every single person who steps inside a Circle to make sure that no one gets hurt and that the energy of the space stays clear and comfortable. Just because the officiants are in charge of a ritual, does not mean that the rest of the participants can slough off and just be entertained. Each individual is responsible for their own health and actions. This is what the Wiccan religion is about, being responsible for yourself.

Respect the organizers of the ritual. The organizers of a ritual are usually very harried individuals. They are normally doing their best with minimal resources and usually even less help from the people in the community. They are giving of themselves for you, so accord them the respect they are due. You don't have to like them, but at least be polite to them, and cooperate with them during the ritual.

Respect the practices of the presiding Tradition. Do not try to impose your personal beliefs or ritual practices on the people leading the ritual. They may be practicing a path that is different from your own. And when you enter their Circle, you are choosing to follow their rules for the duration of the ritual.

If you have any doubts about what will be done during the ritual, find out about the ritual beforehand. If you are uncomfortable with either the actions or beliefs that will be espoused during the ritual, you can choose not to attend. If for any reason you become uncomfortable during the course of the ritual and wish to leave, feel free to do so. But make your exit in as unobtrusive and polite a manner as possible. Many Traditions prefer that you formally request permission to leave, and then the Summoner or High Priestess will "cut you out of the Circle" so as not to disrupt the energies of the ritual.

Wicca is the religion of diversity. There are a tremendous variety of beliefs and practices in our community, so there is the distinct possibility that an individual will find something uncomfortable about how another person interprets their beliefs. This is okay. There is no dishonor in being uncomfortable with something and deciding not to participate, as long as you do so politely with as little disruption as possible. And there is no dishonor to the presiding officiants if someone politely decides not to participate, as long as the officiants do not make a big deal about it. Remember, all participants are entitled to their own opinions.

Respect those around you. Unless you are a member of a very select coven, there will be people circling with you who may have differing beliefs and lifestyles. Remember, the Universe is diverse, and show respect and honor for the diversity of the paths around you. Do not impose yourself or your beliefs onto anyone else. Remember that all paths lead to the Goddess.

Despite the occasional hugging sprees to the contrary, most Wiccans (and most magicians and/or psychically sensitive people in general) are very private persons with a strong sense of personal boundaries. When you see two Wiccans hug, if you watch closely, you will probably see that in any physical contact there is a specific ritual of covert asking and giving permission to touch on both participants' parts. Despite rumors to the contrary, there is very little casual physical contact among Wiccans. So never enter anyone else's personal space without their permission. And never touch anyone's ritual or magickal belongings without expressed permission.

Respect the Goddess and the Gods. A cast Circle is a Sacred Space, no matter who does the casting, whether it is in a person's living room, or out in the forest, or around an emergency medical station during a natural catastrophe. One should always enter every Sacred Space with a clear mind and heart.

It is also very disrespectful and disruptive to enter a Sacred Space either drunk or under the influence of drugs, or to drink or smoke anything during a Circle, unless it is a recognized intentional part of the ceremony.

TOOLS USED IN MOST CIRCLES

While there may be many types of ritual tools available to the magician, Wiccans typically tend to use only a few main ones to put up their Circles, no matter which of the other ones may be used later in the ritual.

While you may already be familiar with some of the descriptions of each tool, there are some things that you may find unfamiliar. Paul has spent the last few years researching what the various tools are used for and has developed some possibly radical ideas. If you find this objectionable, please remember, the following information is only our opinions, based on our continuing research. If, after the examination of the ideas, you believe them to be incorrect we ask you to do your own research into those areas in which you believe we are mistaken. This process of examination can only increase the general knowledge of magick.

The following are the most common tools used in Wiccan Circles:

The Athame. The athame is considered by many to be the most personal tool of the Wiccan or witch. It is described by various sources as a weapon to control and/or banish demons, or a tool to separate "this from that." In many Traditions it is ideally a black-handled, straight-bladed, double-edged dagger. For others, it can take the form of almost any kind of knife, or almost any other similarly shaped object, like a feather or a fan.

Paul's research indicates that an athame is a tool that conducts the body's bioelectric energy (also known as the aura or Chi) in a linear pattern, kind of like a flashlight, laser beam, or a directional antenna. This directed auric energy does the actual "cutting" of psychic energy ascribed to the athame. When one cuts or delineates a Circle (as described later in the Circle ritual), what one is cutting is psychic, spiritual, or astral energy, which is affected very little by any strictly physical object. But once one's focused will is projected down, through, and out a blade, it becomes an extension of your own psychic energy. And psychic energy will cut psychic energy. We introduce an exercise later in the book that will teach you how to project your Chi. (See page 206.)

Paul's research indicates that in order to be a good athame, an object should be physically capable of projecting Chi in a linear pattern that will cut other psychic energy. To project energy linearly, the body of the athame should be composed of a relatively flat, layered material, like the pages in a book. Steel, for example, because of the way it is forged, naturally has a planar crystalline structure. This structure appears to project the energy in a linear, straight-line manner mimicking the shape of the blade. This then metaphorically extends the presence of the blade into the astral realms. The size of your astral blade is limited only to your imagination and the amount of energy you give it. And while the blade of an athame can be of almost any design, a symmetrical shape should produce a more symmetrical energy field.

Also, an athame seems to work best if it is made of the most conductive materials that are practical. In this case, conductive means that the material allows Chi energy to flow easily through it. Now Chi doesn't really act exactly like electricity, even though we try to use contemporary scientific descriptions to explain it. It does appear to respond similarly to electricity when it comes to metals; i.e., a good high-carbon steel blade will conduct both electricity and Chi better than stainless steel because chrome, a major ingredient in stainless steel, is less conductive than iron. Other substances such as wood and leather that were both living tissue at one time will pass Chi through them easily, while being non-conductive to electricity.

Paul began his research to disprove some of the old traditional formulae concerning the size, shapes, and purposes of the tools. He is finding that there appear to be real physical reasons for the traditional practices. In this case, while almost anything may be used as an athame, what appears to work best is the traditional high-carbon steel dagger blade, with either a wooden or leather grip.

As far as symbolism of the athame is concerned, there is disagreement among Wiccans. There are proponents who believe the athame should symbolize the element of Fire or the element of Air. We believe the athame is more connected to the Fire element. Our decision is related primarily to how the energy running through it is used and not due to what it is made of. One of the attributes of the element of Fire is to burst through, or cut. This is how we use the athame, as a cutting tool, to define or cut the Circle.

Other occult aspects associated with the athame (the reasons for which are too numerous to explore here) are as follows: In the Western Ceremonial Magick Tradition, it is connected with "The White Pillar," and is energetically "electric"; and in the Eastern Mystical Tradition, it may be considered to be a "yang" tool. These are comparable descriptions, and both describe what is considered an energetically masculine tool.

And finally, if you do not have a physical athame present when you need one, you can take your strong hand, the one you write with, and make a fist. Then, extend your index and middle fingers together. If you keep visualizing your energy running down your arm, projecting through your fingers and extending out like the beam of a flashlight or laser, you should be able to produce an effect that is equivalent to that produced by other—often fancier—athames, and using this athame can cause no controversy in public. It can also not be taken from you, except by extreme methods.

The Wand. Traditionally, a wand may be almost any round, cylindrical object, extending four inches or more in length. Many prefer it to using an athame because they do not like the threat implied by a knife. While most people feel that the wand and the athame are totally interchangeable, Paul's research indicates that while a wand may be made of almost any material, from a simple wooden stick to something painstakingly constructed of several layers (as in the fantasy book series, *Harry Potter*), a wand is different from an athame, runs energy differently, and can be used for its own special applications.

What differentiates a wand from an athame is that, while the athame is physically made of a planar construction, a wand is constructed of two or more concentric circles. Traditionally most wands were either cut from the limb of a tree, or a piece of a sapling. Or they were built up from the center out, starting with some type of energy conductive core material (for example, silver wire), covered with an insulating layer (for example, the wire is wrapped with silk thread), covered with another conductive layer (wrapped with another layer of copper wire), covered again with some type of insulating material (a silk scarf), and finally inserting everything in some type of case (a piece of copper pipe).

A wand created from the limb of a tree uses the natural growth rings of the wood for its concentric circle construction. The second is intentionally built from the center out. And even if you use one of the new acrylic wands, you still have two concentric circles because you wrap your hand around the body of the wand.

This difference in physical construction appears to cause the wand to project energy more like a magnetic field than the athame's electric beam. You can see how this effect is used in our Gardnerian Circle on page 122. The athame is used to cut the Circle, and the magnetic field of the wand is, at least metaphorically, used to attract the guardians of the quarters.

As is the case with the athame, there is disagreement regarding the element the wand represents. We have chosen to base the symbolism on how the tool is used. Because the "magnetic field" produced by the wand expands to include the whole Circle, we feel that the best elemental symbol for the wand is the element of Air. And because it runs Chi energy that acts similarly to magnetic energy, we view the wand as a "yin," or "feminine" tool.

If you do not have a separate tool called a wand, you can take your "strong hand," the one you write with, and make a fist. Then, extend just your index finger. If you keep visualizing your energy running down your arm, projecting through your index finger and extending out like radio waves, you should have the equivalent effect of any other wand.

The Chalice. Paul has asked if the liquid in the chalice is the reason for the chalice, then why wait till the end of the ritual to drink it? Instead of using the beverage to help with the Working, it is usually used at the end to symbolically ground the energy. But wine (the traditional beverage in a chalice) is not a very good liquid to ground yourself; it is, however, an excellent energy conductor.

In most rituals, the chalice is filled at the beginning of a ritual and sits on the altar until nearly the end of the ritual. Then it is blessed and shared among the congregation.

What is the meaning of these actions? The filled chalice is left on the altar throughout the ritual and becomes a passive energy collector, absorbing excess ambient Chi produced by the ritual and storing this energy in the liquid, a little like a battery does. Toward the end of the ritual, the High Priestess and High Priest use the Great Rite to "charge the chalice." The energy to charge the wine comes from the Chi built up during the ritual. Next the chalice is passed around the Circle for everyone to share. All participants receive a little bit of the energy created by the ritual and stored in the liquid to take with them.

Finally, the High Priestess usually drinks most of what is left, and then pours the last drops out onto the pentacle, which grounds the energy. Theoretically, there should not be any energy created by the ritual left in the Circle. So when the wards are dropped and the Circle is grounded, there will be no psychic evidence that a ritual occurred.

There is very little controversy about what element the chalice symbolizes. Because of the liquid it holds, it is considered to be a tool of the element of Water. And because of the way the chalice is used in the Great Rite, it is considered the penultimate symbolic female tool, as the athame is the correspondingly penultimate symbolic male tool.

If you do not have a special cup to use as a chalice, then you can use your hands as a cup. Some people question why we use tools at all, if you can just use your fingers and hands? All tools are force multipliers. You don't really necessarily *need* anything besides your mind to work magick, but your conscious mind can only work with a few concepts at a time, and if you use a tool, you won't have to consciously concentrate on the job the tool is doing; the tool can do it for you. Also it is much easier for a group to build a group mind-set, if you use items that each individual subconscious mind instantly recognizes and understands. In addition, if you properly dedicate a tool to a specific job, and you use it only for that job, you now have the effect of two "people" doing the same thing (both you and the tool), hopefully enhancing what you both are doing.

The Pentacle. The pentacle is one of the most mysterious of the tools. What is it? It is the representation of a circled five-pointed star on some plate-like object that rests on the altar. It is supposed to be a symbolic representation of the element of Earth, and as we saw with the chalice, you can ground energy through to the Earth with it. How does it do that? Frankly, a piece of rock should make a better symbol for Earth than an inscribed star. The other tools are not just symbols, but have a connected physical function. Why is the pentacle so different? To try to answer these questions, let's take apart the pentacle.

The pentacle is a figure inscribed on some disk-shaped object (in some Traditions wax is used so you can easily destroy it if necessary). Each point of this five-pointed star represents one of the five magickal elements (Air, Fire, Water, Earth, and Spirit) that are invoked in a circle. A circle encloses this star. When the pentacle is properly consecrated, each of the five elements is separately invoked into this tool.

This doesn't sound like a procedure that you really need if you are only producing a symbol for the Earth element. It sounds more like one that might produce a complete warded Circle and Sacred Space within the pentacle.

What would be the advantage of having a warded Circle within a warded Circle? You produce a single warded Circle when you have cast your regular ritual Circle. The pentacle produces a Circle within a Circle, or you could call it a warded gate within your Circle. Once you have put up your Circle and are in a "Place without a place, and a Time without a time," it might be nice if you could have various invited entities or energies come and go (like the Gods for instance), without having to open and close a separate gateway for them each time.

A properly consecrated pentacle provides that gateway. When the High Priestess drains the last of the chalice onto the pentacle, she is not just draining that energy onto a symbol of the Earth, but onto a gateway to the rest of the Universe.

This is also why the pentacle is considered the symbol of the element of Earth, because once the Circle is truly cast, you now exist in a separate place and time. The pentacle is your gateway or connection to the Earth. Or as Astral Travel Theory might state it, the pentacle is your Circle's silver cord (i.e., life line) to the rest of the world.

Salt and Water. The salt and the water are usually kept on the altar in two separate bowls. These, with very little disagreement, are your true physical symbols of the elements of Earth and Water on your altar.

The salt and water are used by the High Priestess. She projects Chi thorough her athame and psychically cleanses the salt. Then she uses a little bit of this blessed salt to cleanse the water.

Salt cleanses in two ways. First, it is an astringent;

it absorbs water, not allowing microorganisms to grow (among other things). But when you place the salt in more water than it can absorb, you take what basically is an insulative material (pure water), and turn that water into a highly conductive material (a saline solution). Or to use a more metaphysical alchemical explanation, you take a little bit of the element of Earth (whose power is to solidify) and mix it with a lot of the element of Water (whose power is to dissolve and transport), and you get a magickal material whose power (when you sprinkle or aspurge some around your Circle) removes unwanted energy out of the aspurged space and transports that energy to ground. Because "like attracts like," you are using a cleansed material that will attract to it any energy attached to the metaphysical elements of Earth and Water. Any stray psychic energies attached to Earth and Water will be attracted to the cleansed Earth and Water and be cleansed so they don't interfere with the Circle energies. You are cleansing your Sacred Space with specially charged bits of the elements of Earth and Water, two of the five elements needed in the Circle.

We have seen a somewhat disquieting trend develop over the last few years. In some Circles, the High Priestess will aspurge either the outside of the Circle, or the participants. However, it's the Sacred Space—inside of the Circle—that needs cleansing, in order to make it a place suitable for the Gods and focused spiritual work, not the world outside. And the participants should be in a properly cleansed and focused state *before* they enter the Circle. They should have left the mundane world behind *before* they enter any Sacred Space. Any officiants of a ritual might want to reconsider whether they want somebody in a ritual who is not prepared for it. If you don't cleanse the inside of your Circle, as far as Working magick or worship-

ping the Gods is concerned, you are just wasting water!

Incense. The most common type of incense used today is stick incense. Many of the original Traditions used powdered incense, sprinkled onto charcoal. You might try the powder and charcoal, but by far the stick incense is the most common and easiest to use.

The incense is used as physical symbols of the elements of Air and Fire. When you light the incense, you are invoking the element of Fire into your Circle. And because the incense does burn, fire remains even though the actual flame may be extinguished. This fire creates smoke, which because most "air" is invisible to us, is the only way we can really see the element of Air.

Fire is cleansing because it transmutes one thing into something else, and the smoke from the incense that has been purified by fire purifies your Sacred Space because the power of air is to expand, and so the purified smoke basically displaces any unwanted energy in your Circle.

You now have cleansed your Sacred Space with Fire and Air, two more of the five elements that are generally invoked into your Circle. Earth and Water, Fire and Air, only adds up to four elements, and originally we did say we needed the five elements.

The fifth element is Spirit. And what is Spirit? *You* are! Every *person* inside the Circle is part of the element of Spirit. Cleansing the Circle with Spirit basically means that you will be filling up the center of the Circle with your combined focused Chi. And this is where a Working gets most of the power to give life to the magick and the will to direct this energy where it is supposed to go.

When the High Priestess draws pentagrams similarly to what she does earlier at each cardinal point to invoke the elemental guardian of that quarter, she is cleansing with Spirit. However, the first of these extra pentagrams is drawn above her head (commonly called "above," it represents the invocation of the higher, or spiritual realms into the Circle), and the second one is aimed at her feet (commonly known as "below," it represents the invocation of the lower, physical realms into the Circle). You and the people working the ritual fill up the Sacred Space with your focused Chi, your combined will.

Some groups perform this filling of the Sacred Space with Spirit during their invocation of the Gods. When the ritual known as "Drawing Down the Moon" (or any similar rite) is performed, the Gods are being invoked into and through the persons of the High Priestess and High Priest. It is not just the Gods' energy that enters the Circle, but an amalgamation of the Gods and the spirits of their Priestess and Priest, and it is this combined melding of Divine and mortal spirit that is used to represent the element of Spirit.

Altar/Shrines. Why do we need altars? And what is the difference between an altar and a shrine? In a Wiccan Circle, four shrines are placed at the four cardinal points. Each shrine is then decorated to represent the elemental guardian that will be invoked at that quarter. Typically, but not necessarily, the element of Air is in the East, Fire in the South, Water in the West, and Earth in the North. Shrines are created for two reasons: to establish a link between each element and the physical space of the Circle, so that when the gateway to the elemental realm is opened by drawing the pentagram in the air at that quarter, and the call is made to the guardian, it is as easy as possible for that guardian to come into the Circle; and to provide an anchor of the essence of that element for the guardian, so that it feels welcome. You are inviting the guardians

to be guests in your Circle so make them feel comfortable.

A shrine is basically a physical place that has been dedicated to a specific God or Goddess or spirit, so that they can more easily manifest themselves in that specific place and time.

When you have cast your Circle, it is worthwhile for you to set the parameters of the world inside your Circle, which is one purpose of the altar. On your altar there are usually examples of the four terrestrial elements—Air and Fire (in the burning incense) and Earth and Water (each in their own bowls)—and there are usually symbolic representatives (commonly statues) of the Goddess and God, the everlasting dynamic polar opposites of energy in the Universe (not to mention whatever spiritual meanings the Goddess and God personally have for you). And it is also where your astral gate (your pentacle) is placed, providing access from your Circle reality to everywhere else.

Metaphysically this is the purpose of the altar. It is not just a handy place to arrange your tools— it is your psychic and/or astral anchor to the normal mundane reality that you understand and are comfortable with.

This sounds like a bit of an oxymoron: you are creating a place that is psychically separate from the mundane world, but you also have a bit of that mundane world with you in that separate place. But because you exist for most of the time in the physical, mundane world, if for no other reason, what you do magickally must be capable of existing in that same mundane reality. Also metaphorically, your altar provides an astral anchor to the real world, so you don't get lost.

It is not coincidence that much of the ritual starts and ends with the altar. It can become a touchstone or anchor for the Working. It is the psychic center of the Circle no matter where your Tradition mandates you physically place it.

Also the altar and shrines help provide visual reinforcement that the Circle is a special place—magickal, separate, and different. Many people decorate them according to what ritual they are performing. These decorations can become one of the most powerful tools you have for setting the stage and creating the right mood for the gathering, and the altar becomes another visual reinforcement for the subconscious that something special is happening, and to pay attention.

Candles. The candles are multifunctional. They are frequently the only light used by many groups. They provide fire for lighting the incense. They can be used as the symbols of the Goddess and God, or as the magickal focus for invoking them. They can be used as the symbols of the elements. They are visual indicators that something different and interesting is going on, another cue for the subconscious. They provide energy, which can be tapped for the ritual.

Candles are also consumed, and thereby can become a ritual sacrifice. There is a saying, "A gift demands a gift." When you work magick, one way to look at the process is that you are asking the Gods to give you something, whether good feelings, information, some sort of tangible results, or spiritual satisfaction. So ideally you should share something with them in return. Yes, you are inviting them to your party, and to have fun with you. But what fun is a party without sharing goodies? When you share the wine and cakes with the Gods they are experiencing these physical pleasures with and through you; using candles can be another type of sharing goodies.

Candles, especially in our electrically lit society, can bring back primal memories of the times when we weren't so technological, when we were closer to nature. Since Wicca is a nature-based spirituality, sometimes the candles become our most tangible link to that simpler, natural world in our urban living rooms. And because they are not normally used, the use of candles can be another signal to our subconscious minds that something special is happening.

The burning candles are also a measure of time, and in many ways, the flames that are produced are living beings. As living beings, the candle flames will react to the environment around them, and if you become aware of these reactions, it is possible to use these reactions as a gauge of what is happening during the ritual. Sometimes the candles burn more quickly or slowly than is usual during a ritual. This can be an indication that you have connected with something outside yourself, or simply that your house is too stuffy (in which case, open a window). And if the candles go out, you have another indication of activities, which may be significant. Either there is a draft, or you might want to set another plate for the ghost who just walked in. Candles react to both physical and psychic effects. But if one of your candles starts acting funny, and you have already determined that there is no physical reason for this behavior, there might be some metaphysical explanation, and maybe you should take appropriate actions.

And finally, because candles come in a rainbow of colors, you can use them for purely decorative purposes. Many groups just use a candle of the appropriate color as the elemental shrine at each quarter. And other groups use variously colored candles to help create a festive mood for certain Sabbats. Others use many more candles than just the "prescribed" number because they enjoy the presence of the many dancing flames. And, there are specific types of spellwork that use candles. (See Candle Spells on page 216.)

Now that we have described the jobs performed by the officiants of a Circle/ritual, and the reasons for the various magickal tools, let's take a look at the ways these jobs and tools work, and how they affect the workings of a Circle.

EXAMPLES OF TWO CIRCLES

We have prepared as examples the scripts for two separate Circles. One is a highly traditional formal Circle that is performed for a single coven of around thirteen people. The other is of a more eclectic style, that is performed out of doors for a gathering of about one hundred people. We feel it will be worth your while to compare these two rituals, decide for yourselves how they differ or are similar, then compare these two with the sample Circle ritual in the first part of this book (part 1, pages 63–72). Together these examples should give you some good ideas about how to plan and write your own Circles.

Example 1: *A Typical Gardnerian Circle*

Below you will find a typical Gardnerian Circle. Our description may provoke some controversy because there are so many versions of the Gardnerian Circle. There may be criticism from some Gardnerians because we are printing this, but the authors have not taken Gardnerian oaths, so cannot be charged with oath breaking, nor can our sources be charged with oath breaking.

One additional note: The words spoken by the various officiants of this ritual are exact quotes, even where they do not agree with the rules of modern American spelling and grammar. We are using these speeches verbatim in accordance with the tradition of copying word-for-word the information an Initiate received from their High Priestess. What reasons there may have been for these spelling and grammar mistakes are unknown to the authors, but some at least seem to have been deliberate. But we honor the tradition, because it retains the flavor of a Gardnerian Ritual.

STEP 1   **Basic tools needed:**
- personal athames
- ritual robes and jewelry
- three candles for the altar
- four additional candles, one for each quarter
- a statue of the Goddess
- a statue of the God
- a wand
- a chalice with wine

- a pentacle with cakes on a plate placed on top
- a bowl with water
- a bowl with salt
- a bell

STEP 2   **Physically set up your Sacred Space:**

Arrange the tools on the altar, as has been described in an earlier section of this book (page 64). Place the four quarter candles at the cardinal points of your soon-to-be Sacred Space. All participants are to perform a ritual bath of purification, then robe themselves and assemble for the ritual. All doors must be properly secured, so there is no thought someone may come in. And begin.

STEP 3   **Consecrating the elements:**

The High Priestess rings the bell to signal the start of the ritual, then she lights the presence candle, then the Goddess candle, and then finally the God candle saying:

> *Fire, flame in the Old One's name, take thee light and burn*
> *thee bright and let the Spell be Cast aright.*

She places the tip of her athame in the bowl of water and says:

> *I exorcise thee O Creature of Water, that thou Cast out from*
> *thee all impurities and uncleanlinesses of the Spirits of the*
> *World of Phantasm, in the name of (insert your Goddess's name*
> *here) and (insert your God's name here); but evermind that*
> *waters purifies the body, but that salt purifies the soul.*

She then places the tip of her athame in the bowl of salt and says:

> *Blessings be upon this Creature of Salt. Let all malignity and*
> *hindrance be cast forth hence from, and let all good enter here-*
> *in. Wherefore I bless thee that thou mayest aid me. In the name*
> *of (insert your Goddess's name here) and (insert your God's*
> *name here).*

A TYPICAL GARDNERIAN CIRCLE continued...

She next places her athame into the incense and says:

> *(Insert your Goddess's name here) and (insert your God's name here), deign to Bless this odoriferous incense so that it may receive strength, virtue, and power to attract the Mighty Ones, and to cause to retire and repel all rebellious Spirits and Demons. I exorcise thee, O Spirit impure and unclean, that thou quit this incense, that it may be Consecrated and Pure.*

She sprinkles some incense into the lit censer and says:

> *I exorcise thee, O Creature of fire, in the names of (insert your Goddess's name here) and (insert your God's name here), so that every type of Phantasm may retire from thee, and be unable to harm and deceive in any way, and I bless and consecrate it so that it may work no hinderance or evil unto those who use it.*

STEP 4   Summoning the elements:

The High Priest will now go to each cardinal point to light the quarter candles. He first moves to the East, lights the candle that is there and says:

> *Eko Eko Azarak, Power of Air, the Power to Know.*

The participants visualize a great wind in the East and they all say:

> *Blessed Be!*

The High Priest moves to the South, lights the candle and says:

> *Eko Eko Zomelak, Power of Fire, the Power to Will.*

The participants visualize a great fire in the South and say:

> *Blessed Be!*

The High Priest now moves to the West, lights the candle and says:

> *Eko Eko Gananas, Power of Water, the Power to Dare.*

The participants visualize a great sea in the West and say:

> *Blessed Be!*

A TYPICAL GARDNERIAN CIRCLE continued...

The High Priest now moves to the North, lights the candle and says:

> *Eko Eko Arada, Power of Earth, the Power to be Silent.*

The participants visualize the green Earth in the North and say:

> *Blessed Be!*

The High Priestess now returns to the altar and says to the High Priestess:

> *My Lady, the Powers of the Elements have been summoned.*

The High Priestess then responds with:

> *And the Circle Binds them all together.*

STEP 5   Casting the Circle:

The High Priest now takes his athame, and with it he traces a nine-foot diameter Circle, starting in the East, walking deosil, or sunwise, around the Sacred Space, enclosing the participants, and returning to the East, saying:

> *I conjure thee Oh Circle of Power, that thou beist a boundary*
> *between the World of Men and the Realms of the Mighty*
> *Ones. A guardian and a protection that shall preserve and con-*
> *tain the Magick Power which we shall raise within thee.*
> *Wherefore do I Bless and Consecrate thee, in the names of*
> *(insert your Goddess's name here) and (insert your God's name*
> *here), The Ancient Ones.*

STEP 6   Cleansing the Circle:

The High Priestess now puts three scoops of salt (using her athame) into the water and stirs it with her athame. She then takes the water bowl to the East, and goes around the Circle deosil, sprinkling the water within the Circle to purify it. Going from East to East.

Then the High Priest takes the censer, and going deosil East to East, censes the Circle with Fire and Air.

A TYPICAL GARDNERIAN CIRCLE continued...

STEP 7   **Invoking the elemental guardians:**
The High Priestess now goes to the East quarter, taking with her the wand with which she draws an invoking pentagram in the air saying:

> *I summon, stir and call thee up, O ye Mighty Ones of the East,*
> *to Guard the Circle and witness our Rites.*

She moves to the South quarter and, with the wand, she draws an invoking pentagram in the air saying:

> *I summon, stir and call thee up, O ye Mighty Ones of the*
> *South, to Guard the Circle and witness our Rites.*

She moves to the West quarter and, with the wand, she draws an invoking pentagram in the air saying:

> *I summon, stir and call thee up, O ye Mighty Ones of the West,*
> *to Guard the Circle and witness our Rites.*

And finally she moves to the North quarter and, with the wand, she draws an invoking pentagram in the air saying:

> *I summon, stir and call thee up, O ye Mighty Ones of the*
> *North, to Guard the Circle and witness our Rites.*

STEP 8   **Closing the Circle:**
The High Priestess returns to the altar and says:

> *In the name of our Lady of the Moon and the Lord of Death*
> *and Resurrection, In the names of the Mighty Ones of the Four*
> *Quarters, the Kings of the Elements: Blessed be this place, and*
> *this time, and they who are with us.*

And all participants reply:

> *Blessed Be!*

STEP 9   **Insert Working here**

A TYPICAL GARDNERIAN CIRCLE continued...

STEP 10   Cakes and Wine:

The High Priestess stands before the altar with her athame. The High Priest fills the chalice with wine, kneels before the High Priestess and offers her the cup. Then the High Priestess holding her athame between the palms of her two hands, dips the point into the wine and says:

> *As the athame is the Male, so the cup is the Female, and con-*
> *joined they bring Blessedness.*

Then the High Priestess puts aside the athame, takes the cup in both hands, pours a libation, then drinks. She then offers the cup to the High Priest to drink, and then accepts it back.

Then all present file in front of the High Priestess, take the cup, drink, bow low, and return the cup.

Next, the High Priest, kneeling, holds the pentacle with the cakes on it out to the High Priestess, who blesses them by touching each cake with the point of her athame moistened in wine. As the High Priest proffers the cakes to the High Priestess he says:

> *O Queen most secret, bless the food unto our bodies. Bestowing*
> *health, wealth and joy, strength, peace, and that fulfillment of*
> *love that is perpetual happiness.*

The High Priestess eats some of the cake and then gives it, first to the High Priest, then to all the participants who sit down to eat and drink.

STEP 11   Ending the ritual:

When all are done feasting and the High Priestess is ready to end the ritual, she drinks most of whatever is left in the chalice, drains the last drops onto the pentacle and says:

> *Witches all our Mysteries being ended, let us thank the Mighty*
> *ones who have graced us with their presence.*
> *Therefore, ere the cock doth crow, I Charge ye to lock away all*
> *secrets within your hearts.*
> *And may the Gods preserve the Craft!!*

And all participants reply:

> *May the Gods preserve the Craft.*

A TYPICAL GARDNERIAN CIRCLE continued...

STEP 12   Dismissing the quarters:

The High Priestess moves to the East quarter, draws a banishing pentagram in the air with her athame and says:

> *Hail, ye Mighty Ones of the East, I thank you for attending,*
> *and ere you depart for your lovely realms we say Hail and*
> *farewell.*

And all the participants reply with:

> *Hail and farewell.*

The High Priestess moves to the South quarter, draws a banishing pentagram in the air with her athame and says:

> *Hail, ye Mighty Ones of the South, I thank you for attending,*
> *and ere you depart for your lovely realms we say Hail and*
> *farewell.*

And all the participants reply with:

> *Hail and farewell.*

She then moves to the West quarter, draws a banishing pentagram in the air with her athame and says:

> *Hail, ye Mighty Ones of the West I thank you for attending,*
> *and ere you depart for your lovely realms we say Hail and*
> *farewell.*

And all the participants reply with:

> *Hail and farewell.*

And finally she goes to the North quarter, draws a banishing pentagram in the air with her athame and says:

> *Hail, ye Mighty Ones of the North, I thank you for attending,*
> *and ere you depart for your lovely realms we say Hail and*
> *farewell.*

And all the participants reply with:

> *Hail and farewell.*

A TYPICAL GARDNERIAN CIRCLE continued...

STEP 13   Opening the Circle:

Lastly the High Priestess moves to the edge of the Circle, first cutting the Circle with her athame, then grounding the athame and says:

> *Fire, seal the Circle round, let it fade beneath the ground, let*
> *all things be as they were, since the beginning of time.*

And all the participants reply with:

> *Blessed Be.*

STEP 14   Put everything away.

– end –

EXAMPLE 2: PAUL'S CIRCLE

This is basically the same personal warded Circle that Paul has been performing since 1981, with changes and abbreviations depending on the space, the time available, the available tools, and the audience. It was originally designed to be performed out of doors, covering a large space, with a minimum of officiants (only one), and a minimum of tools. Despite how it may look at first glance, this Circle indeed includes almost all of the Circle components described above. And it provides a worthwhile contrast to the previous ritual.

As you can see, this Circle uses some fairly poetic phrases, that repeat over and over again. This is to help memorize the words, so you may not need a script, and to allow the congregation to know what is going on, so they can build a group mind.

The visualizations are his own. It is suggested that you not significantly change these visualizations until after you have gone through this ritual once, in order to get a feel for what is going on.

STEP 1   **Basic tools needed:**
- personal athame
- staff

STEP 2   **Set up:**
The congregation forms as large a Circle as is dictated by the number of people in attendance. When they have done this, the officiant goes to the center of the Circle, and meditates for a few minutes until the congregation settles down.

STEP 3   **Personal preparation, grounding, and centering:**
First, you will perform a simple grounding meditation, to connect yourself with the Tree of Life and to center and ground yourself.

To do this, stand in a comfortable position with your spine straight and your staff in your left hand, in the center of the Circle facing North. Now take slow, deep, steady breaths.

As you breathe, you want to visualize your breath reaching from your staff…Down though the grass…Then down through the ground. With each breath you want to visualize your breath going deeper and deeper into the ground…Past the bedrock…Through the Earth's crust…Through the fire until you reach the Earth's core.

Once you have achieved this, you want to change the direction of your breathing and visualize yourself reaching upward from the crown of your head…Into the air. With each breath reaching higher

PAUL'S CIRCLE continued...

and higher…Through the clouds…Through the upper atmosphere…Past the moon…Out into the Solar System…Through the Center of the Galaxy…Until you reach the Center of the Universe.

Now that you have reached both the Center of the Earth and the Center of the Universe, connect the two by visualizing yourself as a tree with your roots deep in the core of the Earth, and your branches reaching up high into Heaven.

Now psychically reach down with your left hand through your staff and visualize yourself *grasping the energy line* that is extending to the Center of the Earth. And psychically reach up with your right hand and visualize yourself *grasping the energy line* that is extending to the Center of the Universe. (This is done by visualization only.)

Now you are going to *switch the Center of the Earth with the Center of the Universe,* by pulling the energy from the Center of the Universe…*Down* with your right hand…Through your body…And down into the Center of the Earth. And at the same time with your left hand, you will be pulling the energy *up* from the Earth Mother…Up your staff…And up out through the Center of the Universe.

NOTE: This meditation takes much longer to read or recite, than it does to perform. Once you have the feel for how the meditation works, it can go very swiftly. What Paul does is

- On his first inhalation, he straightens his spine and centers himself within himself.
- On the exhale, he reaches down to the Center of the Earth, all with one exhale.
- On his next inhalation, he reaches up to the Center of the Universe, all with one inhalation.
- On his second exhalation, he breaths out sharply and switches the energy.
- Done.

STEP 4   Scribing the Circle:
The officiant is still standing in the center of the Circle, facing North, and with the staff still in the left hand. Now the officiant takes the athame in her/his right hand.

Walk to the eastern quarter of the area, outside the Circle formed by the participants. Reaffirm your connection with the Tree of Life and direct the energy you get from this connection (called chi from now on), from your staff through to the athame. Then facing the quarter draw an invoking pentagram with your charged athame, and say:

> *Hail Guardians of the East, Powers of Air. Oh Golden Phoenix*
> *of the dawn. I Invoke and summon you, be with me now.*

PAUL'S CIRCLE continued...

Visualize a yellow and red phoenix flying out of a pink rising sun.

Next, walk to the southern quarter of the area, outside the Circle formed by the participants. As you walk, allow your staff to touch the ground with each step and as you do visualize lines of yellow light springing up from the ground each time the staff touches. Continue this until you have reach the southern quarter, thus connecting one quarter with the next one.

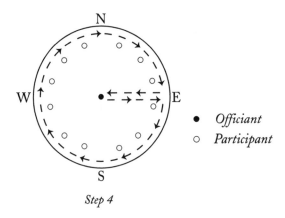

Step 4

You are now facing the southern quarter. Reaffirm your Tree of Life connection and direct Chi from your staff through to the athame. Then draw an invoking pentagram facing the quarter with your charged athame, and say:

> *Hail Guardians of the South, Powers of Fire. Oh Red Lion of*
> *the desert. I Invoke and summon you, be with me now.*

Visualize a lion with a red mane advancing across a sunny plain.

Next, walk around the outside the Circle formed by the participants to the western quarter. As you walk, allow your staff to touch the ground with each step and as you do visualize lines of red light springing up from the ground each time the staff touches. Continue this until you have reached the western quarter, thus connecting one quarter with the next one.

You are now facing the western quarter. Reaffirm your connection to the Tree of Life and direct Chi from your staff through to the athame. Then draw an invoking pentagram facing this quarter with your charged athame, and say:

> *Hail Guardians of the West, Powers of Water. Oh Blue Serpent*
> *of the depths. I Invoke and summon you, be with me now.*

PAUL'S CIRCLE continued...

Visualize a blue and gray winged serpent flying out of an ocean storm.

Next, walk around the outside of the Circle formed by the participants to the northern quarter. As you walk, allow your staff to touch the ground with each step and as you do visualize lines of blue light springing up from the ground each time the staff touches. Continue this until you have reached the northern quarter, thus connecting one quarter with the next one.

You are now facing the northern quarter. Reaffirm your connection to the Tree of Life and direct Chi from your staff through to the athame. Then draw an invoking pentagram facing this quarter with your charged athame, and say:

> *Hail Guardians of the North, Powers of Earth. Oh Green*
> *Dragon of life. I Invoke and summon you, be with me now.*

Visualize a green dragon moving through a forest.

Next, walk around the outside of the Circle formed by the participants back to the eastern quarter. As you walk, allow your staff to touch the ground with each step and as you do, visualize lines of green light springing up from the ground, each time the staff touches. Continue this until you have again reached the eastern quarter, thus forming a complete circle of multicolored lights connecting all the cardinal points around the participants.

Now walk back to the center of the Circle again facing north. Look up, reaffirm your connection to the Tree of Life, and direct Chi from your staff through to the athame. Then with your charged athame visualize yourself drawing a line of white light energy from the eastern quarter to directly above your head. Again, draw an invoking pentagram above your head with your charged athame, and say:

> *Hail mighty Thunderbird, stormy bringer of the lighting. By*
> *the steel in my hand, I Invoke and summon you, be with me*
> *now.*

Visualize a silver-gray Thunderbird flying out of storm clouds. Also visualize a thin line of white light moving out from the invoking pentagram, and trace around with your athame through the western pentagram, around and down until you are pointing your athame at your feet. This connects the upper quarter with the lower quarter.

Remain in the center facing North, look down, reaffirm your connection to the Tree of Life,

PAUL'S CIRCLE continued...

and direct Chi from your staff through to the athame. Then draw an invoking pentagram below you with your charged athame, and say:

Hail mighty Nidhögg, shaker of worlds. By the Staff that I
carry, I Invoke and summon you, be with me now.

Visualize a black dragon moving through the deep rocks. Also visualize a thin line of white light moving out from this invoking pentagram, and with your athame trace a line connecting this lower quarter back around to the eastern quarter, connecting your previously visualized horizontal circle of light, with a vertical one from East, up, West, down, and back to East.

You should also remain aware of a phoenix in the eastern quarter, a lion in the southern quarter, a sea serpent in the western quarter, a green dragon in the northern, a silver thunderbird above your head, and a black dragon under your feet.

STEP 5   Warding the Circle:

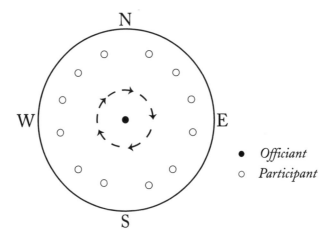

- Officiant
○ Participant

The first four parts of Steps 5, 6, and 7

Still standing in the center of the Circle—where you will remain for the rest of the Circle casting—turn to face the eastern quarter, reaffirm your connection to the Tree of Life, and direct Chi from your staff through to your athame. Then re-draw your invoking pentagram facing this quarter with your charged athame, and say:

Hail Guardians of the East, Powers of Air. Oh Golden
Phoenix of the dawn. Guardian of the East you are, so
Guardian of the East you shall be. I charge you; Ward and

PAUL'S CIRCLE continued...

strengthen the east of this Circle. Protect it and all within from
every evil, real or imagined. Warn me of all transgressions.
And destroy in the whirlwind, all unwanted or hostile spirits
who would disturb the peace of this Ritual.

Visualize yellow light emanating from the eastern pentagram; allow this light to slowly grow larger, to provide a solid yellow barrier, completely enclosing the entire eastern half of the Circle.

Turn to face the southern quarter, reaffirm your connection to the Tree of Life, and direct Chi from your staff through to your athame. Then re-draw your invoking pentagram facing this quarter with your charged athame, and say:

Hail Guardians of the South, Powers of Fire. Oh Red Lion of
the desert. Guardian of the South you are, so Guardian of the
South you shall be. I charge you; Ward and strengthen the south
of this Circle. Protect it and all within from every evil, real or
imagined. Warn me of all transgressions. And destroy in the
inferno, all unwanted or hostile spirits who would disturb the
peace of this Ritual.

Visualize red light emanating from the southern pentagram, allow this light to slowly grow larger, to provide a solid red barrier, completely enclosing the entire southern half of the Circle.

Turn to face the western quarter, reaffirm your connection to the Tree of Life, and direct Chi from your staff through to the athame. Then re-draw your invoking pentagram facing this quarter with your charged athame, and say:

Hail Guardians of the West, Powers of Water. Oh Blue Serpent
of the depths. Guardian of the West you are, so Guardian of the
West you shall be. I charge you; Ward and strengthen the west
of this Circle. Protect it and all within from every evil, real or
imagined. Warn me of all transgressions. And destroy in the
hurricane, all unwanted or hostile spirits who would disturb
the peace of this Ritual.

Visualize blue light emanating from the western pentagram, allow this light to slowly grow larger, to provide a solid blue barrier, completely enclosing the entire western half of the Circle.

Turn to face the northern quarter, reaffirm your connection with the Tree of Life, and direct

PAUL'S CIRCLE continued...

Chi from your staff through to your athame. Then re-draw your invoking pentagram facing this quarter with your charged athame, and say:

> *Hail Guardians of the North, Powers of Earth. Oh Green*
> *Dragon of life. Guardian of the North you are, so Guardian of*
> *the North you shall be. I charge you; Ward and strengthen the*
> *north of this Circle. Protect it and all within from every evil,*
> *real or imagined. Warn me of all transgressions. And destroy in*
> *the earthquake, all unwanted or hostile spirits who would dis-*
> *turb the peace of this Ritual.*

Visualize green light emanating from the northern pentagram, allow this light to slowly grow larger, to provide a solid green barrier, completely enclosing the entire northern half of the Circle.

Remain facing North, look up, reaffirm your connection to the Tree of Life, and direct Chi from your staff through to the athame. Then re-draw your invoking pentagram above you with your charged athame, and say:

> *Hail mighty Thunderbird, stormy bringer of the lighting.*
> *Guardian of the winds and storms you are, so Guardian of the*
> *Upper Reaches you shall be. By the steel in my hand I charge*
> *you; Ward and strengthen the Upper Reaches of this Circle.*
> *Protect it and all within from every evil, real or imagined.*
> *Warn me of all transgressions. And destroy with the thunder-*
> *bolt, all unwanted or hostile spirits who would disturb the*
> *peace of this Ritual.*

Visualize silver light emanating from the upper pentagram, allow this light to slowly grow larger, to provide a solid silver barrier, completely enclosing the entire upper half of the Circle.

Remain in the center facing North, look down, reaffirm your connection to the Tree of Life, and direct Chi from your staff through to the athame. Then re-draw your invoking pentagram below you with your charged athame, and say:

> *Hail mighty Nidhögg, shaker of worlds. Guardian of the deep*
> *earth and Mysteries you are, so Guardian of the Lower Reaches*
> *you shall be. By the Staff that I carry I charge you; Ward and*
> *strengthen the Lower Reaches of this Circle. Protect it and all*
> *within from every evil, real or imagined. Warn me of all*

PAUL'S CIRCLE continued...

> *transgressions. And destroy in your great claws, all unwanted*
> *or hostile spirits who would disturb the peace of this Ritual.*

Visualize black light emanating from the lower pentagram, allow this light to slowly grow larger, to provide a solid black barrier, completely enclosing the entire lower half of the Circle.

STEP 6 Cleansing the Circle:

Standing in the center of the Circle, turn to face the eastern quarter, reaffirm your connection to the Tree of Life, and direct Chi from your staff through to the athame. Then re-draw your invoking pentagram facing this quarter with your charged athame, and say:

> *Hail Guardians of the East, Powers of Air. Oh Golden*
> *Phoenix of the dawn. Lend me your strength to bind this*
> *Shield. Banishing all unwanted or hostile spirits to the Nether*
> *Reaches, to disturb us no more.*

Visualize a wave of yellow light emanating from the eastern pentagram, slowly reaching across the Sacred Space and completely infusing the inside of the entire Circle.

Turn to face the southern quarter, reaffirm your Tree of Life connection and direct Chi from your staff through to the athame. Then re-draw your invoking pentagram facing the quarter with your charged athame, and say:

> *Hail Guardians of the South, Powers of Fire. Oh Red Lion of*
> *the desert. Lend me your strength to bind this Shield.*
> *Banishing all unwanted or hostile spirits to the Nether*
> *Reaches, to disturb us no more.*

Visualize a wave of red light emanating from the southern pentagram, slowly reaching across the Sacred Space and completely infusing the inside of the entire Circle.

Move to the western quarter, reaffirm your connection to the Tree of Life, and direct Chi from your staff through to the athame. Then re-draw your invoking pentagram facing the quarter with your charged athame, and say:

> *Hail Guardians of the West, Powers of Water. Oh Blue Serpent*
> *of the depths. Lend me your strength to bind this Shield.*
> *Banishing all unwanted or hostile spirits to the Nether*
> *Reaches, to disturb us no more.*

PAUL'S CIRCLE continued...

Visualize a wave of blue light emanating from the western pentagram, slowly reaching across the Sacred Space and completely infusing the inside of the entire Circle.

Turn to face the northern quarter, reaffirm your connection to the Tree of Life, and direct Chi from your staff through to the athame. Then re-draw your invoking pentagram facing the quarter with your charged athame, and say:

> *Hail Guardians of the North, Powers of Earth. Oh Green*
> *Dragon of life. Lend me your strength to bind this Shield.*
> *Banishing all unwanted or hostile spirits to the Nether*
> *Reaches, to disturb us no more.*

Visualize a wave of green light emanating from the northern pentagram, slowly reaching across the Sacred Space and completely infusing the inside of the entire Circle.

Remain facing North, look up, reaffirm your connection to the Tree of Life, and direct Chi from your staff through to the athame. Then re-draw your invoking pentagram above you with your charged athame, and say:

> *Hail mighty Thunderbird, stormy bringer of lightning. By the*
> *steel in my hand, lend me your strength to bind this Shield.*
> *Banishing all unwanted or hostile spirits to the Nether*
> *Reaches, to disturb us no more.*

Visualize lighting bolts striking down from above at the cross-quarters, sealing all the joints of the Circle.

Remain facing North, look down, reaffirm your connection to the Tree of Life, and direct Chi from your staff through to the athame. Then re-draw your invoking pentagram below you with your charged athame, and say:

> *Hail mighty Nidhögg, shaker of worlds. By the Staff that I carry,*
> *lend me your strength to bind this Shield. Banishing all unwant-*
> *ed or hostile spirits to the Nether Reaches, to disturb us no more.*

Visualize a wave of black light, rising up and engulfing everything in the Circle. Then slowly subsiding, returning to the Lower Reaches with all unwanted energies.

PAUL'S CIRCLE continued...

STEP 7   Sealing the wards:

Remain standing in the center facing North, reaffirm your connection to the Tree of Life, reaffirm the entities at each quarter. Lift the staff and athame, and start turning slowly sunwise in place. Make at least three full turns and say:

> *Hail all ye Spirits that are here assembled. I charge you, Bind*
> *this Circle, make it one. Protect what we do here.*

Visualize the entities that you invoked in each quarter, spinning in a clockwise direction around and around the perimeter, but at random angles. Faster and faster until they blend together in a white blur. Then visualize a white aura emanating from yourself, growing brighter and brighter until it fills the Circle completely.

STEP 8   Insert Working here:

Insert invoking of the Deities and Working here. After the Working is done, first dismiss the Deities that you called to witness and/or help with your Working.

STEP 9   Banishing the Circle:

Stand in the center facing North, reaffirm your connection to the Tree of Life, reaffirm the entities at each quarter (If you have to strongly reconnect with each entity, re-draw an invoking pentagram at all six quadrants and re-invoke each entity separately). Once you have reconnected with each entity, raise your staff above your head two-handed, swing it around your head at least three times, and plant one end in the ground (possibly with a shout), and say:

> *Hail all ye Spirits that are here assembled. I thank you for your*
> *help. Hail and farewell.*

Visualize the loose end of the staff collecting strands of light from each entity as it is swung around the Circle. As you plant the end of the staff, ground all this energy through the staff to ground.

STEP 10   Opening the Circle:

Finally leave the Circle, take your staff and athame with you, and allow the participants to disperse.

Once you have memorized how to perform this Circle ritual, you can perform it with less and less recitation of the words and physical performance of the actions, as long as you do them in your head. Paul, when he is in a hurry, can stand in the center of the Sacred Space, and put up this entire Circle in less than thirty seconds, just by going through everything mentally, and psychically feeling the Circle go up. He can take it down in five seconds.

There are many ways to do Circles, you can dance them, sing them, invoke them by using horns, whistles, drums, almost anything. You may use almost any kind of poetry or words in your Circle. But be careful, as we have said elsewhere *"Anything may work, but not everything will work."*

In other words, don't be afraid to experiment, but keep track of what you are doing. Then keep what works, and discard what doesn't.

DEITY

CHOOSING A DEITY OR DEITIES CAN BE DIFFICULT for a Wiccan. Other religions have made this choice for you. If you are Christian you worship God the Father and His Son, Jesus Christ. If you are Islamic, you worship Allah, and revere Mohammed as his Prophet. If you are Buddhist or Hindu, you have a few more Deities to choose from, but there is a defined list.

Wiccans have no defined list of Deities we work with. Each Wiccan makes their own choice. And this should be a personal and private one. You don't have to share whom your particular Deities are with anyone else. You can be in a coven with several other people, and each can have their own Deities, and all can work comfortably together.

CHOOSING A DEITY

One way of deciding which Deity to work with is to read and do research about the many pre-Christian pantheons and belief systems. Many of us, for example, are familiar with the Greek and Roman myths. You have probably read or at least been exposed through TV and film to various fairy tales. You may have become acquainted with vari-

ous Deities that way. Anything that might shift your world-view a little closer to the realms of magick and a belief in the spiritual can help.

Sometimes a person encounters a figurine or portrait of a Deity and, through that image, the Deity speaks to them. Occasionally a person receives a vision, and encounters Deity that way. Sometimes all these methods don't work and a person chooses a Deity based upon some favorite culture, or admired attributes of a specific Deity, or some personal interest or whim.

Interestingly, occasionally the choice of Deity is made for you by one or more of these actual Deities, and their criteria for what person would make a good worshipper sometimes appears to be very strange to us poor mortals. One woman in Detroit came to one of Paul's Rune lectures because some "tall blonde white chick" (Goddess) kept coming to her in her dreams and telling her to study the Runes. This apparently was the Norse/Germanic Goddess Freya, and the woman now has a comfortable relationship with her. A tall, skeletal dark-skinned man (God) with polite manners and a top hat appears to Estelle frequently, and she acknowledges and pays homage to Baron Samedi (from the Voudun Pantheon) when appropriate. This cross-cultural phenomenon is discussed in greater detail in the chapter on ritual. There are many ways that Deity can communicate to us. Pay attention to your dreams or attractions and you might just find your Deity that way. Some Wiccans never choose a specific Deity. They just worship an undefined and unnamed Lord and the Lady, or the Lady is worshipped in the guise of the Maiden, Mother, and Crone. Some choose Sky Father and Earth Mother. Those choices can work, and may be the ones a Wiccan lives with for many years. It all depends on what you are comfortable with, and how your "Minds" work (see the discussion on Conscious and Subconscious Minds in the chapter on rituals, pages 147–192).

But eventually most Wiccans will gravitate to some specific Deities. If you progress in certain Traditions and want to get a Third Degree, you have to name yourself as a Priestess or Priest of a specific Deity. That's the Deity you will mainly serve, although that Deity may not necessarily be the only one. There are likely to be others you work with, but these Traditions will expect that you choose one main Deity to dedicate yourself to. And if you are Wiccan and you do Circles and magick and spellwork, eventually some God or Goddess will take notice of you, and then you may choose to work more closely with that Deity, or politely say, no thank you. Our Gods are not jealous nor are they absolute or blindly demanding. You have the right to work with whomever you are comfortable with. You can say no to anyone, but it is usually best for you to connect with a Deity and work with them, because it is easier and more convenient working with specific well-defined and understood Divine partners. You get to know each other, and your effectiveness can increase.

When Estelle teaches beginning Wicca, she insists each student choose a male and female Deity before the year is over. They have to write a short paper explaining why they chose who they chose, and why those Deities will be compatible with them and each other. Choosing Buddha and the Virgin Mary might be justifiable, but the justification would have to be really good, and the individual should really understand the basic concepts of these Deities. Those two aren't from the same culture or pantheon, and one is Christian (though arguably a Great Goddess in her own right), so this pair may be somewhat of an intellectual and spiritual stretch for a Wiccan.

If you like the Greek or Roman myths, choosing Deities from those pantheons might be useful. You certainly can find stories and pictures of them fairly easily. For those of German or Nordic descent, the Norse Deities can work well. Celtic Deities are fairly easy for people of that heritage to understand. But you don't have to be of a specific heritage to choose a pantheon, if you feel a kinship or you have a relationship with a certain Deity that's good enough. Hindu and Buddhist Deities can work. Egyptian Deities may work also. Babylonian, Assyrian, and other cultures had Deities, which adapt well to Wicca, though some of these really should be researched more thoroughly than may be necessary with Deities from other, better known cultures. Directly adopting Deities from the Voudun or Santeria religions usually doesn't work exceptionally well, and can be somewhat tricky for someone who is not an adherent of these religious paths, because they are normally worshipped today with very strict, culturally focused rituals. And Native American Deities are generally best left for those practicing a Native American spiritual path, not Wiccans, again because they are normally worshipped with very strict, culturally focused rituals.

Looking into the stories and histories of many

Freya

Christian saints reveals that they were originally local Pagan Deities. They were later adopted by the incoming Christians as Saints to help facilitate the conversion of the people in that locality. Many Wiccans can sometimes adopt their favorite Saints as their Deities; Saint Brigid of Kildare is a fairly well-known example of a Goddess that was "borrowed" by Christianity. Check out many of the Saints who were de-canonized in the 1980s because there was no verifiable historical person attached to the stories. Those are usually the ones that were canonized Pagan Deities.

We do suggest that you try choosing one or more specific Deities to work with because it is one of the best means of simplifying and developing a clear strong focus for your spiritual work. This choice does not have to be forever binding, nor will it be exclusive. As the years go by and your understanding of yourself and the Spiritual Worlds increase, you may form relationships with other Deities, possibly from several pantheons. Being friends with several Deities, who may be specialists in various separate areas of expertise, can be a nice resource for certain activities. For example, the Greek God Hephaestus works well when invoking car repair issues. He is great with emissions testing also. If you work at a certain profession, choosing a Deity who is associated with that profession can be helpful: the God Hermes for communications and computers; Mars for iron or steel workers; Uranus for electrical workers; Hephaestus or Athena for craftspeople; Artemis, Apollo, or Aesclepius for health care workers. These are all examples from the Greek and Roman pantheons, but you can get the idea. If you choose a Deity and they have a consort, that can be your other choice, or you can choose another Deity from that pantheon.

The Internet has a number of good resources for looking up ancient Goddesses and Gods. Search using the name of the God you wish to research. Be sure to search out all alternate spellings also. Try to access the more ancient myths and stories; these are usually the purest, with the Deity in their most unaltered form. Searching out translated original text material is also valuable. Much is fragmentary, but it can offer valuable clues. And if you get additional insights, more's the better.

HOW TO CHOOSE DEITIES

Below you will find some general guidelines for choosing Deities:

• Choose Deities who are familiar to you and you feel comfortable with.

• Choose Deities who have a body of literature and/or documentation so you have some details of who they are and what they are about. Written material may sometimes be misleading, but if the books say one thing, and you hear from your particular Deity something else, you might want to be suspicious. You shouldn't trust absolutely anything any book or anybody says, but if you have two sources that contradict each other, be careful and try to check things out more thoroughly.

• Have some picture, statue, or symbol of the Deity on your altar, to help you connect with them in your rituals.

• You may or may not choose Deities of your personal ethnic heritage, but try to do some research into the life and times of the original people(s) who worshipped those Deities. If the Deities are still actively worshipped today, look into those people and their religions, lifestyles, and possible mindsets. How are they different from modern life? What things do you have in common with them?

• Get to know what foods your Deities eat, what jokes they laugh at, what they may wear. Their foods, humor, and fashion are related to their original culture.

• If there are things about a Deity you really object to, try to find another Deity, or a variant of that Deity in another time or place. Don't necessarily choose Deities on one criterion, such as you like their colors or their patron bird. Be sure you can live with most of what the Deities are about and what they stand for.

• If you choose a Deity in one pantheon, investigate the Deity's associates. Who are their friends? Who are their enemies? Can you live with those associations and alliances? Ideally you want to like the Deity's spouse (if any).

• If you choose Deities in different pantheons, research whether or not those cultures had contact, whether they were friendly or enemies. Have you chosen two variants of the same Deity in two different cultures? Have you chosen earlier and/or later versions of the same Deity? Were those Deities compatible? Hopefully there will be something they have in common, other than being Deities. Just as not all people necessarily get along, neither do all Deities.

• Realize that for many Wiccans, two Deities just isn't enough. Our Gods are not jealous Gods and they do not necessarily expect their adherents to worship them exclusively. If the Deity is part of a pantheon, they are already used to sharing worshippers.

• If you connect with some Deity no one has ever heard of, and there is no information available about them, be very cautious. There are entities that mask themselves as benign Deities and are not. For a beginner, keep to the tried and true Deities you can read about and others are familiar with.

• Realize that you may absorb attributes or characteristics of your chosen Deity(ies). If you choose a Deity like Bacchus, who drank a lot, and you are a recovering alcoholic, you would do well to reconsider your choice. If you choose a celibate Deity and you like to have close intimate relationships, some accommodation may be in order. If you choose a polygamous or philandering Deity and you are a faithful monogamous person, think again. Pick someone who fits comfortably with your personality and lifestyle. Patron Saints are spiritual guides who had something in common with a person to give them a feeling of familiarity in their spiritual practices. A Deity should also provide a similar feeling of familiarity. It's the same concept and idea, in a Pagan form.

• Don't scatter your energies choosing more than a few Deities, until you have built a solid comfortable relationship with those first ones. They will probably remain your main Deities. Get to know them well before inviting any others into your life and spiritual practices.

• Treat your Deities as friends, allies, spiritual partners, and teachers. Let them become a part of your life, but don't expect them to do everything for you. If you bother them frequently for trivial matters (Oh Great Artemis, I really need a good parking space!), they will not pay as close attention when you call on them for something really important. You can think about them, talk to them, and ask for help and guidance. Sometimes you get a reply, sometimes not. Keeping open to omens and portents can be helpful. If you are worrying about money and you come across a penny in the street, that might be an omen or message, "Don't worry, the money will come." If you are wondering whether the nice guy you just met is "Mr. Right," and you get splashed with mud by a passing taxi, maybe someone is trying to tell you something. Some people will call this superstition, but it is an ancient and valid technique. After all, one person's spirituality is another's superstition, and superstition is the religious practice of a person whose religion you denigrate.

Become more open and aware of seemingly random influences. Put aside your cultural conceptions of what is rational or possibly embarrassing. If you aren't hurting anyone (including yourself) and are relatively circumspect, you have the Goddess-given right to believe in Deity as you see fit. You don't have to talk about your beliefs or practices; in fact, it's sometimes better if you don't. As with magick, there is no coincidence, all things happen for some reason. We might not know why or how, but if we stay aware and open, we can receive a lot more information about ourselves and the world than others can.

COMMUNICATION WITH DEITIES

A very few Wiccans (and others of other faiths) are able to communicate with their Deity almost at will. It is a two-way communication with the person receiving messages from their Deity and also able to speak to their Deity and receive replies. The idea that some people are able to talk directly to their God is ancient and universal. Sometimes they are Priestesses and Priests, sometimes they are just plain people.

When we talk about communication with Deities, we are talking about mystical, faith- and spirituality-related communications. Unfortunately, modern society has decided that people who talk to God, outside a restricted narrow minority, are not sane. Certainly there are people with mental disorders who hear voices, but many normal people without mental disorders also can hear God, and they are not insane. And what exactly is hearing God? Sometimes we are alone and despairing, and we feel a warm comforting hand on our shoulder, which makes us feel valued, protected, and understood. It's a subjective experience and not something that we may be able to replicate, but in that moment we know we have contacted God. Anyone who has felt that knows and understands,

and anyone who has not cannot fully grasp what a soul-warming joy it is to know somebody "up there" cares and takes interest in us. It's subjective but very real, warming, and comforting.

DEITIES AND INITIATION

Wicca is a mystery religion, much of what we feel and believe is experiential. It cannot necessarily be taught in books or even in person. A good Initiation puts you in contact with the Divine in some way. The Initiator arranges the situation and performs the Initiation. It's up to the Initiate to open up to Deity, and experience what is there for them. Occasionally it's traumatic, but usually it's heady, enlightening, and life-changing. And there are occasions when nothing happens. If a person shows they have changed in some fundamental way through actions or mind-set or personality, the Initiation was successful. The change is not drastic, frightening, or traumatic, but a deepening of faith and spirituality, a better grasp of the mysteries of life, a deeper patience for people and their faults, something for the betterment of the person—these are the signs of a good Initiation.

But a Wiccan does not have to have a formal Initiation to contact Deity. If you are lucky, that may have already happened. A common experience is a feeling of need, emptiness, or that something is missing in a person's life. Then they discover spirituality and encounter Deity, in whatever form, and they are no longer needy, empty, or lonely. That contact with Deity is what was missing. The trick is to find a religion, spirituality, and Deity you are comfortable with, that fits your life, that works for you. Wicca allows a person to choose a Deity and many find that ability greatly empowering. Wicca is not for everyone, not by any means. But if you are willing to take the time and invest the energy and do the work, Wicca can be vastly rewarding.

RITUALS

THE CONSCIOUS USE OF RITUALS AND MAGICK distinguish the Wiccan religion from many other belief systems. Many other religions use magick (usually described by them as prayer) and almost every religion uses ritual, but few provide their rank and file members access to the knowledge of how to do magick the way Wicca does. Nor do many expect the degree of participation, even of their newest members, in the design and performance of these rituals the way most Wiccan groups do. Wiccans feel that the prerogatives of designing and using rituals and magick for the betterment of the world should be dictated only by each individual's personal abilities and private ethical beliefs, not by some small ecclesiastic elite part of the community. In Wicca all Initiates are Priestesses and Priests, so all are empowered to be able to do ritual and magick for themselves and others.

The use of magick is the Goddess' given right of every individual, and because of the way the human psyche works, ritual is one of the most effective ways of achieving what one wants through magick. It is also the most practical way of coordinating the efforts of multiple individuals into one focused effort, as well as building a community from diverse individuals. This is very important if you are trying to do some act of group magick.

WHAT IS RITUAL?

A ritual is any act performed either repetitiously or with a focused intent. With this definition, we could include everything from what most individuals do every morning to get ready for their day's activities to the practices of certain serial killers. This definition is too broad for us to use easily. So for the purposes of this book, we will define ritual more specifically. Therefore what we mean when we use the term ritual is a deliberately planned, organized, and executed outcome-oriented spiritual gathering or activity of one or more participants, whether the goal of the gathering is social, celebratory, or magickal.

Examples of social Wiccan rituals include certain rites of passage and some Initiatory rituals, in which either an individual is newly welcomed into a group or community, or an individual's change of status within the community is formally recognized.

Probably the most widely practiced Wiccan

celebratory rituals involve honoring the changes of the seasons, also known as the Wheel of the Year, commonly called the Sabbats. And the most common, strictly magickal rituals practiced by most Wiccans involve attempts at healing either specific individuals or parts of the world in general.

We have described these three types of rituals here for ease of classification, but in reality these classifications tend to blur. One way of determining how accomplished a ritualist any Priest or Priestess is, is by how well they can combine these various types of rituals. For example, how magickal a Priestess can make a Coming-of-Age rite, or how much of a social event and celebratory experience another Priestess can make the healing ritual for a cancer victim, will give you a fairly good idea of how effective that healing ritual or Coming-of-Age rite may be.

WHY DO RITUALS?

Humans do rituals because we are very complex beings. It is very difficult to explain just how our minds and/or spirits comprehend the external world, and it is even more difficult to describe our connection to the metaphysical or spiritual world.

Every individual is (according to several psychological and spiritual doctrines) a conglomeration of at least three separate pseudo-personalities. Some psychologists call these personalities the Ego, Super Ego, and the Id. One set of spiritual teachings calls them the Middle Self, the Younger Self, and the Higher Self. Other teachings call them the Conscious Mind, the Subconscious Mind, and the Soul. For simplicity sake, we will use these last names to describe these internal, spiritual sub-personalities.

Our rational mind, the personality we face the world with, and our short-term memory reside in what we call our Conscious Mind. This, to use

computer terms, is our microprocessor. This is where we assemble all the data from our many sensory and memory systems, where we make most of our decisions, and where the actions that follow those decisions are planned. This is the personality where "We" reside most of the time.

Our Soul is the most mysterious, and like many mysterious things, has a simple description. Our Soul is no more and no less than our connection to the Divine. Every impression or experience that we might have, or have ever had with what is called the spirit world, the astral realms, or any other name for these normally non-physical phenomena, comes from and through our Souls.

And lastly we come to our Subconscious Mind. It is for that part of us that most of the rituals have been performed all over the world throughout all of time. Simply, what our Subconscious Mind controls are our long-term memories, our emotions, and it is the personality that executes the plans formulated by our Conscious Minds. This personality has been described as our two-year-old child. It remembers everything, and it does so in emotional terms.

In order to do ritual to work magick, to have a prayer heard by God/dess, or even to curse someone, you have to get your Soul to do the work. After all, your Soul is your contact with the spirit world, which is the realm in which our prayers or spells work themselves out. The problem is that our Conscious Mind and Soul don't directly communicate with each other. The Soul will only talk to our Subconscious Mind, and the Subconscious Mind is a two-year-old.

The Subconscious Mind is considered a two-year-old because it shares many personality traits with typical children of this age. The Subconscious communicates by emotions and/or pictures, not verbal language. If you must use words a lot, you may find that rhyming your words work best.

The Subconscious remembers everything, especially highly emotionally charged memories and/or injuries, although you will find that it will sometimes hide, or not understand certain memories.

The Subconscious does not understand the concept of no. This means that if you design a major magickal Working that says to the Gods and the Universe in general, "I don't want to be poor anymore!" what your Subconscious will hear and relay to your Soul is "I want to be poor," because basically, it screens out the word "don't."

The Subconscious has the relatively short attention span of a two-year-old. This problem may be overcome during a Working by intermixing periods of intense concentration with short breaks. And you may slowly increase your Subconscious' attention span by practicing certain types of meditation. That's one of the things that meditation was designed for.

The Subconscious hates bad feelings. You can't lie or fool yourself (the psychological concept of conscience comes into play here). If you really think what you are doing is bad, your Subconscious Mind will be unhappy, and you won't get much cooperation from it.

The Subconscious loves pageantry. This is why using fancy robes, magickal tools, colored candles, lyrical repetitive language, ritual theater, and incorporating mythology and fairy stories into your ritual designs works so well and is so common in the rituals of most cultures. Including these things attracts and holds the attention of your two-year-old.

Once your Subconscious understands something, it is capable of performing an almost unimaginable number of functions at once. Martial artists call this your body memory. It is this body memory

that moves your muscles when you walk, without your active concentration. However, communication between your Conscious and Subconscious Minds is not good. Your Subconscious can really only comprehend one communicated concept from your Conscious at a time. Try to communicate any more, and your Subconscious will quickly become confused.

So to get our Souls to understand what we want to do, we have to attract and engage the attention of a two-year-old. And we must effectively communicate with this young child of ours, and make it understand just what we want to do.

So, why do people do ritual?

Human beings perform ritual because it is the only way our everyday mundane personalities can regularly communicate with our Soul, and through our Soul we can communicate to the rest of the Spiritual Universe and the Gods. While we may have instances of spontaneous insight or enlightenment, ritual is our most reliable means of two-way contact with the wonders of the Universe. And without that contact, we live a life devoid of wonder, and of spiritual and occasionally emotional sterility.

WHAT HAPPENS IN RITUALS?

During rituals, we are attempting to contact our Soul, and through that Soul, make the Universe understand what we desire. Some of the other reasons that a magickal Working might not work as we envisioned it (besides the possible ones we've just given you above) is because our Soul either knew that what we really needed wasn't what we said we wanted, so what we got was what we needed (even if we don't consciously recognize it as such). Or the Soul didn't really understand what we were trying to get it to do.

There isn't much we can do about the first

situation. Despite what you may think, your Soul really does know what is best for you, especially in the long run. And you can't fool or lie to yourself. But there are some things that we can do about the second situation that can help improve the communications between "You," your two-year-old Subconscious, and your Soul.

Know what you want to accomplish, why you want it, and how you will go about doing it before you start the actual ritual. In other words, thoroughly pre-plan what you will be doing. And it is important that this planning includes why you are doing the ritual, so that there will be little confusion in both your thoughts and actions.

One hint though: When it comes to the how, it is usually better if you just envision how you want things accomplished as a broad outline. The Soul works best if it is allowed to work any details out by itself. After all, this is its area of expertise. And it seems that micromanaging magick doesn't work any better in the spiritual world than it does in the mundane world.

Cater to as many of your senses as possible. Many disciplines recommend the use of colored candles, silky robes, incense, music, etc. Remember your Subconscious loves to feel good. You want to make your ritual as pleasantly sensuous an experience as you can without distracting from the purpose of the ritual. While it helps to make a ritual as much fun as possible, if you just totally lose yourself in the physical experience you are creating, what you will get is merely good feelings, not a Working ritual.

Restrain yourself from using any mind-altering substance before a ritual (this category includes tobacco, sugar, and chocolate, not just the commonly recognized alcohol and drugs), and limit, under strictly controlled and pre-planned circumstances, their usage during your rituals. If the purpose of your ritual is to get "wasted" (which very occasionally is a valid spiritual goal), use the mind-altering substance of your choice. But if what you want is a consciously directed spell or prayer, keep the substances to specially limited, intentional usages.

Do things that please both your senses and conscience. If it feels right, if what you do makes you feel good, both physically and psychologically, do it! If not, try something else. Remember, your Subconscious doesn't like things that are frightening or make it feel bad or guilty, either physically or psychologically. This is another area where you need to be honest with yourself, because you can't get away with lying about anything to yourself.

Envision what you want as simply as you can. Try to see your desires as pictures; for example, see yourself in your mind's eye, successfully doing or accomplishing what you want. Again, don't try to micromanage the magick. You will only tie your Soul's hands, so to speak.

Do something special to put your Subconscious on notice that something *special* is happening. Some disciplines and/or Traditions use specific costumes, wear special jewelry, or recite specific prayers or chants at the beginning of a Working to announce to their Subconscious that they are going to be doing something that is exciting, interesting, or special.

One additional consideration: If you develop the habit of doing certain special things during your rituals, don't do these special things outside the ritual. Keep the special ritual things special! If you constantly overexcite any of your senses, you will lose the special quality attached to doing something extra nice. In other words, if you use a certain type of incense in ritual, don't use it all the time just because you like it. Then it will become just an ordinary pleasure, and not be special enough to attract the attention of your Subconscious.

Try to envision each concept as metaphors or stories that your Subconscious Mind will understand. If you were brought up in a white, middle-class Swedish-American household, you will probably identify better with paradigms or stories based on a Nordic/Germanic mystical world-view (e.g., dragons, frost giants, etc.) than someone brought up within the Afro-American or American-Indian cultural paradigms would, and vice versa.

Sometimes it is amazing just how similar, or compatible, certain metaphors or archetypes are. We have found, for example, that the Norse archetypal concept of the God Thor, and the American Indian Thunderbird, and the African Orishan God Changó, all seem to work pretty well together. Unfortunately, when it comes to mixing religious metaphors, it commonly takes an exceptional person to successfully mix vastly differing cultural metaphors. For example, try attempting a "Runic Voodoo Ritual." In most cases, the culture one has experienced up to the age of five years is what they will retain all their lives. Successfully adopting other cultural paradigms when one is an adult—so that Subconscious understands them—normally takes much study, practice, and empathy. Thus the old magician's saying: "Mix metaphors at your own risk."

There is one interesting paradox that you should be aware of, however. The societally dominant European-American culture is truly a cultural melting pot, and sometimes reveals itself in unexpected ways. Paul has experienced this firsthand. At the weddings Paul presides over, the Yoruban Goddess Oshún takes a prominent place. Paul is culturally primarily a "Canuck." That is mostly white, French Canadian, and American Indian. And while Paul's father describes their ethnic heritage as "half Eskimo, half doorknob," there was not very much Yoruban tradition present in Paul's upbringing that he knows of. We just figure that Oshún really likes the weddings Paul puts on.

So be aware, while this kind of cultural crossover is not common, it appears to be showing up more and more often, as the various cultures in this country integrate.

Do, don't say. Physically perform as many aspects of the ritual as you can, instead of just speaking aloud or meditating on everything you are doing. The Subconscious is frequently very physically-oriented. Try to use this aspect as much as you can.

Concentrate on only one concept at a time. You can do more than one thing during a Working, but keep each concept discrete and try to minimize the number of each type of concept. Your preparations for the Working is one set of concepts. What you want to accomplish is a different set. What you do to "re-pay" or thank the Gods for their help—i.e., your "sacrifice"—is a third set of concepts. And, what you do to end the Working is another.

Focus mostly on the goal, or final outcome, of what you want to accomplish, rather than on the mechanics of how you think you might want it to be accomplished. Your Soul not only knows what is really best for you, but how to do it better than you do.

Alternate periods of intense concentration (or concepts) with more relaxed periods. You will get farther by interspersing periods of intense concentration with periods where you relax for a while instead of trying to keep the pressure up constantly. Remember your Subconscious' two-year-old attention span.

Use repetition as much as possible, both within a specific Working and between separate, similar Workings. Not only should you repeat what you want to accomplish several times and/or ways during a Working, but you should endeavor to keep the various elements of your Workings consistent from Working to Working. For example, you should evoke the same way, and you should sacrifice the same way, every time you do a specific type of Working.

When you are finished, release your thoughts into the Universe, and then forget it. Once your Soul understands what you want it to do, it works better if you leave it alone to finish the job. You can do other Workings to set up different jobs, but refocusing or re-phrasing your original requests will only confuse matters.

If you must repeat a Working (i.e., to add more energy into a specific request), repeat it exactly, change as little as possible. Otherwise, try to forget all about it. Give your Soul room to maneuver. Generally, micromanaging magick doesn't work.

The above suggestions can apply to any magick or prayer that you may say. They work well with any world-view, cultural paradigm, or magickal system.

BASIC COMPONENTS OF GOOD RITUALS

Many Wiccans appreciate variety in their rituals, so it sometimes seems that anything goes. Fortunately (or unfortunately as the case may be) there seem to be certain principles of ritual design that work better than others. And the larger and/or more complex a ritual becomes, the more these principles seem to apply. Or as one Wiccan saying puts it: "While anything can work, not everything does work."

We have assembled below the principles of ritual design that we have found useful. Please consider these principles as suggestions, not dogma. After all, as with most things, you must also know when to break the rules.

First and foremost, every ritual should have a focus built around a desired outcome. There should be a reason why you are bothering the Gods. And this focus should not wander too far, or too long from the central theme. This focus is frequently achieved by either the High Priestess or ritual designer having a clear vision of the important parts of the ritual, and not letting anyone change that vision beyond recognition. If you do not know what you intend to accomplish, then why bother expending the effort of doing the ritual? Doing a ritual for the sake of doing a ritual, practice, or teaching is a valid reason for doing a ritual. Just make sure you keep that focus as your intent. If you feel funny just putting up and taking down a Circle, why not try a little divination as a Working? A celebratory ritual for a Sabbat or Esbat is also valid. And of course, planning a ritual Working of magick, for whatever purpose, is also valid.

Make sure that you plan into every ritual an obvious beginning, a middle, and an end.

Plan a visible beginning to the ritual where you have set up the physical and metaphysical parameters of your working area. Assemble whatever personnel and arrange any equipment you will be using. Ground and center the participants, cast your Circle, set up your wards, and cleanse your working space.

Invite whomever you wish to be present into the ritual, either corporeal or otherwise. All the physical participants are where they need to be, you have invoked your elemental guardians, and called down your Deities. And, you have explained the ritual's purpose or goal to the group. It is usually best if you explain, both for your mortal participants and your Divine allies, what you are planning to do, and the reasons you are doing this ritual. This reduces confusion and helps to build a group mindset. But please note, in certain rituals you may want to maintain a certain element of mystery, so you need not necessarily tell everyone everything.

The Working—the reason for doing the ritual—is performed in the middle section of the ritual. At this time your sole focus is achieving your desired outcome.

At the end of a ritual you will share whatever party materials you have provided (i.e., the wine and cakes, etc.) with both the participants and the Gods, as a social bonding, grounding after the Working mechanism, and short break before you have to start the work of closing down the ritual.

This section is a good place to add a social aspect to what can otherwise be too serious or boring a ritual. One of the best metaphors we have come up with is that when you perform a ritual you are inviting the Gods to a party. If you can treat this part of the ritual (at least) as a party, without losing your ritual's focus, then you should have a more pleasant and powerful ritual experience.

Thank whomever you invited for coming by and helping with the Working. This includes the physical participants, and whichever Deities, elemental guardians, power animals, angels, etc., that you invoked at the start of ritual. It always pays to be polite.

Remember to dismiss those you "called up" (i.e., the Gods, the guardians of the four quarters, etc.). This part is sometimes either ignored, or downplayed by some ritualists, because they feel it might be disrespectful of the Gods to order them about. But remember, your ritual is a party, and there is nothing disrespectful about making sure your guests go home. And it is very disrespectful to force entities to stay around somewhere they are not welcome. This is what happens if their energy is still confined to your Working area, once you turn your Sacred Circle back into your mundane living room. So don't be afraid to invite the Gods to leave, and make sure

that you fully dismiss any other elemental energy in strong enough terms that all the other participants understand that the energies are dismissed.

Finally, declare the ritual finished. This is another part of the ritual that is frequently overlooked. It may not be necessary to formally say "the ritual is ended," if by your actions (or other understood signal) you can make the participants know that the ritual is ended. It is absolutely necessary for both the proper unfolding of the Working's magickal energies and for the participants to mentally return to mundane reality for there to be a definite ending.

Return the Working area to its normal, mundane, pre-ritual state. Wiccans pride themselves on being capable of performing their rites almost anywhere, not just in some physical temple or other holy site. To effectively do this (unless you are one of the few with some sort of permanent ritual site) everyone must be able to leave the area you work in as psychically unburdened as possible, so you can have a clean slate to work with next time.

Also, Wicca as a religion has strong roots in a past characterized by religious suppression, and a present which embraces the ecology movement. So to paraphrase an ecologist's saying, "Take nothing but memories, leave nothing but echoes."

Make the ritual personal. Cater the message and metaphors to the specific audience. Make them feel as if the ritual was written just for them. This is very important, because if your audience does not truly understand what you are doing, if their Subconscious Minds do not relate to what is going on, you will only get a fraction of the effect you might have had. And frankly, bored or confused participants will look for and find contentment at other rituals, performed by other Priests and Priestesses.

It also helps if you make sure that the ritual is comprehensible to both beginners and experienced participants. It frequently takes practice for a ritual designer to be confident that they can keep an advanced celebrant involved without losing a beginner. Unless you will only be performing rituals for a very small, select group of close friends, you must be capable of reaching an audience of diverse skills and interests.

If at all possible, the celebrants should learn something from the ritual. Not only will you help them develop along their own spiritual path, but also the celebrants will more easily realize that "they got their money's worth" from the ritual.

Try to engage everyone in the ritual. Make the purpose and message of the ritual understandable to everyone. Get as many people involved in running the ritual as possible, either by spreading the workload of the ritual around to as many people as possible, or by having as many of the participants as can, dance, sing, etc.

One way of spreading the workload is to have a different person call and dismiss each quarter or have various people help with preparations, decorations, food, or supplies, or have a group planning session, without losing the intent or focus of the Priest or Priestess.

Dancing and/or singing are good ways to raise energy and engage all the participants. Ideally the songs should either be familiar or taught before the ritual starts. Dancing should also be staged to accommodate those who may not be as physically able as others. Either scale down the dance (like the Granny Step, which is just a simple step to the side, bring your feet together, that can be done by most people), or define an area where some can sit and watch or clap or just move in place. A troop of practiced dancers can look more professional and may create more energy, but having as many participants actively engaged helps raise the energy better. Handing out drums, rattles, tambourines, etc.,

can engage those who do not dance, and clapping is easy and universal.

Use all the senses to reinforce whatever your message may be. Use singing or chanting whenever possible, excite the sense of smell with incense, allow the eyes to see lovely flower arrangements, splendid robes, and colorful candles.

In many ways you are on stage when performing a ritual. Because of this, the things you do or say may not be as clear as most people expect. Allow not only the subject of your ritual to be as large and embracing as possible, but make any movements you perform as big as possible for the available space. Speak as clearly as possible, pronounce your words carefully, and project your voice.

You should also make sure that the ritual flows, that there are no hang-ups. Don't linger too long on any one section, and make sure there is a smooth progression of actions from one section of the ritual to next. You can plan for a quick break between the sections (beginning, middle, and end) of the ritual. It is helpful to be able to stop and take a breath. You do change focus from one section to the next, so plan a break. Achieving the balance between having a breather and disrupting the flow of a ritual takes practice, so do your best, and you will find it all comes more naturally with time.

Show, don't tell. There is little that is more boring than for the members of a group to stand around listening to someone else pontificate. Whenever possible use theater and reenactments to get your message across. Also, Wicca has produced some mighty poets, so take advantage of their words and imagery if you feel you aren't up to what you envision. As long as you credit your sources, it's okay to use the works of others if they suit your purpose. Some examples of actions that we use instead of speaking include:

Sacred drama. Retelling the story of Persephone's

kidnapping by the Greek God Hades has been a popular one among many people to celebrate the coming of winter.

Idolatries (statue, tree, stone). It is much easier for many people to call down the Goddess, for instance, if they have a physical representation of their ideal Goddess to focus on. We frequently use a statute of the Chinese Goddess Kuan-Yin in our rituals.

However, there is a potential problem with physical representation; it is possible that you or some of your celebrants may come to feel that the statue is the Goddess. This is a common problem in our culture—we come to believe that the symbol is the reality. The map is not the territory. Yes, the Goddess will be residing in whatever symbol you choose to invoke Her into, but no more than She manifests Herself in everything. Your specific manifestation will just seem greater because of your own heightened awareness of Her, excited by the calling down.

Great Rite (idea of polarity). Along with the many things that the Great Rite is good for (see discussion of Great Rite, page 358), another profound one is that it visibly demonstrates the concept of the Divine opposites coming together to create.

Song/Music. Accompanying physical activities with music where you can, or singing a part instead of just reciting it when possible, can be powerful tools to keep the attentions of the celebrants focused. One caution, however: If the music or singing you will be performing is sufficiently poor, you may get the reverse result from the one you anticipated.

Sacred dance. This is another area that attracts and holds attention, either by using some specifically choreographed piece for a precise reason in the ritual, or just the standard, chaotic Pagan ecstatic dance that is commonly used to raise energy.

The caution here, which may also be applied to a slightly lesser extent to any music you may use, is that the High Priestess needs to be somewhat in control of what's going on. Otherwise these enhancements to the ritual may take over and become the actual focus of the ritual instead of what the focus is supposed to be. The High Priestess needs to to be able to end these activities when they have done their jobs. So use them, making sure that the High Priestess is the conductor.

Symbolic actions by individuals. These actions can graphically illustrate your message. Paul has used one significant action very successfully to remind people how important fire is to us. During the Yule ritual, all the lights are extinguished so that the room is absolutely dark. Then Paul tries to light a small fire using flint and steel. For those that don't know, this can be a tricky and not always successful operation. But the sparks flashing in the dark and the fire, kindling from a tiny glow to the light of the world, can be very impressive.

Use familiar language and phrases. Wicca has developed its own rhetorical language, like the "Charge of the Goddess," and the "Witches' Rune." And because these poems are familiar, your congregation will recognize and understand the images they evoke. So it is useful to develop a collection of stock phrases, and use them when appropriate. Two standards are Blessed Be! and So Mote it Be! that manifest as statement, then reiteration/response.

Don't be afraid to improvise. For various reasons, many rituals don't go as planned. Either something that you planned doesn't come off as you expected, or possibly the Gods decide to add something to the ritual. Either way, if you try to control all aspects of the ritual, you will feel that everything's totally ruined, and you might as well give up. We can only say, don't. Just because one or more things are not happening as you planned doesn't mean that it's bad. As long as the High Priestess can maintain a vision of the goal of the ritual, the ritual will turn out. Just keep the goal in mind, and improvise around or with whatever the Gods feel they should bless you with. Some of the best rituals we have been in ended up as improvisations, done spontaneously after something happened that not only disrupted the original plan for these rituals, but on occasion actually changed the goal of the ritual. What the ritual became was needed more than the originally planned Working.

Throw out dogma. Wicca is one of the few religions that does not believe in a systematized dogma. We believe people need to reach the truth by themselves. Dogma tends to keep people in the same old ruts, and ruts tend to get in the way of movement. Although it is usually worthwhile to use stock phrases and stock visualizations, if you *have* to use any ritual item or phrase, maybe you should reevaluate what you are doing. If you find that you are stuck with something, you may also become stuck, at least spiritually.

Throw out ego. You should be doing a ritual for some need of your congregation, not because you need the ego boost. If you focus on making each ritual the best you can for your people, we guarantee that you will receive the accolades you need, and you will be a valued member of the community because you get things done. On the other hand, if you focus on how good a performance you are presenting, or to show off, you will not be considered a very great ritualist, even if people are polite to your face.

Control the energy. The High Priestess should have control in the raising of energy, and the direction of the magick. You cannot allow the ritual to just go where it wants to. Besides not getting what

you want done, an uncontrollable ritual occasionally ends up going places that you really don't want it to go. Admittedly, sometimes controlling a ritual may be akin to shooting white water rapids in a canoe. Every so often you just have to paddle as fast as you can and hang on and pray. But if you don't try to keep in control, you will lose it.

Do rehearsals. To perform any ritual well you need to know the ritual. To get to know the ritual, you need to run through it—rehearse—until you understand it. The newer a ritual is, or how unfamiliar the officiants are with each other, will dictate how much rehearsal time you will need to perform a ritual well. Notice we did say need, not necessarily get. It is normally the case that you never get enough rehearsal time. But you should make a point of at least running through your script with the people involved.

If you have a speech, rehearse it beforehand. And have note cards as a backup in case you forget parts of your speech. Nobody says it has to be totally memorized. Use inflection and work with the words, play with them, understand them. If you recite by rote, you will have less energy than if you use emotion and understand the meaning of the words. Moving around as you speak can also help add energy and excitement, provided the space allows for it. Rehearsal and practice are your best allies in this endeavor. Especially if you are planning for a large group, you will have to rehearse to work out who moves where and the timing. If you usually do ritual in a living room, and this ritual will take place in a gymnasium, you will have to allow for extra time for people to move from one part of the Circle to another. If you have a speech that takes ten seconds, and it takes twelve to twenty seconds to get from point A to point B, either you have to write more, or maybe slow down the words, be more dramatic, and take advantage of natural pauses.

Use professionals. Use people who know what they are doing from within the community, such as singers, dancers, flautists, drummers, etc., to lead or provide additional focus. Using people who are practiced and competent with what they are doing can be a big help, and they may even be delegated to plan and run a section of the ritual that they will be contributing to. But make sure that the participants are actively engaged in all parts of the ritual, not just acting as spectators at a performance.

THINGS TO THINK ABOUT DURING THE PLANNING STAGES

Below you will find various things to consider during the planning stages of your ritual. The more of these and other related items that you are ready for, the fewer problems you are likely to have in the long run, and the better you will know your ritual.

Defuse any anticipated problems ahead of time. For example, a first-comer's Circle is a Circle in which there may be a significant number of people who have never attended a Circle before. The presiding High Priestess should give a short explanation of Circle etiquette and what to expect in the Circle.

Is the ritual private or public, closed or open? To what levels? Where are you holding the ritual? Who will be allowed to attend, just close Initiates? Friends? Children? Will the ritual be performed skyclad or robed? Which one, or will it matter? Will there be nonalcoholic or alcohol libations or both? They must be visibly distinguished, one from the other. What's in the cake and chalice? Check to see that what you are using will not cause a major reaction (of any kind) in any one of your attendees, and announce to the assembly what is in the libations before the ritual, so there won't be any surprises.

Will there be a common cup or Dixie cups? With the number of communicable diseases, it is important to determine if everyone will be drinking from the same chalice. The more people you have the more duplication of certain items you will need, or the distribution will take too long. If you have just thirteen people, using one chalice will do fine. Trying to pass one chalice or smudging each person with one smudge stick when you have one hundred people attending will be awkward. Make sure that anything that might get messy is covered.

Announce and teach before starting. Go over quickly what will be done, and teach any necessary songs or speeches before the start of the ritual.

Have contingency plans for twenty people, fifty people, ninety people. Consider what you will do if you plan a ritual for thirteen people and fifty people show up, or one hundred, or just three. Make sure the ritual is in an accessible location (parking, bus line, handicap ramp). Can your people get to the place? Be sure to have accommodations for physically challenged participants. Once they are there, can they get into and move around the place? Will you need mosquito repellent, etc.? Make preparations for the physical environment. If it is out of doors, bring bug spray. If it is out in the sun, bring hats, water, and sunscreen, etc. Be certain everything that is there needs to be there (no clutter). Altars are generally crowded enough as it is, so don't bring anything that is not needed.

Memorize only a few words and improvise the rest based on the outline. A few words are easier to remember and, if you know why and what you are doing, making up speeches as you go along works better than trying to hold complicated speeches in your mind. If you need them, have some notecards with clear, large print with the ritual outline and/or scripts ready as reminders. One hint here: Don't use red ink if you're reading by candlelight. Know any Deity speeches ahead of time. If you must memorize anything, memorize what any Deity will be saying. A confused Deity is very disconcerting. Make sure you remain within the theological boundaries of the Tradition you are doing the ritual for. Having the High Priestess burned at the stake for heresy is not normally considered to be a good ending for a ritual. Keep some mystery. Try to keep some surprises; people get bored if they know everything that is going to happen.

HOW TO PLAN A RITUAL

Now that we have you thinking about what may go into a ritual, let's introduce you to a procedure for writing out your ritual.

As you might expect by now, first you need to figure out why you are doing this ritual, and what the overall goal or outcome should be. Next work out a basic outline of the ritual. This is just a sketch of who is doing what. You don't need any details yet. Just figure out what you want done, and who will be doing what part. Third, try to get at least some of the main participants together and block out the ritual. Figure out what you will need for equipment, props, costumes, and supplies. Who will supply what equipment, supplies, etc.? Where will the altar be placed, and what will be placed where in the Circle? And finally, do a quick walk-through, to make sure that the participants can physically perform what you want them to, and that they don't get in each other's way.

Now write out your full script. This includes what each person will say, as well as simple stage directions. Decide on any songs or music that you want performed. Make copies of the ritual up to this point for the rest of the participants.

Rehearse. At the very least walk through the ritual with all the main participants some time before the ritual is scheduled to be performed. This should help work out any bugs, and you need

to make sure your people know what they are doing.

After the rehearsal, make any last minute changes in the script that were necessary. *Copy* the final scripts and/or song sheets you will need for all the participants, including the list of the items needed, and who is responsible for what item. And just before the ritual, collect in one place all the equipment you will need during the ritual. This will help you make sure that you have everything, and that it all will get to the ritual site.

It might seem that with all the stuff we have been talking about in this chapter, we are making mountains out of molehills. Actually we are not, and while it appears that you could just throw a ritual together, those people who appear to throw together very successful rituals do use some version of the procedures we have discussed above. They don't have to consciously go through everything step by step; they have gone through the process so many times that it is just second nature. Once you have gone through the process a few times, it will become second nature to you too.

SABBAT CELEBRATION OUTLINES

In other parts of this book, we have shown you various parts of the above procedures. We have given you the scripts for two Circles in the chapter on Circles, for example. Here we will show you what a set of basic outlines looks like, and we will do so by outlining a series of rituals that cover the Wiccan Wheel of the Year.

Most of these rituals are designed for groups of twenty or more. They can be adapted for fewer, or for a very large group of one hundred plus. With more people, you will need more Handmaidens and Summoners.

Usually, each ritual can be staged for less than twenty-five dollars. You can spend more if you want. We try to suggest low- or no-cost decorations, usually natural things like leaves, pine cones, etc. Flowers are always nice, but don't spend tons at the florist if you can't afford it. Pictures are also acceptable to set the mood. The costs should be shared by those conducting the ritual. The minimum cost would be for candles, wine, and cakes. The more elaborate the decorations and costumes, the more expensive it can become. Also beware of the special decorations that can only be used at one holiday. Can you store all that for next year, or will it have to be discarded? If you make decorations, sometimes they can be hung in a home, or recycled as quarter decorations for the next ritual. Try to keep the accumulation of holiday-specific decorations to a minimum.

Candles and fire can be problematic. Some places specifically forbid open flames. You can decorate an altar to represent fire by using the appropriate color. You can have unlit candles. You can use colored lanterns or flashlights, battery operated.

The altar should be centrally located and decorated. From the group members who are putting on the ritual you should be able to gather a Goddess and God statue, the usual ritual tools, maybe a pretty altar cloth, some flowers, or other decorations. The altar itself can be a specially made item or just a card table. Just so it's stable and big enough for all you want to put on it. You can store refills for the wine and props under the table, hidden from view by an altar cloth.

You can have separate small altars at each quarter. One group uses small parsons tables with a colored towel and candle on it. The towels are washable, and can collect spilled wax. Each quarter altar can also be decorated appropriately. Air could have a fan, feather, flute, picture of sky or clouds, etc. Fire could have a flame (though ideally each quarter will have a quarter candle of the appropriate color), red flower, a picture of a desert or of flames. Water could have a small bowl of water, a seashell, a picture of lake, a river, or an ocean. Earth could have leaves, a pine cone, a rock, a bowl of earth, a bowl of salt, a picture of a forest or mountains. You can just place candles at each quarter, but we recommend they be raised up off the floor for safety. If children are present, you might want to reconsider the use of candles at the quarter altars, unless they are closely supervised.

In most of the rituals described in this chapter, the altar is placed in the center of the Circle. If another placement works better for you, use it. Rehearsal and blocking should help determine what to place where. Try to get into the space to see it before your ritual. If you can rehearse in the ritual space, wonderful. Some groups rehearse immediately before the ritual. We discourage this because there might be logistical problems, with attendees showing up and getting in the way, or the rehearsal may be cut short because of time constraints. A good rehearsal should take longer than the actual ritual because you need time to work things out, and may need to repeat things until people feel comfortable. The day of the ritual the group should check out the place and make plans before setting things up. If modifications need to be made, setup is the time to discuss that. Everybody should have an idea what to do, and a short run-through of blocking might be in order. This is not a full rehearsal, but just going through the motions without necessarily saying the words.

Each ritual should have an equipment list in addition to the standard ritual tool and supply list. Divide up the stuff, and nobody should be too overburdened. It may take more than one trip to get it all into the space.

Each of these rituals is an example of a possible rite for each Sabbat. None are cast in stone. We offer them as guidelines, so feel free to modify, delete, add, and change them as you want. There are other books with other seasonal rituals in them also. Try some of them if none these appeal to you. Don't be afraid to be creative. The Sabbats are the time for fun and celebration as well as worship.

Samhain—October 31st

Samhain is the biggest Sabbat of the year for Wiccans. Because it is considered the Wiccan New Year, Samhain is presented first. It is a celebration of harvest, and also a time of the root crops and culling of the herds. It is the time when we remember those who have passed on before. It is also the time when the veil between the worlds is thinnest, and so divination can be a prominent part of the ritual. It is also a traditionally intense and often somber ritual, and therefore children are not usually allowed to attend. The Sabbat celebration does not have to replace the traditional "trick-or-treating" or Halloween parties. You can either do the Sabbat at a later hour, allowing the children to have their fun, celebrate Samhain on another evening, or have the partying with the kiddies on another evening. Be flexible. Also, if you follow certain calendars, Samhain should actually be on November 6th, not October 31st.

The ritual presented here is a fairly traditional remembrance of the ancestors. Some groups celebrate with a dumb supper, a feast that is shared with the ancestors. This can get a little long and tedious, so we usually have the feast separately, after the Sabbat. You can adapt and try it as part of the celebration if you choose.

Expect a good crowd, as Samhain and Beltane usually have the biggest turnout.

Divination at Samhain is traditional and tarot is easiest. You can use some other system, if you like, but keep the potential costs in mind. Tarot is the most cost-effective means of divination. If you think you might need more than one deck, have an extra on hand, count people before starting, and shuffle in another deck if needed. Or alternatively you can shuffle in another set of Major Arcana or Minor Arcana. What remains is a partial deck of either Major or Minor Arcana, which can be useful on occasion. If there are few enough people, just use the Major Arcana. If there are more than twenty-two people, use the whole deck.

People should be informed in advance so they can prepare by bringing pictures or remembrances of the ancestors they want to honor at this Samhain. We interpret ancestors loosely; friends, family, people whom the participants admired, all these are considered ancestors, the only requirement being that they have passed on. You don't have to bring a picture or token but it is nice to see the table with all the things on it and the candle burning. You can have each person also bring a votive candle in a glass cup, or the group putting on the ritual can provide a few candles.

This ritual also includes a guided meditation. This can work with almost any size group, but be cautious. Emotions are often stirred by the meditation, so do not be surprised if people cry. Have tissue available, but let them have the emotional release. Usually other participants will make sure that their friends are all right.

SAMHAIN RITUAL

Materials

ALTAR—Usual items, plus a bell, a pre-shuffled deck of tarot cards in a basket (which people will take home with them), a box of tissues.

ANCESTOR SHRINE—An extra table for the Ancestor Shrine, set up in the northern quarter of the Circle, with candle(s) for the ancestors, music, and something to play the music.

Setup

ALTAR—Set up as usual. The basket with the tarot cards is placed under the altar until the end of the ritual.

ANCESTOR SHRINE—People place their pictures and mementos on the Ancestor Shrine table. No candles are lit yet.

Ritual Opening

HIGH PRIESTESS AND HIGH PRIEST—Cast Circle as usual, invoke the Goddess and God, etc.

HIGH PRIEST—Announces that this is Samhain, the feast of the dead, the night when the veil between the worlds is thinnest and that we are gathered to remember loved ones who have gone on before. The High Priest rings the bell three times.

HIGH PRIEST—Invites congregation to light Ancestors' candles, lights his own, then the High Priestess' candle.

HIGH PRIESTESS—Lights the congregation's candles as they file up to the Ancestors' Shrine.

Working

Once all candles are lit and people have settled down, begin playing some quiet gentle music to accompany the guided meditation. The volume should be low and the music somewhat slow and dreamy. It helps mask the little sounds people make in a group and provides a focus for people to follow on their return from the meditation.

HIGH PRIESTESS—Presents the guided meditation taking the participants down the river Styx, to meet and talk with their ancestors, then brings them back home. A quiet, slow, low tone of voice works best for this kind of meditation.

SAMHAIN RITUAL continued...

HIGH PRIESTESS—Rings the bell three times, and says:

> *Because the veils are the thinnest tonight, we might hope for a message from those who have gone before.*
>
> *Follow me to the banks of the river Styx.*
>
> *We may not cross, but we may look across at those who have gone on before, and we may speak to those beloved dead and receive messages from them.*

Everyone should sit or lie down in a relaxed position. Close your eyes and relax.

Allow enough time for everyone to settle down before continuing.

> *Breathe in, hold the breath, release the breath.*
>
> *Again, breathe in, hold, release. And again, breathe in, hold it, and release. As you breathe you should relax your body so you are comfortable. Take another breath in, and as you exhale, feel yourself float downward slowly into the Earth.*
>
> *Float slowly down, past the foundation of the building (or into the ground if outdoors). Past the earth, deep into the rock, until you come to a cavern divided by a deep dark river. This is the river Styx. It is deep and cold, and none but the dead may cross.*
>
> *Yet we are here on the side of the living. The light is dim, but we can make out shapes on the other side.*
>
> *See the shades of those who have gone on before. Can you recognize any? You can call out silently to beloved ancestors, and they may hear your silent call and come to the opposite bank.*
>
> *They may have a message for you, or you may silently speak to them and they can hear you.*
>
> *See the river, and see those on the other side. Call silently, and see who may answer and what they have to say to you.*

HIGH PRIEST—Should be monitoring the crowd in silence. If people cry, give them tissue. Watch to see if some people become restless or bored. The silent part shouldn't drag on too long. Ten minutes at the most. Use your judgment. Be patient.

HIGH PRIESTESS—Once the High Priestess has determined the time is right, start the journey back, by saying:

> *Now we must return back to our world.*
>
> *Bid farewell to your beloved ancestors. Thank them for whatever messages they had for you.*
>
> *Take a deep breath, and as you breathe in, feel yourself rise back up through the earth. Up through the roof of the cave. Up through the rock. Up through the earth. Up through the foundation of this building (or the ground). Up back into your body.*
>
> *Take another deep breath and feel your body.*
>
> *Feel your heartbeat, feel the blood coursing through your veins. Feel the air going in and out of your lungs.*
>
> *Wiggle your fingers and toes, and feel yourself back in your body. Back in the here and now.*
>
> *I will ring the bell three times, and everyone will be back with us by the third chime.*
>
> *Once, feel yourself back in your body.*
>
> *Twice, wiggle your fingers and toes.*
>
> *And the third time, sit or stand and stretch your muscles.*

HIGH PRIEST—Should be monitoring the crowd. If anyone seems stuck or distressed, the High Priest should be available to gently talk them out of it and back home. If a person needs to cry it out, they should be gently led away and have someone stay with them until they are recovered. This is not a common reaction, but it can happen, so be aware and act accordingly.

SAMHAIN RITUAL continued...

HIGH PRIEST—Invites participants to remember their conversations with their ancestors, and talk about them if they want. (This also allows people to gather themselves up and ground out a bit after a possibly intensely emotional experience.)

HIGH PRIESTESS—Takes the basket filled with tarot cards.

HIGH PRIEST—(Rings the bell three times to get people's attention back.) Invites the congregation to come up to the altar and draw a tarot card.

Closing

HIGH PRIESTESS AND HIGH PRIEST—Perform the blessing of wine and cakes, i.e., the Great Rite. Share wine and cakes around the Circle; use multiple chalices and plates if there is a big crowd.

HIGH PRIESTESS—Grounds the energy through the pentacle. Be certain you do a good solid grounding, because big energies have been called up.

HIGH PRIESTESS AND HIGH PRIEST—Thank and dismiss the ancestors, the Goddess and God, and the elements. Close down the Circle. Extinguish candles on the Ancestor Shrine.

CONGREGATION—Feast and visit. (People can wander and view the shrine as they eat, being careful not to touch anything.) Have people take their pictures and mementos back. Clean up. Go home.

Yule—December 21st

Yule is an interesting time for Wiccans because very often we bring so much baggage with us from our previous (frequently Christian) beliefs. Yule is the darkest and coldest time of the year (especially in the more northern latitudes, like Minnesota), and is a special time for many Pagan cultures. So while we like to base our rituals around the needs of the people in the culture, and incorporate many of our culture's more comfortably familiar themes, we try to put our own spin on things. Thus we have the Oak King and Holly King, characters from English folklore, who rule opposing halves of the year. In this ritual, although the Holly King first appears at Samhain, he does not come to power until Yule, and as the Oak King will not reach his full power until the following Summer Solstice, although he first appears at Beltane.

Another possibly unfamiliar character in this ritual is Mother Bertha. She is a Germanic Crone/Old Earth Goddess, and in this ritual takes the roles of both the Goddess and Santa Klaus.

Yule Ritual

Participants

THE HIGH PRIESTESS

THE HIGH PRIEST

OAK KING—Representative of the Light Half of the Year, i.e., Beltane through Samhain. He carries a staff with ivy leaves wrapped around it.

HOLLY KING—Representative of the Dark Half of the Year, i.e., Samhain through Beltane. He wears a holly crown.

MOTHER BERTHA—Germanic Representative of the Crone, and Goddess replacement for Santa Klaus. She wears black, with a shawl, and is old and ugly, possibly with a big warty nose.

CONGREGATION—All those attending.

Setup

ALTAR—Salt and water, incense, reading candles, brazier (light the brazier as soon as possible), broom, sword.

CIRCLE—Eight-sided Sun Wheel with small tables and pillar candles (light the quarter and cross-quarter candles from the brazier as soon as possible).

EXTRA TABLE—For food and pan filled with kitty litter (or sand) that will hold participants' candles later, laundry basket for gifts.

CONGREGATION—Receive candle and holder as they enter Circle.

Announcements

TO PARENTS—There will be candles, so please watch your children with discretion.

TO CONGREGATION—The large laundry basket is for the gifts that were brought.

Ritual Opening

HIGH PRIESTESS AND HIGH PRIEST—Set up Circle, call quarters (High Priest first *North*—then High Priestess *East*. Then High Priest *South*—and High Priestess *West).*

HIGH PRIEST—Stirs the paint by taking the wand and mixing the energies of the quarters to seal the circle.

HIGH PRIESTESS AND HIGH PRIEST—Light the congregation's candles. The High Priestess starts from the *West*; the High Priest starts from the *East,* both going deosil.

YULE RITUAL continued...

CONGREGATION—Sing as the candles are being lit.

Working

OAK KING—The Oak King steps forward with decorated staff and pontificates on the themes of the Sun's departure, and the harvest's conclusion.

HOLLY KING—The Holly King steps forward and Oak King surrenders the staff, then the Holly King pontificates on the themes of the coming dark time and requests that the members of the congregation meditate on their futures.

MOTHER BERTHA—Mother Bertha steps out of the shadows interrupting the Holly King's pontification. She challenges the congregation, accusing that they are not worthy of the God's bounty, because they are lazy, etc.

HIGH PRIESTESS—Answers this challenge for her congregation.

MOTHER BERTHA—Accepts answer.

HIGH PRIESTESS—Invites Mother Bertha to join the celebration.

MOTHER BERTHA—Agrees and offers to distribute "gifts."

CONGREGATION—File up to Mother Bertha, place their candle in the kitty litter pan and accept a "gift" from Mother Bertha, then return to their places after being warned about not opening them.

Closing

HIGH PRIESTESS AND HIGH PRIEST—Perform the Great Rite, unstir the paint by taking the wand and unmixing the energies of the quarters prepatory to taking the Circle down, dismiss the quarters, and open the Circle.

CONGREGATION—Open gifts, feast, celebrate, etc.

Additional Yule Celebrations

For personal or coven rituals there are several additional things that can be done as celebrations. Since Yule is the longest night of the year, you can celebrate with a Yule log. This is a specially decorated log that is burned. The tradition is to light the Yule log before the Sun goes down, and tend the fire all night until the Sun returns in the morning. Make sure you have enough wood to burn all night. You can have a group vigil, always making sure someone is awake and tending to the fire. If you have a home with a fireplace, this is the ideal venue for your vigil. You can do it outdoors, but be sure to get all necessary permits, and make sure you are safe and dressed for the weather. Some groups accompany their vigil with an open house, and other members of the community can drop by anytime during the night to chat and assist in maintaining the vigil.

Some groups gather on the morning after Yule, to greet and welcome the Sun back after his rebirth. They find a place with a good East view, and gather before dawn, huddling and shivering (at least in Minnesota), drinking coffee or hot cider, and when dawn comes they cheer and sing and celebrate. If the weather doesn't cooperate, usually a day on either side of Yule will do.

The Yule tree is a Pagan tradition that many Wiccans cheerfully keep. When the tree goes up and comes down (hopefully not before Twelfth Night) and how it's decorated is a matter of personal taste. Paul and Estelle have a tradition of obtaining some new ornaments each year—suns, moons, stars, snowflakes, animals, and other similar motifs. We even have an ornament of the Wicked Witch of the West, from *The Wizard of Oz,* just for fun.

Wiccans can also exchange gifts at Yule or Twelfth Night, which is the twelfth night after Christmas. January 6th is Twelfth Night, which coincidentally corresponds with Orthodox Christmas. Having the Twelfth Night tradition gives you more time for receiving and exchanging gifts, and also allows you to shop the after-Christmas sales and still be timely with your gifts. Twelfth Night also extends the holiday season, allowing for a few more parties on a few more weekends to fit in the Wiccan celebrations as well as the usual Christian ones, which most Wiccans still celebrate with their non-Wiccan friends and families.

Wassailing is another old Yuletide tradition. A group visits friends' houses to sing and wassail the houses' inhabitants. They are given drink in return, cider and/or wine or ale, and a short impromptu party results. It is possible to visit four or five homes and wassail each for about thirty minutes. Make sure there are designated drivers. The singing and wassailing is a type of house blessing, and the householders give the drink in return for the blessing. This happens during the holiday season, and can be compared to a living, singing, holiday card. Much fun and good cheer.

Candlemas/Imbolc—February 2nd

Two rituals are offered here. Neither is very long or complicated, but each is effective in its simplicity.

The first is a traditional blessing of the tools. Imbolc occurs toward the end of winter, a time when agrarian societies were thinking about spring planting and the growing season. It was a time when the tools for planting were brought out, repaired, if necessary, in preparation for the planting season. Nowadays few of us grow all our own food, but we all do work, which helps sustain and nourish us, and at Imbolc the tools of our trade are blessed. Think symbolic (bring a floppy disk to the ritual, not your entire computer) and inclusive. The tools you bring for blessing can be those you use in the Craft, in your employment, in your teaching or learning, or for fun or other pursuits.

The second ritual is a fire-starting ceremony. Fire was sacred in prehistoric times, and the making of fire was a magickal act in itself. Few modern people have seen fire created from flint and tinder, and this can be a very powerful ritual.

Imbolc Ritual Number One

No extra tools are needed for this ritual. All you need is enough room for people to put their tools. This can be a part of the altar, or a separate table. People should be told beforehand to bring tools to be blessed, and maybe the symbolic and inclusive nature should be stressed—such as bringing a floppy disk rather than an entire computer, or a small hand trowel as symbolic of a dozen or more gardening tools. People can also improvise on the spot with a pencil or pen (for those who write), and other small tokens that symbolize their hobbies and pursuits. Be creative and open and you will be amazed what people come up with.

Setup

ALTAR—Set up as normal, but with an extra table nearby to accept the tools to be blessed.

CONGREGATION—The people gather, and an announcement is made, describing the ritual and inviting the participants to place their tools on the table for blessing.

Ritual Opening

HIGH PRIESTESS AND HIGH PRIEST—Cast the Circle in the usual manner. Invoke the Goddess and God. Then join hands over the tools, and ask the Lady and the Lord to bless the tools, and the people who will use them.

CONGREGATION—Should focus their energy on the High Priest and High Priestess, while the High Priest and High Priestess channel that energy into the tools.

Closing

HIGH PRIESTESS AND HIGH PRIEST—When the blessing is done, dismiss the Goddess and God. Close down the Circle.

CONGREGATION—Feast and party. Clean up. Go home.

Odhinn

Imbolc Ritual Number Two

This ritual has two mystical messages. The first is the acquisition of fire, which is a very important tool for humans, although its importance is frequently ignored because it is so easy for most people in our modern culture to obtain. The second message is, if you live in the northern hemisphere, it becomes visibly apparent around the early days of February that the Sun is really coming back, and we won't dwell in darkness forever. Many Wiccans consider Yule, approximately December 21st, the time of the Sun's return. This is not wrong, just different from what Paul does. For this book, Yule is the longest night, and the Sun returns on February 1st, 2nd, or 6th, depending on which traditions you follow. Because of this, the Sabbat is also called Candlemas.

Equipment

You will need some special tools for this ritual; the most important are flint and steel, cotton wool or similar material for ignition, kindling, small twigs (match sticks) or wood shavings. You will also need something to create a fire in, like a cauldron or other metal container that will not be damaged by fire. Make sure the cauldron (or vessel) is insulated from whatever it is resting on, either with a hot plate, trivet, stone, or other similar non-flammable item. Paul uses a small incense brazier with long legs set in a bowl of water.

Practice starting a fire at home before you try this ritual. If you cannot do it with flint and steel, use something else, like a long butane fireplace lighter.

Setup

RITUAL ROOM—Should be prepared so that it can be made totally dark. Cover the windows, make sure that all the light switches can be easily reached, etc.

ALTAR—Set up as normal with Goddess, God, and lit reading candles. Place the fire-making materials at the center of the altar. Make sure that they are placed in a position that is easy to reach, where nothing nearby will be disturbed. The High Priest will have to find the flint and steel in the dark.

SUMMONER—Should be prepared to extinguish all the lights in the room.

CONGREGATION— Each is given an unlit candle.

Ritual Opening

HIGH PRIESTESS AND HIGH PRIEST—Cast the Circle as usual. Invoke the Goddess and God.

HIGH PRIESTESS—Announces the purpose of the ritual, and announces to the congregation that the room will be dark. As she finishes her speech, the High Priestess extinguishes the reading candle.

IMBOLC RITUAL NUMBER TWO continued...

HIGH PRIEST—Goes to the altar and picks up the fire-making materials.

SUMMONER—After the High Priestess extinguishes the reading candle, he goes around the room putting out all the lights, starting with the largest or furthest electrical light, to each of the quarter candles, to finally the God and Goddess candles on the altar.

Working
HIGH PRIEST—Takes flint and steel and strikes a spark, trying to start a new flame. (If this is done in the dark, it is quite dramatic.) All the people should concentrate on the spark, and will it into a flame. When the flame is started, the High Priest should feed and tend it until it burns unassisted. Then he should use that flame to re-light all the ritual candles, one by one, using a matchstick, a candle, or another tool which carries the flame from the first fire to each candle. Then he lights the participant's candles.

CONGREGATION—Sing appropriate Sun songs, and admire the fire for a moment.

HIGH PRIEST—Gives a speech welcoming the light.

Closing
HIGH PRIESTESS AND HIGH PRIEST—Dismiss the Goddess and God. Close down the Circle.

CONGREGATION—Feast and party with some cooked food, to celebrate what fire can bring us. Clean up. Go home.

Spring Equinox/Oestarra—March 21st
This Sabbat celebrates spring and the returning life that spring rekindles. Easter bunnies and colored eggs have been borrowed by modern culture from Pagan spring celebrations. Even the Christian holiday of Easter is named after the ancient German Goddess Eástre or Ostara. The egg is a symbol of the Triple Goddess, three circles in one: the shell, the egg white, and the yolk, hidden within. This is a good ritual for children, no matter what age. Because this ritual includes children it is strongly advised to have either a nonalcoholic libation (like cider) or have two chalices, one alcoholic and the other nonalcoholic.

This ritual adapts well to any size group. Cook the eggs in batches at least one day before the ritual (no more than a dozen at a time—they can crack) and chill them in the refrigerator overnight. Make sure you have enough hard-boiled eggs and crayons. Have several baskets with eggs and crayons to circulate in the crowd. Twenty-four eggs per basket is a good number for manageability, so gauge accordingly.

You can also have an Oestarra bunny handing out the eggs, another fertility symbol, or organize an egg or candy hunt, if that is appealing. The hunt should probably be separate from the ritual, otherwise it can become quite chaotic.

Oestarra Ritual

Equipment
ALTAR—Set up normally, but with hard-boiled eggs, some of which are colored on, and a selection of colored crayons.

Ritual Opening
HIGH PRIESTESS AND HIGH PRIEST—Cast the Circle as usual. Invoke the Goddess and God.

HIGH PRIESTESS—Describes what Oestarra is about—spring, fertility, etc.—and invites the participants to come to the altar, choose an egg, and decorate it as they desire. The eggs will be collected later to be blessed, and then they will be taken home.

HANDMAIDEN AND SUMMONER—Distribute eggs and crayons to the participants. People are encouraged to share crayons. There is no right or wrong way to decorate the eggs. Be creative and have fun. People may want to display their egg when all are finished. This allows all to admire everyone's efforts. People will want to sit and share crayons and ideas. The noise level is usually high, with people chatting and laughing. This is good. Parents and others may want to help children, but all are encouraged to use their imagination.

HIGH PRIESTESS AND HIGH PRIEST—Should allow for fifteen to twenty minutes of passing out eggs, coloring, laughing, etc. Monitor to see when most of the people are finished. The High Priestess, High Priest, Handmaiden, and Summoner should also color eggs for themselves. Give a five-minute warning so people can finish up. When all are done, reassemble the people in a Circle.

HANDMAIDEN AND SUMMONER—Should re-circulate and collect the colored eggs and crayons in the baskets.

HIGH PRIESTESS AND HIGH PRIEST—The High Priestess takes the egg basket, and together the High Priestess and High Priest bless the eggs.

Closing
HIGH PRIESTESS AND HIGH PRIEST—Perform the Great Rite and bless the wine and cakes. The chalice and cakes are shared by all. Then the energy is grounded into pentacle, the Goddess and God are dismissed, and the Circle is closed down.

CONGREGATION—Feast and have fun. Collect their eggs from the basket. Clean up. Go home.

Beltane—May 1st

Beltane for most Wiccans is the marriage of the Goddess and God. It is a major fertility ritual, and signifies the start of the planting cycle (in temperate climates).

Many groups will perform a ceremony called the election of the May Queen and Green Man. This allows the Gods to choose a representative of themselves for the day. It usually involves some sort of lottery (in some Traditions, this lottery is done by baking some small item—in many cases a pea—into one of a group of cakes. All the cakes are handed around, and the person who chooses the cake with the pea in it is selected.) The newly elected May Queen and Green Man then reign (with whatever rights, responsibilities, and duration acceptable to each particular Tradition) as the symbolic embodiment of the Goddess and God.

This ritual involves dancing the Maypole. This is another ancient fertility rite, and the version we have here is as simple as we could make it. (You can see a fairly elaborate version of this dance, performed by the schoolboys in the 1960s film *The Wicker Man*.) The requirements for this ritual are slightly different than the other outlines we have presented in this chapter. Either it must be performed outside, or in a room with a ceiling high enough to set up at least an eight-foot pole.

Beltane Ritual

Special Equipment

Your Maypole and ribbons are the only extra equipment you will need. The pole's height should be at least eight feet. If you are going to perform this ritual outside, you will need to bury the pole one or more feet in the ground, so the total height of your pole would be approximately ten feet. If you are performing it indoors, you can get a flagpole stand to hold the pole.

Attach ribbons to the top of the pole, using as many gay colors as you can find, and at least one for every participant. And these ribbons should be at least two feet longer than the standing height of your Maypole. You might also want to make a wreath of flowers that will sit on the top of the pole, and big enough to slide down around the pole as the ribbons are wrapped during the dance. Attach the ribbons and wreath while the pole is horizontal, and when all are attached and secured, stand the pole up.

Setup

ALTAR—Should be set up minimally, if at all. The Maypole is your altar for this ritual.

QUARTER SHRINES—Should be set up at each quarter, decorated with flowers, etc. They should be placed far enough away from the central Maypole, so that the participants can comfortably dance around the pole. You can also use the quarter shrines to hold any necessary ritual equipment that would normally be on the altar.

BELTANE RITUAL continued...

MAYPOLE—Placed in the center of the Circle (either dug in if outdoors, or in a stand if indoors), with the ribbons dangling freely and the wreath placed at the top.

CONGREGATION—Should wear their most colorful robes, flowers, and jewelry, and bring drums and musical instruments (if they have any), and light party foods for the feast.

SACRED SPACE—An area out of the reach of any wildly gyrating dancers—but still in the Circle—should be set aside for people who are not dancing and the musicians.

Ritual Opening
HIGH PRIESTESS AND HIGH PRIEST—Except for the altar, cast the Circle and invoke the Gods and elemental quarters as usual.

HIGH PRIESTESS—Describes the purpose of the ritual, and invites participants to choose a ribbon and dance.

Working
CONGREGATION—All participants who want to dance choose a ribbon and arrange themselves around the Maypole. They should try to place themselves around the pole, alternating boy, girl.

HIGH PRIESTESS—Has also chosen a ribbon, signals the music to start (either live musicians, or tapes or CDs), and leads the participants in the dancing. Men should dance clockwise, women counterclockwise, even weaving in and out of each other (though this is usually too complicated for most nonprofessional people to easily do).

The dancing around and around eventually gets tight as the ribbons wrap around the pole down to the ends of the ribbons. There should be fun and gaiety, laughing and merriment. The ribbons can be tied together at the bottom.

Closing
HIGH PRIESTESS AND HIGH PRIEST—After the Maypole has been completely wrapped with ribbons, thank the congregation for their efforts, thank the Gods for their blessings, and dismiss them. Dismiss the quarter elements and close down the Circle. (You may not need to do the Great Rite, because the Maypole dance has already done that.)

CONGREGATION—Feast and have fun. Clean up. Go home.

Summer Solstice—June 21st

Summer Solstice is the longest day of the year, when the Sun is at its strongest. The ritual we describe is called "The Writing of the Boons." People will write out, on a small slip of paper, some wish they have for the future, or state some work that they need help with, or ask for healing for some friend, etc. Then the written boon is given to the High Priestess to be blessed and burned in a cauldron for the Gods to read and, hopefully, answer.

The fire in the cauldron is created for an indoor environment, although you can use an outdoor bonfire if you are performing this ritual in a place that allows it, or a barbecue grill. These papers should be small, not bigger than one-eighth to one-quarter of a standard piece of writing paper, and lightweight, because you want the paper to burn. Do not use fancy colored or foil papers; they don't burn well and may release fumes.

SUMMER SOLSTICE RITUAL

Special Equipment

A metal cauldron with an inch or two of kitty litter (or sand) completely covering the bottom, a dozen small candles, and extra incense.

Setup

SACRED SPACE—Assemble the main altar in the center of the Circle and quarter altars at their respective quarters. Place the cauldron to the South of the altar, and place in the kitty litter (or sand) six to nine candles and a couple of sticks of incense.

CONGREGATION—Someone greets the guests at the doorway and passes out the paper and pencils, telling the participants that they should write their boons on this paper.

Ritual Opening

HIGH PRIESTESS AND HIGH PRIEST—Cast the Circle as usual. Invoke the Goddess and God.

HIGH PRIESTESS—Describes the purpose of the ritual, and describes the events that will take place.

Working

HIGH PRIESTESS—Asks that all the participants fill out their boons for the coming year.

HIGH PRIEST—Lights the candles in the cauldron.

HIGH PRIESTESS—Approaches the cauldron, invites the participants to place their completed boons into the fire, and begins to sing some appropriate song, which the participants will keep going.

SUMMER SOLSTICE RITUAL continued...

CONGREGATION—Members file up one at a time, make a short personal prayer to the Gods, and hand their boons to the High Priestess.

HIGH PRIESTESS—Blesses the boons and hands them one at a time to the High Priest.

HIGH PRIEST—Makes sure all the boons are burned.

Closing

CONGREGATION—After participants have surrendered their boons, they return to their place in the Circle.

HIGH PRIESTESS AND HIGH PRIEST—After all the participants (including themselves) have burned their boons, they perform the Great Rite and bless the wine and cakes. They share the chalice and cakes all around, ground the energy into pentacle, dismiss the Goddess and God, and close down the Circle.

CONGREGATION—Feast and have fun. Clean up. Go home.

Lughnasadh—August 1st

Lughnasadh is sometimes called the first harvest. It occurs at high summer, and was used by many cultures as a sort of vacation time, because it is between the hard work of planting time—which can extend through Summer Solstice—and the hard work of harvest time—which, except for some few crops, has really not begun yet.

The activities performed in this ritual are twofold. One, we will be celebrating the coming harvest with a corn roast. And two, we will be celebrating the Gods with games. These celebrations have been performed by many cultures including the Irish and several American Indian tribes.

The games should be fairly simple, so that most of the congregation can participate, and similar to the games played at a church picnic: three-legged races (two people try to race with the left leg of one and the right leg of the other tied together), egg races (in which a person tries to carry an egg held in a spoon in their mouth, through a simple obstacle course), relay races (several people on different teams trying to complete a course), etc. You should cater the type of games to the people who will be attending. If you are going to have a lot of kids, you should focus the type of games for the median age group. If you have many people who are not very physically active, design your games for their level of activities. If you have a very close-knit coven of consenting adults, you might make the games a little more exotic or sensual (like a clothes race, where teams of couples run a relay race with one set of clothing that they must take off the person in front of them and put on themselves). Play to your audience. Because this is high summer, with the God at His peak, you might want to make sure that you have at least one game of strength, like arm wrestling, to specifically honor the God.

ᏞUGHNASADH ᏒITUAL

Special Equipment

Make sure that you have prepared the equipment and supplies necessary for the games you will be playing. If you are having a tricycle race (where an adult has to race a tricycle), make sure you have several tricycles. If you are playing dodge ball, make sure you have the ball, etc.

Buy some fresh corn—which should be available at this time of year—and prepare it for roasting. You should also plan some way to cook the corn: a fire, a barbecue grill, an oven, whatever is available at your ritual site.

Setup

ALTAR—Because the altar for this ritual will be both the cooking fire and the bodies of the participants who will playing the games, the altar should be kept to a minimum, if used at all.

SACRED SPACE—Because the games aspect of this ritual may take up a lot of room, make sure that you include all the areas that you will be gaming in and the area in which you will be cooking the corn in your Circle and Sacred Space.

CONGREGATION—Make sure that the participants understand before they arrive the nature of the Working so that they will be dressed in clothes appropriate to the games, and they won't ruin their fancy robes. This is one ritual when the fancy robes will be left at home, and standard play clothes will be worn. This ritual can be done at a public park since it is very much like a family reunion or company picnic in appearance.

Ritual Opening

HIGH PRIESTESS AND HIGH PRIEST—Cast the Circle around the entire gaming and cooking areas. Invoke the Goddess and God, and place the quarter elements to cover the entire gaming area.

HIGH PRIESTESS—Describes the purpose of the ritual, and describes the events that will occur.

Working

HIGH PRIESTESS—Blesses the prepared corn, and gives it to a volunteer to cook. Then she announces the beginning of the games. The High Priestess will act as the judge in any game she does not want to compete in.

HIGH PRIEST—Calls for the first game. The High Priest will be the referee in any game he does not compete in. If the High Priestess or High Priest do compete in one or more of the games (and they should if they can), then a designated substitute (Handmaiden or Summoner?) will referee and judge the games.

LUGHNASADH RITUAL continued...

The games should continue until the corn is ready to eat, usually between one-half and one hour.

HIGH PRIESTESS—Calls a halt to the games, gives thanks to the Gods for the corn, and calls the participants to the feast. This is one of the few rituals in which feasting is an integral part of the Working, rather than the primary social and grounding aspect of the ritual.

CONGREGATION—During the feast, the winners of the games receive their accolades, and sometimes small tokens are given as prizes, if the ritual budget allows.

Closing

HIGH PRIESTESS AND HIGH PRIEST—After the feast is finished, perform the Great Rite with only the chalice and wine, giving thanks to the Gods for their blessings. Dismiss the Goddess and God. Close down the Circle.

CONGREGATION—Clean up the mess. Put away your toys. Go home.

Fall Equinox/Mabon—September 21st

At Mabon Wiccans bless and celebrate the harvest. It is similar to Thanksgiving. In this ritual the Gods partake of the feast only during the ritual, and sharing the feast during the ritual is shorter and more symbolic than would be a full meal. Some groups do make the actual feast a part of their ritual, but the feast can drag on, and the energy of the ritual can dissipate as people move around and eat. Then you have to gather everybody together again to perform the Great Rite and close down the Circle. It's best to bless the feast in Circle, maybe have a token feast (at the minimum the Great Rite is a token feast), and have the primary feast after the ritual is over.

This ritual requires a fairly large space. It also requires rehearsal and blocking to ensure that it flows smoothly. You can add music, sung or played, to enhance the ritual.

ᴄᴍᴀʙᴏɴ ʀɪᴛᴜᴀʟ

Special Equipment
- Oats and Indian corn and other decorations
- Metal cauldron with the bottom covered completely with an inch or two of kitty litter (or sand)
- A dozen small candles and extra incense
- Rattle and Jack o' the Green costume
- Special decorations for the four directional quarters: North—pine boughs; South—maple or sumac leaves; East—birch or rowan leaves; West—ivy

Setup

This ritual features a burnt offering. People write what they have to be thankful for on a slip of paper, and these are burned in a fire to send the messages to the Gods. The fire is created for an indoor environment, although you can use an outdoor bonfire if that is possible, or a barbecue grill. These papers should be lightweight and small, not bigger than one-eighth to one-quarter of a standard piece of writing paper. Do not use fancy colored or foil papers; they don't burn well and may release fumes.

Jack o' the Green is a folk figure/God featured in Celtic mythology. His face is often depicted in leafy foliage. This form is also known as the Green Man. He is a God of vegetation and farming, a role that lends itself well to costuming. Dressing in green with leaves, etc., green face paint, and other similar things can add to the fun of this ritual. Jack is a jolly, lively figure, and he can dance while he blesses and eats the feast. Creativity and rehearsal are important to enhance the performance of Jack o' the Green.

ALTAR—Along with the normal altar equipment, have some cooked corn warmed in roaster with butter and salt on or near the altar, cider and Sangria (ice) with ladles, and pre-cut paper and pencils for thanks-giving offerings.

SACRED SPACE—Assemble the main altar in center of the Circle, and quarter altars at their respective quarters. Place a feast table to the North of altar, and create a beautiful display of the food (with potluck offerings from the congregation). Place the cauldron to the South of altar, placing six to nine candles and a couple sticks of incense into the kitty litter (or sand).

CONGREGATION—Have someone greet the guests at the doorway. These people should direct any food contributions to be placed on the food table. Pass out the paper and pencils, telling the participants that they should be writing their thanks offering on the paper.

MABON RITUAL continued...

Ritual Opening

HIGH PRIESTESS AND HIGH PRIEST—Cast the Circle as usual. Invoke the Goddess and God.

HIGH PRIESTESS—Describes the purpose of the ritual, and describes the events and procedures to the participants.

Working

HIGH PRIESTESS—Invokes the Spirit of Jack o' the Green into the High Priest. She should give a speech describing Jack and what he does, and what he will do for the ritual.

CONGREGATION—Should help the invocation with their focused energy, clapping and cheering.

HIGH PRIEST—The newly invoked Jack o' the Green takes his rattle and dances around the Circle once or twice. He then goes to the cauldron and lights the candles and incense.

HIGH PRIESTESS—While Jack o' the Green is performing, she makes a speech about the harvest, and about the coming burning of the paper offerings.

CONGREGATION—Invited by the High Priestess to bring their offerings to the cauldron to be burnt by Jack.

HIGH PRIESTESS—Announces that the harvest brought by the congregation will be blessed by Jack, and that He alone will enjoy the first fruits, "Thus giving the Gods their due."

HIGH PRIEST—Jack o' the Green then asperges and blesses the harvest that is spread out on the feast table.

HIGH PRIESTESS—Holds a special chalice of cider and plate of corn for Jack to bless (this is the Great Rite for this ritual).

HIGH PRIEST—Jack now enjoys a small amount of the blessed cider and corn (with butter and salt), thanks the participants for the harvest, and blesses the congregation.

CONGREGATION—Reply as they feel, with laughter, cheers, etc.

HIGH PRIESTESS—When Jack has finished eating, she thanks him and dismisses the Spirit of Jack o' the Green.

Closing

HIGH PRIESTESS AND HIGH PRIEST—Dismiss the Goddess and God, and close down the Circle.

CONGREGATION—Feast at the now blessed harvest potluck. Clean up. Go home.

ESBATS

Sabbats are the celebrations based on the Solar cycle. Esbats are the celebrations based upon the Moon. When a Wiccan talks about celebrating an Esbat, they are probably speaking of a Full Moon celebration. At the Full Moon, the Moon is brightest and has the most power, and legend has it that magick is easier and more effective. Because the Moon represented the Goddess in many cultures, the Full Moon is the time of the Goddess. The Full Moon energies are good for spellworking, healing, divination, prophecy, and for calling in energies for building and accomplishment (prosperity, etc.). The Full Moon corresponds to the Goddess in all her glory—the pregnant Mother, the powerful and abundant Earth Mother, Queen of the Night.

The New Moon is also a time of power, but of a different kind. A few Wiccan groups also celebrate an Esbat at the New Moon. The New Moon is more in tune with the energies of the Crone—seclusion, secrets, and banishing. Sometimes divination is also an activity that can be effective at the New Moon, as are finding lost or hidden things.

The ceremony of Drawing Down the Moon—invoking the Goddess into the High Priestess—is the classic celebration for a Full Moon Esbat. Ideally this should be done on an experienced Priestess in a Circle with an experienced High Priest. Once the Goddess has been invoked, she can participate in spellworking, divination, or occasionally pure prophecy. Prophecy is a gift from the Goddess, but one that cannot be counted upon. The Goddess enters the Priestess, and then people ask her questions and she may answer. Sometimes the answers are clear and concise, sometimes they are vague and obscure.

Sometimes Esbats are just pure celebration where the people feast, drink, and dance in the joy of the Goddess.

For a Full Moon Esbat, you should decide beforehand what sort of Working or celebration you intend to have. Once you decide that, you can then decide whether or not you will perform the ritual of Drawing Down the Moon. There should be some sort of food and beverages. This can range from just cakes and wine (alcoholic or nonalcoholic) or juice, to a full meal with a potluck, organized or just bring what you will. Partaking of the bounties of the Goddess (the food) is a part of the Esbat celebration.

If you are going to do some spellwork, research, and have your materials ready. If the spell is to consecrate or construct something, have it ninety-nine percent finished before you start the ritual. The ritual is not to actually make the thing (which could take days or longer) but to finish and magickally charge the item.

If you are doing a healing, be sure the person you are healing (whether present or not) is aware of the healing and willing for it to be done. Otherwise you should just send the energy to the cosmos, for the person to use or not as they will.

Ideally there will be one focus for the Working. Having a coven of ten people, with each doing their own separate spell, can get long, tedious, and exhausting. The group should decide beforehand (ideally a week or so, so all can prepare) what they will do. Maybe one coven member really needs a new job. Maybe there is an ecological problem in your area that needs attention and care. Maybe the coven as a whole wants some guidance and direction for their efforts and studies. Esbats are good for the big important spells done by the whole coven. You have the extra energy of the Full Moon and the energy of the group.

If there is no major area that needs attention, divination is a good Working. Each person should bring their tarot deck or other favorite means of divination, and then, for the Working, a common question is asked, and each person does a reading to get an answer. Write down each answer (ideally this is done without comment or consultation to keep each answer uninfluenced by others). Then after the Circle is down, the coven can meet and compare answers and see how they fit together. This can be immediately after the Esbat, or more likely at another date. Since people wrote down their results and possibly journaled the experience after the Esbat itself, there are written records. Examples of questions might be: What will the next month, three months, six months, year bring? What should the coven do to help the community? What can we do to help (your candidate of choice) win the next election? Is there anything anyone in the coven should be especially aware of or look out for? Ideally the divinations should be for things that affect the coven and the community in general. Personal divination can be done, but with the power of a group you can get more, so why not go for the big questions?

Ideally this Circle should be performed outdoors in a secluded, private place. You should be able to see the Full Moon. If you cannot be outdoors, being able to see the Full Moon through a window is highly desirable. If the sky is overcast or you cannot meet in a suitable place, a single candle can substitute for the Full Moon.

Full Moon Esbat Ritual

Setup

SUPPLIES AND EQUIPMENT NEEDED—Your standard Circle supplies. A dark bowl with water. Paper and writing tools. Food and/or drink for all to share.

Ritual Opening

HIGH PRIESTESS AND HIGH PRIEST—Cast the Circle in the manner you are accustomed to. Invoke the Goddess and God. Place the bowl of water on a low table, so it catches the light of the Full Moon.

Working

HIGH PRIESTESS AND HIGH PRIEST—Join hands over the bowl, and charge it with their energy, and that of the Full Moon. Each gazes into the bowl in turn, and sees what they may.

CONGREGATION—Members of the coven, in turn, come up and gaze into the bowl to see what they may.

When all have had their look, the coven members join hands and thank the Lady for her light and her messages.

There may be additional dancing or singing if the coven chooses.

FULL MOON ESBAT RITUAL continued...

Closing
HIGH PRIESTESS AND HIGH PRIEST—Thank and dismiss the Goddess, God, and the elemental quarters. Close down the Circle.

CONGREGATION—Feast and party. Clean up. Go home.

NOTE: Scrying with the water-filled bowl reflecting the moonlight is ancient and powerful. You can substitute another form of divination if you wish. The coven should be silent while each person takes their turn gazing into the bowl. Each person should keep a written record of what they saw in their Book of Shadows.

CEREMONIAL MAGICK

Below we have included two traditional High or Ceremonial Magick rituals, so you can see how they work, and because they are both relatively ancient (as far as Wicca goes) and are widely known. If you can say the words, or visualize them, they work. Try them, see how they feel to you, and have fun.

The Ritual of the Rose Cross

The Rosy Cross, more properly called the "Ritual of the Rose Cross," can produce a very good basic warding and energizing Circle. This Circle is visualized as a ball-shaped web of light, completely surrounding your Sacred Space, which is connected at the cross-quarter directions of the compass (i.e., South East—South West—North West—North East) and directly above and below the center of the Sacred Space (i.e., above and below).

While the imagery was designed by a Christian mystical order, one need not be stuck with the Christian imagery. Almost any God or Goddess name and/or imagery may be substituted, if you understand the imagery you are replacing, and know and are comfortable with the images you are going to use.

The symbol of the Rose Cross itself is a simple equal armed cross within a circle (also known as a Sun Wheel) and is an ancient universally known symbol used throughout the world. Because the Sun Wheel is so universally known, and because the Rose Cross itself is used only as a focus for your attention and your visualized will, we recommend using the Rose Cross unchanged for this ritual. These Rose Crosses are most effectively produced with a lighted stick of incense. Hold the incense in front of you at each quarter of the Circle, draw an equal arm cross in the air, then draw a circle around it three times while chanting *Ye-He-Shu-Aaah*. This chanting can be done silently or audibly, or even by using visualization only. If you can't use incense, you can move your hand as if you had incense.

The Ritual of the Rose Cross

PART 1

STEP 1

Ground and center with three deep cleansing breaths (see the diaphragm breathing exercise on page 203). Light your incense. Start in the Southeast cross-quarter direction. Face outward. Repeat the following directions in each cross-quarter (i.e., SE, SW, NW, NE):

Holding the incense in your right hand, about chest height, starting in the center of where your Cross will be, visualize drawing with the incense a Cross in gold light, by tracing a line of light going up about a foot or so, then down past your center starting point an equal distance, then back up to center.

Then trace another line of light toward the right, about the same distance as your extended vertical arms, then back left and through center, then back to the end of the right arm and pause.

Now draw a circle around your Cross with a clockwise spiral of at least three full circles, ending finally in the center. As you draw the circles, chant:

> *Ye-He-Shu-Aaah*
> (YHShA—Joshua in Hebrew, another name of God).

Intone it loudly. You may feel strange but once you are comfortable, it adds energy.

STEP 2

You will now create a web of energy lines, anchored at the cross-quarters, as well as above and below.

After you have drawn the first Cross, draw with your incense a line of blue energy, from the first Cross, to the place where you will draw your second Cross at the SW corner. Draw the second Cross as you did the first, with the same motions and chant.

Then draw another blue energy line to where the third Cross will be at the NW corner, and so on around your Circle.

The pattern for making the web is; SE, SW, NW, NE, SE, Above, NW, Below, SE, SW, Above, NE, Below, SW, NW, NE, and then the last cross at SE, seventeen in all.

For the last cross at the SE cross-quarter chant:

> *Ye-He-Shu-Aaah-Ye-He-Vah-Shaa*
> (Joshua, and another tetragrammaton).

THE RITUAL OF THE ROSE CROSS continued...

Draw the last Cross and seal it, move up and down, right and left, and also in and out in three dimensions, before drawing the last circles, which binds the whole thing, and activates the bright luminescent silver protective web.

Take a breath and relax. You may end the ritual here, if you want. You have produced a protective energy web, and it is useful when you don't want to be noticed on the astral. You do not need to take this Circle down, as it naturally fades away if you do not keep focusing on it.

If you wish to continue, go on to part 2.

PART 2

STEP 3

Put the incense aside, but keep it burning for its healing aroma. This next part will call down healing light into the Circle and into yourself and/or another person who needs the healing energy. It is adaptable to almost any healing purpose—physical, spiritual, and psychic. It should only be done inside the energy web, as it's not effective otherwise.

When healing another person, they should sit on a stool in the center of the Circle facing East. You draw the energy web, above, below, and around both of you.

Then facing East, stand behind the seated person. (If alone, just stand in the center of the Circle.) Relax, with your feet shoulder width apart.

With your arms straight out to the side, right palm up, left palm down, visualize cosmic energy looping through your body, shaped and directed by your hands, like a figure 8 on its side.

Intone the words:

> *Yod-Noon-Resh-Yod*
> (YNRY in Hebrew—Latinized INRI).

This is another tetragrammaton, acronym for "The beginning, life, death, and the end."

Then, with your right arm straight up, your left arm straight out, making an "L," and head tilted left, say:

> *Virgo, Isis, Mighty Mother.*

With both arms above the head making a wide "V" shape, head tilted back, and looking up, say:

> *Scorpio, Apophis (ah-pahf-iss), Destroyer.*

THE RITUAL OF THE ROSE CROSS continued...

With both arms crossed over your breast, hands on shoulders, and head bowed down, say:

> *Sol, Osiris, Slain and Risen.*

While opening your arms upward to full extension above your head, tilt your head back until you are looking up, and intone:

> *Isis, Apophis, Osiris. Eeeeeeee, AAAAAHH, OOOOOHH.*
> (Resonate the vowels, it adds energy. IAO is the "call of Kether.")

When the resonances have died down, move your arms to the Virgo position (with your arms in an "L") and say:

> *L.*

Then move to the Scorpio position (with your arms in a "V") and say:

> *V.*

Then move to the Osiris position (with your arms in an "X") and say:

> *X.*

(These three positions should be done quickly.)

Then repeat the arm and head motions and say:

> *L-U-X.*

Then raising your arms above your head, say:

> *Lux (Luke's). Light. The Light of the Cross. Let the Light, Descend!*

As your arms are raised you should grab hold of the golden energy shining down from above and draw it down over the top of the head of the person seated in front of you. If you are doing it on yourself, draw it down over the top of your head. Do not push or force the energy, just let it flow down.

This energy is to be taken as needed, poured like honey. Once done, you might do a cleansing breath, and maybe let your hands rest on the person's shoulders. You and the person seated may feel warm, or energized, or a bit buoyed up. This is normal. Ask and make sure the person is okay and centered afterward.

The Rose Cross creates a Circle which does not have to be consciously taken down, but can be allowed to dissipate on its own. For healing, this can be done up to three times a day, morning, noon, and night; theoretically it's most effective at dawn, noon, and dusk. Twice a day is also good, and even once a day is helpful. Try to do it at regular times each day. The healing effects may be only temporary at first, but over time it can be very effective. This ritual works even if you just say the words and go through the motions, or by just visualizing yourself doing it. But doing everything—motions, chanting, and visualizations—helps.

The LBRP or Kabbalistic Cross

The LBRP, or "Lesser Banishing Ritual of the Pentagram," also known as "The Kabbalistic Cross" is included in this book because it is a good general grounding and balancing ritual that produces a reliable safe space. It is fairly complex (when compared to some of the other ceremonies we discuss in this book), with both a standardized verbal script and visualizations, plus a complete set of physical motions. All of the parts of this ritual should be memorized to obtain the best results. It is probably the most widely known single ritual in the Anglo-American magickal traditions. If you say the words and perform the actions, it will automatically work, in spite of anything else you do, or whatever shape you are in.

---

*L*ESSER *B*ANISHING *R*ITUAL OF THE *P*ENTAGRAM

PART 1—THE KABBALISTIC CROSS

STEP 1

Ground and center with three deep cleansing breaths (see the diaphragm breathing exercise on page 203). Let all the tension and outside distractions fade away.

STEP 2

Stand solidly and comfortably facing the East, with your feet shoulder width apart. Using your right hand:

- As you inhale, reach up to the Center of the Universe.
- As you exhale, visualize yourself grabbing a beam of golden energy.
- As you inhale, pull this light down to your mid-chest.
- As you exhale, intone or chant the sound:

> *Ahh-Taay*
> (This is the word ATEH in Hebrew, which roughly translates as *"thou art"*).

LESSER BANISHING RITUAL OF THE PENTAGRAM continued...

STEP 3

With your right hand:

- As you inhale, reach down to the Center of the Earth.
- As you exhale, visualize yourself grabbing a beam of golden energy from below.
- As you inhale, pull this light up to mid-chest height (same place as before, the two beams should meet and join).
- As you exhale, chant the sound:

   Maal-kooth
   (This is the word MALKUTh in Hebrew, which roughly translates as *"the kingdom"*).

STEP 4

With your right hand:

- As you inhale, reach to your right, to the far horizon.
- As you exhale, visualize grabbing a beam of golden energy.
- As you inhale, pull this light from the horizon to your mid-chest, meeting the other two vertical beams of light.
- As you exhale, chant the sound:

   Vaay-Geh-Boo-Rah
   (This is the word VGBRH in Hebrew, which roughly translates as *"and the power"*).

STEP 5

With your right hand:

- As you inhale, reach across your body to the left, to the far horizon.
- As you exhale, visualize yourself grabbing a fourth beam of golden energy.
- As you inhale, see yourself pulling this light from the horizon to your mid-chest, where all four beams of golden energy should meet.
- As you exhale, chant the sound:

   Vaay-Geh-Doo-Lah
   (This is the word VGDLH in Hebrew, which roughly translates as *"and the glory"*).

LESSER BANISHING RITUAL OF THE PENTAGRAM continued...

STEP 6

With both your arms:

- As you inhale, cross them at chest level, hands touching your shoulders.
- As you exhale, bow your head and chant the sounds:

> *Lay-Orh-Lahm, Ar-Men*
> (These are the words LEOLAM and AMEN in Hebrew, and roughly trans-
> late as "*to the ages*" and "*so be it*").

As you do so, visualize sealing the four beams of golden energy together, forming a cross that stretches from horizon to horizon, and from the Center of the Earth to the Center of the Universe. When these four beams combine, you should feel yourself becoming filled with more and more energy, until you have all the power you need.

Together, the five Hebrew words you have chanted, roughly translates as "Thou art the Kingdom, and the Power and the Glory, for ever and ever, Amen."

This first part can be done by itself without including the other parts of the ritual. It is a grounding and centering ritual which can help clear the mind. The second part adds the creation of a cleansed Sacred Space.

PART 2—INSCRIBING THE PENTAGRAMS

STEP 7

Facing East, with the first two fingers of your right hand together, extend and point and visualize yourself drawing a High Magick banishing pentagram in yellow light, in the air in front of you—starting at the lower left point of the star and going clockwise.

As you finish the pentagram, inhale, and point your two fingers into the center of the pentagram. Now, as you exhale, chant the sounds:

> *Yohd-Haay-Vavh-Haay*
> (YHVH in Hebrew—this is known by the Greek word, the Tetragrammaton,
> as the name of God).

This banishing pentagram will open up an astral window, which will then draw all the negative air energy out of your Sacred Space.

LESSER BANISHING RITUAL OF THE PENTAGRAM continued...

STEP 8

Using your fingers/athame, and moving to the South, visualize yourself drawing another pentagram in the air in front of you, this one in red light. As you finish the pentagram, inhale, and point your two fingers into the center of the pentagram. Now, as you are exhaling, chant the sounds:

> *Ah-Doh-Nai-EE*
> (This is the word ADNH in Hebrew, which roughly translates as *"the great and powerful lords"*).

With this pentagram, you are now removing any negative energy of the element of Fire.

STEP 9

Move to the West, visualize drawing a pentagram in blue light in the air in front of you. As you finish the pentagram, inhale, and point your two fingers into the center of the pentagram. As you exhale, chant the sounds:

> *Ay-Hay-Ee-Ay*
> (This is the word EHIH in Hebrew, which roughly translates as *"I am what I am"*).

You are now banishing any negative water energy.

STEP 10

Finally, move to the North, again visualize yourself drawing a pentagram in the air in front of you, in green light. As you finish the pentagram, inhale, and point your two fingers into the center of the pentagram. And as you exhale, chant the sounds:

> *Ah-Gah-Lah-Aah*
> (the word AGLH in Hebrew, which roughly translates as *"thou are great forever oh Lord"*).

You are now banishing from your Sacred Space all negative energy that is connected with the element of Earth.

The third part of this ritual will ward your Circle.

LESSER BANISHING RITUAL OF THE PENTAGRAM continued...

PART 3—INVOKING THE ARCHANGELS

STEP 11

Face the East—stand with your feet shoulder width apart, arms extended out to the sides, right hand pointing up, left hand pointing down. Say:

> *Before me RAAF-AYE-EL.*

While doing this, visualize either the Archangel Raphael in yellow robes, or picture a yellow caduceus appearing in front of you. Then say:

> *Behind me GAB-RYE-EL.*

And visualize the Archangel Gabriel in blue robes, or a blue trumpet appearing behind you at the west quarter of your Circle. Then say:

> *At my right hand MIKH-AYE-EL.*

Visualize the Archangel Michael in red robes, or a red flaming sword appearing at the southern quarter of your Circle. Then say:

> *At my left hand AUR-AYE-EL.*

And picture the Archangel Auriel in green robes, or a green lantern appearing at the northern quarter of your Circle.

STEP 12

The next part is more complicated. First say the words:

> *Around me flame the pentagrams, above me shines the six-rayed star.*

The visualizations are three and simultaneous—this takes practice and you can do one at a time until you become adept at doing it:

- See the pentagrams you made in part 2, which are hanging in space and are connected by a thread of light, flare bright silvery-blue as the Circle seals itself.
- Above your head, you should see appearing a Star of David. This should look like two interlocking triangles, the first one with the point upward in white light, the second one with the point downward in black light.
- And lastly, through your body, shaped and directed by your hands and arms, will appear a cosmic lemniscate—the infinity sign (like a figure 8 on its side)—in gold light. Feel the energy flowing around and around through your arms and body.

LESSER BANISHING RITUAL OF THE PENTAGRAM continued...

All this is occurring as you are saying the phrase, "Around me flame the pentagrams, above me shines the six-rayed star." If you need to, take your time, stabilize the energies, and wait until it is all there. With practice it comes quickly.

In the last part, we will finish and integrate all the things that you have done.

PART 4—THE INTEGRATION OF THE CIRCLE

Repeat Part 1—The Kabbalistic Cross. You can bring the energy beams through your body this time, and have them meet at your heart chakra if you want. You are done.

All the words should be intoned—almost sung. Be loud. The first few times you do it you will feel conspicuous. That's normal, you will eventually get over it. We have our students do this every morning and evening for at least three weeks, and we do it in a group at the start of each class to get us into class mode.

This is an effective grounding and centering exercise. It can be done audibly or (when you have got the hang of things) silently, with or without the actual motion, visualizing only, and it still works. In addition, this ritual should also work if you just say the words and go through the motions without doing the visualizations.

This ritual creates a Circle, specifically for banishing, cleansing, and warding. It should be allowed to dissipate, not taken down. You do not have to cut yourself out when exiting or entering. You can use it to seal hotel rooms when traveling. Estelle also uses it when she cannot sleep at night. It grounds, centers, and shields you from all the noise (both audible and psychic), allowing you to relax and sleep. It also helps cut out extraneous noise, when life gets hectic.

MAGICK

ICCANS USUALLY SPELL MAGICK WITH A "K" to differentiate it from stage magic, prestidigitation, slight-of-hand, illusions, and other entertainments. Many religions overtly or inadvertently use magick. After all, magick is the changing of the world using the force of the will of the individual or the group. Using this definition, the building of the pyramids and Stonehenge were both truly acts of magick, no matter what technology was used in the physical creation, because they were created as acts of will.

What makes the magick used by Wiccans different from the mainstream religious practices in America is that we perform our rites in a warded Sacred Space known as a Sacred Circle. We give our people almost unprecedented access for an occidental religion, not only the right to personally perform magick of all kinds, but to training that will increase their skills and abilities with magick, such as psychic abilities or ESP (Extra Sensory Perception). And, we are very forthright about our belief that our magick works.

To say we believe in magick is not a strong enough statement to make it work. Belief implies a margin of error, a measure of doubt. We *know* that magick works.

If you have been a practicing Wiccan for any length of time, you too may have seen magick work enough times to understand that it does work. We know that magick and psychic powers are not considered real by the scientific community because of "magick's unreliability." But, in the scientific community, to replace an accepted theory with an opposing one (in this case, replacing the theory that "there is no such thing as magick," with "magick works"), you have to compile enough incontrovertible, scientifically acceptable, and reproducible physical proof that those holding the opposing viewpoint are considered extremists, and, sometimes, wait for all the champions of the old theory (especially in places of power) to die.

Because we don't have effective instruments to accurately measure the effects of magick, we must rely on the experiences of people—so-called "anecdotal evidence." This accumulated body of experience is beginning to produce a strong body of knowledge about how magick works. And it usually does work, even though it may appear that someone failed at what they were trying to do. It may not have been a failure, because things don't necessarily work out exactly as we poor mortals envisioned or expected. Occasionally you may get a total flop, just as chief Dan George quotes in the movie *Little Big Man*, "Sometimes the magick works, and sometimes it doesn't." Even the most reliable scientific process doesn't always work, and frankly, when a certain spell fizzles, it may have been the best thing in the long run. You just have to do your spell and *know* it will turn out for the best, whatever that best may be. And as you gain experience in working magick, you, like many other Wiccans, will develop your own bank of knowledge in which you have personally witnessed miracles.

In the past few decades, some scientists have found that the old classical scientific paradigms are not as accurate and stable as they were once thought to be. Quantum physics, chaos theory, and other similar disciplines are now allowing for randomness and inexplicable factors influencing what were once believed to be immutable physical laws. Recently, scientists claimed that they have broken the speed of light, which was considered impossible. We know magick works, and it is encouraging to see science following in our footsteps in its own way.

WICCA AND THE GODS

Some people see magick as a way of petitioning the Gods (who or whatever you may envision them to be) to do something for you. This can be one valid way of looking at it. Another view of this matter is that people and the Gods work in concert.

Many people believe that individual humans are here on Earth to accomplish a task, live a life, and better themselves and others, to learn, progress, and grow into more spiritually evolved beings. Whether or not this growth includes the idea of

reincarnation is a personal matter. Most Wiccans do believe in some sort of afterlife and a continuing series of lives. Where it ("it" is a personality, soul, spiritual entity) started or where it will end is not necessarily defined the same way for all. Many haven't actively thought about the full cycle.

Whether or not this view of the meaning of life is really true does not matter. The opposite opinion that we are just mold growing on a dust speck known as the planet Earth, with no higher reason or purpose than just existence, simply doesn't account for the innate spiritual nature of human beings either. But however you look at it, we humans are on the Earth and we experience Earthly mortal life, warts and all.

What we Wiccans believe to be the "nature" of magick, through the intervention of the Gods, requires some explanation. To develop our explanation, we must begin with a series of assumptions:

Assumption One. We humans have a relatively accurate view of this physical plane and how it works, and may on occasion have glimpses into other planes or other beings that are different, sometimes larger than ourselves. Some of those beings are called Gods.

Assumption Two. We use the term "Gods" to mean Deities of feminine, masculine, indeterminate, and other gender. And whether those Deities are just various manifestations of one All-Powerful Supreme Being, which we humans cannot grasp in totality because he/she/it/they are so far above us, or actual separate entities is subject to individual belief. To a Wiccan that distinction is not important. There probably is some Great Cosmic Entity that created life, the Universe, and everything in it. Wiccans just don't pretend to have the last true and only word on the true nature of him/her/it/them.

Assumption Three. The Gods, from their realms, can look in on the various planes of existence and can affect events there. However, their perspective is quite different from ours on this plane. We are able to perceive clearly the day-to-day details of life on Earth as we see it and as it affects us. The Gods have a larger view, but do not necessarily acknowledge or even recognize the details of physical existence all the time. Therefore, the Gods also rely on our perceptions of physical reality to determine where and how they will intervene in this reality.

In other words, they see the forest, and we report what is going on in just one tree. Occasionally they understand what we are saying, and/or see through our eyes, and agree that things should be changed as we feel that they should. Other times they have other things on their "minds," or don't agree with our assessments.

Some may say that these assumptions, especially Assumption Three, are a cop-out. Either your spell works or it doesn't, yes or no. This is the philosophy of either the skeptic or the engineer. The skeptic tries to disprove everything, because he does not want to believe in anything, while the engineer has to know exactly why things work, and everything has to work one hundred percent of the time. Neither believe in any kind of "Margin for Error." While we, like most other effective magicians of whom we are aware, accept a paradigm similar to that of the technician. A technician doesn't need to know exactly why or how something works to be capable of making something, only that things appear to work in a certain way. They also do not need to have something work one hundred percent of the time, only more times than not. And that is what you have with magick. Certain principles appear to work certain ways most of the time. If you can't live with this, magick isn't for you. If you can, you may have a ticket to the Universe.

To summarize, the use of magick requires the acceptance of the following that we call the "Margin

of Error Factor": The Gods do not necessarily do what you want; the principles or "lore" of magick appears to work in certain patterns; and even if you get everything right, you can count on even your best spells working only more times than not.

It is worthwhile planing on a hefty Margin of Error in the practice of magick. We have found that the more specific you try to make a spell—the more you try to dictate how things will happen or turn out—the lower the rate of success will be. For example, if you do a prosperity spell for a winning lottery ticket, your odds of getting what you want are still millions to one, depending on which lottery you are counting upon winning. On the other hand, if you do a prosperity spell to increase your cash flow so you can pay off some pressing bills, you open yourself up to other avenues of success. You could win the lottery; you could also win a radio contest; you could get offered overtime at work; you could hold a garage sale and sell everything; you could inherit from a rich relative; you could receive an unexpected gift; you could discover a priceless antique at a garage sale for pennies; you could sell a book and make millions; you could get a new job for more money; the list goes on and on. Open yourself up to more possibilities. The Gods have a broader view, and if you call their attention to your need through a spell, you can take advantage of their broader view if you don't presume to constrain their actions.

Of course, the main ingredient for success is that you have done your part. There is an old joke about these two old Jewish men. One says to the other "God promised I'd win the lottery." The other says "Mazel tov! Such good fortune." A week goes by, and no win. The first guy says, "God promised, it's coming." The second guy says "So when?" More time passes and the first guy gets tired of his friend ribbing him about his nonexistent lottery win. He goes back to God and says, "So God, you did promise and I believe and I don't doubt but just when will I win this lottery anyway?" And God answers, "So go buy a ticket already." The point is, God can promise, but it's up to us to do our part also.

The activities of magick require the cooperation of our Conscious Mind, Subconscious Mind, and Soul working together. Please review the discussion of our "three minds" in the Rituals chapter (pages 148–149).

MAGICKAL MIND-SET

A Zen-like quality of mind is necessary in order to effectively work magick. This mind-set seems to contain several contradictions to our normal Western paradigms, among them the suspension of disbelief, letting go of expectations, and releasing the energy to the Universe.

These seemingly contradictory ideas are more familiar to Oriental philosophy than Western, but these and others are all an important part of spellwork. Take the concept of releasing the energy to the Universe, for example. Most books on magick advocate that after you have finished your spell you finish your rite, close the Circle, put away your stuff, and then completely forget about the spell you have just done and do something else that is entirely different, preferably something very ordinary that engages your brain: cleaning house, fixing the car, playing bridge with friends—something everyday, ordinary, and that gets your mind off the powerful Working you have just done. This releases the spell and divorces you from your expectations.

Many people find it difficult to achieve this kind of magickal mind-set. They find it difficult to suspend disbelief, which allows for the endless possibilities that magick offers. The "anything is possible" mind-set also allows for things to occur outside the realm of modern science. Modern society has been conditioned to believe in a solid, provable, rational, scientific paradigm, which doesn't allow for changing reality through the use of personal will.

One way to create the magickal mind-set in yourself is to read magical fiction books because they can introduce your mind to new things, and nothing can engage your Subconscious Mind better than new and exciting things. The *Harry Potter* books by J.K. Rowling, for instance, are a wonderful series of children's novels, which postulate an entirely separate magickal world, coexisting with our normal mundane reality. There are many other books on this and related subjects. We are not alleging that a person, through the use of magick, can create a Harry Potter-like world (though there are many who would dearly love to live in that sort of world); however, you can experience in your mind how it might feel to use magick and work spells, and that fictional understanding can translate to your personal spellwork.

To be an effective magician in our modern world, you have to be able to hold two apparently different and sometimes opposite mind-sets or paradigms simultaneously: first the mind-set that will permit you to perform your magick in the spiritual worlds, and the opposing mind-set that will allow you to live in the modern scientific mundane world. In fact, certain aboriginal tribal magicians, known as Shamans, have been described as effective schizophrenics, because they live and effectively work on several planes of reality at once.

MAGICKAL PERSONAS

To effectively balance the needs of these frequently conflicting magickal and mundane paradigms (without losing one's mind), many people create what are known as "magickal personas." This is an aspect of their personality, which is strong and effective in magick, and not necessarily totally suited for the mundane world. This persona usually has a different name (their magickal name), wears different clothing (their magickal clothing), and operates in a different realm (a magickal circle) from their mundane personality. These mystical requirements that many magickal personas have may somewhat constrain the person (i.e., they can only do effective magick in a Circle with all their stuff), but their effectiveness may also increase. Others, with practice can put on or take off their magickal persona anytime, anywhere, and have less dependence upon the accouterments. How you choose to operate is up to you. It probably will change with time and practice. Most people start practicing magick inside a Circle with their stuff, and as they gain experience and confidence, they can branch out to being able to practice almost anytime or anywhere. Ideally you should be able to be naked in a bare room and still practice good effective magick.

We will now describe one way to develop a "magickal persona." To do this we are going to describe two psychological/magickal concepts or techniques, "true name," and "personality doubling."

True Name

If you read the serious, ceremonial, or certain fantasy books, you will run across the term, "true name." A true name is, in theory at least, exactly what it implies, the actual (possibly primordial) original name of every object or person. The theory states that if you know a person's or object's true name, you can command them or it. There is truth to this belief, but the reality is both simpler and more difficult than this short explanation.

Merely speaking a word, any word, without the knowledge of what you are saying (knowledge of a word impacts psychic power which can be tapped when that word is used consciously with will) is just meaningless sound. When you say a word that you understand, you are subconsciously going over in your mind everything you know about that word. If you, for example, wish to light a match, whether you say the word "fire" out loud or not, your mind will be invoking fire by going over everything that you have ever known and experienced about fire. If you see a friend, your Subconscious Mind, as part of the recognition process, will quickly review every memory that you have involving this friend. It is this automatic subconscious review process that is the true name. Also please remember, it is your Subconscious Mind that communicates with the Soul. Saying a word triggers the reviewing process. So a true name will only work if you truly know what that name means. It is this concept about the nature of physical reality that traditional magicians studied, and why they were considered true philosophers.

Now, because of this truth regarding true names, you will not be capable of effectively developing a magickal persona unless you know who you are in order to have some place to start, and you know what you want your persona to be.

These two things are not as hard as many people believe because most Wiccans normally work on self-discovery, and because there are so many potential magickal role models upon which to base a persona. Now that we have a start at understanding what a true name is, let's outline how to develop a magickal persona.

Step one is getting to know yourself as truly and honestly as possible. Please understand that knowing oneself is a never-ending process, not an absolutely or instantaneously achievable goal. If you have only just started to get to know yourself, that is good enough for now. You will become more self-aware as you progress, and your understanding of your true name will increase.

Step two requires that you decide on a role model for your persona that you are comfortable with. This could be a character out of a book or movie or based on a living person who impressed you, or your magickal persona may be based on your own idealized conception of what a powerful magician should be. Any one you like will do.

And for step three, proceed to personality doubling.

Personality Doubling

We can find references to the psychological technique called "personality doubling" going as far back as the early 1700s. With this technique, one basically develops an intentional, *controlled* alternate personality. To effectively use various alternate personalities, without them eventually controlling you, you need to know your Core Personality. Your Core Personality, in this case, is the same as your true name. The exercise that we describe below not only will help you develop various alternate personas, but will also help you maintain control over who you are because it safeguards a person's Core Personality.

Cast your standard Circle. The following exercise will be the Working for this Circle.

PERSONALITY DOUBLING EXERCISE

STEP 1

In an intentional ritual that you have designed to fit your personal belief system, name yourself (any magickal or mundane name will do) as your *"true name."*

This will be your "Core Personality." What goes into this Core Personality is everything you know yourself to be. Allow your Subconscious Mind a chance to add input here.

STEP 2

Visualize casting another magickal Circle around this Core Personality, and know it to be yourself.

You don't need to lie to yourself about yourself, this should be as honest an appraisal of yourself as you can be. This "true named persona" is going to be your baseline personality.

NOTE: If you already "know who you are," because of various soul-searching techniques that you have already practiced, you can skip this step. Just make sure you periodically check to see that you still "know who you are."

PERSONALITY DOUBLING EXERCISE continued...

STEP 3

Now in a distinctly separate part of the ritual, choose a situation you think you may need to deal with, but feel "Yourself" personally inadequate to cope with.

Pick a role model or personality type that you would like to emulate. This personality should be chosen on the basis of how effective it is perceived to be in coping with the envisioned situation. (For example, basing a persona on the Conan character from Howard's books—not Schwarzenegger's movie portrayal—is worthwhile if you need to destroy some "evil monster." It is not quite so effective a role model if one wants to be an astrologer or mathematician, however).

Build up this persona in your mind and name it.

STEP 4

Now (and these final two points are very important if you don't want to lose "Yourself" in a persona, as we have seen some people do) choose some kind of invoking trigger, some gesture or word that you will always use to invoke this personality. It does not have to be fancy, just consistent.

For example, when many Priestesses don their ritual robes, they trigger a persona that can best be described as their "Priestess of the Goddess" personality. This can be drastically different from their mundane personality.

STEP 5

Finally, choose a dismissing trigger word or gesture that you will then use to turn off the specific personality, when it is no longer appropriate. For one alternate personality of Paul's, he invokes him by tugging on his right earlobe. Paul will then dismiss this personality by tugging on his left earlobe.

This last step is possibly the most crucial, and the one that is most often omitted by many magicians. As one old magickal saying puts it: "One must be able to dismiss what one calls up." And in truth, if you cannot turn off any of these "artificial" personalities at will, then you may well be starting on the road to true clinical schizophrenia.

This is the end of the Working. Close down your Circle as usual.

Then from the end of the above ritual, until you retire your newly created persona, you should conscientiously use these invoking and dismissing triggers whenever you wish to use this personality.

For those with an actor's training and/or experience, these techniques are similar to what an actor does when getting into and out of character. That body of techniques (well documented elsewhere) can also be effective when doubling your personality.

It is possible to create virtually any kind of persona using this personality doubling technique, to deal with virtually any kind of situation. You might also want to later incorporate parts, or all, of these artificial personalities within your Core Personality if you wish to. But remember: If you don't keep these personalities separate from "Yourself," if you don't consciously keep control of when and how these new personalities are invoked and used, if you don't consciously dismiss them when they are no longer needed, then you may find that you might actually lose "Yourself"—or in other words, these alternate personalities may take control of your thoughts and actions when it is inappropriate for them to do so.

Retaining control of all your personalities, incidentally, is one of the reasons for developing your own true name. You will then have someone to compare yourself to, so if you do develop problems with a situation in which one or more alternate personalities tries to take over (or something else as confusing), you can catch yourself and remedy the situation.

If you are reading this book, we assume that you want to be a Practitioner of the Arts Magickal and that you are attempting to develop the awareness that sometimes psychic impressions from outside yourself may try to influence you (i.e., there are thoughts or feelings which try to make you feel or do things that are not you, or what you want). If you consciously know who you really are, you should be capable of recognizing when these "strange feelings" are not you—when they are coming from outside your "Real" or "Core Personality"—and that is a good reason for developing and maintaining a Core Personality. One slick means of then banishing these alien thoughts is to invoke your own true name.

PSYCHIC ABILITIES

Magick is not the same as psychic ability, although psychic abilities can be a strong factor in making magick effective. Most Wiccans believe in and fully accept the existence of psychic abilities and phenomena. Whether or not they personally possess some of these abilities varies.

We believe psychic abilities are a normal part of human existence. That's why the terms paranormal or extrasensory are not often used in the Pagan and Wiccan Communities. We more commonly use the term talents. Psychic ability is just another type of talent people exhibit and use. They are inherent in all of us in different measures. However, like any other talent, they can be practiced, honed, and developed. There aren't many places a person can go to develop their telepathy or precognition. Wicca is one venue for that. Many of the techniques in this book can—as a side effect—help develop psychic talent. Also, it can allow a person to control their psychic abilities, so they are more easily able to operate in the mundane world. Shielding, grounding, and centering are necessary and invaluable tools for magick, and also for effectively living with high psychic abilities.

There are probably a higher percentage of recognizably psychic people in Wicca than in the general population, and one reason is that Wicca accepts, celebrates, and allows for effective use and control of these talents. The boy in the movie *The Sixth Sense* (1999), who sees dead people, is certainly not unique, but he finds his ability frightening because no one else seems to see what he sees, and he cannot control his talent. If he were able to learn to shield himself and control his ability, to harness it so it was subject to his will and control, his life would be less frightening, but then it would also be a less interesting and scary movie.

Part of the paradigm shift frequently required of many people who become Wiccan is to take it for granted that ghosts, spirits, and psychic abilities exist, that they frequently are a normal part of everyday life, and that the skills associated with these phenomena are controllable, usable, and subject to development and improvement. Fear stems from that which is unknown and strange, unfamiliar, or has been declared "impossible." Once these things become part of your everyday life, they lose much of their scare appeal. Remember that at one time both flight and the ability of a human being to breathe while moving at speeds greater than thirty miles an hour were commonly declared impossible.

And How Do I Do This?

How you become psychically open is another one of our "Catch-22" situations. You can't believe it until you've seen it, and you can't see it until you believe it. The process of opening up is, initially, usually a slow one. We have found that a majority of people were psychically open when they were children. But over time, either because their parents or society kept telling them that what they were seeing did not exist, or something frightened them, their Conscious Mind refused to "see" these things any more. Well guess what, your Subconscious Mind still "sees" things, whether your Conscious Mind will believe it or not. This is why even the most mundane people still have "funny feelings," or what is called "intuition" or "hunches."

When something happens that looks, feels, sounds, or smells "funny," don't just automatically dismiss it. Acknowledging unusual phenomena will help you become psychically aware. Allow yourself to explore the possibility that it is a "supernatural" event. Once you have recognized one psychic event, it is easier to recognize another. As you recognize more and more impossible psychic events (no matter what they are), your Conscious Mind will begin to believe and then *know* that these impossible events are real. And finally when your Conscious Mind knows that what your Subconscious Mind has been telling it all these years is real, you will have bridged a large communication gap between your Conscious Mind and your Soul.

The Down Side

Sometimes when people start picking up on large amounts of psychic information they can become overloaded with the data. Similar to what people report who wear a hearing aid after years of less than adequate hearing, suddenly you can hear all the background noise and it becomes necessary to learn to filter out the extraneous material from that which is important and relevant. People start hearing the psychic mice crawling around behind the baseboards (so to speak), and it can be very distracting, and also unnerving.

This is one reason for the "Psychic War Syndrome" experienced by many newly aware people. This syndrome can occur when someone who is newly psychically awake misinterprets anything (and frequently everything) that they now pick up as a "psychic attack." There are such things as psychic attack and psychic war that can occur when someone is either praying or casting spells *against* someone else. But the reality is much less frequent than the imagined instances and it requires personal experience to recognize the difference. Once you open yourself up psychically, you will open yourself up to bad things, but once you've experienced it, you won't have too much trouble distinguishing a "psychic vampire" from a "faery."

And unfortunately, until you have experienced both, you won't know that there is a difference. If you are lucky, you will know some experienced person who can point out which is a pyschic vampire, and which is a faery when it happens. If there is no one to help, you will have to figure out the difference on your own. In this case, trust your feelings. If it feels bad, believe that it is bad. If it doesn't feel bad, just strange, it may only be different, not bad.

As your experience grows, you will be able to distinguish what is important to you from what does not concern you. Just as a city person learns to filter out the random noise of city life, and a country person filters out the natural sounds of their environment, a psychic person has to learn to distinguish between important and irrelevant data. It takes time, but it can be done.

One of the reasons psychic abilities are feared in the mundane world is that it is generally believed they give people some sort of unfair advantage. If all people have these abilities, they are not really unfair. Is it unfair if one person can develop their skill in basketball to the level of a Magic Johnson? If they use it to hurt or harass people, then yes it is. If they use it for their personal betterment, and possibly the service of others (and entertainment is providing a service to the community as a whole), then it isn't unfair. Not everybody can play basketball like Magic Johnson. Not everybody can be highly psychic. But if you have a natural ability, you can work on it and make it better. Practice is the key.

Psychic Exercises

On the following pages are four exercises that are designed to increase your awareness of the psychic world. They are presented in order, so please practice them in the order given, and do not proceed to the next one until you have both an intellectual grasp and a physical feeling of how each exercise should go. In other words, you should know each exercise in turn well enough so that you will only have to read the latest exercise.

The first one is Diaphragm Breathing, and this exercise is the foundation of almost all physical and spiritual disciplines. If you master no other exercise presented here or in other books, master this one.

The second one, which we call Level Drops, is a very commonly taught exercise and is used, in one form or another, in many different metaphysical disciplines. Several of these disciplines (including a few martial arts ones) consider Level Drops their primary metaphysical exercise.

The third one, the Tree Meditation, is a more advanced version of the Grounding and Centering Ritual presented earlier in this book (see page 75). It is designed to not only center and ground you, but to metaphorically connect you to the "world below" and the corresponding "world above." Both of these "worlds" are discussed thoroughly in other books on Shamanism, so we won't take the time here, except to say that they have nothing to do with the Christian concepts of heaven and hell. They are symbolic representations of man's connection to the physical and spiritual worlds. This ritual will help you build up your spiritual power, as it creates an energy circuit between the world below, yourself, and the world above.

The fourth one, Psychic Radar, should be used after you are proficient with the three previous exercises. The procedure you want to follow when performing these rituals is: First practice Diaphragm Breathing until you are very relaxed. Besides practicing this ritual as a pure exercise, we suggest that you get into the habit of doing at least a shortened version of this exercise before you do anything else. And we mean anything, either physically taxing, or metaphysically challenging.

Then do a Level Drop, to prepare yourself both mentally and spiritually.

Next perform the Tree Meditation, to prepare yourself psychically and connect yourself to the astral realms.

Then practice the Psychic Radar, to see what you can pick up "out there."

And lastly, when you are done, do the Grounding and Centering Ritual, just as we described earlier (see page 75), to psychically cleanse and re-center yourself. You don't want to carry extra baggage or unwanted energy from the psychic realms with you, so always make sure you re-center and re-ground yourself after every magickal Working.

Exercise 1: Diaphragm Breathing
Diaphragm Breathing is also known as deep breathing by some disciplines. We include this technique here because it:

- helps develop strong meditative powers;
- supercharges your blood system with oxygen for use during heavy physical exertion;
- is a good vehicle to teach and reinforce visualization practices, because you can physically feel what is going on within your body;
- helps develop and concentrates your internal psychic energy; and,
- it can also be used as a simple personal centering and shielding technique.

DIAPHRAGM BREATHING EXERCISE

STEP 1
First, stand straight, lay flat on your back, or seat yourself comfortably with your spine straight. Then place one hand on your stomach, approximately over your navel, place your other hand on your chest, near your heart, and put your tongue against the roof of your mouth.

STEP 2
Breathe in slowly through your nose. Feel your stomach rise with your hand, but try not to let your chest rise. You are not trying to fill your chest completely with air, to take what is called a big breath. You are trying to get the air as far into the bottom of your lungs as possible. This is called a deep breath.

STEP 3
Next, purse your lips almost as if you were whistling, holding your tongue against the roof of your mouth. Then breathe out slowly through your mouth, pressing your hand against your stomach. Again, try not to let your chest rise or fall.

DIAPHRAGM BREATHING EXERCISE continued...

Step 4

Now keep breathing like this in a rhythmic pattern. This pattern should create a comfortable, but consistent rhythm of *Inhale* —breathe in through your nose as deeply into your lower stomach as you can; *Hold*—hold that breath in your stomach, for as long as it is comfortable; *Exhale* —as smoothly as you can through your lips; *Hold*—don't breathe again for as long as it is comfortable, then repeat.

Repeat the above sequence for at least ten minutes.

How fast, how hard, and how long you continue the action of each phase will determine how high the oxygen level in your lungs will be. Another name for this technique is "Controlled Hyperventilation." Because you will be replacing the carbon dioxide (which most people store in the bottom of their lungs) with oxygen at a considerable rate, you can induce hyperventilation. So be careful, because you could cause yourself to pass out. Some of the signs that your rhythm isn't right for your body (perhaps you are breathing too quickly, or too slowly) are coughing, yawning, or dizziness.

We cannot definitively tell you what each of these signs means; they can vary among people and the needs of each individual's physiology. In Paul's case, for instance, he will sometimes *yawn*, if he is holding too long on the inhale—hold part of the cycle, *cough*, if he is holding too long on the exhale—hold part of the cycle, or get *dizzy*, if he is breathing too fast or too hard. Remember, these are three personal experiences and do not include all the variations that have been noticed. We expect that other individuals will notice other variations in themselves.

Once you become practiced with this technique, you can perform it in any physical state—running, walking, laying down—anywhere. It is an excellent meditative technique, under any kind of physical or psychic distress, because it can automatically center and focus your mind on a behavior pattern that both relaxes your body and prepares it for action.

Exercise 2: Level Drops

Level Drops is a colloquial psychological term to describe the process of entering effective receptive states. It also has been described as a "light self-hypnotic trance." Entering a psychologically receptive state allows you to access your Subconscious Mind more directly. It is much easier to teach yourself new techniques in this state of mind, and it also can be easier for you to become psychically receptive.

Different sources teach a variety of methods to reach varying levels of receptivity (i.e., going deeper). Most of these practices have in common the use of the metaphor of some kind of descent (e.g., going down a tree, down a root, down a river, etc.).

The process we describe will teach you how to drop down two levels. If this style of Level Drop works for you, you can try adding other techniques to go deeper. If this style does not appeal to you, you can try other types of Level Drops until you find one that you are comfortable with. There are many different techniques described in a variety of books on New Age, psychological, psychic, martial arts, and even sports training subjects. Some of these resources are listed in the Resources section at the end of this book.

*L*EVEL *D*ROP *E*XERCISE

STEP 1

Lay comfortably on your back, loosen any constricting clothing, and close your eyes.

STEP 2

Inhale and, while inhaling, tense (as hard as you can) the muscles in your feet. Then exhale and, while exhaling, relax the muscles in your feet. As you relax your feet, say to yourself "Relax."

STEP 3

Repeat this process of inhale–tensing, exhale–relaxing separately with the muscle groups listed below, with the command "Relax":

- Feet — Inhale…Tense your feet…Exhale and Relax.
- Calves — Inhale…Tense your calves…Exhale and Relax.
- Thighs — Inhale…Tense your thighs…Exhale and Relax.
- Hips — Inhale…Tense your hips…Exhale and Relax.
- Stomach — Inhale…Tense your stomach…Exhale and Relax.
- Chest — Inhale…Tense your chest…Exhale and Relax.
- Hands — Inhale…Tense your hands…Exhale and Relax.
- Forearms — Inhale…Tense your forearms…Exhale and Relax.
- Biceps — Inhale…Tense your biceps…Exhale and Relax.
- Shoulders — Inhale…Tense your shoulders…Exhale and Relax.
- Neck — Inhale…Tense your neck…Exhale and Relax.
- Head — Inhale…Tense your head…Exhale and Relax.
- Entire body — Inhale…Tense your entire body…Exhale and Relax.

STEP 4

As you inhale, imagine and feel yourself, your entire body, rise toward the ceiling. As you exhale, imagine and feel yourself sink further and further through the floor, and again say to yourself "Relax." Repeat this process three times: Inhale, rise; Exhale, sink and Relax; Inhale, rise; Exhale, sink and Relax; Inhale, rise; Exhale, sink and Relax.

This should put you in a comfortably relaxed and receptive state of mind. Once you are comfortable doing this Level Drop exercise lying down, try doing it sitting up, then standing, then with your eyes open.

Exercise 3: Tree Meditation

This involves some sophisticated visualizations, but if you have practiced the previous exercises and have become comfortable with them, it should be possible for you to accomplish. If you are uncom-fortable trying it, read through the entire exercise a few times and then do it slowly.

This exercise is designed to connect you with the World Tree, a metaphorical axis from which all the worlds of the psychic or astral Universe branch. Not only does this center and ground you, but it will give you access to psychic energy.

Paul does a shortened version of this exercise before he will do any kind of magickal Working, and frequently he will perform a much more intri-cate version of this meditation, if time permits.

Tree Meditation Exercise

Begin by playing some of your favorite, relaxing music at a low volume. Darken the room so that it seems almost like twilight. Unplug the telephone. Stand or sit comfortably with your back straight. Center and ground yourself using the techniques previously described. When you are fully relaxed:

PART 1—FROM THE WORLD BELOW

STEP 1

Focus your breathing on your lower stomach, by placing your right hand over your stomach, with the thumb of your right hand on your navel. This area is called the lower "Tan-Tien" or "Hara" by martial artists. The lower Tan-Tien is the area where the "energy from the Earth, and the energy from the sky balance each other out." Start there.

Inhale deeply, imagining that you are "breathing power" into your Tan-Tien until you feel relaxed and "power full." It may take one breath, it may take several breaths.

STEP 2

As you exhale, visualize psychically reaching down your spine, from your lower Tan-Tien until you reach your knees, ankles, the soles of your feet. Inhale and relax.

STEP 3

As you exhale, we want you to psychically reach down through your feet, and visualize a line of energy reaching down from your feet past any covering on the floor, through the floor, the

TREE MEDITATION EXERCISE continued...

basement, the surface of the Earth, through bedrock, the Earth's mantle, until you reach the Center of the Earth with this line of energy.

STEP 4

Feel and confirm your connection with the Earth's core. Make it solid, *Know* it is there!

PART 2—TO THE WORLD ABOVE

STEP 5

As you inhale, starting again from your Tan-Tien, visualize yourself reaching psychically up your spine to your diaphragm, your heart, your throat, the center of your skull, to the crown of your head.

STEP 6

As you inhale, psychically reach up through your head, and visualize a line of energy reaching up past the ceiling of the room you are in, and up through the sky, the Center of the Solar System, the Center of the Galaxy, until you reach the Center of the Universe.

STEP 7

Feel and confirm your connection with the Universe. Make it solid, *Know* that it is there!

STEP 8

At this point, you should have a visualized energy connection from the Center of the Earth, up through your Tan-Tien to the Center of the Universe. Feel these connections, *Know* that they are there!

PART 3—BACK AROUND AND TOGETHER

STEP 9

Now visualize the energy that is rising through you from the Center of the Earth, up to the Center of the Universe, then falling back to the Earth, like rain. The energy from the Universe falling back to the Earth is sinking deep into the Earth until it again reaches the Earth's Center. Again feel this energy rise up though you, to meet the Center of the Universe. Again let this energy fall back to the Earth, until you have a solid visualized energy circuit from the Center of the Earth, through you, to the Center of the Universe, and back down again.

(This exercise is called the "Tree," because the energy is rising through your body, up to the

---

TREE MEDITATION EXERCISE continued...

Center of the Universe, and falling back to Earth. Is frequently visualized as a willow tree, drawing energy up from its roots in the Earth, up its trunk, to its branches that span the Universe, and then draping down as willow branches do, once more to the Earth.)

STEP 10

Feel the energy as it rises up your body, out through your branches, and back down to Earth, to be collected by your roots, and sent back up your trunk again. Confirm it, *Know* it is there!

You are now fully a part of the World Tree, and may partake of the energy of all creation through it.

At this point, you should have all the magickal energy you can use. To ground out this energy, repeat the exercise "A Grounding and Centering Ritual" on page 75.

Exercise 4: Using Your Senses As "Radar"
Once you have sufficiently relaxed using the Diaphragm Breathing exercise, opened your senses to the Universe with the Level Drop exercise, and connected yourself to the Universe using the Tree Meditation, this exercise allows you to metaphorically extend your senses a short way up the "Tree," and then out. This is one way of psychically "viewing" your surroundings. We call it "radar," because Paul visualizes this technique by plotting what he psychically senses on an imagined radar screen in his head.

PSYCHIC RADAR MEDITATION EXERCISE

Perform the Diaphragm Breathing and Level Drop exercises.

Perform the Tree Meditation, from Step 1 through Step 10.

STEP 1

Visualize yourself climbing up the Tree, just a little way…past the ceiling of the room you are in, up past the roof, until you are a little way into the sky.

STEP 2

"Reach out" with your senses (either feeling or seeing as you are most comfortable with) and "perceive" what there is to see.

Paul visualizes "reaching out" like psychic radar with a very narrow "beam," that sweeps slowly around in a 360-degree arc. Psychic impressions then come to his attention as various types of feelings. For example, he might feel a sense of electric brightness in one direction, or he might see a Storm Giant in a thundercloud.

These may only be psychic impressions, and may not exist physically. You are using the psychic senses of your Subconscious Mind to perceive these things, so if you react to these impressions as if they were real, you allow your Subconscious to also act as if these impressions are real. Please remember, to your Subconscious these impressions *are absolutely real*.

It's all a matter of perspective. At one festival Paul worked, some sort of psychic energy was affecting the people there, making them very nervous and uncomfortable, and many of them were having similar nightmares of rape and murder. Using the Psychic Radar Meditation, it was determined that there was an upset dragon outside the camp. Some people wanted to destroy the dragon, others didn't feel that such drastic measures were necessary. One person finally asked the dragon what was making him so upset. The dragon responded that people had been throwing trash in his pond, located at the center of the camp. The trash was removed, the dragon went away, the attendees became more relaxed, and their common nightmares of rape and murder went away.

Perhaps you might think this is nonsense, but the fact of the matter was a majority of the attendees at the Pagan festival were becoming more and more agitated, with many of them sharing similar violent nightmares, with no obvious physical cause. Paul performed the Psychic Radar Meditation. The physical response suggested by the results of the meditation was carried out, and the symptoms of agitation of the festival attendees went away. A

positive end was accomplished with minimal fuss and nobody was hurt or upset in the course of the solution.

So whether or not there was an actual dragon that was upset, the exercise worked and brought about a positive result, and all were happy. The trash in the pond had been left by previous groups, not the festival attendees. At the very least the pond was cleaned up, and people stopped having nightmares, both of which were positive results. How that occurred, and whether it was scientifically provable, is a moot point. It worked. That's all that should matter. This pragmatic results-oriented mind-set is how one approaches magick.

Once you become competent with these psychic/magical techniques, you will have the tools needed to investigate and respond to many kinds of psychic/magickal situations, and the best part of it is, with practice these techniques are very fast and can be performed anywhere.

Now let's move from exploring our internal psychic abilities to explaining how one articulates intent so your Subconscious Mind understands and appreciates it.

Spellworking

One of the main reasons many people study the Craft is to learn how to create and cast spells. People want to be able to have significant influence over their own lives. At first, they desire love, security, etc., but, as people progress in the Craft, they frequently find that the personal psychological work (the internal spiritual progress that makes accomplishing the magick possible) becomes more important and fulfilling than the spellwork.

A prayer and a spell are two different things. When a person prays, they are often requesting the Gods to intercede on their behalf, whether requests for something or for someone. A spell is accomplished by the force of the individual's will and/or power, without Divine intervention. We could argue back and forth about whether one can really divorce oneself from the Divine, but the working paradigmal difference is one (prayer) *directly* involves the Gods, while the other (spell-work) does not.

How do you craft a spell? The intellectual procedure that seems to work the best is very similar to the procedure for crafting a ritual for similar reasons. We'll repeat the highlights here for clarity:

- Know *what* you want to accomplish, *why* you want it, and *how* you will go about doing it before you start the actual spell.

- Cater to as many of your senses as possible.

- Do things that please both your senses and Subconscious Mind.

- Envision what you want as simply as you can.

- Do something *special* to put your Subconscious "on notice," that something *special* is happening.

- Try to envision each concept using metaphors or stories that your Subconscious Mind understands.

- *Do*, don't Say.

- Concentrate on only one concept at a time.

- Focus primarily on the *goal*, or final outcome of what you want to accomplish, rather than on the mechanics of how you think what you want should be accomplished.

- Alternate periods of intense concentration (or concepts) with more relaxed periods.

- Use repetition as much as possible, both within a specific Working and between separate, similar Workings.

- When you are finished, release your thoughts into the Universe, and then *forget it*.

One could call a spell a ritual within a ritual. If you are a beginner, we strongly suggest that you follow the above procedure until you become comfortable developing spells. If, however, your intuition kicks in, and you are inspired to do something a certain way, then trust your feelings, and do it that way. Then see how well it worked, and change the next spell you do accordingly.

The "Laws?" of Magick

Over the last few years, certain concepts have been discussed around the magickal community that have been called the "Laws of Magick." These "Laws" describe the working parameters of how magick works. Below are a few of the more reliable of these "Laws"—what we refer to as Magickal Theories—for use in the crafting of your spells. Please note that we call them "Theories," or "Principles," or "Lore," not "Laws," because we feel they are not sufficiently technically describable to be called "Laws."

The primary requirements for working magick are the principles of Knowledge and Self-Knowledge. The more you know about what you are doing, what you will be affecting, and especially about yourself, the more effective you will be.

Cause and Effect means that every time you do something, there will be a result. And theoretically if you do the same thing twice in row, you should get the same effects each time.

Chaos Theory says that everything is connected so any change anywhere affects everything everywhere. This is the reason a competent magician knows that it is impossible to control all the variables. We call this the Domino Effect. When dominos are set up, one next to the other, if you knock one domino over on one end, all the others are knocked over in a cascade. One of the problems with magick generally is that you are not the only person building pictures and knocking over dominoes, and all of these pictures are interconnected all the time.

The Holographic Universe Theory, borrowed from the Chaos Theory, states that everything that exists, exists and is reflected in everything, and that a small change on one level of existence is proportionately reflected on every other level of existence. Another way to say this is "As above, so below."

Synchronicity can be defined as two or more similar events occurring at the same time, and is also called coincidence. One of the aspects of this effect is best described as "The right person being in the right place, at the right time."

The Theory of Association states that if two items have elements in common, then they interact through their commonalties, and control of the common elements of one of these items will grant you control of the other item.

The Law of Similarity, and the following Law of Contagion, were first described by the popular authors L. Sprague deCamp and Fletcher Pratt in their fantasy novel *The Incompleat Enchanter* (Ballantine Books, New York, 1975, pp. 7–8), and their definitions are still considered the standard ones by many people. In this book, they write that "The Law of Similarity may be stated thus: Effects resemble causes. It's not valid for us, but primitive peoples firmly believe it. For instance, they think you can make it rain by pouring water on the ground with appropriate mumbo jumbo."

To describe the Law of Contagion, deCamp and Pratt write: "Things once in contact continue to interact from a distance after separation." In this case, the contact may be either physical or psychic, the strength of the contact will depend on how much energy or attention is focused on the connection, and the separation doesn't matter if it is in time or space.

We will be discussing two opposite and complementary theories here—Positive and Negative Attraction. In Positive Attraction, if you want to create a specific reality, you have to put out a corresponding energy. For instance, if you want to attract love, you must be loving. Negative Attraction can best be explained as "opposites attract." It is beyond the scope of this book to try to fully explain how these two theories interact and, since most of us have been indoctrinated in the Western philosophical theory of Dualism, it is difficult to explain that these two seemingly opposing concepts are actually complements. Perhaps the best way to describe this interaction is for the reader to explore the Oriental concept of yin and yang, which better describes the effects of these two "Attraction" theories.

The last property we will mention is the true name. For an explanation, please see our discussion earlier in this chapter.

There are other "Theories of Magick," but since you don't have to know all the theories to be an effective magician, we will stop here. If you are interested in the other more exotic and complex theories, refer to the Resource Guide on pages 453–460 for additional resources. Working with those theories we have stated here will give you a big boost in increasing your magickal effectiveness.

To illustrate the use of some of these theories, we will describe a healing spell for a friend with a broken arm.

Healing Spell

STEP 1

You want to help your friend's arm heal by strengthening their healing ability and reducing the pain. The first step is to tell your friend what you plan to do and get their permission.

Obviously if your friend is in the hospital unconscious, obtaining that permission may be difficult. But unless it is absolutely impossible to get permission, you need to get the person's permission. Even if they are unconscious and cannot respond, you should still inform them what you plan to do. It is important to obtain permission for two reasons.

If you do not get prior permission to work magick on a subject, most Wiccans would consider your actions unethical, no matter what the reason or eventual result is. It is important to maintain high ethical standards because, if you do not, you devalue what you do, and devaluing your magick in your own eyes is not a good way to make your Subconscious Mind understand how important your magick is.

It is important for the subject to understand what you are trying to do. If they don't, they may resist the spell. If their Subconscious Mind doesn't understand that what you are doing is good for them, then their Subconscious may interpret your actions as an attack and will treat your spell as an attack.

STEP 2

If you are doing this spell from a distance (i.e., you at home, and the subject in the hospital), make yourself a poppet of the subject. A poppet is a doll that is connected in your Subconscious Mind with the subject. (When making a poppet, use as many of the principles of magick as you can. For example, attaching a lock of the subject's hair would involve the Law of Contagion, using a picture would involve the Law of Similarity, making the poppet with an arm that you can fix invokes the Theory of Association, etc.)

STEP 3

Now put up a Circle and prepare yourself for the Working.

STEP 4

Take the poppet, and visualize moving the pain from the subject into something else (a candle perhaps). As the candle burns down, visualize their pain lessening (Theory of Association).

HEALING SPELL continued...

STEP 5

If your poppet has an arm that you can fix, physically fix the poppet's arm (possibly splint it), and visualize the subject's arm being repaired. (What principles of magick are being invoked here?)

STEP 6

Now hold the poppet's fixed arm in your hand. Breathe deeply. As you inhale, will good healing (blue-colored) energy into the subject. And as you exhale, will bad (gray-colored) energy out of the subject.

STEP 7

When you are done, take your Circle down, wrap the poppet up in a scarf, put the poppet in a safe place (you can safely de-construct it later), and visit your friend. Don't discuss the ritual until long after they are healed. If they ask, you can say, "It's being worked on."

Visualization

Visualization is using your imagination to "see" the psychic world. Your mind alone is not equipped to interpret psychic phenomena. It is through the cooperation of your five physical senses (sight, hearing, touch, smell, taste), your Conscious Mind, your Subconscious Mind, and your Soul that imagination occurs. And your imagination only works with pictures. The following exercise will help you improve the pictures your imagination sees.

Visualization Exercise One

Step 1

Create a relaxing, nonintrusive environment, a room with muted lighting, quiet background music, and a faint, pleasant, nonintrusive scent. You want to engage as many senses as you can without distracting you. Sit in a comfortable position.

Step 2

Place a lighted candle approximately six feet in front of you and contemplate the flame. Observe its colors, how the flame moves, see everything about it. Become familiar with the flame.

Step 3

After a few minutes of contemplating the flame, close your eyes, and continue to see the flame in front of you. In other words, recreate the flame in your mind.

After a few more minutes of visualizing the flame in your mind, open your eyes and see if what you have been visualizing is what you see.

Repeat this procedure until you can visualize and accurately see the flame with your mind's eye.

VISUALIZATION EXERCISE TWO

This exercise, in one of several forms, is the basic exercise used by many Traditions to help develop an individual's visualization skills.

STEP 1
Create a relaxing environment as you did in Exercise One, sit comfortably in a chair, and close your eyes.

STEP 2
See before you a totally black, velvet screen. Know that the black screen is there.

STEP 3
See a small yellow dot appear in the center of the screen. Watch the dot grow into a ball. Know that it is there.

Watch the ball form itself into a square, then into a star. See these shapes form. Know that they are there.

Turn the star back into a ball, then into a dot, then watch the dot disappear into the black screen.

Repeat this last step until you are comfortable with it.

As you become more and more proficient with this technique, try visualizing more and more complex pictures.

The ability to visualize what the mind "sees" is very important for spell casting and for divination.

Rhymes and Chants

Rhyming is an ancient technique and some magickal Traditions require that all spells be "spake in rhyme" to be effective. Although rhyming is not required to create effective spells, using rhymes makes a spell easier to remember. The rhymes carry a cadence and timing that can make working the spell easier for some. We do not actively teach rhyming, preferring other methods to create effective spellwork, but if you like rhymes, and they come easily to you, go ahead and rhyme your spells.

Chants and mantras are also very ancient, have some similarity to rhymes, and can be extremely effective. Experiment with them, and see how they work for you. Once you become proficient at a certain ability, such as meditation or grounding and centering, a trigger phrase can often be enough to accomplish the task. If you associate the feelings and techniques you have perfected through practice with a catch phrase (which you have used while you are learning) you can almost instantaneously achieve the state you need for a certain skill by using just the catch phrase, which then becomes a mantra for you. Some people can create a Circle with just a mantra. Some people can do a spell in a similar manner.

Be careful how you use these mantras. Be certain you want the effect you evoke with the mantra.

Perhaps saving these mantras for personal shielding and protection is best.

Practice, practice, practice is the key to effective spellwork and magick. It should feel natural and comfortable. Sometimes rote memorization also helps with certain Circles or spells and techniques. The more you do magick, the better you will become at it. The same applies to psychic abilities.

Candle Spells

Candle spells are some of the easiest spells to do. If you have access to an occult shop, a botanica, or an ethnic grocery, you can find pillar candles in glass containers with pre-printed spells on them. Some have the names of Christian Saints or Santarean Gods on them. When you burn them, you invoke whatever energies are written on the candle, and when the candle is completely used, it is believed that you will get either the spell written on it or what you asked for in general. Pretty easy. These pillar candles are called seven-day candles because you can burn them for several hours over seven days before using them up. Unfortunately, most people lose interest and do not finish the candle spell properly—by burning the candle until it is gone.

Wiccan candle magick is similar to the above concepts.

CANDLE SPELL

STEP 1
First determine the what, why, and how of your spell.

STEP 2
Then select a single taper candle, one that would fit a standard candle holder. Choose a candle of the color that is appropriate for your purpose. The color should have meaning for you. The color you choose can be one of the special colors listed in any of the books that contain magickal correspondence charts, but the color of the candle does not have to be in any of these charts. It can have meaning only to yourself. Ideally the candle should not be scented, unless you can choose a scent that also corresponds to your purpose. You can also use a plain white candle or uncolored beeswax candle. You can then add color to your spell in other ways.

STEP 3
Assemble all the other materials that you will need for your ritual, including the standard ritual tools you use in your customary Circle.

STEP 4
Cast a Circle.

STEP 5
Once the Circle is cast, take the candle and cleanse it with salt and water to remove unwanted influences, purify it with Fire and Air and bless it with oil and/or wine to give the candle the energies you want. Then consecrate the candle for the purpose. This can be done in several ways.

You can carve words into the candle that represent your desires for the spell. Choose positive words (remember the Subconscious Mind doesn't understand no), and make your words brief enough to fit on the candle. One or two word affirmations are best; for example, you could use health, prosperity, love, patience, courage, understanding, sympathy, a good job, an affordable home, learning and knowledge, increase psychic abilities, protection, safe from harm, enemies far away, happy family, etc.

CANDLE SPELL continued...

You can use scented oils to anoint the candle and impart your intent that way. The oils only work if the candle is unscented. Beeswax candles do have a natural honey scent, but it will not cause problems if you add another scent with oil. Use an oil that corresponds with what you want. There are many good books available that list oils and their attributes (see Resource Guide). As you anoint the candle, state your purpose and the oil seals that purpose into the candle. Coat the candle lightly with the oil and rub it in. Do not apply the oil heavily.

You can chant or sing the intent into the candle.

You can tie a ribbon of an appropriate color around the candle, which ties your intent into the candle.

You can combine any or all of the above methods.

STEP 6
Once your candle is consecrated for your purpose you can either light it in the Circle and send the spell immediately, or you can close down the Circle and save the candle for a later date.

The candle itself is charged with your intent. Burning the candle releases the intent into the Universe. Usually it will take several burnings to burn the candle completely. Don't expect to burn it all in one sitting, unless it's a small candle or you have a lot of time. The candle will probably take a few days to burn. When you light the candle, remind yourself of the intent you put into the candle. You should concentrate on the flame as you light it and for a few more moments after lighting. Then let the candle burn, as you pursue other activities.

Never leave a burning candle unattended. Snuff it when you have to leave. You can start it again when you return. Concentrate on your intent when you light it and when you snuff it.

Once the candle is consumed, your spell is done. What happens after that is up to the Universe. You should give the Universe a reasonable amount of time to accomplish your purpose. Burning a love candle and then declaring it a failure after only a week is unrealistic. Candle spells are best used for processes that take time to accomplish. They are also good for behavior or character modification, if you want to change or better yourself. You can repeat the spell, but only after at least a month has passed. If, after a month, you don't notice a change in behavior or attitude, or if the thing sought has not occurred, maybe that thing isn't for you, or you aren't seeing what is offered. Sometimes you may decline an opportunity that you didn't relate to your spell, or maybe you didn't need what you asked for. There are many reasons for what seems like a failed spell. Be honest with yourself, and you will probably find all your spells are answered, just not necessarily the exact way you wanted.

Cord Magick

This type of spell engages the physical senses as well as the mental and emotional. Estelle likes cord magick for weaving protective cords, cords that are connected to certain specific Deities, and spells that are aimed at certain types of character modification. For example, Estelle wanted to be more professional and less emotional at work. She wove a spell into a cord that she could wear at work, under her clothes. It had certain characteristics woven into it, which helped promote her ends. It worked. Eventually you find that you have no more need of the cord, and you can stop wearing it, because you have absorbed the instructions woven into it.

We illustrate two different types of cord magick spells here. While they do not differ greatly in difficulty or the type of ritual or material they use, they do differ significantly in what parts of the brain they engage. One uses a spoken chant, while the other uses focused visualization. We suggest you try both, and see which style works best for you.

Materials

You will need some sort of cord or yarn. We recommend silk or satin polyester—sometimes called rat tail, mouse tail, or bug tail—in three different widths. It comes in many bright colors and is usually available at fabric or craft stores. You can use yarn, but you usually cannot find short lengths and you have to buy a whole skein. Ribbons, narrow and relatively flat, can work, and can be bought in specific lengths. Macramé cord will also work well.

The colors you choose should be connected to the spell you are hoping to weave. These colors should have meaning for you, but don't necessarily have to apply to anyone else. The more cords you are weaving together, the more colors you can use, but only three are recommended at first. You can use any combination of colors for the three cords—different, three similar shades, two of one color, etc. The colors should be bright or strong, and, as you weave them together, the colors will help you add energy to your spell. If you are making a cord for a Deity, use their colors if you know them. You are looking for colors that evoke an emotional response and connect you to the spell you are going to weave. If you are weaving a spell for another person, you can ask for their input, but remember, you are the one weaving the spell.

What length you choose is up to you. The longer the cord, the longer it will take to weave, but the more spell energy you will be able to put into it. The maximum length we recommend is nine feet (three yards). Three feet is the minimum, because it takes some time to develop the rhythm of the spell, and shorter lengths are tougher to work with. Also, you probably will not be able to tie a cord braided from three-foot lengths around your waist (it gets shorter when braided). On the other hand, you can place a short cord in your pocket or purse more easily than a longer one. Either way, the spell will still work.

Cord Knotting

In the first spell, you will be knotting the spell into a cord. This type of spell is very ancient and a variety of cultures have used some form of this kind of spell knotting for centuries. You can do this knotting in any pattern you wish. For this spell, we have chosen to use only a slightly complex pattern. Some people have been known to use Cat's Cradle or macramé patterns when doing this type of Working. How complex a pattern of knotwork you use is up to you. Unless you are experienced with macramé or complex knots, we recommend you start simply, and with practice and success, move into more complex knots.

Cord Spell Number One

Step 1

Decide before you begin the why, what, and how of your spell, and choose the material, color, and length of cord you will use.

Step 2

Put up a Circle. Invoke whichever Deities you are comfortable with. Consecrate the cord by passing it through incense. Cleanse it with salt and water, and anoint it with oil.

Step 3

Sit in a comfortable position in the center of the Circle. Pick up your cord. Visualize what you want knotted into the cord, and say:

> *By knot of one, the spell's begun.*
> (Tie a knot in the center of the cord.)

> *By knot of two, this spell is true.*
> (Tie a knot halfway between one end of the cord and the center knot.)

> *By knot of three, a thing for me.*
> (Tie a knot halfway between the other end of the cord and the center knot.)

> *By knot of four, open the door.*
> (Tie a knot halfway between knot number two and your center knot.)

> *By knot of five, the spell's alive.*
> (Tie a knot halfway between knot number three and your center knot.)

> *By knot of six, my spell I fix.*
> (Tie a knot halfway between knot number two and the end of the cord.)

> *By knot of seven, we'll go to heaven.*
> (Tie a knot halfway between knot number three and that end of the cord.)

> *By knot of eight, this work is great.*
> (Tie a knot on one end of the cord.)

CORD SPELL NUMBER ONE continued...

By knot of nine, my goal I'll find.
(Finally, tie a last knot on the other end of the cord.)

So Mote It Be.
(Dip the knotted ends of the cord into the melted wax of a candle, sealing the power in.)

8   6   2   4   1   5   3   7   9

Knotted Cord

STEP 4
Thank the Gods. Close down the Circle. End the ritual.

Cord Braiding

This spell is done without a specific chant, and you will be braiding, instead of knotting, the spell into your cords. Rather than writing down exactly what you will say, we recommend you have a good idea of what you want to accomplish, and compose some simple chant or mantra that will help you focus on what the spell is about. Estelle usually uses words or phrases that describe in a positive way what she wants. For the job spell mentioned above, she said, "professional, career-oriented, objective, diplomatic, comfortable, excellent, hard worker." She didn't

say, non-emotional, because the Subconscious wouldn't hear *no* (or negatives) and would have interpreted that as emotional. Instead she used professional and objective as alternative ways to express non-emotionality.

You may want to stay with a simple three-cord braid for your early efforts with this type of spell. You want your energy to go into the spell, not into maintaining a complicated pattern. There are macramé books which teach various types of braiding when you wish to get more elaborate.

Cord Spell Number Two

STEP 1

Decide beforehand the why, what, and how of your spell, and choose the material, color, and length of cords you will use.

STEP 2

Put up a Circle. Invoke whichever Deities you are comfortable with. Consecrate the cords by passing them through incense. Cleanse them with salt and water, and anoint them with oil. Then run the ends of the cords into melted wax to prevent fraying before you start braiding.

STEP 3

Anchor one end of the cords to something solid, and braid out from that solid object. Estelle uses a handle on a chest of drawers. Estelle weaves the cords onto a ring, the kind used for a key chain. They are inexpensive and easy to find at hardware stores. You can just knot the ends also.

STEP 4

Now visualize the goal of the spell, and start working, chanting the mantra or words loudly or whispered as you braid. Say and form the words with your lips, even if you don't fully voice them. You are "chanting" your spell into the cord as it's braided. As you braid, other words or phrases might occur to you. If they fit, are appropriate, and positive, use them. You can improvise your words, and probably will as the cord grows. You don't need to remember exactly what you said after the cord is finished. As you braid, you will probably enter a state of "no-mind," not fully conscious of what you were doing while chanting. The repetition is what makes this type of magick effective—repetition and concentration, both on the weaving and on the words.

Estelle is a fast braider, and a nine-foot cord can take as little as twenty to thirty minutes. If you are slower and more meticulous, it will take longer. Try to adjust your time and length. If you braid more slowly, use a shorter cord; if you are, fast a nine-foot cord may be for you. Allow enough time so you can finish the cord in one sitting. If your arms and shoulders cramp, you can certainly move and work out kinks, but do not let go of the cord until you are done. You can pass the cord from one hand to another, while stretching. Just don't let go, because the braiding may unravel, and you want to maintain an energy contact with the cord until your spell is all tied up and finished.

CORD SPELL NUMBER TWO continued...

STEP 5
Once you are done, you may want to drip melted wax onto the knots at the ends to help seal them. Sometimes satin cord can be notoriously slippery and doesn't want to hold knots.

STEP 6
Close down your Circle. Clean up your area, putting all your materials away. Then go about your regular business. And when the time comes, take the cord, and use it.

The finished cord is energized by your braiding and the words woven into it. It is always aligned to whatever purpose you wove into it. It is an instant spell, which you can invoke simply by wearing or handling it, while recalling the intent you wove into it. And when you are done, you remove the cord to return to your normal everyday state of mind.

What to Do with the Cords
Estelle has a whole bunch of cords, woven for many purposes, and she carries them in her traveling ritual kit. She stores them in bags, and pulls out whichever ones she needs at any time. Most of the cords are Deity cords, and she uses one or more whenever she does a ritual or attends a Sabbat.

We do not recommend wearing spell cords continuously. First of all, you can become dependent on them. They should be a reminder. Eventually you will adapt and absorb your intent, so it becomes automatic and you don't need the cord anymore. If you use a cord for protection and shielding, it can be very effective, but it can also become a crutch. You should be able to ground, center, and shield by yourself. A cord should be saved for times when you have to do other things, and perhaps need the additional shielding the cord provides. The cord will shield for you, freeing your energies for the other things. Occasionally you can loan a cord to people who haven't yet learned how to effectively shield themselves. They can then experience what it feels like to be shielded, and it can help them learn.

Estelle once wove a full Circle into a set of cords, six in all, one each for Air, Fire, Water, Earth, above, and below, each in their appropriate colors. These cords, when placed around a room while mentally invoking each element in their appropriate area (Air is East, etc.), and asking their help to guard the Circle, become a portable Circle, and when mentally connected with energy, it seals and protects a room just as effectively as a cast Circle does. Woven into cords, this kind of Circle can be set up very quickly (in a couple of minutes) and requires no special supplies. When Estelle is finished with this Circle, she "disconnects" the energy, gathers up the cords, gives thanks to each element for protecting the Circle, and wraps them for storage for the next time. Each time they are used, they are re-energized.

You can also weave cords dedicated to various

Deities, saying their name(s), attributes, etc., as they are woven. These cords can be used for protection by that particular Deity, for accessing qualities or attributes of that Deity, or just as a symbol of that Deity in a Circle.

You can weave healing spells into cords. But once the person is healed, the cord should be destroyed, usually by burning. It has served its purpose. You don't necessarily have to destroy other spells, but healing cords should be destroyed because they can become infused with the energies of the healed person, and that can adversely affect another person if the cord is re-used.

Spell cords can be used to create a symbol for a coven. The coven receives a name and each person contributes cords in a color of their choice. Then the cords are woven together and contain the energies of all the people in the coven. For example, in a five-person coven, each person contributes five cords of their color in the agreed-upon length. At a coven meeting, each person gives a cord to the others, and keeps one for themselves. Then the coven, as a group ritual, braid their cords at the same time; the pattern is an individual choice. The finished cords contain the energies of each coven member, and they can be worn during coven meetings and rituals, or as a badge of membership in that coven or in other ritual settings. Weaving group cords is a good ritual for a coven to do to begin building a group mind-set.

Divination

Divination is ancient. Samples of tortoise shells used for scapulomancy dating to around 7500 BCE have been found in China. Other cultures have documented various techniques over the millennia. Divination is an attempt to receive a message from the Gods. Another way of looking at divination is that it is the reverse of spellworking. With spell-

working you are trying to change the Universe, while in divination, you are trying to perceive what the Universe actually is. These skills are complementary—the better you can "read" the Universe (divination), the better you can "write on" the Universe (spellwork). We are not going to detail the mechanics of any specific method of divination, but rather we will explain how divination can become an integral part of your spiritual life.

Many people think divination is about "telling the future," predicting what will happen. Most people do not do divination for themselves, but go to a fortuneteller to find out what the future holds for them. Some books and teachers even discourage people from doing readings for themselves. We disagree.

The best person to know about you and your situation and your future is *you*. We could predict that you will be in a car accident, but if you don't drive and take the bus, then that prediction is useless. We don't know about you or your situation, you do. However, you are intimately involved in your own life and can lack the perspective you might need to interpret the meaning of the reading. For example, you might do a reading for yourself and see some misfortune on the horizon. You think about the leaky plumbing in your house and attribute the misfortune to that. Then Aunt Hepsibah comes into town and camps on your sofa for a week, totally disrupts you life, and you forget to pay a bill until you incur a hefty late charge, at a time when you are already chronically short of money. Misfortune happened, but not in the way you envisioned.

You have to cultivate a twofold mind-set when doing divination—a reading—for yourself. You have to be simultaneously aware of yourself and your situation and life, yet also be open to possibilities you hadn't entertained before. This takes skill and practice but can be attained.

Divination can also be used as a spiritual guide and soul development tool. Asking about what you should work on, what you should study, how you can improve yourself are all good questions to ask using almost any divinatory system.

What divinatory system you choose is up to you and your resources. Some systems are relatively inexpensive and easy to learn and use. The pendulum is one of the easiest. Just hang a weight from a chain or cord so it can move freely. Hold it until it is still. Ask it "What is your yes?" and note the movement. Then ask "What is your no?" and note the movement. Then ask your questions, and depending on how the pendulum moves, you have your answer. Moving in a way different from yes or no may indicate you asked the wrong question, or the answer is more complicated than yes or no. Asking more narrowly focused questions or additional questions may clear up the uncertainty. You can buy special pendulums that show which direction means what, but we prefer the simple, easy, personal way, and it's cheaper too. Always be sure to thank the pendulum and whoever is helping you after your session.

Tarot

The primary divinatory system for Wiccans is tarot. Most Wiccans have a familiarity with tarot, even if they don't actively practice it themselves. There are hundreds of tarot decks available. The Internet has a number of good sites, which display and review decks, to help you choose a deck for yourself. Many Wiccans have several decks that they use interchangeably for various purposes. Estelle uses a *Robin Wood Tarot* for regular questions, and she also likes the *Rider-Waite* deck she has had since she was fourteen. She likes the *Voyager Tarot* for more spiritual and soul development questions, because of the many different images each card contains. The *Osho*

Zen Tarot is another good spiritual deck. Paul uses a *Fantasy Tarot* for readings, which many other people find almost impossible. Some Wiccans find *Rider-Waite* or any of the Waite decks to be too Christian in symbolism. Many like the *Aquarian Tarot*. You should look at a few decks, making sure you see most of the cards, and take your time deciding on which deck is for you. Check out the books on each deck to get an idea of its focus and the symbolism it uses.

Tarot works by using pictures and colors to capture the attention of the Subconscious and getting it to concentrate on what question you have asked. Images are powerful, but they also have strong cultural ties. A star may mean different things to a Christian, a Wiccan, and an African animist. You want to pick a system and symbology that speaks to you, clearly and in a way you find comfortable to work with. Tarot decks are widely available, so finding one you like and can use shouldn't be too difficult.

Don't expect to be able to do perfectly clear readings from the start. Use the book that usually accompanies the cards or find a good general book on tarot (see Resource Guide, pages 453–360). Be prepared to go outside the book's interpretations and meanings if a certain image speaks differently to you. Practice on yourself. You can read in a Circle, it will help cut down on outside noise and interference. You can also just center, ground, and relax before you read. Always try to read in a quiet private place. You might light a candle to give a signal to your Subconscious that something special is going to happen, and meditate to clear out the mundane thoughts before you actually do the reading. Keep records of the date, your question, the exact cards you get, and possibly a short interpretation. This can be a part of your Book of Shadows. You can go back at a later date and see how accurate you were. Your interpretation might be off, but with hindsight you might easily see what the cards were trying to tell you.

Other Types of Divination

Some Wiccans become proficient in several divinatory systems. This can be a spiritual quest in its own right. Just using and working with different systems opens you up to differing mind-sets and paradigms. The Norse Runes certainly stem from a different culture and mind-set than tarot. Tarot shares similarities with astrology, and there are a number of varieties of astrology (though ninety-five percent of the commonly available materials are about Western astrology). Numerology is a stand-alone, organized system of divination, although elements of it are found in tarot, astrology, and other systems.

Part 3, A Wiccan Glossary, contains entries on a myriad of divinatory systems, some still practiced today, many not. Some involve various forms of sacrifice, which are illegal, and, of course, are not recommended at all. Some are not practical, like using an axe and dancing around a fence post. Not many people have axes anymore and few have fence posts, and those that do probably don't want to drive an axe into them.

You can certainly buy slick commercially created divinatory systems, some of which guarantee results with a minimum of fuss and study. These are cute, but for the serious student, they become boring rather quickly. The systems which have stood the test of time have done so because they are accurate, can be learned by reasonably intelligent people, and provide a complexity of interest which can make for sustained study through the years. We recommend the more traditional, study-oriented, tried-and-true systems (tarot, etc.) rather than slick pre-packaged commercial fads. If you are in doubt, look through a book or two about the system you are contemplating. If there are several or many books on that topic, you have a good chance that it's solid and will stand the test of time for you.

Various Uses

There are many ways that divination is used in conjunction with worship. In some groups each individual takes a tarot card at Beltane and/or Samhain. This card gives some indication of how the next year (or six months) will go. You can use the symbols as a focus of meditation, and see what you get out of it. You can use symbols as focus for energies in spellworking. Choose a symbol that corresponds to what you want, thereby adding the energy of that symbol to your Working. You can study tarot cards alone, in pairs, in sequence, as groups, whatever you like. You can take two different decks and compare and contrast them. How are they different, how are they similar? What decks seem derived from each other?

We have used the tarot as our primary example of a divinatory system, but other systems also lend themselves to this sort of study. Tarot is very popular because the pictures speak to almost everyone, which makes them easy to use and generally yields good results.

When you work with and learn a divinatory system, you are also absorbing the paradigms, mind-set, and symbolism of that system. When you learn another separate system you are not only absorbing and learning that system, but you are also subconsciously comparing and contrasting it with the first system you learned. It can be difficult to learn the first system, but often the learning becomes progressively easier with each additional system if they are from a similar paradigm and culture. Tarot, astrology, Kabbalah, and numerology all derive from the same cultures and mind-sets. They interrelate, and people have consciously integrated elements of each into the others. The Norse Runes is a system unto itself, because it comes from a cultural paradigm that differs from the Mediterranean mind-set behind the tarot and Kabbalah. I Ching, Feng Sui, Nine Star Ki, and other Oriental systems are similar but, of course, quite different in focus and underlying philosophy from the ones mentioned before. All forms of astrology have similar elements, though they can differ strongly in philosophies and mind-sets.

Most tarot decks are based on one model, though some are more exotic than others. And many card systems are not tarot (Spirit guide or angel cards, for example) and use their own paradigms and symbology. Know the culture the system is based upon, and commonly used in (for they might not be the same), and you have a good handle on working with the system.

Flexibility and learning to make correlations, find similarities and differences, all have bearing on working magick. The more you do it, the easier it is to "bend your mind" into new and different ways to make your magick more effective. Sometimes the endpoint isn't in learning the divinatory system itself, sometimes the exercise is in opening up your mind to new and different things, and thereby becoming more effective and flexible in your magick. It all works together.

Divination Systems Not for the Beginner

There are some divinatory systems we do not recommend, and, in fact Estelle forbids her First Degree students to practice some systems. One is using the Ouija™ board, which is a modern version of spirit spelling or table tapping. There are other variations on this theme, but usually you ask some question and have a mechanism like a pointer or a wine glass that spells out answers on a board. You are *not* using cards or symbols or an object (like a crystal ball) as a focus, or using your mind to interpret something. You just let your mind go and allow "whatever makes it work" to give you spelled out answers.

How Ouija™ boards work is a subject for much debate. Some feel it is your Subconscious or your Higher Mind. Some feel it is your guardian angel. Some feel it is your dead Aunt Sally. Some feel it is demons. Some feel it is the Gods. Unfortunately any or all of the above can be possible. And our work with these systems shows that what is most consistent about them is their unreliability and inaccuracy. In a nutshell, *"The spirits can lie!"* Frequently you receive the message or answer you want, or what something or someone (who knows which) thinks you want to hear, but not the truth. The spirits that contact you may frankly not know any better than you do what's going on. Usually these systems are used in an air of party or fun and not serious spiritual quest. They are also almost idiot-proof, almost anyone can make them work, and they require little effort, knowledge, or training.

Unfortunately, some people have been hurt emotionally using these systems. They can become psychically opened up to entities or energies that may be in the "astral neighborhood" (good and bad), while having no training or awareness of what is happening to them or how to deal with it. They can become dependent upon these systems, almost like alcoholism. In very rare cases they can open themselves up to possession by some discarnate entity. Or, more likely than any of the above, people can become angry or frustrated when what they were told does not come to pass. Then they become bitter and decide that all divinatory experiences are worthless.

Estelle does allow her more advanced students to try Ouija™ boards, etc. Occasionally she encourages it. Then several sessions are spent asking all sorts of questions and getting answers, and eventually the inaccuracy and false statements become glaringly apparent. Then it's fun no longer, and serious study replaces the pastime.

Choosing a Divinatory System

When researching a divinatory system for your personal use, you can try to discover which systems were from the cultures of your chosen Deities. However, many ancient techniques aren't easily adaptable to the modern world. The Oracles of the ancient world, for example, were organized systems but many of the Priestesses used psychotropic substances to help them achieve a trance state. They also needed a Priest, who was specially trained to help interpret their messages. Most of us don't have a temple system to support us, nor a special Priest (or Priestess) to help with the messages and interpretations, and using most psychotropic substances is illegal. However, the system of augury—reading the flight of birds and their calls—is easily adaptable to modern usage.

Sometimes relying on your personal impressions and interpretations are just as valid and of equal or of greater value than the books and instructions of a divinatory system you purchase. For example, dream interpretation books have many interpretations of various symbols that are adaptable to many different things, including dream interpretation—another ancient method of divination. If, to you, a crow means company and the arrival of people, don't be concerned that it means death to the author of a book or to your friend. Your symbols are personal to you. Books can give general meanings, but these are usually superseded by your personal meanings. Your life experience will naturally color the meanings from other sources. If you are extremely afraid of dogs, the interpretation that dogs mean faithfulness and loyalty isn't appropriate for you. If you are a geologist, and you see a rock in a vision, you will naturally want to investigate what kind of rock it is. For example, is it in situ or was it transported from its native terrane? What age is it? How weathered is it? What other rocks does it associate with and what mechanism formed that rock? As a geologist, you have specialized knowledge that makes the symbol of "rock" take on many more levels of meaning than it would to a non-geologist. The Subconscious communicates with pictures, and if your Subconscious has specialized knowledge because of your life experiences, then it will use that specialized knowledge to make pictures which incorporate that special knowledge.

At the most basic, divination is the interpretation of symbols to receive a message. No matter how you receive those symbols—through cards, runes, scrying, or dreams—the symbols are what convey the message. Choose a system that is comfortable to use. Choose a system that gives you reasonably clear and accurate messages over time. Choose a system that fits with you as you are now, the culture you come from, and what paradigms you work with. Choose a system that is reasonably obtainable and relatively easy to learn. Practice, practice, practice, and keep records of your readings.

If you follow these simple steps, eventually you will master a system of divination. Then you are ready to tackle another system, and another, and another. On the way you will gain insight into yourself, other people, and the world in general.

DEDICATION

Wicca is a mystery religion with many activities within Wicca referred to as mysteries. Some Wiccans believe that certain words of power and/or God names are secret, feeling they are imbued with certain power and exclusivity. In the past, when these words or names have been revealed to others outside the group, the words have been changed. Some believe certain techniques or practices are "secret," most of them related to raising power. Some people feel the techniques for developing psychic abilities taught within a Tradition should be secret, and traditionally any techniques or formulas concerning magick have been treated as special, secret, and possibly dangerous.

However, there are certain mysteries that can be shouted from the rooftops, and paradoxically, still remain secret. These are the secrets derived from experiential practices. In the ancient world, the Eleusinian Mysteries was a widely popular cult, with its center at the Temple of Demeter, outside Athens. The actual rites and practices of these mysteries are still secret, partly because initiates had to swear an oath not to reveal what they saw, and also because it was an experiential process. We know the

rites had to do with death and resurrection, and a sheaf of grain. But exactly how the mystical experience was accomplished has been lost to time.

In Wicca the experiences of Initiation, and to a lesser extent Dedication, are mysteries. Many different rituals for Dedications and Initiations have been published, but just reading a ritual in a book can never impart the mystical experience that a good Initiation and/or Dedication will impart, and two people properly initiated by the same person with the same ritual will probably have different experiences.

PRIVACY ISSUES

There are few penalties within Wicca and those that exist usually relate to secrecy and individual privacy issues. In general, we don't mind if you disseminate our teachings or use our spells or recipes. But we do mind very much if you publicize or disseminate in any form just who is Wiccan, where they live, and where the covens meet. Wiccans call this outing, and other Wiccans will ostracize you for betraying this private information. The oaths of secrecy within Wicca require that you maintain privacy by not revealing the names of the people in Wicca, and where they live and meet.

Some Wiccans have chosen to be public, or at least not hide their beliefs. These people are "Out" or "out of the broom closet." That's their choice, and we celebrate those who are courageous and secure enough to make this choice, but most Wiccans are not Out. They prefer to be private about their beliefs.

Traditionally Wiccans feel they are the "Secret Children of the Goddess." As a result, there has always been some element of secrecy and mystery surrounding our beliefs and practices due partially to the experiential nature of some Wiccan practices, and partially because Wiccans believe that some things are best taught one on one and not widely publicized. In the wrong hands with the wrong intent, Wiccans believe that magick can be dangerous, particularly to the practitioner, because certain techniques can occasionally lead to undesirable results. Wiccans believe that people should learn how to use tools—and magick is a tool—properly and responsibly, and learning to use a tool properly takes time and practice. To become proficient with any tool takes time and commitment and magick is no exception.

WHAT IS DEDICATION?

Dedication is similar to either baptism or confirmation in a Christian church. The Dedicant has done some preliminary investigation, understands something about the religion of Wicca, and has decided that Wicca is a possible life path for them. The Dedication is the ceremony whereby the person contacts the Gods and declares their intention to learn more about Wicca. This ceremony can be public, private, or solitary. The intent is to declare—out loud—to oneself and the Gods (and

any others present) that this person has consciously chosen to pursue a course of study on the religion and practices of Wicca. This is not a sealing into Wicca. It is not a lifetime commitment, it is not a sacred binding oath to be Wiccan forever, it is just a promise to learn and study Wicca to see if it is something with which the person might want to become more involved, and possibly later make a more binding oath.

Wicca does not advocate proselytizing. To be Wiccan is not necessarily an easy path. Certainly it is in some ways outside the mainstream. Even in our mysteries, we make sure a person is fully informed and aware before we ask them to take any binding oaths. If a Dedicant studies and decides that Wicca is not for them, that's the end of their commitment. All that is required of a dedicant is to make the effort to read, learn, and practice. There is no penalty if a person decides not to become an Initiate. There is no penalty for moving on to another life path. There is no penalty for abandoning Wicca. The person, although they have decided not to pursue Wicca, is better informed about what Wicca is and what it means to be Wiccan.

We will describe two Dedication rituals. The first Dedication ritual is performed in a coven setting. Prior to the Dedication, the candidate will take a ritual bath either at the covenstead or at home and dress in sort of ritual garb, either their own or borrowed from a member of the coven. If the Dedication will be performed skyclad (naked), this should be decided before the Dedication. In Estelle's beginning classes the Dedication is on the fourth class day, which gives the students time to learn a little about Wicca and what Dedication is and obtain ritual dress. In the event that within your coven Dedication is performed skyclad, be consistent—everyone or no one.

Nudity

There are several reasons for performing the ritual of Dedication—and Initiation—skyclad. First, it symbolically represents birth, and since a Dedication and/or Initiation is a form of rebirth, skyclad helps reinforce that idea to the Subconscious Mind. Secondly, skyclad displays to our covenmates and/or the Gods that we have nothing to hide or fear, that we are open and ready to accept a new life. Skyclad helps reinforce trust. Thirdly, the energy of the ritual feels different when we are unclothed. That doesn't mean that energy cannot be good or effective if people are not skyclad, but the energy of the ritual is definitely different, even stronger and more effective when we perform ceremonies skyclad. Fourth, being skyclad in our ceremonies sets Wicca apart from other religions and requires a degree of commitment that is different from other religious groups, and as you enter Wicca you will experience a number of paradigm shifts. Since the nudity taboo is very strong in American society, learning to relax those inhibitions is one way of helping change those paradigms.

A female candidate should not be in her menses when the Dedication ritual is performed because the female energy during menses can be quite different, and is not necessarily desirable for a Dedication or Initiation.

Names

Each candidate picks a Craft name. Choosing a Craft name provides you with an opportunity to name yourself, something we usually don't get to do, and it allows you to begin establishing your magickal persona. Some people choose their mundane name as their Craft name, but most people choose something different.

Try to avoid names that are really common in the Craft community. Rowan and Robin are good names, but they are used by many people. If you want one of these names, try to have a modifier, like Red Rowan, or Robin the Merry.

Some people choose God or Goddess names, but that creates links to that Deity and can also invoke that Deity. Some consider it to be hubris.

Choose a name that is easy to pronounce, or you may end up with a nickname. Some Celtic and Welsh names are quite beautiful, but are unfamiliar to American ears and either will be mispronounced or shortened.

You can choose a name that is completely magickal—for example, Riefus Stardancer, or Janelle Twohearts—or one that is mundane, but has magickal significance.

You are not tied to your name forever, but each time you change your name, others will have to learn your new name, and some people will continue using the old choice. Some people choose one name and add other modifiers to it later, for example, Edgar becomes Edgar of Starshine Coven or Edgar Starshine or Edgar Shining Star.

Baby naming books have many interesting names and usually give the national origin, other national variants, nicknames, and the meaning of the name.

You can use physical characteristics or nicknames you already have, like tall or dark or bear. Be cautious about choosing a name for character traits. Sometimes that links you to that character trait (like lost or lonely) or can elicit comment (like the wise or the good) if people perceive you are not living up to your chosen name.

Sometimes translating a word or phrase or your name into another language can provide an interesting name; for example, Horse in German is Pferd.

Try to avoid titles or positions for your name, unless they relate to your mundane profession and you don't mind others knowing. King, Queen, etc., generally have no meaning in Wicca, but people might think it is improper to call yourself King Sean the Mighty. The titles Lord and Lady are used in certain Traditions, so avoid using them for yourself until you have more knowledge and understand what those titles imply.

Sometimes you can use a name for a place, real or legendary, such as Meaghan of Avalon. Be sure you have researched what that place is and/or was so you know the meaning of the place and what that meaning holds for you.

Above all, research your name. Belenos may sound nice, but it has the same root as belligerent. Do you want to tie yourself to that energy? Even a name you think you have made up can mean something in a foreign language. For example, Drek sounds like a good name, but it means shit in German and Yiddish.

Once you choose your name, try it out for a while. Write it down, meditate on it. Do divination on it. Think about being known as that name for a very long time. If it fits, great. If not, try again. Be patient and your name will come to you.

DEDICATION RITUALS

Dedication Ritual for a Group

Read through the following Dedication ritual at least twice before you attempt to do it. And perform at least one rehearsal before you decide to change anything.

The ritual should be performed by the person with the most expertise. Traditionally it is performed cross-gender, male performs for a female and female performs for a male. Eclectics do whatever is expedient and are not bound by this. If a number of people are being dedicated at one time, officiants can trade off between people, so no one person does all the work. But one person should perform the Dedication for one person, not several people for one person.

DEDICATION RITUAL FOR A GROUP

Setup

TOOLS NEEDED—You will need the standard Circle tools and supplies of the presiding High Priestess. You will also need some oil to anoint the candidate. The oil can be scented or unscented. Test it by placing a drop on the candidate's inner wrist to check for possible allergic reactions. Pure almond or olive oil usually causes no reaction. Do not use vegetable cooking oil.

THE CANDIDATE'S TOOLS—You should wear ritual garb of some sort, and should have chosen a Craft name. Additionally, the candidate should bring a candle—a single taper of whatever color they choose.

PRE-RITUAL—The candidate is sequestered in another room to sit quietly and meditate upon their coming experience. They should not see or hear the Circle being put up. You can dedicate several people in succession, bringing each candidate out in turn. Candidates are silent except when questioned.

Ritual Opening

HIGH PRIESTESS AND HIGH PRIEST—Cast a Circle. Invoke your favorite Goddess, God, and elemental quarters.

SUMMONER AND HANDMAIDEN—Escort the robed candidate to the edge of the Circle, and announce their presence.

Working

OFFICIANT—(Ideally of the opposite sex from the candidate, though this is not required) asks:

> *Is it your desire to gain knowledge of the Craft and its ways?*

CANDIDATE—Dedicant replies in the affirmative. The Dedicant and their escort are then cut into Circle. (See page 305 for explanation of cutting in and out.)

OFFICIANT—Welcomes the Dedicant saying:

> *A full Circle has been cast, and we are here with you. Have you brought the item requested?*

CANDIDATE—The Dedicant's candle is put on the altar.

OFFICIANT—Says:

> *At this time, we require you swear an oath of confidentiality.*

DEDICATION RITUAL FOR A GROUP continued...

> *We require you keep secret the names of your brothers and sisters*
> *in the Craft and the location of this and any other covenstead.*
> *Do you so swear?*

CANDIDATE—Dedicant replies in the affirmative. (If at any time the answer to a question is negative, the ritual stops.)

OFFICIANT—Says:

> *Though the knowledge of the Goddess and God, and of their*
> *Craft are available to all, there are mysteries we would have*
> *you keep secret, so they cannot be profaned by those not in the*
> *Craft. Do you so swear?*

CANDIDATE—Dedicant agrees.

OFFICIANT—Says:

> *You come into the Craft as you entered the world. Do you wish*
> *to proceed and dedicate yourself to the learning of the Craft and*
> *its ways?*

CANDIDATE—Dedicant agrees.

OFFICIANT—Says:

> *Then remove your robe, and present yourself to the Goddess and*
> *God as you were when you were born—skyclad.*

CANDIDATE—Dedicant removes robes, and Handmaiden places them aside.

OFFICIANT—Says:

> *You are here to dedicate yourself to the Goddess and God and*
> *the learning of their ways.*
>
> *Blessed be thine eyes that have seen this day.*
>
> All respond: *Blessed Be.*
>
> *Blessed be thine ears that hear the words of the Goddess and God.*
>
> All respond: *Blessed Be.*

DEDICATION RITUAL FOR A GROUP continued...

> *Blessed be thine lips which shall speak of the Blessings of the*
> *Goddess and God.*

All respond: *Blessed Be.*

> *Blessed be thine feet which have led you in these ways.*

All respond: *Blessed Be.*

> *You have chosen a name by which you would be known to the*
> *Goddess and God and to your brothers and sisters in the Craft.*
> *What do you wish to be called?*

CANDIDATE—Responds with their new name. All should make sure they understand, and have it spelled and/or written down if necessary. The High Priest(ess) pronounces the name.

OFFICIANT—Escorts the candidate to each quarter—East, South, West, and North—and presents them to the elemental guardians in turn by saying:

> *Guardians of the Watchtowers of the <direction>, creatures of*
> *<element>, we present to you, <name of candidate>, who is*
> *dedicating her/himself to learn of your ways and the ways of*
> *the Craft. Protect and instruct her/him.*

OFFICIANT—Escorts the candidate to the center of the Circle, and says:

> *Lady and Lord <or substitute coven Goddess/God names or*
> *alternatively use Earth Mother, Sky Father>, we present to you*
> *<name of candidate> who is dedicating her/himself to learn of*
> *your ways and the ways of the Craft. We ask you bestow upon*
> *her/him your blessings, and protect, guide, and instruct her/him.*

HIGH PRIESTESS—Takes the salt and water from the altar.

HIGH PRIEST—Takes the lighted incense from the altar.

HANDMAIDEN—Gets the anointing oil and holds it for Officiant.

SUMMONER—Gets candidate's candle and holds it for Officiant.

HIGH PRIESTESS—Anoints the candidate's forehead, throat, and heart with salt and water, saying:

> *I anoint you with salt and water to purify you.*

DEDICATION RITUAL FOR A GROUP continued...

HIGH PRIEST—Takes the incense and censes candidate's forehead, throat, and heart (by gently blowing incense onto candidate), and says:

> *I anoint you with Fire and Air to cleanse you.*

OFFICIANT—Anoints the candidate's forehead, throat, and heart with oil, saying:

> *I anoint you with oil to bless and consecrate you in the Craft.*

HIGH PRIESTESS—Purifies the candidate's candle with salt water.

HIGH PRIEST—Purifies the candidate's candle with incense.

HIGH PRIESTESS—Consecrates the candidate's candle with oil.

HIGH PRIEST—Carves a pentagram into the candidate's candle.

OFFICIANT—Holds the consecrated candle and says to the candidate:

> *We present to you this anointed and inscribed candle—a symbol*
> *of knowledge and life. Light this candle from our altar.*
> *Meditate upon this candle and offer through its flame a short*
> *prayer to the Goddess and God—things you would change about*
> *yourself—things you need in your life. When you are done with*
> *your short prayer, extinguish it here, but keep it safe. Take it*
> *home with you and privately burn it all to offer your prayers to*
> *the Gods. Do this when you have time to meditate undisturbed.*

CANDIDATE—Lights their candle and offers prayers—silently or aloud—and extinguishes the flame when finished.

OFFICIANT—Says to the candidate:

> *Now you may don your robes, as a symbol of your Dedication.*

Candidate's robes are returned to them and the candidate dresses.

OFFICIANT—Declares:

> *Welcome sister/brother in the Craft!*

CONGREGATION—Group hug! Congratulations, etc.

(If there are several Dedications, the candidate is escorted back to meditation place and the next candidate is brought in. After all have been dedicated, all are brought back and cut into the Circle.)

DEDICATION RITUAL FOR A GROUP continued...

CONGREGATION—All hold hands in center of Circle.

HIGH PRIESTESS—States:

> *Welcome to all. New sisters and brothers, I will tell you a mystery. We are ALL students of the Craft. We all learn together and will teach each other to the best of our abilities. So Mote it Be!*

> All respond: *So Mote it Be!*

Closing

HIGH PRIEST AND HIGH PRIESTESS—Perform the Great Rite and bless the wine and cakes. Chalice and cakes are shared by all. Ground energy into pentacle, dismiss the Goddess and God, and close down the Circle.

CONGREGATION—Feast and have fun. Clean up. Go home.

Solo Dedication Ritual

This ritual is designed for a solitary candidate to dedicate themselves. While certain Traditions refuse to recognize any but their own Initiation rituals, there are many Wiccans that consider solo Dedication valid.

Setup

Tools Needed—

- standard Circle tools and supplies
- ritual garb of some sort
- a candle, single taper, of whatever color candidate chooses
- oil for anointing (this can be scented or not, but you should place a drop beforehand on your inner wrist to test for possible allergic reaction. If there is a reaction, change oils. Pure almond or olive oils usually cause no reaction. Do not use vegetable cooking oil.)

Altar—Prepare your altar and quarter shrines as carefully and completely as you can. Remember, you can only perform a First Dedication once. Make it special for yourself.

Dedicant Preparation—You should have meditated on the coming changes in your life. How will this Dedication affect your relationships? your attitude toward your job, etc.? And you should have chosen a Craft name.

Ritual Opening

Candidate—Cast your standard Circle. Invoke your favorite Goddess, God, and elemental guardians.

Working

Candidate—Once your Sacred Space has been completely consecrated and warded, stand in the center of your Circle and say:

I have come before the Goddess and God to declare my intention to gain knowledge of the Craft and its ways.

I swear I shall keep the secrets of any fellow Craft brothers and sisters I shall meet along the way. I swear I shall keep secret the location of this and any other covenstead.

SOLO DEDICATION RITUAL continued...

> *I swear I shall keep secret any mysteries that shall be revealed to me, so they cannot be profaned by those not in the Craft.*

> *I present myself to the Goddess and God as I was when I was born—skyclad.*

CANDIDATE—Remove your robes, and place them aside. Then say:

> *I am here to dedicate myself to the Goddess and God and the learning of their ways.*

> *Blessed be mine eyes that have seen this day.*

> *Blessed be mine ears that hear the words of the Goddess and God.*

> *Blessed be mine lips which shall speak of the Blessings of the Goddess and God.*

> *Blessed be mine feet which have led me in these ways.*

> *< your new Craft name> is the name I have chosen to be known by to the Goddess and God and any brothers and sisters in the Craft.*

CANDIDATE—Walk to each quarter, East, South, West, and North, and present yourself to each of the guardians in turn, and say:

> *Guardians of the Watchtowers of the <direction>, creatures of <element>, I, <Craft name>, dedicate myself to learn of your ways and the ways of the Craft. Protect and instruct me.*

CANDIDATE—Move to the center of the Circle, and say:

> *Lady and Lord (or substitute your favorite Goddess/God names, or alternatively use Earth Mother, Sky Father), I, <Craft name>, dedicate myself to learn of your ways and the ways of the Craft. I ask you bestow upon me your blessings, and protect, guide, and instruct me.*

SOLO DEDICATION RITUAL continued...

CANDIDATE—Move to the altar. Take the salt and water and anoint your forehead, throat, and heart, while saying:

> *May this salt and water purify me.*

CANDIDATE—Take the incense and cense your forehead, throat, and heart, while saying:

> *May this Fire and Air cleanse me.*

CANDIDATE—Take the oil and anoint your forehead, throat, and heart, while saying:

> *May this sacred oil to bless and consecrate me in the Craft.*

CANDIDATE—Purify your candle and with salt water. Then purify the candle with incense. Now consecrate your candle with oil. And lastly carve a pentagram into candle, while saying:

> *I, <Craft name>, purify, consecrate, anoint and inscribe this*
> *candle—a symbol of knowledge and life.*

CANDIDATE—Light the candle from the altar and offer your prayers to the Gods, meditating for a short time on what has happened. Extinguish the flame when you have finished meditating. Save the rest of the candle for later meditations. Then dress yourself in your robes, saying:

> *I, <Craft name>, reclaim my robes as a symbol of my*
> *Dedication. May the Goddess and God protect and guide me as*
> *I learn and grow in the Craft. So Mote It Be!*

Closing
DEDICANT—Perform the Great Rite and bless the wine and cakes. Thank the Goddess and God, and dismiss them and the elemental guardians. Close down the Circle. Clean up. Celebrate.

INITIATION

Initiation is a ceremony that can be compared to being ordained into the priesthood or ministry in a Christian religion. The first ceremony in which each Wiccan participates is Dedication. After at least a year-and-a-day following Dedication, the Dedicant may be initiated into Wicca.

Traditionally there is a year-and-a-day between Dedication and Initiation (and the other degrees), because there is a lot to learn, not only book learning, but also experiential learning. You can read about the Circles and Sabbats, but until you have experienced them and done a few yourself, you can't really understand them. Becoming Wiccan requires changes in your mindset, outlook, priorities, and values and these changes do not happen in a few days or after reading a book or two. You have to have time to integrate these changes into your everyday life.

Also, it is important for each prospective initiate to experience the Wheel of the Year. Each Sabbat within the Wheel has a certain place in the grand scheme of the year and is tied to the seasons. It's an endlessly repeating cycle, but no one year is identical to the last or the next. As the yearly cycle mirrors the seasons it is also an allegory for the lives of the Goddess and God, and for the person new to Wicca, it requires a full year to have their first experience of the Cycle of the Seasons, and understand the rituals and meaning of the Sabbats.

WHAT IS INITIATION?

Whereas Dedication is a promise to learn and study Wicca, Initiation is a sealing into Wicca. The Dedicant has studied and practiced and determined that Wicca is for them, and they are willing to commit their life to being Wiccan. Obviously, not every Wiccan Initiate stays Wiccan forever. People do change their religions from Wicca to other religions, similar to changes in the various Christian denominations. However, Initiation should not be undertaken lightly. It is a big step.

For many Wiccans, this First Degree Initiation is the only Initiation they will undergo. They may not move on to higher degrees. That's perfectly okay. But Initiation does indicate a Wiccan is willing and able to act as Priest/ess for themselves. Initiates have the knowledge, training, and experience to do their own Circles, perform Sabbats, do magick, and do whatever else they feel they need to live a full and healthy spiritual and religious life. Sometimes it seems that a year is too short to learn all you need to know, but an Initiate never stops learning, practicing, or growing. In Ceremonial Magick the ultimate goal is self-perfection through magickal pursuits. In Wicca self-perfection and soul growth are also the ultimate goals, but these goals are practically unattainable. As soon as a person reaches one level of skill and mastery the Gods turn the heat up a notch and the tasks become more difficult. Thus the Initiation can be compared to the first step on the long and limitless road of being a Wiccan.

Not all Wiccans are dedicated, and the First Degree Initiation may be the first time the candidate formally commits themselves to Wicca.

WHEN SHOULD SOMEONE BE INITIATED?

If you are in a group, the leaders and teachers have standards and guidelines to decide when a person is ready for Initiation. A person should be familiar with the Wheel of the Year and understand the meaning and rituals of the Sabbats, and have participated in putting on at least one Sabbat themselves. A prospective Initiate must have working knowledge of Wicca and where to go for the answers to questions and concepts with which they aren't familiar. Knowledge and practice of magick is helpful. Some Traditions do not practice magick, but most do. Again, mastery is not required, but familiarity and understanding of the underlying principles and basic practices is necessary.

Knowledge of self is essential for an Initiate. You must formulate a personal code of ethics and realistically understand your strengths and weaknesses. It is important for a prospective Initiate to understand some basic attitudes and beliefs held by Wiccans: 1) Taking responsibility for one's actions and inactions is vital. In Wicca there is no confession, absolution, or salvation. Wiccans make their own place in the afterlife or the next life. 2) We reap what we sow without requesting Divine intervention to wash away sins, mistakes, and bad deeds. 3) We have more freedom to choose for ourselves, and we are not bound by any established holy book, code of behavior, or rules to live by other than our own. 4) Our moral code dictates honesty, respect, and loyalty. We tend to be more ecologically conscious than average and take active roles in causes we support. We vote and support the democratic system in which we live.

WHAT WILL INITIATION DO FOR ME?

Initiation can trigger deep fundamental personal transformation or can acknowledge that the change has already occurred. Initiation is profoundly personal and mystical—the subjective experience of the Initiate.

If the actual Initiation ritual doesn't move the earth for you, don't despair. Deep mystical bonding might have already happened, or might be coming shortly. In practical terms, the Initiation might start a process which can last for a while, at least a month or more.

Some Traditions believe that Imbolc is the time for Dedication and/or Initiation. In general, though, people are initiated at almost any time of the year, whenever they are ready.

THE INITIATION RITUAL

The Initiation ritual described is a First Degree Initiation. A person can perform it solo or have it performed for them by another Initiate. Craft lore has it that an Initiate can initiate others up to the degree they hold. A First can initiate Firsts, a Second can initiate Firsts and Seconds, and a Third can initiate Firsts, Seconds, and Thirds. (Of course, the ultimate philosophical question is "Who Initiated the First Wiccan?" The answer is the Gods did.) As far as we know, there are no rituals available to self-Initiate to the Second and Third Degrees. Certainly it is possible. But if you are a solo practitioner, you don't need a Second or Third, for those degrees are for people who are responsible for others and for the community as a whole. We do not describe Initiation for the Second and Third Degree. That is beyond the scope of this book. Second and Third Degrees generally work within a group and, once a Wiccan is ready to move to Second and Third Degree, they tend to make their own path. There are few agreed-upon standards for what a Second or Third needs to know.

One thing not specifically mentioned in the Initiation ritual we describe is the examination of the potential Initiate's Book of Shadows. Some Traditions make this an integral part of the Initiation itself. It's easier and more practical if it is separate, either just before or at another time and place than the Initiation. Some people don't examine the Book of Shadows as a whole, but rather review bits and pieces of it as the year of learning progresses. Whatever the method you choose, each Initiate should have a Book of Shadows which contains the basics for being a Wiccan. What you consider to be a part of that Book of Shadows is up to you. Some teachers accept books and materials from others as okay to include in a Book of Shadows, since this is how much of the Wiccan teachings are disseminated in the modern world. Some feel only material written by the Initiate or copied by them to be valid, basing this requirement on the old tradition of hand-copying all passed-down writings.

Whatever your criteria are, the Initiate should have a body of written lore to which they can refer. This will not be complete at the First Degree level—ideally it will never be complete—but it should contain most of the elements discussed in this book. And if something is missing, the Initiate should have enough knowledge, experience, and material to collect what they need, or the understanding of the resources to be able to go to find it for themselves. A Book of Shadows should be at a minimum a relatively full folder and a couple of notebooks.

Personnel

The people (or person) who are in charge of the Initiation should be at least First Degree or higher. Other witnesses or guests (usually not members of the coven) may be present, all of whom should also be First Degree or higher. The other witnesses or guests can be invited by either the High Priestess, High Priest, or candidate, with agreement by all principals involved. Possible guests or witnesses might include the teacher or mentor of the presiding High Priest or High Priestess, a community elder, the significant other of the candidate, if First Degree or higher, or a coven-sibling of First Degree or higher. An Initiation is not an entertainment, it is a serious religious ceremony performed for the benefit of the candidate. Witnesses and/or guests are usually invited to attest to the validity of the Initiation, to give their personal seal of approval to the Initiation by their presence, or simply to be present to share in the energy and joy of the new Initiate.

If the Initiate has Craft friends with whom they want to share the celebration, they may come to the feast afterward. They don't have to be of any special degree, but if they are not at least Firsts, then nobody should speak of the Initiation in specific terms.

Hermes

Dissecting the Initiation Ritual

The candidate should bring their personal tools (athame, wand, chalice, and pentacle), as well as their robes and a new single taper candle with them to the group Initiation. They can also bring other tools and personal items like jewelry, etc., but do keep the number of items to a minimum because all items must be consecrated and the more you bring the longer the Initiation will take. This Initiation usually involves skyclad work. Each Initiation is highly individual, and the ordeal the Initiate must go through should be personalized to each candidate. In a group, the teachers have had a year to get to know the person.

Ordeal or Not Ordeal?

The traditional ordeal is a hot seat, which involves a thorough questioning of the candidate about their knowledge and intentions in Wicca. It is usually quite detailed and can be emotionally intense. During the time of the Inquisition, people who felt they might be called before the Inquisitors practiced by experiencing a hot seat in case there was hostile questioning. The Inquisition is no more, but there are many real-world situations where the ability to operate coolly under stress is invaluable. Estelle was subpoenaed and underwent a deposition in a lawsuit. She appreciated her hot seat experiences because she felt they really helped during the ordeal of deposition. So even though it may be unpleasant and stressful, there are real-world applications for learning to handle yourself during a hot seat. Of course, we hope you will never have to use those skills, but if you do, you will be that much better prepared.

Other types of Initiation ordeals might try to explore a person's weaknesses to get them to open up to new experiences or ideas. The purpose of an ordeal is to create a mental change in the person, so

be creative. Here are some ideas to help you decide what types of ordeals would be suitable in specific situations.

One candidate who believed they weren't creative and had no artistic ability was given modeling clay and told to create a Goddess figurine.

One candidate who was very uncomfortable being skyclad was asked to dance with the others in a ring, while all were unclothed. This helped break down a barrier and initiate a paradigm shift.

One candidate was challenged strongly in a hot seat about life choices they had made and the possible consequences for their thoughtless actions. The candidate ended up in tears, but realized there is a consequence for every action or inaction and they became more self-aware and understood they were in charge of their life, not other people or circumstances.

An ordeal or hot seat is meant to make the candidate uncomfortable and undergo some stress, but it is a controlled situation with people who are on the candidate's side. You want to design the ordeal so it will be challenging, yet attainable. You don't want the person to fail. You also have to be adaptable and willing to change as circumstances dictate. Remember, sometimes things don't go as planned, so be ready to improvise.

Sometimes it can help if the Initiation is held in a place where the candidate has never been before, which can create an out-of-balance psychological state. You should always make sure the place is private and secure, without the possibility of intrusion by outsiders. It is nice to perform this ritual outdoors, but again, privacy is necessary, so it should be held on privately owned land with the permission and blessing of the owner. Make sure there are no roads or paths that might allow inadvertent access to outsiders.

Taking the Measure

Taking the Measure is a Wiccan ritual in which the candidate is "measured" skyclad using some kind of cord (such as the material used in macramé) that is usually white. It is a ritual that symbolically "binds" the candidate to the coven. You will need a long spool because you must take seven measurements—the candidate's head, chest, hips, height, arm length, wrist and thumb (strong or dominant hand)—without cutting the cord. At the end of the process you will have a rather long rope with a series of knots in it.

Measure the circumference of the head (usually forehead) and tie a knot. From that knot measure the chest and tie a knot. Next, measure the hips and again tie a knot. Then, measure the candidate's height. Tie a not. Measure the arm length of the dominant arm (right- or left-handed, whichever is used to write with) and tie a knot. Measure the circumference of the wrist and tie a not. Measure the circumference of the thumb (of the dominant hand) and tie a knot.

Once finished, the cord is cut from the spool just after the last knot. You might want to dip the ends of the cord in melted wax to prevent fraying. The measure becomes the property of the coven, and binds that person to the coven. If a person leaves the coven before further Initiation, the measure is returned to the person, symbolically severing the ties between the candidate and the coven. After the Initiation, the cord stays with the coven as long as that person is a member. A measure taken at the First Degree Initiation can be used for other purposes, but these are associated with the Second and Third Degree Initiations and are not included here. If you like, you can also take a second, separate measure that is given to the candidate at the conclusion of the Initiation. It then can be woven into a cord that becomes the symbol for the First Degree.

Ritual Bondage

Usually a candidate is tied and a blindfold is used during the Initiation ritual. Binding and blindfolding symbolize the former unenlightened state of the candidate. The binding should not be excessively restrictive. Some people only tie the candidate's hands, others also bind the feet, but the candidate must be able to walk, to negotiate stairs, etc. If the candidate is physically challenged in any way, be sure to take that into account. Be adaptable, should the need arise.

Death Drink

The purpose of the Death Drink is to allow the candidate to "taste their death" (a bitter experience) and it reminds them of their mortality. It is also an implied peril because those who approach Initiation under false or frivolous circumstances are supposedly in peril for their lives. The so-called "Death Drink" is traditionally made from some bitter, possibly unpleasant-tasting herbs. It should *not* contain any substance the candidate is allergic to, or anything that might be hallucinogenic or toxic. One Death Drink recipe starts with instant coffee (the cheaper the better), with only as much water as needed to make it a drinkable liquid. Then lemon juice and vinegar with oregano and other spices are added. This thick, bitter drink, although it smells and tastes terrible, is completely nontoxic. Unsweetened cranberry juice also tastes terrible and can be a good base from which to create the Death Drink. The candidate should drink only one ounce (a shot glass) or less. Be sure to take into account any gastric disturbances the candidate might have.

Ritual Challenges

Traditionally, the Challenge at the edge of the Circle is done at sword point. If you don't have a sword, any pointed blade will do. Since the candidate is blindfolded, you have to put the blade against their chest so that they feel it. But do not apply pressure that might break the skin. Pressing the blade against the skin at an acute angle (forty-five degrees) will depress the skin without causing injury. Because of the candidate's heightened emotions during an Initiation, the process will likely be magnified in their mind. If you feel it is too traumatic or you object to the use of a blade, you can press your palm firmly against the candidate's chest to stop progress. The candidate only needs to know they cannot proceed without impedance or injury. The purpose of the process is to heighten the importance of the challenge.

The candidate is challenged to say the appropriate password to enter the Circle, which you have told them in advance. If they forget the password due to the heightened emotions of the moment, tell them again. You are not setting the candidate up to fail, but you are challenging their skills, knowledge, and courage. Make it a test, but one they can pass.

Escorting the Candidate

Bringing the candidate into the Circle may sound complex, but it is simpler in actual execution. After the kiss, the High Priest or High Priestess puts their hands on the candidate's shoulders or upper arms and gently rotates the candidate and themselves in a complete clockwise circle while moving and guiding them into the Circle. Be careful to guide gently and slowly because the candidate is blindfolded and may be bound, making them disoriented.

Within the Circle, the candidate is guided from place to place. Be sure to hold the candidate firmly but gently and guide their movements, don't push or jerk. If necessary, you can tell them when movement is needed. It is very important that the people who conduct the Initiation are aware and sensitive to the candidate's reactions. They can make things run more smoothly and adapt movements if necessary. Since the candidate will have to kneel and rise at different times during the Initiation, they may need assistance, and the Handmaiden and Summoner are there for that purpose. It is appropriate to let the candidate know when they are required to kneel or rise.

Consecrations

The five-fold blessing is another Wiccan mystery. We have altered the traditional blessing for this Initiation, because it is difficult to include all the possible ways to perform this blessing in a book, and we feel that some mysteries are best taught person-to-person.

Traditionally, the candidate is consecrated by drawing a pentagram on their forehead with a finger that has been dipped in liquid. You can also write their Craft name on their forehead with wine. When you consecrate the candidate with a kiss, it is a chaste kiss on the lips.

The Initiate will consecrate their own tools at the appropriate time, first with salt water (from the altar), then with incense (also on the altar)—by moving their tools through the smoke—(if another stick needs to be lighted have one handy and do so), and anointing the tools with oil and wine (also on the altar). If an item could be damaged by liquids, running the finger over the tool without touching it is acceptable. The Initiate may also anoint their tools, then wipe them off. Occasionally an Initiate freezes, so subtle prompting is acceptable.

The process of anointing the candle is the same as in the Dedication: first cleansing with salt water, then with incense, anointing with oil and wine, and carving a pentagram into it.

The Officiant presents the candidate their robes (and cords if a second set has been made), wand, athame, chalice, and pentacle and briefly describes the purpose of each. Descriptions should be short, reinforcing what the candidate has already been taught.

Scripting

The ritual is a long one, usually sixty to ninety minutes, and there are lengthy passages that are spoken during the Initiation. The Officiant should practice their lines before they say them. Use a written script and make marks to show emphasis or pauses. Say the words with meaning. Understand what you say. If some of the words seem strange or their meanings aren't clear, change the words to fit you, but be careful not to deviate too far from what is written here.

Plan a whole evening (or morning or afternoon) for an Initiation. It can take up to four hours from setup to cleanup. Because of the time required for a single Initiation, only one person can be initiated at a time. Also plan to have a bit of a feast afterward, even if it's just snacks and drinks. This will help the Initiate ground and also to help ease them back into the mundane world. Allow some time for the person to assimilate what they have been through before making them go back out into the world. Make sure a candidate is well grounded and back to normal before they leave, or have someone drive them. Keep the alcohol to a minimum. You don't want to muddle the experience with alcohol.

After the Initiation, check up on the Initiate during the following few days and weeks. Sometimes Initiation triggers big changes, and the Initiate may need help dealing with the energies. Sometimes Initiation opens a person to new realms and it can be confusing. Let the new Initiate know you are available to talk and to answer questions if necessary, and you should also be prepared to act in the very rare cases where Initiation triggers emotionally difficult experiences.

First Degree Initiation Ritual

Setup

TOOLS NEEDED—Standard altar setup and equipment, Officiant's boline, blindfold, and shackle cord, anointing oil, cord for taking measure, herb concoction (Death Drink), basket to hold candidate's robes and personal effects.

CANDIDATE—Brings all their ritual tools, any jewelry, and (possibly) their Book of Shadows.

PRE-RITUAL—The candidate is sequestered in a separate room with instructions to robe, adorn themselves with any jewelry they may have, gather their tools, and to meditate. During this time alone the candidate is asked to write down on two separate slips of paper their mundane name and their new Craft name.

FIRST DEGREE INITIATION RITUAL continued...

Ritual Opening

HIGH PRIESTESS AND HIGH PRIEST—Cast a standard Circle and invoke your favorite Goddess, God, and elemental quarters.

SUMMONER—The Summoner approaches the candidate in their sequestered room and offers the First Challenge. (Are you prepared for what is to come?, etc.) If the candidate agrees, the Handmaiden enters the room carrying the basket containing the bitter Death Drink, which she then hands to the Summoner.

HANDMAIDEN—Offers the Second Challenge by saying:

> *Have you prepared yourself?*

CANDIDATE—Responds. If you get a positive response, continue with the ritual. If at any time you get a negative response, the candidate is not ready—do not proceed.

HANDMAIDEN—Upon receiving a positive response, says:

> *Do you willingly submit yourself to our mercies?*

CANDIDATE—Responds.

HANDMAIDEN—Opens her arms wide and says:

> *I am your death! Come and embrace me!*

CANDIDATE—Embraces the Handmaiden.

HANDMAIDEN—Requests the slip of paper with the candidate's mundane name written on it. She destroys it by burning and says:

> *I destroy your identity!*

HANDMAIDEN—Takes the slip of paper with the candidate's new Craft name written on it, and hands it to the Summoner, who places it in the basket, and says:

> *I take your secret self!*

HANDMAIDEN—Takes all of the candidate's jewelry, hands it to the Summoner, who places it in the basket, and says:

> *All your wealth is dust!*

FIRST DEGREE INITIATION RITUAL continued...

HANDMAIDEN—Takes all of the candidate's ritual tools, hands them to the Summoner, who places them in the basket, and says:

>*All your power has fled!*

HANDMAIDEN—Asks the candidate to disrobe, hands the robes to the Summoner, who places them in the basket, and says:

>*Naked you came into the world and naked you shall leave it!*

HANDMAIDEN—Takes the candidate's Measure: (height, span, head, chest, hips, wrist, thumb (once or twice), and says:

>*Around the thumb; tie a knot. Around the wrist; tie a knot.*
>*Around the hips; tie a knot. Around the chest; tie a knot.*
>*Around the head; tie a knot. From finger tip to finger tip; tie a*
>*knot. From toe to crown; tie a knot.*

HANDMAIDEN—When she is done, she hands one or both Measures to the Summoner, who places them in the basket, and says:

>*Gone are your dimensions!*

HANDMAIDEN—Blindfolds the candidate, and says:

>*Alone, in the dark, you are lost!*

HANDMAIDEN AND SUMMONER—Symbolically take the candidate's freedom by binding or loosely tying the candidate's hands. (Note, this step is optional, depending on circumstances, especially if some other ordeal is prescribed.) While the candidate is being tied up, the Handmaiden says:

>*For all the good it does you, you may as well not move at all!*

SUMMONER—Whispers into the candidate's ear:

>*I give you two keys: Perfect Love and Perfect Trust.*

HANDMAIDEN—Gives the candidate a sip of the Death Drink, and says:

>*Taste your death!*

HANDMAIDEN AND SUMMONER—Move to each side of the candidate, with the Summoner carrying the basket, and prepare to escort the candidate to the Circle. As they leave the place of meditation, the Handmaiden says:

FIRST DEGREE INITIATION RITUAL continued...

> *Only by passing through the doorway, into the great*
> *Unknown, can you attain the next Cycle!*

HANDMAIDEN AND SUMMONER—Carefully lead the candidate to the Circle. The Officiant awaits them at the Circle doorway (Note: Initiations should be performed cross-gender whenever possible. The High Priestess should perform the entire Initiation for a male candidate, while the High Priest should perform the entire Initiation for a female candidate. The person who performs the Initiation is the Officiant.) The Summoner then knocks three times at the entrance.

OFFICIANT—Responds with:

> *Who knocks at this door?*

HANDMAIDEN—Answers:

> *I bring one who would be an Initiate.*

OFFICIANT—Says:

> *Ask and it shall be given unto thee. For none can be refused by*
> *one who has the power. But, we ask thrice of the candidate, if*
> *they be truly prepared for this assay, for if they are not, they*
> *have only themselves to blame and may be caught between the*
> *worlds, unable to return to the world of men as they were, and*
> *unable to advance to the world of the Gods. For they claimed*
> *that which was not theirs. Know, that in magick, to claim that*
> *which is not yours is to bar your attainment of it.*

OFFICIANT—Places the edged weapon against the candidate's chest and challenges the candidate for the third and final time by saying:

> *O thou who standeth on the threshold between the pleasant*
> *world of men and the dread domains of the Gods, hast thou the*
> *courage to make the assay?*

CANDIDATE—Responds.

OFFICIANT—Says:

> *For I say verily, know that it is better to rush upon my blade*
> *and perish, than to make the attempt with fear in thy heart!*
> *With what keys do you have to admit you to our Circle?*

FIRST DEGREE INITIATION RITUAL continued...

CANDIDATE—Should respond with the passwords they have been given: "Perfect Love and Perfect Trust." (If they don't remember them, the Summoner may prompt the candidate.)

OFFICIANT—Answers:

> *All who bring such keys are doubly welcome.* (Officiant then removes the sword.) *I give you a third key, a kiss.* (Officiant now kisses the candidate chastely on the lips.)

Working

OFFICIANT—Brings the candidate into the Circle and moves them around the Circle once, turning deosil, and says:

> *This is the way all are first brought into the circle, always moving Sunwise, from darkness towards light.*

OFFICIANT—Brings the candidate to the center, facing the East, and says:

> *O thou who has declared intent to become one of us, hear then that which thou must know to do. Single is the race, single of men and Gods. From a single source we both draw breath, but a difference of power in everything keeps us apart. Yet in the greatness of minds, we can be like the Gods.*
>
> *Though we know not what goal, by day or in night; the fates have written that we shall run beyond all seas and earth's last boundaries, beyond the spring of night and the heavens' vast expanse, where lies a majesty which is the domain of the Gods.*
>
> *Those who would pass through the gates of night and day, into that sweet place which is between the worlds of men and the domain of the Gods, know that unless there is truth in thy heart, then every effort is doomed to failure.*
>
> *Hear then the Law:*
>
> *That thou lovest all things in nature,*
> *That thou suffer no innocent to be harmed by thy hand or in thy mind.*

FIRST DEGREE INITIATION RITUAL continued...

That thou walkest in the way of the Gods,
That thou shalt learn contentment through suffering, from long
years, and from nobility of mind and purpose.

And if among the vulgar, some discoveries should arise concern-
ing some maxims of thy beliefs in the Gods, for the most part
keep thou silent. And when someone shall say to thee: "Thou
knowest not," and it bites thee not, then knowest thou, that
thou hast begun the work. Even so: Do not display the maxims
to the vulgar, but rather the works which flow when they are
absorbed and understood.

By what name will you be known in the Craft?

CANDIDATE—Responds with their chosen Craft name.

OFFICIANT—Leads the candidate to each quarter in turn, and says:

Take heed, O Mighty Ones of the <direction>, creatures of <ele-
ment>, that <name>, properly prepared, will be made Priest/ess
and Witch!

OFFICIANT—Returns to center of the Circle with the candidate, and orders:

Kneel.

CANDIDATE—Kneels.

OFFICIANT—Rings the bell eleven times. Then orders the candidate:

Rise.

In other religions, the postulant kneels as the priest/ess claims
supreme power. But in the Craft we are taught otherwise, and
we kneel and say:

(The Officiant now kneels at feet of candidate.)

Blessed be thy feet, that have brought thee in these ways.
Blessed be thy knees, that shall kneel at the sacred altar.
Blessed be thy (loins/womb), from which springs forth life.

FIRST DEGREE INITIATION RITUAL continued...

> *Blessed be thy breasts, formed in (strength/beauty).*
> *Blessed be thy lips, that shall utter the sacred names.*

OFFICIANT—Removes the bindings and blindfold from the candidate.

CANDIDATE—Performs any other ordeal, if something other than binding has been planned.

OFFICIANT—Declares:

> *Thine ordeal is done. Thou hast done well.*
> *Art thou ready to swear that thou wilt always be true to the Craft?*

CANDIDATE—Responds.

OFFICIANT—Says:

> *Art thou always ready to help, protect, and defend thy brothers*
> *and sisters of the Craft?*

CANDIDATE—Responds.

OFFICIANT—Says:

> *We demand no oath of you to never reveal the secrets of the*
> *Craft, requiring only that you swear to keep secret the names of*
> *your brothers and sisters, the location of the covenstead, and the*
> *items of business communicated within the Circle.*
>
> *Instead we ask of you an oath in your own words, stating your*
> *commitment to the Craft, and to the magickal knowledge, to*
> *your brothers and sisters, that you stand ready to give your*
> *magickal help if properly called upon, to serve always with*
> *honor the Wicca and the Gods, to work in peace and trust with*
> *your brothers and sisters in the Craft; and if you feel out of*
> *harmony with us, you will ask to withdraw, but still keep your*
> *oath.*

CANDIDATE—Swears to keep the oath and then gives their personal oath in their own words.

OFFICIANT—Consecrates the candidate with the various elements in turn, while saying:

> *I consecrate thee with water and earth, that thou may be pure*
> *in thy workings with the Craft.* (Aspurge the candidate with
> salt and water.)

FIRST DEGREE INITIATION RITUAL continued...

I consecrate thee with fire and air, that thou may be fervent in thy workings with the Craft. (Cense the candidate with the burning incense.)

I consecrate thee with oil to anoint thee into the service of the Craft. (Anoint the candidate with the oil.)

I consecrate thee with wine, that thou may be steadfast toward the Craft. (Anoint the candidate with wine from the chalice, in the same way you anointed them with the oil.)

I consecrate thee with my lips, that thou may give in love and truth to the Craft. (Kiss them chastely on the lips.)

To obtain magickal power, learn to control fixed thought. Admit only ideas which are in harmony with the end desired. Fixed thought is a means to an end. Pay attention to the power of silent thought and meditation. The material act is but the outward expression of thought. Thought is therefore the commencement of action. If a chance thought can produce the effect of action, what cannot the fixed thought produce.

Establish yourself firmly in the equilibrium of forces, in the center of the cross of the elements. Learn both the power of thought and the power of restraint, that thou control thy thought and action. I shall now present you with the working tools of the Witch.

OFFICIANT—Presents the candidate with their robes, cords, wand, athame, chalice, and pentacle, briefly describing each one's purpose, and says:

I now salute you in the names of The Lady and The Lord, newly made Priest/ess and Witch. By which names do you honor each?

CANDIDATE—Responds.

OFFICIANT—Says:

I will now write your magickal name on your forehead. I will you <say their name>. (Trace the candidate's name on their forehead with wine from the chalice.)

FIRST DEGREE INITIATION RITUAL continued...

> *Now it is your task to study the practice of the Craft. Know,*
> *however, that in true religion, there is no sect. Take heed that*
> *thou blaspheme not the name by which another knoweth their*
> *Gods. Think ye not that a little knowledge give you mortal*
> *authority. Remember the ordeal, and know that it is through*
> *discipline and suffering that the soul is purified.*

OFFICIANT—Now cleanses and anoints the candidate's candle with salt and water, fire and air, wine, oil, and carves a pentagram in the side. Then the Officiant lights the candle and hands it to the candidate, saying:

> *Take this lighted candle to symbolize the divine light that is*
> *within thee. Nurture that light within, and protect it as you*
> *must protect the candle flame from passing drafts.*

CANDIDATE—Is now invited to consecrate their tools. (Unless you have a great deal of extra time, or the candidate has very few tools, they should be encouraged to choose only one or two tools to consecrate. These consecrations are meant to show the assembled congregation that the new Initiate is capable of performing the duties of an Initiate.)

Closing

HIGH PRIESTESS AND HIGH PRIEST—Perform the Great Rite. The chalice is passed and grounded.

OFFICIANT—Places the newly Initiated Witch in center of the Circle, and standing behind them, turns them and themselves to face each quarter in turn, and declares:

> *Hear ye O Mighty Ones of the <direction>, creatures of <ele-*
> *ment>, that <give their Name> has been consecrated a*
> *Priest/ess of the Craft, and a (brother/sister) of the Wicca.*

CONGREGATION—Offer greetings and welcome for the newly ordained Witch.

HIGH PRIESTESS AND HIGH PRIEST—Thank and dismiss the Lady and Lord, the quarters, and take down the Circle.

CONGREGATION—Relax and make merry. Clean up mess. Go home.

SOLO OR SELF-INITIATION

Solo or self-Initiation is a controversial subject within Wicca. Some Traditions feel that there is no such thing as a self-Initiation, that a person can only be initiated by another Initiate. In Eclectic Wicca, in general, self-Initiation is recognized as a valid path, but the status and authority of the self-Initiated person depends on the group with which they are associated. Some treat a self-Initiate as they would any other Initiate, but others do not. Nonetheless, if a person has no teachers except themselves and no one to be initiated by, then they sometimes will Initiate themselves.

Self-Initiation requires that the prospective Initiate have at least a year of study and practice. The learning and accomplishment requirements are the same. It may take longer to reach the stage at which you feel ready and competent to become initiated due to lack of resources, but you will be more independent and self-reliant. Some people self-Initiate and then later after hooking up with a group, may choose to undergo another First Degree Initiation with that group.

When to Self-Initiate

How do you know when you're ready for your Initiation? That's not always easy to tell. It is difficult to explain, but when you feel a sense of calm assurance, a steady grounded feeling that indicates to you that you know what you need to know but also know you still have a lot to learn, when, in some unexplainable way, you realize it really doesn't matter whether or not you go through the actual Initiation ritual, for you calmly, detachedly, and maturely know you have reached that level of knowledge and skill—then, paradoxically, you are probably ready for Initiation. If you long for and crave it, the time is not right. If you know you have

accomplished some and are ready to learn more and go on to the next level, you are probably ready.

You have to be brutally honest with yourself and examine your feelings and ideas closely. If you Initiate yourself too early, you probably will not get much out of it, although you won't expose yourself to something which can cause harm because you don't have the skill or understanding to get to that next level.

If you have been contacted by Deity, that's good. If not, keep trying, but you should have chosen a Deity or two for yourself before you Initiate. (See the chapter on Deity, pages 141–146.)

This solo Initiation is designed, as the term implies, for one person alone. You could adapt it for a small group, but if the others haven't been through an Initiation, it won't be as effective or meaningful for them. If you are part of a small group, one person in the group should probably self-Initiate, then, if the rest of the group wants to self-Initiate they can, or perhaps adapt the Initiation for a group to suit their needs.

A good Initiation opens a person up to the Divine. Hopefully you will have done the groundwork to accomplish that for yourself.

Parameters for the Ritual

As with the Initiation performed in a group, a solo Initiation should take time: at least an hour for the ritual with setup and cleanup time added to that. Make sure you are not rushed. It's best to have no clocks to see so you are not distracted. Lock the door, turn off the phone, and close the curtains to eliminate distractions. Leave yourself enough time to do it, and also to relax and unwind afterward.

Remember the time you spend after the Initiation cleaning up and doing other mundane tasks is important because it allows your Subconscious Mind and your Soul to process the experience without distraction. Go shopping, hang out with friends, see a movie, pay bills, clean the closet, work on crossword puzzles, do a good workout, something entirely different that will take your mind off of the experience. This is not a good time to sleep; try to "get mundane" before going to bed.

Taking the Measure in a solo Initiation is somewhat different. Take your Measure by measuring your height three times, knotting between each.

Make sure there is no slack in the cord and stand straight and tall. Measure from under your food to the top of your head. This cord will be braided and become the symbol of your First Degree. White or red are the customary colors.

Your ordeal in this case is the study and practice you have done for the last year-and-a-day. You have shown discipline, perseverance, patience, and determination. That is ordeal enough.

First Degree Solo Initiation Ritual

Setup

TOOLS—Your standard altar tools, equipment, and Book of Shadows, plus anointing oil, cord to make your Measure, and a basket for your robes and personal effects.

PRE-RITUAL—Prepare yourself by gathering all necessary materials, and purify yourself with a ritual bath. A ritual bath is a quick bath performed with intent. The bath water should be a saline solution, so either use the salt you normally use in ritual, or else some bath salts, and perform the same consecration sequence that you use for blessing the salt and water for your Circle.

When the bath is completed, robe yourself, adorn yourself with whatever ritual jewelry and personal tools you own. Lock the doors. Turn down the lights. Unplug the phone, and begin.

Ritual Opening

CANDIDATE—Cast the Circle in your customary manner, invoking your favorite Goddess, God, and elemental guardians. Once the Circle is cast, meditate upon what you are about to do. You should write down on two separate slips of paper your mundane name and your new Craft name.

When you are ready, stand in the center of your Circle and say:

> *Hear ye oh Mighty Ones!*
>
> *I have prepared myself through learning, practice, and accomplishment. I have studied for at least a year-and-a-day. I am ready, and I approach this ritual freely and of my own choice. I submit myself to what the Gods shall put before me. Through*

FIRST DEGREE SOLO INITIATION RITUAL continued...

> *my free will I shall take what they offer. I am ready to declare*
> *myself Priest/ess and Witch, and claim all that goes with the*
> *title.*

CANDIDATE—Take the piece of paper with your mundane name written on it and burn it in the altar candle, saying:

> *I destroy my old identity!*

CANDIDATE—Take the piece of paper with your Craft name written on it and lay it safely aside, saying:

> *I take my secret self, and put it in a safe place!*

CANDIDATE—Remove any jewelry and place it in the basket, saying:

> *All my wealth is dust!*

CANDIDATE—Place all your ritual tools in the basket, saying:

> *All my power has fled!*

CANDIDATE—Remove your robes and place them in basket, saying:

> *Naked I came into the world, and naked shall I leave it!*

CANDIDATE—Take the cord and measure your height three times, tying a knot between each measure saying:

> *Gone are my dimensions!*
>
> *I understand that only by passing through the Doorway, into*
> *the Great Unknown, can I attain the next Cycle!*

CANDIDATE—Knocks three times, saying:

> *I knock at the Door to show my intentions to become an Initiate.*
> *I have prepared properly for this assay, I have studied and*
> *learned and accomplished. I come to claim that which is mine.*
>
> *I understand that if I be not truly prepared for this assay, I have*
> *only myself to blame, and may be caught between the worlds,*
> *unable to return to the world of men as they were, and unable*
> *to advance to the world of the Gods. I know, that in magick, to*
> *claim that which is not mine is to bar my attainment of it.*

FIRST DEGREE SOLO INITIATION RITUAL continued...

> *I who stand on the threshold between the pleasant world of*
> *men and the dread domains of the Gods, for the last time I*
> *state that I have the courage to make the assay.*

Working

CANDIDATE—Walk once around the Circle, deosil, return to the center of the Circle, face East, and say:

> *Single is the race, single of men and Gods. From a single*
> *source we both draw breath, but a difference of power in*
> *everything keeps us apart. Yet in the greatness of minds, we*
> *can be like the Gods.*

> *Though I know not what goal, by day or in night; the fates*
> *have written that I shall run beyond all seas and earth's last*
> *boundaries, beyond the spring of night and the heavens vast*
> *expanse, where lies a majesty which is the domain of the Gods.*

> *I would pass through the gates of night and day, into that*
> *sweet place which is between the worlds of men and the*
> *domain of the Gods. I know that unless there is truth in my*
> *heart, then every effort is doomed to failure.*

> *I make my oath to the Gods:*

> *I shall love all things in nature,*
> *I shall suffer no innocent to be harmed by my hand or in my*
> *mind.*
> *I shall walk in the way of the Gods,*
> *I shall learn contentment through suffering, from long years,*
> *and from nobility of mind and purpose.*

> *And if among the vulgar, some discoveries should arise con-*
> *cerning some maxims of my beliefs in the Gods, for the most*
> *part I shall keep silent. And when someone shall say to me:*
> *"Thou knowest not," and it bites me not, then have I truly*
> *begun the work. I shall not display the maxims to the vulgar,*

FIRST DEGREE SOLO INITIATION RITUAL continued...

> *but rather the works which flow when they are absorbed and*
> *understood.*

> *My Craft name shall be <say your Craft name>!*

CANDIDATE—Next move to each quarter in turn, saying:

> *Take heed, O Mighty Ones of the <direction>, creatures of <ele-*
> *ment>, that I, <Craft name>, properly prepared, will be made*
> *Priest/ess and Witch!*

CANDIDATE—Return to center of your Circle and kneel. Ring your bell eleven times and then stand in center of your Circle and say:

> *In other religions, the postulant kneels as the Priest/ess claims*
> *supreme power. But in the Craft we are taught otherwise.*

> *Blessed be my feet, that have brought me in these ways.*
> *Blessed be my knees, that shall kneel at the sacred altar.*
> *Blessed be my (loins/womb), from which springs forth life.*
> *Blessed be my breast, formed in (strength/beauty).*
> *Blessed be my lips, that shall utter the sacred names.*

> *I present my Book of Shadows as proof of my studies and*
> *accomplishments. I swear I shall safeguard the knowledge You*
> *have given to me, and shall not share it with any save those*
> *who are ready and able to use it in a manner that shall be*
> *proper and safe.*

> *I swear that I shall always be true to the Craft.*

> *I am always ready to help, protect, and defend my brothers and*
> *sisters of the Craft, whoever they may be.*

> *I swear I shall keep secret the names of any brothers and sisters*
> *in the Craft, the location of any covenstead, and the items of*
> *business communicated within the Circle.*

> *I shall serve the Wicca and the Gods always with honor, I shall*
> *work in peace and trust with any brothers and sisters in the*

FIRST DEGREE SOLO INITIATION RITUAL continued...

> *Craft; and if I feel out of harmony with any, I shall withdraw,*
> *but still keep my oath.*

CANDIDATE—Give any personal oath. Then consecrate yourself by anointing your forehead, lips, and heart with each of the following elements, saying:

> (Salt and water) *I consecrate myself with water and earth,*
> *that I may be pure in my workings with the Craft.*

> (Incense) *I consecrate myself with fire and air, that I may be*
> *fervent in my workings with the Craft.*

> (Oil) *I consecrate myself with oil to anoint myself into the*
> *service of the Craft.*

> (Wine from your chalice) *I consecrate myself with wine, that*
> *I may be steadfast toward the Craft.*

> *I swear with my lips, that I may give in love and truth to the*
> *Craft.*

> *To obtain magickal power, I must learn to control fixed*
> *thought. I shall admit only ideas which are in harmony with*
> *the end desired. Fixed thought is a means to an end. I shall*
> *pay attention to the power of silent thought and meditation.*
> *The material act is but the outward expression of thought.*
> *Thought is therefore the commencement of action. If a chance*
> *thought can produce the effect of action, what cannot the fixed*
> *thought produce.*

> *I shall establish myself firmly in the equilibrium of forces, in*
> *the center of the cross of the elements. I shall learn both the*
> *power of thought and the power of restraint, and control my*
> *thoughts and actions.*

> *I now claim the working tools of the Witch.*

CANDIDATE—Reclaim and re-garb yourself with your robes, cords, wand, athame, chalice, and

FIRST DEGREE SOLO INITIATION RITUAL continued...

pentacle, etc., briefly going over in your mind what they are for. Once you are fully dressed and ready to continue, say:

> *I honor the Lady and Lord with the names <insert your*
> *favorite Deities' names>. I write my magickal name on my*
> *breast, to engrave it into my heart forever.* (Write your new
> Craft name over your heart in wine from the chalice.)

> *In true religion, there is no sect. I shall not blaspheme the name*
> *by which another knoweth their Gods. A little knowledge can-*
> *not give me mortal authority. It is through discipline and suf-*
> *fering that the soul is purified.*

CANDIDATE—Cleanse and anoint your candle, carve a pentagram in it, then light it from one of the altar candles, saying:

> *This lighted candle symbolizes the divine light that is within*
> *me. I shall nurture that light within, and protect it as I must*
> *protect the candle flame from passing drafts. I reaffirm all I*
> *have sworn this day, and may the Gods do with me as they*
> *will should I break my oaths. So Mote It Be!*

CANDIDATE—Re-consecrate any or all of your tools, as you feel appropriate.

Close

CANDIDATE—Perform the Great Rite. Ground the chalice. Now stand in center of your Circle, turn to face each quarter in turn, and declare:

> *Hear ye O Mighty Ones of the <direction>, creatures of <ele-*
> *ment>, that I <Craft Name>, have been consecrated a*
> *Priest/ess of the Craft, and a (brother/sister) of the Wicca.*

INITIATE—Thank and dismiss the Lady and Lord, the quarters, and take down your Circle. Clean up. Relax and make merry.

RITES OF PASSAGE

*I*NITIATION IS ONLY ONE OF SEVERAL RITES OF passage Wiccans may experience in their lives. Below are descriptions of some of the important rites of passage celebrated by Wiccans. The rituals for these rites of passage are not carved in stone, but can be changed and modified to fit your specific purpose.

NAMING/WICCANING

When a child comes into the community, by birth, adoption, or fostering, that is a gift of the Goddess. After the family has settled down, the time comes to present the new child to their community. There is no specific rule as to when a Naming must be performed. Some wait a year or more. A Naming is not a sealing of the child into Wicca. Since Wiccans do not proselytize, Wicca is a religion that must be chosen freely, and most children are not equipped to freely choose their religion. A Naming introduces the child to the Gods and the community. It places all on notice that this child is precious and valued and should be cared for and watched over. The child is placed under the protection of the Gods and the Wiccan Community, in addition to

their parents and family. There is usually a party and possibly gift giving afterward. This ritual should be relatively short and simple because few children will be still and/or quiet for a long drawn-out ritual. This is not an Initiation or even Dedication, so little strong energy should be raised. And non-Wiccan family members may attend.

This can be a wonderful introduction to Wicca for non-Wiccan friends and family, since through education fear and prejudice are dispelled. It is not an intense ritual with unfamiliar language and practices and illustrates how Wiccans love and value their children. And we also welcome others to see who we are and what we are about.

If outsiders are present, expect them to be nervous and uncomfortable. Reassure them that this is a ceremony to welcome the child into the family and community. Explain what the ritual consists of and what will happen. Explain there will be a sharing of wine and cakes, and if they feel uncomfortable or their beliefs forbid it, they will not be required to partake. Show them how to honor the cup (hold it and raise it up), if they choose to not partake. Make sure there is room for all, and perhaps seating as well. Try to have the non-Wiccans included in the group, not off to one side or apart. They should be a part of the Circle, and if they object to a magickal Circle, then perhaps they should leave. You do not want guests present who will be actively hostile to what you are doing. Emphasize this ritual is for the child, and to show love and support for the child and their family. Tell guests that this ritual is to allow family, friends, and community to welcome the child into their midst. Answer any questions patiently and cheerfully. This may be their first exposure to Wicca, and you want to make it a positive experience.

In planning this ritual, the presiding Priest or Priestess should meet with the family and get acquainted with the child. The family and the Priest or Priestess together should choose Deities who will watch over the child as they grow. These Deities should be oriented to children. Do research. If the parents have Deities, maybe those can be used, or others of the same pantheon. For example, Hecate is a Great Goddess, but a bit forbidding for a child. Try to obtain pictures or statues of the Deities. These will belong to the child, so they should be sturdy and not expensive. One family we know of keeps the Deity figures in the child's bedroom, so that when the "boogie man" comes, the Gods will protect the child from harm. And, it works. If you can get a stuffed toy or other familiar object to symbolize the Deity, that's good also. As the child grows, let them know those Deities are watching over the child and will protect them from harm.

The Priest or Priestess should prepare a short speech about each Deity for the child and participants. Sample speeches are included, but you should make your own to customize to the Deities chosen. The explanations and blessings should be written out and put in the script or on 3 x 5 cards.

One variation on this ritual was done for children who were adopted from a foreign country. The children started the ritual dressed in their native costume. Then during the ritual, they removed their native costume (down to their underwear) and re-robed in American clothing. These children were older, so they helped participate in choosing both costumes. It also helped illustrate their transition from their native country to becoming Americans, and allowing the children to participate in the planning helped increase their interest and involvement in the ritual.

You can also include blessings from the witnesses for the child. This should be only one short sentence. The blessings should begin with someone in the crowd who is prepared and can speak to give the non-Wiccans an idea of what to say. Blessings help include all participants in the ritual. But if there is a large crowd, this process can get long. If you explain before the ritual starts what will be expected, and provide a couple of sample blessings (for example, may this child grow in strength, health, and love; may this child be blessed with love and security; may this child be happy and well cared for), people will usually get the idea. The gifts (if any) should be left until after the ritual.

Another personal touch can be to include pictures of relatives who have died, but are still fondly remembered in the family. You can introduce the child to the relatives, and maybe say a phrase about each. Remind the child that these family members are also watching over the child.

The Circle is much simpler than the other Circles in this book. It is still effective, but shorter and less imposing than that of the more intense rituals. You are encouraged to substitute an athame or staff for the sword, and substitute your fingers for an athame in calling the quarters if you feel it would be better.

$\mathcal{N}$aming $\mathcal{R}$itual

Setup

ALTAR—Have salt/water, incense, presence and reading candles, oil, wine/cider. Have the statues or pictures of the chosen Deities arranged in a prominent place on the altar.

Ritual

HIGH PRIESTESS—Sweeps around the Circle deosil with the broom, outside the Circle of participants.

HIGH PRIEST—Draws the Circle with the sword, again moving deosil, outside the Circle of participants.

HIGH PRIESTESS—Aspurge Circle with salt and water, while saying:

> *I cleanse this Circle with water and earth that all impurities be*
> *cast forth and all goodness enter within.*

HIGH PRIEST—Censes the Circle with incense, while saying:

> *I cleanse this Circle with fire and air that no evil may defile*
> *this Circle, and that you may protect this Circle with love.*

OFFICIANT—Calls the quarters by saying:

> *Guardians of the Watchtowers of the <direction>, creatures of*
> *<element>, I welcome you to our Circle. We ask that you wit-*
> *ness this rite, and guard this Circle and all within. Hail and*
> *Welcome!* (The response *Hail and Welcome* from others is
> optional).

HIGH PRIEST—Makes a pass around the Circle with the wand, stirring the paint and sealing the Circle.

Both the High Priestess and High Priest now declare:

> *The Circle is cast. We are in a time which is no longer a time,*
> *in a place which is no longer a place, for we are between the*
> *worlds and beyond. May the Gods protect us on our magical*
> *journey. So Mote it Be!* (The response *So Mote it Be* by par-
> ticipants is optional.)

NAMING RITUAL continued...

Once the Circle is cast, bring the child into the Circle with parent(s).

OFFICIANT—Welcomes the child into the Circle by saying:

> *We are here to welcome <child's name> into our community*
> *and ask the Gods' protection and blessing for him/her as he/she*
> *grows up among us.*

OFFICIANT—Greets the child. Then blesses and purifies the child with salt and water, incense, oil, and wine, by anointing the child's brow, hands, and feet.

Then guides or carries the child to each quarter and introduces the child to each quarter, and says:

> *Guardians of the Watchtowers of the <direction>, creatures of*
> *<element>, I <your name> Priest/ess and Witch do bring before*
> *you <child's name>, son/daughter of <parents' names>.*
> *<Additionally include Grandparents, Uncles, Aunts etc., if*
> *appropriate> Know that he/she is come under our guidance and*
> *protection, and we ask you add your protection to ours, so he/she*
> *may grow and thrive in his/her life here with his/her family,*
> *friends, and community. So Mote it Be. (All respond So Mote*
> *it Be.)*

OFFICIANT—Tell stories about the chosen Gods—for example, Ana, Dagda, Brigit, and Cernunnos. Officiant also shows the child the statues and/or pictures of chosen Deities with each story. (These are just examples; you can choose whichever Gods you and the parents feel are appropriate.)

> *Ana is the Great Mother, Mother of Ireland, nourisher of the*
> *Tuatha Dé Dannan. Her name means wealth and abundance.*

> *Dagda is the "Good God" of the Celts. He is Father of all, the*
> *lord of great knowledge. He is owner of the great cauldron of*
> *abundance, with which none shall go hungry.*

> *Brigit, whose name means the exalted one, is the daughter of*
> *Dagda. She is Goddess of the hearth, fire, smithy, fertility, cat-*
> *tle, crops, and poetry. She is a mother and grandmother.*

> *Cernunnos is the horned God, Lord of nature, animals, fruit,*
> *grass, and prosperity.*

NAMING RITUAL continued...

OFFICIANT—Brings blessing of the Gods onto the child by saying:

> *We call upon the Great Mother Ana to watch over this child, and*
> *bring her blessings upon <name> that he/she may grow, thrive,*
> *and prosper. Nourish this child that he/she may grow strong and*
> *healthy. Care for this child and protect him/her from harm.*
>
> *We call upon Dagda, the Father of All, to watch over this child*
> *and keep him/her safe from harm, from within and without.*
> *Grant <name> peace and plenty. Let Dagda fill this child with*
> *a love of knowledge and learning. Let this child be fed from*
> *Dagda's cauldron of plenty.*
>
> *We call upon Brigit, the exalted one, to watch over this child.*
> *Gift <name> with your skills and love of work. Let this child*
> *learn to be clever and accomplished.*
>
> *We call upon Cernunnos, the horned God, to watch over this*
> *child and grant him/her strength, endurance, and perseverance.*
> *Let <name> come to love nature and animals as Cernunnos*
> *does. Grant <name> prosperity.*
>
> *Welcome to our community!* (All respond with *Welcome!*)

OFFICIANT—Then continues with:

> *May this child grow and prosper with his/her family. May you*
> *find love, acceptance, and nurturing for your life. May you take*
> *the best of all you encounter in your life and blend them so you*
> *may be a complete, fulfilled, happy person, prosperous and secure*
> *in your place in your family, your community, your country, and*
> *the world. In the name of the Gods, Ana, Dagda, Brigit, and*
> *Cernunnos, I call their blessings down upon <name>. So Mote*
> *it Be!* (And all respond with *So Mote it Be!*)

OPTIONAL The parent(s) take child and show them pictures of their ancestors and introduces
him/her to them.

NAMING RITUAL continued...

OFFICIANT—Then the Officiant guides or carries the child around the Circle, directing everyone to offer personal blessings by saying:

> *As a token of our love and commitment to see this child grow*
> *strong, healthy, caring, and wise, let us each give this child our*
> *personal blessing.*

OFFICIANT—Hands the child back to their parents.

HIGH PRIEST AND HIGH PRIESTESS—Perform Great Rite, while saying:

> *As the cup is the female, and the athame the male, together they*
> *are one, and the source of all life.*

HIGH PRIESTESS—Blesses the cakes, while saying:

> *May these cakes be blessed by the Gods that we may partake of*
> *their bounty.*

HIGH PRIESTESS—Passes around the wine and cakes (in this case, possibly fruit juice and cookies), letting all partake or just honor the cup as their beliefs dictate. After everyone has had a chance to partake of the wine and cakes, she finishes the wine and grounds the chalice on the pentacle.

HIGH PRIEST—Moves around the Circle with the wand, unsealing the Circle.

HIGH PRIESTESS—Dismisses the quarters by saying:

> *Guardians of the Watchtowers of the <direction>, creatures of*
> *<element>, we thank you for your presence at our Circle. May*
> *there be peace between us, now and always, and as you depart*
> *we bid you, Hail and Farewell!* (All respond with *Hail and*
> *Farewell!*)

HIGH PRIEST—Opens the Circle by walking widdershins with the sword, and grounding the energy, while saying:

> *The Circle is open yet unbroken. Merry meet, merry part, and*
> *merry meet again.*

CONGREGATION—Present and open their gifts to the child, feast, and celebrate.

COMING-OF-AGE (PUBERTY)

In ancient societies, puberty marked the time when a person moved from being considered a child to an adult. Sexual maturity was usually closely followed by parenthood. In modern society we have arbitrarily chosen eighteen years of age as the time of entering adulthood, and in most states, one may not legally drink alcohol or enter into certain legal agreements until the age of twenty-one. For some, the ability to drive a car at sixteen is emancipating and is almost the only overt symbol of adulthood in our prevailing culture. In Judaism, the Bar or Bat Mitzvah usually coincides with puberty. Since Wicca is an Earth- and fertility-centered religion, it makes sense to celebrate fertility and puberty. For girls the time is clearly demarked: at menarche, when a girl has her first menstrual period. For boys, the time is less clear. Some determine male puberty to begin when a boy starts displaying secondary sexual characteristics: deep voice, beard, body hair, thickening of the muscles, or from a boy's first nocturnal emission, also called a wet dream.

Puberty celebrations are by no means universal among Wiccans. There are still a lot of negative cultural connotations surrounding sexuality, puberty, body image, and functions. Women are often reluctant to mention when they are in their menses, having their period. Women are taught by some Christian denominations that menstruation and menstrual and birth pain are the curse of Eve or just the curse: God's punishment of all women for Eve's first transgression against God. Sexuality and sex are regulated by law and custom. Boys are taught that nocturnal emissions are caused by evil demons (succubi) who tempt a boy into impure ungodly thoughts. Masturbation is a taboo not to be talked about even though it is widely practiced.

Wiccans are trying to resurrect some of the older paradigms about sexuality and body functions.

Many Wiccans worship nude (termed skyclad). Some Wiccans go about skyclad at private festivals and gatherings as another clothing style option.

In prehistoric times it is surmised that menstruation was a major mystery. What bleeds but does not die? Females do. In a society where bleeding wounds could bring death, nearly half of the population bled regularly and suffered no apparent ill effects from it. And the timing of this cycle with the phases of the Moon was readily noted. Some Wiccans refer to menstruation as a woman's Moon time or Moon blood. Every woman contains within her all three phases of the Goddess: Maiden, Mother, and Crone. Each is associated with menstruation: Maiden by menarche, Mother by the cessation of menstruation, which accompanies pregnancy, and Crone who has ceased to menstruate and has experienced menopause. These three aspects are linked with fertility and childbearing.

All this makes a girl's first period a natural time of celebration. However, there are still problems. First, many feel no young person can reasonably be expected to make the major life choice of a religion at such a young age, and some females are starting to menstruate at the age of nine and earlier (attributed by some to the growth hormones currently in food). The average time of menarche is still around twelve, but that is considered still quite young and immature in our prevailing cultures. If a young woman chooses to be Wiccan, she still has to have the approval of her parents, because children are legally the responsibility of their parents until eighteen. Because of these constraints, the puberty celebration is for young women who are in a Wiccan household already.

Some people in the Craft are actively exploring resurrecting women's and men's mysteries. Since the Dianic movement, women's mysteries are pretty well established. Celebrating a young woman's first period is done more often, and not just in Wiccan and/or Dianic circles. The women's movement has resulted in women feeling better about themselves and their bodies. The gay men's movement has individuals actively exploring reclaiming men's mysteries. In some societies, men's mysteries were associated with hunting. Although some Wiccans actively hunt, many do not. Because of the mixed feelings about hunting and killing of animals in general (whether for food or other reasons), this is not necessarily popular. Some are substituting camping, woodlore, and survival skills for hunting. Others are consciously exploring male sexuality and role models as templates for Coming-of-Age rituals.

Whatever ceremony you create for a Coming-of-Age ritual, personal responsibility and personal pride should be strongly emphasized. Sexual maturity doesn't mean free license to have sex. In our modern society, irresponsible sex can kill. AIDS kills, but so can other sexually transmitted diseases. And some sexually transmitted diseases (STDs) that do not kill can be with us for life and require massive lifestyle changes; for example, herpes. In ancient times pregnancy was usually the penalty for irresponsible sex. Now it's pregnancy plus a whole bunch of STDs which range from merely annoying to lethal.

Teaching the young person about sex, sexuality, birth control, and personal responsibility is something which can either be a part of the Coming-of-Age ceremony or separate, but it should happen. Your family's personal values and beliefs will of course dictate what you will tell your young adult. Some Wiccan parents go so far as to take the young adult to a doctor for an adult checkup and also to obtain birth control. At least some education on the subject is in order, even if it's just don't do it until you are married.

Another touchy subject is personal pride and body image. The predominant culture creates an ideal body for males and females, which changes over time. Marilyn Monroe was considered a perfect female in her time, yet today she looks plump and out of shape. Johnny Weismuller looks a bit soft and pale. Today's fit and trim tanned athletic body will certainly give way to whatever is coming next. In Renaissance times, a plump, Rubenesque figure was considered sexually alluring. In ancient times, a fat person meant they were rich, and therefore desirable as a mate.

Body image causes much pain and anguish in modern society. Wiccans feel every body is beautiful. We are all Children of the Goddess, and She loves all her children. Our body also houses our soul, which is always beautiful. However, that does not eliminate the fact that many Americans are overweight, due primarily to living in a rich culture with many exciting food choices and not enough mandatory exercise.

Then there is the issue of body type. People come in all shapes, sizes, and colors. We can diet or work out or even have surgery to modify our bodies, but there is little a person can do if they're 6'7" and they want to be 5'10", or if their skin is very pale white and they would rather be black, brown, yellow, or red. The trick is to be content, and even happy, if possible, with what nature and your parents' genetics handed you. Make the most of what you do have, and don't waste time pining for what you don't or can't have. Even the beautiful people usually have insecure self-images. If you are content with your body, eat well, exercise regularly, and make the most of what you have, you are way ahead of ninety percent of the people in our culture, which breeds insecurity about body images through advertising and multimillion dollar industries that rely on creating needs to sell their products.

Wiccans in general try to be less susceptible to such messages and also try to focus their attention on personal awareness and personal responsibility.

All these issues unfortunately converge at puberty, which is a time of hormonal, body, and emotional changes, and a time of high stress. The new emotions and feelings and urges are so strong and powerful, it can be difficult to restrain yourself. Falling in love for the first time is special, and the emotions are so intense and real. Young adults are learning courtship, mating, and socialization rituals and behaviors. Life is hectic and full and add to that fads and cliques and boy- and girlfriends and all the rest, and it's a wonder any of us survive.

So Coming-of-Age is a time when all these changes occur. It peaks at about nineteen (or so), but never truly dies, for even after the hormones aren't flowing the socialization we learned is still operating powerfully. It is a time of celebration, but also sadness. Childhood is over, and it's time to start shouldering responsibilities in preparation for being independent and on our own. The Coming-of-Age ritual should incorporate some of the excitement of the new phase in life, but also emphasize the responsibility and choices, which come with growing maturity. Keep the scary speeches about sex, etc., for another time. They probably have already heard it anyhow. Be receptive and a good listener. Be available and a resource for accurate information. If you don't know, say so, and then go look it up together. Adolescence is the time when young people discover their parents aren't the infallible demi-Gods they appeared to be when they were children.

For the ritual, it's customary that only guests of the same sex be invited. This is a modern re-creation of women's and men's mysteries, and those were always same sex-only ceremonies. Children under five are usually considered to be unaware of sexual dynamics and therefore can attend no matter what

sex, if a parent cannot arrange for care. Have relatives come, if they are open and it's appropriate. Gifts are encouraged, but not big items. Or conversely, each person can contribute a small amount and pool the money for one big gift. This should be decided beforehand, possibly with the input of the young person. In some Wiccan families, this is when the young person gets their first proper athame, or all their ritual tools. Hopefully the gifts will include something lasting that will not wear out or be used up but be some sort of lifelong keepsake.

Maybe some new adult course of study can be undertaken. Estelle started learning astrology with her mother around menarche, and she is still practicing, learning, and studying. Most Wiccans find, looking back, that they started or did something around puberty, which had a profound and lasting impact or impression on their life. It's a magickal time, and therefore worthy of celebration. This is the time when young people begin their introduction to adult life and all the adult things that our society has to offer.

The ritual should not be planned like a surprise party. The young person should know what is coming and why, and be encouraged to help in the planning and preparation. Awareness is one lesson you are hoping to teach, and having a surprise party is sort of contrary to this message. Also, because of the body changes, it might take the young person a while to be comfortable with the whole idea of celebrating sexual changes, etc. Let them deal with some of it before putting them in the spotlight.

Make sure the family members of the other sex are out of the house and away for the duration of the ritual. For single parents with opposite sex children, this is when your brothers and sisters in the Craft can help. Hopefully the young person will be familiar with some adults of the opposite sex, and maybe someone will have taken them under their wing as a sort of adopted aunt or uncle. That person is the one who would hopefully take over and plan and execute the ritual for the young person, in consultation with the parent.

Keep it light and fun. A feast is certainly in order. Games or contests can also be fun.

Coming-of-Age Ritual

Below is a short outline of a Coming-of-Age ritual. We don't spell out everything for you here because we feel that would be unfair to the girl-woman or boy-man whose ritual this is to be. We don't know their family situation. We don't know who their friends are, who your friends are, or what is important to the girl-woman or boy-man. As an example, if the young person is a computer geek, a ritual based on camping might not work very well. Hopefully with the ideas we have discussed above, you should be able to fill out this outline and produce a satisfying ritual.

COMING-OF-AGE RITUAL

Setup

Prior to the ritual, discuss with the adolescent the significance of this ritual, going over with them the major points of what is going to happen. Allow them some input about what will be done. Also ask them to decide on some article from their childhood that they will symbolically give up, and also a suitable symbol to represent the entrance into adulthood (an athame, car keys, etc.) should be decided upon and prepared.

The High Priestess or High Priest (depending on the gender of the ritual's subject—this ritual is performed by an officiant of the same sex as the adolescent) will set up the altar, Circle, and Sacred Space as they deem appropriate. If the ritual is in a private temple in someone's home, there could be a full Ceremonial Circle cast. If, on the other hand, at least part of the ritual is being held in a public restaurant, or with a mixed Wiccan and non-Wiccan group, you might want to be more circumspect. This should be planned out with the parent, High Priest or Priestess, and adolescent beforehand.

Ritual

After all the planned preparations are made, and all guests are in their places, the Officiant announces the purpose of the ritual, and the significance of passing from childhood to adult responsibilities.

The Officiant introduces the adolescent to the group, asking if the adolescent understands the step they are about to take, and whether they are ready to take that step.

ADOLESCENT—Responds.

COMING-OF-AGE RITUAL continued...

OFFICIANT—Asks the adolescent if they have a symbol of the life they are leaving behind, HP/HPS receives the symbol from the adolescent, shows it to all the congregation (who are witnessing the change from childhood to adulthood), then places the symbol aside. This symbol may either be publicly destroyed, or placed away as a memory of the subject's childhood, either one will do as long as there is a conscious break with it acknowledged by the adolescent.

The Officiant describes some of the responsibilities and/or privileges that the adolescent will now be expected to shoulder, and asks the individual members of the group for any advice they have to give. This should be in the form of short sentences. You might start with someone who is well-versed in the ceremony, or give examples beforehand so the ritual does not drag on endlessly.

When this is done, the Officiant will invest the adolescent with whatever symbol of adulthood has been prepared. The new adult is then introduced to the group, and the party begins after the Circle is taken down.

HANDFASTING

Handfasting is the public joining together of a Wiccan couple. It differs from a wedding in some significant ways. It is usually not a legally recognized ceremony, does not require a state licensed minister or justice of the peace, and may be performed by any Wiccan Priestess or Priest. Also, because the government does not have a say in this ceremony, Handfastings can be held for relationships that are not considered legal, as between same-sex or multi-partner (three or four person, what is popularly called poly-amorous) relationships. It frequently has a built in and pre-agreed time limit, and is not considered "forever," unless those are the terms. A year-and-a-day is a common prearranged time for Handfastings. After this time, if the couple desires it, they can re-Handfast for the same or a longer period.

If a couple wishes to legally marry, there are a few Wiccan clergy around. Then the Handfasting can also be a legal marriage. Sometimes a couple will Handfast for a few years, and then decide to legally marry. There is little social stigma anymore with living together, so Handfasting without legal marriage can be a way to declare the partnership when moving in together for romantic reasons. People who intend to only share living space and be roommates shouldn't Handfast. Handfasting is for committed partnerships. A couple can also Handfast to each other privately, with or without a presiding Priest/ess.

The Handfasting is a religious ceremony, acknowledging the couple's commitment to each other before each other, their Gods, and anyone they want to invite. Marriage is a legal contract recognized by governments and other legal entities. You can have one, the other, or both.

The Horned God

HANDFASTING RITUAL

PARTICIPANTS—The Bride and the Groom.

WITNESSES—A friend of the Bride, of legal age, to back her up. A friend of the Groom, of legal age, to back him up.

OFFICIANT—The presiding Priest, Priestess, or Minister.

Setup (Previous to the Day of the Wedding)

The participants should write their vows to each other, and anything special they would like to have done or said during the ceremony. There should be a rehearsal with the all the participants and their family, possibly the weekend (or evening) before the ceremony. The rings (or some other token) that are going to be exchanged (if any), should be in each individual's possession for at least a week (i.e., the Groom will be carrying the ring he will be giving to the Bride, and vice versa).

Prepare the wedding cord, which is a two- to three-foot cord made out of ribbon or any other appropriate material to which the rings are tied. If the cord is intended to be passed around to the couple's friends and family for them to braid in good luck, then it should initially be three pieces, at least three feet long. Some traditional colors are red or white.

The Groom decides on and acquires the wedding cordial (the wedding cordial is any libation the couple chooses: alcoholic like wine, liquor, or beer, or nonalcoholic like cider or sparkling grape juice) and chalice.

The Bride decides on and acquires the wedding bread and basket.

Setup (The Day of the Wedding)

PARTICIPANTS—Spend some time alone to meditate on why and what they are about to do.

OFFICIANT—Sets up a standard ritual altar (whatever that is, on a small table). In addition there should be the following items available: a broom, a bell, the rings which have been tied into the wedding cord, the Bride's basket with the wedding bread, and the Groom's chalice with the wedding cordial.

OFFICIANT—Prepares and consecrates the Sacred Space.

WEDDING PARTY—Consists of the participants and the witnesses; all should be waiting off-stage for the Officiant to come and get them.

HANDFASTING RITUAL continued...

Site Preparation

OFFICIANT—Once the Sacred Space has been created, and all the guests have taken their places, the Officiant thanks the guests for attending and announces the start of the ceremony, emphasizing the start and other important places in the ceremony with the bell, then describes what the Sacred Space is and asks all attending to take a few moments to pray for whatever spiritual guidance they might want to be present.

Remember, there may be guests at this ceremony who do not understand what Wicca is, so if there are a significant number of non-Wiccans present, a question and answer session might be in order before or after the ceremony.

Processional

OFFICIANT—Summons the participants and witnesses, who have been waiting off-stage, to conduct them to the place of the wedding. (This is a good place to start any musical accompaniment.) The Officiant will challenge the participants for the first time when he greets the wedding party and asks if they are ready.

These challenges are similar to what is given in the Initiation ritual (see page 248). The first challenge should be given in private, to give an uncomfortable participant a chance to withdraw in private. The other two should be before the attending guests, so everyone may witness that both participants are entering into this union of their own free wills.

During the procession, the Officiant stops at the entrance to the Sacred Space, and issues the second challenge there, with the guests as witnesses.

The Ceremony (Introduction)

OFFICIANT—When the participants, witnesses, and the Officiant have taken their places at the altar, the Officiant will introduce the wedding party to the guests, and explain the purpose of the witnesses.

The Officiant announces the purpose of the ceremony, exhibits and explains the purpose of the wedding cord and passes it around the circle of guests for the immediate family to bless, explains the practice of "jumping the broom," discusses the meaning of the ritual, etc.

When the cord has been passed around, the Officiant retrieves it, asks a special blessing on it from the Gods (however best fits the audience and the preferences of the participants), and then issues the participants their third and final challenge.

HANDFASTING RITUAL continued...

Declarations

OFFICIANT—Asks the participants to declare their vows to each other and their community before these witnesses.

BRIDE—First declares her vows to her Groom while holding the wedding cord and rings.

GROOM—Then declares his vows to his Bride while holding the wedding cord and rings.

The Binding of the Marriage

OFFICIANT—Recovers the wedding cord and the rings. Unties the rings from the cord, and hands them to their respective participant.

PARTICIPANTS—Exchange their rings, possibly with one further promise to each other.

OFFICIANT—Binds the marriage by wrapping the participants' dominant forearms together with the wedding cord, tying a simple knot and handing each of them an end. The Officiant may discuss the concept of "Only if you both hang on, will the relationship remain intact, etc."

The Officiant blesses the wedding bread and cordial, and holds them out for the participants.

THE PARTICIPANTS—Feed each other some bread, and share some cordial using their weak hands. This not only symbolizes their nourishing each other, but also symbolizes, by using their free, generally weaker hands, that they will have to depend on each other to accomplish this task.

Solemnization of the Marriage

OFFICIANT—Now performs the "Sweeping Dervish" with the broom, a rite in which a circle is swept around the couple, symbolically sweeping all bad luck away from them.

Then the Officiant thanks the witnesses for their part in the wedding and hands them the broom to hold for the couple to jump. The couple will "jump the broom" with their hands tied and the Officiant may want to imply the possibility of the witnesses holding the broom unsteadily for dramatic effect.

Lastly the Officiant thanks the guests for attending.

PARTICIPANTS—"Jump the broom."

OFFICIANT—Will then cut the cord at its center, leaving the knot intact, declares the couple married, ends the ceremony, and closes down the Sacred Space.

Some Notes on Handfasting

Following are some ideas relating to various Handfasting and/or marriage traditions, some of which are mentioned in the above ritual that we feel are worth explaining in greater depth.

Exchanging rings, or some similar token, while considered to be an old tradition, is not as ancient as it appears. It has only been in the last few centuries that people in this culture could generally afford rings. To instruct couples to be joined to carry the ring that they will give their beloved, preferably on their person, possibly on a string around their neck, for at least a week before the ceremony, gives the rings a chance to attune to the giver, so that what they place on the finger of their beloved is really something that was theirs, and not something that was just bought at a store, with no connection to the person giving it.

Rings, though popular, are not the only tokens possible. We have seen bracelets, necklaces, even complementary tattoos. They are symbols of the couple's commitment to one another.

The mingling of blood (and joining of the hands that follows it) is not done very often anymore, but this is an old rite of physically joining two family lines together. Each person basically adopts the other partner into their own family. If you really want to perform a mingling of the blood, make sure that all possible safety measures are considered. Clean the site of the cuts with a sanitary alcohol scrub. Make sure you use sterile scalpels, etc., and that you have bandages ready. For this rite, the common place to make the incisions is the heel of the couple's strong hands, because they will be immediately joining hands, and you want to make sure that the cuts match, and, of course, you don't want to cut any tendons or major blood vessels. Remember, this is supposed to be a happy occasion, not a trial by combat.

The vows or oaths that the couple make to each other should be something that they have agreed upon together. It could and/or should include some of the terms of the Handfasting (if there is an understood time limit, whether they plan on spending every waking hour possible in each other's company, etc.), some type of statement of enduring love for each other, and the people and/or spiritual entities (i.e., God, etc.) that they wish to witness their vows to each other.

As examples of these types of oaths, we have included parts of Handfastings at which we have been Officiants. As you can see, there are quite a variety of oaths available, from the simple to sublime. And there are many books available on the market that will give you other ideas for vows.

Examples of Handfasting Oaths

Example 1

Bride and Groom together:

> *By the setting of the Sun,*
> *by the rising of the Moon,*
> *I, (X), take you, (Y), to my hand.*

Example 2

Officiant:

> *Speak now, (X) and (Y), before the Gods, your ancestors, and*
> *before this company of good friends and family, your vows of*
> *love and commitment to one another. And place upon your*
> *beloved's finger the ring that is the Circle of Eternity.*

Bride:

> *It is a wonder to find in this lifetime someone who completely*
> *understands you, and truly takes all of your goals and interests*
> *to heart.*

Groom:

> *It is a wonder to know someone who can look into your eyes*
> *and see your soul, delighting in the knowledge you are there.*

Bride:

> *It is wonderful to be completely happy, free of doubts, and cer-*
> *tain of someone's love.*

Bride and Groom together:

> *I (X/Y) question no part of your commitment, recognize no*
> *darkness we cannot vanquish with open hearts, and accept you*
> *as my partner above all others. I pledge before this company to*
> *love and cherish you forever as my (husband/wife) in acknowl-*
> *edgment of the miracle of us.*

HANDFASTING OATHS continued...

Example 3

Bride and groom together:

You cannot possess me for I belong to myself. But while we both wish it, I give you that which is mine to give.

You cannot command me for I am a free person. But I shall serve you in those ways you require and the apple will taste sweeter coming from my hand.

I pledge to you that yours will be the name I cry aloud in the night, and the eyes into which I smile in the morning.
I pledge to you the first bite from my meat and the first drink from my cup.
I pledge to you my living and my dying, each equally in your care.
I shall be a shield for your back, and you for mine. I shall not slander you, nor you me.
I shall honor you above all others, and when we quarrel, we shall do so in private and tell no strangers our grievances.

This is my wedding vow to you. This is the marriage of equals.

If blood is not your thing (see the discussion on mingling of blood on page 279), but you still want to bind the hands, you will need a cord at least two to three feet long. Have the couple join dominant hand to dominant hand—the ones they write with. Part of this tradition is not only symbolically joining two people together, but also to illustrate how dependent each will be on the other. Having one's dominant hand confined not only makes one do everything with the hand they don't use as much but as their partner moves, they commonly pull their partner slightly off balance. This reduces their self-confidence. In the above ceremony, each will have to feed their partner a piece of the bread, and hold the chalice for them to drink, not particularly difficult tasks, but still not practiced. Remember the couple is being watched by their family and friends and they will be very conscious of embarrassing themselves, which will add to the tension. They may also have to later "jump the broom" with their hands tied. This also reinforces the idea of them having to cooperate.

The wedding cord can be made of almost any colorful cord or ribbon. You can also attach flowers and other decorations, as long as you do not make the cord too stiff to tie a knot in it.

We "tie the knot" literally (does this saying give you an idea of how old this practice may be?) by having the couple join their strong hands at the forearms, then we wrap the cord around their hands two or three times, and tie a simple square knot. Or you might do some fancier knot if you want. Then one end of the cord is given to each partner to hold, with the admonition that only if they both hold on, will their relationship last. Then when you wish to release the couple at the end of the ceremony, we suggest that you cut the cord at the center. Do not untie the knot. The ribbon or cord which binds the hands should be preserved with the knot intact and kept preferably near the couple's bed. Unknotting the cord would symbolically undo the Handfasting (something that you perhaps might consider for a Handparting ritual).

The couple publicly "shares a plate and a cup," which, in several cultures, is the public announcement of a couple's union. In these cultures sharing a plate was all that was required to make a marriage. In the above ceremony, the Bride provides the bread (as a symbol of her skills as a homemaker) and the Groom provides the cup and the liquid (as a symbol of his abilities as a provider). We realize that these symbols may be too patriarchal for some people's tastes. This is why we are mentioning them, so you can change them to whatever you feel is appropriate. Whatever you do, because of the ancient lineage of the original traditional practice, you should consider having the couple feed each other. Further pledges between the Bride and Groom may be offered here, or the participants may offer their own toasts as well wishes for the happiness of the couple.

The kiss is another public acknowledgment of the marriage. In ancient Celtic culture, a practice called a "Shivaree" was conducted at this part of the ritual. This (depending on the individual group) could include physically putting the couple in bed and actually witnessing the consummation! But more commonly it is escorting the couple to the bridal chamber (or tent as the case may be) and serenading them with drunken songs for the rest of the night. And the rest of the ceremony then continues at dawn the next day.

While some version of the Shivaree has been conducted at Wiccan weddings, unless you prepare a proper physical environment (most commonly available only during a camping event), a public kiss should be adequate.

Bedecked with ribbons and flowers, the broom is first used to sweep away ill fortune around the newly handfasted couple to the four winds (this is the "Sweeping Dervish"). Then as a fertility charm (which, as most other traditional wedding practices, goes back to ancient times) the couple "jumps over the broom." Alternatives to the broom, also of ancient traditions, have been a sword, a candle, or small bonfire.

The couple jumps the broom with their strong hands still bound. This invokes a strong subconscious mutual interdependence. The Bride's Maid and Best Man hold the broom, to show the support of their friends. These acts, like the rest of the ceremony, may be changed as you feel appropriate. Maybe the couple's parents should hold the broom? Perhaps this part of the ceremony could be used to give an active part to any children from one or both of the couple's previous relationships.

The Great Rite is another symbolic sex act that can be used to both finish the ritual and close down the ritual. Grounding out any leftover energy is one thing that the Great Rite is traditionally used for. An additional use of the Great Rite, when you are joining a High Priestess with a High Priest, is to let them perform this rite to demonstrate their commitment as working partners, on top of their handfasting commitment.

One last comment, a Handfasting is usually designed for some specifically agreed time period. A year-and-a-day, for five years, for as long as our love will last, etc. If the couple getting handfasted starts talking in terms of forever (called Soulfasting), you may wish to seriously discuss whether this is what they really want and mean. Because if they vow that they will love each other forever, their vows will last that long whether their love does or not.

Vowing to love each other forever (or any other similar commitment) is not just a sweet romantic nothing. In a serious magickal ritual, it is a serious personal commitment. Instigating a karmic bond that can last well after the couple should have gone their own ways is not necessarily desirable. Sometimes the bond only needs to last seven years, or perhaps seven lifetimes. And vowing to love each other forever makes the bond that much harder to break, and adds possible additional karmic consequences. Be aware of the vows that the handfasting couple plan to make to each other. Incidentally, Wicca is not the only religion that believes in Soulfasting, also known as Celestial Marriage. Any couple attempting it should really know what they are doing.

HANDPARTING

In this age of divorce and multiple marriages, a Handparting can be as important as a Handfasting. Handfasting is not just a religious ceremony, it is also a magickal binding of two people to each other, for whatever span of time they have chosen. When the relationship ends, a magickal unbinding is in order, to help bring closure to the couple.

Sometimes, in the case of acrimonious divorce (or possibly also if the partner dies), it is not possible for both parties to be present at a Handparting. The ceremony should still be done with the one partner speaking their peace to the absent partner. This is a magickal severing of the ties that were magickally bound in the Handfasting. This ceremony is not a time for acrimony and recrimination. It is a sacred magickal act, telling the Gods, witnesses, and the former partners that they are no longer partners, that each has chosen to go their own separate way. No fault is assigned, no blame is laid. The rings may be removed, but each should retain their own.

If there are children involved, they may or may not be included in the ritual, according to age and as the parents wish. The parents may want to make a promise to the children that they will always be loved and cared for, that even though the parents are no longer married, the children will always be loved, cared for, and valued.

This is one ritual which probably does not end with a shared feast.

Some Notes on Handparting

The Handparting is performed backwards. Ill will is swept away from the couple, still joined by the knot; they jump the broom backward (a traditional action), and in the opposite direction; they then sever or untie the knot and part hands. The rings may be removed, though not exchanged. You might give each partner half of the severed wedding cord to do with as they will. Some will burn the cord to symbolize the end of the relationship. Some may save their half in remembrance of the relationship. What each partner does with their half is their business, and should be saved for a further private ceremony.

In the case of a Handparting with an absent partner, the absent partner's half cord could be sent to them, to symbolize that the Handparting was performed. If one partner is dead, their half cord could be buried with them, or kept as a keepsake of the relationship. Sometimes a stand-in for the absent partner can be used. Ideally this would be either the Bride's Maid or the Best Man who was present at the original Handfasting. Otherwise a High Priest or High Priestess could take the part.

When you perform a wedding, your responsibility does not end with the ceremony or reception. As Officiant, you are responsible for that couple's joining. Hopefully you are also able to help if the couple runs into trouble down the road, usually in the form of advice or counseling. Sometimes you can point the couple to other resources if your skills are not adequate to deal with whatever problem presents itself. And sometimes it comes in the form of being able and ready to perform a Handparting, if requested. You can't always keep track of the people you have married, but it is responsible to try your best. In performing the Handfasting, your energies are also bound up in the partnership.

ELDERING OR CRONING

Some Initiation rituals are performed by the Gods, some are performed in hopes of the Initiate growing into their new duties, and others are a public recognition of already reached achievements. Thus is the usual case with the Eldering or Croning ritual. This is a ceremony that is performed even less frequently than a Coming-of-Age ritual, as there are fewer older people in the Craft. Sometimes you hear of someone in their forties or even thirties being called an Elder or Crone, but technically an Elder is someone who is near retirement age, someone who has been around for a while and is no longer active, has a lot of life experience, ideas, and advice.

For women the traditional time of Croning is at menopause. This is generally around the age of fifty. Alternatively, you can time the Eldering ceremony with retirement, now sixty-five. If a person retires early, this might also be a good time for the Eldering ceremony.

In primitive societies, Elders were a community resource, valued and cared for. They had quite a bit of life experience, and had carried the memories passed down from other departed Elders. They may not have been as active in the hunting and gathering, but their accumulated knowledge, experience, and wisdom made up for their lessened productivity. The Elders also helped watch the young children when their parents were out working or getting food. The Elders were the storytellers and Priests and Priestesses. They also helped pass the tribe's history and lore on to the next generations. Their wisdom and experience helped guide parents and children into the life paths that were best for them and their tribe.

Unfortunately, today our culture is very youth-oriented. Age is seen as the enemy to be disguised, denied, and avoided at all cost. Old people are considered old-fashioned, resistant to change, and backward. Their skills and knowledge are outmoded because of technology, and they just aren't as valuable as new younger (and often cheaper) workers. All this contributes to the frightening statistic that approximately fifty percent of people who retire will have some major health crisis in the first year after retirement, often resulting in death.

In Wicca we are trying to reverse this appalling trend. First of all, because Wicca is a recreation of older pre-Christian traditions, we try to consciously value our Elders. Those Elders are also our magickal ancestors, and they were the ones who started this trend. If not for them, we would not be Wiccans. That they are still alive and available to tell the stories of the good old days is highly valued. They are repositories of living history.

Also, we practice certain skills and disciplines in Wicca that aren't mastered in a few weeks or months or even years. A person can literally devote their life to the study of magick, ritual, tarot, and other things, and still have new things to learn and discover. We try to actively encourage teaching and mentoring within Wicca, and other disciplines. Elders make natural teachers and mentors. And Wicca itself is still very much a growing, evolving movement. We try to honor our past, remember it, and use those lessons to build a better future. And our Elders have insights or ideas that are invaluable. Eldering can mark the time when a person gives up active leadership and gains a seat around the council fires.

The Eldering ritual is similar to a Naming and a Coming-of-Age. It isn't an intense ritual, it's more of a celebration and recognition of achievement. Non-Wiccans are also starting to celebrate this similar phase in life, at least among women. A retirement party, which celebrates leaving a job, profession, or career, is not an Eldering ritual. The Eldering celebrates your life and experiences, all of it, not only your job. It celebrates the possibilities of the rest of your life, and what you have accomplished which makes for the foundation of your future. Eldering celebrates what you now can do which you didn't have time, resources, or inclination to do before.

Eldering Ritual

Below is a very short outline, not because this ritual is unimportant, but because an Eldering ritual should be an individualized ritual, one that is constructed with the needs and practices of your individual community as the primary focus.

ELDERING RITUAL

Setup
The High Priestess or High Priest (depending on the gender of the ritual's subject, as this too can be a gender-specific ritual, like the Coming-of-Age ritual) will set up the altar, Circle, and Sacred Space as they deem appropriate. The future Elder might be waiting off-stage for a processional (similar to the Handfasting ritual). Presents from the community and some symbol of the Elder's status should be prepared beforehand. This could be a new robe, a staff, or possibly a medallion or coronet to be worn at ceremonial occasions. You could also have some permanent token that symbolizes wisdom and experience. You might solicit input from the Elder's friends, family, and community. Thought and love should guide your choice. You can choose a humorous gift, but also have a serious one as well. This is one ritual that *might* be performed as a surprise party. It all depends what is considered best for all the participants, the Officiants, and the subject.

Ritual
After all the planned preparations are made, and all guests are in their places:

OFFICIANT—Announces the purpose of the ritual, and the significance to the community of one of its members achieving Elder status.

ELDERING RITUAL continued...

The Officiant and a suitable delegation of the community leaves to escort the Elder into the Circle to a place of honor (either next to the altar or possibly to a prepared throne) and then introduces the pending Elder to the congregation, asking the Elder if she or he understands the step they are about to take and its implied responsibilities.

PENDING ELDER—Responds.

OFFICIANT—Asks the congregation if they understand the potential resource an Elder represents, and the implied privileges of this position in the community.

CONGREGATION—Respond.

OFFICIANT—Gives a short recitation of the Elder's achievements (prepared beforehand) and displays to the congregation, and invests the Elder with the symbol(s) of their new status.

CONGREGATION—Members of the congregation may now come forward and say whatever they feel appropriate.

OFFICIANT—When the congregation has finished speaking to the Elder, the Officiant should invite the newly recognized Elder to say whatever they feel appropriate. This should not be abbreviated. This is their moment. Let them enjoy it.

Then close down the Circle and celebrate.

DEATH RITES

Many books have been written about death and dying. In general our present day culture is uncomfortable dealing with these issues. Because of the youth-oriented nature of the culture, death is largely ignored or relegated to special industries, which take on the responsibility and get it done for us (usually at extravagant prices).

In Wicca, death is seen as a natural part of the life cycle. It is the other half of life. When Wiccans die, we are sad, we miss them, we weep and mourn. However, we also know that there is more to life than our physical existence on this Earth, and probably there will be other lives to come, certainly there have been other lives before this. Reincarnation is a part of Wiccan belief that is widely shared, although not universal. Most Wiccans believe the soul lives after death, and contact between the living and dead is an accepted principle.

In general Wiccans believe the soul goes to a place called the Summerlands, a pleasant place, and souls eventually return to Earth in another body to further their soul development.

The body is a vehicle for the soul, a container we use when on this Earth, and when we die, it is no longer needed. Special treatment of a body is considered illogical. Some Wiccans who are gardeners have expressed the wish to be composted, so they can help their gardens grow. This is, of course, not possible in modern society. Some Wiccans have become donors, so their organs and tissues can be used by others after their death. Many Wiccans feel cremation is a sensible balance between conservation of resources and disposal of the dead.

The modern funeral industry operates with mindsets that many Wiccans find uncomfortable. Filling the body with a toxic substance—embalming fluid—is not ecologically sound. Spending great amounts of money on a fancy casket that is airtight to delay return of the body to the Earth doesn't seem logical. Unfortunately, the funeral industry will not deviate from their standard embalming and funeral arrangements unless the relatives make a point of requesting something different. Many Wiccans have requested they be buried in the traditional pine box. This saves resources and money. Depending upon the municipality, Wiccans may or may not be able to forego embalming. Cremation is considered by many as the way to go.

There are few specifically Wiccan cemeteries. Most Wiccans were originally members of some other religion, and usually their families take over at death (unless their spouse or children are Wiccan) and they are buried in the religious tradition they were born into. Some Wiccans are not Out to their families, and this can extend to death and beyond.

Some Traditions mandate that a Wiccan's Book of Shadows, tools, and other Wiccan artifacts either be destroyed or disseminated among their coven after death. The lore has it that within twenty-four hours of a Wiccan's passing, there should be no evidence in their home or anywhere that he or she was a Wiccan. This lore probably comes from the Inquisition, and the fact that a witch could be tried after death and condemned to hell or their family could come under suspicion if it was discovered he or she was a witch. There was also real belief that witches could and did still operate after death, sometimes more powerfully than when they were alive.

Nowadays most of those superstitions are gone. But because of the secretive nature of Wicca and Wiccans, there are still customs that derive from the old days.

If a person was openly Wiccan, all the rites and funeral arrangements can be openly Wiccan if the family wants it. Most funeral directors will be accommodating of a family's wishes, as long as they are firm about what they want. There are Wiccan clergy, and any competent High Priest/ess should be able to perform some sort of funeral/memorial ritual/ceremony.

Because Wiccans consciously celebrate death and dying yearly, at Samhain, they probably have considered their own death, and at least expressed their wishes to their families and loved ones. If they are unusually foresighted, they have written down their wishes, so there is no ambiguity. But because Wiccans are also people and live in the real world, many aren't any better prepared than the rest of society for their death.

However death meets Wiccans, they will probably leave behind friends and loved ones in the Craft. Perhaps they were members of a coven. Maybe they were a member of a Wiccan organization or church. Funerals are not so much for the dead person, but for those who were left behind. A memorial service is designed to comfort, offer solace, and reassure loved ones, to confirm that although the deceased is not physically present, the person is still alive in our memories, and in the afterlife, however each may envision that. The service may also be the only time, other than weddings, when a family may come together and interact. And it may be the only time, outside of weddings, when the (birth) family meets and interacts with the friends of the deceased.

The ritual presented here can be used as a funeral service or as a memorial in a Craft-only setting. It can be adapted as you see fit. There are good Wiccan books available on the subject, so what is presented is an overview. There can be more than one memorial for a Wiccan. Their coven may want to do some private ceremony. Their larger Circle may want to gather and remember the Wiccan. If they are in a Wiccan organization, something may be planned there. Any or all of these may be in conjunction with the official public ceremony, or not.

If a Wiccan was not in a Tradition that mandates what is to be done at death, here are some possible guidelines.

The Wiccan's personal cords should either be buried with them, or burned. If the coven holds a separate cord, that cord should be treated similarly. No coven should keep the cord of a deceased member, for it may prevent the soul from moving on.

If there is a coven, the coven should have discussed the disposal of any collectively owned items.

The Wiccan's Book of Shadows should either be destroyed or stay within the Craft. If the Wiccan was not Out to their family, this is quite important, for it protects the Wiccan's privacy after death. Hopefully the Wiccan will have made arrangements beforehand. If the family moves in before this can happen, a small delegation might be in order to gently explain the situation and respectfully request the return of the Book of Shadows to the Craft.

The Wiccan's tools should be disposed of as they requested. There are several options: They can be destroyed or buried or dropped in a large body of water; they can be buried with the Wiccan; they can be passed on to family or friends in the Craft; they should *not* be sold or passed on to the public-at-large; they should *not* become museum pieces or objects of curiosity.

The Wiccan's robes and other paraphernalia, which are not specific magickal tools and the like, can be disposed of either by the Wiccan's wishes, a Craft giveaway, a Craft garage sale, or least desirable, given to the (non-Wiccan) family or sold at a non-Wiccan garage sale.

Books and other written materials (other than the Book of Shadows) can be disposed of as above, but as most books were bought commercially, there is less danger if they end up with non-Wiccans. A Craft sale is possible, and used bookstores usually welcome occult and metaphysical materials.

Any pets and/or familiars should be kept within the Craft if possible. Hopefully the Wiccan will have made arrangements. It is not uncommon for some familiars to pass on shortly before or after their Wiccan companion. Otherwise volunteers may approach the family, to assure that the Wiccan's pets/familiars find a good Craft home.

Other non-Wiccan possessions should be dealt with as law and custom provide. If the Wiccan left a will, they might have provided for a bequest to their church or local organization.

The ritual presented here is a straightforward memorial ritual. It probably will not differ from a standard memorial service except that a Circle is cast, and wine and cakes are shared. It can be altered or adapted as the family and circumstances dictate. If there are non-Craft people present, the Circle can be cast before the crowd arrives, and taken down after they leave, saving the wine and cakes for a private few just before the end.

You can include an inspirational reading if that seems appropriate.

Memorial Ritual

Materials

ALTAR—Set up as usual, plus a bell, box(es) of tissues.

MEMORIAL SHRINE—An extra table for the Memorial Shrine, set up in the northern quarter of the Circle, with a candle for the deceased. Possibly also memorial cards with the name of deceased, dates of birth and death, an inspirational saying or poem, a pretty picture. Something to personalize and take home as a memento.

Setup

AT ENTRANCE—There should be a guest book to sign and possibly also memorial cards. The body may or may not be on display. It should be near the Memorial Shrine, if possible. If there is no body, the Memorial Shrine is the substitute for the body. The Circle should include the body and shrine.

ALTAR—Set up as usual. Altar should be to the side—the focus is on the body and/or Memorial Shrine.

MEMORIAL SHRINE—Pictures and mementos of deceased on the Memorial Shrine table. No candles are lit yet.

Ritual Opening

HIGH PRIESTESS AND HIGH PRIEST—Cast Circle as usual, invoke the Goddess and God, etc. The Circle might be modified (i.e., no actual quarter tables or candles, more of a generic Circle, etc.) if non-Craft people are present. Use your judgment and have it planned out with the family (if present) beforehand.

HIGH PRIEST—Announces that this is a memorial rite for (name of deceased):

> *We are gathered to remember <name>, and pay our respects to*
> *<name>.* (Then rings bell three times).

HIGH PRIESTESS—Lights the candle(s) on the Memorial Shrine.

Working

HIGH PRIESTESS—Once the candle is lit and people are settled down, she thanks people for their presence, and says a few words about death and dying. She may or may not talk about the

MEMORIAL RITUAL continued...

Summerlands. She reminisces a bit about the deceased and invites the High Priest to reminisce. Then she invites members of group to reminisce. There should be some sort of talking stick that can be passed back and forth to signal who has the floor. Briefly explain how talking sticks work. Reminiscences should be short and sweet. People may cry. Have tissue available and pass it around as needed. Usually an hour is all most people will easily tolerate for the whole ritual. When the time is nearly up, the High Priestess should take the talking stick and invite the members of the congregation to share other stories after the ritual is over. Encourage the people to sign the guest book, and take home a memorial card.

HIGH PRIEST—Rings the bell three times.

Closing
HIGH PRIESTESS AND HIGH PRIEST—Perform the blessing of wine and cakes, i.e., the Great Rite. Share the wine and cakes around the Circle. You might want multiple chalices and plates if a there is a big crowd. Have the Handmaiden and Summoner help with the distribution. If it is a mixed Craft and mundane crowd, maybe Dixie cups are in order. Have a primary chalice for the High Priestess and High Priest, and pass the Dixie cups and cakes on trays after they have been blessed.

HIGH PRIESTESS—Grounds the energy out in the pentacle. Be extra sure to do a good solid grounding, for strong emotional energies have been called up.

HIGH PRIESTESS AND HIGH PRIEST—Thank and dismiss the Goddess and God and the elements. Close down the Circle. Let the candles burn out on the Memorial Shrine if possible. If not, the High Priestess or other close friends of the deceased should take the candles home to finish burning them.

CONGREGATION—Feast and visit. People should be encouraged to take the memorial cards with them. Clean up. Go home.

Burial Ritual

Cast a Circle around the gravesite. A small portable altar with very few tools might be the setup, no elaborate statues or candles.

The grave should be cleansed with salt and water, purified with incense, anointed and consecrated with oil and wine. The coffin can be cleansed, purified, and anointed as well. A short blessing should be said. People can leave flowers or tokens of remembrance.

The coffin is lowered, and the Circle taken down. The energy is grounded in the coffin and the earth. No wine and cakes, just take the Circle down and ground into the earth.

Alternatively, the Circle can go up before and be taken down after the people come and go. Then the cleansing, purifying, and anointing ceremony is performed along with the short blessing.

Tips, Techniques, and Ideas

In this chapter, we have collected a combination of topics that didn't fit anywhere else. We hope these tips will make things easier for you. Some of the topics are rarely discussed in other books. They were acquired through experience, and we hope you can benefit from our mistakes.

ALTARS

Some Traditions require that the altar be placed in the center of the Circle, some in the East or North. Usually the altar is placed by expediency, where it fits best. See what layout of your room or ritual space works best with what you have available. Don't be afraid to try different layouts. Do what works best for you.

What makes a good altar? There is no one answer to that question. One of the most useful items is an old dresser or cabinet. The top surface is usually at a convenient level for working. There are drawers and/or cabinets to put your tools in for storage between Workings. You can have your statues and the rest on the top as decorations or knick-knacks between Workings. You can keep your altar set up, if your living space allows. Of course you have to have room for a big piece of furniture.

Some people like to use a steamer trunk. These are large trunks that can be used for storage. They also can be used as the altar itself. You have to remove and replace your stuff each time you use it, but it has the advantage of doubling as a coffee table or it can be moved into a closet when not in active use, and you can store your tools, etc., inside.

Some people use a chessboard or other stone or wood item as their altar. This is smaller, and more portable. You also have less room for tools and other items. But placing the chessboard on another table provides an altar and more space for other items. If you want to get elaborate, some people carve a pentagram on the underside of the board, and then their pentacle is a part of the altar itself, and it can be easily camouflaged for those who are not Out. On one side it is a chessboard, and on the other an altar with the pentacle. Boards made of marble and alabaster can be easily carved with dental tools.

A pretty scarf or cloth can also be used as an altar, placed on another surface, or on the floor or ground. Ideally it should be made of silk, but any sturdy material will do. You can sew or decorate the cloth as you see fit, and when you are not performing Workings it can be folded and stored easily. You can also have an additional altar cloth on top of your regular altar, but the cloth alone can be a substitute.

A briefcase or old hard-sided suitcase is another variant on the steamer trunk. You can pack your tools inside, and if you pack carefully, you have a portable altar along with your traveling kit. You can use the closed case as the altar surface, perhaps with a cloth on top. This also stores easily in a closet or under the bed.

Storing your magickal tools is something each Wiccan should plan. It is easiest when you are planning a Working if you have all your stuff in one place. Some people have their tools in different places, but it makes it a bit of a hassle when planning a Working.

Modern storage containers are the Wiccan's friend, from small jars and Tupperware for herbs to larger plastic tubs for other items. We do not recommend that you use a plastic tub as an altar. Plastic is a manmade substance and not very magickal, and it does not conduct energy properly for use as an altar. Store your stuff in plastic, but use something more natural for an altar.

Some Wiccans like to use a flat rock for their altar. If you have one that is portable, well and good. Marble tabletops (especially when broken) are not uncommon and sometimes they are cheap. Stone tiles or flagstones are also usable. Portability and ease of use are the key here. You can make or get a "coffee table" with an elaborate stone top, which will be used as an altar. Marble can stain, so if you use red wine, be warned. Sometimes cemetery marker companies have sample slabs of granite and other decorative stones that are inexpensive. If one is too small, consider putting a few together for the altar surface.

If you have a plastic or Formica table, putting something on it that is more natural—wood, stone, cloth—can make it nicer for an altar.

TOOLS

Most Wiccans have a hard time finding their first tools. A good guideline is get the best you can afford. Some people get what they can afford at first, and then move up to something fancier or of better quality later on. The important thing is that the tool works well for you. It does no good to get the fanciest, flashiest biggest knife you can find, and then discover you cannot wield it safely without danger to yourself or others. Some people find a fancy decorated tool to be more satisfying and more effective for them. Some prefer a simple but elegant model. How the tool works for you, how it runs energy, and how it fits in with your style of ritual and magick should be the criteria for choosing a tool, not how expensive it is, or who made it, or who it will impress.

Size can be a factor. If you are a small person with small hands, you probably would not want to choose a sixteen-inch bowie knife for your athame, nor a large brandy snifter for your chalice. Make sure you can physically handle the tool comfortably and safely (especially the athame.) Some people have two sets of working tools, one of which is fancier and more elaborate, which are left at home. These are the main formal tools. The other set is generally smaller, lighter, more portable, and perhaps less valuable. These are the tools which are used elsewhere, carried and stored in a bag. Most Wiccans, if they work outdoors or outside their home, have some sort of traveling altar kit which is packed and ready to go as needed. Athletic bags work well for this purpose, will have room for robes, and are inconspicuous.

Some Traditions mandate that all tools should

be hand-made, even the athame. This is not as impossible as it sounds. Several businesses have knife-making kits or supplies. You can get a blade, and custom fit a handle, pommel, and the rest. Then you polish and finish it. Making your own tools gets you better tools for the money, and you have put your own personal energy into the tool as you construct it. A hand-made tool, though possibly less elegant or fancy than a professionally made one, can be more comfortable and effective, simply because you made it yourself. Some of the old grimoires have elaborate instructions for making tools. Some of the old instructions for making athames begin with: "Take a suitably sized piece of meteoric iron, and forge it into a blade." Few people have the facilities, skills, or patience to do that, let alone access to a big enough iron meteorite. But starting with a good kit, and customizing, can give you a very nice looking well-made personalized blade.

Many people just don't have the time or skills to make their own tools. Where can a person go to buy their magickal tools? Until someone establishes Diagon's Alley, the magickal shopping mall in the *Harry Potter* books, we have to be more creative. Most New Age, occult, metaphysical, or magickal bookstores sell some tools and items. There are many online stores that supply magickal needs; www.magusbooks.com is one. If you don't see what you want listed, sometimes an e-mail inquiry will produce results. Their e-mail address is store@magusbooks.com, and their toll-free number is 1-800-99MAGUS (1-800-996-2487). This is one store that the authors are personally familiar with. They provide good service and have a wide range of books and items. There are many other stores which sell occult, Wiccan, and magickal books and supplies.

Keep an open mind when looking for tools. The Museum Store, the Nature Conservancy, and other similar stores have items that can be used for magickal purposes. Garage sales are a boon to Wicca. If you go to enough of them, you can find literally anything eventually. Gun and antique shows are a good place to get knives and an amazing variety of other items. So are sporting goods stores. There are many catalogs that contain items that can be used magickally. Once you have a resource, keep track of it in your journal. Have one journal of resources, where you can get herbs, athames, incense, etc. Keep track of where and when you got certain items, and how much they cost. You might want to store those catalogs in your Book of Shadows.

Goddess and God images can be trickier. You can, if necessary, photocopy a picture and use that. Laminating the picture at one of the self-service copy stores makes it more durable. Keep your eyes open for small statues, figures, and the like. Sometimes if the Deity has a symbol associated with it, like Athena and the owl, you can get the symbol more easily than the Deity. Be creative, be open to ideas.

Few Wiccans start with a full set of tools, statues, etc. They get what they can when they can and improvise until they obtain what they need. For wooden items, a good ecologically compatible way to get what you want is to take wood from storm-downed trees, or use wood from trimmed or pruned trees. Try *not* to take wood from living trees in public places. Most urban trees are found in parks, and damaging public property is not the way to go for good karma.

For general supplies, be flexible and keep an open mind. Garage sales, flea markets, dollar and thrift stores all have things which can be used for rituals. Occasionally, if you need something for a specific ritual, try saying a prayer for finding what you need (need not want) or a short finding spell before going out shopping. And shopping with intent, going out with a specific goal (or goals) in mind, can work to your advantage. If one of your Deities is connected with commerce (like Hermes), then call on them for their guidance and help. And if you do find that bargain, don't forget to say thanks, either immediately or after you get home. The magick words please and thank you also work with the Gods.

SWORD AND ATHAME ETIQUETTE

Conscious care and handing of cutlery is important, so we have decided to discuss the sword and athame in fuller detail than the others. It is not that we consider any of the other tools (the wand, chalice, pentacle) any less important, but they are much less physically dangerous in the hands of an overly enthusiastic novice. Because we don't have the space to go into the differences between the athame and sword (this is the subject of a book in itself), we will discuss them together. There are significant differences, but as for as this book is concerned, don't worry about it. The following are some of our suggestions concerning the responsible use of blades.

The first, and most important thing one needs to know and understand about both the athame and sword is that they are primarily, and physically, weapons! They must be treated with the care and respect that weapons are due, at all times.

In some instances, Pagans, because they were uncomfortable with the concept of blades as weapons, use athames made out of "non-dangerous" materials. This is an extremely dangerous practice for two reasons. It allows the athame's bearer to become careless. Even if your athame is made out of a real feather, it can still hurt someone if you put it in their eye. It permits the athame's bearer to be lazy and slipshod with their magick. If you do not have

respect for your tool as the real physical object it is, how can you respect it as the symbolic ritual tool you will want to do magick with?

The potential problems of people unthinkingly waving around naked blades aside, we can think of very little that is more useless (not to mention unpredictable and potentially troublesome) than a careless, lazy, and slipshod magician.

You are responsible for knowing where the edge and point of your blade is at all times! We have seen some members of the Society for Creative Anachronism (a mediaeval/fantasy recreation group) cry "clear" as they pull a sword, and then expect all the passersby to get out of the way. If you carry a blade, you are responsible, because only you can control it.

Paul was at a Pagan festival some years ago. A martial artist was practicing with her sword in a location that she thought was totally isolated. Part way through a cut, a four-year-old child ran out of the bushes right at her, and the only reason the child merely received a creased nose instead of a split skull was because the martial artist was good enough to stop herself in mid-swing.

Take care of the blade. How much respect are you showing if you let your athame rust? Or if there is the sticky wine residue of who knows how many Great Rites left to accumulate on the blade? Again, if you do not care for and respect your ritual tools, any ritual tool, how can you expect to do magick that works? Magick, like many other endeavors, starts with respect, respect for yourself, respect for your tools and equipment, respect for your Working partners, and respect for your abilities. Without these, you might as well be playing monopoly.

Another point of etiquette to keep in mind is to never touch a blade with your fingers—not yours, not someone else's, not one you are considering buying. Your fingers have oil and residues on them, and these are transferred to the blade. We have seen many fine blades ruined with rusty fingerprints up and down the blade, because people unsheathed them and touched the blade, then sheathed it again without wiping it off or cleaning the blade before they sheathed it again. When looking at a blade, if it needs holding or support, rest it on your sleeve and examine it by turning it around as it rests gently on your arm.

If you want to protect your blade from moisture and casual handling, use Turtle Wax, the car wax polish. Just follow the directions on the container, and you can have blades which are fairly well protected from rust and casual handling. You still want to wipe it off after using it for the Great Rite. That's why the handy altar towel is there. You may need to re-wax your blade every year or so.

Choosing a Blade

How do you decide which blade is right for you? There is much more to a sword than looks, and this also applies to athames, despite their smaller size. Many of the knives and replica swords available today are basically poor-quality weapons. We have found that a true, high-quality weapon usually makes a better Working, ritual tool than something that is a flashy, chrome-plated display piece. Also, it is usually best if you can find something that you can physically handle. The heft, balance, and length are very important. You have to be able to move the thing about, usually in a limited space.

Heft is a property of weight. If the thing weighs ten pounds and you will have to hold it up through a five-minute calling of each quarter, you'd better start working out with weights right now. Pick a weapon that has enough size and weight to remind you that it is there, but not too much to make it a burden to use. It is more effective and impressive to be able to wield a smaller blade well.

Balance is a property of how the weight is distributed. Two blades might weigh the same, but one may be balanced more toward the tip, which will probably make it tougher to move easily and hold for long periods of time. We recommend that you try to find a sword that has its point of balance approximately a hand's span from the hilt. Most knives are balanced just in front of the guard.

We feel the best length for a ritual sword is a weapon approximately as long as your arm (between twenty-four and thirty inches for most people), or smaller. There are some possible occult reasons for this, which we haven't the space to delve into here. One practical reason, however, is that it will not be too long to easily move around in a ritual Circle. An athame should have a blade not much bigger than the span of your hand (between six and seven inches). A blade longer than that has the effect of a sword, not an athame. The size of the grip can also be important. Try to find one that feels comfortable in your hand, and if you plan on holding a sword out for any length of time—in dramatic ritual gestures—you may want to get one with a grip that is long enough to hold two-handed.

A blade made from finely tempered, high-carbon steel, with brass hand-guard and leather-wrapped grip, will probably make a better ritual tool than a piece of aluminum. Even if the steel blade is somewhat old and rusty, it will serve better than aluminum or even cheap stainless steel. Two rules of thumb Paul uses are as follows: "If you could use a blade for real, you can use it for ritual." And: "The better a blade would be for combat, the more effective it can be in ritual." In other words, the properties that would help a real weapon survive the stresses of live combat are the same ones that produce a tool that will conduct energy well.

The more aesthetically pleasing the blade, the more pleasing it is to your Conscious and Subconscious Minds, but sometimes people place too high a value on looks, to the detriment of heft, balance, and construction. There is a wide variety of flashy, fancy-bladed things, which are totally useless in the real world, and are just as useless in the magickal world. Gold plating or metallic, plastic-coated finish should be a secondary consideration to the quality of the blade, the heft, balance, the grip, and how useful it will be. A plain well-made blade, handled well, is far more impressive (and effective) than any of the "Conan the Barbarian" implements available.

Collector's value may be a consideration. There are many blades that have historical value, which can be used effectively in ritual. This will depend on your interests and pocketbook, for you may pay more for a good collector's blade than you will for a mass-market commercially made item. Having an historical blade with a legitimate provenance can add to the mystique surrounding your ritual sword or athame. One such historical weapon, currently being used in ceremonies by a group of Native Americans of Paul's acquaintance, was taken from a cavalry trooper of General Custer and was used in the massacre at the Battle of Greasy Grass (more commonly called the Battle of the Little Big Horn).

You have to heft and hold a lot of blades to appreciate the wide range of possible ritual tools available. We suggest that you visit a few shows or conventions and hold as many knives and swords as you can, always asking permission first. Once you have held a few, you will have a better understanding of what might or might not work for you. Rarely does a person find the perfect blade the first time out. Be prepared to be patient and you should eventually get what you want.

Sheaths

Some people might feel that the sort of covering you use for your athames or swords is a side issue, but as the Japanese have been known to say, "Only the very poorest swords are kept without a scabbard." The kind of sheath you choose is important for reasons of safety and respect.

For those who may be confused by the terms "sheath" and "scabbard," a sheath is commonly made out of leather and is somewhat flexible, and a scabbard is usually rigid, generally made with a core of either wood or metal.

Whatever name one calls a sheath, or what it may be made of, is really not too important. What *is* important is that you have one, even if you have to make one using cardboard and duct tape. One of Paul's Living Swords is kept in such a cardboard and tape scabbard. To not use a scabbard indicates a lack of respect in the blade's user for their tools. For both an athame or sword, a sheath has several practical uses. It protects the blade from accidental damage, it protects you (and other people) from the edge, and it allows you to conveniently carry your blade on your person.

The sheath also has magickal uses because it helps shield the blade from unwanted psychic influences and can appear to "put the blade to sleep" (as one Tradition puts it) when you do not need it. This sleeping mode can be very important if you happen to have a weapon with a strong personality or soul. There are times when you don't want a demon (if you are using one of the legendary bad blades that likes hurting people) loose in your Circle. On the other hand, unsheathing (or unleashing) a demon at an appropriate point in a ritual can be very effective.

Legal Considerations

In some legal jurisdictions a magickal sword or athame may be considered an assault weapon.

While it is generally legal to use an athame or sword at legitimate religious functions, some police departments will arrest you for openly displaying or wearing one of these tools while traveling to or from the ritual site. They can also arrest you for carrying a concealed weapon, if you try to hide it, for instance, in the folds of your clothing or a pocket.

To combat this problem, not only sheathe your blade, but place it in an additional, separately closed case, and then carry the case in a way that makes it difficult to immediately access (like a car's trunk). If you are walking to the ritual site, wrap your sheathed blade in your robes, then place them in the bottom of a backpack (with everything else packed on top), then close the pack and wear it strapped to your back (the longer the blade, the larger the pack). An alternative is to carry the blade in a locked case. Musical instrument cases are ideal for this purpose, and many swords will easily fit into the average trombone or guitar case. A standard suitcase can also be used, and many sword collectors and dealers have been using hard-sided, locking gun cases for years.

It is better to err on the side of legality and caution than to be loud and proud about asserting your rights under the First Amendment. The law does not allow for religious exercise if it can be proven to be harmful to the society at large, and many communities feel carrying around concealed or edged weapons is harmful, no matter what the intended purpose. Usually one can work around or with the regulations and still have a usable magickal tool. So remember, each tool is but an extension of the magician's energies, it does not create the energy itself. You should be able to make do with what you are allowed, which is one real-world test of a magician's effectiveness.

Where Can One Find a Good Blade?

If you decide that a good-quality blade is for you, you should make your selection carefully. Some people wait for years before they find their sword or athame. Others just buy whatever they find without really evaluating the possible options. One problem in finding an ideal working sword is that they are not a commonly available item, and no matter where you get them, a good sword will likely be a major purchase. There are several places where a person can expect to find a selection of blades.

The first is a gun show. Most moderate-sized gun shows often have a truly impressive variety of handmade items, and will usually have various kinds of knives, plus a sword or two for sale. Gun shows can be ideal places to see and hold swords and knives (athames), in addition to buying them. If nothing else, you can ask the various dealers and collectors about the weapons they carry. Most will be happy to discuss the attributes of edged weapons with potential customers and fellow collectors. This is one of the best ways to educate yourself about the idiosyncrasies and qualities of various types of edged weapons.

There are a number of custom blade workers in the United States, and if you are in the market for a special blade, personalized just for you, a gun show, Renaissance or Pagan festival, or various addresses on the Internet are places to hook up with the people who can make it for you. Be prepared to wait and be patient, for custom work can take a long time. And it will be expensive, but you will probably get quality far beyond the average mass market sword or knife.

A third way to buy a blade is from a mail-order catalog specializing in edged weapons. Two of the best companies are Museum Replicas and Arms & Armor Inc. Museum Replicas is one of the largest of these mail-order companies, and carries some of the finest quality reproduction bladed weapons available in today's market. They can be reached at:

Museum Replicas Limited
Box 840
Conyers, Georgia 30012-0840
1-800-883-8838
www.museumreplicas.com

Another company that carries quality reproduction swords is Arms & Armor Inc. They can be reached at:

Arms & Armor Inc.
1101 Stinson Blvd.
Minneapolis, Minnesota 55413
1-800-745-7345

A third company which deals through a mail-order catalog is W. Fagan & Co. They deal in quality antique items. If they sell a reproduction, it is usually a one-hundred-year-old copy of a much older item. They deal in many, sometimes very old, antique collections, with items from all over the world. And while they may be considered expensive by some people, where else might you find an authentic Egyptian necklace, Roman spear head, or a Yoruban ceremonial mask, with authentication papers dating to 1862? There is the possibility that you might acquire something that you might be psychically uncomfortable with, but in this case: "You pays your money, and you takes your chances." You can contact them at:

W. Fagan & Co.
22952 Fifteen Mile Road, Suite B
Mount Clems, Michigan 48043
(313) 465-4637

The drawback to buying from a catalog is that the item may look great in the picture, but you cannot feel or hold it to see if it's right for you. Check with the firm's return and/or exchange policies before buying. Minimally you will have to pay shipping both ways. But most reputable companies will work with customers until they are satisfied. And if your purchase arrives damaged or defective, you usually can work out a refund or exchange with either the company or the shipping agent. Be sure to keep all documentation and paperwork. You might also write down when you ordered, who you spoke to, what you ordered, and what things they told you about the item or policies, etc. Having a paper trail helps immeasurably in getting satisfaction.

Other venues for buying blades are various conventions around the country, whether they are science fiction, Pagan, Renaissance, or re-creationist in focus. Most conventions have dealers who sell some sort of knives and/or swords. These are often the same ones you can get from a catalog, but you can hold them and feel the balance. You might also get to see some special items that are kept for the special customers. There are also a number of custom blade makers who sell at conventions; their work is quite nice and they can customize for your personal needs and tastes.

There are other places you can get swords and knives, and other items usable as magickal tools. Antique shops, flea markets, and garage sales are all possible places, but you have to know what you want because many times the people selling the items know little or nothing about them. Also the prices can range from wonderful bargains to exorbitant, depending on the knowledge and expertise of the seller. The Cutlery, and other chain stores that sell knives in malls, do carry a few swords. You can ask if their selection is not to your liking. The prices tend to be higher than the catalogs, and the quality of the blades they offer tends to be on the poor to fair side. Import shops, especially ones that specialize in things from India, often carry swords, but most tend to be poor quality. Some occult shops also carry swords and/or athames, and you might be able to see a catalog and choose from a wider selection. Gun stores may carry knives, but few carry swords. Pawn shops might have the odd sword or two, but it's strictly buyer beware. Again, prices can range from cheap to ridiculous depending on the knowledge of the seller.

PRACTICAL IDEAS FOR CIRCLES

Whenever you have candles or open flame present, you should also have some method to extinguish the flames should a mishap occur. Home fire extinguishers are relatively cheap and can be unobtrusively placed. Alternatively, you can substitute non-flammable light sources for candles, if conditions do not permit open flame. Using small hurricane lamps can also minimize the fire risk.

Have some light source available for reading scripts, notecards, etc. If it is a candle, make sure there is some holder that will catch the wax so it does not drip on people, rugs, floor, tools, etc. If it is a flashlight, make it small and make sure it works before you start. Do not count upon ambient lighting to be enough to read by, especially if it's just a few candles. Let people use their glasses if necessary. Don't write in red or other colored ink; use plain black on white. Use a computer to print out large-type versions of speeches or the entire ritual, if it will make things easier. If you memorize, always have a backup script handy. Have the Handmaiden be the light carrier and script holder, or designate another person for that task.

If the ritual is long, and the officiants few, allow congregants to sit during parts of the ritual. Be aware of the physical limitations of congregants and officiants. If someone cannot stand for long periods, have a chair available.

Test all oils, incenses, and smudges with every-one in your group for possible allergic reactions. When in doubt, don't use it, find a hypoallergenic substitute. Almond or olive oils are generally good to try with allergic people. Try switching brands of incense, if someone reacts. Most incenses from India are not as pure as those made in the United States. You could alternatively light the incense for a short time, and put it out when you don't actively need it anymore. Beeswax candles seem to create fewer allergic reactions than standard paraffin ones. Candles with no dyes or perfumes are the best for sensitive people. To make sure the candles are placed in the correct locations in your Circle, tie a ribbon of the appropriate color, or put it in or on a colored holder to designate the quarter.

Plan the Working to fit the area available. It does no good to have the High Priestess be carried in on a sedan chair if you have a ten- by twelve-foot room to work in. Realize a lot of people in a tight place with candles burning will get hot and close. Have a fan available or window open if fresh air is needed. Have a chair for people who feel faint. Don't plan a long complicated Working in a close hot room.

Make sure people dress appropriately if the ritual is held outdoors. Have alternative plans if the weather turns bad. If you are outdoors, having a few designated people who act as Tylers, to keep outsiders away from the Working, may be appropriate. This is not like a palace guard, but more like a lookout. They can gently let outsiders know a private celebration is taking place, and when it might end. If there is another way to go around, they might guide the outsiders. If not they can inform the coven so things can be hidden or suspended for the time the outsiders are present. If you are outdoors, in a public park, get all appropriate permits, know and follow the rules, and clean up after yourselves. If you are outdoors on private property, make sure you will not be disturbed and you have the permission of the owners. If you are outdoors on public unowned land, do not assume you are okay. Some jurisdictions claim all unowned land for themselves, and any trespass is illegal. There are unfortunately few wide unclaimed spaces anymore. If you suspect the police might patrol, call them first and let them know you will be holding a religious celebration, and what it will consist of. If that makes you uncomfortable, stay indoors at home.

It is wise to ascertain beforehand if there are any food/beverage allergies/problems. If anyone cannot or does not wish to drink alcohol, either provide a nonalcoholic substitute (two chalices can be passed), or allow for a way to honor the cup which does not involve imbibing alcohol. Minors may partake of alcohol in a religious setting if their parents are present and consent. This means a small sip from a chalice, not indiscriminate drinking. Mixing alcohol half-and-half with water makes it easier for minors to handle, cuts the taste of cheap, rough wines and can make the wine go farther. It is an ancient practice. If a person has a cold or other communicable disease, either provide them a separate chalice (or paper cup), or just have them honor the cup and do not drink. The Gods do not want us to share diseases. Nor will the Gods magickally protect us from any diseases just because we are in a religious setting.

Keep a towel (more aesthetic than a roll of paper towels and more environmentally friendly) on or near the altar to wipe up spills, etc. This can be something like a kitchen or hand towel, not as large as a bath towel.

Use 3 x 5 cards to write your notes for rituals and Sabbats. Always have a written script available, even if you have memorized text, because there are times when people freeze and blank and cannot even remember their names. It's a good idea to have a designated script holder, a person who, in a large group ritual, holds the script for the High Priest and High Priestess so they can read, leaving their hands free. This person stands to the side and slightly behind whoever is reading, and holds the script at a comfortable reading distance for the reader.

When you print a script, using a computer, be generous with large type and bold lettering. We make spoken words large and bold so they can be easily read in less than full lighting (like candlelight). Also, it helps distinguish spoken words from text and stage directions, which are not meant to be read aloud. Have extra copies so you and others can have their own, for use and also for archive and their Book of Shadows. Those old rituals and Sabbats can be resources in the future. They also become a record of what you have done.

BOOK OF SHADOWS TIPS

What does a Book of Shadows contain? Ideally the Book of Shadows will have all the information you need to be Wiccan. Practically it will mean you have a standard Circle, rituals for consecration, blessing, healing, the Sabbats and Esbats, Dedication, Initiation, and other rites of passage. There should be some material on magick and spellwork. You should include some history of the Craft, what it means to be Wiccan, what Wicca is. This book is a good start for a Book of Shadows. It is not complete, and ideally no Book of Shadows is ever complete or finished, because you are always learning, growing, exploring.

Compiling your Book of Shadows is a never-ending process. The structure is what you choose to make it. Wiccans often have folders or notebooks with materials that are written or handed down, like photocopies or catalogs. Some people include books they have purchased in their personal Book of Shadows. Most have a personal library as an adjunct to the notes, handouts, and other materials they have collected. Ideally you will have several notebooks on various topics: one for readings, one for class or lecture notes, a dream journal, recipes, a timeline of what you have done, what Sabbats or festivals you attended, what magickal acts you performed, one for research, a personal journal of your thoughts and ideas about Wicca and magick. When one notebook is filled, it is filed for reference, and a new one is started.

Keep a running log of what you have done in the Craft, rituals and/or Sabbats you attended, festivals, classes, or workshops, etc. Also record your own Workings there, not in great detail but more like one-line explainers—did a reading about work—so you have some record. Keep this current; it's really easy to forget and things go by the wayside.

If you are totally computerized, back up everything on floppies. Have a file of floppies for old or outdated stuff, just so you can refer to them. If you upgrade with new software, convert old files to the new format at the upgrade. It's a pain, but you lose less data that way. Nothing is more frustrating than having a disk with good stuff you cannot access because you are one or two formats behind. We try to keep stuff in hard copy as well as on disk. It can kill trees, but paper is still one of the best permanent storage systems there is. You also have another copy, and you can photocopy if you want to share.

Look through your old notes and journals once in a while. This can be incorporated into a personal annual (or more often) ritual. Imbolc adapts well to that. Set aside time now and then to update and reshuffle your Book of Shadows.

Estelle has a cabinet of shadows. She has a catchall pile for the general stuff, and every few months when the pile is large, she sits down and sorts the catchall pile, files the materials into the specific folders, and maybe reviews and rearranges materials at that time. It's an evening's work, but it is pleasant and satisfying to see the Book of Shadows grow, and to review materials which have sat for a while. Old materials are good idea generators. It can be satisfying to see just how far you've come and just how much you've learned and absorbed, and you can be reminded of old projects which were abandoned or laid aside. This task is good for times when Mercury is retrograde, an astrological tip for those who are astrologically inclined.

Looking through your Book of Shadows should make you feel good. You have a tangible record of what you've done, where you've gone, and how much you know. That's a solid achievement. Be proud of it.

Be cautious about sharing your Book of Shadows with people other than covenmates or those you can trust implicitly. There is probably private stuff there (or should be if you journal properly) and you want to be circumspect about who sees that material. When you are oathbound, note so on the paper. You have the right to journal about your experiences and feelings, but if you swore an oath not to reveal it, then write that down. Don't expect to remember all that perfectly. When humanity converted to keeping written records, the techniques for rote memorization died slowly. Many people write it down just so they don't have to clutter up their brains with that information.

CHILDREN

Children are fun and can add magic to a ritual, especially at Yule with a gift exchange and Mother Bertha handing out gifts. Mother Bertha is a German folk character who is an ugly crone. She rides a giant goat with an enormous beard, named Gnasher Skeggi. She hands out gifts, but she can take away naughty children also. It adds a bit of a Halloweeny atmosphere to Yule. It's safe, scary fun.

Be sparing with candles and incense when children are present, because they really are fascinated by fire. Keep an eye on ritual tools, especially the knives, for children are tempted and sometimes just "no" isn't enough. If you bring children, be responsible for them. Do not allow them to run wild. Do not expect other people to discipline your children. Do not expect other people to watch out for your children. They are likely to help with all these things, but if nothing else, it is bad manners to expect or rely on others to take over your responsibility. Bring extra clothing in case of accidents.

The following is an excerpt from a set of suggested guidelines for children in ritual that were formulated for our Wiccan church. Hopefully they can give some idea of the issues inherent in allowing children into ritual:

Divide the children into age categories, because what might be appropriate for one age level might not be appropriate for another. These categories are not hard and fast, but general guidelines, and individuals may vary:

Babes in arms—Infants who must be held/carried and are generally incapable of much independent movement, usually from birth to one year or so.

Toddlers—Small children who are able to walk, (also crawl), and who do not have to be held, from one to five years old.

School age—Children who are attending grade school and can manage with an age-appropriate amount of autonomy and understanding, from five to twelve years.

Adolescent—People who have entered puberty, and although they may physically be adults, they are legally still considered as children. There is a measure of maturity, autonomy, and understand-ing but tempered with inexperience and the emotional turmoil of puberty, from twelve to eighteen years.

Babes in arms are generally exempt from ritual restrictions. They are held, and in general, sleep most of the time. If an infant becomes fussy or disruptive, the parents should quietly solve the problem or cut themselves out of the Circle and remove the disturbance.

It is a good idea for people who are planning rituals to rate the ritual for age-specific considerations; some children are able to attend, but not others. Guided meditations might be okay for adolescents, possibly also school-age children, but certainly not toddlers. Parents are also encouraged to be aware of the maturity level and temperaments of their children, and they should gauge their children's participation accordingly.

Certain rituals have elements that might make them inherently inappropriate for children. To help you determine how appropriate a ritual is for children, following are descriptions of three categories of ritual elements:

Appropriate for children: Open ritual, non-Initiates okay; High Priest/High Priestess will decide if children will be present; storytelling, age-appropriate material; if parent/guardian accompanied (i.e., there be some responsible adult). Wine in a chalice as a sacrament is acceptable for children, and is legal in most states with or without parental consent.

Inappropriate for children: Heavy Working (may or may not include Samhain, depending on the specific ritual used); nudity—legal issue (filmy or revealing clothing where there is partial nudity is also under the nudity category); non-sacramental alcohol in any form.

It depends: Participating in a ritual (calling quarters may be okay, invoking, evoking, etc. This is case by case—play it by ear); pointy objects (athames/swords)—Initiates okay, age-appropriate substitute if necessary (sticks or plastic for athames); under eighteen Initiates may not be present with nudity—it's the law; Samhain—depending on the individual ritual at the discretion of High Priestess/Priest and parents, if in doubt leave them home; guided meditations, age-appropriate ratings.

Below are some guidelines outlining the responsibilities of various people in the community relative to children in ritual situations:

High Priest/Priestess—Should include in ritual announcement if children are allowed. Use rating system or age levels if necessary; if it might be appropriate for some ages but not others, think about the ritual. If rituals allow children and alcohol is to be used in the chalice, use wine or beer and not hard liquor. Or, alternatively, have a non-alcoholic chalice. If you choose to allow children, be prepared for a higher distraction level than normal.

Parents/Guardians—Be responsible for your children. If they are acting up, calm them down or remove them from the Circle and be prepared to leave if you have to. Be able to handle the children you bring—adult/child ratios—for example, one parent with eight rambunctious children won't be able to keep proper control. Don't leave your children—you must accompany your younger children at rituals. It may be okay to leave teens if they're reliable and mature, but this should be discussed with High Priestess/Priestess beforehand. You should instruct your children in minimal Circle etiquette (for example, be quiet if it's quiet time, don't run around yelling, etc.). Be prepared for any psychic disturbances your children might experience. You can't always predict a child's reactions to the ritual atmosphere. Be aware of mobility issues of others; restrict jump-

ing, running, horseplay, etc. Be aware of privacy/confidentiality issues. Are the children able to understand "not telling?" Know where your children are at all times.

Children—Be polite and on company manners. Pay attention to the ritual and what others are doing. Understand Circle etiquette and behave in an age-appropriate manner. Know where your parents/guardians are. Don't touch anything, but looking is okay. Ask questions at an appropriate time if you're wondering about something that occurs during the ritual. Afterward, only discuss the ritual with parents/guardians and family—don't talk about it at school or with your friends.

Community—Be prepared to forgive minor breaches of behavior in an age-appropriate manner. Be prepared to live with the noise levels. Be instructive and teaching if needed, not scolding or repressive. Be prepared for a slightly higher chaos level. Help keep a community eye on the children present. If you don't like children and can't deal with them, stay home.

Privacy is a big concern. There are members of the Wiccan community who are not Out, and children have lower maturity levels, and may not understand the seriousness of the privacy issue. Additionally, they could inadvertently place their parents and family in jeopardy if they talk about the Witches ritual they attended last night in front of an uninformed teacher. Child protection could be alerted, and in that case it is up to the parents to prove no harm was done. It is understood that children cannot be held to oaths of secrecy like adults. Also how individual parents deal with the privacy issue with their children can change the situation. Children are inherently less discreet. It is up to the parents to evaluate how their children deal with privacy issues. If the children cannot be discreet or do not understand privacy and keeping a secret, maybe the children should be left at home.

Age is an issue when dealing with privacy. Babes in arms and toddlers aren't a problem. They are not sufficiently sophisticated in speech and understanding to describe or reveal much of the events they observed. School-age children and adolescents are a different matter. Unfortunately, our religion is not popular in certain areas of society, so our beliefs have to be more discreet, and children are not always able to fully appreciate the need for discretion.

Additionally, the issue of ritual nudity and children cannot be emphasized enough. Some people feel because it is religious, anything goes. That is definitely *not* the case. The U.S. Supreme Court has ruled definitively on this matter in Employment Division v. Smith (494 U.S. 872 (1990)) ("the peyote case"), among others. And since the Religious Freedom Restoration Act—RFRA (42 U.S.C. Section 2000bb et seq. (Supp. V 1993))—was declared unconstitutional in June 1997, there are still strong restrictions as to what behaviors are legally protected in a religious context. If there is a mixed group of children and adults, *nobody* may be nude, and that includes children and/or adults. Any dress that reveals body parts which are considered sexual and/or genital is nudity. This can endanger every adult on the premises and threatens every family present.

This is a heavily debated issue in some Wiccan circles, with some people maintaining that if the ritual is on private property (and in some cases rented property can be considered private), then mixed-age nudity is okay. Although the authors are not lawyers, we do follow closely the cases concerning religious freedom and expression in the United States. The preponderance of law indicates that if an activity can be considered harmful to society at large, no matter what the setting, religious or secular, public or private, it is not legal. Of course, a complaint has to be made for an activity to be prosecuted, but the Wiccan Rede states, "An ye harm none, do what ye will." Harming none includes endangering fellow ritual participants by your actions or behavior. And that means legally and morally as well as psychically and magickally. If you are with your family at home, there is little possibility of complaint, unless you practice with the shades open, but in any sort of group or community setting, the chances for complaint rise greatly. You can never know just who is at your community ritual, unless you personally know every soul present.

Paul and Estelle found out some months after the fact that a magazine reporter was present at a Samhain ritual put on by another group by reading an article about the ritual in a prominent regional/local magazine. This was quite a shock, and an excellent object lesson for those who feel to enter a Circle in perfect love and perfect trust is all the protection they need.

Certain jurisdictions have mandatory laws requiring that certain professionals—health professionals, teachers, clergy, and others—report any abuse or illegal behavior that endangers a child or vulnerable adult they witness. They are *required* by law to report the behavior, or they are subject to prosecution. So, be sensible and err on the side of caution and discretion.

CUTTING IN AND OUT OF CIRCLE

Sometimes you just have to leave a Circle while a ritual is going on. Maybe your toddler just decided *now* was the optimum time for a temper tantrum. Maybe you feel sick and must leave the Circle. Maybe something is going on in the ritual you do not wish to participate in. Maybe you are a High

Priest or High Priestess and you want to admit someone outside the Circle to the inside.

This is accomplished by the technique called cutting in and/or out (depending on which way you are headed). It is a simple technique and, when done properly, does not disrupt the energies of the Circle. First, if you need to leave, try to catch the eye of the High Priestess, High Priest, or other officiant. Try to get permission, and be as unobtrusive as possible. It is best if you allow the people putting on the ritual to cut you out. If you cannot, then cut yourself out.

Take your athame, either the actual blade or your universal athame of two fingers extended together, and "draw" a doorway from the ground, up to roughly your height, and to the ground crossing to your starting point, creating an opening roughly shaped like a door with a rounded top. If you project energy while drawing the door, you have created a magickal gateway in the Circle, while still allowing the Circle energy to flow around the doorway you have cut. Exit or enter the Circle, then "undraw" the doorway, by re-tracing your pattern and withdrawing the energy you used to cut the doorway. You may then "smooth" the Circle energies with your hand to help reestablish the completed Circle. You have just allowed yourself to cross the Circle boundary without disrupting the Circle's energies.

Once you are cut out, you should leave as unobtrusively as possible. You can wait elsewhere for the ritual to end and to recover your belongings if necessary. Be prepared to explain politely why you had to cut yourself out. Some High Priests or Priestesses may object and not want you to attend any of their Circles again. Be prepared to handle that also. Conversely, if you are sensitive to what other people do, maybe you should be assertive about finding out about the ritual beforehand, so

you don't have to cut yourself out if things get to a point where you are not ethically comfortable. And if you have doubts, maybe you shouldn't be a part of that ritual. Of course, the best option when you find something about the ritual personally objectionable is to shield yourself from energies you find unpleasant and wait for the ritual to end. You may be surprised to find something you thought would be awful turns out to be interesting or even nice. Reserve cutting yourself out of a Circle for true crises, not just a whim.

There are situations that arise in which an Officiant must cut themselves out to deal with something that occurs outside the Circle. Wait patiently, and let the people in charge deal with it, it's their ritual.

CRASH GROUNDING

Sometimes a ritual is disrupted by unforeseen circumstances. It is useful to know about crash grounding, a quick and almost instantaneous closing down of a Circle. You mentally gather up all the energies invoked, called up, and generated, and then in one fluid motion gather them into your strong hand and pull them down, into the Earth, by forcibly placing your hand on the floor (or ground). Keep concentration until you feel all the energies drain back into the Earth. The Circle should be down, all the Gods and Goddesses have left, and the elements sent back home. Nothing should be left of the energies of the Circle. Then you and others can scramble to pack up all the tools and equipment and leave quickly. In this circumstance, make sure all the ritual elements are taken away quickly and quietly. Sort out who owns what at a later date. This crash grounding is best left to the official High Priestess. If she won't do it, the High Priest is next in line, then the Tyler.

RITUAL ROBES

Where can a person obtain ritual garb? A very simple ritual robe is a caftan, a simple length of cloth, twice your height, folded, a hole cut for your head, and the sides sewn together with spaces left for arms. Use a material you like and which is appropriate for your ritual style, and you are set.

You can sometimes buy old costumes that look like robes. You can add a hood to a store-bought garment. You can go to second-hand clothing stores and usually find clothes adaptable for ritual use. Estelle and Paul like to use kimonos, available at second-hand shops. They are silk and look good, and usually fit well while allowing easy movement.

Sometimes you can buy a cape or cloak at a Renaissance festival or other place where medieval and/or Renaissance clothing is available.

If you sew, Folkways Patterns have a number of interesting options. Check out the costume section of other pattern companies also. Most have some cape, cloak, and hood patterns. A few shops do sell off-the-rack ritual robes, but be prepared to pay a hefty price. If you get to a festival or gathering, maybe you can find robes there. Be open-minded and creative, and you will find something that can be adapted to ritual use.

KNOW YOUR RIGHTS

Being a member of a religion gives you certain protections in most governmental jurisdictions in the English-speaking world, but those protections vary widely from country to country, state to state, and locality to locality. Know the local, state, and national laws about religion and religious practice for the place you live.

Part of being Wiccan is to be self-aware and to be able to take responsibility for your actions. Wicca is a religion recognized by the federal government, but just to say you are Wiccan, and expect that to stand up with any legal authorities is not enough. There are several things you can do to help "validate" your religious beliefs and practices.

Be a dues-paying member of a legally recognized religious organization. Paying dues, and having the canceled checks and receipts to show for it, helps establish your sincerity in the eyes of the law.

Have some resources to explain what Wicca is, for example, this book. The organization you join may have materials available to members. The *Army Chaplain's Manual* has a section on Wicca, specifically Gardnerian Wicca.

Know your local laws. Wiccans use athames as a sacred tool. Unfortunately most law-enforcement personnel will just see a big knife, and will believe it is a weapon. Some states (California and Massachusetts) and localities mandate that any double-edged blade is illegal. So in those places, you might have a wonderful athame, but if it's double-edged it is also illegal. United States federal law has mandated that anything that poses a threat to the greater good of society may be declared illegal, regardless of whether it infringes upon religious exercise. This means athames, drugs, alcohol for minors (though this is usually exempt in a sacramental setting), some nudity, certain sex acts, and whatever you might do in ritual that might ordinarily be illegal if performed in the middle of Main Street at noon.

Always get the appropriate permits; if you are using public facilities for your rituals, pay the fees, and know and follow the rules. If you are uncertain, contact the local police and inform them of who you are and what you will be doing and when. Know your local concealed weapon laws; an athame in a ritual bag may also be considered a concealed weapon. If you have a sheath, to be safe, store it in a bag, and place the bag in a trunk or locked compartment for transport. Many swords are by definition illegal. Three inches or less is the usual maximum length for a legal blade.

Be a good citizen and don't give cause for suspicion. Don't look for trouble. Some people just cannot be silent in the face of injustice, or feel they have to protest what they believe to be morally or legally wrong. Do what you feel you need to do, but don't make a point of being Wiccan about it. This can harm all other Wiccans. If a police officer's only experience with a Wiccan is in a protest line, with angry words and possibly violence, that person will have that experience tied with Wicca until something more emotionally forceful comes to replace it. Be considerate of your fellow brothers and sisters in the Craft, and make Wicca something people will respect and feel is beneficial.

Keep your paranoia in check. If you are wearing a pentagram and a clerk treats you rudely, don't automatically assume it is because you are Wiccan. Most people will not even notice the pentagram, or if they do, not understand it means you are Wiccan.

Not every bad thing that happens to you is due to prejudice. Be mature enough to realize that prejudice is due to fear and unfamiliarity. Remember this maxim, "Don't attribute to malice that which can be blamed upon sheer stupidity." It works.

Don't expect special or preferential treatment because you are a member of a minority religion. Throughout its existence members of the Wiccan religion have had to adapt to prevailing cultures that ranged from hostile to indifferent. If you choose to be Out and fight for your rights, do so in a professional, dignified, and mature way. Remember, you represent other Wiccans.

Educate yourself about religious freedom and the current legal climate in the locality, state, and country in which you live. This can take time, but it frequently proves valuable. And at the very least you will be better informed, and can be an informal resource for others. But remember, unless you are a lawyer specializing in this type of law, your opinions are just that.

PART III

WICCA A TO Z

$\mathcal{A}$ WICCAN GLOSSARY

INTRODUCTION TO THE WICCAN GLOSSARY

With the growing popularity of occult, metaphysical, and magickal things and the revival of the pre-Christian Pagan religions that has created a subculture all its own, people are encountering many unfamiliar terms. This work seeks to combine definitions of these terms into one volume. Because of the dynamic culture of Paganism, these definitions cannot be cast in stone. They may not even be totally consistent from one end of North America to the other. However, with the rise of the Internet there has been some standardization of the usage of terms. And an effort has been made to cull out those terms which are archaic or have been corrupted through time or purposeful misdirection. Some definitions will differ markedly from the original due to the Christianizing influences of translations of pre-Christian works into English. There is a great deal of cross-referencing between various works in the last fifty to one hundred years. It is almost amusing to see who borrowed what from whom, and what different slants each new author chose to use in compiling their material.

This work also has a bias derived from the authors, but hopefully one that tries to be truer to the original materials than some of the Victorian scholars were. Where there are variant spellings, we have attempted to communicate that, although with translations there can be several spellings. Sometimes we suspect some variants are actually misspellings perpetuated by various authors through the decades. Where possible, we have offered the original language derivations and their root meanings.

Wicca is a subculture, and therefore it has developed a group of terms and word usages that are Wiccan/Pagan specific. Sometimes it can be confusing for an outsider or a person who is new to Wicca to understand what some words mean. Many Traditions require a year-and-a-day of study before Initiation, and one reason for this is to allow time to assimilate the terms and word usages.

The popular media tends to lump Wicca in with the occult, supernatural, strange, and sensational. When researching Wicca one can come across an amazing number of references, some apply, some are merely coincidental, and some are purposefully misinformation. We have included many references that might seem "non-Wiccan" because these terms are encountered in association with Wicca, and it is useful to know which are valid and which are not. Hopefully, using this glossary, you can look up a term which might be associated with Wicca and find its meaning along with information regarding its specific application in the Wiccan subculture.

The terms are defined so that someone not familiar with Wicca can understand them. We often use analogies to concepts that are familiar to a general audience, hence the number of Christian, Buddhist, and Hindu analogies.

We have also included a number of divinatory systems, some archaic, some still practiced. Divination is important in the Wiccan world and it is interesting to see just how many systems have been developed through the millennia. It is also interesting (at least to us) to see which systems have been derived from others that preceded them.

This glossary compiles various diverse sources into one more-or-less comprehensive volume. There are probably things we have inadvertently overlooked, and for that we apologize.

We have deliberately avoided certain subjects except in the most general form—astrology, tarot, Kabbalah, Ceremonial Magick, alchemy, etc.— because there are many good works that cover those subjects well. We also avoided including the names of various Deities because, again, there are other good works available.

Some of the most famous personages and magickal organizations through the ages have been included to lend historical perspective. Again, those included and those left out are solely the choice of the authors and not intended to slight any person or philosophical path.

A

abracadabra—1) The special word that makes the magic happen. Nowadays more of a cliché than anything else. 2) An ancient Roman charm of protection, repeated over and over, eliminating one letter from the end each time. When you reach "A" the spell of protection is completed. 3) A Kabbalistic charm possibly deriving from Ab, Ben, and ruach a Cadesh—Father, Son, and Holy Ghost.

abraxas, abrasax—1) A Gnostic term, meaning hurt me not, this word was inscribed on an amulet and worn for protection. 2) A word gematrically equivalent to 365 and linked with the Solar cycle, it is symbolized by the image of a man with a cock's head holding a shield and a whip. This hermetic image is found on amulets, carved in a gem or stone.

abraxas gem—Amulet used to ward off witchcraft.

abuse—1) Actions that cause harm to the self and/or others. 2) Speech that is insulting, intimidating, loud, or overbearing. Abusive behavior is frowned upon in the Pagan Community, but the usual remedy is to leave the group in which the abuse is perpetrated, rather than confronting the abuser(s). Confrontative behavior is also sometimes considered abusive.

actorius—A magical stone, found in chickens (capons). Worn around the neck it confers courage.

Adam Weishaupt—An eighteenth-century Magus, he was supposedly the predecessor who helped maintain and preserve the knowledge eventually passed to the Golden Dawn, and from them to occultists everywhere.

adept—One who is skilled in magick, mysticism, or arcane knowledge. A general term that can be used about any magickal practitioner, including Pagans or Wiccans.

ADF, An Driaoch't Fein—An organization of Druids.

adjuration—In Ceremonial Magick a formula by which a demon or spirit is commanded in the name of the Christian God to do as the magician commands. Can be used in invocation or exorcism.

adytum—Greek, the holiest portion of a temple. Used to connote the holiest area of an Initiation place. BOTA (Builders of the Adytum) is an occult ceremonial magical organization.

aeromancy—1) Divination using atmospheric conditions, clouds, storms, winds, etc. Sometimes synonymous with nephelomancy. "Red sky in the morning, sailors take warning, red sky at night, sailor's delight" is one form of this. 2) Scenes or visions in the sky that have been witnessed by many and are not typical heavenly appearances. There is a folk tale that peasants across Europe, in the late Spring of 1914, saw a large sword in the sky while cutting hay, which was said to presage W.W.I. 3) A branch of geomancy in which a question is asked and then dirt or seeds are thrown into the wind. The shape of the cloud and/or the pattern of the material as it falls provides the answer.

afreet, afrit—Persian/Arabic, a demon, the soul of a dead person. More of a trickster but can be persuaded to be helpful.

Age of Aquarius—Due to a wobble in the Earth's axis of rotation, the Vernal Equinox (the point at which the Sun crosses the celestial equator moving from south to north—spring in the northern hemisphere) "precesses" backward over the millennia. From roughly 2260 BCE to 100 BCE this point was in the constellation Aries (Age of Aries). From roughly 100 BCE to 2060 CE it is in the constellation Pisces (Age of Pisces). From roughly 2060 CE to 4420 CE it will be in Aquarius

(Age of Aquarius). It takes about seventy-two years to move one degree (a sign has 30 degrees in it—twelve signs times thirty degrees each equals 360 degrees, a full circle.) The dates are not precise because, although it is understood that the span of one entire cycle is 25,900 years and the average length of one age is 2160 years, the points where each constellation begins and ends are not universally agreed upon. Therefore modern literature has the Age of Aquarius beginning anywhere from 1860 CE to 2680 CE. The constellation lines in the astronomy books are arbitrary boundary markers decided upon in the 1760s and have nothing to do with astrology. Not all astrologers or astrology systems agree on the size and component stars of each constellation. Most do agree that these present times are near the end of the Age of Pisces and the beginning of the Age of Aquarius. The Age of Aquarius is believed to herald a time of peace, love, and universal brotherhood. The term has come to signify a resurgence in spiritual, occult, and metaphysical teachings and practices, and the mainstream acceptance of same.

AGLA—A Kabbalistic name, a tetragrammaton, four-letter name of God. An acronym for Atheh Gabor Leolam Adonai—Thou art great and powerful, oh Lord. Used as a charm or mantra to secure blessing and protection from God, particularly against satanic forces. Used in Ceremonial Magick for invoking archangels, Watchtowers, etc.

agnostic—From the Greek *a-gnosis* (without knowledge); one who has no certain knowledge about spiritual, mystical, or religious matters; one who doesn't know whether or not there is a God. One can be agnostic and still be Wiccan.

akasha—Magickal life force, similar to the Oriental concept of Chi. All-pervading spiritual ether usually considered to be violet or ultra-violet in color.

A Hindu and Buddhist concept popularized in the West by Madame Blavatsky and the Theosophist movement in the 1870s.

Akashic Chronicles, Akashic Planes, Akashic Records—From the Sanskrit *akasha* (primary substance). A higher ethereal plane where the records of all time are recorded.

Edgar Cayce was able to access these Akashic Records while in trance and thereby make health assessments and diagnoses as well as comment upon past and future lives of individuals.

Rudolf Steiner claimed to have accessed these records for his descriptions of the lost civilizations of Atlantis and Lemuria. Books of records are kept in the Akashic Library and it is believed that each soul has its own book that contains all the information about each soul's incarnations, past, present, and future. The Akashic Records are what is judged in determining each soul's karma.

Albertus Magnus—(1193–1280 CE) A.k.a., the Universal Doctor; theologian and Bishop of Ratisbon. Occultist and alchemist, he was said to possess the philosopher's stone. He left many volumes of writings on alchemy and other subjects. His writings are still studied by modern alchemists.

alchemy—An ancient forerunner of chemistry, it originated in Alexandria, Egypt, and China during the first century CE. The object of alchemy was the fusing of base metals into gold and the creation/discovery of the philosopher's stone—originally a Chinese concept which was brought to the West in the eighth and ninth centuries CE. Some alchemical practitioners believed this objective goal of alchemy was its primary purpose and created many interesting and dangerous compounds by methods that have been developed into chemistry. Other practitioners believed these goals to be metaphorical, and interpreted them to mean the refinement of the base metal of their soul into spiritual gold and thereby the refinement of the personality and soul. Astrological calculations were used in this endeavor because it was believed that the placement and influence of the planets needed to be correct for the transmutations to be successful. Once the scientific revolution occurred, the alchemical methods were co-opted and the science of chemistry was born, using these principles for the analysis and refinement of elements and compounds for practical use, and the spiritual practices were dropped. Still practiced by some, alchemy can also be practiced to search for an elixir of youth, a universal cure for all disease, the attainment of eternal life, and other accomplishments.

Some famous alchemists and authors of alchemical treatises were al-Razi (886–925) and Avicenna (980–1036), Persian physicians; Arnold of Villanova (1240–1313), Roger Bacon (1214–1294) and Albertus Magnus (1193–1280), medieval scholars and translators of earlier materials; and Philipus Aureolus Paracelsus (1493–1541), a German physician.

Many alchemical experiments created useful formulae. Roger Bacon created a recipe for gunpowder and instructions for constructing a telescope. Arnold of Villanova described the distillation of wine. Paracelsus changed medicine by using alchemical compounds to fight the causative agents of disease, and thereby changed the emphasis of alchemy from creating the philosopher's stone to making medicines.

alectromancy—Predicting the future using celestial, atmospheric, or weather conditions. In ancient Egypt, an early form of astrology in which comets, shooting stars, and eclipses were used to foretell the future either of individuals or the state. Sometimes equated with astro-meteorology, it is the astrology of weather prediction and use of comets, shooting stars, and eclipses to predict the future.

alectryomancy—Greek *alectruon* (cock) and *manteia* (divination). 1) Divination by means of a cock, black hen, or a bird, that pecks at grain placed on a figure of letters of the alphabet. 2) Divination by reciting letters of the alphabet and when the cock crows during the recitation of a letter, the letter was considered significant. 3) In Babylon, water was splashed three times on a sleeping ox's head. There were seventeen recorded possible reactions of the ox which would predict the future. 4) General divination by the behavior of animals. The Hittites circa 1600 BCE–1200 CE studied the movements of an eel in a tank of water. Ants, jackals, beetles, and groundhogs are also used.

aleuromancy—Greek *aleuron* (flour) and *manteia* (divination). Divination with flour. Messages were placed in dough and baked, and the message found in the baked dough was a prediction of the future. Chinese fortune cookies are a modern form of this. In one version of this practice a coin or bean was baked into a cake and the recipient was granted a wish or was chosen as Lord of Misrule for winter celebrations. Medieval and Renaissance midwinter celebrations often included choosing a Lord of Misrule, who behaved frivolously and could order people to perform foolish or uncharacteristic acts; similar to a prankster master of ceremonies.

alomancy, halomancy—From the Greek *halo* (salt) and *manteia* (divination). Divination with salt.

alphitomancy—From the Greek *alphitomansis* (divination using barley). A type of trial by ordeal. Wheat or barley cakes were given to a suspected person, and if they could not swallow them, they were considered guilty and condemned by their own actions. Based on psychological principles, it was believed that a guilty person would be more nervous and have a dry mouth.

altar—1) Center of sacred rites. 2) Place of sacrifice. 3) Place where one's ritual tools and other items needed for a Working can be laid out. Can be permanent or portable. Usually made of some natural substance like stone or wood or the ground is used. Altar placement is not standard within Wicca. Some traditions mandate which quarter the altar will be in (usually East or North or Center), others have guidelines, others leave it up to the individual and the vagaries of the space used. Altar placement can lead to hot disagreement among Wiccans.

altar cloth—Consecrated cloth that covers an altar and on which ritual tools are placed.

altrunes—German "old runes."

amniomancy—1) Divination by observation of a caul over the head of an infant at birth. It is believed by some that a child born with a caul has the second sight. 2) Also a general set of lucky or unlucky omens that were used at the birth of a child to predict the child's future and/or character.

amulet—From an Arabic root meaning to carry, an object, drawing, image, or inscription charged with energy to bring about a desired end. It is usually used as a "good luck charm," and can also be used for protection, shielding, grounding, and other purposes. Amulets can be made or found, some are found and then altered. An object worn as a protective charm against evil or specifically the evil eye, some amulets are inscribed with magickal words, formulae, or sigils. Simple amulets are items that are unusual, eye-catching, or rare, like a four-leaf clover. Amulets are generally worn around the neck or in a ring. See also talisman, charm, and fetish.

Angelical Stone—A stone used for scrying by Dr. John Dee, who claimed it was given to him by the archangels Raphael and Gabriel, it is now in the British Museum.

angels—An immortal spiritual being that acts as an intermediary between God and humanity. In Judaism, divine messengers. In Christianity, inhabitants of heaven. Angels also are recognized by other religions and have various attributes and functions. They are good beings and are created by God for his purposes. Fallen angels are beings created by God who turned away from Him and now use their powers to do evil and thwart God's plan. Wiccans generally do not deal with angels, preferring to work with their Gods or other nature spirits. Dionysius the Areopagite in the early fifth century CE classified angels into a hierarchy in his *De Hierarchia Celesti* into three triads (from "lower to higher"): 1) Seraphim, Cherubim, and Thrones in the first circle; 2) Dominions, Virtues, and Powers in the second circle; 3) Principalities, Archangels, and Angels in the third circle. Emmanuel Swedenborg and Rudolf Steiner claimed to have communicated with angels.

anima—The spiritual force. The presence of Deity, life force, or the cosmic creative principle found in all living things.

Anima Mundi—From Latin, soul of the world. Ancient philosophical term referring to the divine essence that surrounds and energizes all life in the Universe.

animal magnetism—An organic magnetic force that can be transmitted from one person to another and produce healing. Term popularized by Austrian doctor Franz Mesmer who developed therapeutic techniques utilizing this force in the late eighteenth century.

animate, inanimate—Turning inanimate objects

into living creatures and then back into inanimate objects. A golem is one sort of animate construct.

animism—The belief that all things have souls or spirits. All things were created by Deity, therefore all things retain some portion of that primal Divine spark.

ankh—Egyptian hieroglyph meaning life. In heraldry (and Christianity) known as the Crux Ansata. Used as a protective symbol, and symbol of immortality. Known as the "cross of life." Used as an occult symbol for the life principle and also a charm against death.

Ankh

anointing oil—Ancient formula consisted of vervain or mint crushed and steeped in olive oil, then squeezed though a cloth several times to purify it. Used in magickal ceremonies and Initiations.

anthropomancy—From the Greek *anthropos* (man) and *manteia* (divination). 1) Divination practiced by ancient Egyptians and Greeks employing human sacrifice and divination by dissection of bodies. May have continued sporadically during the Roman Empire. 2) Divination by reading the intestines of sacrificed people (generally children), attributed to Emperor Julian the Apostate (ruled 361–363 CE), as a successor of Constantine the Great (ruled 306–337 CE). Julian was said to have practiced necromancy and other depraved practices. Julian also attempted to revive and reestablish the Pagan religions in Byzantium after Constantine mandated that Christianity become the official state religion in 313 CE. Once Julian was murdered his successors suppressed the Pagan religions. 3) General divination by means of the entrails of sacrificial victims. Used in many cultures throughout the ancient and not-so ancient world. 4) Divination using bodily fluids, especially blood, but not involving death. In the Middle Ages, spontaneous nosebleeds were indicative of good or bad luck depending upon circumstances.

anthropomorphic—To ascribe human characteristics to something not human.

anthropophagism—Cannibalism, the eating of human flesh. In the Middle Ages witches were said to practice this, and some states passed laws mandating fines for such practices.

anthroposomancy—See phrenology.

antidote—A remedy or cure for a curse, spell, poison, or disease. May be purely magickal, magickal and herbal, or solely herbal in composition. Pharmacology was derived from herb lore and magickal potions designed to cure various ills.

antinopomancy—Similar to anthropomancy with children as the main sacrificial victims.

apantomancy—1) Divination by an oracle who would go to a certain sacred place and then wait for some sort of symbol or message to be imparted by the Gods, usually through the appearance of an animal, bird, or natural phenomenon. 2) General divination using chance encounters with animals. 3) Divination by observation of the behavior of animals, especially for weather and seasonal predictions.

Apollonius of Tyana—Greek philosopher of first century CE who traveled widely in search of esoteric knowledge and gained a great reputation as a formidable thaumaturgist. In Asia Minor he was considered a Deity and temples were dedicated to him. In the Middle Ages his name was associated with legends and stories with magical themes, and Apollonius was considered the Archmagus.

aporrheta—Greek, esoteric instructions revealed to initiates during secret ceremonies in Greek and Egyptian Mystery Schools.

apotheasis—Deification, becoming Goddess.

apothecary—Ancient version of the modern drug store. Originated in ancient Greece, many physicians prescribed certain herbs and antidotes and the patient brought the prescribed formula or prescription to an apothecary to be filled, alleviating the doctor of the need to have a large collection of herbs on hand. Many apothecaries were midwives or herbalists. In China apothecaries still thrive. Generally an apothecary works directly with the natural substances, and a pharmacy with the refined, processed, and packaged modern derivatives.

apotheosis—Deification, becoming God.

apparition—An appearance of paranormal phenomenon. Includes ghosts, spirits, poltergeists, ectoplasm, clairvoyant images, visions, or materializations of inanimate objects, possibly also dreams, especially of the dead or the future. A ghost is an apparition of a dead person. Generally accompanied by a feeling of cold, strange smells, or displacement of objects.

apport—Psychic manifestation of objects, shapes, sounds, or smells by a medium. Some feel these are created by the medium, some that they are merely revealed and were always there but invisible. These manifestations can be faked and have been considered suspect, as these phenomena were faked to help "prove" the efficacy of mediums.

Aradia—1) *Aradia, Goddess of the Witches* (1899), by Charles Leland (1824–1903), the modern translation and version of a book circa 1353 that described a medieval witch cult that was feminist and formed in reaction to and as protection from the Catholic Church. Described to Leland by a female Gypsy Witch. 2) Supposedly a female mystic, viewed as a Christ figure who taught in Italy circa 1353. 3) Divine daughter of Diana (Goddess of the Moon) and Lucifer (God of the Sun) considered to be the Queen of the Witches.

4) A popular Goddess with Wiccans, sometimes known as the Goddess of the Wiccans, though this is by no means universal. The name Aradia appears in chants and rituals descended from Gardnerian Wicca, hence the popularity among Wiccans in general.

arcane—From Latin *arcanus*, closed things. Secret, mysterious, occult.

arcanum, pl. arcana—That which is arcane, hidden, occult. Can be a general term to describe all esoteric wisdom or occult lore. More specifically used to refer to the tarot; specifically the trumps as the Major Arcana and the suit cards as the Minor Arcana.

archangels—Spiritual beings of the sphere of Mercury that guide the spiritual destiny of groups of people and nations. In Christian iconography the Archangels are often pictured with models of cities in their arms. In Judaism and Christianity the seven most important Archangels, which are each assigned to one of the spheres of heaven (and the corresponding planet therein), are Gabriel, Raphael, Michael, Uriel, Joophiel, Zadkiel, and Samael.

archetype—1) Jungian, a basic pattern or idea in the collective unconscious within which things of the same class or idea are represented. 2) Fundamental elements of the collective unconscious that determine patterns of thought and behavior but cannot be directly defined, only approximately suggested through symbols. Dream symbols are usually archetypes. The signs, planets, and houses of astrology are archetypes. Some feel the Gods are archetypes. The symbols used in divination are archetypes.

Ardanes—A set of rules by which a coven is run. Originally compiled by Gerald Gardner and his followers, they have been added to, annotated, commented upon, and refined by many people through the years. Even though they are supposed to be Tradition secret, they are fairly similar from Tradition to Tradition and branch to branch. Some groups only use them as a guideline, some use them as absolute mandates, some do not use them at all, preferring to make up their own rules. They range from some sensible interpersonal rules to some very restrictive mandates. Used mainly by Gardnerians and Alexandrians, and groups that are offshoots of those.

AREN—Alternative Religious Educational Network, formerly WADL, Wiccan Anti-Defamation League. A group of people who support and help Wiccans and Pagans who need legal help. Generally make use of the First Amendment, anti-discrimination, and hate crime laws to aid Wiccans and Pagans with legal matters that may be prejudiced by their religion.

Their resident attorney has been admitted to practice before the United States Supreme Court, which allows AREN to plead Pagan cases before the highest court in the United States, if necessary.

The dissolution of WADL and rebirth of AREN was necessitated by a lawsuit from B'nai Brith and the JADL (Jewish Anti-Defamation League) for infringement of copyright.

ariolater—Latin. From Latin *ara* (altar) or possibly Sanskrit *hira* (entrails). A diviner, one who tells the future from omens. The Romans had a College of Augurs who were trained and held important positions in society. No important event could take place without the auspices and omens being taken and interpreted. A priestly occupation.

ariolist—Divination by means of an altar.

arithmancy, arithmomancy—From the Greek *arithmos* (number) and *manteia* (divination). Divination using numbers. Numerology and vertical sequences are two examples.

Armageddon—The final conflict between good and evil that will result in the destruction of the world and the Final Judgment, it is a Christian concept. Wiccans generally do not believe in any Armageddon.

armanen—German (noble). 1) The name of a Runic alphabet that was devised by the Pan-Germanic scholar Guido von List in 1902 CE. List channeled this alphabet and it is partially based upon older historic Runic alphabets. 2) Circa 1900, a colloquial term for a movement and groups arising from that movement that attempted to develop a Pan-Germanic culture, this concept was later co-opted by the Nazi Party and the Third Reich. Through its association with the Nazi Party, the movement was discredited.

armomancy—1) Divination by observation of the shoulders of a sacrificial animal. 2) The art of choosing sacrificial candidates by visual inspection, especially for defects or impurities.

asperge, aspurge—To sprinkle with holy water for purification, to cleanse with consecrated water.

aspergillis—A sprinkler for holy or consecrated water.

aspidomancy—1) Divination by sitting on a shield in a magickal Circle. The diviner pronounces certain spells, falls into a trance, and then prophesies. 2) Divination by allowing oneself to be possessed by a demon, angel, or other supernatural being in a magickal Circle. When returning to the natural state the magician writes down what was revealed during the possession.

asport—Psychic disappearance of objects unhindered by physical barriers like walls, usually during a seance under the agency of a medium. Can be faked, which caused this practice to be suspect since these phenomena were faked to help "prove" the efficacy of mediums. Can also take place through the activities of a poltergeist. Opposite of apport.

Association, Law of—The magickal Law of Association, which states that an item still has a link to the person from whom it came or to whom it belongs or even whoever touched it last. Using that energy link a magician can gain information about the person, perhaps discern their location, or use the link to influence the person in some way. Can be used in white and black magick. Using a personal possession or item of clothing or hair as a focus, one can find a lost person. See also psychometry.

astragalomancy, astragyromancy—From the Greek *astragalos* (dice or knucklebone) and *manteia* (divination). Divination by means of knucklebones (later dice).

astral, astral plane(s)—Derived from Latin *astra* (star). 1) The planes of higher consciousness. The non-corporeal continuum where dreams, magick, astral travel, and other mystical actions take place. An alternate reality that intersects with this plane only through magick, dreams, or the mind; the level of reality intermediate between the physical and the mental. It is the level of the emotions and instincts. 2) The fabric of the heavens.

astral body—Spiritual appearance of a person in the astral realms. One's astral appearance can be different from their everyday appearance. One can appear ageless, vital, and powerful, regardless of actual physical age and/or infirmity. Some adepts appear in certain color robes or special magickal garb, or sporting jewelry, sigils, or tools.

astral projection, astral travel—Non-corporeal travel in which a person's spirit body leaves their physical body and travels to other places. Can be a way people "check up" on others without actually going there. Also can be used to describe "dream travel" in which a person flies to different places in their dreams. It may be involuntary or deliberate.

astrology—Divination and determination of character based upon the positions of the planets at birth. Can also be used to make predictions in non-personal spheres. There are many branches of Western astrology:

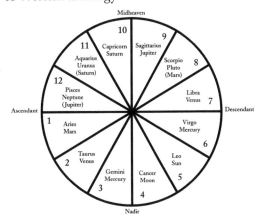

Mundane Chart

1) *Horary astrology* is the astrology of divination in which a question is asked of an astrologer, and the astrologer does a chart for the day, time, and place for that question (may be in person, on the phone, or by mail). The answer is contained in the chart. Before modern times this was the most common form of astrology practiced.

2) *Electional astrology* is used when a person wants to plan a future event (like a wedding or real estate closing) and has an astrologer search for a time that will ensure success in the matter. The flip side of Horary, often the two are practiced together.

3) *Natal or Genethelical astrology* is the astrology of birthcharts and personal horoscopes. Ninety percent or more of all modern astrology deals with this branch.

4) *Mundane or political astrology* is the astrology of nations and natural disasters, and analyzes the charts of nations, national rulers, eclipses,

equinoxes, and natural disasters and interprets events based on these charts. One of the oldest forms of astrology.

5) *Astro-meteorology* is the astrology of weather prediction and the use of comets, shooting stars, and eclipses to predict the future, now made obsolete by meteorology.

6) *Uranian astrology* is a modern construct developed in Germany in the 1920s and has been expanded and built upon. It makes use of special charts and measurements to interpret personality and events.

There are three main schools of astrology:

1) *Western or Tropical astrology* is a form of astrology popular throughout the West. It is based on a zodiac which begins at 0° Aries which is located at that point on the ecliptic where the Sun crosses the equator moving northward. This is commonly known as the Vernal Equinox and does not correspond to the constellations in the sky (see Age of Aquarius). It is the astrology of over ninety percent of all popular books available.

2) *Hindu, Vedic, Jyotish or Sidereal astrology* is based upon the practices and traditions of the Sanskrit Vedas. That zodiac is based upon the stars' positions and is currently about 23 degrees "behind" the tropical zodiac. This astrology also utilizes the 27 lunar mansions or nakshatras as additional divinatory placements, augmenting the signs of the zodiac.

3) *Chinese astrology* is based upon the twelve Chinese zodiacal signs, but also utilizes time portions of the day and the year one is born, in a sixty-year cycle.

astromancy—Divination using the planets, Sun, and Moon in connection with other conditions. Precursor to astrology which depended upon mathematical calculation of horoscopes. Survives as sayings such as "red sky at morning, sailor's warning, red sky at night sailor's delight."

athame—Pronounced in a variety of ways around North America (*ATH-e-may; a-THAM-ee; a-THAH-may; a-THAME*. British pronunciation; *ath-AY-mee*), it is traditionally a black-handled knife (although in modern practice it can have any color handle) that is an important—for some the main—sacred tool of a Wiccan. Symbolizes the element of Fire or Air. Symbolizes the masculine aspect in the Great Rite. It directs energy and is used to draw a Circle, make pentagrams, cut or take down a Circle, and has other uses for controlled directed energy. It is a sacred tool, not a cutting instrument. An athame should be double-edged (to show that power cuts both ways), and have a blade of at least four inches. A

Athame

sheath protects the blade from rust and wear. Some Wiccans decorate the hilt and blade with magickal symbols and sigils, some do not. Tradition says each person should make their own athame, but most people buy them either from catalogues or gun shows.

Some Wiccans feel if an athame draws blood, it is no longer fit to be used as a sacred tool. Some feel it should be a strictly personal tool, belonging to and used by one witch. Others believe that an athame may be shared in class or coven situations. In Ceremonial Magick, the athame is an important sacred tool, sometimes more intensely personal than Wiccans view it. Some ceremonial magicians feel one must construct one's own athame, preferably from meteoric iron. The athame does not have to have a sharp blade, as it only cuts energy.

atheist—From the Greek *a-theist* (no God), one who believes that no Deity exists, or ever existed.

Atlantis, Atlantean—The mythical continent which is believed to have occupied the area that is now the Atlantic Ocean. Legend has it that the Atlantean culture was very advanced but the inhabitants made some great mistake and caused their land to be destroyed in a series of explosions and natural disasters over several centuries.

In modern folklore Atlanteans (people of Atlantis) were responsible for building the pyramids, the Sphinx, and other ancient monuments. They were also believed to be the founders of some or all of the great ancient civilizations. Some people believe that land near Bimini that appears to contain ancient artifacts of buildings is a remnant of ancient Atlantis.

Belief in the existence of Atlantis (and also Lemuria and Mu, other ancient legendary civilizations) is popular in modern culture. The degree to which Wiccans believe in the existence of Atlantis varies widely. Some people feel (and Edgar Cayce stated in his readings) that today's modern technological society is due to the reincarnation of many Atlanteans in this time and place and that many who live today remember their former technological knowledge and skills. Use of crystals is believed to be a holdover from Atlantis.

The energy vortex called the Bermuda Triangle that can cause disruption in electrical equipment and mental disorientation in some people is believed to be associated with Atlantis. Exactly where the Triangle is located (other than the West Atlantic bordering on the Caribbean) and what places lie within it is widely disputed.

Atlantis was first mentioned by Plato around 350 BCE, who recounted tales told by Egyptian priests 200 years earlier. It was reported that the Atlanteans sought to dominate the Mediterranean world more than 9,000 years before Plato. Both Helena Blavatsky and Rudolf Steiner mentioned Atlantis in their writings. Legend has it that Native Americans are descendants of refugees from Atlantis. Modern archaeologists have equated Atlantis with the Minoan civilization that was disrupted and partially destroyed when the island of Santorini/Thera in the Mediterranean erupted in a volcanic explosion around 1450 BCE.

augur—Derived from Latin *avis* (bird). 1) A soothsayer or diviner. 2) A Roman priest who interpreted omens from the behavior of birds, and other phenomena of the sky, or the reading of entrails.

augury—Generically, divination by whatever means is at hand. More specifically, divination by the movements and sounds of birds, or divination by the reading of entrails.

aura—Biomagnetic energy field that surrounds all living things. Similar to Chi. Some feel the inner bands of the aura are etheric in substance and serve as a link between the physical and astral planes. Some people can read auras, and can determine the health, mood, temperament, and spiritual development by the colors, size, and shape of an aura. Theoretically anyone can learn to see auras, it just takes practice. Kirlian photography supposedly photographs auras.

austromancy—Divination using the direction and force of winds, and the shapes of clouds. Used to predict the weather (a primitive form of meteorology) and also the fate of nations or individuals.

automatic writing—A form of spirit communication by which a person allows a discarnate being to partially possess them and write using their hand. Usually the handwriting is markedly different from that of the person's usual handwriting.

The person is usually not aware of what they are writing. May be performed in or out of trance, may be voluntary or involuntary. Some messages have been received in foreign languages or have been written backward so they must be read in a mirror. Ruth Montgomery practiced automatic writing for many years and published a series of books based upon the teachings she received. It is generally not recommended, as it is a form of possession and you cannot be sure just who it is you are allowing to use your hand.

avatar—Derived from Sanskrit *aloatara* (descent). 1) In Hinduism a God who has incarnated into a human or animal form to experience mortal life and help those less enlightened to attain nirvana. 2) A person who has gone through a course of training to help them achieve enlightenment and spiritual elevation to live a better, more effective, and enjoyable life.

axinomancy—Greek *axine* (axe) and *manteia* (divination). Divination by means of an axe. 1) To determine a guilty person, suspend an axe from a string, put all the possible culprits in a circle, spin the axe, and when it stops it will be pointing at the culprit. 2) Heat an axe head, set it upright, place a marble or agate on the head and slowly rotate the head until the marble rolls in the direction of a guilty person, or treasure. 3) Drive the axe blade into a post and let it waver while people dance around the post. When the axe falls, the handle is supposed to point to the culprit if present, otherwise it will point in the direction he took when he fled.

B

BCE—Before Common Era, less Christocentric term for years previously numbered "before Christ" or BC.

backward magick—Reciting certain spells backward to reverse their effects, or counteract the effects of another. In Satanism (of the reverse Christianity type) the mass was said backward, especially the Pater Noster, Lord's Prayer, or certain psalms, and was supposed to invoke Satan.

baculum, baculus—Latin, staff or stick. Term for a wand used in Wiccan rituals in some Traditions.

balefire—1) A.k.a., witchfire. An ethereal fire that may exist within a material fire or alone. Sometimes synonymous with swampfire, which is the ignition of methane gas that can occur in swamps as a byproduct of decay. Otherwise it can occur when there is ethereal activity and it is considered a proof of the presence of the little people or fey folk. 2) A bonfire that is lit in celebration of a Sabbat, usually the Great Sabbats, Imbolc, Beltane, Lughnasadh, and Samhain, although it can accompany the lesser Sabbats also.

bane—A source of harm or undoing causing sorrow or death, a curse.

banishing—1) An act by which unwanted psychic and/or magickal influences are removed. Can be as elaborate as an exorcism or as simple as burning incense, depending on the influence and intensity of the banishing. 2) Short for "banishing the Circle," or taking down a Circle after it has served its purpose. 3) Expelling a witch from a coven for an offense; a witch who has been expelled either may reapply for readmission after a year-and-a-day or may be permanently exiled if the offense is great.

banshee—From Old Irish *ben sidhe* (woman of the fairy folk). A spirit of Scottish or Irish families, it is said to wail at the death of a family member. In Nordic folklore, a benevolent spirit. In modern usage, a baleful spirit that is said to terrify travelers, especially at night.

Baphomet—Probably a corruption of Mohammed. The Knights Templar were accused of blasphemous worship of this demon, which was one of the charges used to justify the attack and elimination of the Order by Phillip of France in 1307. A goat-headed God with androgynous qualities, he is depicted in Ceremonial Magickal lore. Popularized by the writings of Eliaphas Levi, he is revered as a Deity, although mysteries surround this being. In popular lore this image of the goat-headed God is used when one illustrates Devil worship and Satanism. Baphomet is one of the Deities revered by some Satanists. Christians view this entity as a demon. Some Wiccans revere Baphomet, usually in direct proportion to their involvement in Ceremonial Magick.

Baphomet

bard—A level of Initiation in the Druidic Tradition; also a person who is a singer and storyteller, as well as a magician.

Bath-kol—Hebrew (daughters of the voice). A Divine voice announcing the Will of God. A method of divination among the ancient Jews in which one would appeal to Bath-kol, and the first words uttered after the appeal were accepted as prophetic.

Bavarian Illuminati—See Illuminati.

Beelzebub, Baalzebub—Beelzebub is a Hebrew variation of Baalzebub and roughly translates as "Lord of the Flies." Baalzebub is derived from the ancient Syrian God Baal and means Lord of the High House. An alternative name for Satan, sometimes separately considered to be the leading representative of the fallen Gods. In Matthew 12:24 he is mentioned as Prince of the Devils.

bell—Tool used in casting, cleansing, and/or closing a Circle. Also used during certain rituals. Hand bells, struck bells, gongs, singing bells or bowls, and small chimes are all used as bells. A clear tone can be cleansing. Also used to engage the sense of hearing when making magick. Certain tones have magickal correspondences and influences.

belomancy—Divination using arrows. 1) Toss an arrow to determine the direction of the path to follow. 2) Take three arrows, one black, one white, and one uncolored, and choose one when blindfolded while asking a yes/no question. The black arrow signifies no, the white arrow signifies yes, and the uncolored arrow signifies ask again later. 3) Herodotous (circa 450 BCE) described Scythian soothsayers using arrows as divining rods. 4) Several arrows can be inscribed with sayings, etc., and the message on the arrow drawn at random is viewed as the answer asked or the advice to take.

Beltane, Bealtaine—The Great Sabbat also known as May eve, May Day, Walpurgisnacht, etc. Celebrated either April 30th or May 1st. The original meaning is Bel-fire after the Celtic God known as Bel, Balar, Balor, or Belenus. Traditionally this holiday represented the union of the Goddess and God, and was a fertility festival to ensure a good growing season. Bonfires were lit, people danced naked, and couples would lay together in the plowed fields to ensure fertility of the land and a good growing season.

berserk, berserker—From the Norse *bare sark* (bare chested). A state of Divine ecstasy that occurred during battle in which a warrior would fight on and on impervious to pain or injury. Considered a form of Divine protection against injury and should death result it is a guarantee that the warrior would be transported to Valhalla. Sometimes the berserker would fight anyone who came across his path, friend or foe. It is believed to be a mental state of uncontrollable rage and hyper-adrenaline activity. Berserkers were revered for their Divine madness but also feared because they were unstoppable until their madness left them. Often most berserkers were not conscious of their actions. The concept is known in many cultures under various names and associated with various Deities. Sometimes also associated with the belief that a person would be transformed into an animal during battle, usually a bear or wolf.

Besant, Annie—(1847–1933) English social reformer and Theosophist. Crusader for free thought, birth control, and women's rights. Member of the socialistic Fabian Society. Converted to Theosophy in 1889, and moved to India. Traveled in the United States and Britain with her adopted son Krishnamurti, whom she presented as a new messiah, a claim he later renounced. President of the Theosophical Society from 1907 until her death. Wrote widely on Theosophy and many of her works are still in print and used for esoteric instruction.

besom—From Old English *besema* or *besma* (a bundle of twigs). A witch's broom, used in Wiccan rituals. See also broom.

bezoar—A precious stone found in the entrails of certain animals that possessed magickal properties.

bi-location—The ability to be in two places at once. Accomplished using astral travel, but the person retains awareness of their surroundings, of their physical body, and awareness of their astral self. A type of out-of-body experience.

bibliomancy—Divination using books. Specifically divination using the Bible. Other sacred texts as well as classical books (especially Shakespeare) are also used. One thinks of a question, closes their eyes, allows the book to fall open, and places their finger on a page. Some also use a pin to pinpoint the passage. Whichever passage or paragraph is indicated is the answer to the question. A form of divination approved by most Christian sects. Also called rhapsodomancy when poetry is used. Stichomancy or stoichomancy is divination using a random passage in a book.

bigghes, beighes—See witch's jewels.

binding—1) The sealing of a Working. "Thus we are met, on a night which is not a night, in a place which is not a place, at a time which is no longer a time. May the Gods protect us on our magickal journey," is the binding on a Circle as it is being created. 2) A spell which is designed to restrict a person or thing to limit its actions. Considered black magick by some, only done when there is an urgent necessity, and in the least restrictive manner possible. 3) In certain Traditions binding is used in Initiations, the actual tying of hands, hobbling of feet, or other bindings. This practice is borrowed from Masonry.

birth stones—In many occult sources, including the Bible, precious stones are linked with the signs of the zodiac, Lost Tribes of Israel, and other things. Precious stones and their associated meanings can be used in talismanic magick or in amulets.

These correspondences are the basis for the tables that list birth stones for the various months, a practice popularized by the jewelry industry since the early 1900s. Often these lists are altered depending on price, availability, and popularity of various gem stones and materials. These lists are commercially driven and have little psychic or magickal basis. There are older, less economically driven lists, but here too availability is a consideration, as is workability and durability. Unfortunately, most of these correspondences are suspect because the descriptions of the stones can mean various minerals or gemstones depending upon time period and/or geographic location. Ancient names for materials may not correspond to modern equivalents. In the ancient world the name "lapis lazuli," for example, may have been applied to any gem material of a blue color, which includes what we now call lapis lazuli, sodalite, azurite, turquoise, blue sapphire, blue zircon, aquamarine, and various other opaque and transparent materials of a blue color. In addition, the same name may have been applied to two different materials depending upon availability. And, conversely, the same material may have gone by two or more different names in neighboring localities (in space or time).

bisba—A modern form of character reading by the size and shape of a woman's breasts. The underlying belief is that a woman's breasts reveal more of her character than any other feature.

Black Arts—Medieval term referring to practices that included summoning and controlling of demons, necromancy, possibly witchcraft, almost any form of divination, as well as the general practice of magick. Generally any occult and/or arcane lore or practice that was frowned upon or forbidden by the Church. By practicing the Black Arts it was presumed by the Church that one risked one's immortal soul or was already damned.

Black Book—Alternative term for a Book of Shadows. Term used before the term Book of Shadows was introduced by Gerald Gardner. See Book of Shadows.

black magick—See magick.

Black Mass—A deliberate and obscene travesty of the Christian Mass for black magick purposes, which strictly speaking can only be performed by an unfrocked or corrupt priest. It was created during the Spanish Inquisition, and was fed by mass delusion and also unscrupulous persons who wanted to shock and defy society (like Sir Francis Dashwood and the Hell Fire Club in England in the 1700s). Modern reproductions appear in satanic literature, in varying guises and levels of mockery. This rite has never been a part of genuine Wicca.

Blavatsky, Madame Helena Petrovna—(1831–1891) Medium, spiritualist, and founder of the Theosophical movement in 1875 in New York with Colonel Henry Steel Olcott. Theosophy was a forerunner of the Golden Dawn and other occult organizations. She was a natural medium and exhibited extraordinary psychic abilities, some of which were tested and verified under scientific conditions, others that were considered highly suspect. She went to Tibet for some years and returned to England in 1870 and then traveled to America. She was charismatic and had many followers. Theosophy is a blend of Hindu, Buddhist, occult, and mystical elements and is still practiced. Blavatsky wrote many books, many of which are still in print and are used as texts for esoteric knowledge.

bless/blessing—1) A prayer said over something to keep it sacred and safe from harm or unwanted influences or a prayer said over a person to keep them safe from harm and under the protection of the Gods. 2) Blessing: the act of using psychic energy for benefit. Prayer is a specific type of blessing.

blessed—Something that has been made sacred or magickally protected.

Blessed Be—A phrase used between Wiccans as a greeting, farewell, and blessing. Sometimes abbreviated as BB.

blighting—The use of psychic energy to harm or destroy a living thing. Considered by some to be black magick.

blindfold—1) Some Traditions blindfold candidates for Initiation; it is a practice borrowed from the Masons and can also be used as a technique to either enhance or block psychic ability. 2) In some cultures animals and birds are blindfolded while hatching and rearing young. This supposedly bestowed upon the offspring the abilities to find gold, treasure, or certain plants or herbs useful in magick.

blood of the Moon—See Moon Blood.

boline, bolline—A white-handled knife or a small sickle. A sacred tool used for various mundane functions: cutting cord, scribing words or sigils on items, slicing food, harvesting herbs, etc. Known as a Kerfan in Welsh Traditions. The athame is used only to "cut energy" and the boline is used for the cutting/chopping tasks. Can be as simple as a steak knife, a paring knife, a jackknife, or a hunting knife. The traditional boline is single-edged. Some Wiccans do combine their athame and boline in one blade, keeping it sharp and using it to cut mundane things as well as energy.

Bolines: Sickle and Straight

Book of Changes—See I Ching.

Book of the Dead—A series of ancient Egyptian religious and magickal texts detailing the soul's journey after death, giving advice and magickal aid to ensure safe passage through Amanti (the Egyptian Underworld). This document was buried with all those who died, but there were three common versions, short, medium, and long. These were written in a scribe factory, leaving blanks for the deceased's name. One's relatives purchased a copy that fit their pocketbook, the name was filled in, and it was buried with the deceased during the funeral rites. When it was translated in modern times it became an esoteric text. In the 1970s, the original papyrus scroll that was given to Joseph Smith by the Angel Moroni, and from which he was able to "translate" the Book of Mormon, was determined to be a middle-length unused version of the Book of the Dead. At the time Smith was translating the papyrus, hieroglyphics was an unknown language and his translations predated the discovery of the Rosetta stone. The papyrus has since disappeared and the Mormon Church denies all accounts of this information.

Book of Shadows—A.k.a., Grimoire or Black Book. It is a Wiccan's book of things they have learned. It is a combination notebook, journal, memoir, spell book, cookbook, encyclopedia, and general journal for information magickal and Wiccan. A compendium of Wiccan and magickal lore, it was originally held in common by a coven or Tradition, written by the High Priestess. When a new coven formed, the new High Priestess would hand-copy the Book of Shadows so her new group would have its own copy. Today, most Wiccans have their own Book of Shadows.

As Wicca has no Holy Bible, each person is encouraged to keep a Book of Shadows that they use in their religious activities. This becomes their guide for how to be a Wiccan. Some Traditions require that the Book of Shadows be hand-copied from one's teachers. Computerized Wiccans have a Disk of Shadows, keeping their notes on disk or hard drive. Today xerography is also widely used for disseminating information. Much of the material that was formerly only in Books of Shadows and passed from Initiate to Initiate is now published, so a library can also be an adjunct to a Wiccan's Book of Shadows.

Some Traditions require that the Book of Shadows be kept secret and only shown to students and fellow Initiates. Some require that the Book of Shadows be destroyed when the owner dies. Some require that the Book of Shadows be passed on to successors in the coven. Originally each book was hand-copied by its owner and passed on for safety, since, if it was in your handwriting only you were responsible for its dissemination. At present, due to desktop publishing and photocopying it is now virtually impossible to trace materials to any specific source, so fewer and fewer Traditions mandate all materials be hand-copied.

boomerang effect—Slang for the Law of Three, whatever you send out will return to you three-fold. May specifically refer to a psychic attack that meets with a stronger defense.

botanica—Occult store that caters to the needs of the Afro-Catholic practitioners of Voudun, Macumba, Santeria, etc. May also carry more "generic" occult materials. Botanicas stock herbs, spells, charms, votive candles, images of saints, etc. There may also be a practitioner in residence who can help those in need and possibly tell fortunes.

botanomancy—Divination by burning branches of brier and vervain that are inscribed with questions.

bracelet—In some Traditions a cuff bracelet is a mark of a Third Degree Initiate. The bracelet may be engraved with certain symbols or dates. Women may have a silver bracelet, men a gold or brass one.

brazier—Incense burner or thurible. Made of non-flammable materials like ceramic or metal with sand in

Brazier

the bottom to absorb heat and hold incense in place. Loose incense can also be placed on top of charcoal briquettes. It may also hang from a chain.

broom (besom)—A sacred tool, it can be used to cleanse an area by sweeping away all the negative influences, literally and figuratively. In handfasting/wedding ceremonies, the couple "jumps the broom" to signify that they are setting up housekeeping and leaping into a new future together.

Brothers of the Shadow, Dark Brothers, Grey Brothers—Name sometimes used for those who follow the left-hand path or practice black magick. Not the same as the Men in Black.

brutch—An area of psychic distortion in local space/time, such as the Bermuda Triangle, it is generally much larger than a gate.

Bulwer-Lytton—(1831–1891) An English writer who was an occultist and acquainted with Eliaphas Levi, and helped bring the esoteric knowledge to those who eventually founded the Golden Dawn, he is also the author of the immortal first line "It was a dark and stormy night," in whose honor a bad prose contest is held each year.

Burning Times, The, the burning—Refers to the witchcraft persecutions in history, sometimes specifically those of the Catholic Inquisition, sometimes generally used to describe any religious persecution of Pagans, heathens, heretics, or followers of "the Old Ways." Wiccans feel these martyrs are their spiritual ancestors, and are quite adamant about not allowing this form of religious persecution. "Never again the burning" is a cry that is understood personally by Wiccans, too many of whom have suffered modern persecutions for their religious beliefs. In actuality witches in England were customarily hanged, not burned, and other methods of torture and death (pressing and drowning) were also used more widely than burning. It is the idea that witches and/or Pagans were persecuted, tortured, and killed by the early Christians and others for their beliefs that is the meaning behind the cry, "Never again the burning."

C

CAW, Church of All Worlds—A Neo-Pagan organization that is non-denominational. Local branches are called "Nests," and it is based upon the ideas presented in Robert A. Heinlein's novel *Stranger in a Strange Land.* The magazine *Green Egg* is the official church magazine, and the magazine is read by many others who are interested in Wicca and Neo-Paganism. The church was inspired by science fiction as mythology, and dedicated to the celebration of life, the maximal actualization of human potential, and the realization of ultimate individual freedom and personal responsibility in harmonious eco-psychic relationship with the total biosphere of Holy Mother Earth. A catalyst for the coalescence of consciousness. Ecosophyl world-view.

CE—Common Era, less Christocentric term for years formerly numbered "after Christ" or AD (Anno Domini—the "year of our Lord" in Latin).

COG, Covenant of the Goddess—An organization of witches, some are Wiccans, others are not. COG is an international corporation, an ecumenical umbrella organization of witchcraft covens that provides legal corporate status for member groups. Originally founded on more of a Dianic and Eclectic model than at the present time. Open to females and males equally, in COG local covens are members of the larger organization with local branches called "coun-

cils." There are various levels of participation and elevations. The organization holds a Grand Council every fall called Merry Meet (usually around Labor Day weekend) at which time officers are elected and group business conducted. The site of Merry Meet moves from region to region in the United States annually in a set pattern. Has councils in the United States, Canada, Australia, and New Zealand.

Cabbala—see Kabbalah.

cacodaemon, cacodemon—From Greek *kakos daimon* (evil spirit), it is a term used by medieval and ancient astrologers to describe the twelfth house, traditionally a house of misfortune, imprisonment, undoing, ruin, and other calamities. This fatalistic interpretation is rejected by modern humanistic astrologers.

caduceus—The name given to a number of different symbolic wands, first appearing in Mesopotamia circa 2600 BCE, and later in a number of different cultures. The wands consisted of two serpents or basilisks entwined around a rod. The serpent entwined winged staff was carried by Hermes/Mercury. The white wand was carried by Roman heralds suing for peace. In Hindu and Buddhist esoteric teachings it symbolizes the kundalini energy encircling the spine. In Masonry it symbolizes

Caduceus

the harmony and balance between negative and positive forces, the fixed and the inconstant, the continuity of life and the decay of life. Adopted by the medical profession as a symbol of their craft, it is a healing symbol, and also a symbol of magick.

Cagliostro, Count Alessandro, born Giuseppe Balsamo—(1743–1795) An Italian magician and adventurer born in Palermo, Sicily, he was initiated into the Knights of Malta at twenty-three where he studied Kabbalah, alchemy, and occult subjects. Later in London he joined the Freemasons. He traveled Europe performing feats of magick and selling an elixir he called elixir of life. He was framed and was subsequently tried for fraud. He was eventually released and went to Rome where he attempted to start an Egyptian Freemasonry Order. He was imprisoned by the Church, questioned by the Inquisition, and sentenced to death in 1791. His sentence was commuted to life in prison. His psychic abilities included psychic healing, alchemy, and scrying. After his death, rumors that he escaped and was alive persisted in Europe, Russia, and America.

cantrip—A written spell or charm that reads the same forward or backward.

capnomancy—Divination using wreaths of smoke. 1) Used by European peasants until modern times, a sacred bonfire was lit on certain holidays, and the smoke of that bonfire was used for the divination. Usually used to predict weather for a season, the smoke allowed observation of air layers and thus could show meteorological conditions. 2) Indoors, burnable substances were thrown on a hearth fire and the smoke was used to interpret questions or messages. 3) Psychotropic substances were burned in a fire, the smoke inhaled, and the ecstatic state used for divination.

cartomancy—Divination by reading playing cards, specifically, divination by reading tarot cards. There are many methods of divination using cards, and many types of cards: a standard deck of playing cards, tarot cards, specialized decks of cards based on non-card systems (mah jong, runes), individually created card decks, sometimes erroneously also called tarot.

Cassandra—1) In classical Greek mythology the daughter of King Priam and Hecuba, she won the love of Apollo by her beauty and he gave her the gift of prophecy in exchange for her love. When she refused Apollo's advances he cursed her so that, although she retained the gift of prophecy, no one would believe her prophecies. She was a major figure in the *Iliad*. 2) A female who is a prophet or seer, sometimes one who is not believed but whose prophecies are found to be true after the fact.

cast—A creative act with intent, as in cast a Circle or cast Circle (create Sacred Space); cast a spell (gathering, focusing, and then sending mental energy); or cast out all impurities (cleansing with intent).

catoptromancy, catoxtromancy—Divination using a magic mirror. It is a form of scrying; the mirror was either suspended in water or angled to catch the light of the Moon. In modern versions a black mirror is used. Some speculate that in the Middle Ages concave mirrors were used.

cattabomancy—Divination using bronze vessels. In ancient China (Zhou dynasty eighth to fifth centuries BCE) many varieties of specially shaped bronze vessels were used for sacred and divinatory purposes.

cauldron—From Old French *caudron* or *chaudron*, derived from Latin *caldaria*, a kettle for hot water. In English before 1330 it was called a caudrun, after it was caldron or caudrona. A black metal pot used for various magickal purposes, traditionally it is made of cast-iron, has three legs, and a handle. It can be used for making potions and herbal brews or cooking; or used (with sand in the bottom) as a portable "fire" with candles inside; it symbolizes the womb and thus can be termed "the cauldron of rebirth," used in rebirthing ceremonies. Also used in ceremonies as a term referring to the Goddess' womb of rebirth, which has the power to both create and destroy, and is needed for the perpetuation of life. Traditionally used to restore the dead or bring fertility to the crops.

Cauldron

causimomancy—Divination by fire. When objects thrown into a fire did not burn, it was considered a good omen.

Cayce, Edgar—(1877–1945) A.k.a., The Sleeping Prophet—An American trance channeler who was able to access the Akashic Records directly (psychically), diagnose illness, and prescribe cures, often locating the remedy in hidden places in forgotten back rooms. Originally merely a gifted reader and healer, he later revealed a Christian doctrine of reincarnation and a hidden Christian tradition that stretched back to Atlantis and accounted for Jesus' "lost" years. A photographer by profession, Cayce never charged for his readings and was constantly on the verge of bankruptcy. Most of his readings were transcribed first by Cayce's wife, Gertrude, then later

by his secretary Gladys Davis. This mass of material still exists and is the basis for the Association for Research and Enlightenment (ARE), headquartered in Virginia Beach, Virginia. Many books have been written about Cayce (pronounced "casey") and his work did much to bring psychic abilities to the attention of the public.

celebration—A Sabbat, Esbat, or other event in which a Circle is created for the purpose of entertainment or to celebrate a holiday or other non-spell type event. Can be combined with spellwork, but the main intent is for celebration, not accomplishing a specific spell-related magickal goal.

censer, cense—See brazier.

centered—The condition of being psychically aware and yet contained within yourself. Psychically relaxed and ready.

centering dome—A place (often a tent) at a festival near the medicine tent where volunteers are housed who are skilled in helping people who have problems coping with the energy generated at such an event. Also a psychic neutral zone and safe spot, and a place where people with psychological problems can go and talk.

ceramancy, ceromancy, ceroscopy—Divination by interpretation of melted wax. Wax is melted in one vessel and then poured into a bowl of cold water and the resulting shapes are interpreted. Shapes and their interpretation are well documented, and these interpretations are the basis for tasseography.

ceraunoscopy—Ancient divination method employing meteorological phenomena, thunder, and lightning.

Cernunnos—A Celtic God; little is known about this Deity other than his name and image, which is that of a stag-horned male that was found on the Gundestrap Cauldron circa 250 BCE. The cauldron was made by the Celts and found in the Balkan area. Modern lore has filled in a mythology and attributes. A popular God with Wiccans, sometimes known as the God of the Wiccans, although this is by no means universal. The name Cernunnos appears in chants and rituals descended from Gardnerian Wicca.

Cernunnos

chain of being—An ancient concept that proposes an immutable order and hierarchy of creation from the Throne of God to the lowest beings of Earth. The chain of being stretches from the highest heaven to the Center of the Earth. Developed by Plato and continued by Aristotle and the Neo-Platonists, this idea is the basis for many cosmologies, including that of the Catholic Church. Dante popularized this concept in his books *Inferno*, *Purgatorio*, and *Paradiso*, known as *The Divine Comedy*.

chakra—Sanskrit, wheel, a center of biomagnetic energy in the human body. There are many systems of chakras, but the "standard" system has seven chakras. Similar to the idea of Chi in Oriental martial and spiritual arts. To "open one's chakras" is to allow the free flow of psychic energy in the body and allows one's psychic awareness to become enhanced. Having a "blocked chakra" can inhibit an individual's ability to manipulate energy, and affects spiritual, emotional, mental, and/or physical health. Each chakra corresponds to an area of the body, a life condition, and a color. Raising the Kundalini Serpent refers to an opening of the chakras and a flow of energy that can attune a person to the infinite. One can reportedly cleanse one's or another's chakras with energy, crystals, meditation, exercises, and other psychic and spiritual techniques. The seven chakras are: first or base, which is red and centered at the base of the spine; second or root, which is orange and centered in the sexual organs; third or solar plexus, which is yellow and centered in the stomach or diaphragm; fourth or heart, which is green and centered in the heart or center of the chest; fifth or throat, which is blue and centered in the throat; sixth or third eye, which is indigo and located in the center of the forehead; and seventh or crown, which is violet and located at the top or just above the top of the head.

chalcomancy—Divination by striking bowls of copper or brass. The Oracle of Dodona employed this as one method of divination, giving meanings to the various tones produced. It is associated with the music of the spheres.

chalice—From Greek *kylix* (see also cup), a consecrated ceremonial cup used in ritual. Usually a stemmed goblet, although any shape can be used. Symbolizes the element Water, used to hold the sacred libation. Symbolizes the feminine aspect in the Great Rite.

Chalice

chalk—A natural substance from the decomposed skeletons of marine organisms, it is used for drawing and scribing Circles. Considered to be magickal because of its animal origin, it possesses natural energy, and residual life force that can aid magickal Workings.

challenge—Some Traditions require that each prospective participant in a Circle be challenged upon entrance to the Circle. Usually a blade is placed at the throat or chest and a verbal challenge is made of the participant. With a satisfactory answer, the blade is removed and the person welcomed into the Circle. Also used in Initiations.

Symbolizes the importance of keeping the secrets of the Tradition. Borrowed from Masonry.

channeling—A "New Age" term, it is also called mediumship, and was called Spiritualism in the nineteenth century. A trance-like condition in which one person allows their personality to step aside and some other entity use their body for communication. Not recommended for those who are either untrained or frivolous in their intent, as it can lead to possession if it is not done in a carefully controlled setting (as in a Circle) with strong safeguards and people who know how to handle any problems that arise. Invocation of a Goddess or God is a type of channeling, which requires careful training. It is not common for a Deity to speak through a Priest or Priestess, although it does happen on occasion. Channeling in various forms is universal throughout history. Shamans, ancient Egyptian priests, Greek Oracles, prophets and saints of Jewish, Christian, and Islamic traditions and many others have practiced various forms of channeling and received messages from Deities. Madame Helena P. Blavatsky is one of the most famous modern mediums. J.Z. Knight, who channels Ramtha, is a popular "New Age" channeler.

chaomancy—Divination using atmospheric conditions in general. Can be a general term for the more specific methods of atmospheric divination. Used as a method of weather prediction, and survives in various aphorisms and superstitions. An example of an aphorism associated with chaomancy is the following:

"When the wind is in the east,
'tis neither good for man nor beast,
when the wind is in the north,
the skillful fisher goes not forth.
When the wind is in the south,

it blows the bait from the fishes' mouth,
when the wind is in the west,
then it is the very best." (traditional)

Charge, The Charge—Short for the Charge of the Goddess (or God). This is the traditional address of the Goddess to her followers, delivered by the High Priestess. The most common version is one which was compiled by Gerald Gardner reportedly with help from Doreen Valiente and others, incorporating materials from Crowley and other sources. At present, there are many other "charges" written, of the God, Crone, Dark Goddess, and others, all adapted from and modeled after Gardner's original Charge, which was based upon passages from Apuleus' classical allegorical tale, *The Golden Ass*, and passages from *Aradia, Gospel of the Witches*, by Leland.

charge—1) To imbue or infuse with magickal energy. 2) To instruct or assign, as in the Charge of the Goddess.

charged—That which has magickal energy within and can be used for magickal purposes.

charm—From Latin *carmen* (song). 1) A spell; spoken, sung, or written magickal words. 2) Object carried for magickal powers or protective properties. See fetish and amulet.

chartomancy—Divination by written inscription. One can write or interpret inscriptions. When revealed, inscriptions written in invisible ink are one form. Greeting cards are a modern descendant of this art.

cheresmomancy—Divination by the utterances given by a person in an ecstatic frenzy. This method was used by the Oracle at Delphi. The oracle would breathe the smoke from sacred (and probably hallucinogenic) herbs, and the priests would interpret what she said. Similar to glossalalia.

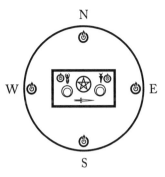

Circle with Altar and Quarters

Chi, Ki, Qi—Chinese/Japanese pronounced "chee." Life force energy that can be used in martial arts, healing, and psychic disciplines. Etheric energy that can be harnessed and controlled to produce amazing effects. An energy that pervades all living things, including animals, plants, rocks, the Universe, and all things in it. Similar to prana.

chiromancy, cheiromancy, chironomancy, cheirosophy—Palm reading. Also known as palmistry. Divination by interpreting the lines of the hand. Also the shape of the hand, fingers, nails, etc.

chrystallomancy—See crystalomancy.

chthonic—(*k'-THON-ick*) From Greek *chthon* (Earth). Of or pertaining to the depths of the Earth. Caves, volcanoes, deep rift valleys above and below water, almost any place which is below average ground level. Deities that inhabit these places can be referred to as chthonian.

cingulam—See cord; a magickally charged cord worn around the waist and used for binding, measuring, and counting.

Circle, circle—1) The usual shape of Sacred Space. 2) An area of Sacred Space. Some Traditions require that a Circle must be nine feet in diameter, and measured out with a cord, drawn with chalk on the ground. Others make the Circle as large or small as space and need dictates. 3) "Put up a Circle" means to perform a ritual and define an area of Sacred Space for a Working. 4) As a verb, it is the act of putting up a Circle, as in, will you Circle with us tonight? 5) Three or more people who gather together to work ritual or magick (see coven). 6) A gathering of Wiccans and/or Pagans. 7) A level of degree attainment in the Church of All Worlds. In CAW, there are nine circles and to advance requires study and reading and tests knowledge and abilities.

circlet—A thin metal band worn around the head. Usually silver, it denotes one who is a High Priestess or High Priest. It can also be the mark of an Initiate or an Initiate of a certain degree. Also used as a mark of rank in the SCA (Society for Creative Anachronism). Different Traditions have different customs and rules for who may and may not wear a circlet and other marks of Initiation and/or rank. See also crown.

Circlet

clairaudience—From the French, clear hearing, the ability to psychically hear events that are remote in space and/or time, or not discernible to normal hearing.

clairsentience—From the French, clear sensing, the ability to psychically sense things that are remote in space and/or time, or not discernible to normal senses. A general term that can include clairaudience and clairvoyance but also includes smell, taste, touch, and emotional sensations.

clairvoyance—From the French, clear seeing, the ability to psychically see events that are remote in space and/or time, or not discernible to normal sight. Also used as a more general term for any psychic ability by which a person senses things from afar.

classical planets—The seven classical planets are Saturn, Jupiter, Mars, Sun, Venus, Mercury, and Moon. These planets are visible to the naked eye and were known throughout the ancient world. When older works refer to "the planets," it is the classical planets to which the term refers. Uranus, Neptune, and Pluto were not discovered yet. Modern transcriptions of these older works sometimes have changed the term "planets" to "classical planets" to clear up any confusion that might arise if the reader does not understand the distinction. (See also modern planets.)

cleanse, cleansed, cleansing—To remove unwanted or stray influences, to magickally make pure. See also purification.

cledonomancy—Divination by interpretation of utterances in a trance state, similar to glossalalia, or speaking in tongues.

cleidomancy, clidomancy—From Greek *kleis* (key) and *manteia* (divination). 1) Divination using a key suspended by a string tied to the finger. This has evolved into pendulum divination. The key was also used in connection with books, especially the Bible. By holding the key over a page it would indicate a passage for guidance or divination. 2) In one form a person holds a key in one fist and offers both closed fists to a pregnant woman. If she chooses the hand with the key, it indicates her child will be a girl.

cleromancy—1) Divination by the drawing of lots. 2) Divination by means of throwing dice or other small objects.

climaterics—Certain critical years in a person's life. Generally considered to be the years evenly divisible by seven: seven, fourteen, twenty-one, twenty-eight, thirty-five, etc. Associated with the Lunar and Saturn cycles in astrology and popularized by Madame Blavatsky and Rudolf Steiner.

closed—In magickal usage this term is used to indicate something is not open or available to all who are interested. Opposite of open. When used in reference to a Circle, a "closed Circle" is a Circle that is restricted in some manner to certain participants only, all others are excluded. When used in reference to a group, "this group is closed," means there is no provision for new members, at this particular time. Generally not used for exclusivity but for reasons of safety, benefit for participants, or expediency. For example a women's mysteries ritual would usually be closed to men. An Initiation ritual would be closed except for participants and/or observers of that Tradition of a certain degree level and above, except for the candidate.

cloud dissolving—A supposed demonstration of psychokinetic ability, causing clouds to dissolve or change shape at will. A form of weather Working.

collective consciousness—A group mind that can be created by a number of people working together over time. Ideally manifests as a single consciousness, but in practice a group in which the participants are so familiar with each other and how they work magickally together that there is no need for instruction concerning roles or duties. This is one goal of a coven.

collective unconscious—Jungian, the collective symbols and the understanding of the symbols that underlie a society and possibly all of humanity. The collective memory and knowledge of a group that accumulates over time and can be accessed through dreams, meditation, and psychic techniques. Archetypes are manifestations of collective unconscious. Dream interpretation is based upon universal symbols that are part of the collective unconscious.

color correspondences—In magick there are a number of color correspondences that relate to a variety of ideas and/or objects. In Kabbalah and Ceremonial Magick, there is the King's list and the Queen's list of color correspondences as well as myriad other interpretations passed down since ancient times. Modern psychological theory has supported some premises of ancient sources (red as a color of passion, lust, anger, and aggression as well as energy.) There is no one all-inclusive correct list of meanings or correspondences. *777* by Aleister Crowley is a very good source for lists of correspondences.

community—The total Wiccan population of a designated area, a community can be a neighborhood, a city, a state, a country, a continent, the world. The greater Wiccan (or Pagan) Community generally refers to a nationwide group of people very loosely affiliated and loosely in contact through the Internet, various zines, newsletters, group affiliations, and festivals. There are many more Wiccans out there than is generally known because there are a large number of solitaires and small groups that are isolated and unconnected to the greater Pagan Community. Because of secrecy one can have a good friend who is also Pagan and never know it until you meet by chance at a festival, for example.

cone of power—A magickal construct that is raised by a magickal Working; the combined psychic energy of the participants, constrained by a magickal Circle, directed by a single will (usually the presiding Priestess or Priest), released at the peak of the Working to accomplish the aims of the Working. The energy raised within a Circle. Used to aid the magick work for healing or celebration. It can be visualized as a cone whose base is the Circle of people working and the apex is above the center of that Circle.

conjure, conjuration—The act of summoning up or creating nonphysical entities or spirits. Sometimes generically used for working magick.

consecrated—Dedicated to magickal service. Dedicated to the service of a Deity. Also applied to magickal tools or items that have been blessed in ritual.

consensus—Arrival at a decision by agreement. Many Pagan and Wiccan groups use consensus to make the decisions of the group, although, in some cases, authority and responsibility are clearly defined. It requires more time and conversation than voting, but it can result in less dissension and more cooperation.

Contagion, Law of—Things or entities that have been in physical or psychic contact can continue to interact with each other after separation in space or time. For example, one can use a personal object to "tune in" to the owner, no matter where they are.

cord—Long flexible material like string or rope. Used as a tool in magickal acts such as binding, or knotting and/or unknotting a spell to focus intent. Can be braided and/or in certain colors to indicate attainment of degrees.

Braided Cords

cords—A (usually) braided belt of three or more strands that symbolizes the Initiate's degree of attainment within the person's Wiccan Tradition. Often a braided belt that is used to carry one's athame. A braided belt that has a spell or intent woven into it. Generally an item of magickal use and intent, part of a Wiccan wardrobe. In some Traditions the length of cords is specified, and that length is used as a radius to measure the size of a standard Circle for that particular Tradition. See also cingulam.

correspondences—In magick and the Craft there are many systems of correspondences, in which a variety of attributes can relate to the larger concept. In Kabbalah, each of the ten sephiroth have numerous correspondences, including colors, attributes, emotions, qualities, incenses, plants, numbers, and many more. There are many correspondences in tarot, runes, astrology, and other systems as well. The book *777*, by Aleister Crowley, is a book of lists of myriad correspondences. Some people have tried to "force" cross-correspondences between systems—runes and astrology, for example—some systems work with cross-correspondences (astrology, tarot, and Kabbalah, for example), some do not (runes, for example). Each symbol (rune, tarot card, sephira, astrological symbol, etc.) is more of a concept or idea than a single thing, and the correspondences allow a person to more fully grasp the whole concept symbolized by the thing. The more correspondences one learns, the better one can grasp the ideas underlying a specific concept or discipline.

Council of Themis—In the late 1960s to early 1970s a Pan-Pagan Council (not affiliated with the festival Pan Pagan) was formed in California. Various Pagan leaders banded together in a loosely organized group to communicate and represent a number of smaller groups. Because this conglomeration was too eclectic and the various groups had little in common, the Council dissolved within a few years due to factionalism. It was a precursor to the Covenant of the Goddess (COG).

coven—From Latin *conveniere* (to agree, to be of one mind, to come together). A Wiccan group that has come together to work magick and study Wicca and related subjects. In many ways it can be compared to a Bible study group. Traditionally there are up to thirteen members, but covens can be as large or small as the members want. Groups much larger than thirteen are awkward and with more than twenty members groups tend to break up into smaller groups. Three members is generally the minimum. Often the number is dictated by the space in which the coven meets—commonly someone's living room. The internal hierarchy, rules, and operation are decided by the members.

Covens are formed for many reasons: teaching or training covens teach or train new people; a working coven is a group of Initiates who meet and work magick and study Wicca and related topics. Covens are also subsets of various denominations of Wicca, i.e., a Gardnerian coven is a local "branch" of Gardnerian Wicca. A coven is often led by a High Priestess and a High Priest, though this is not mandatory. In some Traditions, a coven is an Inner Court group.

covenant—A document or verbal agreement detailing the rules by which a particular coven is run. Can be as elaborate as the United States Constitution or as simple as a few verbal rules. Each coven decides how it runs, who is in charge, what purpose the coven is established for, how new members are brought in, what the mechanism is for having members who wish to leave, how to maintain order, etc. Many of these questions are only implicitly addressed; ideally, all are at least acknowledged and discussed. Usually the coven does not establish a written covenant until there have been interpersonal problems within the group, and the covenant is in response to those problems. The Ardanes probably started as a covenant and there are groups that use the Ardanes as a covenant for their group.

Covenant of the Goddess (COG)—See COG.

covendom—Geographical area of a coven.

Traditionally, each coven covered an area of one league (about three miles) in any direction, a circle of about six miles in diameter. Today, with so many different Traditions and urban Pagans this is generally ignored.

covenstead—The home site for the coven, the place where a coven meets, usually someone's home. May or may not be the home of the High Priestess or High Priest. Not all covens have a covenstead.

cowan—Non-Pagan or non-Wiccan person. A term borrowed from Masonry by Gerald Gardner.

Craft—An alternate name for Wicca, as in The Craft or "the craft of the wise." Crafter is a colloquial term for a person who practices Wicca. Today it is considered an abbreviation of witchcraft, though not all Wiccans consider themselves witches, and not all witches consider themselves Wiccans.

Craft name—The name one chooses for oneself that is used within Wicca. Can also be a magickal name or just an alternative name. Many Wiccans know each other only by their Craft names.

Creatrix—Female creator. Goddess.

credentials—In Wicca there are few academic or religious credentials awarded. Certain Traditions grant degrees, although these are often unrecognized by other Traditions. Ministerial credentials issued by state or local authorities are valuable, but rare; few Wiccan churches have tax-exempt status or the authority to grant recognized ministerial credentials. ULC, Universal Life Church, is sometimes used by Wiccans desiring ministerial credentials. The UU (Unitarian Universalist) Church has offered to give people the opportunity to receive ministerial credentials through completion of their seminary course. Some Wiccans have taken the courses, and CUUPS (Congregation of Unitarian Universalist Pagans) have sprung up in various parts of the country. Some Wiccans have university degrees in magic, comparative religion, or feminist studies. However, the majority of Wiccans are self-taught or taught by others with few or no recognized credentials. Word of mouth is the best way of ascertaining whether a person is knowledgeable, and talking to the person and judging for yourself may be best. A university degree does not necessarily mean a person has knowledge or competence in Wiccan ways or magick. There is little academic snobbery in Wicca, but being a published author can sometimes substitute for a degree in terms of status and authority in the Wiccan Community.

crime solving—Psychic abilities and forms of divination have been used by modern law enforcement to solve crimes. Occasionally psychics have come forward of their own volition, but usually there is a person "on call" who is consulted in difficult or dead-end cases. Valuable information can be obtained by psychics, and at times they have given tips or leads which have led to discovery of victims or evidence. This work is difficult for most psychics, as it involves violence, dark emotions, injury, and death. Many do not do it for any length of time, and law enforcement agencies are reluctant to use psychics unless there is no other alternative, usually because they fear negative publicity. However, there is a good success rate, so this method is still pursued by enlightened law enforcement departments.

crithomancy, critomancy—Divination using grain in sacrificial rites. Patterns made by the grain or its flour or the dough or cakes baked from the dough are studied. Also includes the behavior of the dough and quality and features of the baked products which are produced.

cromniomancy—Divination using planted onions. Names or events are written on onions and then ceremonially planted. The first to sprout contains the answer. A long-range method of prediction.

Crone—The third face of the Goddess, the aspect that represents maturity and wisdom, a female who is past her childbearing years—after menopause. Also a title of great respect for a woman. One who has been through a Croning ceremony.

Croning—A ceremony for a woman celebrating menopause and the end of childbearing, it can be a rite of passage or a ceremony honoring a leader who has passed into an advisory and/or mentoring role. It can celebrate the time of taking a seat around a council fire and possibly retiring from active leadership.

cross-quarters—The directions between the cardinal quarters: SE, SW, NW, and NE. Also slang for the four great holidays: Beltane, Lughnasadh, Samhain, and Imbolc (as opposed to the holidays celebrated on the quarters—solstices and equinoxes—which are less important, and which some Traditions do not celebrate at all).

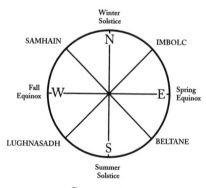

Cross-quarters

Crowley, Aleister, nee Edward Alexander Crowley—(1875–1947) The self-styled "wickedest man in the world," a.k.a., "the Great Beast 666" and the "Beast of the Apocalypse." Crowley, born in England, is a prominent figure in Western Magick in the twentieth century. He was a member of the Hermetic Order of the Golden Dawn (1898–1907?), founder of the A.A. (Astrum Argentum—Silver Star—1911), and member of the OTO (Ordo Templar Orientalis—Order of the Temple of the East—1912), all of which were Ceremonial Magick groups. Crowley's parents were members of the Plymouth Brethren, a fundamentalist Protestant Christian sect, and they raised him in an atmosphere of strict discipline, repression, and religious bigotry. He was extremely rebellious and his mother in sorrow and exasperation christened him the Beast after the Antichrist. In Cairo in 1903, Crowley's personal guardian angel, Aiwass, appeared to him and dictated *The Book of the Law* (1904). This is the basis for the Thelemic magickal system, the basic premise of which is the Law of Thelema: "Do what thou wilt shall be the whole of the law. Love is the Law. Love under Will."

Crowley worked with magick and occultism and wrote a number of books on various topics, the most prominent of which is *Magick in Theory and Practice* (1929), which was the basic text for generations of Ceremonial Magicians. He also wrote *Moonchild* (1929), a fictionalized account of his attempts to beget a magickal child, and *The Book of Thoth* (1944). Crowley was also an adventurer, sexual compulsive, and drug addict, the latter due to his chronic lifelong affliction with asthma. He is rumored to have been initiated into the old style witchcraft of Old George Pickingill. Whether Crowley actually ever met Gerald Gardner, or whether he initiated Gardner into his style of Wicca or gave Gardner any magickal or Wiccan materials, is a controversial Craft legend. Crowley's written material has left a sound magickal and occult legacy that is used widely within Wicca as well as other magickal groups.

crown—A silver circlet with a crescent moon, or a triple moon, it is the badge of rank of a High Priestess, Witch Queen, or May Queen. A Horned Crown is the mark of the High Priest or Green Man. Usually the crowns are worn only in Circle during Sabbats and other coven activities. Various Traditions have rules and customs regarding who may wear what crowns and circlets and when they may be worn. To "put on the crown" or "put on the horns" is slang for taking the part of May Queen or Green Man in Beltane celebrations, or taking the part of High Priestess or High Priest.

Crown

Horned Crown

crystal(s)—Minerals in one of several specific structural configurations. They have various properties, but can be identified using specific mineralogical tests and techniques. Colloquial term for almost any "pretty rock" that is believed to have psychic and/or spiritual properties. A psychic tool for energy work. Crystals are presumed to have certain vibrations or energies inherent in them and these energies and/or vibrations can be tapped or harnessed for psychic work. There are many books available that supposedly describe the psychic properties of minerals, crystals, and rocks (usually including organic specimens like amber, coral, jet, ivory, and others). Unfortunately, no two books agree about what each specific mineral is used for. Wiccans may use and collect crystals, but they are used by Wiccans primarily as tools, not as objects of worship. Wiccans do not become dependent on tools or objects but use them to manipulate energies. Wiccans tend to use caution when attributing meaning and uses to specific crystals.

crystalomancy, chrystallomancy—Divination by looking into a crystal or crystal ball. Probably a descendant of catoptromancy, mirror gazing. A form of scrying.

cubomancy—Divination by use of thimbles. An ancient Greek technique also practiced by the Roman Emperors Augustus and Tiberias.

cult—From Latin *cultus* (a system of worship). The rites of a religion. Also more recently a negative term used to describe religious or pseudo-religious organizations that exploit and practice some form of mind control upon their members. A very subjective term used to describe any religious group that is "objectionable." Colloquially used by some fundamentalists as synonymous with occult. P.E.I. Bonewits developed the "Advanced Bonewits' Cult Danger Evaluation Frame" (ABCDEF for short) (see appendix 1) that allows a person to evaluate an organization using fifteen questions and determine how cult-like it is. This questionnaire is used throughout the occult and law enforcement communities. Most Pagan and Wiccan groups score very low on the questionnaire, which is the opposite of cult-like behavior. Generally groups that score very high or very low are viewed as suspect by mainstream society.

cup/chalice—Sacred tool for holding the wine during a ritual. Used in the symbolic Great Rite. Symbolizes the feminine aspect in the Great Rite. A cup or other bowl-like container may be used to hold water for cleansing, but this is a separate vessel from the wine cup or chalice.

curse—A spell used to cause hurt or harm. A spell of blighting. A spell of black magick. The use of magick to effect a negative result.

cyclomancy—Divination using a spinning device. 1) The jury wheel was an ancient device to pick members for a jury by writing their names on a wheel and spinning the wheel until the jury was filled. 2) The roulette wheel is a modern wheel of fortune that is spun and lands on prize-winning numbers. 3) An object (like a top) is spun in a circle of drawings or letters, and where it falls determines the answer. 4) An object like a top is inscribed with symbols and spun, and whichever side lands up when it stops determines the answer, like a dreidel. Spinning arrows may be used instead of a wheel or top.

cypher—Some people write their Book of Shadows in cypher—secret code—to protect them from outsiders. Some Traditions have special cyphers which are shared. Similar to a magickal alphabet.

Cypher Manuscript—A magickal book, translated by S.L. McGregor Mathers of the Golden Dawn, which contained the nucleus for many of their rituals and practices. It is available in reprint, with translation. The origin of the Cypher Manuscript is clouded and somewhat controversial. This is a manuscript relevant to Ceremonial Magick and is not directly tied to Wicca or Paganism except as modern Wicca is descended from people who were also active in Ceremonial Magick. The cypher of the Cypher Manuscript can be used as a magickal alphabet.

D

dactyliomancy—From Greek *dakterlios* (finger ring), and *manteia* (divination). Divination using a finger ring. 1) A form of charm, rings were inscribed with sayings that were supposed to bring good fortune or bestow certain abilities. Gems could also have special meanings and, when set in a ring, would give the wearer certain abilities or protections. Also rings of specific metals could be worn on certain fingers to bestow astrological benefits. 2) A ring suspended from a string could be used in various ways, for example, as a pendulum. 3) A ring is dropped into a bowl of water and how it falls and where it lands indicates the answer.

daimon—Greek, divine power, fate, or God. Ancient Greek concept of a spiritual entity that was believed to accompany and watch over each living soul. Less powerful than angels, they could be sent from the Gods to bestow good or evil fortune as the person's life merited, or merely according to the whims of the Gods.

daphnomancy—An ancient Greek method of divination in which yes/no questions were answered by throwing sacred laurel leaves on the sacred fire of Apollo. The louder they crackled, the more emphatic was the yes. Silence meant no.

Dark Moon—See New Moon.

dark side—The side of life associated with death, decay, entropy. The side of life that is not happy, sweet, or pleasant. "Dark siders" are people who revel in the darkness and celebrate that aspect of life. Most Wiccans do acknowledge that there is a dark side to life, and although they do not wallow in it, they do celebrate it as a necessary part of existence. Samhain is, in many ways, a celebration of the darkness, as is Yule (the longest night). Death, destruction, war, illness, calamity, all the negative events that can happen to an individual are relegated to the dark side. Wiccans realize that there must be a balance between darkness and light, but Wiccans strive to live in the light, and also realize that to progress each person must deal with and in some way conquer their dark side. The dark, while unpleasant, is not inherently evil, though evil can take on aspects of that which is dark. See also evil. For example, the television and movie characters, the Addams Family, were dark, though certainly not evil.

days of power—Sabbats, but also days with astronomical and astrological occurrences, one's birthday, the days of a woman's menstrual bleeding, anniversaries of Initiations, and other special days. Broadly, days when magickal power is greatest, either generally and/or personally.

death—The cessation of organic life. The condition in which a living organism becomes entropic.

death and life, death and rebirth—Two sides of the same coin; many Wiccans feel you cannot have one without the other. An example of the belief that life is cyclic, illustrated by the Wheel of the Year or the cyclic nature of seasons or the belief that death leads to rebirth, a manifestation of reincarnation.

death panorama—The replaying of the life that a newly departed spirit experiences after death. Reported by people who have had near-death experiences.

death prayer—1) Prayers said for the soul of the departed to either speed their journey, obtain intercession for that soul, or obtain help from that soul for the living. 2) A form of black magick in which prayers are said for a living person as if they were already dead. A Requiem Mass said for the living is a form of curse to hasten a person's demise. A prayer to demons said by a black magician to kill a certain individual. A prayer for the

death of another. Supposedly, black magicians are able to curse a person to death.

Dedication, Dedicant, Dedicate—1) A ceremony in which a person is introduced to the quarters and the Goddess and God and declares their intent to study and learn about Wicca. This is not an initiation, but many Traditions demand a person go through a Dedication (and thereby become a Dedicant or Dedicate) before the person will be accepted into a training group. Most Dedications are performed with the candidate skyclad (naked). Being dedicated does not guarantee or demand that a person will become an Initiate. 2) A level of attainment in certain Traditions, may or may not equate with Initiation. Varies among Traditions. 3) The opening statement at the beginning of a ritual that declares the ritual's intent and purpose.

Dee, Dr. John—(1527–1608). Author of *Liber Mysterium* (*The Book of Mysteries*), Dee was an English mathematician who also studied astrology, alchemy, and other occult subjects. Imprisoned (1555) for allegedly casting horoscopes and using enchantments against Queen Mary of England (reigned 1553–1558), he became a courtier under Queen Elizabeth (reigned 1558–1603) and was said to have been sent to continental Europe to conduct a service for the government of a delicate and secretive nature. His associate, Edward Kelley, was a shadier character and charges of chicanery were brought against him. Dee's book is the basis for the Enochian magickal system.

degree, Degrees, First, Second, and Third Degrees—Levels of Initiation. Most Wiccan Traditions have three degrees of Initiation. A First Degree is a person who has studied for the traditional year-and-a-day and understands the basics of Wicca. They can conduct themselves in a Circle and understand the language and basics of the practice of Wicca as prescribed by their Tradition. A Second Degree has studied for at least another year-and-a-day and is more skilled and proficient in knowledge and practice. Many Traditions expect a Second to have some specialty or area of knowledge and study, and also teach what they know. A Third Degree has studied for at least another year-and-a-day (usually longer) and is highly skilled and proficient in knowledge and practice. They are the High Priestesses and High Priests of Wicca. Most Traditions allow only Thirds to start their own covens. These three degrees may have other names or titles in various Traditions, and the requirements can vary widely among Traditions.

Deity—Goddess or God. A generic term for God that is less sexist than "God," and shorter than "Goddess or God." A spirit of great power.

demon, demons—From Sanskrit *div* (to shine) and from Greek *daimon* (spirit or Divine power). 1) In Christianity, beings who are servants of Satan or the Devil. Lesser or fallen angels. According to Johann Weyer there were 7,405,926 demons serving under 72 princes. Evil spirits. 2) Spirits evoked from the human Id. 3) Low-level spirit that interacts with the material world. The classical notion of a daimon was an intermediary spirit between humans and the Gods.

demonic sins—A.k.a., the seven deadly sins, Christian mythology ascribes seven specific demons to the seven deadly sins. Lucifer—pride; Mammon—avarice; Asmodeus—lechery; Satan—anger; Beelzebub—gluttony; Leviathan—envy; Belphegor—sloth.

demonology—1) A branch of black magick that employs conjuration and control of demonic entities and forces to accomplish the magician's will. 2) A body of lore, spells, and incantations that are reportedly used to summon, control, and banish demons. A form of negative Christianity not practiced by Wiccans.

demonomancy—Divination by evoking demons to ask them questions and obtain their answers. However, since demons are difficult to recognize and notorious for deception, it is difficult to get a reliable answer. Medieval authorities determined there were precisely 1,758,064,176 lesser devils constantly at large in the world ready to appear in almost any form at the slightest wish. Some Christian sects consider all forms of divination to be accomplished with the aid of demons and/or spirits.

deosil, deiseil, deasil—(pronounced variously *DEE-oh-sill*; *JESS-ill*; *JESH-'ll*) Latin (sunwise); clockwise movement, forward movement. Most Wiccans consider deosil movement to be invoking in nature, and will only move in a clockwise manner while in a Circle so as not to destroy the energy built up in the Circle. Opposite of widdershins. A deliberate change in spelling from "deasil" as in *Webster's*.

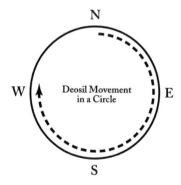

Deosil Movement

destiny—Western concept that a life path is preordained according to a specified set of rules determined by God, the Universe, or Deity, etc. Not connected to past lives or past actions. A cosmic involuntary life assignment that cannot be escaped or ignored.

deva—Sanskrit (shining one). 1) Hindu and Buddhist, exalted spiritual beings or Gods. 2) An occult term popularized by Madame Blavatsky who defined devas as types of angels or Gods who were progressed entities from a previous planetary period and were here to aid humanity in its spiritual development. 3) A type of nature spirit, who may help people.

Devil—From Sanskrit *devi* (little God). Also shortened from the French *Homme d'Evil* (man of evil). Also derived from translating the Hebrew Satan into the Greek Diabolos. In Christianity, the chief adversary of God (Yahweh) and Jesus; the personification of evil; ruler of hell; chief of the demons. The popular depiction of the Devil as a half-beast horned anthropomorphic being is a corruption of the depiction of the Pagan God Pan. This entity as the personification of evil has many names including Beelzebub (lord of the flies), Asmodeus (creature of judgment), Abaddon, Behemoth (beast), Belial (without a master), Diabolos (two morsels, or Greek downflowing), Demon (cunning over blood is supposedly the meaning of "demon," like Lucifer is light bringer), and Satan (adversary). See also Baphomet, Lucifer, Satan. This entity is a Christian concept and is not part of the Wiccan belief system.

Devil's mark—See witches' mark.

Devil's Night—American secular "holiday" that takes place on October 30th, the night before Halloween. Originated in the Detroit area during the 1960s, it is a night of burning, looting, and general vandalism and destruction and has no relationship to Wicca. It may have evolved from the traditional secular Halloween pranks done to those one did not like or as "punishment" for those who didn't have treats for Halloween revelers. In recent times this "holiday" has been abandoned for the most part and the number of arson fires on October 30th is similar to those on other days of the year.

dharma—A Buddhist religious precept of reaping one's past merit. One lives out one's dharma in response to the karma one has built up over previous lifetimes.

Dianic—A feminist Tradition of Wicca that generally acknowledges only the Goddess as Deity. Most Dianics believe only women can be witches.

direct writing—Written communication from the spirit world without the use of a corporeal agent, as opposed to automatic writing. For example, an unfinished communication is completed in a different unknown hand or on a typewriter, blackboard, or even computer. May be benevolent or malevolent.

directions—(See quarters.) The cardinal directions, North, South, East, and West. The four Watchtowers. Most Circles are oriented to the cardinal directions, and many groups mandate in which quarter one begins casting the Circle and/or placement of the altar. There is no universal standard for starting, altar placement, or even which quarter symbolizes which element.

discarnate—Opposite of incarnate. A state of being of a spiritual entity that is not "in the flesh." Can manifest as a ghost or spirit, but Deities are also discarnate beings.

divination—From Latin *divinare* (to foresee), and also Latin *divinus* (Divine or pertaining to the Gods). To tell the past, present, or future through indirect means either using a focus or with pure psychic talents. Obtaining information about a person or situation though psychic or magickal means. Clairvoyance using tools, such as tarot cards, a crystal ball, a pendulum, etc. Some claim divination is merely a manifestation of synchronicity and should be used as a Jungian technique of self-exploration.

In the ancient world there were two types of divination—direct or natural divination, consisting of dreams, necromancy, oracles, and prophets, and indirect or artificial divination which was divided into two categories: 1) the observation of animate phenomena, haruscipy (divination by reading the entrails of sacrificed animals), augury (the flight patterns of birds), and the observation of human birth deformities; and 2) the observation of inanimate phenomena, such as casting of lots and dice, observation of weather phenomena, observation of terrestrial events (like earthquakes), or observation of celestial phenomena, from which arose astrology. In the ancient world it was generally presumed that women practiced direct divination, and men practiced indirect divination.

There are many divinatory systems encountered in Wicca, as well as in the mundane world. Tarot cards, astrology, runes, numerology, scrying, augury, palm reading, tea leaf reading, phrenology, physiognomy, handwriting analysis (some dispute this is divination), Ouija™ boards, crystal balls, etc., are all methods of divination. Wiccans can use divination as a tool for self-development and personal improvement. Some Wiccans practice divination to augment their income and/or for helping others. Wiccans do not worship the objects or systems that they use for divination, i.e., tarot cards, astrology, etc., but rather use these as tools and a focus for psychic skills.

Divinity—1) Goddess and/or God. Spiritual entity that dwells on a higher plane and may or may not be accessible or understandable by incarnate beings. 2) The moment of consciousness in which a person feels that they are one with Deity, which can result in a personal transformation of a positive nature.

djinn, djin, genii, genie—Arabic, demon or spirit. Legend says that King Solomon imprisoned all the djinn in bottles so mankind would be free of their tricks and torments. Aladdin's lamp was supposedly a djinn bottle.

doll—See poppet.

dolmen—A standing upright stone in an ancient holy place, usually in Britain or Europe. A stone placed as a part of a stone circle, a noncircular pattern, or alone.

Dolmen

doppelgänger—From the German, double goer or double walker. The spiritual twin of a living person can so closely resemble the person as to fool those who encounter the double. Lore has it that if a person actually meets their doppelgänger they will die. A doppelgänger can be distinguished from a living person because it floats above the ground.

Dorothy, Old Dorothy—Woman who headed the New Forest Coven and who initiated Gerald Gardner into Wicca. Also known as Old Dorothy Clutterbuck. The exact identity of Old Dorothy has not been proven, but research has revealed there could have been such a person. Supposedly Dorothy's tradition was a Fam-Trad. Dorothy was supposedly an upper-class woman of means and property who was also a witch and headed an hereditary Wiccan coven descended from Old George Pickingill.

double—Apparition of a person that may manifest as a result of astral travel or other out-of-body experiences. Can be an indication of the imminent death of the person. The Irish term is fetch, the German term is doppelgänger.

dowsing, dowser—Colloquially "water witching"— a method of finding water or other commodities in the Earth by using a forked (or y-shaped) willow wand, bent wire, or pendulum. The ends of the fork were held and the desired commodity was concentrated upon, an area was walked and if the commodity existed on that plot of land the tail or "y" of the wand would eventually point to the spot in the ground to dig for the commodity. One can also use a map of an area and get

Dowsing with a Willow Wand

good results. The technique was used in ancient Egypt, ancient China, and medieval England and Europe and has been practiced in the United States since colonial times. Once a very popular way to find water and determine where to dig a well, which was often an expensive and sometimes frustrating process. Nowadays dowsing is also used to find oil, other minerals, and sometimes used in the same way one would use a metal detector, looking for lost valuable objects. Used in W.W.I and Vietnam to locate mines and other hazardous things without injuring the seekers. See also pendulum.

Drawing Down the Moon—A Wiccan rite to invoke the Moon Goddess. The Goddess aspect is invoked—drawn down—into the High Priestess by the High Priest. A document of this rite has been passed down and widely distributed. The original text was found in Apuleus' *The Golden Ass*, but was modified, expanded upon, and embellished over the years. Originally adopted by Gardner and possibly expanded and modified by Doreen Valiente, it is Craft lore and widely used throughout Wicca and Paganism. It is also the title of a book by Margot Adler (1979,

revised and expanded 1986, and again 1999) that details the practices and practitioners of Wicca and Paganism in the present day United States.

Drawing Down the Sun—A Wiccan rite to invoke the Sun God. Invocation of the God aspect into the High Priest by the High Priestess.

dreams—In the ancient world, a person could receive information directly from the Gods through dreams. In the modern world, a natural trance state in which one can use symbols to process life's events and work through problems or situations. A tool for psychological healing and/or self-development.

drugs—The use of psychoactive drugs as a means of achieving altered states of consciousness and as a means of contacting the Divine is an ancient worldwide practice. Many Wiccans are predominantly opposed to drug use, believing that ecstatic states are best achieved through self-induced means rather than through the use of a psychoactive substance. There are a few Wiccans who use drugs in controlled ritual situations, but they are very careful and practice privately. Ecstatic drug use is in general a shamanic technique. There is an awareness that use of mind-altering substances in a sacred setting is to be honored, understood, and performed in a sacred manner.

Druid—Gaelic, Oak Man, or knowing the oak tree. A person who follows a revived ancient Celtic religion and Tradition. A Pagan, but not Wiccan Tradition. People can be Wiccans and Druids simultaneously. The original Druids were a powerful Celtic priesthood and magickal Order who worshipped in oak groves and held mistletoe to be sacred. The social and political power of the Druids (and the Celts in general) was destroyed by the Romans in their conquest of the ancient world. Little is recorded of their rites and the cult was actively hunted and destroyed by the Romans because the Druids were the center of resistance to Roman conquest.

drum, drumming—Many Pagans celebrate by drumming and dancing. Like Pagan celebrations of old, Pagan drums can be used to achieve altered states of  consciousness by listening to them, dancing to their sounds, or playing them. Used in rituals. In some usages, it is sacred dancing as a way of celebrating. Drumming and dancing can also be used to raise power in a ritual.

Drums

Dryad—Greek, a tree spirit, generally regarded as feminine.

dualism—The doctrine that for every principle there is an opposing, separate, and irreconcilable counter-principle. Usually viewed as a good-evil dichotomy. Wicca is generally not dualistic, although it does recognize the dark and evil, and sees duality as forces of nature or humanity rather than cosmic principles.

E

Earth magick—Magick practiced for, by, and with cooperation from the Earth. Can be ecological in focus. Also magick using natural places, occurrences, or rocks and stones. Sometimes Gaia (the Earth Mother) is invoked for her help or healing. A system of magick that relies more on shamanic techniques and natural items and places than manufactured items or buildings. The celebration of the primeval and unspoiled Earth.

Earth Mother—1) Greek, Gaea or Gaia. 2) The personification of the Earth, its biosphere, and all things arising from that, the original fertility Deity. 3) The feminine principle of Deity, it is equated with Mother Earth and Mother Nature. Most Wiccans acknowledge that the Earth is our Mother. 4) A generic representation of The Goddess.

ecliptic—The apparent path of the Sun as it moves through the sky. The constellations the ecliptic crosses make up the zodiac. (See also zodiac.)

ecology—Belief in the practice of ecology and ecologically sound living is a central tenet to most Wiccans' world-views. Renew, reuse, recycle is taken to heart. Avoidance of toxins is desirable. Pagans prefer to buy Earth-friendly products (including natural and organically grown) if possible.

ecstatic—Latin (out of the body), transcendental joy. Type of spiritual practice that produces a mental state that seems to bring people out of themselves and into contact with something greater than themselves. Can be achieved through several means, from the purely mental (meditation), to the use of music, dance and/or song, to the use of drugs, to the use of sensory deprivation, and other techniques. Generally used as a way for an individual to commune with Deity.

ectoplasm—1) The etheric, translucent, luminous material that emanates from the body of a medium, usually from some natural orifice. A white viscous substance with an ozone-like smell, it has been photographed in recognizable shapes that have been molded by spirits. 2) The material out of which ghosts and other spiritual beings are constructed.

ego—The conscious, individual part of the human psyche; includes individual personality traits.

elaeomancy—Divination by means of a liquid surface. Generally not just water (see hydromancy), but also using oil upon water, oil, or other liquids.

Elders—Third Degree and Second Degree members of a coven or group. Generally the people in the Craft who have been with the group for an extended period of time, have life experiences to share, and have gained some wisdom and maturity through their experiences and knowledge. Can function as unofficial advisors in the Pagan Community.

elemental—A spirit of one of the four elements: Earth—gnome; Air—sylph; Water—undine; Fire—salamander. Also a term used in role-playing games like Dungeons and Dragons, etc., that refers to similar entities who are considered "monsters" and can be harnessed or fought. An elemental being is not viewed as adversarial in Wicca; the elements and their manifestations are considered allies or servants. In Ceremonial Magick, the goal is to control and dominate the elementals and their manifestations to carry out the magician's purpose. This is one of the primary philosophical differences between Wicca and Ceremonial Magick. Nature elementals are creatures such as fairies, brownies, leprechauns, dryads (tree maidens), dragons, etc. In some instances, elemental is used in a way similar to thought form.

elements—The classical Greek elements of Fire, Air, Water, and Earth. These are not interpreted literally but allegorically as representations of passion and zeal—Fire; knowledge and inspiration—Air; emotion and life passages—Water; and manifestations, the tangible world—Earth. There is also a fifth element—Spirit (sometimes ether or aether) that represents the magickal, spiritual, and unseen-but-felt presence of the Gods. The elements can also symbolize the four states of matter: Earth—solid; Water—liquid; Air—gas; and Fire—plasma. The periodic table of the elements is not to be confused with the "magickal" elements. Both types of "elements" have their place in Wicca.

elixir, elixir of life—A liquid or occasionally a powder which, when applied or ingested, miraculously heals a mortal wound and extends life indefinitely. Widely represented in various magickal traditions. The Holy Grail can be seen as an elixir of life. Some interpret the elixir of life to be the philosopher's stone.

Elvish—An invented language and alphabet sometimes used as a magickal alphabet. Invented by J.R.R. Tolkien and used in his novel *The Hobbit*, and the *Lord of the Rings Trilogy*.

embrace—Power or psychic energy can be transmitted, sent, or received, through an embrace or touch, sometimes willingly, sometimes unknowingly by transmitter or receiver. Also a way a psychic leech can be transferred from person to person. (A psychic leech is a psychic entity which feeds on psychic energy, a parasite that must be attached to a host to survive, also can be called a psychic vampire.) Many Wiccans and other sensitives will not embrace or even touch unless the person is known to them and they feel secure in their presence. Exchanging energy without the willing consent of both parties is considered a form of psychic attack.

Emerald Tablet—A tablet made of a great emerald of the finest quality, on which the essence of all magick is revealed. Legend has it that it was found by Alexander the Great in the tomb of Hermes and was supposedly written by Hermes.

emetic—Chemical agent that induces vomiting when ingested. Sometimes used when attempting to expel an evil spirit possessing a person. Also used as a trial by ordeal, if a person vomited easily after taking an emetic, it was proof of innocence. If they experienced vertigo or lost self-control it was a proof of guilt.

empathy—Sensing of the emotions of another, a psychic ability.

empyromancy—Divination by observation of objects placed in a sacrificial fire.

enchantment—1) A spell designed to place a person in a magickal thrall—see fascination. 2) An item that is charged and kept secret, may be used to contact Deities or spirits, or may be used to affect a person's aura. *The Picture of Dorian Grey* is a fictional example of this form of enchantment. One can use a gem or written charm as an enchantment.

entity—A being, spirit, living creature, or personification. Something with a Divine spark of spirit or soul.

equality—Most Wiccans believe in absolute equality of the sexes, races, abilities, ages, and can extend to species, animals, plants, rocks, planets, stars, and all things in the Universe.

equinox—From Greek *aequus* (equal) and *nox* (night). The two days of the year when the length of day and night are equal. Spring Equinox is around March 21st and Autumnal Equinox is around September 21st. The moment when the Sun's path, the ecliptic, crosses the Earth's equator. Astrologically Spring Equinox is the 0° Aries point and Autumn Equinox is the 0° Libra point. Spring Equinox is the lesser Sabbat of Oestarra and Autumn Equinox is the lesser Sabbat of Mabon.

eromancy—Divination technique in which a person puts a cloth over their head and speaks questions over a bowl of water. Any rippling of the water is taken as a positive answer. Practiced in the Orient.

Esbat—From Old French *esbatment*, to divert oneself or an amusement. Margaret Murray (1863–1963) first used this term to describe mundane (non-Wiccan) gatherings of witches. Now used for celebrations at a Full Moon and/or a New Moon. Holy Days based upon the Lunar cycle (as Sabbats are based on the Solar cycle). Some groups celebrate only Full Moons, some only New Moons, and some both. Some groups celebrate each quarter Moon as well. Esbats tend to be more Goddess-oriented. Can also refer to the regular (weekly, bi-weekly, monthly) meeting of a coven or group, when worship, magick, or healing is performed, and/or also any group business is taken care of.

ESP, extrasensory perception—See extrasensory perception.

ether—The medium by which magickal energy is transmitted. Another term for spirit.

etheric body—A noncorporeal structure intermediate between the astral body and the physical body. It is an energy network that links the physical body to the corresponding astral, mental, and spiritual bodies, and thus literally keeps it alive. The aura is a manifestation of the etheric body. Sometimes equated with the etheric double.

ethics—A personal guide for one's behavior concerning good and evil, right and wrong, how to relate to other people, moral dilemmas, and other life situations. Personal propriety. Principles of behavior and right conduct imposed from within that govern thought and behavior. As Wicca has no set doctrine or creed, and has no imposed morality, each Wiccan must formulate their own code of ethics by which they live. Ethics is a large part of Wiccan training and each student is expected to think about what rules they live by and why they have adopted these rules. Ethics is considered a more active system of personal life rules than morals, which are imposed from outside by a society and not usually subject to personal choice.

evil—An obsession to destroy, inflict pain and cruelty, either for the intent of gaining power over others or for its own sake. Anti-life, anti-evolution, anti-consciousness. Generally evil has intent behind it, as in the deliberate acts of a person or group, or the byproduct of deliberate acts. The dark can also be destructive; for example, a flood is a natural process, and is considered dark but not evil.

evil eye—The ability to send malicious or evil intent to cause harm with a look or penetrating stare. Casting an evil spell with a look. Can also be a bewitching look that causes the person bewitched to be bound to the caster. A universal concept throughout history in many cultures. Many charms and amulets are worn specifically to avert the evil eye. Especially talismans with eyes are made to specifically avert the evil eye. German—*boser blick*; Italian—*malocchio*; French—*mauvais veil*; Latin—*fascinum*.

evoke, evoking, evocation—1) Calling up. 2) Calling something out from within. 3) Calling a Goddess or God not dwelling within a Priest or Priestess, similar to inviting them to the party as another guest. 4) To call forth or to summon as in calling an elemental to a Watchtower. 5) The summoning of a non-material entity of a lower order of being than oneself.

exorcism—The expulsion, by psychic means, of an unwelcome possessing or influencing entity from a person, place, or thing. A ritual designed to banish a spirit, ghost, or discarnate entity. A universal concept in most cultures throughout human history, exorcism is a form of intense cleansing and banishing, specifically designed to remove some entity, rather than just unpleasant energies. Can be performed by a Catholic priest or other magickal practitioners including some Wiccans. Can involve invoking the authority of a higher power.

extispacy—Divination by the means of entrails of a sacrificial victim, usually animal. The extipices of the Roman religious colleges were the auspices or augurs.

extrasensory perception, ESP—The ability to receive data by other than the five senses (sight, hearing, touch, taste, smell). Colloquially called the sixth sense.

Psychic or PSI phenomena, psychic abilities, or psychic talent are grouped into four main categories: 1) Telepathy—mind-to-mind communication. 2) Clairvoyance—perception of events and people remote in space and/or time or which are not discernible to the normal senses. 3) Precognition—knowledge of events in the future. 4) Retrocognition—knowledge of events in the past of which the person has no previous knowledge.

Parapsychology is the study of ESP. Because of the impossibility of accurate reproducible results, the case for scientific proof of PSI phenomena is still controversial, although some excellent studies have documented its existence and effects. Wiccans generally accept the validity of these abilities, although they recognize that the skill and levels of ability can vary widely among individuals.

To develop and harness one's ESP is one goal of studying Wicca. Most Wiccans believe that everyone has some ESP ability, but what kind, how strong the ability is, and how trained a person is makes the difference. ESP is believed to be a natural phenomenon, available to everyone who cultivates it. Much of the Wiccan training involves techniques and disciplines for developing ESP which lends credence to the belief that Wiccans are "more psychic" than normal people, but this is a fallacy. Wiccans tend to work at developing and using their ESP more than the average.

Eye of Horus—Also called an utchat, magickal charm of the ancient Egyptians worn as a protection against evil. Stylized eye of the falcon-headed sun-sky God Horus. Associated with regeneration, safety, health, wisdom, and prosperity.

Eye of Horus

F

fadic number—A number that recurs in a person's life and is considered influential or fatalistic. May be obtained through numerology, or birth dates, license numbers, number of letters in a person's name, etc. Numbers can be combined and used in different orders so a person with five letters in their name born on the seventh, sixteenth, or twenty-fifth could have the numbers 5, 7, 57, and 75 as fadic numbers.

faery—1) The folk of the fey—the little people—supernatural beings that coexist occasionally in this plane of existence and can interact with people. May be friendly or neutral—the Seelie or Seelie Court; unfriendly or antagonistic—the Unseelie or Unseelie Court. 2) A name used by two Wiccan Traditions, Radical Faery (sometimes spelled Radical Fairy) and Faery Wicca.

fairy—Miniature winged beings who display magickal abilities and properties. May help or hinder people. See also faery. Fairies generally are con-

sidered more appealing and engaging than the faery, although in folk tales they can also be fearsome and evil.

fakir—(pronounced *fah-KEER*) A Hindu holy man who has practiced yoga and similar mind and body control techniques and is able to perform supernatural feats, such as lying on a bed of nails, walking over hot coals, and live burial. Sometimes certain "feats" are produced by sleight-of-hand and other trickeries. May be the root from which fake and faker derive.

Fam-Trad—Short for Family Tradition. An hereditary tradition of magickal, esoteric, or herbal lore passed down through the generations. May or may not be identified with witchcraft.

familiar/pet/animal friend—From Latin *familiaries*. Alternative names were Roman *magistelli* and *martinelli* and Greek *paredrii*. 1) Animal companion that helps with psychic, magickal, and religious matters. A nonhuman entity, usually an animal, with which one has an empathic and magickal bond. More active and immediate than a power animal. A pet is not necessarily a familiar, nor is a familiar necessarily a pet, although usually they go together. Wiccan lore states that cats are able to move in and out of a Circle without disrupting the Circle. Dogs usually will not cross a Circle, and are aware of the magickal barrier. Any animal can become a familiar, although the cat is most common. For example, Sybill Leek had a jackdaw named Mr. Hotfoot Jackson. Cats, dogs, and horses in particular are very sensitive to negative influences, and can give early warning or corroborative evidence. 2) Certain kinds of deliberately created and maintained thought forms may also be called familiars. Derives from English witchcraft handbooks of the early seventeenth century, and do not appear in continental European witchcraft trials or literature.

family—People living together in one economic unit. Wiccans are more inclusive about family composition than is the mainstream society. May or may not include minor children, may or may not include married partners.

fascinate, fascination—from Latin *fascinare* (to enchant). 1) The act of charming a person using the evil eye. 2) A spell that clouds a person's judgment and causes them to act in a manner contrary to their character, wishes, or better judgment. 3) A spell or charm that causes the recipient's gaze to be directed toward a person or object so that the recipient becomes fixated upon that person or object. Generally considered to be a form of black magick.

fast, fasting—Technique of altering consciousness by means of abstaining from food and/or water for a specific period. Fasting is reported to clarify the mind, possibly enhance psychic abilities, and make a person more receptive to the ethereal planes. Can be used to aid divination or magickal workings. A technique used widely in the world's religions.

fate—The concept that certain events are preordained and nothing can change that. Contrasts with free will. This concept is central to certain religious systems and is the reason for certain Christian sects' existence (fate vs. salvation). Wicca generally postulates free will and the concepts of karma (you reap what you sow) as opposed to immutable fate.

felidomancy—Divination by observing the actions, moods, and behaviors of a cat. Dates to the Middle Ages.

feng shui, feng sui—(*fahng SHWAY*) Chinese, "wind" and "water"—An ancient Chinese study of wind and water, and more specifically that the currents of energy flow over, in, and around the Earth. Used to choose propitious sites for living, burial, and religious practices. Many contemporary books emphasize the correctness of living places and offer remedies to negative feng sui. Still widely practiced in the Orient, it is gaining popularity in the United States. Similar to the use of Chi and study of ley lines.

fertility—The ability to procreate. The ability to raise or grow food, both crops and animals. The ability to be creative on any plane a person wishes: physical, mental, psychic, spiritual. Wicca is a fertility religion, and actual fertility is recreated in the Great Rite, which is symbolic procreation. However, modern Wiccans recognize that not everyone is cut out to be a farmer or a parent, so fertility in all guises and planes is celebrated, and is not limited solely to physical procreation.

festival (alternatively gathering)—A meeting of Pagan and/or Wiccan believers for group activities, workshops, large group rituals, buying and selling, meeting people, and fun. A cross between a Wiccan/Pagan church camp and a Wiccan/Pagan conference and trade show. Most are strongly teaching/learning- and workshop-oriented. Usually there are merchants at these gatherings that sell items, homemade and commercial, that are of interest to the attendees. Originally all festivals were held outdoors and most people camped at the site, but today several gatherings are held at motels similar to trade shows. There are dozens of festivals held all over the United States each year. Most festivals are open to anyone who is interested in attending, but there is little advertising except in Pagan publications. Also used to describe one of the eight seasonal Sabbats.

fetch—1) The apparition, double, or wraith of a living person. 2) A projected astral body or thought form deliberately sent out to make its presence known to another person. May be used by an individual as a sort of astral familiar. 3) The collective astral projection of a magickal group. 4) Another term for Summoner.

fetish—Possibly from Latin *factitius* (made by art), or Portuguese *feitico* (charm or sorcery). A created object that has magickal powers or has been invested with magickal energy in contrast to an amulet, which may be found or created. Fetishes usually have some organic animal product that empowers them—an eye of newt, gallstones from a sheep, or hair and/or nail clippings. Sometimes considered to represent spirits and create a bond with the supernatural world. Generally fetishes are considered to be more primitive and superstitious than a charm or an amulet.

fey—Of or pertaining to faery or fairy. Magickal, supernatural, sometimes tricksterlike.

Fifth Degree—See Fourth Degree.

First Quarter, Diana's Bow—Moon phase when the waxing Moon is ninety degrees in front of the Sun. Used for magick which is invoking in nature. Can be used for timing Circles. Symbolic of the Goddess as Maiden.

Phases of the Moon:
First Quarter, Full Moon, Third Quarter, New Moon

fivefold kiss, fivefold salute—A ritual salute used during a Circle. Traditionally used as a method of saluting the Goddess and God dwelling within the High Priestess and High Priest. Also used during Initiations and other formal rituals. Most traditionally done only man to woman or woman to man, Eclectic Wicca has abandoned this stricture. There are two versions used today. The first version salutes with kisses on each foot, each knee, the lower belly, each breast, and the lips; eight kisses in all. The second version salutes with kisses on each foot, the lower belly, each breast, the lips, and each eye; again eight kisses in all. Not a sexual or prurient act.

floromancy—Divination by observation, collection, planting, and harvesting of plants and flowers. This also includes size, color, and shape of flowers, time of planting, time of sprouting, and places where plants may grow unexpectedly. The belief that a four-leaf clover brings good luck arose from this body of lore.

flying ointment—A medieval concoction of varying recipes. Generally believed to be a psychoactive drug that induced a state of euphoria and made users believe they were flying. Psychoactive drugs are not generally used in Wicca anymore; euphoric states can be achieved without drugs. Without drugs the practitioner is more in control of the experience and also more skilled in achieving altered states of consciousness.

Fortean, Fortean phenomena—Named after Charles Fort (1874–1932), an American journalist who collected and catalogued descriptions of odd phenomena such as rains of frogs, fish, stones, dead birds, and snakes; paranormal phenomena, floating balls of light, spontaneous human combustion, cases of stigmata, and other unusual occurrences that seemed to defy explanation. He wrote *Book of the Damned* (1919), which was a partial catalogue of these phenomena. He used the examples, which he never attempted to explain, to show the limitations and shortcomings of scientific knowledge and the inherent danger of accepting natural laws dogmatically, without leaving room for such strange occurrences. Fort challenged the scientific method of accepting a phenomenon as genuine only if it could be proven and independently duplicated.

Fort catalogued numerous "sky oddities" dating back to 1779, which has evolved into the search for UFOs. Modern researchers have continued Fort's work in many fields. Psychic phenomena fit in the category of Fortean occurrences.

fortunetelling—Witches along with Gypsies and others were said to earn their living in part by telling fortunes and predicting the future. How much of these practices consisted of actual psychic talent and how much is astute psychological observation and attentive listening is a subject for much discussion. Today some Wiccans still tell fortunes at psychic fairs, etc. It is generally a less desirable term as it has negative connotations; most reputable practitioners prefer the term reader and readings.

Fourth Degree, Fifth Degree—Mythical Wiccan Initiations that supposedly contain blood oaths, sacrifices, and/or Dedication and swearing of allegiance to Satan. This information is propaganda promulgated by people who believe Wiccan Traditions are satanic in nature.

Fourth Quarter, Last Quarter, Hecate's Sickle—Moon phase when the waning Moon is ninety degrees behind the Sun. Used for magick that is banishing in nature. Can be used for timing Circles. Symbolic of the Goddess as Crone.

Fraudulent Mediums Act—A British law that, in 1951, replaced the anti-witchcraft laws, which had been on the books since medieval times. The law was enacted to protect the public from shady practitioners of various mediumistic and magickal schemes designed to separate the public from its money by use of fraud, trickery, or psychological coercion. Most communities in the United States and Canada also have similar statutes that nominally criminalize most forms of divination in exchange for money or other goods. In practice many readers display a sign— "for entertainment only"—and circumvent the laws in that way. Some organizations of readers and astrologers have formulated ethical standards and certification to reassure the public that their members are honest and do not engage in such criminal activities. These efforts have met with mixed success, mostly being ignored by the public through lack of publicity and also apathy.

free will—The concept that a person is in control of their life and can choose to change themselves, their outlook, and their circumstances and supports the belief that nothing is absolutely predetermined. This concept has been handled differently by various religions throughout time. Karma is not fatalistic, but allows that actions of exceptional merit can erase negative karma and cause a person to avoid certain unpleasant consequences of past-life actions, which adds a certain element of free will to a concept that is often misunderstood. Modern thought leans toward the free will model. Wicca postulates free will, which allows a person to change themselves and their life for the better.

Freemasonry—Secret and fraternal organizations whose Grand Lodge in London was founded in 1717. Masonic lore has it that the Masons' ceremonies and rites evolved from the medieval guilds of the stonemasons, but the order supposedly has esoteric secrets passed down through the millennia from Old Kingdom Egypt. Gerald Gardner was a Mason and many of the Initiations and ceremonies of Wicca are borrowed from Freemasonry, omitting the secrets. Because of the secret nature of the rites and degrees, and the fact that only men are allowed to become Freemasons (though legend has a few women becoming Masons through various accidents), there is a great deal of suspicion and distrust of the organization, which is unwarranted. All that is required for membership is that a man be an upstanding citizen and believe in God, though no particular religious faith is mandated. The aims of the organization are to enable men to meet in harmony, promote friendship, and be charitable. The Shriners is a Masonic offshoot. Lodges (the local branch) exist all over the world, and the papal ban on Catholics' membership was rescinded in 1983.

fringe—1) Marginalized class of people. Wicca is considered a fringe belief and lifestyle. 2) Loose threads on a border of a cloth. Some traditions consider a fringe to have magickal properties. In Judaism the Lord told Moses to order the children of Israel to fringe the borders of their garments, which survives as the fringed tellis worn during prayer. Today, in applications other than the tellis, it is a form of decoration, although if a fringe is applied with intent, it can have magickal effect.

Fringed Cloth

Full Moon—Moon phase when the Moon is opposite or 180 degrees away from the Sun. Supposedly the most powerful time for the Moon's energies. Esbats are usually celebrated at Full Moons. Symbolic of the Goddess as Mother. Symbolic of a woman during ovulation.

fundie—Colloquially, a fundamentalist Christian or people who have closed minds about Wicca and believe the misinformation spread about Wicca, the occult (pronounced *AWK-kult*), and Satanism. Not a complimentary term, though usually more neutral than nasty.

Futhark—The runic alphabet, the name is derived from the first six letters ("th" is one character) of the runic alphabet. There are several versions of the Futhark that have been used by various Germanic tribes at various places and times. Also used as a magickal alphabet. Also a reference to the lore and body of Norse mystical teachings.

G

Gaia, Gaea—Greek Goddess of the Earth, a.k.a., Mother Earth or Earth Mother. Primeval entity that was the mother of all the Gods, Titans, and humans. Invoked in rituals with an ecological theme. Sometimes said to be the Goddess of the ecologists.

Gaia Hypothesis—Scientific paradigm that links geology, biology, ecology, evolution, oceanography, atmospheric studies, and cosmology into a unified theory to explain the Earth, its history, and evolution from cosmic dust to mankind and present day technologies. It is an interdisciplinary study that believes the Earth is a living entity, that we are a part of that entity, and that the Earth is the product of a series of scientific events that shaped the Earth and its life in all its forms. Often called by critics a Pagan philosophy, there is a great deal of scientific data to support and explain the multitude of changes the Earth has undergone in response to various forces. The Gaia Hypothesis emerged as the result of the marriage of the ecological movement with more traditional scientific fields. It is not a religious belief system per se, although it has many parallels with Pagan beliefs.

Gaian—Generic term for a Goddess worshipper. May be a feminist but is not necessarily one.

Gardner, Gerald—(1884–1964) A retired British civil servant who helped codify the practices of Wicca, and also publicized and popularized the revival of the religion of Wicca, he was the founder of Gardnerian Wicca. Author of the novel (under the pseudonym Scire) *High Magic's Aid* (1949) and the non-fiction book *Witchcraft Today* (1954), among others. Reportedly, Gerald Gardner was involved in various occult groups and was invited to join a Wiccan coven in the New Forest area (the New Forest Coven) run by a woman named "Old Dorothy" (Dorothy Clutterbuck) just before W.W.II. This group was supposedly a descendant of the Craft as practiced by Old George Pickingill. Gardner took the teachings and practices of this group, added elements of Masonry, Ceremonial Magick, and other occult practices and teachings, and codified these into a complete system. When the witchcraft laws were finally repealed in England in 1951 (to be replaced with the Fraudulent Mediums Act), Gardner went public with what has come to be known as Gardnerian Wicca. He gained the appellation "The Official Witch of England" from the British press and enjoyed a long relationship with the press, which caused mixed feelings from other Witches both in his groups and in other groups. Gardner trained and initiated many people who brought Gardnerian Wicca to Ireland, the United States, Canada, Australia, New Zealand, and Europe. He took over and ran a witchcraft museum on the Isle of Man.

Gardnerian—A Tradition of Wicca descended from Gerald Gardner or one of his High Priestesses. First coined by one of Gardner's enemies in the press, the title stuck and now is the "official" title for his Tradition of witchcraft.

garlic—A charm against vampires or the evil eye, also used as an immunity booster, and, of course, a great seasoning for food.

garter—Worn by a Witch Queen as a symbol of her rank. Traditionally of green leather (snakeskin) backed with blue silk. One large silver buckle symbolizes the original coven and other smaller buckles symbolize each of the daughter covens which have hived off of the original group. Worn on the left leg, just above the knee.

Garter

gastromancy—Literally "stomach divination." Divination by hearing voices that are unexpected, like from the stomach but also from trees, brooks, etc. The voices seemed to emanate from places where the diviner pointed. May refer to ventriloquism, but also speaking through trance possession and glossalalia.

gate—1) An opening to other dimensions; a localized area of psychic distortion; an area where those in other planes can pass into our own. Usually characterized by a feeling of cold, distortion, or a shimmering as one passes through. May act as a lens or window into other planes. 2) Also called a doorway, an opening in a magickal Circle where participants can pass in and out without disrupting the Circle's energies, its position may or may not be indicated in the Circle. Sometimes created as a part of the Circle, sometimes created for immediate need and closed afterward.

gathering—See festival.

geas—A magickal spell that binds a person to perform a particular act or task, which can be self-imposed or imposed from without either by mortal or supernatural means. Theoretically the person is hampered or restricted in their daily activities until the geas has been carried out. The Quest for the Holy Grail was a geas of sorts for those knights who committed to the quest.

Geller, Uri—(1946–) Israeli psychic who demonstrated his psychokinetic abilities on television during the 1970s. He was also reputed to be tele-pathic and tested well for ESP, though tests of his psychokinetic abilities were inconclusive. In the late 1970s Geller retired from public life and now consults on a private basis, including dowsing for minerals and oil.

gelomancy—Divination through interpreting hysterical laughter. Similar to glossalalia, this may have arisen from the ancient Oracles who usually burned hallucinogenic substances and inhaled the smoke to induce trance and visions. Results could be unpredictable.

Gematria—A Hebrew study of the alphabet and the numerical correspondences for each letter. Words whose letter values add up to the same total are said to be similar in essence and some level of meaning. This is a Talmudic teaching that has been adopted and adapted for modern and sometimes non-Hebrew use. Numerology in the Western tradition is an offshoot of Gematria. Each letter of the Hebrew alphabet has a numeric value assigned to it, and by adding these values one comes up with the numeric equivalent of the word. The Number of the Beast of Revelations—666—was determined in this way.

geomancy—1) Divination using earth, stones, sand, or dirt. 2) A specific divinatory system with Italian roots, sometimes tied with astrology. 3) A divinatory system practiced by driving stakes in the earth at random points, connecting them with string, and interpreting the resulting shapes.

ghost—A disembodied spirit, a discarnate entity, a phenomenon that indicates an excess of psychic energy and some emotional or psychic disturbance that triggers the "apparition." Ghosts can also be otherworldly creatures (fairies or elementals). Used generically by the mundane population, Wiccans tend to be more specific in describing psychic disturbances.

ghoul—From Arabic *ghul* (to seize). 1) A person who eats the dead. 2) A person excessively fixated on things morbid and negative. 3) An Arabic demon with one eye, wings, and an animal shape that eats flesh.

glossalalia—Also called speaking in tongues—1) The phenomenon of a person uttering words that are in an incomprehensible language, which can be in an actual foreign or ancient language, or in a language that is unknown. The person may or may not be in a trance-like state. Sometimes seen as a form of possession. May be a communication from the spirit world. 2) A Christian practice that is said to indicate the presence of the Holy Spirit within the person, usually done in a charismatic or evangelical setting.

glyph—A written or drawn symbol. Sacred or magickal symbol. Can be used as a symbol of a person or group or tradition. Can be used like a magickal name. Can be invested with magickal energy or carry psychic energy on its own (like the runes). One can use a glyph to mark one's magickal items. Can also be used like a spell, to call forth certain energies when used or viewed.

Gnome—An earth elemental.

Gnomes of Zurich—Supposedly one group of Illuminati who control the Swiss banking system and also possibly the financial systems of the entire world, a favorite target of Aryan and Nazi groups.

gnosis—Greek, meaning knowledge. The theological concept that each person is responsible for making their own connection to Deity, whatever that may be.

Gnostic, Gnosticism—A pre-Christian, Pagan, Jewish, and early Christian belief system (second century BCE to third century CE) based upon mystical and spiritual teachings and the adherent's direct connection to and dialogue with God.

An early Christian heresy. There are many Gnostic documents contained in the Dead Sea scrolls and the Nag Hamaddi collections, all of them early religious and mystical writings discovered in the Middle East in 1945 that date from about 200 BCE to about 150 CE. These writings are the remnants of small religious groups that lived in isolation in an attempt to attain enlightenment. Wiccans readily adopted the Gnostic principle that the individual is free to seek Deity in their own way.

Gnosticism also presents a strongly dualistic belief system, good/evil, light/darkness, spiritual/physical. Asceticism and rites of Initiation were believed to liberate the immortal souls of believers from a prison of physical existence. In the ancient Middle East, Gnosticism was practiced by Pagans, Jews, and Christians alike.

In the early Christian church there were fierce political battles between the Gnostics and those who later became the Catholics, because the two viewpoints were incompatible and much was at stake. The proto-Catholics eventually won, and the Gnostics were either wiped out, converted, or forced into hiding. The surviving accounts were written by the Catholics, so it is likely that much of what is written is a distortion of Gnosticism, with some blatantly propagandistic and scurrilous practices attributed to the original Gnostics. There are Gnostic elements in the Coptic Church, Nestorian Christianity, and other small remnants of those early splinter groups, but for the most part these ideas were declared heretical. When they invariably reappeared every few centuries or so in various guises the adherents were ruthlessly eliminated, because one cornerstone of the Catholic religion is the need for a priest as intermediary between man and God. Carl Jung felt that the reintroduction of Gnostic ideas would benefit mankind, and explored alchemy to discover some of Gnosticism's long-hidden concepts.

God—Deity manifest as the masculine gender. Also used as a generic term for Deity, though Deity is less sexist.

Goddess—Deity manifest as the feminine gender.

Goetia—An occult book by Aleister Crowley. The term is derived from Greek and is used to mean witchcraft.

goetic—Magick that involves evocation and binding of evil spirits to accomplish the will of the magician.

Golden Dawn, Order of the—An occult order founded in 1887 by three members of England's Rosicrucian Society, it became a major influence in Western ritual magick and is an occult ancestor of modern Wicca. Through the efforts of its members much of the Western esoteric tradition was resurrected, codified, and built upon, and eventually publicized. Some of its prominent members were S.L. MacGregor Mathers, Moina Mathers, W.B. Yeats, Israel Regardie, Dion Fortune, Annie Horniman, Florence Farr, Maud Gonne, A.E. Waite, and Aleister Crowley (who was eventually expelled). Its purpose was "to prosecute the Great Work: which is to obtain control of the nature and power of my own being." It broke up around W.W.I, and was revived afterward, but in a somewhat diminished form. Various groups claim to be the modern day successors of the Golden Dawn Tradition. Its rituals are basically Kabbalistic, with elements of the Chaldean Oracles, the Egyptian Book of the Dead, and Blake's prophetic books.

golem—A Hebrew creation, a man-sized figure formed from clay and animated by a rabbi with magick and prayer. On its forehead is written *emet* (life, in Hebrew). Once created it obeys the commands of its creator, is supernaturally strong, and cannot be injured. To stop the golem, one must wipe off the first letter, making the word *met* (death in Hebrew). The Rabbi Judah Loew of Prague supposedly created a golem to protect his people during pogroms in the Jewish ghettos in the sixteenth century. A golem is reported to have protected and aided the Jews in the Warsaw ghetto uprising against the Nazis during W.W.II.

Grand Grimoire—A collection of spells, invocations, and magick attributed to King Solomon. The manuscript actually dates from the sixteenth century and is an interesting compendium of magickal thought and techniques used at the time.

graphology—Handwriting analysis to determine character. Once considered to be in the realm of fortunetelling, it is now a highly respected adjunct to the psychologist's arsenal of character analysis techniques.

Great Rite—Ritual sex within the magickal Circle. The sacramental blessing of the wine and cakes at a Wiccan ritual. The words "as the cup is the female and the athame is the male, together they are one," followed by thrusting the athame into the filled chalice to consecrate the wine, symbolizes the act of love and procreation—sex. The Great Rite is symbolic sex, and well illustrates that Wicca is a fertility religion. Fertility is meant in many ways, but actual procreation is also included in that fertility. "The Great Rite in actuality" refers to actually having sex, usually within a Circle or in connection with a private ritual at home. Some traditions require that only a married or committed couple may celebrate the Great Rite in actuality. Wiccans do not celebrate with public or group sex and there are no ritual orgies.

Priestess and Priest Performing Great Rite

Great Work—The culmination of all magickal work, this is the process of refining the mind and soul to create as perfect and effective a human as possible. Through magick and other means a person is constantly refining their soul and character, examining flaws and shortcomings, and working to become whole, effective, and perfected. This concept originated in the Hermetic system, but has been adopted by Wiccans and others who engage in magickal self-development.

Greater Sabbats—The Sabbats celebrated at the cross-quarters—Beltane, Lughnasadh, Samhain, and Imbolc—are sometimes referred to as the Greater Sabbats because many people and cultures are familiar with them, whereas the Lesser Sabbats are not always celebrated, even among Wiccans.

Greco-Egyptian Magick—A magickal and religious system practiced from the first century BCE into the second century CE, and possibly beyond. A blending of Greek and Egyptian theology and magick combined with other mystical and philosophical elements. Much of Ceremonial Magick draws heavily upon the Greco-Egyptian traditions and writings, with the addition of elements from Hebrew and Kabbalistic practice. The Hermetic Tradition is believed to be a descendant of these practices. Masonic legend also traces Freemasonry through this magickal tradition.

Green Egg—A national Pagan magazine and official organ of the Church of All Worlds (CAW), a Pagan church with nests (branches) in the United States, Canada, New Zealand, and Australia, it is the most widely circulated and best known Pagan magazine of the twentieth century. It has a listing of festivals, local CAW groups, and letter columns as well as articles and artwork.

Green Man—1) A.k.a., Jack o' the Green, John Barleycorn—God of vegetation and agriculture. 2) A person (usually male) chosen at Beltane to represent the God, either for the day or for the year in some Traditions. Generally chosen by a lottery.

Green Man

gremlin—Mischievous spirit causing minor problems that are difficult to track down and repair. Popularized during W.W.II and thereafter as an explanation for strange inexplicable problems in technological equipment. The female counterpart is a fifinella.

grimoire—A.k.a., Gramerie. (See also Book of Shadows.) A magickal compendium of spells, herb lore, charms, recipes, and other information. May be handed down in a hereditary manner or may be hand-copied by each recipient of the knowledge. A medieval term for a book or grammar of magickal procedures, the most famous of which is *The Greater Key of Solomon the King*, colloquially known as the *Key of Solomon* or the *Grand Grimoire*. Sometimes mundanely defined as a satanic book of black magick. In Wicca, the term is used generically and sometimes interchangeably with Book of Shadows and the older Black Book. Other famous grimoires are the *Grimorius Serum*, *The Lesser Key of Solomon*, *Heptameron*, *Enchiridium*, *Grimorium Verum*, and the *Grimoire of Honorius*.

grounded—The state of being fully "in the world," not disoriented. Also having psychic equilibrium and not being unduly affected by stray psychic influences. Being grounded makes you more stable and confident, and also less subject to emotional and psychic upset.

You can ground yourself through various means and/or ground another person. Grounding can be achieved through learned techniques, chants, rituals, objects created or energized for the purpose, eating a heavy meal (greasy fast food can give you a "crash grounding"), literally lying on the ground, taking a bath or shower, using salt in various ways.

grounding and centering—The act of grounding and centering one's self, creating within yourself stability and shielding yourself from psychic influence, upset, or harm. Wiccan training includes many techniques for grounding and centering, and it is desirable to ground and center both before and after a ritual to get the best results. Some groups and Traditions require each participant to be grounded and centered before any Working is started.

group mind—A gestalt created by a number of people working together doing magick and psychic work. A collective awareness that can be either conscious or unconscious. It is the group mind that enables a group to work magicks that are more powerful than any of the individuals could accomplish either individually or collectively.

grove—1) A local Druidic group. 2) A group of people gathering together to study. 3) (archaic) A coven of more than thirteen members. Also similar to an Outer Court of a hierarchical Traditional coven.

Gurdjieff, George Ivanovich—(1872?–1949) Spiritual leader and founder of a movement based upon the attainment of enlightenment through meditation and heightened self-awareness. He established an Institute for the Harmonious Development of Man at Fontainbleau in France. Gurdjieff employed techniques of hypnotism and taught the necessity of obedience to a teacher who has achieved enlightenment (a Man Who Knows). Constant self-observation, physical labor, demeaning tasks, intense emotionalism, exercise, and dance routines were all employed to help a person attain a higher state of self-awareness, to transcend mechanical existence, and commune with the true soul. Also known as the Third Way, there are many adherents of this system throughout the world.

guru—A Hindu term, an enlightened teacher, one who has superior mystical knowledge, skills, and training. Although Wicca is generally taught in a small-group setting, there are few real gurus. Most Wiccans are not comfortable with the idea of becoming a devoted follower of anyone for any length of time. Wicca teaches strong self-determinism, self-reliance, and healthy skepticism.

Gypsy, Gipsy, Gypsie—Short for Egyptian. Around 1100–1300 CE a group of Aryan peoples migrated to Europe from the East. When asked where they came from, the answer was understood to be "from Egypt," which was a legendary land to the Europeans at the time, so the people came to be called Gypsies. The name they use for themselves is The Rom or Romany, which means The People. Gypsies are nomadic and never settle in one place but make a living traveling from place to place, doing odd jobs such as tinkering, selling herbs and potions, and telling fortunes. In some areas the name Gypsy is synonymous with witch. They are insular and secretive and have retained much of their original culture and language.

During W.W.II the Nazis launched a systematic campaign to wipe out the Gypsies as well as Jews, homosexuals, and mental defectives, and, in many countries, the entire Gypsy population was wiped out.

At the present time Gypsies are still viewed with suspicion, as some have been known to perpetrate frauds and shady dealings as well as outright thievery if the need arises. Some European countries have instituted policies that require the Gypsies to settle down and establish themselves in one community.

Gypsies are believed to have a high incidence of psychic abilities among their people and have a long tradition of herb and spell lore. Some prominent Wiccans claim Gypsy ancestry. Much of medieval and Renaissance witch lore was formulated to cast suspicion on Gypsies as well as "native" witches. Gypsies have been romanticized over the centuries, and it is possible that much of their lore and teachings have been adopted by modern Wicca, sometimes deliberately, sometimes unknowingly. Legend has it that the Gypsies are the direct descendants of the ancient European Pagans and still practice some or all of those Pagan religions.

gyromancy—Divination by spinning. 1) A person spins around and around while chanting certain incantations. When the person falls to the ground they will have an oracular vision. 2) A circle is drawn on the floor that is divided into various segments, often twenty-four. Each segment is marked with Hebrew letters, Kabbalistic symbols, astrological symbols, etc. A person spins around and around, sometimes chanting, and the segment of the circle where they stumble or fall is then interpreted for answers and messages. 3) A circle of letters is drawn on the floor and the practitioner walks around and around the circle until they become dizzy. The letters they step on as they stumble in their dizziness are said to be prophetic.

H

hag—An old woman, usually ugly and possibly evil-tempered, often widowed, or never married. In many places the name Hag was synonymous with witch, giving rise to the belief that all witches were old and ugly.

hag-stones, mare stones—Stones with holes worn as an amulet to prevent nightmares.

hair—A medieval belief holds that magickal potency resided in the hair. Witches were shorn before torture to protect the torturers. Hair is also used as a charm to bind a person or charge a poppet.

Halloween, All Hallow's Eve—Secular name for the Sabbat Wiccans celebrate as Samhain. Generally celebrated October 31st.

Hand of Fatima—A charm of protection in the form of a hand with mystic symbols inscribed on the palm. Generally depicted as either hand, that is, there is no distinct thumb.

Hand of Fatima

Hand of Glory—Traditionally the severed hand of a hanged criminal, it was dried, steeped in various salts, and then either dipped in wax and the fingers lit or candles placed between the fingers. It was used by burglars as a charm to keep a household asleep while they burgled. It

Hand of Glory

entered occult lore and has become a powerful black magick device for causing harm and befuddling an enemy. Probably much rarer than the literature suggests, there are modern candle replicas which sometimes show up around Halloween that are made in China. The use of the candle replicas is supposedly an intent to harm and should not be taken lightly.

Handfasting—From Middle English *handfasten* or *handfesten*. Medieval term for a wedding not sanctified by the church. A Wiccan ceremony and life passage in which people commit to a partnership. Handfastings can be between two people (of opposite or same sex) or occasionally more than two. Can be a legal wedding, or just a religious ceremony. Handfastings can be for a specific length of time (a year-and-a-day is the usual minimum) or "until we part" either by death or choice. Handfastings can be renewed or ended usually at the will of the parties involved. One can be handfasted without being married. Wiccans do not require that partners be legally married to be recognized as a committed partnership within the Wiccan Community.

Handmaiden—A person in a ritual who helps the High Priestess, usually female. Also a coven office. Sometimes an High Priestess in training. The Handmaiden helps organize, sets up the altar, and may be in charge of the use and storage of ritual items. During a ritual the Handmaiden may hold a reading candle, hold scripts, keep the chalice filled, and perform other housekeeping duties necessary during a ritual. The actual duties of the office vary from Tradition to Tradition and coven to coven. May be a permanent or temporary appointment.

Handparting—A Wiccan ceremony in which a committed partnership is ended. Can be the same as a divorce, but not always. Ideally all parties to the partnership take part, but sometimes it is only one. It is considered a necessary part of ending a relationship in order to gain closure and be free from the restraints and emotions of the broken relationship. Divorce is a legal procedure, Handparting is the religious ceremony.

haruspex—Possibly from Sanskrit *hira* (entrails). Latin term for diviner. May derive from the Etruscan method of divination of reading the entrails of sacrificial animals. Extispicy is a synonymous term.

haunt, haunting—Supernatural occurrences attributed to the actions of ghosts or spirits, generally associated with a traumatic or sudden death. May occur to a person, place, thing, or structure. Generally considered to be an unpleasant thing.

Many hauntings have become famous, even tourist attractions. Phenomena of hauntings include apparitions, noises, smells, tactile sensations, temperature extremes, movement of objects, etc. In some famous hauntings, the spirits follow floor plans and room levels that existed when they were alive, and have been subsequently remodeled. This results in spirits walking on air or on a floor level below the present floor, as well as walking through walls that were formerly doors. Not all people can sense a haunting, only those with certain psychic abilities. Many merely feel uncomfortable or a sense of oppression or dread.

An exorcism is a ritual used to rid a place of a spirit and end a haunting, usually by sending the entity on to its proper plane. Hauntings may be momentary, continue for a few days, weeks, months, years, or even centuries. Scientific investigation of hauntings began in the late nineteenth century and have continued with mixed success ever since. Since the phenomenon is subjective it is often difficult or impossible to document or replicate.

head blind—A person who has no psychic abilities. Being head blind does not disqualify one from practicing Wicca. Some feel one who is head blind should not practice any magick. Some Ceremonial Magick techniques do not require psychic ability.

heathen—"Of the heath," a person living in the country, on the heath where the heather grows. Originally used for a non-urban person but later came to mean non-Christian. Heathen religion has come to mean the original Pagan beliefs that were superseded and later wiped out by Christianity. The term originally referred specifically to rural Pagans in the British Isles. Some modern followers of pre-Christian religions prefer to call themselves Heathens rather than Pagans.

Hebrew alphabet—Sometimes used as a magickal alphabet. Hebrew is written from right to left; or the reverse of English and most modern languages. There are numerical correspondences for each letter of the Hebrew alphabet. By using the spelling of words and adding the numerical equivalents one can find further correspondences. This study is called Gematria, and is a Hebrew teaching that has been adopted by magicians as well. Aleister Crowley in *777* used Gematria and other works to derive his correspondences.

Hecate, Hekate—An ancient Greek Goddess (though she existed well before the ancient Greeks, her origins are in the Black Sea area), she is considered by some scholars to predate the Universe or alternatively the Greek Pantheon.

She was the Goddess of magick, witches and witchcraft, darkness, chaos, and other primal pre-civilization forces. She was triple-headed, and the serpent was one of her symbols. Many statues of Hecate are all but indistinguishable from statues of Athena, and both claimed the owl as a patron bird. In medieval and Renaissance times Hecate was considered a demon, patroness of witches and witchcraft.

hell—A Christian concept of a place of torment where people go after they have died when they have not been proper Christians or are not right-eous or have forsaken the Lord (meaning Jehovah and/or Jesus) and his ways. Wiccans do not believe in Hell or Damnation.

Hell-Fire Club—A.k.a., Medmenham Fran-ciscans, Order of St. Francis, Brotherhood of St. Francis at Wycombe, Dashwood's Apostles. A satanic order founded around 1742 by Sir Francis Dashwood, it was devoted to Satanism, licen-tiousness, politics, and debauchery. There had been Hell-Fire clubs devoted to Satanism in varying forms in England off and on since the late 1600s, and they also sprang up now and again as late as the 1880s (and possibly since), but Dashwood's is The Hell-Fire Club.

This group was comprised of prominent members of British government and some royal-ty, and much of the politics of England in the 1750s through about 1770 was conducted at meetings of the club. There was certainly satanic activity, but whether it was in earnest, a parody of polite society, or just an attempt to escape the boredom of conventionality is in dispute. That the meetings usually ended in orgies is not at all disputed. Occult lore has the group tied in loose-ly with Masonry, the American Revolution (sup-posedly Ben Franklin was an honored guest when he was in England), and the loose chain of occult groups which has preserved and enhanced occult lore through the centuries.

henge—A sacred enclosure for outdoor rituals, usually stone, but wood markers can also be used.

henotheism—Belief in or worship of one God without denying the existence of others.

hepatoscopy—Divination by means of a sheep's liver.

herald—1) A person who functions as a public address system, spreading messages and announcements at a festival; a town crier. 2) To act in the capacity of a herald, calling out announcements. Also can be one who carries messages and greetings from one group to the next.

herbs—An aromatic plant of temperate climate, used for seasoning and also possibly medicinal pur-poses. Also used for magickal and spiritual purpos-es. Herb lore was a mainstay of witches of old. Along with midwifery, witches were the female (and male) healers of the common people, and their pharmacopoeia was assembled from herbs and other things that were harvested at certain times for best effects. At various times being an herb woman was synonymous with witch.

Hereditary—1) A person who was brought up in the Craft, as in an Hereditary. 2) A person who follows the older Fam-Trad forms of the Craft, the pre-Gardnerian traditions. 3) A person who claims a historical continuous family Tradition of Witchcraft.

heresy—A religious belief opposed to or differing from the orthodox doctrines of a church, especial-ly beliefs that have been denounced by a church. The Christian church has declared a number of beliefs heretical during its history and what is a heresy in one century can become orthodoxy in another. Generally Pagan beliefs and practices are considered heretical.

heretic—A church member who holds beliefs opposed to church dogma.

Hermanubis—A Greco-Egyptian Deity who was an amalgam of Hermes and Anubis. He was the God of magick and mystical studies, guardian and opener of the gateways to the other realms, guide to astral travelers. Later he was adopted by medieval and Renaissance magicians as their God or demon of magick and mystical lore. He was the main Deity of Hermeticists, and through those teachings he became a prominent figure in Ceremonial Magick.

Hermetic, Hermetica—The occult tradition based upon the teachings of Hermes Trismegistus (Thrice Great Hermes), a medieval alchemist and magician. Also used as an alternative term for the alchemical arts. Combined with Kabbalah this body of lore was the foundation of Western occultism. The original multi-volume book *Corpus Hermeticum* or *Hermetica* survives in fragments and is said to have been originally written on papyrus and stored in the great library at Alexandria. Most of the original volume was lost when the library was destroyed, but fragments were supposedly preserved in secret caches in the desert by initiates. Disputes over the origin and authorship of Hermetica have existed at least since the Renaissance, and modern scholars assume a series of anonymous early Christian to medieval and possibly Renaissance authors wrote the work.

Herne, Herne the Hunter—Celtic God, Lord of the Wild Hunt. A God revered by many Wiccans of Celtic traditional descent. In a British television program about Robin Hood, aired in the United States in the late 1980s to early 1990s, Herne the Hunter was a Deity who granted Robin and his followers aid and protection in exchange for their worship. This series postulated Robin and his band were Pagan worshippers who were being persecuted by the Christian Normans.

Herne the Hunter

Hesperus—Greek, the West. Term used with Venus—Venus Hesperus—when Venus is an evening star—setting after the Sun.

hexagram—1) A six-pointed star, formed either by two interlacing equilateral triangles (for example, the Star of David or Magan David that has been adopted as one symbol of Judaism) or one single line (the unicursal hexagram, invented by Aleister Crowley). The hexagram has been used as an occult symbol since ancient times, and it symbolizes the Hermetic principle "as above, so below." 2) The six-line figures of the I Ching, composed of two trigrams.

Magan David, Unicursal Hexagram, I-Ching Figure

hieromancy—Divination through sacrifice or preparation for sacrifice when performed by specially designated priests or initiates in accordance with established rites and custom.

High Priest—Abbreviated HP. 1) A male Third Degree Wiccan Initiate. 2) The male who co-runs a coven with a High Priestess, though not all covens have a High Priest. 3) The male who officiates at a large public Circle or a Sabbat or Esbat.

High Priestess—Abbreviated HPS. 1) A female Third Degree Wiccan Initiate. 2) The female who runs a coven with or without a High Priest. 3) The female who officiates at a large public Circle or a Sabbat or Esbat. Usually in a Circle or group the High Priestess is the final authority and head of the group. The High Priest helps her and carries out her orders as necessary. Not all covens have a High Priestess or a High Priest.

hippomancy—Divination by observation of a horse's pace, usually during special parades or ceremonies.

hive off, hive, spin off—1) When a coven becomes too large to operate easily, some members may elect to split off from the original group and start a sister coven elsewhere. Or if a faction within a coven is displeased with the group for whatever reason, they may also split off and start a separate group elsewhere. 2) A ritual in which one leaves the Circle of their training in order to form or join a new Circle.

hocus pocus—Possible corruption of Latin *hoc est corpus* (this is the body), a phrase used during the Catholic Mass. Magic words, magic spells, incantations, magical misdirection, or tomfoolery. Not used to describe legitimate magickal Workings. Modern colloquialism that implies that activities are less than honest or not fully disclosed.

holism, holistic, Holistic Universe Theory—This theory asserts that the Universe is mirrored in all its parts. It is a modern version of the old Hermetic saying, "as above, so below."

Fractals, mandelbrot sets, and Julia sets are mathematical equations that can be converted into visual images, which, when reduced or enlarged, eventually look the same as the starting point. This is a mathematical and visual illustration of the holistic theory.

Once theoretical physicists started investigating quarks and other sub-atomic particles and their properties, this theory developed and it was found to apply to many areas outside the field of theoretical physics. The science of chaos is also tied to these theories and constructs. This theory is being used to "explain" astrology, magick, and many other paranormal phenomena, which on the surface have no direct tie to objective reality, yet work consistently. Macrocosm and microcosm are older terms used in explaining these ideas.

Holly King—The God of the waning year who reigns from Summer Solstice to Winter Solstice.

Holly King

horns, horned crown—Symbol of the God as a stag, commonly equated with Cernunnos, the horned God. Worn by some as a symbol of the role of High Priest or Green Man. To take or wear the horns is to act as High Priest or Green Man. Ancient symbol for male Deity used in modern times. When Christianity supplanted the original Pagan beliefs, the horns were demonized and became attributes of Satan or the Devil, which was the antithesis of the Christian God, in an attempt to suppress the Pagan rites that often continued covertly alongside the new Christian practices. The phrase "to give a man horns," which is slang for cuckolding or marital infidelity, may also descend from the Pagan rites, which were not necessarily monogamous.

hot seat—An ordeal, usually part of an Initiation where the candidate is closely questioned and challenged about their beliefs, what they have learned, and/or their commitment to the Craft. Can also be used as a screening process in a class. Traditionally, it was used by witches as a preparation for possible inquisition, should the person be caught and revealed to be a witch. Generally it can range from mild questioning to very heavy verbal challenges and possibly hot confrontative behavior to deep psychological probing, the goal of which is to determine if the person has the strength of their convictions to stand up to a strong challenger and not back down.

hydromancy—1) Divination by gazing into a water surface. May be a bowl, pond, lake, stream, or ocean tides. Stones may be dropped into a still pool or a twig or leaf floated down a small stream, and the resulting patterns or paths interpreted. A fountain may also be used. 2) Divination by invoking water sprites or spirits, and either hearing their messages or reading their messages in the water. 3) Divination by casting objects into water and interpreting them from their behavior. If they sink it is a good omen, if they float off before sinking it is a bad omen. Throwing coins into a fountain for luck or making a wish may derive from this practice. 4) Divination using a bowl of water which, when activated by spirits at the command of the diviner, vibrates to the point of boiling and thereby makes sounds that are then interpreted by the diviner.

hypnosis—An altered state of consciousness of lowered brain wave frequency (alpha-theta) and heightened suggestibility. Similar to the dream state, but induced rather than spontaneous. Some guided meditations take the form of a hypnotic session, and the person or group is guided by the leader of the meditation. Hypnosis in itself is not a specifically occult technique, and should be used cautiously and only by persons who are skilled and experienced. Most past-life regressions use hypnotic induction. Officially discovered by Dr. Anton Mesmer in the 1770s, who called it animal magnetism. It was historically called mesmerism, after Mesmer. Actually, hypnotic techniques have been part of occult lore for millennia, under various guises and techniques.

I

I Ching, the Book of Changes—The oldest Chinese book in existence. It is a book of divination that contains 64 figures (hexagrams) made up of six lines each, broken (yin) or unbroken (yang). Lines may be "moving" or "fixed." Moving lines have two interpretations, their initial character and the character they change into which creates a new hexagram. Each hexagram has meanings derived from component parts, and additional meanings are derived from moving lines (if any). One can obtain each line in many ways, throwing yarrow sticks is the traditional way, but modern practitioners usually substitute coins, which are thrown. The philosophy underlying the I Ching is Confucian and patriarchal, but it can give good advice and when used properly and with reverence can seem like one is being counseled by an ancient sage.

The origin of the I Ching is not clear, but as a divinatory system is said to date from 3000–5000 BCE. It is surmised to be a refinement of scapulomantic techniques, and many tortoise shells and shoulder bones with cracks and written interpretations have been found in ancient Chinese sites. Legend has the original text dating from the First Emperor Fu Hsi, 2852–2738 BCE. King Wen and his son Duke Chow (circa 1150 BCE) are said to be the main authors of the present text and Confucius and his disciples (circa 500 BCE) authored the commentaries.

icon—A sacred image or representation. Wiccans are liberal in the types of symbols that can be used to represent the Goddess and/or God. The black and white candles on the altar are often symbols for the Goddess and God. Rocks, feathers, or other natural objects can be used as well as pictures, statues, and the like. There are many popular images which are generic in depiction, as well as images of specific Goddesses and Gods.

icthyomancy—1) Divination using the entrails of fish. 2) Divination by observation of a fish's movements and behavior.

idolomancy—Divination by use of an idol. Some cultures had large hollow statues in which priests would hide and speak as if the Deity were speaking to the seekers. Otherwise the idols were used as a focus, in dream imagery, and other ways.

Illuminatus, Illuminati—Latin, enlightened one(s). 1) A trilogy of books authored by Robert Anton Wilson that are supposedly thinly disguised fictionalized accounts of a secret occult/fraternity/cabal/conspiracy that is covertly running the world as the "powers behind the throne" in many arenas of world politics and commerce. A game of the same name was developed which is fun and quite silly, putting many of these theories in perspective. A popular occult conspiracy theory pre-dates the books, but was widely popularized by them. 2) A level of initiatory attainment in several secret societies. 3) Order of Illuminati a.k.a., Bavarian Illuminati, founded in 1776 by Adam Weishaupt in Bavaria, who wanted to become a Mason and did so in 1777.

Scottish Rite Masonry supposedly has many elements of the Illuminati, which include anti-monarchialism, and republicanism. In 1784 Masonry was denounced to the Bavarian government as politically dangerous, and the Masons, Illuminati, and other secret societies were suppressed. The attempted placement of the Prince of Lorraine on the throne of France, thereby restoring the Hapsburgs to dominance in rulership of Europe, was one reason this group was considered politically dangerous. 4) Propaganda maintains that Wicca is created and/or controlled by the Illuminati; however, Wicca is real, the Illuminati are not. 5) Illuminatus is also a title of adeptship, used in Ceremonial Magick and occasionally in some Wiccan Traditions.

Imbolc, Imbolg—Gaelic, in the belly, also known as Oimelc, Immilch, and Candlemas. The Sabbat celebrated around February 2nd. Astrologically 15° Aquarius.

immanent Divinity—The idea that nature includes Divinity; that Divinity is a quality, not a separate entity and may be found within, as well as without. An idea broadened and popularized by the New Age.

incantation—A chant used to help cast a spell, usually said or sung in rhyme and easily memorized. The phrase "out goes the bad air, in comes the good" is a simple example of an incantation. Usually an incantation is used together with other techniques and is chanted while preparing or making something. It helps the mind focus on the task and is spoken in order to help engage all the senses in the spell being worked. The more of the senses one engages, the more effective the spell will be.

incarnate—Latin, to enter into flesh, to be born and take on a body, to have a physical body, to be in a physical body on the material plane.

incarnation—One life in a series of lives through which an individual soul can learn, progress, and grow, and eventually develop to the point that the process of incarnation becomes unnecessary and the soul can then merge with the Divine. An Eastern concept. To incarnate again and again is referred to as reincarnation.

incense—Substances that release a smell when burned used in religious and magickal ceremonies. Incense can be used for purification, cleansing, or offering. There are myriad correspondences between various incenses and attributes. Incense is used to help engage the sense of smell and, with repeated use, the smell alone can help trigger certain responses. The more of the senses that are engaged, the more effective a spell or Working will be.

Incenses come in many forms and varieties. Use of a charcoal briquette (which is specially made) with loose incense sprinkled on top has the fewest artificial ingredients. A bundle of dried plants that are burned is called a smudge. Cones and sticks are manmade and may contain more artificial ingredients, even some that may cause allergic reactions. Some incenses from India and the Orient are notorious for containing unwanted oils and resins that can be particularly irritating. It is best to try out an incense before using one to see if it causes any allergic reactions. Some herbs and spices when burned can produce mildly hallucinogenic effects; the ingredients in a smudge or incense should be disclosed before subjecting people to the smoke.

individuality—The immortal reincarnating portion of a person, roughly equivalent to the soul. Individuality is immortal, but the personality changes from incarnation to incarnation.

Initiate—1) A person who has gone through a magickal ceremony designed to acknowledge skill levels and also open them up to greater awareness and abilities. An Initiation can be formal or informal. Many Wiccan groups will not recognize the Initiations of another Tradition, requiring each member to take the Initiations of that Tradition. Not all Wiccans are Initiates, nor do all Traditions require or even offer Initiation. One can also self-Initiate, which may or may not be acknowledged by others. 2) A new member of a coven. 3) A First Degree Wiccan.

Initiate's Circle—Circle for Initiates only. Exclusive for a variety of reasons: a Tradition's custom, the emotional content of a ritual, or the nature of secrets being revealed. Some Traditions only practice magick in an Initiate's Circle.

Initiation—A magickal metamorphosis. A magickal ceremony in which a person is elevated to a higher degree of understanding and knowledge as well as skill and ability. A ritual that represents a final test of a person's qualifications for a certain degree or position. The ritual is an acknowledgment by the initiator(s), witnesses, and also the Goddess and God. Most Wiccan Initiations contain the same elements: a challenge, an oath, imparting of knowledge, and a symbolic death and rebirth. Initiation into First, Second, and Third Degrees are common in Wicca, though not universal.

There are many traditions associated with Initiations: they must be at least a year-and-a-day apart; they may not be performed on a child; they may not be performed on a woman in her menses (during her period); they may not be performed on a woman who is pregnant or within three months after giving birth; the candidate should have no foreknowledge of the actual text or ceremonies of the Initiation; they must be performed by a person of equal or greater degree (this varies widely among Traditions); there should be a change in the person to show the Initiation has been successful; the actual "secrets" of the Tradition are passed on; an oath is required and must be adhered to; a challenge is offered and must be met and overcome.

Most Wiccan Initiations are modeled on Masonic Initiations for their First, Second, and Third degrees. Most Wiccan Traditions offer Initiations, though not all grant degrees.

In self-Initiation one performs the ceremony alone after training and practice. This can also be acknowledged as valid (see Cunningham's *Wicca: A Guide for the Solitary Practitioner* for a solo Initiation), although many Traditions refuse to acknowledge Initiations that are not performed within that particular Tradition. "Initiation by the Gods" is a term used to acknowledge learning and growth through a series of personal life crises that are resolved and acknowledges the wisdom gained thereby. This can be considered as valid as a traditional Initiation.

There is a saying, "The Gods initiate, we just officiate," that can be used to justify/explain a non-standard Initiation, but can also explain why people never react exactly the same when initiated. Some feel someone cannot call themselves a witch unless they have been initiated.

inner court—In certain traditions, Wiccan and otherwise, there is an outer court and an inner court. The inner court is composed of the higher-level Initiates who have access to more of the secrets of the Tradition and perform Workings and projects that require more skill, knowledge, discretion, and responsibility. The High Priestess and High Priest are at the center (or apex) of the hierarchy and thus are also part of the inner court. The inner court Initiates may be the teachers and mentors for the outer court people, helping them learn and overseeing their studies and progress.

Members of the inner court are insiders in the Tradition, and the inner court is usually oath-bound not to reveal secrets to the uninitiated.

Being a member of the inner court requires years of study and commitment to the Tradition, as well as being oathbound to be loyal to the Tradition. It also usually requires exclusivity, that is, one cannot be a member of any other group or coven, and must direct one's energies to that Tradition only.

inner planes—Levels of being and consciousness other than the physical or the normal ego-consciousness. Some examples are the dream state, the meditative state, etc.

Inquisition—An office of the Catholic Church established in the thirteenth century and developed for the discovery and suppression of heresy and the punishment of heretics. The accused were presumed guilty until proven innocent. Torture was a valid method for the extraction of confessions and the confirmation of information. Originally developed as a method to be used rarely and under specialized circumstances for discovering heretics within the Church, as the centuries passed the practice became more widespread and indiscriminate. The formal office of the Inquisition was finally dissolved by Pope John Paul II in 1991. Originally solely a Catholic office, as the Protestant reformation spread and grew, inquisitions by Protestants as well as Catholics became more common. The Salem Witchcraft Trials in the 1690s were a form of Protestant inquisition.

Witchcraft became a heresy during the Middle Ages, and during the Renaissance witchcraft trials were a convenient way for some to make money and get rid of rivals and enemies—the accuser was usually able to confiscate the lands and property of the accused after giving a "gift" to the inquisitors and/or the church.

The popular notion that nine million European women died due to the Inquisition and witchcraft trials may be an exaggeration. Most victims of the inquisitions died either in prison or under torture. The actual number burned at the stake was small. Many committed suicide (a heresy in itself) rather than face the inquisitors. In England the usual punishment was beheading or hanging. The modern phrase "never again the burning" refers to the fervent wish that Pagans never again be subjected to any inquisitions, or other forms of religious persecution.

intent—Performing an act with effect and concentration, with a clearly focused statement of will and purpose. When you do a task as commonplace as washing the dishes with intent you do more than wash the dishes. It becomes a ritual that includes cleansing and consecration. Intent is necessary to make a spell or Working effective.

invoke, invoking, invocation—1) Calling up. 2) Calling something in from without. 3) Calling up a Goddess or God to dwell within a Priestess or Priest. The Goddess or God shares the body of the Priestess or Priest with permission under carefully controlled circumstances for a fixed length of time. 4) To petition for help and support. 5) The summoning of an entity that is noncorporeal and of a higher order than oneself.

Ipsissimus—A title and/or degree of magickal attainment, supposedly the penultimate. Used in Ceremonial Magick.

iridology—Determining health and illness or imbalance in the body by interpretation of color and irregularities in a person's irises. It is descended from ancient Chinese teachings. In medical diagnosis the eyes are checked for various disease symptoms. For example, if the "whites" of the eye are yellow it often indicates jaundice is present.

K

Kabbalah, Cabalah, Qaballa, QBL, and other variations—Derived from the Hebrew root to receive or to accept, it is a mystical Hebrew system in which the Universe is symbolized by a diagram called the Tree of Life that consists of ten spheres (sephiroth) and the paths or lines connecting them. Kabbalah is more than just the study of the Tree of Life diagram, but the Tree of Life is the part of Kabbalah most studied and used in Wicca and Western occult lore. Adapted and adopted by medieval magicians and carried over into modern times, Kabbalah is a field of study popular with people of many religious traditions who are interested in mysticism. Gematria is a tool of Kabbalistic study in Hebrew tradition and is associated with Kabbalah.

There are many spellings of the word, as it is originally a Hebrew word, and there is no exact correspondence in English. The letters used to spell Kabbalah in Hebrew are Qoph, Beth, Lamed—hence the QBL.

Modern Kabbalah is a direct descendant of the ancient Hebrew system of esoteric philosophy, but is not the same. The Kabbalah has probably had the largest single influence on Western occultism of any mystical discipline. Kabbalah was codified and written down during the twelfth and thirteenth centuries CE, but is said to have derived from a much more ancient oral tradition, possibly descending from the time of Moses or before and always linked to the Old Testament. Medieval and Renaissance Christian and Arabic scholars have also used, studied, and added to Kabbalistic lore through the centuries since Kabbalah was written down by Jewish mystics.

karma—Sanskrit, work, action, deed, or cause and effect. Originally a Hindu and Buddhist concept, it has become an integral part of many paths of modern mysticism and esoteric thought. Karma is the merit one accumulates from one's conduct in previous incarnations. Karma is not fatalistic, actions of exceptional merit can erase negative karma and cause a person to avoid certain unpleasant consequences of past-life actions. Karma can be good or bad, depending upon the actions over past lifetimes, and can be used to explain problems, handicaps, special gifts, and other life circumstances that may seem to have no direct cause in the present life. Some of the modern interpretations of karma are inappropriate or even offensive. For example, in modern parlance the notion of "instant karma" has become popular as a sort of moral justification for "what goes around, comes around" and "shit happens." Karma has also been used as a moral justification for any unpleasantness in your life. Since you have brought it on yourself, you should not complain, but take it as a blessing and be happy you can have the opportunity to overcome your negative karma, rise above your situation, and make yourself a better person. Generally Wicca teaches personal responsibility for one's actions, but also acknowledges that life isn't always fair; however, that does not imply that one should welcome or bless adversity. Not the same as destiny, which is a Western concept and is not linked to any past actions, karma is regarded as the fruits of past action.

Keltria—An organization of Druids.

kerfan—See boline.

Key of Solomon—1) A sigil that is attributed to Solomon the King used to imprison all the demons loose in the world. Also a magickal figure that is protective in nature and is used on amulets. Ceremonial Magick. 2) Medieval grimoire on magick (*The Key of Solomon the King*), theoretically ancient and attributed to the biblical King Solomon, widely used and passed down through the centuries. One of the most widely quoted "original" sources of magickal lore.

Sigil Key of Solomon

King of the Witches—1) A title that is not used by Wiccans. Covens are autonomous and different Traditions have no ties between them, so there is no person who is elected, designated, or acclaimed King of the Witches. There is no person who is the Wiccan equivalent to the Pope. 2) A title adopted by Alex Sanders for himself, but not recognized as valid outside his Tradition. 3) Title of Alex Sanders' biography by June Johns.

Kirlian photography—Named after Semyon Kirlian, a Russian electrician and inventor. Kirlian photography is a technique by which one can photograph subjects in the presence of a high-frequency, high-voltage, low-amperage electrical field, and obtain a photograph that exhibits glowing multicolored emanations. The emanations change with changes in emotional states and life energy. What these photographed emanations are is a matter for conjecture and controversy. Popular lore has it that Kirlian photography captures pictures of auras. Brought to the West in the 1960s, this technique is commercially available. There have been scientific studies of this phenomenon, and acceptance is mixed.

kitchen witch—A colloquial term for a person who practices Wicca in a more or less low magick style, who uses herbs and common everyday things as magickal tools. Also someone who uses food and herb magick (like chicken soup curing a cold, etc.).

kleidomancy—See cleidomancy.

knots—Used in magickal spells. Knots are used to tie a spell into a cord, then one knot is untied each day until the spell is complete. Knots were used to remove a curse or cure various ailments. Also used in binding spells. Knot designs are widely represented in many

Knotted Spell Cord

cultures and are usually given magickal or spiritual significance. The terms "binding" and "tying knots" were synonymous for the practice of magick in general.

kundalini—From Sanskrit, serpent energy, a Hindu concept derived from teachings about the chakras and personal bioenergy. The kundalini serpent is coiled at the base of the spine and with meditation, yoga, or other tantric disciplines it can be unleashed and the energy released through the body, opening the chakras and theoretically promoting

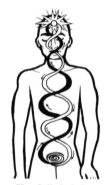

Kundalini As It Manifests in the Body

enlightenment and a glimpse of the Universe. Unleashing this energy without proper preparation and training has been known to cause psychic shock, so it is best to work with an experienced teacher or guru. Modern usage equates this energy with Chi.

L

labrys—Double-headed axe. Symbolizes the Goddess and the Moon. In some ancient cultures, a symbol of feminine mysteries, and men were expected to avoid areas where the labrys was dis-

played. Also in some cultures it was thought to symbolize the Gods' thunderbolt. A sacred weapon, can be used similarly to an athame or sword.

Labrys

labyrinth—A maze design, found throughout the world. Can be used as a symbol for the path of Initiation or can walked to create

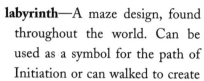

an altered state of consciousness and help trigger an initiatory response. Many ancient sites contain labyrinths which may be places of power. Serpent Mound in southern Ohio is a labyrinth, though in a different design from European ones. "Walking the labyrinth" was sometimes used as an ordeal for a potential Initiate and, if successfully completed, the Initiation was celebrated. Many Christian churches included labyrinths in the mosaic floor designs, sometimes purposefully, sometimes as a design. In the present day, walking the labyrinth is considered a spiritual experience. See also maze.

Labyrinth

Lady—1) Title used by some Traditions to indicate a Third Degree female Wiccan, or the title used by the High Priestess of a coven or Tradition. 2) A term used generically to denote the Goddess when no specific Goddess is specified. Sometimes referred to as the Goddess of the Wiccans. Generally a generic term for female

Deity. 3) A title sometimes adopted by Wiccans and used as a part of their magickal name.

lampadomancy—Divination using the flame of a lamp.

Last Quarter—See Fourth Quarter.

laughter—An outward expression of mirth or merriment, happiness or joy. "Mirth and reverence" is a quote from the Charge of the Goddess and some groups take that dichotomy more seriously than others. It is believed by some that the less laughter allowed within a group, the more potential for harm and destruction is present. There is another perception that most practitioners of black magick (however a person might chose to define that) have little or no sense of humor in general, and that is one way to spot them.

Law of Three—"That which you send out will return to you threefold" is a saying that essentially teaches those who work magick that they should consider what energies they are projecting. If you send out love, you will get threefold love in return, and if you send out negativity you will also get threefold negativity in return. A cosmic law that should raise awareness—for whatever you project, consciously or unconsciously, will return threefold—therefore, it is best to be conscious about all you project. A similar idea is expressed in the Golden Rule, "Do unto others as you would have them do unto you."

lecanomancy—Divination by dropping gems into water and interpreting messages and omens.

left-brain function—Linear, logical, analytical, "masculine" functions that are generally governed by the left hemisphere of the brain, which controls the right side of the body. Generally one needs both left- and right-brain functions to successfully practice magick.

left-hand path, Path of Shadows—1) Followed by those who work toward destruction, manipulation, and evil. Some equate the left-hand path with black magick, and the right-hand path with white magick. 2) In Oriental disciplines the left-hand path is a physical path toward enlightenment, as in martial arts, tantra, Tai Chi, and other physical disciplines that also have a spiritual component. The right-hand path is a purely spiritual path characterized by meditation, renunciation, and fasting. In modern occultism following the left-hand path is considered to be "bad" and the right-hand path is "good." This stems from the Western world's embrace of Christianity and the doctrines of prayer, renunciation, denial of the flesh, and denigration of this world while glorifying the spiritual world and the promise of redemption and an eternally blissful afterlife. 3) Sometimes used in reference to those who practice Satanism in its various forms. Also used to characterize those who practice magick for personal self-aggrandizing ends, rather than self-improvement or aid to others or the cosmos.

Lemuria, Lemurian—Lost continent located in the Indian Ocean said to be the original Garden of Eden and cradle of the human race. Older than, though thought to have existed during the same era as Atlantis. The lost continent theory arose in the eighteenth century to help account for the existence of lemurs in India, Malaysia, Madagascar, and Africa, land masses that in the modern world are not connected. At the present time the theory of continental drift adequately explains how these land masses were connected some 85 million years ago.

Occultists connected the continent of Lemuria to a main center of activity in the early history of humanity. Madame Blavatsky mentioned Lemuria as the home of the Third Root Race of mankind and it became part of Theosophical lore. It is hypothesized that when their continent was destroyed, the surviving Lemurians migrated to Atlantis where they evolved into the Fourth Root Race. When Atlantis was destroyed, those survivors migrated to other lands and gave birth to the present Fifth Root Race.

Lesser Sabbats—The Sabbats celebrated on the quarters: Oestarra, Midsummer, Mabon, and Yule. In many cultures Midsummer and Yule are fairly well represented; however, Oestarra and Mabon are not widely represented. Even some Wiccan groups do not celebrate Oestarra and/or Mabon.

Levi, Eliaphas; real name Alphonse Louis Constant (1809–1875)—French magician and scholar who published many magickal correspondences and laid the groundwork for Ceremonial Magick and the rituals used by the Golden Dawn and others. It is not known where Levi received his mystical knowledge, but some feel he conceived the ideas himself, and some feel it was passed down to him by earlier Initiates in some unknown Tradition. Levi was the first to link the tarot trumps and the paths between the sephiroth of the Kabbalah, now considered to be an "ancient," magickal correspondence.

levitation—A manifestation of psychokinesis. The phenomenon by which objects, animals, or people rise into the air and float or fly without any known physical means. Levitation can occur in connection with mediumship, mystical trance, magick, hauntings, and possessions. Some levitations have been proven fraudulent, but many remain unexplained. An ability also attributed to mystics, holy people, and adepts of many religions, races, and paths.

ley lines—Lines of force or energy that connect places of magickal or natural power. A natural phenomenon, ley lines are discernible by those who are sensitive to these energies or have magickal training. The ley lines can be used as power

sources although the power spots they connect are better sources of energy. In England the ancient stone circles were built on power spots, connected by ley lines. The energy can be equated with Chi and other natural energy forces. Places where ley lines intersect are reportedly prone to supernatural phenomena.

libanomancy, livanomancy—Divination using the smoke of incense.

life—The condition of an entity that is vital and capable of performing certain functions related to metabolism, growth, and reproduction. A system exhibiting negative entropy. Being "in the flesh."

life passages—The various stages of life often celebrated in similar ways by different societies. Wiccans celebrate more life passages than does modern American society: birth, the Naming (or Wiccaning) of the child, puberty (the beginning of participation in the women's or men's mysteries), Initiation, marriage (or Handfasting), divorce (or Handparting), Eldering (sometimes coincident with menopause or retirement, sometimes separate), dying, and death. Some of these passages follow different orders, and some may never be experienced (Handfasting, Handparting, birth of a child, etc.), but these are the life passages which Wiccans recognize.

lineage—Line of magickal descent, one's magickal ancestors. When someone is initiated to the Third Degree a lineage or list of one's magickal ancestors is recited. The lineage usually ends with "and all those nameless ones who have gone before." In the United States most lineages are traced back to Gerald Gardner and his Initiators, but some lineages are derived from other sources. Comparing lineages is one way Wiccans determine the legitimacy of others' Initiations. One's lineage is memorized and, by tradition, never written down, but it must be passed on if the Initiate later initiates another—with their name first, followed by the names of the previous Initiators, possibly back to Gardner and beyond. Some Traditions have lineages for Second and occasionally even First Degrees. One uses magickal names when passing on a lineage, and may or may not know the mundane identity of the people in their lineage. Not all Third Degree Initiates are given a lineage. Some lineages have been lost, broken, or forgotten.

lithomancy—Divination using stones. Can refer to stones of unusual origin, which inspire visions or speak to a diviner in words or symbols only they can understand or interpret. This can range from meteorites to geologic anomalies. Also used as a general term for various specialized forms of divination using stones, such as lecanomancy.

logarithramancy—Divination using mathematics and logarithms. This form of divination has essentially been supplanted by the use of computers.

Lord—1) Title used by some Traditions to indicate a Third Degree male Wiccan, or the title used by the High Priest of a coven or Tradition. 2) A term used to denote the God generically, the Lord, when no specific God is intended or wanted. Sometimes referred to as the God of the Wiccans. Generally a generic term for male Deity. 3) A title sometimes adopted by Wiccans and used as a part of their magickal name.

loup-garou—French for werewolf.

love—The condition that exists when another's happiness is essential to your own. Devotion with commitment. The universal force that drives magick, as in "Love is the Law, love under will."

Lucifer—Latin, light bringer. 1) Term used with Venus—Venus Lucifer—when Venus is a morning star, i.e., rising before the Sun. 2) Another name for the Devil, Satan, Beelzebub, etc.

Lughnasadh—Celtic for the "Festival of Lugh" or colloquially the marriage of Lugh. The Sabbat is generally celebrated July 31st or August 1st. Also known as Lammas, Lunasa (Irish Gaelic), Lunasda or Lunasdal (Scottish Gaelic), Laa Luanys or Laa Lunys (Manx). It is a harvest festival. Games and contests are one way of celebrating this holiday.

Lunar Mansions, Moon Mansions, Mansions—Astrological term referring to 27 or 28 divisions of the zodiac roughly based upon the Moon's daily movement of 13° or 13° 20'. In Western astrology there are 28 lunar mansions, which have devolved into critical (or psychic) degrees at 0°, 13°, and 26° of the cardinal signs (Aries, Cancer, Libra, and Capricorn), 9° and 21° of the fixed signs (Taurus, Leo, Scorpio, and Aquarius) and 4° and 17° of the mutable signs (Gemini, Virgo, Sagittarius, and Pisces). In Hindu astrology there are 27 separate asterisms each exactly 13° 20' that are used in a similar way to the astrological signs with names, symbols, attributes, qualities, rulerships, and other correspondences. These operate side by side with the twelve astrological signs and give another level of meaning.

The biblical passage "in my father's house are many mansions" (John 14:2) is sometimes thought to refer to Lunar Mansions, and thought to indicate that Jesus was an initiate and adept in many forms of esoteric teachings. It is believed that Jesus spent his "lost" years from the age of twelve or thirteen to the beginning of his ministry at thirty studying the esoteric teachings. In Ceremonial Magick some attention is paid to Lunar Mansions and their esoteric meanings and significance.

lustral bath—See purification.

lycanthropy—From Greek *lukos* (wolf) and *anthropos* (man). The transformation of a person into a wolf, usually at the Full Moon, or the general phenomenon of a person being transformed into some animal, usually of a savage and ferocious nature. Many societies have tales of people who are transformed into various animals. Medieval Europeans believed witches could transform themselves into animals and wander at night, performing deeds, both good and evil.

lychnomancy—Divination using flames from three identical candles set in a triangle and lit. How the candle flames interact as well as how the candles burn with respect to each other determines the answer.

M

macharomancy—Divination using swords, daggers, and knives.

macrocosm—The Universe is the whole, the microcosm is a detailed manifestation thereof. A human being is an example of a microcosm, based on the Hermetic principle, "as above so below." See Holistic Universe Theory for a more modern version of these same concepts.

mage—1) A general term for a person practicing magick, in any style or system. Used more for those who are active practitioners rather than those who are "researchers." Short for Magus. 2) Sometimes also a title for a magickal degree of attainment in various organizations or Traditions.

magi—Zoroastrian priests. Powerful practitioners of magick and related disciplines. Later used for powerful magicians of any type. Singular Magus.

magic—1) Stage magic, illusion, prestidigitation, entertainment, escape from reality. Not using psychic ability or will or intent. The use of illusionary techniques to catalyze an experience of wonder. 2) Psychic creation of an altered feeling without focused intent. 3) The use of ritual action to bring about the intervention of supernatural force for a specific purpose, either natural or in human affairs.

The use of magic in human societies has existed universally since prehistoric times, generally arising before religion and the recognition of Deity. Most magical practices were considered secret and handed down either in families or from master to apprentice. Various terms have been used throughout history to designate magical folk practitioners: witch doctor, wizard, diviner, witch, shaman, wise woman, cunning woman or man, sorcerer, magister, mage, etc. Generally as organized religion arose, the priestly class took over all magical practice. See magick.

magic candle—Candle made from the fat of a hanged criminal. It was used in conjunction with a hand of glory to discover hidden treasure.

magic square—A figure of boxes usually at least nine (3 x 3), although it can be larger, with numbers in each box; the sum of the numbers added vertically, horizontally, and diagonally is the same. Considered a magickal charm. Each classical planet has its own magic square. Today considered mathematical curiosities, they are still used as protective charms.

8	58	59	5	4	62	63	1
49	15	14	52	53	11	10	56
41	23	22	44	45	19	18	48
32	34	35	29	28	38	39	25
40	26	27	37	36	30	31	33
17	47	46	20	21	43	42	24
9	55	54	12	13	51	50	16
64	2	3	61	60	6	7	57

Magic Square

magician—A practitioner of magick or magic. Occasionally magickian is used to differentiate and indicate a practitioner of magick, but it is clumsy and awkward. It is usually apparent from the content of the action what is intended.

magick—From Greek *magikos*, the arts of the

Magi, the controlled use of will to effect a change in surroundings or circumstances. "The Science and Art of causing Change to occur in conformity with the Will." (Aleister Crowley) The ability to shape reality in accordance with will by methods that cannot be explained by the current scientific paradigm. ("Any technology sufficiently advanced is indistinguishable from magic."—Heinlein) Spelled with a 'k' to differentiate from stage magic (originated by Aleister Crowley). To will, to know, to do, and to be silent are the four elements of magick.

Magick is a component of the Wiccan religion, though not all Wiccans practice magick. The practice of magick should not be attempted lightly or with frivolous or unfocused intent. There are cases of unskilled or ignorant practitioners causing severe harm to themselves, others, and the environment around them. Usually, however, the results are less dramatic and range from a headache to no effect at all. Generally it is believed that a person needs a teacher, mentor, or guide to become safe, effective, and skilled in magick.

The following are various styles and subsets of magick:

High Magick/Ceremonial Magick—Interchangeable terms for a specific magickal system characterized by such groups as the Golden Dawn, OTO (Ordo Templar Orientalis), and others. Uses specific formulas and rituals and generally calls on angels, archangels, and other God-forms. Use of Hebrew, Kabbalah, and some Egyptian God-forms. Not necessarily Wiccan, you can be Christian, Jewish, or adhere to another religious tradition and also be a Ceremonial Magician. Gardnerian and Alexandrian Wicca tend toward the High Magick systems. In some ways High Magick depends upon the magician having a strong will and being able to order astral beings to do their bidding.

low magick—More free-form and less structured and ritualized form of magick. High Magicians tend to do the same rituals and Circles every time. Low magicians do whatever seems right at the time. Eclectic Wiccans and kitchen witches practice styles of low magick. Low magick is more dependent upon spur of the moment creativity and a good imagination. It is not formulaic and has as little or as much structure as the practitioner wants as opposed to High Magick that is, in general, a structured system of practice. There are as many ways of practicing low magick as there are practitioners. Low magicians tend to use elements, spirit guides, and astral beings as allies and work with them rather than ordering them to do their bidding.

black magick—Magick that is used to cause a person to do something without their willing cooperation, or magick that is used upon a person against their will. Black magick is also that which is done for an unpleasant or restrictive purpose, including sending energy to an unwilling or unaware target. Wiccans generally frown upon black magick, preferring to work for people rather than "on" people or work toward a positive common good. What specifically constitutes black magick can be highly subjective depending upon the practitioner and circumstances.

white magick—Magick that is done for a willing participant; magick that is done for self-improvement or a positive purpose; magick that is done for healing; magick that is done to help others who agree to it. Generally, if a change is desired and magick is used for a person who is not aware or willing, the energy of the magick is sent by the practitioner to the cosmos (or the

Gods) and the practitioner requests the cosmos to order things as they need to be, which includes the possibility of nothing happening. This then circumvents the prohibition of sending energy to an unwilling or unaware target. Wiccans practice white magick.

Some other "colors" of magick are as follows: **blue magick**—Used for emotional work, peace, spirituality; **green magick**—Used for work with vegetation, as in gardening, fertility, also healing, health, and wellness, and wealth and prosperity, money; **orange magick**—Used for pride and courage, heroism; **purple magick**—Used for wealth and good fortune, prosperity, also psychic studies; **red magick**—Used for physical work as in healing, passion, also energy work; **yellow magick**—Used for mental work, meditation, intellect, memory.

magick Circle, magickal Circle—An area in which magick is practiced, and a safe zone for the magickal practitioner. The area in which Wiccans practice magick and hold rituals. It is "drawn" with an athame (or sword) and imbued with energy, and can be visualized as a "cone of power" or a sphere of energy that surrounds and defines an area. Within a properly constructed magick Circle one is "in a place without a place and a time without a time, for you are between the worlds and beyond." The Circle is a created doorway or gate between dimensions. Even in a permanent temple space, the Circle is created anew each time it is used. Once finished with the Working, the Circle is taken down. Ideally there should be no trace, either physical or psychic, that a Circle was ever in place. Over time a permanent site can build up energies that makes putting up a Circle easier.

magickal alphabet (or language)—An alphabet, either tied to a culture or created, in which each letter has an esoteric and exoteric meaning. Most ancient alphabets were considered magickal, writing itself was considered magick and a gift of the Goddess, and the letters were believed to be imbued with energies and meanings apart from the words in written form. Most ancient cultures considered language and writing to be a Divine gift. Some people write their Books of Shadows in an alphabet different from English to keep their secrets from outsiders.

There are several common magickal alphabets used by people in the Craft and other magickal systems. Some are even available as computer fonts. Theban or Honorian is a created alphabet first used by the Golden Dawn. Runes based upon various Futharks are used by some. Ogham or Ogham Bethluisnion is based upon an ancient Celtic alphabet. Angerthas or Elvish was invented by J.R.R. Tolkien in his novel *The Hobbit* and the *Lord of the Rings Trilogy*, and is used as a magickal alphabet by some. Malachim or Language of the Magi is sometimes used. Passing the River and also Angelic or Celestial are mainly used by Ceremonial Magicians. There are others, including personally invented alphabets.

Some of these alphabets (most notably Runic) are phonetic in nature (i.e., not having a letter for letter correspondence, but sound for sound) so "fish" and "phone" would start with the same character because both start with an "f" sound, even though they are spelled differently, and "th," for example, is usually one character, rather than two.

magickal name—A name used when practicing magick. Usually a chosen name—although some are bestowed—which is used within a Circle for the purpose of identifying oneself to the Deities, Watchtowers, quarters, and any other magickal/ spiritual entities. Can be used to identify oneself as part of a lineage. This name is usually kept secret and used only within a coven or during Initiations if others are present. Some Traditions believe that knowing the true name of another gives you magickal power or control over them. The use of magickal names is ancient, and the modern usage is derived from High Magick. Some Pagans also take an outer name they use in Pagan contexts, such as festivals, in group rituals, and among Pagan friends.

magickal persona—A personality one uses in magickal situations that may be different from one's "ordinary" persona; the persona one adapts and/or uses along with one's magickal name in Wiccan situations.

magister—Witch master, an archaic usage, it is generally used for a male witch who is in charge of a large group or several groups, sometimes the founder of a Tradition.

magus—1) A powerful practitioner of magick and related disciplines. A male occult-adept. 2) A Second or Third Degree male witch (more in Gardnerian and Alexandrian traditions). 3) A courtesy title used by the High Priest of a Witch Queen. 4) *Magus, The* (1801), a book by Francis Barrett (1764–?) that detailed the life and activities of a magickal practitioner of the times. An occult classic.

mahatma—From Sanskrit, great one. True masters of esoteric knowledge, who have achieved perfection and act as gurus and teachers to humanity. Borrowed from Hindu and Buddhist cultures through Theosophy, as in Mahatma Gandhi.

Maiden—1) The aspect of the Threefold Goddess which represents youth, freedom, independence, and the season of spring. Corresponds to a female who is at the start of her sexual awareness and menarche. The Maiden has a great deal of vitality, energy, and stamina, but has yet to learn the lessons of life and experience. These will be gained as she progresses from Maiden to Mother to Crone, and then is renewed in the springtime to become Maiden again and start the process anew. 2) Some groups use this term for a Handmaiden, an assistant High Priestess for ritual purposes who may or may not be the High Priestess' deputy in leadership. 3) In an archaic usage the term was sometimes used as High Priestess is today.

malefica—Latin, evil doings, a medieval term that referred to unfortunate occurrences not attributable to any immediate cause, therefore supposedly caused by witchcraft and the work of the Devil. Sometimes the term was synonymous with witch.

Malleus Malleficarum—Latin, Hammer of the Malefactors, a Renaissance book on witchcraft, it contained instructions on how to identify a witch and methods for torturing and extracting information from witches. Published in 1486, the authors were two German monks, Heinrich Kramer and Jakob Sprenger, Professors of Theology of the Order of Friars Preachers. Malleus became the text for witch hunters well into the eighteenth century.

Man in Black—See Summoner; different from Men in Black.

mana—Polynesian, psychic energy. The sum of all one's personal, psychic, charismatic, and physical energies. Similar to Chi.

mandala—From Sanskrit "circle." An image used as a focus for meditation. An associational device used as a focus for meditation that can trigger certain meditative states. Usually drawn in a circular design. Mandalas appear in Hinduism, Buddhism, Chinese, Japanese, and Tibetan Buddhism; Christianity, Gnosticism, Mythology, alchemy, and other disciplines. Mandalas can symbolize the Universe, various Deities, magickal symbols, natural forces. Some temples have mandalas either built into their structure or inlaid in floors or walls. Mandalas can be drawn or painted on cloth or paper. Tibetan Buddhist monks create mandalas with colored sands and the creation is a magickal act accompanied with chants and prayers. Once completed, the mandala is destroyed to effect the intent of the mandala, and also to symbolize their belief in the impermanence of the physical world. Jung considered mandalas as archetypal, mythological representations of the self. Mandalas are used in modern psychotherapy as a therapeutic tool.

mandrake, mandragore, mandrake root—The root of the mandrake plant (*mandragora officinarum*), it grows in the shape of a human. Used as a charm or amulet, it can also be used as a poppet. Member of the potato family. Used most often in love potions.

manifestation—1) A tangible result of magick. 2) Something that is discernible on this plane as an analog for something that exists on another plane. Ghosts and poltergeists are manifestations of activity or disturbances on the astral plane. 3) A mirror for a higher plane entity in this plane, as the Earth is a mirror of the Mother Goddess, or Nature is a mirror of creative Divinity.

mansions—See Lunar Mansions.

mantra—A phrase or word used as a meditational device. "Om mane padme Om" is a Hindu mantra used to focus the mind and create a meditative state. With use a word or phrase can trigger a meditative state simply by reciting it. Certain Christian prayers can act as mantras, among them the Lord's Prayer and the Hail Mary.

margaritomancy—Divination using a charmed pearl placed in a lidded pot. Names of possible thieves or other types of criminals are recited and upon the utterance of the name of the criminal, the pearl will fly up and strike the lid of the pot making a noise. Pearl was used, as it is a gem that was created by a living organism and is considered to be imbued with a residual life of its own. Theoretically some form of deception is required to make this system work, and therefore it may be considered suspect.

Masonry—See Freemasonry.

materialization—The appearance of objects out of thin air, associated with psychic or paranormal activity. A phenomenon of spiritualism and seances, popularized in the late nineteenth and early twentieth centuries. Sometimes accomplished by fraud and sleight of hand, it is a suspect phenomenon, however, many reported materializations have never been exposed as fraudulent. Some mediums could dematerialize and then rematerialize parts of themselves during a seance.

matriarchy, matrilineal—Society in which the women are the dominant gender. Property descends through the mother or other female relatives; paternity is either not known or is irrelevant. In matriarchal societies women own the land and are in charge of cultivation, and men are partners and helpers of the women and also hunters. Paganism is believed to have developed during matriarchal times and for that reason a Mother Goddess figures prominently. Wiccans believe they are spiritual descendants of an ancient matriarchal religion and society. In Wicca, matriarchy is considered peaceful, cooperative, consensus modeling, and positive; patriarchy is considered warlike, conquering, power politics, aggressive, and negative. In reality Wiccans are theoretically striving for a society that is neither matriarchal or patriarchal but egalitarian affording equal power and value to both (or all) sexes.

Maypole—A pole stuck upright in the ground with streamers or ribbons tied to the top, around which a dance takes place. The dance is a braiding dance with women moving in one direction, and men in the opposite direction, each person holding a ribbon as they weave in and out, braiding their ribbons around the Maypole as they dance. Sometimes a ring or circlet of flowers around the Maypole descends as the braiding progresses down the pole. This is a fertility ritual and the Maypole is a prominent feature of many Beltane rites.

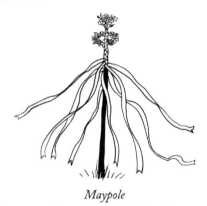

Maypole

May Queen—A.k.a., Queen of the May—a person (usually female) selected at Beltane to represent the Goddess either for the day or for a year in some Traditions. Generally chosen by lottery.

maze—A complex pattern that can be used as a magickal aid. In ancient times a maze was symbolic of the route traveled to achieve Initiation. Some ancient mazes were built on power sites and, as a person "walks the maze," they experience the energies of the place and can undergo an Initiatory experience. Serpent Mound monument near Locust Grove in southern Ohio is a maze. Some cathedrals have mazes set in mosaic in the floor, and the devout walk the maze as a sign of devotion or as an active meditation. A spiral dance is a sort of active moving maze as people dance in and out of the spiral. One type of ritual that is effective for groups is to create a maze and have participants walk the maze. Sometimes a maze is also a mandala. See labyrinth.

measure—During Initiation various physical bodily dimensions are measured with thread or cord and the lengths ritually recorded. May be used to make a cord, may be kept by the coven, sometimes both (if two measures are taken). Can also be hair clippings or some other physical memento. The measure becomes a magickal tie between the Initiate and the coven, and a tie of loyalty. To "take a person's measure" is the phrase describing this process. Some Traditions return the measure if the Initiate leaves the coven or moves on to another place; some covens keep the measure forever. Traditionally the measure is destroyed upon death.

Medea—In classical Greek mythology, daughter of Aeetes, King of Colchis, a sorceress and Priestess of Hecate. When Jason and the Argonauts came to Colchis in search of the Golden Fleece, Medea fell in love with Jason and agreed to help him secure the Fleece if he would marry her and take her with him. She aided their quest and escape using her magick. They married and had two children, a boy and girl. Later when Jason deserted Medea to marry another princess, Medea revenged herself by killing his prospective bride and their children, then fleeing in a winged chariot sent by Hecate. She later married King Aegeus, had a son Medus, who was the founder/father of the ancient tribe/kingdom Medes. Still later she returned to Colchis with her son, and restored her father to the throne by magickally murdering the usurper, his brother Perses.

She is seen as an archetype for rejected first wives. She is also an archetype for a powerful effective magickal female, who makes her own destiny. This mythological tale from an earlier, matriarchal Goddess-centered tale was changed and corrupted by the patriarchal classical Greeks, and as a result she was demonized.

medicine wheel—A Native American construct within which religious rites are practiced. Has similarities to a Wiccan Circle. Can be used as a mandala. Some people have incorporated certain Native American religious practices into Wiccan and other Pagan and New Age practices, but the spiritual paths are distinct and such mixing is viewed with unhappiness by Native American religious adherents. The Red Path—a Native American spiritual practice—is separate and distinct from Wiccan Traditions, and should be regarded as the sole legacy of the Native Americans, and not used by practitioners of other paths.

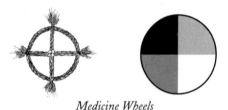

Medicine Wheels

meditation—A mental technique through which one clears the mind of the everyday inner chatter and allows one to experience the still small voice within. One can meditate either quietly sitting or lying down, or achieve a meditative state through movement, practices like martial arts, Tai Chi, jogging, or even just ironing, essentially any physical activity that doesn't require active thought and engages the body while freeing the mind. In some spiritual paths meditation is an end in itself.

For Wiccans meditation is a technique that allows the practitioner to clear the mind and prepare for magick or divination. That which is accessed through meditation is empirical—some feel it is God, or the Gods, some feel it is one's subconscious, some feel it can be characterized as

the collective unconscious, some think it is the Devil. Meditation is pan-denominational; most great religions have some sort of tradition and techniques that utilize meditation and detail the spiritual benefits of it.

medium—A person who can channel discarnate entities, usually a person who will allow you to talk to those who have passed on before. The person goes into a trance state and allows the entity to possess their mind and/or body. Mediums have existed in many cultures throughout time. Many names have been given to people who function as mediums: oracle, soothsayer, wizard, cunning woman or man, wise woman, witch, medicine man, sorcerer, shaman, fortuneteller, witch doctor, mystic, priest, prophet, and channeler. Many mediums communicate with the spirits through a control, another spirit guide, or an entity that remains permanently with the medium. Mental mediums use clairaudience or automatic writing to communicate. Physical mediums use rapping, apports, levitation, and other paranormal phenomena to communicate.

Wiccans generally do not practice mediumship, preferring to either work directly with their Gods or just use their innate psychic abilities rather than communicating with discarnate entities.

Men in Black, MIB—1) Term used to denote a supposed secret brotherhood of adepts who oversee all magickal operations. For example, when someone is performing actions that are "forbidden" or dangerous to others or humanity as a whole, it is reported that this group visits the practitioner, warns them about their action and, if the warnings are ignored, reportedly the Men in Black will take action against the practitioner to ensure they will not continue their practices. This can range from a magickal restraint, full binding, causing mental instability or insanity, to actual death.

Theoretically this brotherhood is very old and has been overseeing the spiritual, occult, and magickal development of humanity for millennia. Theories abound about who they are: extant people descended from Atlanteans, ancient Egyptians, or Tibetan monks, spiritual beings who can assume corporeal form, to some sort of magickal guardian angels. There are people in various magickal communities who have reported that they were visited by the Men in Black, their supposed secret activities were described in such detail and they were warned in such a forceful manner that they abandoned whatever they were doing and shifted their activities into less dangerous lines of research. 2) A colloquialism for government agents who dress in dark clothing who seek to keep secret details about UFOs including suppressing survivor accounts, proposing plausible everyday theories for sightings (the classic weather balloon), and generally keeping the peace so as not to panic the populace about aliens among us. Humorously depicted in the popular science fiction movie of the same name, the actual Men in Black are not nearly as benign as the movie depicts, if accounts of those who have supposedly been visited by them is to be believed. The Men in Black appear primarily in the United States, although accounts of their activities are reported in Europe, Australia, and South Africa.

Merchant's Row—Area at some festivals where the merchants set up shop.

Mesmer, Franz Anton—(1734–1815) Discoverer in modern times of hypnotism (also called mesmerism), and used it as a part of his techniques of animal magnetism. The full range of techniques were designed to influence the magnetic energy in the human body to effect healing. He used magnets, laying on of hands, hypnotism, and waving a magnetic wand. He was accused of being a magician and charlatan by contemporaries. Today, hypnosis is a valid and accepted therapeutic technique.

metaphysics—More "politically correct" term for what used to be called "occult." The study of the relationships between underlying reality and its manifestations. Psychic studies and related disciplines.

meteormancy—Divination by observing shooting stars, and interpreting their size, brightness, duration, and path. A branch of astromancy. Roman augurs also included thunder, lightning, eclipses, and other sky-related phenomena.

meteorology—Prediction of the weather and seasonal conditions. Originally a form of divination, it is now practiced professionally by people with at least a Master's degree and much training in higher mathematics and computer modeling. Satellite imagery, long- and short-range monitoring, and surface and upper air mapping are all used to gather information by which the meteorologist makes an assessment and then makes a prediction. Meteorological prediction is generally eighty percent accurate within a twenty-four hour time period or less, or fifty percent accurate for three days or less; the longer range the prediction becomes, the less accuracy is exhibited. The *Old Farmer's Almanac*'s long-range meteorological predictions—that use still secret methods (though astro-meteorology is supposedly relied upon)—are frequently as accurate (or inaccurate) as the National Weather Service's seasonal forecasts.

metopomancy, metoposcopy—Divination of a person's future by reading the lines on their forehead. It combines astrological lore with physiognomy. The forehead is divided into seven equal strips that correspond to the seven classical planets, Saturn at the top and Moon closest to the eyebrows. A line in the area of a planet bestows characteristics similar to the planet.

microcosm—See macrocosm.

millennium—The date the calendar year changes from 2000 to 2001—January 1, 2001. As there was no year 0, the end of the first 2000 years occurs on January 1, 2001. Also colloquially considered to start January 1, 2000. The end of the first 2000 years and the beginning of the next 1000 years. A momentous time in world history.

mirror—1) A magickal tool for scrying, divination. Also used as a tool for repelling evil. A black mirror (or plate) is a divination tool. (A mirror can also be used as a psychic window to look into a person's home.) 2) A black and white mirror is not an object but a self-help tool created by an individual. It is a list of positive and negative traits used as a device for self-examination and self-improvement.

In ancient times, mirrors were an item of luxury and seldom seen or used by the average person. To accurately see one's reflection as others see us (and even then it is opposite) is somewhat magickal. Some cultures believe that a mirror is able to capture a person's soul, much the same as the belief which some cultures have, that a camera can steal a person's soul. One cultural belief states that to see one's reflection, either in a dream, vision, or reality, presages death. Many cultures feel all mirrors should be removed from a sickroom to avoid the soul being stolen or weakened by the mirror. Theoretically vampires, witches, and demons cast no reflection in a mirror. Using the evil eye can shatter a mirror. If a person breaks a mirror superstition holds that seven years of bad luck will follow. Mirrors can also reflect or return the evil eye and other spells and enchantments. Some cultures felt mirrors were evil and a tool of the Devil, and had all sorts of rules about their use: they must be covered at night; one must not gaze into a mirror by candlelight; one's soul can be captured by the Devil if you gaze into a mirror at night.

modern planets—Uranus, Neptune, and Pluto are the modern planets discovered in the modern age with the use of telescopes and sophisticated mathematical calculations. (See also classical planets.)

moles—1) Placement, size, shape, and color of moles on the body were used as a divinatory system. The Zohar (a medieval Kabbalistic text) equates moles on the body to stars in the heavens, and magicians developed a system to examine a person's skin for prophetic markings. 2) Moles, rashes, and other skin imperfections were considered witches' marks by the Inquisition, especially any skin imperfection that was prominent was considered a witches' pap, a place where the witch could suckle a demon.

"Pricking a witch" was a method of determining if a person was a witch. The Inquisitor would take a needle and poke or prick the mole, and if the subject did not bleed or react they were considered to be a witch. Often this was performed after the subject was forced to lie naked upon a stone floor, and by the time the pricking was done, the subject was so numb, they probably could feel very little.

molybdomancy—Divination using melted lead. The lead was dropped on a flat surface or into water and the resultant shapes were "read." The sound of the lead hissing as it hits the water can also be used for divination.

monologos, monologous—A religion that has one supreme Deity with many different attributes or aspects. Kemet, the religion of ancient Egypt, was monologous. Netcher was the supreme God-form and all the "Gods" of the Egyptian pantheon were aspects of Netcher in various guises and roles. The ancient Egyptian religion, although it appeared to be polytheistic, was not.

Some Pagans tend to view God in this manner, one Supreme Being with various aspects and attributes, some of which are called Jehovah, Athena, Thor, Freya, Vishnu, Buddha, Allah, Jesus, Virgin Mary, Kwan Yin, Diana, etc.

monotheism—The belief that there is only one Deity who created and rules the Universe, believed to be omnipotent, omniscient, omnipresent, pre-existing, and eternal. A religion that has one all-powerful God. Judaism, Christianity, and Islam are all monotheistic religions.

Moon—Satellite of Earth. The Moon is considered to be magickal and the source of magickal power. Much magickal lore surrounds the phases of the Moon, and also takes into account other astrological—especially Lunar—effects. Many cultures still use a Lunar calendar to track time.

The Islamic calendar is a strictly lunar calendar and the most accurate Lunar calendar in existence. The Chinese and Jewish calendars are Lunar/Solar; they have Lunar months, with a thirteenth month added every three years to keep the calendar corresponding roughly to the Solar cycle. Otherwise, the holidays would move around the seasonal year, as the Islamic holidays do over a 33- to 34-year cycle.

Geologists postulate that the Earth would not be what it is and life would not have developed if Earth had no companion satellite. The Moon proportionally is the largest satellite in the Solar system, far larger proportionally than any other companion satellite and because of its size it exerts much more gravitational influence upon its primary. One can become moonstruck—enchanted or vulnerable to the influence of others by the rays of the Full Moon. Mania is ecstatic revelation caused by the Moon. Lunacy means possessed by the spirit of Luna, somewhat deranged or not normal. In Hindu astrology the Moon is considered the more important planet, in contrast to the Sun in Western astrology. Vampires and werewolves supposedly are controlled by the Moon's phases.

Moon Blood, Moon Time, Blood of the Moon—Menstrual period. The time during a woman's menstrual cycle when she is bleeding, it is considered to be a time when a woman is especially psychic and magickally powerful if she is a magickal practitioner and acknowledges her personal power.

Moon Mansions—See Lunar Mansions.

morals—Social customs and conventions. Principles of right conduct imposed by society, family, etc., that govern thought and behavior.

Mother—The second aspect of the Goddess, Mother represents fulfillment, creativity, nurturing, sensuality. It is represented by the Full Moon. The Mother is the mature, capable, active, and powerful feminine force. It corresponds to a female who is fertile and either pregnant or who has given birth and/or is raising young.

Maiden, Mother, Crone

muggle, muggles—1) Term used by J.K. Rowling in her *Harry Potter* books to denote a person who is not a wizard, i.e., non-magickal. 2) Modern Wiccans have adopted this term as the equivalent to mundane, a person who is non-Wiccan, non-Pagan, non-magickal, rapidly supplanting the term mundane when referring to non-Wiccan people.

mundane—Latin, worldly, that which is of the ordinary everyday world; non-magickal, non-psychic, ordinary. Wiccans use this term to mean things or people non-Wiccan, non-Pagan, non-magickal. For example, "I have to change into my mundane clothes (or mundanes) before I go to work," "My family are nice people but they are really mundanes." See also muggle.

Museum of Magic and Witchcraft—Established by Cecil Williamson after W.W.II in Castleton on the Isle of Man, Gerald Gardner entered into partnership with Cecil Williamson in 1951. Soon after, a clash of personalities caused them to sever their partnership, Williamson taking half of the artifacts and moving elsewhere. Gardner ran the museum until his death. The contents, which included many early Gardnerian documents and artifacts, were auctioned off after Gardner's death.

music—Pagan and Wiccan rites often involve singing and sometimes dancing. Most of the songs are modified folk songs, with rounds and chants very popular. Some songs are specifically Pagan, others are re-worded "mundane" songs, such as "Mother Bertha's Coming to Town," a Pagan rewrite of "Santa Claus Is Coming to Town." Many of the "original" Pagan songs are in a minor key, and the singing can range from very lively and professional to droning and dirge-like. Some festivals prohibit non-Pagan music, preferring to keep the Pagan atmosphere free of modern and/or mundane influences. Some mainstream artists have songs of a definite Pagan flavor and are widely favored, for example, the songs of Loreena McKennit.

music of the spheres—Ancient Greek cosmological concept carried over into alchemy and Ceremonial Magick. Musical notes are attributed to each sphere of the planets. (See sphere of the planet.)

myomancy—Divination using rats or mice and their appearance, movements, sounds, and actions.

mystery—From Greek *myein* (to close), it refers to the closing of the lips and the eyes. The central mystical tenet of a religion that is partially experiential and partially symbolic of a greater cosmic truth. Communion is a mystery for the Catholic faith. Some Wiccans consider Initiation to be a mystery. Mystical metaphors revealed only to the initiated. In classical times the mystes, or Initiate, was required to keep secret what was revealed during the inner rites.

mystery religion—A religion that relies on subjective experiences for Divine revelation. Wicca is considered by some to be a mystery religion, and the exact rites and teachings are sometimes kept secret from non-Initiates. Most mystery religions require oaths of secrecy of their Initiates and practitioners. The Eleusinian Mysteries was a well-known classical mystery religion. Its rites were ended in 414 CE by the Christian Church after being practiced since around 1600 BCE. Because of the oaths of secrecy the exact nature of the Eleusinian rites and teachings are still unknown, although it is believed that the teachings promised eternal life in the afterworld, rebirth, and/or redemption. The cult was devoted to Ceres (Demeter) and her daughter Persephone (Kore, Proserpine). Their main festival took place in autumn and was believed to have celebrated death and rebirth, symbolic of the harvest as well as the human cycle of life.

mystic—A person who relates to the supernatural worlds; a person who uses their psychic abilities for healings, fortunetelling, predicting the future, etc., a person who has direct experience with the Divine, who has revelations.

Mystic Oracle—A.k.a., Napoleon's Book of Fate.

Legend has it that Napoleon possessed an ancient Egyptian papyrus that was translated and was the Mystic Oracle that combined symbols and a series of numbered questions. One asked the question and then randomly chose a symbol. A table in the book cross-referenced the symbols and question numbers, and by using the table, one was referred to a series of pages with one-line answers. By looking up the symbol on the appropriate page one determined their answer. Several modern versions of this have been marketed over the years.

mysticism—The religious side of magick.

myth—Metaphor with a plot and cast of characters. A religious teaching of an extinct religion. A story of the Gods and far-off times. A teaching tale. Generally a theology that is not part of the dominant culture of the time is called myth.

mythos—A system of metaphors within a society or culture. A system of beliefs and cosmology that is relatively whole, internally consistent, and related. Sometimes used interchangeably with pantheon.

N

NROOGD, New Reformed Orthodox Order of the Golden Dawn—A Wiccan organization that satirized the Golden Dawn with its name, but has little to do with the Golden Dawn. Founded by Aidan Kelley and others in the late 1960s in California.

Napoleon's Book of Fate—See Mystic Oracle.

nature—The forces of weather, geology, climatology, and the effects of the flora and fauna that shape the environment of the Earth, exclusive of the changes that have been caused by humanity and humanity's effects upon the planet. Wicca is a nature religion that worships and celebrates the Sabbats, Esbats, and life cycles. Practicing ecology, recycling, and living gently upon the Earth are also viewed as a way of worshipping nature by Wiccans and Pagans.

near-death experience—A psychic phenomenon that is universally reported, although more widespread since the advent of modern medicine and its extraordinary lifesaving revival techniques. People on the brink of death report that they see a bright light and experience a transcendent or rising feeling. They may also have an out-of-body experience and witness themselves being administered to by a medical team. Generally the person rises to some supernatural place and may or may not speak with God or some other spiritual being, but then feels as if they are falling or being drawn back to Earth and into their body. Some people who have near-death experiences believe their experience is proof that God exists and/or that there is an afterlife. It can be a life-changing experience and is usually very emotional.

necklace—A necklace with a pentagram or some other symbol can be a symbol of a High Priestess or a Witch Queen. Many Wiccans wear a necklace with a pentagram as a symbol of their Wiccan faith, much as a Christian would wear a cross. A necklace can be worn in Circle as a symbol of rebirth.

necromancy—1) Greek, (corpse divination), raising spirits of the dead, especially for divination. In ancient times it was one way a person could receive messages directly from the Gods. It was very popular in the Middle Ages where it was practiced along with sorcery and alchemy as well as the summoning and control of demons, and was considered one of the "black arts." 2) Also applied to certain black magick practices that use a corpse as a centerpiece for ritual, or which involve killing as a means of raising power. This is an uncomplimentary term in modern usage.

Neo-Pagan—Modern Pagans and the modern revival of various Pagan religions. There are many Neo-Pagan religions, some of which are Wicca, Druid, Witches, Kemet (the religion of ancient Egypt), Asatru societies (Norse pantheon worshippers), Odinists (followers of Odin), Native American religions, modern American versions of Buddhism, Zen, Taoism, and other more mainstream Pagan religions. All of these religions are versions or recreations of ancient religions adapted for modern life. Some feel to be a truly Neo-Pagan religion a religion had to die out completely (like Kemet) for the modern practices to be a true revival. Others maintain some of these religions never truly died out (like Wicca), but just went underground and this is a resurgence.

neophyte, postulant—A newcomer to a coven awaiting Initiation or possibly Dedication, depending upon the Tradition. More formal and narrowly used than newbie.

nephelomancy—Greek *nephele* (cloud) and *manteia* (divination). Divination using clouds, their shapes, formations, color, etc.

nest—A local CAW group.

New Age—A term that came into use in the 1980s to describe a mainstream philosophical movement that is spiritual, eclectic, and non-specific in nature, practice, and ideology. New Age beliefs encompass spiritualism, astrology, mysticism, occult studies, reincarnation, parapsychology, ecology, planetary awareness, and alternative medicine. New Age proponents explore a variety of philosophies and disciplines, including crystals, channeling, past-life regression, reincarnation, divination, etc., but have no specific religion that unifies their beliefs. Occasionally a liberal Christianity accompanies New Age beliefs and practices. The New Age is a result of the occult revolution and resurgence of the 1960s.

Wicca is frequently viewed as a New Age practice, but Wiccans generally do not consider themselves a part of the New Age philosophical movement because they have a specific religion that began before the start of the New Age (at least 1949 and Gerald Gardner). The New Age proponents often feel that they are participating in something new, and Wiccans are under the impression they are doing something that is very old. Neither is totally correct. Wicca saw an explosion of seekers at the height of the New Age revolution, but many left Wicca because 1) Wicca was a religion that required study and dedication to follow, and 2) Wicca required an appreciable effort to understand and practice.

New Moon, Dark Moon—Moon phase when the Moon is conjunct the Sun and invisible (except during a solar eclipse). Symbolic of the time between death and rebirth. Some cultures consider the dark of the moon to be a time of change and differentiate it from the New Moon, considering the New Moon is when the crescent first appears in the sky at sunset, about thirty-four hours after the actual conjunction. Some groups celebrate New Moons as Esbats. Some consider the New Moon to be symbolic of the Goddess as Crone, others believe the Fourth Quarter is the Crone. Also symbolic of a woman who is menstruating.

newbie—New person; also called neo. Term for someone new to Paganism and/or Wicca.

nightmare—Frightening dream that evokes unpleasant or strong emotions. Some cultures believe nightmares are caused by black magick. Early European Christians attributed the cause of nightmares to demonic forces. Today, nightmares are viewed by mental health professionals as signs of psychological or emotional distress.

In the second century CE the physician Soranus of Ephesus concluded that nightmares were the result of physiological and or medical conditions. Many cultures believed specific spirits could cause nightmares: ancient Greece—Ephialties; medieval clerics—Incubi and Succubi; Germany—Wüarger (strangler); Russia—kikimara; France—cauchemar; Switzerland—chauchevielle; Balkans—Vjeschitza (a female flame-winged spirit).

Nostradamus; Michel de Nostre-Dame—(1503–1566) French astrologer, mathematician, magician, courtier, and advisor to the court. He was very famous and was renowned for his astrological prediction skills. He wrote a number of predictions which spanned the eras from his present to beyond the year 2000. Because of the potentially sensitive nature of some of his predictions, he wrote them in poetry, and used archaic French, his native Renaissance French, idiom and many astrological terms, and then obscured the predictions with imagery and foreign words. He even went so far as to scramble his stanzas by throwing them in the air and picking them up at random. His randomized verse was published as *Centuries* in 1555. His prophecies, in four-line stanzas (quatrains), were arranged randomly in groups of 100 (centuries). An expanded version of *Centuries* was published in 1558. He used astrological imagery, and he refers directly in his writing to the Jupiter-Saturn conjunction of May 27, 2000. The predictions supposedly foretell events up to the year 3797. As is often the case, the accuracy of his predictions is usually discovered in hindsight. Some have made use of Nostradamus' predictions to justify everything from World War III to winning the Super Bowl.

numerology—The divinatory system that assigns a numerical equivalent to each letter of the alphabet and, by adding the totals and then adding the digits together, a name can be reduced to a single-digit equivalent. Each digit—one through nine—has a distinct meaning and can be used to determine one's character as well as good and bad days. Western numerology is derived from Gematria. Pythagoras felt all creation ultimately could be expressed mathematically— "all things are numbers"—and felt the universe was mathematically constructed. He developed the concepts of divine proportion and the Golden Mean, mathematical expressions that are the basis of everything from the ideal human form to nature and natural cycles.

nymph—Colloquially a pre-pubescent female. The female Goddess has three forms, Maiden, Mother, and Crone. A child is acknowledged as a Deity, but many older girls/pre-menarche young women don't like the term child and are not yet Maidens, so this category was created and occasionally used to describe teens and pre-teens in Pagan Traditions.

O

oaths—Affirmation sworn in a sacred context. Most Wiccans are required to take various oaths in the course of their Initiations. Oaths of confidentiality are common, usually used to protect fellow Wiccans. There are also oaths of secrecy to protect secrets of the Tradition. People also swear oaths to their Gods.

object link—To use an item—like a lock of hair, a piece of clothing, or a personal possession—to forge a magickal line or tie between the magician and the person to whom the item belongs. An application of the magickal Law of Association, which states that an item still has a link to the person from whom it came or to whom it belongs or even whoever touched it last. Using that energy link a magician can obtain information about the person, perhaps determine their location, or use the link to influence the person in some way. Can also be used to effect a spell without the recipient of the energy present, as in an absent healing.

occult—Latin, hidden, it refers to magickal, metaphysical, and esoteric studies, sometimes as unpopular or incompatible with scientific or religious thought. Occult knowledge has, in general, been hidden knowledge because the keepers of the knowledge did not feel others were ready or able to understand it. Occult can also refer to the hidden truths behind many mystical groups and doctrines. At the present time, the term is not generally used, practitioners preferring the term "metaphysical." Through abandoning this term, some feel they are avoiding the negative connotations "occult" has picked up over the ages; some are affirming that such knowledge should be free and open to any who would learn and study.

Occult Conspiracy Theories—Modern lore grants much time, paper, and energy to various occult conspiracy theories. These range from UFOs to black helicopters, to secret breeding experiments, to Illuminati theories. The basic theme of all these theories is that there is some giant secret governmental or extra-governmental group that has a special agenda for mankind and has manipulated world economies, politics, and/or the media to further their ends. These theories incorporate magick, occult lore, Christian lore and mysticism, parapsychology, ESP, various racial pseudo-scientific hypotheses, Masonic world domination, the IMF, Pagan lore and legend, anti-Semitism, aliens from outer space, angels, and other concepts or beliefs popular at the time. Much ancient, medieval, and Renaissance occult lore is being resurrected as "proof" of a variety of conspiracy theories coupled with some reputable archaeological and historical data. Some of the research is excellent, though the conclusions may not be as valid. Groups exist that are dedicated to various of these movements, some more serious and earnest than others.

Some of these theories are merely the retelling of old legends dressed up with modern historical and archaeological data. Some are based upon actual events and reports by witnesses. Some are based upon newly discovered original documents. These groups are not religions in the formal sense, though the belief and adherence to the material presented can be compared to faith. Sometimes these groups form a subculture in which one adopts these beliefs and from that springs a certain lifestyle or world-view that is different from mainstream society. Since many theories of the past were later proven to be valid and gained wide acceptance, one cannot totally dismiss this body of data out-of-hand.

oculomancy—Divination by studying a person's eyes. Iridology is a more up-to-date version of this ancient system. Could be considered an early form of hypnotism, and a type of fascination.

oeonisticy—Divination using the flight of birds.

Ogham—A magickal alphabet based on an ancient Celtic alphabet, thought to be a descendant of the runes.

oinomancy—Divination with wine used as a libation to the Gods, by using the color, appearance, smell, and taste. One poured wine for the Gods in attempt to appease or garner favor. In ancient times, when drinking in a formal setting, it was considered proper to pour the first drops for the Gods to give thanks, similar to saying grace.

ointment—A compound made of an oil or an unguent that is applied to the body, or an object to impart magickal powers, curses, or cures. May be used in connection with an amulet. Flying ointment is an ancient concoction that was reported to cause visions and help unleash psychic powers. Flying ointment may have contained hallucinogenic components in some of its formulae. Perfumes are modern descendants of ointments used as love spells.

Old George; "Old George" Pickingill—(1816–1909) Hereditary Magister (witch master) from the village of Canewdon in Essex. Reported to be the founder of the "Nine Covens" of which Old Dorothy's coven was a descendant, and therefore Gardnerian Wicca descends from Old George through Old Dorothy. Claims have also been made that Aleister Crowley was initiated by Pickingill into the Craft in 1899, and that Crowley initiated Gardner in 1946 and shared his Book of Shadows with Gardner, which helped form the basis for Gardnerian Wicca. That George Pickingill existed is a matter of fact. Whether he was a Magister or worked with Crowley or others is a matter of controversy.

Old Religion—Paganism in its many forms. The religions that existed before Judaism, Christianity, and Islam. Some modern Neo-Pagans claim they are resurrecting (or continuing) the practices of the Old Religion.

oloygmancy—Divination using the howling of dogs.

omen (and/or portents)—An occurrence or phenomenon foreshadowing a future event, or a message from the Gods. Omens can include natural events (plagues, eclipses, comets, or volcanic explosions), everyday happenings that are considered significant (planning a party and discovering all your wine had turned to vinegar), and divination.

omoplatoscopy—See scapulomancy.

omphalomancy—Divination through the contemplation of one's navel. Used in connection with yogic disciplines and spirituality.

oneiromancy, oniromancy, oneiroscopy—Divination through the interpretation of dreams. This can be symbolic or literal, as in actually dreaming of a future event and having it happen exactly as envisioned. Dream symbol analysis has been adopted by psychologists and other mental health professionals and the symbols and their meanings are universal. Dream symbology, as found in many good dream dictionaries, can be used in many other divinatory systems like scrying, tasseography, nephelomancy, or any other system that bases interpretations on shapes or pictures discerned by the diviner. Dream interpretation can be used as a tool for psychological healing and/or self-development, as well as determining the future.

onimancy, onyomancy—Divination by reading the fingernails, noting the size and shape of the moons and any spots or irregularities, a subset of palmistry.

onomancy, onomatomancy—Divination using names and the letters of which they are composed. Can be used for persons, places, or things. The Naming of a person, place, or thing is also considered significant and by carefully choosing a name it is believed that one can predetermine the future for the person (or thing) named. Choosing a magickal name can be considered a part of this discipline.

onychomancy—Divination by using the reflection of sunlight off a person's fingernails and interpreting any resulting symbols. A type of scrying.

oomancy, ooscopy, ovomancy—Divination using eggs. 1) In this form of divination, a pregnant woman would incubate an egg between her breasts and, when hatched, the sex of the chick would predict the sex of her child. 2) An egg would be broken into boiling water and the resulting shapes interpreted. 3) Eggs would be colored and then the intensity and shapes of color would be interpreted. The practice of hiding and then finding colored eggs may be a modern variation of this practice.

open—A term used to indicate something is available to almost anyone who is interested. When used in reference to a Circle—"open Circle"—means that this Circle is available to any who might wish to join it. When used in reference to a group—"This group is open"—means there is room for and interest in new members. Opposite of closed. In practical terms, open usually has a few restrictions, such as for friends and vouched-for guests, for those who have heard about the activity. The term as it is generally used by Wiccans refers to those who are already in the community in some way, and open rarely means open to the public-at-large.

ophiomancy—Divination using serpents as divine agents.

oracle—Greek. A person who is directly inspired by a God without any perceptible intermediary, moving into an altered state with or without the use of psychotropic substances. An oracle responds to an inquiry, usually asked at a sacred site or within a ritual context. (See also prophet— one who experiences spontaneous or unsolicited visions.) The Oracle at Delphi and the Sibylline prophetesses were famous ancient oracles and priesthoods that lasted for centuries. In general a priestess was the oracle, although her answers might be interpreted by a priest or other person. Some oracles used ecstatic substances to induce a trance, some went into a spontaneous trance.

Usually the message was cryptic and could be misleading or useless. For example, when a famous general consulted the Oracle at Delphi to ask about the outcome of a forthcoming battle, the Oracle said that a great general and his army would fall in that battle. Of course the general who asked the question assumed the Oracle meant it was his opponent's army that would fall. However, it was that general who fell, since both men were considered great generals. Written records of the oracles were kept and some still exist.

ordeal—A situation in which an individual must participate, either willingly or unwillingly, and persevere despite opposition or obstacles. A hot seat is a specific type of ordeal. Challenging life occurrences can be viewed as an ordeal. Sometimes an Initiation may require that the candidate undergo some ordeal to prove their worthiness.

Order of the Knights Templar—See Templars.

Order of the Rosy Cross—See Rosicrucians.

orniscopy, ornithomancy—Divination by observation of birds, their flight, songs, and feeding habits. The ancient Romans theorized that since birds flew high in the heavens, they might be aware of the intentions of the Gods who dwelt there or be dispatched as their messengers. Changes in weather and seasons can be foretold easily by the observation of birds (and other animals and insects).

osculum obscenum—Latin, obscene kiss. In Inquisitional lore, the way witches honored Satan was through the osculum obscenum, kissing the Devil's anus. As this information was obtained under torture at the insistence of inquisitors, whether this was an actual practice is highly questionable.

Ouija™ Board, William Fuld Inc.—From French *oui* (yes) and German *ja* (yes). Pronounced *WEE-jah* or colloquially *WEE-gee*. Trademark game developed in the late 1890s by American William Fuld, it is a descendant of spirit spelling, a spiritualist practice that can put people in contact with discarnate entities. See also spirit spelling. Many denounce Ouija™ boards as demonic, satanic, or just potentially dangerous.

out-of-body experience (see also astral travel)—Also known as an OBE, or oobe (pronounced *oo-bee*, rhyming with doobie). The experience of having one's spiritual self travel to another place while one's body rests in a meditative state.

outer court—In some traditions, there are two groups of people—the inner court and the outer court. The outer court is made up of the lower-level Initiates and the newer people, perhaps Dedicants, people who are still in the learning and studying phase. Their studies and activities may be restricted to specific topics and levels. The secrets of the Tradition are usually reserved for inner court Initiates, and a person cannot progress from outer court to inner court until they have been a member for a certain length of time and studied and passed certain skill levels. What the exact requirements are for entry into the inner court varies from Tradition to Tradition. Usually just to become a member of the outer court (and not just a friend or associate of the Tradition) requires oaths of commitment and secrecy.

outing—Borrowed from the gay community, it means to reveal one's Wiccan affiliations against one's will. Many Wiccans prefer to keep their religion private. Inadvertent outing is accidentally outing someone, but is still inappropriate and thoughtless. Purposely outing someone is a form of black magick and occasionally the perpetrator is declared warlock and shunned.

ovomancy—See oomancy.

P

P.C.—Abbreviation for Politically Correct, using language in a conscious effort to grant equality and value, for example, disability rather than handicap. Often the brunt of jokes, the intent of this form of language is positive. If words have power—and they do—then it is important to consciously use language in a positive way.

pact with the Devil—In medieval and Renaissance Christian belief, in order to be a witch one had to make a pact with the Devil to gain power, and such a pact allowed the witch to order demons and imps to do their bidding. According to Christian doctrine, this pact could be accomplished in a variety of ways: from attending a witches' Sabbat to elaborate written documents signed in blood and accompanied with magical workings and mutual guarantees. At the heart of the pact was the guarantee that the witch would gain earthly power in exchange for their eternal soul, which became the property of the Devil. Popularized by the Faust legends and literature, elaborate rituals and magickal acts were written and are still published today. The *Compendium Maleficarum* (*Witches Manual*) by Francesco Maria Guazzo is a seventeenth-century treatise on witchcraft that details these contracts and ceremonies. Various contracts of the time still exist that prove some people believed the lore and attempted to use it for their own ends. Lore also indicates that the soul can be redeemed by recanting these contracts. A tool of the Inquisition. See also Fourth Degree.

Pagan—From Latin *paganus*, peasant, or generally a country dweller. An ancient word that has evolved to mean one who follows a religion other than the Judeo-Christian, and more specifically, one who follows indigenous or native pantheistic folk religions and cultures, either as originally practiced or as a recreation and modernization of ancient ways. Also includes those who worship nature and life as sacred. In Wicca, it includes Wiccans and also those of other Neo-Pagan religious paths. One possible derivation of the term may come from its use by early Christians who considered themselves soldiers of Christ, and *paganus* was used to describe a civilian, so early Christians adopted the term to refer to non-Christians. Another theory is that as Christianity spread more quickly in the cities, the country dwellers were often converted last, sometimes partially or incompletely, and the term was used to refer to unconverted rural people much in the same way as "hick" is used today.

Pagan Grove—See outer court.

Pagan space—At a festival the common living space and community that develops as the result of many Pagans living together, also a free feeling and relaxed state of mind that develops at a festival or within a coven. The freedom of this space is frequently expressed at outdoor festivals that are "clothing optional." There even are signs at some festivals at the exit gate, "You are now leaving Pagan space, do you know where your clothes are?" Another saying is "Pagan space, where men can put their skirts on and women can take theirs off."

Pagan standard time, PST (outside the Pacific time zone)—An expression that represents the propensity in many Pagan gatherings for a relatively loose interpretation of promptness. For example, if a ritual is scheduled to begin at 7 PM, it can often start at 8 or 9 or even 10 o'clock or when everyone shows up and is ready.

palmistry—Divination by studying the hand and its lines as well as the shape of the hands, fingers, nails, etc. The oldest existing Chinese palmistry texts date from around 3200 BCE. Palmistry is a general term that includes the more ancient and specific disciplines of cheiromancy—divination using the lines on the hands; cheirognomy—divination by the shape and general formation of the hands and fingers; onyomancy—divination by study of the fingernails.

pantacle—See pentacle.

pantheism—Greek, all divine. The belief that divinity is inherent in and manifests through nature; all things natural (deriving from nature) are considered divine and holy, nature worship.

pantheon—A religious system that includes a hierarchy of Deities, for example, the Greek, Roman, Norse, Celtic, Egyptian, Hindu, Buddhist pantheons. Usually a Wiccan worships Deities in one pantheon, but this is not restricted; a Wiccan could have as their major Deities Buddha and the Virgin Mary (thereby combining Christian and Buddhist pantheons). Wicca does not have a standard group of Deities that are worshipped. One is free to seek Deities one feels comfortable with, and worship those one is called to worship. Some Traditions require that their adherents worship specific Deities, but most allow their members freedom to choose.

Paracelsus—(1493–1541) Name adopted by Swiss-born German physician and alchemist Theophrastus Bombastus von Hohenheim. A controversial (at the time) medical reformer who introduced a new theory of disease, employed alchemical techniques to refine the active ingredients in herbs and synthesize new compounds, he helped create chemical medicines. He condemned traditional natural science and medicine. Paracelsus believed disease was caused by outside agents, not imbalance of the body's natural humors. He used his chemicals as therapy to kill those outside agents and restore health. He changed the emphasis of alchemy from finding the philosopher's stone to making and discovering medicines, helping to found pharmacology. He was also a student of occult lore and wrote, among other things, instructions for creating a magical mirror, which was used to view future events.

paradigm—A pattern of reality, a shared reality, a system of belief shared by a group, culture, or ethnicity.

paradigm shifting—Change in world outlook to cause a change in reality, mirrored by a change in one's actions and beliefs.

paranoia—An emotional state in which a person feels they are constantly watched and/or that someone is out to get them. When a person begins to open their psychic channels they can become paranoid because they become aware of the "unseen world" and the entities that populate it. Grounding, centering, and shielding can help alleviate these feelings. Paranoia can be a normal growth stage for people beginning the study and practice of Wicca. Paranoia can result from fear of persecution. Paranoid feelings are often reduced or eliminated through practice and familiarity with the psychic world.

paranormal—That which is unusual or supernatural, not explained by the current scientific paradigms. ESP, UFOs, vampires, magick, etc., are often viewed as representatives of this term. Paranormal phenomena are often viewed judgmentally, although those who work with these phenomena view them as different facets of the Universe. A term not generally used in Wicca.

parapsychology—The study of the mind's ability to perform feats that are often unexplainable by modern science, and also the study of psychic phenomena. An outgrowth of the spiritualism movement in the late 1800s. The first scientific parapsychology groups in the 1880s studied mediums to determine whether their activities were genuine or fraudulent. In 1927 psychologist J.B. Rhine of Duke University in North Carolina pioneered the first rigorous scientific study of psychic abilities. Rhine, and later his followers, used Zener Cards—a specially designed deck of 25 cards, made up of five sets of five cards with a star, square, circle, plus sign, or wavy lines on each. The deck was shuffled and various types of tests were employed with subjects to determine if they could predict which card would come up, and the results evaluated to determine if they varied from statistical probability. There were other methods used to test other psychic abilities. Unfortunately results often were not replicable—a requirement for scientific proof—so despite strong statistical anomalies, these studies did not present concrete proof that psychic abilities exist. The discipline is still studied, though not intensely nor with the funding it received prior to the end of the Cold War. The Russians, during the Cold War era, conducted tests and their studies were published in the 1970s.

partners—People who are in a committed relationship, usually sexual in nature. Wiccans generally recognize many different types of partnerships including same sex partnerships and multiple partnerships. Some Wiccan Traditions, most notably Gardnerians and Alexandrians, do not allow same sex couples to work together in their Traditional teachings. Eclectic Wicca allows almost any type of partnerships. Radical Faery Wicca is, for the most part, a gay men's tradition and Z Budapest's followers, although not necessarily Wiccan, welcome lesbian couples. Many Dianic Wiccan groups are strictly feminist and can also be lesbian.

password—Some Traditions have a special password that is used when entering a Circle. Some require elaborate passwords to aid in the identification of members. Passwords can also be words of power. May also be meaningful sayings or phrases.

past life—A life lived by a person prior to the present one. In reincarnation a person is presumed to live many lives as they learn, grow, and progress. Theoretically information from these past lives is accessible and can be used to help someone in their present life to explain situations, problems, and associations.

past-life regression—An hypnotic technique in which a person is encouraged to delve into their past, before their birth, and possibly get information about previous lives. Purely subjective, it can offer insight into present problems, situations, and associations. Sometimes viewed as a "proof" of reincarnation, rarely does a person receive information that can be researched. It became popular in the mid-1960s after the publication of the Bridey Murphy materials in which a woman under hypnotherapy for an emotional condition was accidentally regressed to a previous life. Not a technique for beginners or the inexperienced.

path—A method, system, or approach to magickal, mystical, or spiritual knowledge. The Red Path, for example, specifically refers to Native American spirituality and lifestyle. Choosing a path can include changing a lifestyle, especially if a person chooses a Pagan path. A term to describe the general tenets and areas of interest of an individual, or to describe areas of interest and study pursued by adherents of various Traditions.

paths/pathways—The term used to describe the "lines" drawn between the sephiroth of the Kabbalah. These paths correspond to the twenty-two trumps of the Major Arcana of the tarot. There are also "hidden pathways," paths that exist but are not shown on the standard diagram of the Kabbalah.

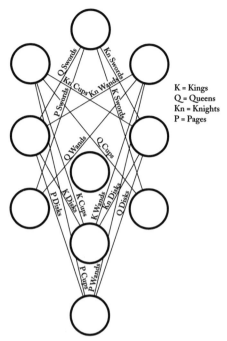

K = Kings
Q = Queens
Kn = Knights
P = Pages

Hidden Pathways of the Tree of Life

pathworkings—The process of study and meditation upon the Kabbalah, the sephiroth, and the pathways that connect them. A practice of active or guided meditations based upon the Kabbalah. A way to gain deeper understanding of Kabbalah, tarot, and their correspondences.

patriarchy—A male-dominated society, such as Western culture, has been the case for up to and including the twentieth century. The patriarchy is often viewed by Wiccans as an undesirable symbol and Wiccans work to restore true equality between the sexes, in which neither is exalted, and people assume roles that suit them, rather than conforming to societally prescribed roles.

patriarchialist—Uncomplimentary term for someone who is a proponent of patriarchy and sees the oppression of women, gays, minorities, and other non-male supremacist groups as the norm.

peace bond—Securing a weapon (usually a sword, although can be done to athames as well) so it cannot be drawn without elaborate unbinding. Usually accomplished by tying a weapon into its sheath. Often done for reasons of safety. Some festivals require all weapons be peace bonded except when used in ritual. When ritual items are transported in public it is often mandatory to transport items in this manner or they could be considered weapons.

Peace Bonded Blade

pedomancy, podomancy—Divination by reading lines on the sole of the foot, similar to palmistry. Widely practiced in China.

pegomancy—Divination by observation of a fountain or spring. A type of hydromancy. Changes in color are especially significant. The flow and shapes of the water as it moves are observed and interpreted.

pendulum—A weight hanging from a hand-held cord, sometimes with a point at the bottom. A pendulum weight can be made from a wide variety of objects, often a gemstone. When suspended, the swinging motion is used for divination. A person asks yes/no questions and after determining which directions signify yes and no, the swinging motion of the pendulum is observed to receive the answer. Also a pendulum can be placed over a map or picture and its motion observed to determine direction or location or other information. A very simple, inexpensive, and easy method of divination. Related to dowsing.

Pendulum

pentacle—A disk with a pentagram inscribed on it, it is similar to the symbol for the suit of Pentacles in a tarot deck. It can also be inscribed on a plate, plaque, or jewelry item. On a ceremonial altar it is a "plate," and symbolizes the element Earth, and

is sometimes used to hold cakes or bread. Generally if it is filled in and on a circle, the pentagram is a pentacle. Some groups paint one side black and the other white, and it can be used as both a shield and magick mirror. Pantacle is a variant spelling, said to be a deliberate misspelling by Eliaphas Levi to see who plagiarized his works. Some Traditions distinguish the pantacle—altar plate, from the pentacle—pentagram with a circle around it.

Pentacle

pentagram—The five-pointed interlaced star that is the symbol for the religion and faith of Wicca, much as the cross is the symbol for Christianity, the star and crescent for Islam, or the Star of David for Judaism. The five points symbolize the five elements: Air, Fire, Water, and Earth, with the top point symbolizing Spirit. It is also used as a mandala and magickal symbol in various magickal and/or spiritual Traditions. It also symbolizes a person, with the head at top and outstretched arms and legs as the other four points. The pentagram (or five-petaled "flower") is also an ancient symbol of the planet Venus, related to its orbit and its pattern in the zodiac, retrograding five times in eight years.

In the ancient world, the pentagram was a magickal symbol and represented certain mathematical and geometric principles well. Pythagoras revered the pentagram in a similar manner to his golden rectangle. The pentagram was the secret symbol of the Pythagoreans, who used its proportions to explain many mathematical ratios, properties, and theories.

In Wicca the pentagram is used with the point up to symbolize one's mastery over desires, and the process of self-improvement as in the Great Work. In Satanism it is displayed point down, which symbolizes yielding to man's desires. The satanic inverted pentagram symbolizes a goat's head with horns, ears, and beard/chin. Some Wiccan Traditions use an inverted pentagram to symbolize various degrees or Deities but, in the United States, the inverted pentagram is usually a satanic symbol and generally avoided by Wiccans. In Britain, Satanists tend to use an inverted cross, so the inverted pentagram doesn't have the same negative connotations it can have in North America. Many Wiccans favor any five-pointed star motif as symbolizing the pentagram, and indeed it is one way for Wiccans who are not "Out" to be able to wear a pentagram without attracting undue attention.

Pentagrams are also drawn in the air as a method of invoking or banishing magickal forces during a Circle. Magickal pentagrams are drawn in various ways, starting at various points, moving in various directions depending upon the type of magick and Tradition practiced. Ceremonial Magick, other than Wiccan, relies heavily upon the pentagram in magickal ceremonies, but it is often used in a different way than in Wiccan Circles. There is no one standardized way to use pentagrams and so this practice varies widely among Wiccans depending upon Tradition, training, and preferences.

Pentagram, Inverted Pentagram, and Pentagram with Human Figure Superimposed

pentalpha—Five-pointed design created by the interlacing of five capital As. Used in Ceremonial Magickal rites. An illustration of the sacredness of alphabets and writing.

Pentalpha

personality—That portion of a person adopted by an individual or soul during a specific incarnation. The personality dies with the body and is only a small portion of the totality of the individuality. A specific personality may be adopted in order to work on certain issues during a specific lifetime. The astrological chart reflects the personality adopted during a particular incarnation, although there is evidence that the chart lives on after the death of the body.

pessomancy, psephomancy—Divination using pebbles. One method of divination is to draw pebbles from a pile or bag, and interpret the meaning of the order and type of pebbles. Marbles can be used as a modern substitute.

petchimancy—Divination by brushing clothes. Before modern laundries and dry cleaning, fine clothing was "cleaned" by brushing the soil off.

philtre—A spell in which a charm is woven into a potion. Can be used for transferring one's powers to the object of the spell. Also an aphrodisiac or love spell, generally in imbibable form. A potion credited with magickal power.

phrenology—Reading character by interpreting the size and placement of the bumps on the head. Developed by Franz Joseph Gall in Vienna in the nineteenth century, by the end of that century it had degenerated into a pseudo-science and was viewed as quackery. Phrenology machines that measured a person's head and produced a character analysis (an early mechanical computer) were made and marketed around 1900.

phyllorhodomancy—Divination by clapping rose leaves against the side of the hand and interpreting the sounds they make.

physiognomy—A.k.a., anthroposomancy. Face reading. Divination of character by reading the features on a person's face. Dating back to the Zhou Dynasty (1122–221 BCE) in China, a popular treatise was published in the Sung Dynasty (906–1279 CE). In the West it is treated as a subset of phrenology, although it is not. The size, relative placement, proportions, and shape of various facial features are used to determine the character. Scars or other facial injuries also play a part in the interpretations. Hair color and condition can also be a factor. Ancient Greeks practiced the custom. Japanese use ninso—person aspect—and take into account the shape of the face, skin quality, eyes, and hair as well as coloring to determine mood and character. How modern plastic surgery modifies a reading has not been determined.

planchette—1) A mounted pencil on casters, used for automatic writing. 2) A device on felt "feet" that allow the device to slide easily, upon which one, two, or more people rest their hands; used in spirit spelling. Used with a Ouija™ Board. Replaced the upturned wine glass that had been used before the planchette was invented.

planes of existence, planes, higher planes, lower planes, astral plane—Realms of existence that co-exist but do not usually interact, they may be interdependent or independent. Also called the unseen realms or realms of the spirits and/or demons and/or Gods, it is in this arena that magick is worked. The homes of various spirit entities. The physical/material Earth is only one of many realms or planes of existence. When one practices magick one enters magickal planes to work magick which then manifests in the material plane, sometimes referred to as "the real world." Wiccans view the spirit planes as just as real as this material plane and can take offense at the reference to the material plane as the "real world."

Spirit realms can be referred to as either higher and lower than the Earth plane, primarily related to vibratory frequency. Practically one can determine whether one has "connected" to a higher or lower plane by the temperature; higher planes are warmer than normal, and lower planes are cooler than normal. Generally it is believed that entities on the lower planes are less evolved and/or aware than we are, and entities on the higher planes are more evolved and aware than we are. Ghosts are a lower plane discarnate entity. The Gods are higher plane entities. When one leaves the body (astral travel), the spirit travels to the astral plane. The astral plane can refer to the plane of higher knowledge, where one can access the cosmic records, or Akashic Library, or whatever name one gives to the arena of higher knowledge that can be accessed by psychics, mediums, and readers as well as those who meditate or study magick. Some consider the astral plane to be the realm of magick. It can also be viewed as parallel worlds that are reached through occult or magickal means.

poison oracle—Divination performed by feeding an animal poison to determine a true answer. If the animal dies, the answer is "No." Then the test is administered again to another to corroborate the answer. Usually the questions are phrased so that one animal must die and the other be spared to receive two corroborating answers. Both animals are given the same dose of the same substance.

poltergeist—German, noisy ghost; from German *poltern*, to knock, and *geist*, spirit or ghost—recurrent spontaneous psychokinesis. Can be a spirit that likes to create mischief, especially noise. Can also be a manifestation of psychic skills untrained and uncontrolled. Poltergeists can manifest in a home in which a girl is undergoing puberty and possibly experiencing emotional upheavals. Once the girl's hormone surges stabilize or she leaves the home, the poltergeist may spontaneously disappear. Can also be exorcised, but this takes skill.

To discourage a poltergeist from remaining in the house put up a list of chores and tell it that if it is to remain in the house it must earn its keep, and here are the chores it is expected to do. If it does not, then you will bring in an exorcist. This method, when presented forcefully and with intent, has effectively caused spirits to leave a house rather painlessly. Occasionally you even get some chores done! Most poltergeists' presence in the home is manifest by strange noises or smells, objects moving or thrown objects, and occasionally objects disappear, only to turn up later unexpectedly.

Psychological profiles have shown that mental and emotional distress, personality disorders, phobias, repression, obsessive behavior, and schizophrenia are linked to poltergeists. In some cases, psychotherapy and/or medication has eliminated the poltergeist activity.

polytheism—Belief in the existence of many Deities. A religion that has an original group of Gods is polytheistic. Ancient Greek and Roman religions were polytheistic. Many Pagan religions are polytheistic in nature, and many Pagan religious paths advocate or tolerate polytheistic worship.

poppet—A small image of a person, made of cloth, wax, or plant materials, that is used in a magickal act. The "voodoo doll" is a non-Wiccan type of poppet. A poppet can be used as a focus for healing when the person is absent. Some lore believes that it is necessary to have something belonging to a part of a person in order to "charge" the poppet and make it effective; others feel if it is made with intent that is enough.

Poppet

portent—See omen.

possession—The condition in which a person's personality is moved aside against their will by a discarnate entity or an ecstatic occurrence in which the personality is overwhelmed and replaced by a non-corporeal entity. Use of Ouija™ boards without appropriate controlled conditions can lead to possession. Possession can be demonic but usually a person is possessed by a personality that wants to be in the mundane world, and does not adhere to karmic rules and guidelines. Sometimes an exorcism is required to end a possession. Literature about possession reports that the possessed person's voice and occasionally appearance may change. In some religions, communication with and voluntary possession by various Deities is central to worship, as in Voudun (voodoo). Invocation and Drawing Down the Moon or Sun are forms of voluntary possession, but are rituals performed under strictly controlled conditions with appropriate safeguards. In Pentecostal Christianity voluntary possession by the Holy Spirit is encouraged and can cause those possessed to "speak in tongues," perform faith healings, and other manifestations.

potion—An herbal brew used as a homeopathic remedy together with psychic healing. Can also refer to poisonous concoctions made in a magickal or psychic context.

power—Energy, specifically magickal energy. Also the state of being powerful, having political influence, and the ability to get things done. Also used as in power-over, being dominant in a dominant/subservient relationship.

power animal—People who practice shamanic techniques can have a power animal that acts as a spirit guide in the shamanic world. This animal can also serve as a mascot and/or character model. This concept is one that has been borrowed from Native American and other teachings. Generally a person will have one primary power animal, but can also have several other allies or guides in the spirit world.

power spot, power place, power point—Natural areas that have an unusually large amount of energy, sometimes psychic, sometimes also associated with natural phenomena (like a whirlpool, volcano, geyser, mountain, spring, cave, etc.). Some power spots have manmade structures that may enhance, dampen, or channel the energies of the power spot. Most ancient Pagan temples were built in conjunction with power spots, and when Christianity removed these Pagan temples, often a church or cathedral was built over the ancient site and the church was then imbued with the energies of the power spot. Indigenous religions treated power spots in various ways; the Native American traditions generally left those places as natural as possible, but used them for teaching and Initiations. Stonehenge is built over a power spot.

It is believed that power spots are connected by ley lines. There are many intensities and qualities of power spots, and not all are bright, good, or beneficial, and it is important to ascertain the type, quality, and intensity of the energy before experiencing the energy of the place. Local legends may develop around power spots, and those local legends are a very good place to begin researching what kind of power spot it is. Since the power in one place may not affect all people equally, it is best to be cautious when exploring such sites.

prana energy—A Hindu term that describes the life force that surround us. It is inhaled with the air and can be utilized for healing, psychic work, and generally revitalizing the body and spirit. There are various breathing techniques used to enhance one's intake of prana and allow more effective use of it. It is the vital force of the cosmos as it operates on the etheric level. It is similar to Chi, and believed to be peach-colored.

precession of the equinoxes—See Age of Aquarius.

precognition, abbr. precog—Latin, foreknowledge, the ability to perceive events before they occur in present time and space. Contrast with clairvoyance, which is perceiving events that happen in present time, but in a different place. With precognition, the perceived event is in the future, and may or may not occur in the same place as the perceiver. Colloquially synonymous with ESP.

premonition—An intuition about some possible future event, it is less certain or clear than precognition. Theoretically all persons exhibit a certain amount of premonition, but only those who heed and develop the ability can achieve any degree of certainty. For example, a person may have a premonition that if they drive through a certain intersection they will have an accident, and, if one follows the premonition, then the intersection should be avoided until they feel safe about it again. If they go through the intersection and have an accident, then the premonition was true. If they avoid the intersection, and there is no accident, then the premonition was presumably also true. Of course if they go through the intersection and there is no accident, then it is presumed the premonition was false, but the accident could still be in the future. Sometimes called superstition.

pricking, "pricking a witch"—Moles, warts, rashes, and other skin imperfections were considered witches' marks by the Inquisition. Especially any skin imperfection that was prominent was considered a witches' pap, a place whereby the witch could suckle a demon.

"Pricking a witch" was a method of determining if a person was a witch. The Inquisitor would take a knife or needle and poke or prick the skin, and if the subject did not bleed or react they were considered to be a witch. Often this was performed after the subject was forced to lie naked upon a stone floor, and by the time the pricking was done, the subject was so numb, they probably could feel very little. Hysteria at being singled out by the Inquisition could also cause adrenaline levels to rise and thereby cause the subject to feel no pain when pricked. Some witch finders would use trick devices, such as a knife whose blade would retract into the handle when pressed, giving the illusion of passing into flesh and being withdrawn, but causing no wound and drawing no blood.

Priest, Priestess—Male/female who officiates at a Circle. The title is rightfully claimed by any male/female Wiccan Initiate. A man/woman dedicated to the service of a Deity. He/she may maintain temples and altars, administer sacraments, conduct and preside over rites, rituals, and Initiations, pastoral counseling, and other duties. He/She may also serve as a direct or indirect channel for Deity.

primary relationship—A one-to-one relationship between two people. The following are varieties of primary relationships encountered in Wicca: a committed partnership, possibly including marriage or Handfasting; a working partnership, magickal, and/or High Priestess/High Priest relationship; co-authors or co-creators of art, music, crafts etc.; a kinship relationship as in parent/child, birth siblings or coven siblings, relatives or in-laws; a teacher/student relationship possibly including Initiation; a sexual relationship of some length of time; a peer relationship of close friendship and common interests and/or activities; a counseling relationship, as in mundane counseling or peer counseling or divinatory counseling; an administrative relationship as in co-officers of an organization or running a festival together; a business relationship as in being co-owners of a business; etc. Wiccans do not limit themselves to only one primary relationship, for few couples, if any, can be all things to each other. Generally a primary relationship is of some time's standing in which the participants have a feeling of commitment and responsibility and "ties of kin" to each other as well as (hopefully) ties of affection or at least common interests. These primary relationships are what makes the associations among Wiccans a web of relationships and can sometimes be seen as the cement which holds a community together. Some maintain only active relationships can be primary relationships; the majority feel that once a primary relationship has been established, though it may dissolve, the energy ties are still there and the relationship can be reestablished if the parties are willing, sometimes in the same way, sometimes in a different form. The idea of "six degrees of separation" takes on a whole different perspective when you start tracing primary relationships between Wiccans.

Principles of Wiccan Belief—A document written by the Council of American Witches (an organization that no longer exists) and adopted April 14, 1974 at Gnosticon in Minneapolis, Minnesota. These principles have been accepted as a working definition of Wicca by several organizations, including some branches of the United States government:

Principles of Wiccan Belief

The Council of American Witches finds it necessary to define modern Witchcraft in terms of the American experience and needs.

We are not bound by traditions from other times and other cultures, and owe no allegiance to any person or power greater than the Divinity manifest through our own being.

As American Witches we welcome and respect all Life Affirming teachings and traditions, and seek to learn from all and to share our learning with our Council.

It is in this spirit of welcome and cooperation that we adopt these few principles of Wiccan belief. In seeking to be inclusive, we do not wish to open ourselves to the destruction of our group by those on self-serving power trips, or to philosophies and practices contradictory to ours, we do not want to deny participation with us to any who are sincerely interested in our knowledge and beliefs, regardless of race, color, sex, age, national or cultural origins, or sexual preference.

1. We practice Rites to attune ourselves with the natural rhythms of life forces marked by the Phases of the Moon and the Seasonal Quarters and Cross Quarters.

2. We recognize that our intelligence gives us a unique responsibility toward our environment. We seek to live in harmony with Nature, on ecological balance offering fulfillment to life and consciousness within an evolutionary concept.

3. We acknowledge a depth of power far greater than that apparent to the average person. Because it is far greater than ordinary, it is sometimes called "supernatural," but we see it as lying within that which is naturally potential to all.

4. We conceive of the Creative Power in the Universe as manifesting through polarity—as masculine and feminine—and that this same Creative Power lives in all people, and functions through the interaction of the masculine and feminine. We value neither above the other, knowing each to be supporting of the other. We value Sex as pleasure, as the symbol and embodiment of life, and as one of the sources of energies used in magical practice and worship.

5. We recognize both outer worlds and inner, or psychological, worlds—sometimes known as the Spiritual World, the Collective Unconscious, the Inner Planes—and we see in the interaction of these two dimensions the basis for paranormal phenomena and magical exercises. We neglect neither dimension for the other, seeing both as necessary for our fulfillment.

6. We do not recognize an authoritarian hierarchy, but do honor those who teach, respect those who share their greater knowledge and wisdom, and acknowledge those who have courageously given of themselves in leadership.

7. We see religion, magic, and wisdom-in-living as being united in the way one views the world and lives within it—a world view and philosophy of life which we identify as Witchcraft, the Wiccan Way.

8. Calling oneself "Witch" does not make a witch - but neither does heredity itself, or the collecting of titles, degrees, and Initiations. A Witch seeks to control forces within him/herself that make life possible in order to live wisely and well, without harm to others, and in harmony with Nature.

9. We acknowledge that love is the affirmation and fulfillment of life, in a continuation of evolution and development of consciousness, that gives meaning to the Universe we know, and to our personal role within it.

10. Our only animosity toward Christianity, or towards any other religion or philosophy of life, is to the extent that its institutions have claimed to be "the only way" and have sought to deny freedom to others and to suppress other ways of religious practice and belief.

11. As American Witches, we are not threatened by debates on the history of the Craft, the origins of various aspects of different traditions. We are concerned with our present, and our future.

12. We do not accept the concept of "absolute evil," nor do we worship any entity known as "Satan" or "The Devil" as defined by the Christian tradition. We do not seek power through the suffering of others, nor do we accept the concept that personal benefit can only be derived by denial to another.

13. We acknowledge that we seek within Nature for that which is contributory to our health and well-being.

Priories of the Elders of Zion—1) One group of supposed Illuminati who control political systems through subtle and possibly illegal means. Theoretically these people are Jewish and covertly advance Jewish causes and agendas at the expense of the Aryan races, with the control over and assistance of the blacks. A favorite target of

Aryan and Nazi anti-Semitic groups. 2) A document created by the czar's secret police as a propaganda device for rationalizing the pogroms against the Jews starting around 1900. Still used today as an anti-Semitic document. See W.I.C.C.A.

projection—1) Short for astral projection. 2) A psychological term used to characterize the assignment of character traits or actions to another that are really present within the self, it often has a negative connotation. Sometimes when one has a bad magickal experience, or bad dream, it can be a form of projection, and the "demons" one encounters are merely those aspects of one's dark side that have not been dealt with and integrated into the psyche.

prophecy—Visions and predictions about the future. Divinely inspired vision or revelation of the future. Some feel any type of fortunetelling is a form of prophecy. Also a written record of predictions about the future.

prophet—From Greek, a person who is directly inspired by a God without any perceptible or known intermediary. A prophet made their pronouncements without any prompting or questioning and experienced spontaneous or unsolicited visions. See also oracle. Some prophets were believed, admired, and became famous (or legendary) like Tiresias; others were disbelieved, like Cassandra, whose curse was to be a prophet and always be correct, but not believed. Prophecy was one way the Gods sent messages directly to mankind (dreams, necromancy, and oracles were the others). A person who speaks for a Deity or other powerful spirit, usually about future events.

psychic, abbr. psi (or the Greek letter psi Ψ)—Of the supernatural, the "unseen realms," the "other world." Mental powers or talents that can affect or alter reality by nonphysical means, psychic abilities include clairvoyance, telepathy, divination, scrying, or other methods. Although many Wiccans have some psychic abilities, it is not at all necessary to be psychic to be Wiccan or to be an effective magician or ritualist. Theoretically everyone is psychic in some way, but it requires training and practice to effectively employ these abilities.

psychic archaeology—See psychometry.

psychic attack—Psychic energy sent to an unwilling or unaware target. The use of magick or psi to harm or destroy a being. A type of black magick. It is common in the Wiccan and magickal communities for people to misinterpret psychic influences as psychic attacks, when, in fact, these energies are not directed at them. When one opens oneself to psychic influences, it is important to learn how to ground and shield oneself so these influences do not interfere with everyday life, which requires practice and training. Some unethical people engage in active psychic attacks, which can cause some unpleasant results. Use of "voodoo dolls" and pictures of a target are varieties of psychic attack, as is attempting to psychically communicate with someone who is unwilling or unaware. Sometimes even healing a person without their knowledge or consent is considered a psychic attack. Praying for someone's salvation against their will is also a form of psychic attack.

psychic barometer—A person who is sensitive and can pick up the mood of a group or place and is affected by it. Can be useful in group dynamics or ghost busting, however, it can be difficult for the person who is such a psychic barometer because they feel the emotions of others and can be overwhelmed by these feelings. Learning how to shield themselves can make these people more relaxed and settled. People who are psychic barometers usually stay out of large crowds.

psychic black hole, psychic vampire—See vampire.

psychic criminology—See crime solving.

psychic reading—See reading.

psychic surgery—Surgery performed by psychic means, it includes the ability to open and close the body and remove afflicted tissues usually by laying on of hands, or by manipulating energy fields to promote the body's natural defenses to concentrate upon the afflicted area and stimulate patients to heal themselves. Patients who experience psychic surgery remain fully conscious and report that they experience no pain. It is a form of psychokinesis. Some instances of psychic surgery have been exposed as fraud, but in some of those cases have been some therapeutic effects. There are documented cases of psychic surgery that are unexplainable and have effected cures that were considered miraculous.

psyche—The nonphysical aspects of a person.

psychokinesis, abbr. PK—The use of pure mind power (psi) to move matter and/or energy. Also known as telekinesis, abbr. teke (pronounced "*teek*"), or TK. This psychic ability was researched, encouraged, and developed by the Russians during the Cold War, and there are films that show people moving match sticks and metal filings solely with mind power. According to accounts, most of the Russian telekinetics died of various cancers. Theoretically any natural healing skill is also a form of psychokinesis.

psychomancy—Divination using purely psychic abilities. Includes clairvoyance, precognition, automatic writing, spirit spelling, etc., and other techniques with no connection to Deity or spirit entities. It can be indistinguishable from divinations derived from non-corporeal entities and has been linked with necromancy. Theoretically only the practitioner can tell the difference, though a sensitive might be able to discern the presence of a non-corporeal entity.

psychometry—The ability to pick up images or information psychically from an object. For example, a psychometrist holding an antique watch might be able to "see" all its owners and possibly report information about the owners. Related to using an object link, it operates through the Law of Association. Sometimes a psychometrist can tell if an item was stolen, where the owner is, or where the item was made. These skills have been useful in criminal investigations. Some archaeologists have used psychometrists to help locate buried artifacts. A psychometrist can also obtain sociological information from an ancient object and help identify it.

psychopomp—A spiritual guide between the worlds of the living and of spirit. Hermes, Anubis, and Vanthe were all Divine psychopomps who brought the newborn into the world and/or escorted the dead into the afterworld. A shaman who attends a soul during its journey to "the other side" is acting as a psychopomp.

purification—1) A.k.a., lustral bath. A ritual bath or cleansing prior to a Circle, Working of magick, or Initiation. Some Traditions require each member to take a ritual bath (usually with salt and/or herbs in the water) prior to entering the Circle. 2) A type of cleansing designed to remove malign or unwanted influences, it can be done with salt, water, incense, herbs, smudging, etc.

Pythia—Ancient Greek Priestess and prophetess of Apollo at Delphi who was a medium for the oracular messages of the Gods. Often the Pythian messages were ambiguous and required interpretation by a Priest.

pyromancy—Divination by watching a fire and the smoke arising from it. A wide range of practices are covered by this term: 1) A sacrificial fire is ignited, how quickly it catches and how it burns is interpreted. 2) Substances are thrown into an ordinary fire and the more quickly they burn, the better the omen. 3) Sparks, colored flames, curiously shaped flames or smoke, and logs that burn in unexpected ways are all considered omens.

Q

QBL, Qaballah—Alternate spelling Qabala, Cabala, Kabala, etc. See Kabbalah.

Qliphoth—(pronounced "cliff-off") In Kabbalah the Qliphoth is a reverse Tree of Life that begins at Malkuth (or sometimes Tiphareth) and descends down in a mirror Kabbalah of dark or evil correspondences, but ultimately ends at Kether, as does the Tree of Life. It can be used as a method of follow-

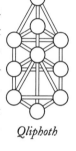

Qliphoth

ing a dark or evil path to a good end in order to gain enlightenment. Sometimes viewed as a left-hand path to enlightenment.

quarters—The four cardinal directions in a magickal Circle, quarters correspond to the four elements. Not every Wiccan Tradition assigns the same elements to the same quarters, nor are the colors used consistent. In the most widely accepted set of correspondences East is Air and yellow, South is Fire and red, West is Water and blue (or purple), North is Earth and green (or brown or purple), and Center is Spirit and white (or clear). Also refers to the Watchtowers.

Queen of the Sabbat—See Witch Queen.

Queen of the Witches—1) A title that is not used among Wiccans. Covens are autonomous and different Traditions are not connected, so there is no one person who is elected, designated, or acclaimed Queen of the Witches. 2) A slang term sometimes derisively used in connection with

Alex Sanders, who called himself King of the Witches. Since he was bisexual, he is sometimes called "Queen of the Witches."

querant—1) An archaic term referring to a person who consults someone for a reading. The more general term client has replaced this term in modern usage. 2) In Horary astrology the person who asks the question.

quesited—1) The person or thing asked about in a reading. An archaic term. 2) In Horary astrology the thing or person inquired about must be precise so that the astrologer can accurately determine which house or planet to look to for the answer.

quintessence—The fifth element of the cosmos, equivalent to Spirit, or the alchemical term elixir.

R

radiesthesia—The ability to locate commodities or detect energy by using a forked stick or wand. A form of telekinesis. A modern scientific term applied to abilities that were previously called dowsing or rhabdomancy.

raise power, raise energy—The act of gathering magickal energy within a Circle for a magickal or celebratory purpose. The act of building mental focus and emotion. There are many ways of raising power—drumming, dancing, singing, sex, use of will, and concentration, etc. Generally in performing a ritual a Circle is constructed, energy is raised within the Circle, the energy is directed to accomplish the purpose desired, and then the Circle is taken down. Wiccans raise power for magick, healing, or celebration.

read, reader, reading—When a person practices a psychic art for purposes of advice, divination, or gaining knowledge, it is known as a reading, whether done for oneself or for another, for money or not. The person doing the reading is known as the reader. Readings are done by practitioners of many disciplines; the term is generic and not tied to any specific divinatory or psychic system. Synonymous with the older, and less desirable, term fortunetelling.

real world—A subjective term used to refer to either the mundane, non-magickal material world or the magickal, psychic, ethereal world, depending upon one's point of view. Unambiguous terms like mundane and magickal worlds are preferred.

reality—The perceptual field, either subjective—one's personal sensory experience, verifiable only to the one experiencing it—or objective, an inferred hypothetical field underlying group perceptions, verifiable only by apparent consistency of experiential or observational data. The present state of existence that has the ability to affect and change us. How one perceives reality determines how one will act. Consensual reality is an agreed upon, shared, group metaphor. See paradigm.

Red Path—Native American practices and lifestyle, especially the spiritual practices, teachings, and traditions. Some have co-opted certain Native American religious practices and amalgamated them with Wiccan and other Pagan and New Age religious practices, but the paths are distinct and such mixing is viewed with unhappiness by Native American religious adherents and discouraged by most Wiccan teachers.

Red Priest—A Wiccan Priest who is designated to serve as special assistant to the High Priest, similar to a Summoner.

rede, the rede—(pronounced "reed"), the Wiccan Rede. The word "rede" is medieval and means counsel or advice. Ethelred the Redeless (modernly pronounced *ready-less)* is not Unready, but rather without advice or counsel.

reincarnation—The belief that a soul or individual personality resides in several human bodies over several lifetimes in order to progress and grow in wisdom and spirituality and work through its karma. Most Wiccans believe in reincarnation. Not to be confused with transmigration, in which a spirit inhabits the body of a human, animal, or insect over successive lifetimes—specifically a Hindu concept. The goal of reincarnation is to progress spiritually with each successive lifetime and eventually re-merge with God or the great creative force. Reincarnation is a concept shared by many religions including Buddhism, Hinduism, Gnosticism, and others.

religion—From Latin *religio* (re-linking). A body of expressions of sacred myths, metaphors, observances, and practices in a given cultural context designed to connect individuals with their conception of the Divine. Some Wiccan Traditions are solely a religious tradition, and do not practice any form of magick. Religion in Wicca is the worship of the Goddess and God (in whatever form or guise) and the celebration of the Sabbats and Esbats and the Turning of the Wheel. Also included are the various life passages and other ceremonies and beliefs one expects of a religion. Divination, viewed as a type of magick, is usually considered acceptable for members of religious-only traditions. Actual spellworkings are considered magick and are not done by strictly religious Traditions. Wicca is a recognized religion in the United States and Canada, and there are recognized active Wiccan churches and Wiccan clergy throughout North America.

remote viewing—Seeing or sensing objects or people at a distant location, through clairvoyance, astral travel, or other means. Remote viewing has been practiced since the eighteenth century, and people can be trained to remotely view people and places, although they have not demonstrated any other psychic abilities. Scientific studies of remote viewing and remote sensing have yielded some positive results.

retrocognition—Knowing about an event after it has happened, although the person has no known way of receiving the information.

rhabdomancy—1) Divination using an arrow and target. A number of answers are attached to a target and the Priest shoots an arrow at the target. The answer pierced by the arrow is the correct one. Pinning the tail on the donkey could be seen as a modern corruption of this divination technique. 2) Divination using a wand, it may have been used as a confirmation of another system. It eventually developed into dowsing.

rhapsodomancy—See bibliomancy.

right-brain function—Intuitive, image forming, synthesizing, sometimes called "feminine" functions that generally belong to the right hemisphere of the brain, which controls the left side of the body. Generally one uses both left- and right-brain functions to successfully practice magick.

right-hand path—Followed by those who work toward construction, persuasion, and good. In Oriental disciplines the right-hand path is a spiritual path characterized by meditation, renunciation, and fasting. The left-hand path is a physical path toward enlightenment, as in martial arts, tantra, Tai Chi, and other physical disciplines that also have a spiritual component. In modern occultism following the right-hand path is considered to be "good" and the left-hand path is "bad." The terms originated in the Western tradition through medieval Ceremonial Magick and Kabbalism. Modern usage can imply judgment, but with more widespread knowledge of Oriental techniques there is a better awareness of the physical versus spiritual distinction.

ring—A ring has had mystical significance since prehistoric times because it symbolizes the sacred Circle. It is considered a powerful amulet, and when set with a stone or engraved with words it becomes more powerful. In Greek mythology, Zeus reportedly invented the ring as a means of perpetual penance for Prometheus after he was released from his torment. Other cultures have invested the ring with the attributes of divinity, sovereignty, strength, power, unity, and protection. Worn on certain fingers, it adds additional meaning. The Romans used a ring as the symbol of citizenship.

rite—A ceremonial act or series of acts.

ritual—A magickal or Wiccan celebration, rite, or Working. Ritual is a general term that includes most types of Circles and Workings. Ritual can also specifically refer to a religious rite or celebration.

ritual abuse—Physical, sexual, or emotional abuse perpetuated in connection with specific and systematic use of symbols, ceremonies, or in a religious context. Generational Satanism associated with ritual abuse and discovered through recovered memories of victims is a controversial subject and has been shown by some investigators to be false and created by some members of the psychotherapeutical community (see *Satanic Panic*, 1993, by Jeffrey S. Victor).

However, there are still types of ritual abuse that can be encountered by a person in connection with Wiccan and Pagan groups. The most common ritual abuse encountered is a sexual relationship at the insistence of a teacher between a teacher and a potential student or Initiate. Ethical teachers will not engage in this practice. Some consider scourging (ritual flagellation) a form of ritual abuse, others feel it is merely another way to raise power.

Generally any sort of activity that can be construed as harmful when imposed upon an unknowing, unwilling, or unaware subject in a religious or magickal context is considered ritual abuse. The term is also used to describe those who use a religious context to achieve dominance and power over others. Can be characterized by isolation, fear and intimidation, emotional dependence, financial or labor demands, threats, or curses for those who wish to leave the religious group and other undesirable practices.

ritual garb—Special clothing worn only during rituals. Generally a part of the preparation for a ritual is to change into ritual garb (or disrobe if you work skyclad) as a part of preparing yourself mentally, emotionally, and psychically for the entrance into the magickal world. Traditionally ritual garb is made of natural fabrics, silk being the most desirable, though cotton, linen, and wool are also used. What form the ritual garb takes varies widely, from a hooded robe, to specially made garments, to specially purchased clothing worn either altered or unaltered. Different Traditions require various types of ritual garb as well as colors, etc. Generally ritual garb is cleansed, blessed, and consecrated before use, and stored separately from other clothing. Some prefer the all black hooded robes, but there is a wide variety of ritual garb encountered in the greater Wiccan Community.

Full Ritual Garb

Rosicrucians, Order of the Rosy Cross—A worldwide esoteric society, their symbol is a rose with a cross superimposed on it. The legendary founder of the order is Christian Rosenkreutz, reportedly born in 1378, but who is thought to be an allegorical figure. The society is reported to have been founded in medieval times, but three anonymous pamphlets—*Fama Fraternitatis* (Account of the Brotherhood, 1614); *The Confessio Fraternitatis* (Confession of the Brotherhood, 1615); and *The Third Chemical Wedding of Christian Rosenkreutz* (1616)—gave the group publicity and impetus. Scholars believe these pamphlets were written by the German Lutheran pastor, Johan Valentin Andreae (1586–1654), to promote Protestant ethics and criticize the Pope. In the eighteenth century, publications announced the existence of The Brothers of the Rosy Cross, and groups in Russia, Poland, and Germany claimed Rosicrucian origins. In 1694 the first Rosicrucian Society in the United States was founded in Pennsylvania. In 1909 Harvey Spencer Lewis founded The Ancient Mystical Order Rosae Crucis (AMORC); its present headquarters is in San Jose, California.

The goal of the Rosicrucians is to develop mankind's highest potentials and psychic powers. The Rosicrucians were responsible for keeping much esoteric lore alive and disseminating it in the United States during the early twentieth century. Their lessons and books are still widely available, although their style is somewhat outdated. The Rosicrucian lore is strongly Christian but with esoteric and mystical elements.

rune—1) A letter of the alphabet of the Norse and Germanic (Teutonic) cultures as described in the Eddas, perhaps descended from Etruscan, perhaps sharing a common origin with Etruscan. The Futhark is the name for the entire runic alphabet (derived from the first six letters). Many different versions of the runic alphabets were used in Northern Europe at various times and places from classical times through the Middle Ages. Originally the runes were used for writing, magick, and divination. Several different alphabets have existed, the most familiar is the twenty-four character Eldar Futhark. The use of runes died out in the fifteenth century with the rise of Christianity and the decline of Pagan beliefs and practices. German occultists revived the runes in the late nineteenth century, and their studies were later incorporated by the Nazis, who used runic symbols, among them the swastika and symbol for the SS. At present the runes are used for magick and divination, and as a magickal alphabet that is phonetic in nature. 2) A modern divinatory system loosely based upon the Futhark. 3) A magickal song or chant as in the "Witches' Rune." The word "run" (pronounced "roon") means secret or mystery in Old Norse, Old English, Irish, and Scottish Gaelic.

runestones—Magickally charged stones marked with letters of a runic alphabet and used for divination, known as casting the runes.

S

Sabbat—From Hebrew *shabbath*, rest. 1) One of the eight major solar holidays of the year. The eight Sabbats are Imbolc (Immilch, Oimelc, Uimelc, Candlemas, Bride, Brigid, Brigantia, Lady Day, Feile Bhride)—February 1 or 2 (astrologically Sun at 15° Aquarius); Oestarra (Spring Equinox, Eostre, Eostar, Alban Eiler)—March 21 (astrologically Sun at 0° Aries); Beltane (Bealtain, Beltain, May Eve, Walpurgisnacht, May Day, Cetshamhain)—May 1 (astrologically Sun at 15° Taurus); Midsummer (Litha, Summer Solstice, Alban Heruin)—June 21 (astrologically Sun at 0° Cancer); Lughnasadh (Lammas)—August 1 (astrologically Sun at 15° Leo); Mabon (Harvest Home, Fall Equinox, Alban Elved)—September 22 (astrologically Sun at 0° Libra); Samhain (Hallowmas, All Hallow's Eve, Halloween, Calan Gaef, Nos Galan-Gaeof, and colloquially Witches' New Year)—October 31 (astrologically Sun at 15° Scorpio); Yule (Winter Solstice, Alban Arthuan)—December 21 (astrologically Sun at 0° Capricorn). 2) Generally a celebration of a religious or spiritual nature.

Sabbat, witches—In written information about the Inquisition a witches' Sabbat is described as a weekly meeting of witches who honored Satan, had a feast and orgy, and usually engaged in obscene or forbidden sexual practices. In these reports Satan would appear in the form of a black goat to preside over the festivities, and might have intercourse with attendants (thereby adding bestiality to the festivities). The food presented at the feast was usually described as vile-smelling and tasting, and sex with demons was described as icy and painful. These descriptions were extracted under torture through the prompting of Inquisitors, so it is more than likely that these practices only existed in the minds of the Inquisitors.

sacrament—A thing that is inherently holy; an item or act. Sacramental rites include seining (baby blessing), rites of passage, communion, marriage, purification, confession, and rites of the dead. Sacramental substances include wine and bread, blessed and shared at a sacred rite.

sacred—Something relating to or deriving from Divinity.

Sacred Space—Holy ground within a Circle. Can be permanent as in a building or outdoors, or temporary, lasting only as long as the Circle is up. Wiccans create Sacred Space each time they put up a Circle, hence Wiccans do not require the permanent buildings other religions use as places of worship. This can be difficult for non-Pagans to understand, especially those of most organized religions who have permanent places of worship. When a Circle is up, Wiccans consider that area to be as holy and sacrosanct as a church, no matter where it is, indoors or outdoors, owned by the group or rented. Because there is no permanent structure, a person might accidentally invade a Sacred Space and disrupt a ritual, which can cause acrimony and misunderstanding.

sacrifice—An offering for the Gods. Something that is offered up in propitiation or homage to a Deity, and can be a person, animal, or object. Some rituals require that a portion of the wine and cakes or the feast be set aside "for the Gods." Sometimes an action or task is considered a sacrifice of time or energy. Sometimes a person donates money or goods as a form of sacrifice. Wicca does not require or condone any form of live sacrifice of animals or humans.

salamander—A Fire elemental.

salt—Used as a symbol of the element Earth. Used for cleansing and protection. In water it becomes a cleansing fluid. Sprinkled in an unbroken ring around something malign it can seal that thing from influencing anything outside the Circle. Salt can also be used to define a Sacred Space.

Samhain—May be derived from Gaelic *samhaim*, to quiet down, become silent. The Sabbat celebrated on October 31. Associated with the feast of the dead, the veils between the worlds are thin on this day. Can be the day when one contacts the dead. This is colloquially known as the Witches' New Year. A holiday that celebrates death and rebirth, it can be a celebration of the death and/or funeral of the God.

Satan—Hebrew, adversary. In Hebrew mythology the entity who was in charge of testing man's relationship with God. Related to the Egyptian Set and Roman Saturn, both harvest Gods. During the Middle Ages the name became equated with the Devil, the archenemy of the Christian God and ruler of the Christian under-world, Hell. Also seen as a "fallen angel" who rebelled against Jehovah and was condemned to rule in Hell as punishment for his rebellion. Satan in its present usage is a Christian creation, and not directly applicable to Wicca, since Wicca is not a Christian religion.

Satanism—Worship of Satan. It developed through many mechanisms: propaganda; the Inquisition; disaffected intellectuals who wished to parody Christianity; those who wanted to live outside society; a means to shock respectable people, etc. It is a mirror image and the dark side of Christianity but essentially shares a similar world-view, that of the mythology and history of Christianity.

In essence a person who practices Satanism has chosen to support evil rather than good as the means of creation, a concept that is encountered in the Christian mythos.

Early Gnostic forms of Christianity were eventually declared heretical and satanic by orthodox Christianity. Medieval dualistic Christian cults, like the Bogomils and Albigensians, were considered satanic. Some asserted that any sect or group that was declared heretical was *de facto* satanic, as it was counter to the orthodox Christianity of the time.

Satanism became a convenient label to use against any unpopular or oppositional group in religio-political arenas, for example, the Templars. In the eighteenth century, the Hell Fire Club was a pseudo-satanic group of English nobles who were more interested in orgies and sexual license than in the worship of Satan. Their escapades were disguised as a sort of reverse monastic order in which licentiousness and debauchery reigned.

In the twentieth century, several satanic groups have arisen from several diverse sources. The most widely known is The Church of Satan founded in 1965 by Anton Szandor LaVey in San

Francisco, through his books, the *Satanic Bible*, and others. According to some, several satanic cults operated in the inner circles of the Nazi party in Germany and elsewhere before and during W.W.II (and perhaps since). The Temple of Set founded in 1983 by Michael Aquino is a splinter group of LaVey's Church of Satan. The Church of Satanic Liberation founded by Paul Valentine, as well as The Church of Satan and The Temple of Set, is a legal religious entity in the United States.

Luciferians worship Lucifer (Greek "light bringer") as a Deity and share some similarities in philosophy with Satanists, though they tend to stay away from the elaborate trappings of other forms of satanic worship. Modern satanic philosophy varies with each group, but most share a doctrine of enlightened self-interest, combined with social Darwinism. Whatever feels good is okay, and those who are strong enough to make their own way and not be subservient or intimidated by others are worthy as equals. One's birthday is held to be a sacred holiday.

Many fundamentalist Christian groups teach that any religious path (including Wicca) that is not specifically Christian (or Jewish) is by definition satanic, as it is not of God and Jesus.

There is a great deal of confusion about Satanism and Wicca, with many in the general public erroneously thinking that all Wiccans are satanic, and therefore worshippers of Satan. Wiccans maintain that since Satan is a Christian construct, he has nothing to do with Wicca, which is not Christian or anti-Christian.

In North America, the inverted pentagram has been adopted by various satanic groups as their religious symbol. In Europe and especially Britain, Satanists use an inverted cross as their religious symbol. Modern Satanists refer to their groups as Grottos or Pylons, not covens.

Inverted Pentagram and Inverted Cross

scapulomancy, spealomancy—1) Divination using the markings on the shoulder bone of an animal, especially a sheep, sometimes heated over a fire. 2) Divination using a shoulder bone or tortoise shell. One heats a poker and then presses it into the bone or shell and interprets the resulting cracks. Practiced widely in ancient China, the I Ching supposedly descended from this method of divination, where the yin and yang lines replaced the cracks.

scarpomancy—Divination of character by examination of a person's old shoes. A modern method of divination.

sciomancy—Divination through the observation of shadows. One could observe the shadow of a living person, or call back the "shadow" or shade of a person who died, and question it about future events. The latter is a form of necromancy. Since an attack on one's shadow was believed to be able to cause death or illness by injury to the soul, this could also be considered a form of black magick.

scion—An elder in CAW.

scourge—A ritual whip that symbolizes firmness, in contrast to the wand that symbolizes mercy. Generally the scourge has a handle and multiple thongs, usually of silk. It may be used as a symbol only or as an actual tool. Scourging is a technique used to excite and stimulate awareness, not to injure or cause pain.

scourging—Ritual flagellation. Some Wiccan Traditions use scourging as a means of inducing altered states of consciousness. Light scourging (no bruising or breaking of the skin) can produce altered states of consciousness and it releases endorphins. Eclectic Wiccans have, for the most part, dropped scourging as a part of their rites. It is still a practice within some Wicca Traditions, and, if done, is done in private ceremonies. In print "$" is used as a symbol to indicate the scourge, and/or scourging. Bondage and discipline or sado-masochism (BDSM)—being bound and/or engaging in ritual flagellation, by mutual consent, for sexual excitation—is not a magickal, religious, or Wiccan path but an alternative lifestyle choice and should not be confused with the practice of scourging used in some Wiccan Traditions.

scry, scrying—Divination by gazing into an object called a speculum. Objects used can be diverse as a crystal ball, a mirror, a bowl of water, a crystal, fire, a candle flame, smoke or incense, random patterns on a TV screen, a moving stream, or waterfall. One focuses one's awareness on the object and allows the mind to drift (either randomly or concentrating upon something—a question or person) attending to the influences that are "seen" in the object, and then the images are interpreted by the "seer." On occasion, dream imagery figures are considered with the images perceived, but the messages are highly subjective and interpreted by the "seer" using their own experience and judgment. A general term, there are many specific forms of divination that can be considered scrying.

scyphomancy—Divination using a drinking cup. 1) In ancient Egypt a cup was filled to the brim, a question was asked, a God was invoked, and a libation poured to honor them. The answer was then sought in the cup. 2) Small particles of tinsel or some other substance were dropped into a cup of water, and the shapes they made were interpreted. Tea leaf reading derived from this practice.

seance—Derived from Latin and French words for sitting. A gathering presided over by a medium during which the medium contacts the spirit world. The contact with the spirit world is accomplished in a variety of ways. Also, the general gathering of people with the purpose of contacting the spirit world, or a gathering of people to investigate paranormal or psychic phenomena. Seances were referred to as circles in the past because participants—called sitters—sat in a circle and linked hands, believing that the linked circle would increase the effectiveness of the exploration. More of an archaic term. Some nineteenth-century mediums resorted to tricks to simulate spiritual appearances. Because of the air of fraud that surrounded the practice—although there are many genuine mediums—the term is not considered complimentary or desirable. Today the terms sitting, or occasionally reading, have replaced seance.

Seax Wicca—1) A Wiccan Tradition. See Traditions. 2) A magickal alphabet derived from the runes (Futhark) for the use of the Seax Wicca Tradition.

second sight—Colloquial term for psychic abilities, usually clairvoyance or precognition.

secrets—The mystical and hidden truths that are associated with magickal study, in certain groups, the higher levels of Initiation, some metaphysical areas of study (like Kabbalah or tarot). Primarily, there are two schools of thought concerning esoteric secrets: 1) that the secrets are important, confer power and knowledge, and are to be jealously protected at all costs; or 2) that you could announce the secrets on a billboard, for example, and only those who were ready and able to use them properly would pay attention or understand them.

With the proliferation of books about the occult or metaphysical, few esoteric secrets are hidden anymore; however, some secrets are not "hidden truths," so one must be able to discern what is true from what is not. Some Traditions still have secret words of power, which are jealously guarded, and are changed if they are revealed to the uninitiated.

sect—A subdivision of a larger religious group or system. Similar to denomination.

seelie, seelie court—The branch of the faery that is friendly or neutral to humans.

seer—One who can see the hidden, a diviner.

sefira, sefiroth—See Sephira.

selenomancy—Divination using the aspects, phases, and appearances of the Moon.

sensitive—A person who can attune himself or herself to psychic influences. Sensitivity can manifest as psychic abilities, but can also manifest as intuition, second sight, hunches, or having a propensity or attraction to objects, places, or things. People who are sensitive can act as a psychic barometer and should learn shielding to help maintain their psychic equilibrium.

Sephira, plural Sephiroth (sometimes spelled sefira or sefiroth)—One of the ten spheres in the Tree of Life in Kabbalah.

septagram—A seven-pointed star. It can be constructed in two ways. The one with shorter arms symbolizes the seven classical planets in astrology. Both types of septagram are ancient occult symbols.

Septagrams

Serpent Biting Its Tail

serpent—Ancient sacred symbol of the Goddess and/or Great Mother. The serpent shedding its skin was an illustration of reincarnation. Symbol of wisdom.

sex—Wicca is a nature and fertility religion, so sex is considered a sacrament. "All acts of love and pleasure are sacred to the Goddess." The Great Rite is a symbolic sexual act, but some Wiccans do celebrate the Great Rite—sex—in private. There are no orgies at Wiccan rituals. Wiccans condemn any non-consensual sexual act in general and abhor any violent sexual act in particular. Sex with a minor and public casual group sex is prohibited; however, Wiccans are generally liberal concerning sex between consenting adults in a committed partnership. Heterosexuals, homosexuals, and groups of committed people are all found within the Wiccan Community. No reputable Wiccan teacher will require a student to have sex with them as part of receiving a degree. If a teacher and student do fall in love, it is considered proper form to either break off training and get another teacher or wait to start up the romance until the training period is over. Some Traditions require Third Degree Initiates to celebrate the Great Rite in actuality as a part of the Initiation, and if the Third Degree is awarded to couples, partners celebrate privately.

shadow—Psychiatric term for the more negative or unpleasant aspects of one's personality, the more unpleasant or negative aspects of life, or the buried unconscious elements of the human psyche. Wiccans believe you must deal with your shadow to progress and improve yourself. This is an important part of the Great Work and part of the process that leads to Initiation.

shaman, shamanic—1) A person who has a direct ongoing contact with their Gods or spirit guides or both. 2) A tribal priest or priestess who communicates with the inner planes by self-induced trance. 3) A person who practices magick in a style that is reminiscent of Pagan practices. 4) A person who may use drugs or other mind-altering substances in a religious/sacred manner to allow them to open up more quickly to the psychic world. 5) A person who follows Native American spiritual practices. A medicine man or woman. 6) A role in a tribal Pagan culture that combines the roles of healer, religious leader, diviner, magician, teacher, psychopomp, and counselor.

Shamans use altered states of consciousness to produce, guide people through, and control psychic phenomena, and also to travel to and from the spirit realm, generally with spirit guides (or power animals). Wiccans can work shamanically—without Circles, rituals, etc.—but generally the practice of Wicca is not shamanic in nature. There are many similarities between shamanism and Wicca, most notably the use of herbs, incenses, roots, and berries for healing. Today, the term has come to mean one who is an adherent of any religious path and who, through intensive training, can assume the roles traditionally considered to be those of a shaman (see #6 above). It is a description of how a person works, not a specific religion.

sheath—Covering for storage and transport of an edged weapon, usually a sword or dagger (athame). Also a sheath can be used when peace bonding a blade.

shield—A psychic energy barrier that blocks unwanted energies and influences. A thought form or psychic barrier of protection. Can also keep energies in as well as out. Shields are created mentally and magickally and can be around people, places, or objects and usually need attention and work to keep them up. Shields can be temporary or permanent and help block psychic noise.

shrine—A holy place, it can be a created place of worship or a natural place. A shrine can be centered around a sacred relic or natural phenomenon, either *in situ* or brought to that place, or it can be constructed on a site of power or sacred energies. Can also be an alternate term for a home altar, usually focused on sacred pictures, objects, or figures.

sideromancy—Divination practiced by dropping straws on red-hot iron, and interpreting the shapes made as the straw burns, as well as the quality and speed of burning.

sigil—A design that has magickal significance and/or an identifying design for people in a certain group or Tradition. Sacred or magickal symbol. There is no registry or copyright of sigils in the Wiccan Community, but some are acknowledged to "belong" to certain groups and are not infringed upon. A person may adopt a sigil as their own upon attainment of certain degrees in Wicca, depending upon their inclination and Tradition.

silver cord—An astral phenomenon that links the physical body to the astral body and/or soul. When one is out-of-body this silver cord links you to your physical body, and by following it or gathering it up you can return to your body from the astral realm. If the silver cord is severed, death results as the "soul's" tie to the body is severed.

Sky Father—1) The primal consort of the Earth Mother. Greek Ouranos. 2) A generic representation of the God. Most ancient societies have a primal Goddess and God who are essentially Earth Mother and Sky Father. Many Great Goddesses are Earth Goddesses and many Kings of the Gods are Sky Gods. There are a few notable exceptions, but the Earth as feminine and the Sky as masculine is a widespread ancient belief.

skyclad, sky-clad, sky clad—Naked, nude, without clothes (though some do wear jewelry, cords, and other magickal accouterments). Nudity not used in an enticing or lascivious way. 1) Ritual nudity. The Charge of the Goddess includes the phrase "And as a sign that you be truly free, ye shall be naked in your rites."

Some Wiccan groups work skyclad, some do not. Most Initiations involve some skyclad work because it is believed that clothes can interfere with the flow of energy. Used to symbolize rebirth. Sometimes used as a symbol of freedom. Used as a matter of tradition. Also it is believed to have been used in the old times because clothing was a mark of rank and in a Wiccan Circle, all are equal. Legend has it that during the Burning Times witches wore no clothes in Circle, but wore masks, so the parts that were normally hidden were uncovered and the parts usually seen were covered, which ensured anonymity and safety in a Circle. 2) Casual nudity. Many outdoor festivals are clothing optional, and people can wear fewer than normal or no clothes at all. Nudity is viewed differently in Wicca, and the body is celebrated as a thing of beauty, not something to be hidden away. Wiccans tend to consider casual nudity as just another clothing style option, rather than something that is sexual or enticing.

slate writing—A medium for automatic writing popular for use with an audience.

smudge—A bundle of herbs that are burned and used for purification. The most common herb used is sage, however, many other plants can also be used alone or mixed with others to make a smudge. At a large ritual an easy and effective way to ritually cleanse a group of people is either to pass the burning smudge and or smudge participants as they enter the Circle. The composition of a smudge should be disclosed because some plants have a mildly hallucinogenic effect when they are burned and some people can also be allergic to certain plants. A practice adopted from Native Americans, though evidence indicates Native Americans have used the practice for only about a hundred years.

solitaire, solitary—A person who practices Wicca by themselves alone, either by chance or by choice. Most Wiccans begin their practice of Wicca after reading a book. Some Wiccans may choose to "go solitaire," dropping out of a Wiccan Community to practice on their own for a time. A solitary Initiation is an Initiation a person gives themselves upon attainment of various levels of skill and knowledge. Some Traditions recognize solitary Initiations, others do not and require each Initiate go through the course of training mandated by the Tradition.

Solomon—An ancient Hebrew king in the Bible, although also much non-biblical lore exists about this real, but also mythical magical figure. He was said to have used his Seal of Solomon to imprison all the demons. Reputed author of the magical grimoire the *Book or Key of Solomon*. A wise king who was also an accomplished and renowned magician, it is reported that in his later years he turned from the worship of Jehovah to the worship of other Gods at the behest of some of his 1000 wives. Reputed author of the *Song of Solomon*, one book of the Old Testament. There is much occult folklore and legend in both the Middle East and Europe surrounding Solomon. The Seal of Solomon is still considered a potent magickal construct.

Solstice—From Latin *solstitium*, from *sol* (Sun), and *statum* (standing still). Point in the Sun's path when it is at its most southern or northern declination, and the length of day or night is the largest. The Summer Solstice, or North Solstice is around June 21st (astrologically 0° Cancer) and the Winter Solstice or South Solstice is around December 21st (astrologically 0° Capricorn). In the northern hemisphere the Summer Solstice is the longest day, and the Winter Solstice the longest night. These are reversed in the southern hemisphere (as are the seasons). Wiccans celebrate the Solstices as minor Sabbats.

Sons of Light—Name sometimes used to denote those who practice white magick.

sorcerer—A male occult adept, may or may not be bound to Satan in exchange for his knowledge and skill, especially with respect to controlling demons. Sorcerers are said to have a hypnotic gaze and their power is intact as long as their feet are in contact with the ground. A term that is not used often by modern occultists; sometimes used as a derogatory term.

sorcery—Thaumaturgical arts. Sorcery is considered to be a darker type of magickal practice. Sometimes it is used synonymously with necromancy, sometimes used to indicate coercive or unethical magick.

sortilege—Divination by the casting of lots. Includes rhabdomancy, belomancy, and other similar techniques.

soul—The eternal spirit that contains the essential spark of being, and that animates the body. The soul is seen as eternal, the body as mortal. Some believe the soul originated with Divinity and will eventually return to merge with Divinity, after various conditions are met, which differ widely depending upon one's specific religious beliefs. Many Wiccans believe in reincarnation that teaches that a soul evolves through many lives in various bodies and, after experiencing many kinds of lives and cultures, the soul will eventually progress spiritually and re-merge with Divinity and "step off the wheel" of reincarnation.

soul mates, twin souls—Souls that are paired in several incarnations in various relationships in order to work out shared karma. Once the shared karma is resolved, souls no longer need to be paired as soul mates. In present day usage, the term is sometimes used to explain love at first sight or the instant recognition of a person who was formerly a stranger. Also used as a way to describe a deep, intense relationship.

spacey—The condition of being ungrounded and uncentered, not really paying attention.

spatulamancy—Scottish version of scapulomancy.

Spear of Destiny—A book by Trevor Ravenscroft (1973) which put forth the theory that Hitler and the Nazis had obtained the spear which killed Christ, and using its magickal energy were able to gain control of Germany and later most of Europe. That Hitler and many high-ranking Nazis engaged in various magickal rituals and ceremonies is more-or-less accepted by historians, but the exact nature and magickal system/s used is under dispute. This lore ties in with many occult conspiracy theories and is sometimes used by Aryans and Nazis for their own political ends.

specialty (as in Seconds have some specialty)—A person's area of skill or expertise within Wicca. In general, Second Degree Wiccans are expected to have some type of specialty. A specialty can be expertise in a divinatory system, skill at organizing and putting on a festival, skill in arts and crafts, specialized knowledge, ability to work with children, ability to plan and execute large-group rituals, etc. A specialty may or may not relate to a person's job or career, can be a true vocation, or just a hobby.

speculum—An object or construct with a shiny surface used for scrying. Can be as varied as a crystal ball, a shiny polished stone, a mirror, a bowl of water, a lake, or pool.

spell—An interwoven set of mudras, mantras, and mandalas, designed to achieve a magickal purpose. A clearly focused intent that is directed through a ritual raising of energy. Spells can be very simple or extremely complex with many parts. Many spells use text that rhymes, both as a mnemonic device and also to help aid concentration and more easily access the subconscious.

spheres of the planets—In classical cosmology each planet was believed to be attached to an actual sphere. The cosmos was made up of a series of nesting spheres: Earth at the center, then the weather and atmosphere, the Moon, Mercury, Venus, Sun, Mars, Jupiter, Saturn, the fixed stars surrounding all, with God, and the plasma of the Universe (depending on the culture and cosmology).

The fixed stars were usually believed to be "holes" in the farthest sphere with the light of God leaking through.

Each sphere rotated or vibrated at a specific frequency and this produced certain effects, one of which was a musical tone which became the music of the spheres. This concept of nesting spheres was adopted by early Christian cosmology and was built upon by Dante Allegheri in his works *Inferno*, *Purgatorio*, and *Paradiso* (*The Divine Comedy*).

sphondulomancy—Divination using spindles.

spiegelschrift—German, mirror script. Some automatic writing is done in mirror writing to "prove" its authenticity. Also used as a form of cypher to keep secret journals.

spin-off—A ritual in which one leaves the Circle where one has trained to form or join another Circle. See also hive off.

spiral—Ancient Goddess symbol of emergence. Can also symbolize moving inward to a center. Can be used as a maze.

Spiral

Spiral Dance—1) A Wiccan dance utilizing spiral symbolism. Symbolizes the "dance" of life. 2) A book by Starhawk, originally published October 31, 1979, 2nd revised edition 1989, 3rd revised edition 1999.

spirit—A discrete consciousness, it can manifest apart from an obvious physical body. If the spirit is the soul of a dead person, it is usually called a ghost. If it is the soul of a living person, apart from their physical body, it is considered a manifestation of astral projection.

spirit spelling—A form of communicating with spirits by using either a wine glass that is turned over and handwritten letters on a table or a commercial board and planchette. Usually at least two people are required, but can be done solo. The participants concentrate and then speak aloud a question and the spirits guide the indicator to spell out words and communicate messages. Not a recommended method because it can allow entry to discarnate entities, and the information obtained is usually notoriously misleading or wrong. Can also open a person to possible possession, but this is rare.

Spiritualism—A religion based upon the belief in life after death and communication with the "dead" through mediums. Theosophy is a spiritualistic path started in Hydesville, New York, in 1848 by Margaret Fox and her sisters, who were able to produce spirit rappings in answer to questions. The group later moved to Rochester, New

York. The Fox sisters became famous and traveled widely. Many imitators sprang up, and Spiritualism claimed over two million followers by the mid-1850s. Later in life Margaret Fox claimed she had produced the rapping noises by manipulating her joints.

Spiritualism has waxed and waned in popularity, but never died out. Channeling is the modern version of this phenomenon, and some channelers are able to contact extraterrestrials, angels, powerful spiritual beings, and entities from ancient mythical societies, as well as the dead.

spirituality—The feeling of closeness and connection to God (or the Gods) and the practices that help promote this feeling. Spirituality is separate from religion (although it can be experienced through religious practice). Wicca is both a spiritual path and a religion. One can be on a spiritual path or exploring their spirituality and not be religious or an adherent of any specific religion. In modern Wiccan parlance, being spiritual is considered more desirable than being religious.

splanchomancy—An Etruscan method of divination using sacrificial victims, and studying their entrails. A form of anthropomancy.

splodge, splodging—To psychically pollute. To be unshielded and allow your negative energy to impinge on others. To create negative vibes.

spodomancy—Divination by examination of ashes, particularly the ashes of a sacred fire.

sprite—A nature spirit, usually tied to a specific area like a glade or waterfall. A sometimes visible manifestation of an elemental being.

spudomancy—Divination using the cinders from a sacrificial fire.

staff—1) A wooden rod the length of a cane or walking stick or longer. Can be used as a cane or walking stick. Used as a repository of magickal energy and an aid to spellwork. Some think of a staff as a large wand, some feel it is a separate tool. The staff is one of only two common tools which is supposed to touch the ground in normal use (the altar is the other). 2) A wizard's primary magickal implement. It should be the same height as the wizard, and contains,

Person with Staff

directs, and focuses magickal energy. The staff embodies the wizard's personal energy, and usually it may not be used by anyone else.

Steiner, Rudolf—(1861–1925) Austrian philosopher, scientist, artist, and educator, the founder of Anthroposophy, a Christianized version of Theosophy. The Anthroposophical Society was founded in 1912, and has branches throughout the world.

Anthroposophy teaches that humans possess spiritual cognition, or pure thought that functions independently of the senses, and aims for maximum development of this ability. Steiner published over 350 books and articles. His occult philosophy helped inspire many and his accomplishments had many mundane-world effects: his teachings inspired the Waldorf school movement and led to schools for handicapped or maladjusted children; his agricultural methods inspired chemical-free organic farming; he created eurythmy, a form of expressive movement to music and speech; he formulated guidelines on holistic medicine and pharmacology that are still widely respected. He also wrote articles about Atlantis and Lemuria as well as on a wide range of other occult topics.

stirring the paint—A ritual step, after calling the quarters and part of binding the Circle, in which the High Priest uses the wand to mix the energies of the quarters and seal the Circle. Unstirring is the opposite function performed as part of taking down the Circle, before dismissing the quarters. Not a universal Wiccan practice, it was developed by Paul Tuitéan in the 1980s and is used in Eclectic Circles in the Midwest.

stichomancy, stoichomancy, stolcheomancy—See bibliomancy.

stolisomancy—Divination by observation of a person's manner of dress.

Strega—Italian or Sicilian witch. There are several authentic works detailing the Italian and Sicilian "Wiccan" Traditions and the practitioners call themselves Strega. Some Strega do not feel they are a Wiccan Tradition, but rather that Wicca is a variation of Strega-like spirituality.

student—One who is learning about Wicca, the Craft, magick, or any of the many assorted disciplines associated with occult or metaphysical studies. Not necessarily a newbie, one can be a practitioner of the Craft for many years, decide to learn something new, and become a student of someone who is expert in that discipline. The role of student requires that the person will dedicate a certain amount of time and energy for a length of time—specific or open-ended—to learning what the teacher has to teach. The student will make the effort to be on time, ready to learn, and do the work and assignments. The student also acknowledges that in the specific subject being studied, the teacher is the master, and will abide by their rules and be respectful of their expertise.

student stealing—A practice that is considered unethical in which a teacher attempts to entice students of another teacher to leave that teacher and study with them. It is considered cowardly and underhanded. Most reputable teachers will not take another teacher's student—even if that student is dissatisfied with the original teacher—unless the original teacher-student bond has been formally dissolved.

Summerland, Summerlands—A spiritualist term adopted by Wiccans. A place on the astral plane where Wiccans go after death. "We will meet again in the Summerland" means we will be together again after we have died. It is viewed as a place of eternal Summer, a pastoral place with woods, parks, and gardens, etc. It can also be a place where souls rest between incarnations and assimilate what they have learned and decide where to go next. A common but not universal Wiccan belief.

Summoner—1) Usually a male person in a ritual who helps the High Priest. Also a coven office. Sometimes a High Priest in training. The Summoner helps organize, and helps maintain order. May issue the challenge upon entering the Circle. During a ritual the Summoner may hold a reading candle, hold scripts, keep charge of the ritual sword until it is needed for use, and other duties necessary during a ritual. The actual duties of the office vary from Tradition to Tradition and coven to coven. May be a permanent or temporary appointment. 2) A.k.a., Man in Black or Black Man—In ancient times covens were notified of the time and place of the Grand Covens or Grand Councils by the Man in Black or the Black Man who was also a Summoner, who went from group to group informing each High Priestess of the gathering. If a person was drummed out of a coven for outing or other offenses, the Man in Black would also go to each High Priestess and inform her of the person, the crime, and the action taken, so that person couldn't find refuge in any group affiliated with the aggrieved group. The Man in Black performed his duties in disguise so none but the originating High Priestess knew his identity. A position of immense trust, because only he and the originating High Priestess knew about other groups, their location, and their High Priestesses.

sunwards, sunwise—See deosil.

Sun Wheel—The eight-spoked wheel. Symbolizes the Wheel of the Year, can also be depicted with the eight Sabbats drawn on it. An ancient symbol also depicting the Gods, gaining wisdom through life and renewal.

supernatural—A term describing those entities, energies, etc., that exist above, beyond, or outside of nature. To mundanes, psychic phenomena are "supernatural."

superstition—Acts or beliefs that defy ordinary logic; frivolous, trivial, and irrational. Any spiritual, religious, or philosophical beliefs outside one's personal world-view.

Swedenborg, Emmanuel—(1688–1772) Founder of the Swedenborgian movement. Swedenborg was a Swedish scientist, theosophist, and mystic. He was a scientific theorist and inventor, and wrote several scientific works. He was also a scientific visionary, anticipating technological and scientific advancements by more than a century.

In 1745 Swedenborg experienced a mystic illumination and claimed to have glimpsed a spiritual world that directly underlays the natural sphere. He later had dreams, ecstatic visions, and trances in which he claimed to have communicated with Jesus Christ and God. The vision he received concerning the order of the Universe was radically different from teachings of the Christian Church. He resigned his job to devote himself to transcribing and publishing his visions and revelations. He proposed an approach to spiritual reality and God or Christ through material nature, which was contrary to the usual mystic's rejection of the material world in favor of the spiritual.

Swedenborg's brand of mysticism has been described as an intellectual and scientific view of spirituality and God. Much of contemporary angelology can be traced directly to Swedenborg's works and ideas. His ideas gained popularity through his writings and Swedenborgian societies, as well as his New Church. In the nineteenth century, Swedenborgian ideas and beliefs were incorporated into Spiritualism and disseminated in the works of William Blake, Samuel Taylor Coleridge, and Henry James. Johnny Appleseed, whose legend is based on the life of a real person, was a Swedenborgian, and disseminated Swedenborg's ideas as well as apple seeds.

sword—An edged blade longer than a dagger, usually greater than fourteen inches, used as a ceremonial weapon to defend the Circle from unwanted influences. Many groups have a group sword. It is used like a very large athame. It is also used for large rituals in place of an athame so all can see it and help maintain the group mind focus. A group's sword can also be a symbol of the group itself. Symbolizes Air or Fire, depending upon the Tradition. The Key of Solomon describes how a magical sword is to be made and inscribed, which may or may not be followed by any particular group or Tradition.

Magickal Sword

sychomancy—Divination using leaves. 1) Divination by writing names, questions, or sayings on leaves and waiting for the leaves to dry out. The faster the leaves dried, the worse was the omen. Originally fig leaves were used. 2) A more modern version used ivy leaves that were placed in water for five days. If after that time the leaves were fresh and green, the person named on the leaf would have good health; if spotted or darkened, illness and/or misfortune would be in proportion to the number of spots or dark areas.

sylph—An Air elemental.

sympathetic magick—Magick by association or imitation. The laws of sympathetic magick state that the effect resembles the cause, and that which is done in the microcosm is reflected in the macrocosm. Using a poppet to symbolize a person is a form of sympathetic magick.

synchronicity—Simultaneous occurrence, meaningful coincidence. Used to explain the effectiveness of magick. Things happening at the same time are somehow connected and mutually influence each other—a Jungian principle.

synergy—The combined effect of several qualities or actions or events such that the whole is greater than the sum of its parts. A synthesis in which new properties emerge that were not contained in any of the original components.

T

table lifting—A form of levitation exhibited by a medium as proof of spiritual activity. May be accomplished with or without the medium's fingers touching the table. The table may rise off the floor, tilt, and/or rotate. Since this can be faked, it is often viewed with great skepticism. May be performed by a person in or out of trance and in or apart from a seance.

table tapping—A method of communication between a medium and the spirit world in which spirits communicate by tapping on a table. The process is as follows: a group of people hold hands, the medium enters a trance state and makes the connection to the spirit world. Usually these techniques are suspect because often unscrupulous mediums had elaborate mechanisms to rig their tables and produce the tapping sounds.

taboo—From the Polynesian, kapu, tabu. Something that is socially proscribed, dangerous, or forbidden. A taboo may be magickal, or a matter of taste or morality. If supernatural, a taboo is imposed either to protect society from forbidden and dangerous practices or to protect sacred and/or secret teachings or practices. Sometimes colloquially synonymous with superstition. In modern Wicca and occultism there are many taboos, which can vary widely from one group and/or Tradition to another. Occasionally used to make a group exclusive. Sometimes used to differentiate groups as in one group practicing ritual scourging and another forbidding or at least discouraging it.

talent—A natural ability or skill that is expressed at levels above average. Sometimes used to denote psychic ability.

talisman—A manufactured amulet or mandala carried on one's person. Generally designed and constructed for one person with a specific purpose. Many grimoires devote much space to the making and charging or consecration of talismans.

tantra—A spiritual practice that utilizes techniques for direction and control of sexual energy. Can be used in a magickal context. In general tantra is a discipline studied to learn to control and harness the energy raised by sexual acts and used to change oneself or the world at large, not a discipline used to achieve greater sexual satisfaction and intensify orgasms; often actual orgasm is turned inward with physical techniques and the energy redirected for outer purposes.

tarot/tarot cards/tarot deck—A deck of cards used for divination, the tarot deck contains seventy-eight cards consisting of four suits of fourteen cards each (the fifty-six Minor Arcana in the suits of wands, cups, swords, and pentacles, numbered ace to ten with four court cards, Page, Knight, Queen, and King) and twenty-two extra cards called trumps (the Major Arcana, individually named and numbered one to twenty-one with the Fool Major Arcana card left unnumbered or numbered zero). The cards are usually individually illustrated and contain a vast amount of arcane symbolism. Considered by some to contain the sum total of all occult knowledge.

Tarot and modern playing cards are descended from a common ancestor, but which came first, the playing cards or the divinatory cards, is controversial. The earliest known examples of tarot cards date from the thirteenth century. Modern playing cards evolved from the full tarot deck and now consist of four suits of thirteen cards each (wands became clubs, cups became hearts, swords became spades, pentacles became diamonds, and the knight was eliminated from each suit) and an extra wild card or Joker added (derived from the Fool, the only trump to survive the change). There are currently dozens of tarot decks available. The term tarot generally refers to any type of deck of cards used for divination, including Kabbalah Cards, Mah Jong Cards, I Ching Cards, Shamanic Animal Guide Cards, and many other variations of divinatory card systems that are not strictly tarot.

tassel—Amulets with a tassel or fringe are said to protect against the evil eye or discarnate spirits. Most worry beads have a tassel, and they help protect the user when they are used.

tasseomancy, tasseography—Tea leaf reading. The tea is drunk until only the dregs or used leaves are left in a little liquid. One thinks of a question while swirling the cup and upends the cup into the saucer. The cup is allowed a few moments to drain, is lifted, and the leaves remaining in the cup are inspected for pictures or shapes, and the shapes are interpreted.

tattoo—1) Permanent design inscribed into the skin with needles and some sort of dye or ink. A practice that has been used since prehistoric times. Can be a symbol of Initiation, attainment, or magick. 2) A patterned drum beat, or coordinated drumming designed to inspire and/or excite.

tattooing—Many Wiccan Traditions require that upon attainment of Third Degree (or at each degree) the Initiate get a tattoo on their body as a mark of attainment. What the design is and where it is to be placed varies widely. Some Traditions require "secret marks"—tattoos hidden on parts of the body that will escape casual sight; others require some permanent marking and leave the design, size, and placement up to the Initiate. Some Traditions will accept a piercing or scarification as a substitute for a tattoo. Body art is celebrated in the Wiccan Community, though it is usually an individual choice whether or not to have a tattoo.

teacher—A person who has knowledge and expertise in a subject area and is willing to impart that knowledge or those skills to others—their students. The teacher-student relationship is considered sacred, and there are conventions that must be observed (according to many Traditions) in order for the relationship to be rewarding and successful for all parties.

The teacher's responsibility is to be fair and understanding of the student(s) and help them learn in the best way possible for each student. The teacher is obligated to present the material in a way that imparts knowledge without condescension and without making the student feel inferior. The teacher must be prepared to help motivate the student when interest flags and make sure the student does their share of the work, by using stern lectures if necessary. The teacher is in a position of authority and must be careful not to abuse that authority—especially in the area of sexual and/or romantic relationships. Many Traditions have strict rules forbidding sexual or romantic contact between teachers and students. If one member of a committed couple wants to learn, and the other member can teach, it is still mandated that the potential student find another teacher, and not take training from their significant other. A teacher is under no obligation to give degrees or elevations, but they are responsible for the student if the student is studying for a First Degree (and some mandate after that First Degree—until the student gets a Second Degree and is then answerable only to themselves). Teaching is a sacred task and duty, and is also a source of great joy and learning for the teacher.

Teaching is usually done in small groups—a teacher can have just one student, or have six (or more)—but rarely is Wicca taught in a classroom setting with one teacher for ten (or more) students. Wiccan training is very intensive and personalized, two or three to one is the usual ratio of students to teachers. And if a person is learning some specialized knowledge, the relationship might be more like an apprenticeship, rather than a classical classroom learning experience. A teacher can have several students at any time, each learning different things and at varying levels of experience.

telekinesis—See psychokinesis.

telepathy—Mind-to-mind direct communication without verbal or visual cues. Can be done over short or long distances.

teleportation, TP—Instantaneous movement from one place to another. Can be done by a person or a person can teleport an object. This is the rarest of the psychic abilities, and there are few, if any, substantiated cases of teleportation.

Templars, Knights Templar, Knights of the Order of the Temple of Jerusalem—A medieval religious order of warrior knights established in 1118 by Hugh dePayens, whose original mission was to protect pilgrims on crusade, and help regain the Holy Land for Christendom. In 1128 Pope Honorius II officially recognized the Templars as a separate Order and conferred upon them unprecedented autonomy: they were responsible only to the Pope, not to any secular rulers; were exempt from local taxes and judicial authority; and were solely responsible for clerical appointments. After 1291, and the fall of Palestine to the Muslims, the Templars withdrew to Europe and their main activity turned to money-lending.

During their existence they amassed vast wealth, and by the fourteenth century their wealth and power rivaled that of Rome. King Phillip IV (the Fair) of France together with Pope Clement V (in Avignon) conspired to capture and kill most of the Templars and split their wealth and holdings. This secret plan was executed throughout France and France's possessions on Friday October 13, 1307, which is the origin of the present day belief in the unlucky nature of Friday the 13th. Similar attacks were mounted against the order in Spain and England. The Templars were charged with abandoning Christianity, idolatry, sacrilege, and compulsory sodomy as well as witchcraft, blasphemy, Satanism, and committing a variety of other depraved and evil religious and magickal practices, were declared heretics, excommunicated en masse and separately, and the order dissolved in 1312. The Grand Master of the Templars Jacques deMolay was imprisoned, repeatedly tortured, and eventually burned at the stake in 1314. Those Templars who managed to escape either went into hiding or were eventually captured and either recanted or were tortured for information about their legendary hidden wealth.

Supposedly the Templars had also amassed a vast repository of magickal and spiritual lore and practices that was used for beneficial purposes, especially healing. Many magickal practices were believed to have been saved by those few Templars who escaped. Masonic lore states that surviving Templars banded together in Scotland (which was under interdict and therefore did not recognize the excommunications) and eventually established the basic tenets of Masonry, which was based upon their "secret" spiritual and possibly magickal teachings. Rosicrucian lore states that escaping Templars lent their knowledge and helped found Rosicrucianism.

temple—1) Ritual meeting place of a coven that is used for no other purpose. It is not necessary to have a temple since a Circle can be cast anywhere. 2) A consecrated ritual meeting place for a magickal group that is used for no other purpose other than magick. Ceremonial Magicians find a permanent temple quite desirable for their Workings, as the magickal energy builds up over time with each Working. 3) An organization within a specific Tradition that includes two or more groups (or Circles), usually a coven (an outer circle or court), and a grove (an inner circle or court). Generally the coven is more open to the public and the grove is for more serious students and Initiates.

Temple of Set—Founded in 1983 by Michael Aquino as a splinter group from LaVey's Church of Satan. Incorporates materials which are satanic, Neo-Nazi, Norse, and strongly self-deterministic, it is more intellectual and studious than the Church of Satan. Aquino was a high ranking officer in the United States Army when he founded the Temple of Set, and managed to have it (as well as the Church of Satan) included in the *Army Chaplain's Manual* as a recognized religion. Aquino has since retired from the Army, but the Temple of Set continues.

Ten thousand years of the Goddess—A popular conception in Pagan circles that Goddess worship emerged around 10,000 BCE or alternatively 10,000 years ago, roughly 8,000 BCE. It is believed that the current time of patriarchal worship and societal dominance is only a phase in the Goddess' cycle, and soon (the time varies widely among adherents) She will re-emerge to again take Her rightful place as Great Goddess. It is believed that the Goddess led humankind into agriculture and civilization and most ancient societies credited the Goddess with the gifts of letters and writing. This conception also has adherents who date time with an extra digit, 1999 becoming 11999, adding the extra 10,000 years of the existence of Goddess worship. Also the extra digit reminds people that civilization and religion have existed longer that the 2,000+ years with which we number our calendars.

tephramancy, tephromancy—Divination using the ashes of a sacred fire, sometimes by writing in ashes. Similar to spodomancy.

tetragrammaton—A four-letter name of God in Hebrew. INRI, YHVH, and others are all tetragrammatons. Most are acronyms for longer prayers to the glory of God. Used to invoke angels, Watchtowers, banish evil, and other magickal purposes. Used in Ceremonial Magick and Kabbalah.

thaumaturgy—The performance of miracles, specifically by magick. The use of magick to effect changes in outer reality, as opposed to magick performed for changes within the self.

thealogy—Intellectual speculations concerning the Goddess and Her relations to the world in general and humans in particular.

Theban—A magickal alphabet used by the Golden Dawn and perpetuated by others.

theology—Intellectual speculations concerning God and His relations to the world in general and humans in particular.

theomancy—1) Study of the sacred writings, a branch of Kabbalah. If the Kabbalah is mastered, the scholar, through theomancy, has power over angels and demons, the ability to see into the future, and the ability to perform miracles. 2) A study of sacred writings for hidden messages contained therein, encoded or by other secret means. 3) Divination through direct appeal to a divinely inspired oracle. Special chants and formulae were employed for making the appeal.

Theosophy—Derived from Greek *theos* (God) and *sophia* (wisdom). Term means wisdom of or about God. 1) Generally used to refer to one or several groups espousing various occult and/or mystical philosophies, often pantheistic in nature. Theosophy is loosely derived from Hermeticism, and is based upon various hidden spiritual/religious traditions passed down in succession from the ancients, and/or revealed to more modern mystics. Theosophy is thought to provide a key to nature and humanity's place in the Universe. 2) The Theosophical Society, founded in 1875 in New York City by Madame Helena Blavatsky and Colonel Henry Steel Olcott. The Theosophical Society combined elements of Theosophy, Spiritualism, Hinduism, and other occult and mystical paths. Three fundamental beliefs underlie the doctrines of Theosophy: 1) That there is an omnipresent, boundless, and immutable principle that transcends human understanding, which has been identified as God in various human cultures; 2) the law of periodicity as found in nature and recorded in science is universal and applies in many contexts—morning, noon, night, and then morning, birth, life, death, and rebirth, and reincarnation governed by the laws of karma; 3) all souls originated from and are still attached to the universal Oversoul, so that brotherhood is a fact of nature and reincarnation is a path for all souls to evolve and eventually re-merge with the Oversoul. Buddha, Jesus, the mahatmas are perfected individuals and universal beings.

After the death of Madame Blavatsky in 1891, there was a battle for leadership of the Theosophical Society. Annie Besant emerged as leader in Europe and Asia, and W.Q. Judge led a splinter group in the United States. The Society flourished under Besant and, in 1911, she presented a young Indian, Jiddu Krishnamurti, as a World Teacher. She founded the Order of the Star around Krishnamurti, which provoked Rudolf Steiner, a prominent member, to leave and later found his own Anthroposophical Society along with a number of followers. There are various groups that trace their roots to Theosophy, and are still active around the world.

theriomancy—Divination through messages relayed by imaginary animals such as a salamander playing in a fire, or a sea serpent riding a wave.

theurgy—The use of magick to effect changes in inner reality, i.e., within the self. Contrast with thaumaturgy which uses magick to change outer reality. Magick used to accomplish the Great Work.

third eye—A colloquial term for the chakra centered in the middle of the forehead, usually the sixth chakra. It is a personal energy point usually considered the center of one's consciousness or soul. Meditative techniques can be used to open the third eye, which can endow a person with

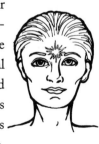

Third Eye

psychic abilities. It can be used to "see" psychic energies, auras, and other psychic phenomena not generally perceptible by average people. Sometimes depicted in art, it does not represent an extra eye, but is meant to represent spiritual enlightenment.

thurible—From Latin *thuribulum* (censer). A consecrated ritual incense burner.

tiromancy, tyromancy—Divination by observation of the process of cheese making from coagulation to final product. With pasteurization and automation this system of divination is not often practiced successfully.

totem—A plant or animal that has an ancestral relationship or affinity to a tribe, clan, family, or individual. Also an item that depicts such an entity.

touch—Energy can be exchanged through touch. Laying on of hands is a form of psychic healing using touch. Some Wiccans and sensitives will not touch another person without express permission in order to protect themselves, the other person, or both. Unwilling exchange of energy through touch is considered a form of psychic attack.

toxic prayer—Prayer that is unpleasant or for ends that the target of the prayer has not agreed to. For example, praying for the salvation of someone who does not wish to be saved, or praying for misfortune for an individual, or praying for a negative or harmful end.

Tradition, abbreviated Trad.—1) A generic term synonymous with denomination or sect. A style or variety of practicing Wicca. May be new, created, developed from a book, outlined in a book, passed on from person to person, generational, or passed on within a family. 2) More formally, a system of religion, spirituality, and/or magickal teachings passed down relatively unchanged through three or more generations of students.

3) Generally a Tradition is an established system of Wicca that is disseminated through teaching, hiving off, schisms, family, generations, or books.

There are a large number of Wiccan Traditions, some you can find in books, some you have to be allowed into, some are public, some are secret. Some Traditions are open to anyone who expresses an interest or reads the book associated with the Tradition. Some Traditions are closed; one must be invited to join. Most Traditions' requirements are between the two extremes; a person may discover some of the practices and beliefs, but must be accepted into a training group to attain degrees, become a full member, or advance. A person who starts a Tradition (at the present time this is most effectively accomplished by writing a book about it) is considered important and often is accorded some respect in the greater Wiccan Community. Whether the importance comes from founding the Tradition or whether there is interest in the Tradition because the person is published can be debated. Fam-Trad—an abbreviation for Family Tradition—is a Tradition that is hereditary, i.e., you were born into it or initiated into it by a family member. Most Fam-Trads are closed to all but blood relatives or those who marry into the family.

Traditional—Witches who follow Traditions that were in existence before the Gardnerian revival. May or may not be Fam-Trads.

Traditions—Wiccan Traditions can be named after the founder (e.g., in homage to the first publicized Tradition—Gardnerian Wicca was named after Gerald Gardner, although he did not "coin" the name). For the most part, Traditions are named by the practitioners, not the founders. Some authors, for example, have objected to their works becoming the basis for a Tradition. But people who read the books use the material as they see fit, and often the author has little to say once the material is public. Some Traditions are named by the founders, and those names stick—Seax Wicca and Pecti Wicca were named by Raymond Buckland in his books. Others are descriptive names—like Caledonian Tradition or Teutonic Wicca. Some Traditions are known by different names in different parts of the United States. Because Wicca has little set doctrine, people feel free to incorporate whatever works for them into their practice of Wicca. When those practices and teachings are passed on to others, it becomes a Tradition. A partial list of some of the Wiccan Traditions follows:

1734 Tradition—Based on the magickal and spiritual philosophy of Robert Cochrane. The number 1734 and the component digits have symbolism and meaning for those in this Tradition.

Alexandrian Wicca—The first schismatic Wiccan Tradition in the modern Wiccan movement. Founded by Alex Sanders around 1960, he claimed he was initiated by his Wiccan grandmother at eleven years old when he inadvertently interrupted her during a Working. Sanders was briefly a member of a Gardnerian coven and met Gardner. Shortly thereafter Sanders left and started his own group. Alexandrian Wicca is similar to Gardnerian Wicca. *What Witches Do*, by Stewart Farrar, describes the beliefs and rituals of Alexandrianism.

Blue Star—A Wiccan Tradition started by Tzipporah Klein, based loosely upon a closed Fam-Trad. Mainly a religious Tradition with little magickal practice other than prayer or healing.

British Traditional—An amalgam of Celtic and Gardnerian beliefs and practices. The International Red Garter is a well-known branch of this Tradition. Janet and Stewart Farrar documented much of this Tradition in their many books. This is a structured Tradition that trains Initiates and grants degrees in covens that contain both sexes.

Caledonian Tradition—A.k.a., Hecatiae Tradition, it is of Scots origin and strives to preserve the unique traditions and festivals of the Scots in a magickal Wiccan context.

Celtic Wicca—Combines Celtic and Druidic teachings with some of Gardnerian structure and methods. The emphasis is on healing, horticulture, stone lore, and contact with elemental spirits, gnomes, fairies, and the little people. There is also a magickal body of lore.

Church of the Eternal Source—Egyptian recreation group who celebrate July 14th as the birthday of Osiris. Early (around middle 1970s) Pagan group with clergy, but not Wiccan.

Dianic—1) A.k.a., Dianic Feminist. Refers to a wide range of loosely related Traditions that emphasize the Goddess, sometimes to the complete exclusion of any male Deities. Generally all-female, some have lesbian proponents. Most Dianic groups are oriented toward empowering women in various ways. The ritual emphasis is upon women's spirituality, building self-worth and self-esteem, celebrations, singing, dancing, and drumming. Feminist and environmental activism is common. 2) A group founded by Morgan McFarland in Dallas, Texas, with her Dianic covenstead. Stresses awareness of self and kinship with nature, strong emphasis on creativity, psychic skills, and sensitivity.

Elite (pronounced Ee-lite)—A Tradition founded by a man who called himself Eli, it started in Minnesota and expanded to include groups throughout the United States. An extremely secretive Tradition, even from other Wiccans. Believed to be an offshoot of

Gardnerianism, with elements from Mormonism, Ceremonial Magick, and other sources. There were reportedly three men who held the title Eli in succession.

Fairy Wicca, Faery Wicca—A Tradition dedicated to exploring the interface between humankind and fairy or the fey, as depicted in many mythologies and folklore traditions. Depicted in the book *Faery Wicca*, by Francesca DeGrandis, although this is not the only source.

Feraferia—A group that was founded in California in the mid-1970s, and led by a man who was a gifted artist, this group has many rituals and beautiful statues, but they are not witches or Wiccans.

Gardnerian—The descendants of the practitioners of Wicca as formulated and rediscovered by Gerald Gardner and his associates. There are many Gardnerian groups and covens in the United States. Not all acknowledge each other as legitimate. British Gardnerians may not consider any American Gardnerians as legitimate. There are several Gardnerian lines in the United States named for geographical areas, although they are not confined to those areas. In the strictest sense, Gardnerians are those who were initiated by Gerald Gardner or one of his High Priestesses, and their initiatory descendants. If one's lineage of Initiation descends from any of these people, one has a Gardnerian lineage, although one may not necessarily be a practicing Gardnerian. There are also people who practice Gardnerian Wicca who do not possess Gardnerian lineage, and occasionally these people are fully accepted as Gardnerian by others. Skyclad worship, a nine-foot Circle, three degrees, and a coven led by a High Priestess are characteristics of this Tradition. Neo-Gardnerians are people who follow Gardnerian ritual but do not have any direct link with Gardner's original coven.

Georgian—(named after the late founder George Patterson of Bakersfield, California) Eclectic revivalist Tradition that is an amalgam of Gardnerian, Alexandrian, and Traditional Wicca with additional original material. Great emphasis on individual freedom and members are encouraged to write their own rituals and learn from all available sources. Generally work skyclad.

Hereditary Wicca—A.k.a., Fam-Trad or Traditional, a person who follows the Craft through family ties. Most are born into the Tradition but a few have been adopted into the Tradition either through marriage or through interest and sincerity. There are reportedly many Fam-Trads, but they are very secretive and most of the teachings are oathbound so little is known directly by those outside each specific Tradition. Some modern Traditions are descended from or based upon the teachings of Fam-Trads.

kitchen witch—One who practices the more practical side of the Craft, usually in connection with herbs, cooking, hearth, and home. More of a style than a Tradition in itself.

Livingtree—An Eclectic Tradition practiced by Robin Wood and others, it has three degrees and two levels, Pagan Groves (for beginners and non-Initiates), and Initiates' Circles, where magick is practiced.

New Reformed Order of the Golden Dawn, NROOGD—Founded by Aidan Kelly and others in Northern California in the early 1970s, this Tradition has nothing to do with the Golden Dawn. Members use ritual drama in public ceremonies. Kelly himself has been in and out of Wicca several times and is a very controversial figure in the Wiccan Community.

The People of Goda—the Clan of Tubal Cain—
A Tradition that was followed by Robert Cochrane, it is the name of the group he led in Britain.

Pecti Wicca—A Pictish Wiccan Tradition as outlined in the book *Scottish Witchcraft; The History and Magic of the Picts*, by Raymond Buckland, 1992. A Scottish style of witchcraft that is attuned to nature in all animal, vegetable, and mineral forms. Mostly a solitary path with much magick and little religious emphasis.

Pow-Wow—Based upon 400+ years of elite German Magick, it has migrated to America and evolved into a group that practices faith healing and use of Pennsylvania Dutch "Hex" symbols as well a simple herb lore. Documented by Silver Ravenwolf in her book.

Proteus—A Gardnerian offshoot. Based in New York it was originally a Gardnerian group that then hived off. It was formed in reaction to certain practices in Gardnerian Wicca. Hierarchical and degreed members teach and practice magick.

Radical Faery, Faery Wicca—A gay men's Tradition founded in 1979 in Tucson, Arizona that explores men's mysteries through sharing feelings and experiences. Celebration, music, and dance are components. Similar to Dianic Traditions, for gay men.

Reclaiming Wicca—A Dianic Feminist Tradition based upon the practices outlined in Starhawk's book, *Spiral Dance* (1979, 1989, 1999). Members sponsor "Witchcamp" workshops across North America. No degree system is recognized.

School of Wicca, Church and School of Wicca—Members are sometimes referred to as Frosties. Founded by Gavin and Yvonne Frost and based in North Carolina, the group adver-tises in many magazines and offers courses and degrees in witchcraft and Wicca. There are some major differences between the School of Wicca and "standard" Wicca and is considered Pagan but not necessarily Wiccan by mainstream Wiccans. Teachings have been modified over the years to bring them more in line with standard Wicca, but differences still remain. The Frosts are controversial figures and enjoy a mixed reputation in the greater Wiccan Community. They charge money for their correspondence courses and degrees, a practice supposedly against Wiccan Tradition, which has caused some controversy.

Seax Wicca—A Saxon Wiccan Tradition detailed in the book *The Tree: The Complete Book of Saxon Witchcraft* (1974), and others by Raymond Buckland. A Tradition of Wicca with Saxon roots that is based on Gardnerian teachings without breaking any Gardnerian oaths, it has eliminated some aspects of Gardnerian Wicca that have been considered controversial. It seeks to have practitioners enhance their lives in a positive direction. Similar to Gardnerian Wicca, but has a High Priest (not Priestess) in charge of the Circle and the Tradition allows self-Initiation.

Shamanic Wicca—Groups that emphasize methods of shamanism in their practices, including exploring altered states of consciousness. Groups use European, Native American, or both forms of shamanism. Selena Fox's Circle Sanctuary in Wisconsin uses Native American forms.

Starhawkian Tradition, Starhawkian Wicca—A style of Wicca based on Starhawk's books, especially *Spiral Dance* (1979) and others. This Tradition was not founded, endorsed, or encouraged by the author. Groups of people in isolated areas used the book to formulate their own style of Wicca. These groups have little or no connection with Starhawk herself or the Reclaiming Tradition. Because of the wide dissemination of *Spiral Dance*, it has become a standard Wiccan text and is used by many as the basis for their Wiccan practices. The book is enormously popular which is a tribute to the power and beauty of Starhawk's message.

Strega—Italian hereditary Tradition described in the book *Aradia, Gospel of the Witches* by Leland in 1899. Mainly a Tradition for women who wanted to have some power and retaliation against the power of the male-dominated Catholic Church. Practitioners still exist today, but which of them are true hereditary Strega and which have adopted the Tradition is not always clear.

Teutonic Wicca, Nordic Tradition—People who practiced a type of Wicca in areas where the Germanic languages were spoken. Included the cultures of the English, Dutch, Icelandic, Danish, Norwegian, and Swedish, it is a modern recreation of this Tradition, blending elements of all those cultures and the Norse Runes.

Traditional—Groups that emphasize the folklore, legends, and forms of various cultures rather than the more common forms of the mainstream Wiccan revival. Traditional covens follow Welsh, Irish, Saxon, Celtic, Scottish, Greek, Egyptian, and other cultures. Traditional covens do not usually work skyclad, and may adopt clothing appropriate to the culture they are following. People who follow Family Traditions may refer to themselves as Fam-Trads, though not all Traditional covens are Fam-Trads. Membership may be restricted by ethnic origin or interest, depending upon the individual group.

Wichan (pronounced weech-enn)—A Wiccan Tradition in central California that is secretive and reclusive. Probably an early (1960–1963) coven of Gardnerians, their newsletter is the *Red Garter*. They claim *wee-cha* is the correct pronunciation of Wicca.

Others—American Celtic Wicca, the Church of Y Tylwyth Teg, "Coven of the Forest, Far and Forever," Deboran Wicca, Maidenhill Wicca, Northern Way Wicca, Nova Wicca, and Algard.

trance—A mental state of disassociation and withdrawal during which brain wave activity is slowed down to eight cycles per second or less. Meditation can induce a trance state. For Wiccans, trance can be the start of a spiritual exploration, rather than an end in itself. Trance, throughout human history, has been a method used to contact the inner places, spirit planes, and/or the Divine. Some cultures have developed extraordinary physical abilities and practices (for example, sleeping on a bed of nails) through the use of trance and controlled perception of stimuli. Some practitioners can slow heartbeat and breathing, as well as other autonomic activities through controlled trance. Psychologically the term trance can also refer to states initiated by hypnosis, trauma, or drug use.

transataumancy—Divination by things seen or heard accidentally. Trifling mistakes were seen as omens by the ancient Romans. In modern times Jungian theory has postulated that there are no coincidences or accidents and everything has a purpose, even if that purpose is not understood by the perceiver. The saying, "See a pin, pick it up, all the day you'll have good luck" comes under this category.

transmigration—The Hindu doctrine that believes that souls inhabit many types of creatures, not only as they undergo human successive incarnations. You might be reborn as an animal, insect, fish, etc., as well as a human. This is related to the belief in reincarnation, but belief in reincarnation does not necessarily require belief in transmigration. Most Wiccans believe in some form of reincarnation but do not believe in transmigration.

Tree of Life—1) A name given to the Kabbalistic diagram depicting the ten sephiroth and the paths between them, it is a Kabbalistic diagram of cosmology. Originally depicted as an actual tree, by the fourteenth century the diagram that is now in common usage was somewhat standardized. 2) Symbolic representation of the emergent evolution of life forms. Represents the umbilical cord of Mother Earth.

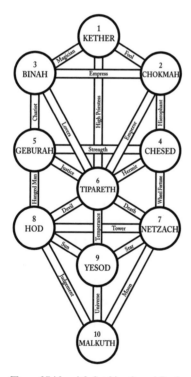

Tree of Life with Sephiroth and Paths

triad—Maiden, Mother, Crone is the sacred triad of the Goddess. Many ancient Goddesses are represented as sacred triads. A generic way to worship the Goddess.

Sacred Triad

trial by ordeal—A medieval method used to test facts, a person's innocence, the validity of an oath, the abilities of a witch, or to decide between two parties in a dispute. The person (or persons) was subjected to an ordeal that if successfully completed, would prove that the person was in the right or had God on their side. Usually successful completion meant the person emerged unharmed. A guilty person would succumb to the ordeal and be harmed or die. Some trials by ordeal were surprisingly astute: in one type a person was tested by feeding them a dry barley cake. If they choked or couldn't swallow it was believed that the person was lying or guilty. This method was believed to be effective because a guilty person would be more nervous and have a drier mouth. Other trials were more dangerous and potentially deadly: walking through fire or coals, trial by combat, ordeal by water (ducking or swimming), poison, or torture. Accused witches were usually subjected to some type of trial by ordeal. Today a trial by ordeal is usually a series of difficult tasks or events that, when completed or mastered, confers a certain ability or wisdom upon the person. It can be used in Initiations, or it can be a substitute for a formal Initiation. Today ordeal is the term used for these type of experiences.

Triple Goddess—Maiden, Mother, Crone. The three faces of the Goddess as manifest in the ages of a post-pubescent female. A generic way to worship the Goddess.

Triple Goddess

triskelion—A three-part symbol used by Celtic druids to symbolize all sacred triads, such as the Triple Goddess. Used in the ancient Mediterranean as a protection against the evil eye, and also symbol of the Triple Goddess. Also used as a generic symbol of the Triple Goddess by Pagans in general.

Triskelions

tuathal—Widdershins.

turifumy—Divination using sacred smoke.

Tyler, ritual Tyler—Person in a ritual who is responsible for keeping the Circle and participants safe from outside influences, corporeal or not. Borrowed from Masonry. The Tyler may be inside or outside the Circle. Usually used for larger group rituals, though may also be an officer of the coven, similar to Summoner. The Tyler can protect people inside the Circle, the Circle as a whole, or people outside the Circle from stray energies leaking out from the Circle. The Tyler protects the group from outside influences so the High Priestess and High Priest can concentrate fully on the ritual. To tyler is to act in this capacity. Some magickal tool or weapon is usually used to aid in tyling, most commonly a staff or sword.

twin souls—See soul mates.

U

UFO, Unidentified Flying Object—something that appears in the sky and cannot be explained as a natural or manmade phenomenon. Popularly used to describe aliens and their spacecraft and other phenomena caused by them. Wicca is a spiritual and religious path and has nothing in common with UFOs or UFOlogy although individual Wiccans may believe in UFOs. Popular media has a tendency to combine all supernatural phenomena, so some television shows or books may treat Wiccans and space aliens similarly.

unconscious—That part of the human psyche not available to the conscious ego. The unconscious mind can be divided into two parts: the collective unconscious that all of the human race holds and is the home of the archetypes, and the personal unconscious that contains all the hidden elements of the personality. To do the Great Work is to strive for the improvement of communication between the ego and unconscious.

unctions—1) Occult term that refers to various anointing oils used in Ceremonial Magick. 2) Inquisitors used the term to refer to the legendary flying ointment that enabled witches to fly to the Sabbat. Inquisitorial lore stated that these oils were produced from rotting corpses or the boiled bodies of sacrificial infants.

undine—A Water elemental.

ungrounded—The act or state of not being grounded, being psychically adrift, or possessing no psychic equilibrium, or being "spacey" without conscious attention to the here and now. A common way to become ungrounded is to encounter a strange, eerie, or frightening psychic event without the ability to remain calm and balanced.

Sometimes a person can experience physical symptoms when ungrounded, especially if they are subject to physical/medical conditions that are exacerbated by emotional upset. It can also lead to fright, fear, panic, and/or anxiety if the emotional upset is not dealt with.

Wiccan training usually includes techniques for grounding and ways to avoid psychic/emotional upset in yourself and in others. One must be grounded in order to successfully practice magick, and Ceremonial Magick has many rituals and techniques to achieve grounding and centering. Being ungrounded is generally an undesirable state, although some metaphysical groups (usually non-Pagan) may actively pursue it to enhance their experience of psychic phenomena. Some may mistakenly confuse being ungrounded with being open and aware. One can be open and aware and still be grounded, so that unusual experiences will not upset the perceiver, which can often happen if one encounters psychic phenomena while ungrounded. Generally being ungrounded also intensifies emotions, and emotional reactions.

unguent—A salve or pasty potion. Similar to a modern creme. Can be used for curing, charm, or bewitching purposes. Similar to an ointment.

universal balm—A magickal ointment that reportedly could heal all wounds, cure every sickness, and reverse every adverse spell. A concept widely represented in many magickal Traditions, it could not restore life or bestow immortality. See elixir of life.

unseelie, unseelie court—The branch of faery that is unfriendly or hostile to humans.

urban legend—A term to describe a popular story that spreads swiftly by word of mouth and other means and is soon accepted as truth. The hereditary Satanic Cults is a widespread and damaging urban legend of the late twentieth century. The book *Satanic Panic* details the phenomenon from beginning to end.

Wicca is unfortunately included in many urban legends, among them: The Satanic Conspiracy Myth—that Wicca is a front for Satanism; The W.I.C.C.A. Letters Myth [The Witches International Coven Council (of America)]— there is a secret group with an agenda to take over the world, based upon the Protocols of the Elders of Zion—an anti-Semitic forgery that first appeared in Russia in 1903; The Illuminati—a secret semi-occult organization that seeks to gain world control and is supposedly a descendant of the Templars and the Masons; The Palladists or Order of the Palladium—a shadowy satanic group with possible ties to Masonry and the Templars; The Black Mass Myth—Wiccans celebrate some sort of perverted or reverse Christian rite, mostly based upon Inquisitional materials; Ritual sacrifice myths— Wiccans perform blood sacrifices, based upon Inquisitional materials; and others. The existence of these groups or myths is not truthful, but has been created to expose Wicca and others as dangerous and an immediate threat to modern-day orthodox beliefs and institutions.

V

Valiente, Doreen—(1922–1999) One of Gerald Gardner's High Priestesses, Valiente was also a prolific author who wrote about Wicca and Paganism in general. Doreen Valiente rewrote much of Gardner's original material, making it beautiful and poetic. She also removed from Gardner's work much of Crowley's writings that were borrowed by Gardner. She is credited with finalizing the Charge of the Goddess. She broke with Gardner in 1956 over the issues of publicity and coven management. She was a practicing Wiccan until her death.

vampire, vampirism, psychic vampire, psychic black hole—1) Draining an individual's psychic energy by another, it can be conscious or unconscious. It is considered a type of black magick, especially if it is consciously done. People who are psychic vampires (also known as psychic black holes) can drain a group's energy just by their presence. One way to spot a vampire is to observe them. Generally they will arrive down, tired, listless, depressed, or in a bad mood. As they "feed" on the ambient energy, they will perk up, becoming more lively, happier, and more animated while others become drained, tired, listless, crabby, and/or depressed. Sometimes this process can be very subtle and hard to detect. Generally most Wiccans and magickal practitioners do not allow psychic vampires in their groups because they hinder magickal Workings. With training, vampirism can be eliminated, but it is difficult and takes willing work. 2) In folklore, a malevolent being that refuses to be dead, but instead takes possession of a body in order to enjoy the pleasures of the living. In contemporary cultures, a vampire is a supernatural being that is undead, drains blood for sustenance, cannot abide sunlight, exists mainly on film and in books, and does not exist in the mundane world, although there are those who emulate these creatures and affect their habits, dress, and mannerisms. Based loosely upon the legends of Count Vlad Tepes (colloquially Count Dracula) who dispelled the Turks from his native Transylvania in the fourteenth century and was canonized for his efforts. Occasionally one encounters Satanists who also model their ideas, dress, and practices on vampirism.

vegetarian—Many Wiccans are vegetarian to one degree or another. Some will only eat meat (red meat) on Holy Days (usually Samhain).

veil—Some Wiccan Traditions mandate that a female Third Degree Wiccan may wear a veil in Circle as a mark of her rank.

vertical sequence—A type of divination using year dates added in sequences to create other numbers. One adds up the digits in the birth date, (for example, August 1 would become 8 + 1 = 9) and adds that total to the birth year (9 + 1932 = 1941) to obtain another year of significance. A technique of numerology.

veve—A sigil specific to the religion of Voudun. A drawn design used to summon the various Loa ("Gods") of Voudun.

vibes—A slang term for energy, usually the ambient energy in a place or surrounding a person. One can sense "bad" or "good" vibes.

voice calling—Direct vocal communication of warning by a spirit. Can be from a dead relative or just a disembodied voice. Not a psychic ability or telepathy. Can warn of accident, danger, disaster, financial ruin, war, societal collapse, evil spirits, etc.

voiding the coven—When a coven hives off for a time, the new coven avoids working with the original coven in order to establish their new identity.

voodoo—Colloquial term for the religion of Voudun, as well as any sort of black magick or possibly spells or potions that are generally used in a non-technological society. Not a complimentary term, as it implies superstitions and possibly anti-scientific beliefs and practices.

vortex—A flow of energy around a center, pulling into that center all that surrounds it.

Voudun—A.k.a., voodoo—Originally, a black tribal religious tradition that is an amalgam of indigenous African spiritualities combined with some characteristics of Christianity, usually Catholicism. Developed in the Western Hemisphere, predominantly in Haiti, by enslaved Africans, in an effort to safeguard some of their indigenous beliefs. They "sanitized" them by combining them with Christian symbology so they could still practice without causing alarm from or drawing the attention of their white Christian masters.

The rites involve ecstatic possession by ancestor archetypes (Loa) and raising power to do magickal Workings. Some forms of animal sacrifice are practiced in a sacred context. In Voudun, the work of the left hand includes practices such as creation and control of zombies. Not strictly a Pagan Tradition, there are many elements very similar to those of Pagans and some Loa and activities of Voudun have been borrowed by Pagans. Voudun is similar to other Afro-Catholic amalgams such as Santeria in Cuba, Macumba in Brazil, and Obeah or Obi in Jamaica.

In an important legal action, the Church of Babalu Aye vs. Hialeah, members of the church were being prosecuted under animal cruelty laws for sacrificing chickens and other animals for religious purposes, which was a common and long-standing practice of this religious group that has ties to Voudun. In 1992, the Supreme Court of the United States decision stated that this group had the right to practice their religion as they saw fit, even to sacrificing live animals, a landmark religious freedoms case.

W

WADL—Wiccan Anti-Defamation League. See AREN.

W.I.C.C.A.—Witches International Coven Conspiracy (or Council) of America. A mythical organization that does not exist that supposedly runs and/or controls all Wiccans, Pagans, and occultists and opposes Christianity. It is a deliberate anti-Wiccan, anti-Pagan, anti-occult hoax that promotes rumors of an international Wiccan conspiracy and "proves" that people who call themselves Wiccan are in reality trying to take over the world and wipe out all Christians and Christianity.

WPPA—the Wiccan Pagan Press Alliance—A united group of Wiccan/Pagan publishers of magazines, zines, newsletters, and Web sites who adhere to certain standards of quality and content. Those publishers that are a part of WPPA display a large pentagram and WPPA as their symbol.

Walpurgis Night—See Beltane.

wand—A consecrated short stick used to store and/or manipulate energies and possibly to store spells. A magickal tool used to invoke or conduct energy. Symbolizes the element of Air or Fire. A wand can be made from many materials (wood, glass, crystal, plastic, metal, etc.), depending upon its uses. It can be plain, or fancy with paint, inscriptions, crystals, feathers, beads, and other decorations. Generally they are handmade, although there are commercial magic wands that do work well magickally. Some Traditions use a wand in situations where it would be inappropriate to use a blade.

Wand

ward, wards—A temporary psychic shield of protection erected around an area or a person, it can also refer to consecrated and/or charged objects that, when magickally connected, produce a shielded area within. Wards are more defensive and active than shields. One can set wards around one's home or living space for extra protection.

warlock—From Anglo-Saxon *waer loga* (traitor or deceiver). A popular culture term for a "male witch." In the Craft the word is highly uncomplimentary and used when someone has broken an oath, usually by revealing secrets or "outing" someone. It can indicate a person is pariah and to be shunned. During "The Burning Times" the term was used for a witch who betrayed others to the Inquisition. Can also be used by Wiccans to refer to an Initiated witch who turns against the Craft.

Watchtowers—Guardians of the quarters of a Circle, usually one each for Fire, Earth, Air, and Water. Can be symbolized by archangels, spirit animals, colors, the element itself, etc. The four directional points of a Circle, into which elementals are called to be guardians for the duration of the Circle.

water of life—Translation of Gaelic *usquebaugh*. Early alchemists believed it was the elixir of life. The derivation of the modern word whiskey, used to designate doubly distilled alcoholic spirits.

water witching—See dowsing.

wax images—Figures made of beeswax were said to have special magickal properties since beeswax was believed to be the anima substance of the animal kingdom. People could make an image of themselves in beeswax and it would increase their magickal powers and/or sexual stamina as long as the image was not damaged in any way. Since these wax images could be used against their creators or destroyed, it was important to keep them in a safe place. See also poppets.

weather worker, weather Working—A person who does energy and/or spellwork to influence the weather. A weather worker cannot "create" weather, but they can work with prevailing conditions and affect the development and flow of the weather accordingly. At festivals weather workers have worked to divert the worst of storms and other possibly dangerous weather from the festival site itself. Some people feel they can affect weather patterns over a large area like a city or county with long-term effects. A Native American rain dance is a form of weather Working.

web—1) Worldwide web, the Internet. 2) The model for Wiccan affiliations, structure, and organization. Wiccans try to avoid hierarchical models, and the way people and groups are interconnected (outside a small coven) is more like a web of affiliations, friendships, and alliances. Similar to the "six degrees of separation" idea, though there are probably fewer than six degrees of separation among Wiccans all over the country. In a way the Wiccan/Pagan Community is like a small town, with people living closely (although not necessarily in proximity) and everyone in the community aware of the activities of others. 3) The pattern of all energies that interweave and interconnect all living things and the cosmos. The web of life. Borrowed from ecology.

werewolf—In European folklore, an affliction or disease that causes a person to be transformed into a wolf either at night or during the Full Moon. Lycanthropy is the more generic term for a person who can shape shift into various animals. The ability to shape shift is associated with witchcraft, though it has existed in many cultures over time.

Wheel of the Year—The cycle of the Sabbats and Esbats throughout a year, and also year after year. Can be equated with a macrocosmic magickal Circle.

whistle up the wind—A form of weather magick, a person can literally whistle and create, intensify, or change the direction of the wind.

white-handled knife—See boline.

Wicca (alternative spelling Wica)—From Old English *wiccacraeft*. The name used for the practice of the Craft of the Wise, the "Old Religion." The word has several possible origins: 1) from Anglo Saxon *wik* or *wit* meaning wise or learned, as in "the Craft of the Wise"; 2) from Anglo Saxon *wicce*, meaning to turn, bend, or twist; 3) from proto Indo-European *weik* (pronounced *way-ick*), pertaining to magic and religion. Originally in Old English wicca (then pronounced *wee'cha*) meant a male witch and wicce a female witch. Wicca as a religion is also known as the "Craft."

Wicca is a religion recognized by the United States federal government and all Wiccans enjoy the same protection and rights under the United States Constitution as does a member of any other religion practiced in the United States. Wicca is a recreation/revival/continuance of pre-Christian European spiritualities. It is a religion that worships nature, is fertility-oriented, and is the major faction of the Neo-Pagan religious movement. Organized by Traditions, and practiced in almost as many ways as there are practitioners. The modern revival began in the early 1930s in England and spread to the United States in the late 1950s to mid-1960s.

Wiccae—Plural of witch or Wiccan. Also refers to things Wiccan. Term used in some Traditions, but is not universal.

Wiccan Rede (pronounced "reed")—"Eight words the Wiccan rede fulfill, An ye harm none, do what ye will," these are the final lines of a much longer poem, and is a saying that mandates how Wiccans are to live their lives. A person must think about what actions they take and do not take in life, and their consequences. Those who abide by the Wiccan Rede should act in ways that cause the least harm, to themselves, to others, and to the Earth and its inhabitants. By using the Rede as a guide, each Wiccan must develop their own ethical system and act from those beliefs.

Wiccaning—The ceremony of Naming a child and placing it under the protection of the Goddess and God until the child can choose for themselves the life path they wish to pursue. Not a sealing into Wicca. Some call it the Wiccan equivalent of a Christening.

widdershins—German, against the way; counter-clockwise, moonwise, backward movement. Gaelic equivalent is Tuathal. Many Wiccans believe that to move widdershins is banishing in nature. Most Wiccans will not move widdershins during a ritual except when banishing energies, otherwise they might cancel out the energies that accumulate in a Circle during a ritual. Some feel widdershins movement is indicative of chaos.

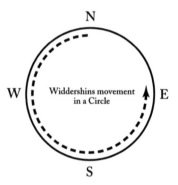

Widdershins Movement

wild hunt—In Celtic mythology it is the dark time of the year between Samhain and Beltane, when the wild hunt is abroad. The wild hunt is a supernatural group of beings that mimic a hunting group, but can hunt people or faery. One can become caught up by the wild hunt, become a participant, and disappear only to return years with no visible signs of aging. Sometimes a way to explain mysterious disappearances, it was believed that solitary travelers at night were attacked and killed by the wild hunt. The change in emphasis from an agrarian lifestyle that is practiced during the summer, to a hunter-gatherer lifestyle that occurs during the winter is explained by the wild hunt and the Oak King and the Holly King, the "Gods" of summer and winter respectively.

wild talents—Psychic abilities. The theory that psychic ability is natural and bestowed by a "wild" and yet unidentified gene and therefore a product of evolution.

witch—1) Medieval unisex term for a person who practices magick. Derives from wicca, an Old English word meaning a male witch, wicce is a female witch. Mundanely a modern term for a female practitioner of magick. 2) A magickal shaper of reality. Many Wiccans consider themselves witches, but not all witches consider themselves Wiccans. The term is unisex; there are male and female witches. A witch uses magick and casts spells and may practice divination. People from Z Budapest's Tradition consider themselves feminist witches, but are not Wiccan. Sometimes a title claimed by an Initiate of Wicca who is schooled in the practices and mysteries of their Tradition. A term that not all are comfortable using or claiming, regardless of the usage in their particular Tradition. The term has societal connotations that some are fighting to lose (as in "wicked witch," or a polite euphemism for "bitch," among others), while others use the word purposely to shock and call attention to themselves. Some consider the term synonymous with Wiccan, but this is not so. Most Wiccans do identify with the witches of the past who were persecuted and killed, especially those killed by burning. Historically witches specialized in herbalism and midwifery, and were mostly women, sometimes single women.

witch finder, witch hunter—One who uses their abilities, natural or supernatural, to seek out witches and expose them to the existing and interested authorities. Sometimes, in the past, a captured witch would be forced to act in this capacity in return for their life and the lives of their family and relatives. Historically, fees were paid for discovering a witch, so the position could be highly lucrative for those who chose voluntarily to take up the profession. Matthew Hopkins was Witchfinder General for England and, in 1645 at the height of his power, was responsible with the help of his pricker, John Stearns, for the exposure and hanging of several hundred witches.

witch hunt—1) Modern term used to indicate a campaign of persecution based upon spurious or falsified information. The Army-McCarthy Trials on Communism in the United States during the 1950s was called a "witch hunt" by some. May be against an individual, a few individuals, a group, or a class of people. 2) Late medieval and Renaissance social phenomenon that was a vehicle for ridding society of witches, evil, social outcasts, and malcontents.

The first major witch hunt occurred in Switzerland in 1427. The *Malleus Maleficarum*, the classic witch-finding text, was published in 1486. Persecution of witches in Europe reached its height between 1580 and 1660, and witch trials became almost universal throughout Europe. Germany, Austria, and Switzerland were the center of witch burning, but few areas were untouched by the persecutions. Torture was prohibited in England and only about twenty percent of accused witches there were executed by hanging. Few witches were persecuted in the Dutch republic, and Ireland seems to have escaped the witch trials altogether.

Many witch trials were provoked by quarrels among neighbors or greed. If a person found and denounced a witch, they were entitled to up to half of the convicted witch's property and possessions, with the local government or church authorities getting the other portion. This made witch hunts very lucrative, and often it was enough to be conspicuously wealthy and without political protection to be accused of being a witch.

In the Americas the witchcraft persecutions lagged behind those in Europe. In the French and Spanish colonies witchcraft cases were under the jurisdiction of the church, and no one was put to death on that charge. In the English colonies about forty people were executed for witchcraft between 1650 and 1710. The Salem Witch Trials of 1692 were responsible for the deaths of twenty people. In Europe witch trials declined after 1680. A late wave of witchcraft persecutions affected Poland and other areas of Eastern Europe, but ended about 1740. In England the death penalty for witchcraft was abolished in 1736, though it was still considered a crime until 1951. The last legal execution of a witch occurred in Switzerland in 1782.

About eighty percent of all accused witches were women, especially single, widowed, or independent women. Since women had little political power they could not muster the same means to defend themselves as men, and women were the traditional repositories of herb lore and magick, as well as the midwives. Some communities considered any form of herb lore, especially that dealing with contraception and abortion to be witchcraft. The occupation of midwife was considered one that was especially desirable for a witch, because she had access to infants for sacrifice, could consign infants to Satan as they were born and before they were baptized, and she was familiar with sex, the act of procreation, and the intimate parts of a woman, said by the church to be the most polluted and vile parts of humans. Some feel the witchcraft persecutions were nothing more than a campaign against women and women's power. (See also the Burning Times, Inquisition.)

Witch King—A title that is not used among Wiccans. Covens are autonomous and different Traditions have no ties between them so there is no person who is elected, designated, or acclaimed King of the Witches. The High Priest of a Witch Queen is sometimes called Magus, as a courtesy title.

witch mark, witches' marks—1) A.k.a., Devil's Marks. Skin imperfections that can indicate the person is a witch and are generally believed to be insensitive to pain or impervious to bleeding. In medieval and Renaissance times any birthmark, mole, or other skin imperfection could be called a witches' mark if the inquisitor so deemed it. Generally a red or blue spot supposedly tattooed upon the witch by Satan or one of his minions. See pricking, "pricking a witch." 2) Today, many Traditions mandate that some sort of tattoo or other permanent mark be made upon attainment of various degrees. What the design of the mark might be, where it is placed, and when it is to be made all vary widely depending upon the Tradition.

Witch Queen, Queen of the Sabbat—1) A person who has founded a Wiccan group and two or three other groups have subsequently hived off from that original group. A person who has founded three or more Wiccan groups, of some permanence. 2) Less commonly used in a derogatory manner about Wiccans who allow ego to drive much of their public activities.

witch's jewels—The jewels that are worn by a Witch Queen to distinguish rank. Also known as Witch Queen's bigghes. The silver crown, a band of silver with a crescent moon, the garter, bracelet, and necklace are the tokens of rank worn in Circle.

Priestess with Jewels

witch's ladder—A string of forty beads or a cord with forty knots, used as an aid for concentrated repetition without actual counting. Similar to a rosary.

witches' teats—A wart, mole, boil, or other raised skin imperfection that was considered to be a teat to suckle Satan's imps by the Inquisition. A mark of witchcraft.

witchcraft—The lore and practices associated with being a witch. Sometimes synonymous with Wicca (also known as the Craft). In ancient, medieval, and Renaissance times witchcraft usually included herbalism, healing, midwifery, and other folk cures, and may also have included spells, charms, and/or curses. Some witches were knowledgeable about poisons and abortifacients.

Witches Anti-Defamation League, WADL—A modern organization to legally combat slander and libel about witchcraft, the WADL collects and stored stories from the media about witches. (See AREN.)

Witches Rune—A power-raising chant accompanied by a ring dance. The most common version was written by Gerald Gardner and revised by Doreen Valiente.

wizard—From Anglo Saxon *wyzard*, wise one. A solitary practitioner of magick and dispenser of arcane lore, a lore master, generally a masculine term. Sometimes synonymous with sorcerer.

words of power—In some Traditions there are secret words that are used to raise power and aid in magickal Workings. Over the years some words of power have been published, and they have subsequently been changed. These are some of the "secrets" of various Traditions, and are very jealously guarded. Some feel that these words of power are invested with the energy and character of the Tradition, and for others to use them

dilutes the energy and in some ways dilutes the Tradition.

work—To do magick, to work magick. For example, "he's at work" means he is in the middle of working magick or performing a Circle or spell or some other magickal/psychic act.

Working—1) A magickal act; 2) A Circle used for a tangible end such as a spell or healing or divination. Contrast with celebration, that usually has no tangible end other than to honor the Gods or celebrate a Sabbat or Holy Day. Workings and celebrations can be combined. A magickal spell done to accomplish an end.

working center—Performing the function of High Priestess or High Priest for a ritual.

working partner, working partners, working partnership—A magickal partner; a person who habitually performs magic with another; two people who perform magick together. A High Priestess and High Priest of a coven are working partners. Two people who teach a Wicca year-and-a-day class together are working partners. People who perform only one ritual together are working partners for that particular ritual. A handfasted couple may or may not be working partners, each may have a separate person with whom they usually perform magick.

In the Wiccan Community people can be "associated" in many ways, and being part of a working partnership is one way to be associated, almost as strong as being married or handfasted, yet different in duties, responsibility, and scope. It is very rare for two Wiccans to be able to meet all of each other's needs, and the Wiccan Community has various mechanisms for allowing other needs to be met without sacrificing the committed partnership. It is less common for a High Priestess and High Priest to be committed married partners than for each to have a "home life" relationship with someone else, who may or may not be coven members. See also primary relationship.

world tree—Ygdrassil, the Norse representation of the nine worlds and the bridges between them. A Norse diagram of cosmology. Sometimes contrasted and compared with Kabbalah, but there is no historical evidence that the two systems were ever practiced together before the modern age.

Ygdrassil

worry beads—A string of beads which is worked with the fingers to absorb nervous energy. Can be used as a spell or charm against evil or calamity.

worship—Communion with and honoring divinity, however that is defined by the worshippers.

wortcunning—Anglo Saxon word meaning root, herb, or plant knowledge. Herbal lore.

X

XTian or Xtian or X-Tian—Wiccan or Pagan abbreviation for Christian, in the same way Xmas is an abbreviation for Christmas.

xenoglossy—The ability to speak in an unfamiliar foreign language, associated with past-life recall, trance, hypnosis, and mediumship. Similar to glossalalia, but the language spoken is an actual language, although its historic existence may require research to discover. Usually manifest by a person reciting words and phrases in the unknown language, but very rarely does it happen that a person is able to converse in that unknown language.

xenophobia—A fear of strangers. A fear of that which is new, different, or strange.

xylomancy—Divination by wood. Several methods are known: 1) Divining with the I Ching using the yarrow sticks; 2) Reading signs made by wood-eating (xyolphageous) animals; 3) Reading woodpecker markings on sacred trees; 4) Reading the placement and positioning of sticks encountered along a forest path chosen at random or encountered in a dream; 5) Interpreting the positions and actions of logs burning in a fire.

Y

Ygdrassil—See world tree.

yin and yang, yin/yang—The symbol for the practice of the Tao (the way). Yin is the female, negative, dark, and passive principle in the Universe and yang is the male, positive, light, active principle. The symbol, which contains two dots in each side, symbolizes that there is nothing that is pure yin or pure yang, each carries a bit of the other within it, and the combination of these two principles make up all that is in the Universe, in varying proportions. This dualism underlies much of Chinese philosophy, religion, medicine, science, and magic.

Yin/Yang Symbols

yoga—Indian tradition, specifically in Hinduism, a series of mental disciplines that object of which is personal identification with consciousness. Also a series of exercises and meditative practices. It became popular in the West in the 1960s and is still used widely as a way to keep limber and stay fit, especially for persons who might not be able to participate in more strenuous and jarring exercise regimens.

Yule—Sabbat celebrated at the Winter Solstice,

usually December 21st. Generally celebrates the re-birth of the Sun God or the longest night.

Z

Zen—The undefinable made manifest. An Oriental spiritual path, encountered in Zen Buddhism. A teaching system that is not taught in a classroom but rather by the teacher who either asks questions or guides the student through experiences designed to promote enlightenment. It is an experiential enlightenment that is difficult to communicate to those who do not practice it, cannot be caused or forced, but only guided and pointed out. A few Wiccans use Zen techniques to teach, but generally it is not a Wiccan path.

Zener Cards—A specially designed deck of twenty-five cards, composed of five sets of five cards each with a star, square, circle, plus sign, or wavy lines on it. The deck is shuffled and, through various types of tests, subjects are evaluated to determine whether they can predict which card will come up, the results are recorded, and variation from statistical probability is evaluated. It is used as a way to test psychic ability in the psychological community and it not a form of divination.

Symbols of Zener Cards

zine—(pronounced *"zeen"*) Short for fanzine, which is an abbreviation of fan magazine. Small press privately published newsletter of widely varying quality on a narrowly defined topic. There are many Wiccan and Pagan zines. A newsletter can also be called a zine. Zines are topic-oriented usually with a single editor in charge. They are usually distributed by the editor to friends, members, and other interested parties, and do not in general charge a subscription fee. The Internet with bulletin boards and Web sites has replaced some zines, although many still exist on paper.

zodiac—The classical band of twelve constellations situated roughly along the plane of the ecliptic (the Sun's path across the sky) through which the Sun, Moon, and planets move across the sky. The exact constellations making up the zodiac have varied over time in Western cultures. The band of the ecliptic is universally recognized, but the Western constellations were codified, drawn up, and boundaries demarked in the 1700s by the IAU (International Astronomical Union). It was this body, in their demarcation of the constellations (shown by the boundaries visible on star maps), that made the ecliptic cross fourteen constellations (adding Cetus and Ophiuchus), rather than the classical twelve acknowledged by astrologers. The IAU demarcation is a modern convenience for astronomers and has nothing to do with astrology. Ancient research indicates that the zodiac once consisted of only ten constellations, those we now call Virgo, Libra, and Scorpio being one giant constellation symbolizing the Great Goddess. This was later broken down into two constellations, Virgo (roughly the same as today) and Scorpio, with what is now Libra called the Chelae (claws in Greek), the claws of the scorpion. In early classical times this separate area was re-designated as Libra and given the pictorial representation of a balance, thereby becoming the only inanimate object in the classical zodiac.

zombie—A soulless corpse reanimated by a practitioner of Voudun, supposedly under the thrall and control of the animator. Modern research has indicated that people who were made zombies may be victims of poisoning by administration of a powder derived from the puffer fish, which is a strong neurotoxin that first causes the victim to enter a near death state, and then later revive. This neurotoxin contains chemical inhibitors that kill any initiative and depress the memory and motor functions. This exotic poison is tropical in nature and reportedly does not work outside its native environment.

To be cursed and be made a zombie is the ultimate threat a Voudun practitioner can make, and supposedly the fear helps keep followers compliant. Some feel that threat and fear can cause the "death" and reanimation as a zombie, purely through the power of suggestion.

zoomancy—Divination by observation of the actions and/or appearance of various animals, especially strange, unusual, or erratic behavior.

$\mathcal{A}$PPENDIX I

THE ADVANCED BONEWITS'
CULT DANGER EVALUATION FRAME

INTRODUCTION

Events in the last few decades have clearly indicated just how dangerous some religious and secular groups (usually called "cults" by those opposed to them) can be to their own members as well as to anyone else whom they can influence. "Brainwashing," beatings, child abuse, rapes, murders, mass suicides, military drilling and gunrunning, meddling in civil governments, international terrorism, and other crimes have been charged against leaders and members of many groups, and in far too many cases those accusations have been correct. None of this has been very surprising to historians of religion or to other scholars of what are usually labeled "new" religions (no matter how old they may be in their cultures of origin). Minority groups, especially religious ones, are often accused of crimes by members of the current majority. In many ways, for example, the "Mormon" were the "Moonies" of the 19th century—at least in terms of being an unusual minority belief system that many found "shocking" at the time—and the members of the Unification Church could be just as "respectable" a hundred years from now as the Latter-day Saints are today.

Nonetheless, despite all the historical and philosophical caveats that could be issued, ordinary people faced with friends or loved ones joining an "unusual" group, or perhaps contemplating joining it themselves, need a relatively simple way to evaluate just how dangerous or harmless a given group is liable to be, without either subjecting themselves to its power or judging it solely on theological or ideological grounds (the usual method used by anti-cult groups).

In 1979 I constructed an evaluation tool which I now call the "Advanced Bonewits' Cult Danger Evaluation Frame," or the "ABCDEF," a copy of which was included in that year's revised edition of my book, *Real Magic* (Samuel Weiser Pub.,

1989). I realize its shortcomings, but feel that it can be effectively used to separate harmless groups from the merely unusual-to-the-observer ones. Feedback from those attempting to use the system has always been appreciated. Indirect feedback, in terms of the number of places on and off the Net this ABCDEF has shown up, has been mostly favorable. For example, it was chosen by and is now displayed on the website of the Institute for Social Inventions, who paraphrased it for their "Best Ideas—A compendium of social innovations" listing.

The purpose of this evaluation tool is to help both amateur and professional observers, including current or would-be members, of various organizations (including religious, occult, psychological or political groups) to determine just how dangerous a given group is liable to be, in comparison with other groups, to the physical and mental health of its members and of other people subject to its influence. It cannot speak to the spiritual "dangers," if any, that might be involved, for the simple reason that one person's path to enlightenment or "salvation" is often viewed by another as a path to ignorance or "damnation."

As a general rule, the higher the numerical total score by a given group (the further to the right of the scale), the more dangerous it is likely to be. Though it is obvious that many of the scales in the frame are subjective, it is still possible to make practical judgments using it, at least of the "is this group more dangerous than that one?" sort. This is if all numerical assignments are based on accurate and unbiased observation of actual behavior by the groups and their top levels of leadership (as distinct from official pronouncements). This means that you need to pay attention to what the secondary and tertiary leaders are saying and doing, as much (or more so) than the central leadership—after all, "plausible deniability" is not a recent historical invention.

This tool can be used by parents, reporters, law enforcement agents, social scientists and others interested in evaluating the actual dangers presented by a given group or movement. Obviously, different observers will achieve differing degrees of precision, depending upon the sophistication of their numerical assignments on each scale. However, if the same observers use the same methods of scoring and weighting each scale, their comparisons of relative danger or harmlessness between groups will be reasonably valid, at least for their own purposes. People who cannot, on the other hand, view competing belief systems as ever having possible spiritual value to anyone will find the ABCDEF annoyingly useless for promoting their theocratic agendas. Worse, these members of the Religious Reich will find that their own organizations (and quite a few large mainstream churches) are far more "cult-like" than the minority belief systems they so bitterly oppose.

It should be pointed out that the ABCDEF is founded upon both modern psychological theories about mental health and personal growth, and my many years of participant observation and historical research into minority belief systems. Those who believe that relativism and anarchy are as dangerous to mental health as absolutism and authoritarianism, could (I suppose) count groups with total scores nearing either extreme (high or low) as being equally hazardous. As far as dangers to physical well-being are concerned, however, both historical records and current events clearly indicate the direction in which the greatest threats lie. This is especially so since the low-scoring groups usually seem to have survival and growth rates so small that they seldom develop the abilities to commit large scale atrocities even had they the philosophical or political inclinations to do so.

Isaac Bonewits

THE ADVANCED BONEWITS' CULT DANGER EVALUATION FRAME

FACTORS		1 2 3 4 5 6 7 8 9 10
		Low High
1. Internal Control: Amount of internal political power exercised by leader(s) over members.	**1.**	1 2 3 4 5 6 7 8 9 10
2. Wisdom Claimed by leader(s): Amount of infallibility declared or implied about decisions or doctrinal/scriptural interpretations.	**2.**	1 2 3 4 5 6 7 8 9 10
3. Wisdom Credited to leader(s) by members: Amount of trust in decisions or doctrinal/scriptural interpretations made by leader(s).	**3.**	1 2 3 4 5 6 7 8 9 10
4. Dogma: Rigidity of reality concepts taught; amount of doctrinal inflexibility or "fundamentalism."	**4.**	1 2 3 4 5 6 7 8 9 10
5. Recruiting: Emphasis put on attracting new members; amount of proselytizing.	**5.**	1 2 3 4 5 6 7 8 9 10
6. Front Groups: Numbers of subsidiary groups using different names from that of main group.	**6.**	1 2 3 4 5 6 7 8 9 10

7. **Wealth:** Amount of money and/or property desired or obtained by group; emphasis on members' donations; economic lifestyle of leader(s) compared to ordinary members.

7.   1 2 3 4 5 6 7 8 9 10

8. **Political Power:** Amount of external political influence desired or obtained; emphasis on directing members' secular votes.

8.   1 2 3 4 5 6 7 8 9 10

9. **Sexual Manipulation:** Of members by leader(s); amount of control exercised over sexuality of members; advancement dependent upon sexual favors or specific lifestyle.

9.   1 2 3 4 5 6 7 8 9 10

10. **Censorship:** Amount of control over members' access to outside opinions on group, its doctrines or leader(s).

10. 1 2 3 4 5 6 7 8 9 10

11. **Dropout Control:** Intensity of efforts directed at preventing or returning dropouts.

11. 1 2 3 4 5 6 7 8 9 10

12. **Violence:** Amount of approval when used by or for the group, its doctrines or leader(s).

12. 1 2 3 4 5 6 7 8 9 10

13. **Paranoia:** Amount of fear concerning real or imagined enemies; perceived power of opponents; prevalence of conspiracy theories.

13. 1 2 3 4 5 6 7 8 9 10

14. **Grimness:** Amount of disapproval concerning jokes about the group, its doctrines or its leader(s).

14. 1 2 3 4 5 6 7 8 9 10

15. Surrender Of Will: Amount of emphasis on members not having to be responsible for personal decisions; degree of individual disempowerment created by the group, its doctrines or its leader(s).   **15.**   1 2 3 4 5 6 7 8 9 10

16. Hypocrisy: Amount of approval for other actions (not included above) which the group officially considers immoral or unethical, when done by or for the group, its doctrines or leader(s); willingness to violate group's declared principles for political, psychological, economic, or other gain.   **16.**   1 2 3 4 5 6 7 8 9 10

$\mathcal{A}$PPENDIX II

RESOURCES

THERE ARE MANY PLACES TO FIND INFORMATION ABOUT DIFFERENT ASPECTS of the Wiccan and Pagan religion. When inquiring, always include a self-addressed stamped envelope to keep the costs down for the organizations. Some information resources are online. Make sure you include a reply address if you want a reply. And don't be disappointed if your ten-page rambling request is answered by a form letter, or possibly not at all. You are not the only person inquiring, so keep the inquiries short and to the point.

There are several national groups which offer membership to Wiccans. There may even be a local group near you, or you might want to start a local chapter with a few friends.

COG, acronym for The Covenant of the Goddess, is a national religious tax-exempt organization with branches in many states. They can be contacted at:

> **The Covenant of The Goddess**
> Box 1226
> Berkeley, CA 94701
> www.cog.org

The Northern California Council of COG also runs an excellent website, with links to many useful places with information about Witchcraft: www.conjure.com/COG/cog.html

There are two nationally available magazines with articles and information for Wiccans and other Pagans in general. One is *Circle Magazine*. This is published by Circle Sanctuary, a nonprofit religious organization—one of the oldest in the country. They also publish a contact list with people, groups, organizations, and businesses that cater to Wiccan and Pagan interests. They also do phone counseling and referrals. Their address is:

Circle Sanctuary
P.O. Box 219
Mt. Horeb, WI 53572
www.circlesanctuary.org

The other is *The Green Egg*. This is the newsletter for The Church of All Worlds, a Pagan, but not Wiccan, organization. However, they have good articles and material and there are contacts there as well. Their address is:

Green Egg
32 East San Francisco Ave.
Willits, CA 95490
707-456-0332
www.greenegg.org

The Church of All Worlds can be reached directly on the Internet at www.caw.org

Another NeoPagan organization that you might want to contact online is called CUUPs. The Covenant of Unitarian Universalist Pagans, a subsidiary of the Unitarian Universalist Church, encourages membership by Pagans and Witches and the worship of the Divine in Nature. They can be reached at www.cuups.org

If you are online, there are many places to find out about Wicca and purchase materials and tools, but be cautious about giving out information on the Internet, especially your credit card number. Also, remember that not everything you find online is necessarily accurate or valid for you. Use your instincts. If you do not have access to the Internet at home, most libraries have online resources.

We are not providing a long list of resources because we encourage people to look on their own, and we cannot guarantee these entities will be around forever. Also, because we list them doesn't mean we endorse them unreservedly. Our experiences have generally been positive, but that is no guarantee for you.

Below are two book lists, one nonfiction, one fiction. Being Wiccan means you read lots of books on a wide variety of subjects. We have included books which we particularly like or feel are important. With some we have described what we like about them. This list is by no means exhaustive. We have included books on topics which are not necessarily Wiccan, but which are adaptable to Wiccan life and practice. There are a few books on tarot, Kabbalah, astrology, and other occult topics, as well as some on Ceremonial Magick. We also recommend you check out books on mythology, comparative religions, ethics, and self-exploration.

In the self-exploration category, the Kiersey Temperament Sorter or the Meyers-Briggs tests are excellent. These tests measure your individual operating preferences and are not mental health measures. There are books available as well as many Web sites devoted to the subjects. The Internet might be a better resource for this material.

Some of these books are out of print. They are still obtainable by diligent searching at used bookstores, online, or through specialty stores that have rare or out-of-print books. Our favorite used bookstore (and supposedly the largest in the world) is John K. King. They also deal by mail. Their address is:

John K. King
901 West Lafayette
Detroit, MI 48226
313-961-0622

GENERAL NONFICTION BOOKS

Adler, Margot. *Drawing Down The Moon: Witches, Druids, Goddess-Worshippers, & Other Pagans in America Today*. Beacon Press: Boston, MA, 1979, 1984, 1999.
This is a general overview of the Wiccan and Pagan communities in this country. It has been periodically updated.

Amber K. *Covencraft: Witchcraft for Three or More*. Llewellyn Publications: St. Paul, MN, 1998.
A good guide to working and living in a coven.

_____, *True Magick: A Beginner's Guide*. Llewellyn Publications: St. Paul, MN, 1996.

Banzhaf, Hajo and Anna Haebler. *Key Words for Astrology*. Samuel Weiser: York Beach, ME, 1996.
This is a good reference, which has good interpretations of the planets in the signs, houses, and key phrases for aspects. Easy to use and understand, accessible to beginner and advanced.

Benares, Camden. *Zen Without Zen Masters*. Falcon Press: Phoenix, AZ, 1988.
Introduces you to alternative philosophies without you consciously realizing
it because it is a Zen joke book.

Bonewits, Isaac. *Real Magic: An Introductory Treatise on the Basic Principles of
Yellow Magic* (Revised Edition). Samuel Weiser: York Beach, ME, 1989.
This book was the author's master thesis in magick. It is dense and not an
easy read, but it has good material. Look through it before buying.

Brown, Tom Jr. and Brandt Morgan. *Tom Brown's Field Guide to Living with the
Earth*. Berkley Books: New York, 1989.
This is one of the best books of a great series dealing with basic survival, and
back-to-nature subjects. It is a good example of how "Pagan" a "non-Pagan"
can be.

Buckland, Raymond. *Advanced Candle Magick: More Spells and Rituals for Every
Purpose*. Llewellyn Publications: St. Paul, MN.

_____, *Buckland's Complete Book of Witchcraft*. Llewellyn Publications: St. Paul,
MN, 1986.
This is colloquially known as "Buckland's Big Blue Book," and was the standard text for eclectic Wicca for many years. It is not complete, but provides a
framework and some good information.

Covey, Stevens R. *The 7 Habits of Highly Effective People*. Simon & Schuster:
New York, 1989.
This book illustrates some disciplines and personal habits that are generally
worthwhile to cultivate.

Crowley, Aleister. *777 and Other Qabalistic Writings of Aleister Crowley*. Samuel
Weiser: York Beach, ME, 1977, 1993.
This is an excellent book for magickal correspondences.

Cuhulain, Kerr. *The Law Enforcement Guide to Wicca* (3rd Edition). Horned Owl
Publishing: Victoria, B.C., 1997.

_____, *Wiccan Warrior: Walking A Spiritual Path in a Sometimes Hostile World.*
Llewellyn Publications: St. Paul, MN, 2000.
Kerr Cuhulain is a law enforcement officer who is also Wiccan. His books
are must-haves for dealing with the real world and common sense practice of
Wicca.

Cunningham, Scott. *Living Wicca: A Further Guide for the Solitary Practitioner.*
Llewellyn Publications: St. Paul, MN, 1993.

_____, *Wicca: A Guide for the Solitary Practitioner.* Llewellyn Publications: St.
Paul, MN, 1996.
Cunningham was a prolific writer and these are only two of his many books on
Wicca, Magick, and the occult. His books are basic and simple, but his infor-
mation is solid and usable. For someone starting out, they are good resources.

Curott, Phyllis. *Book of Shadows: A Modern Woman's Journey into the Wisdom of
Witchcraft and the Magic of The Goddess.* Broadway Books: New York, 1998.

Daniels, Estelle. *Astrologickal Magick.* Samuel Weiser: York Beach, ME, 1995.
This book was written to give astrology back to the Craft and magickal practitioners. There is no other like it available yet, and using the techniques and
an almanac you can time your workings by the Moon.

Denning, Melita & Osborne Phillips. *The Llewellyn Practical Guide To: Psychic
Self-Defense and Well Being.* Llewelllyn Publications: St. Paul, MN, 1994.
This is a classic, and a must-have for any Wiccan.

_____, *The Magical Philosophy Series.* Llewellyn Publications: St. Paul, MN,
Vol. I 1974, Vol. II 1974, Vol. III 1975, Vol. IV 1978, Vol. V 1981.
A five-book series that covers most basic ideas of the western Occult system
of magick.

Elgin, Suzette Haden. *The Gentle Art of Verbal Self-Defense.* Barnes & Noble,
Inc.: New York, 1993.

Farrar, Janet and Stewart. *The Witches' Goddess: The Feminine Principle of Divinity*. Phoenix Publishing, Inc.: Custer, WA, 1987. Also *The Witches' God*. These are excellent resources for people choosing a Deity.

———, *The Witches' Way: Principles, Rituals & Beliefs of Modern Witchcraft*. Phoenix Publishing, Inc.: Custer, WA, 1988.
This is possibly the single most complete, current work on "traditional" Alexandrian Wicca.

Fortune, Dion. *Psychic Self-Defense: A Study in Occult Pathology & Criminality*. Aquarian Press: Wellingborough, Northamptonshire, UK, 1965.
This is another excellent book, though perhaps a bit dated. Any of Dion Fortune's other books are also good resources, and she wrote some good fiction as well.

Gardner, Gerald Brosseau. *Witchcraft Today*. Magickal Childe Publishing, Inc.: New York, 1954.
This is difficult to find, but it is the original nonfiction work on modern Wicca, and is historically important.

Gerwick-Brodeur, Madeline & Lisa Lenard. *The Complete Idiot's Guide to Astrology*. Alpha Books: New York, 1997.
Despite the title, it's a good introduction to learning astrology.

Gimbutas, Marija. *The Civilization of the Goddess: The World of Old Europe*. Harper Collins Publishers: San Francisco, CA, 1991.
Gives a more modern view of the ancient Goddess cultures.

Greer, Mary K. *Tarot Constellations*. Newcastle Publishing: North Hollywood, CA, 1987.

———, *Tarot for Your Self*. Newcastle Publishing: North Hollywood, CA, 1984.
These are two good general tarot books which go a bit beyond the "this card means this" basic information. There are many spreads, exercises, and ideas listed, which adds up to a good general overview of tarot. It also has numerological information.

Grimassi, Raven. *The Wiccan Magick: Inner Teachings of the Craft*. Llewellyn
Publications: St. Paul, MN, 1997.

_____, *The Wiccan Mysteries: Ancient Origins & Teachings*. Llewellyn
Publications: St. Paul, MN,1997.
Grimassi has several good books on specific Wicca topics, and Strega-Italian
Wicca in particular.

Harner, Michael. *The Way of the Shaman: A Guide to Power and Healing*. Bantam
Books: New York, 1982.
The most familiar introduction to Shamanistic techniques.

Harrow, Judy. *Wicca Covens: How to Start and Organize Your Own*. Citadel Press:
Secaucus, NJ, 1999.
Another good book on covens.

Hopman, Ellen Evert and Lawrence Bond. *People of the Earth: The New Pagans
Speak Out*. Destiny Books: Rochester, VT, 1996.
This is out of print, but it includes a wide variety of people and gives insight
into how varied being Pagan can be. It is more a book of personalities and
different types of Paganism.

Hutton, Ronald. *The Triumph of the Moon: A History of Modern Pagan Witchcraft*.
Oxford University Press: New York, 1999.
A very good recent attempt at describing the complete history of English
Craft, from its Ceremonialist beginnings through Gardner and others.

Kempton-Smith, Debbi. *Secrets From a Stargazer's Notebook*. Bantam Books: New
York, 1982 (and through 1997 or so).
This is a great book full of useful astrological information, both general and
specific. It has tables to figure out some of your own chart, and is easily read-
able. There is a newer, more expensive edition with updated tables, but you
can still get the little purple paperback used. If you only have one astrology
book, this should be it.

King, Francis and Stephen Skinner. *Techniques of High Magic: A Manual of Self-
Initiation*. Destiny Books: New York, 1976.

This is a standard beginning text on High or Ceremonial Magick. It can be stuffy, but it is quite complete.

King, Serge Kahili, Ph.D. *Urban Shaman: A Handbook for Personal and Planetary Transformation Based on the Hawaiian Way of The Adventurer.* Simon & Schuster: New York, 1990.
A somewhat better introduction to Shamanism as it relates to most city dwellers.

Parfit, Will. *The Elements of the Qabalah.* Barnes & Noble: New York, 1991.
This is a good beginning Kabbalah book. Parfit has written other Kabbalah books, all of which are excellent, but they are British, so may be hard to find.

Quin, Daniel. *Ishmael.* Bantam Books: Bantam Books, 1996 (also *The Story of B* and *My Ishmael*).
Not exactly a trilogy of books, but they deal with the same themes from different perspectives. These books are wonderful for starting to think about the world and your place in it differently. They are nominally fiction but they illustrate alternative philosophies so well that we included them in this section.

RavenWolf, Silver. *To Ride a Silver Broomstick: New Generation Witchcraft.* Llewellyn Publications: St. Paul, MN, 1996.
A good general description of what most contemporary American Wiccans believe and practice, illustrating current trends.

Reed, Ellen Cannon. *The Witches' Qabala*, also published as *The Goddess and the Tree.* Llewellyn Publications: St. Paul, MN.

———, *The Witches' Tarot.* Llewellyn Publications: St. Paul, MN, 1989.
Both these books are classics on Kabbalah and tarot.

Ryall, Rhiannon. *West Country Wicca: A Journal of the Old Religion.* Phoenix Publishing, Inc.: Custer, WA, 1989.
Describes a pre-Gardnerian "Fam-Trad." This work is generally illustrative of the pre-High Magic Craft. There are many similar Fam-Trads, usually in rural areas of the U.S. and U.K.

Slater, Herman. *A Book of Pagan Rituals*. Samuel Weiser: York Beach, ME, 1974.
This was one of the first books of collected modern Wiccan rituals. It is still worth having to generate ideas.

Somé, Malidoma Patrice. *Ritual: Power, Healing, and Community*. Penguin Books: New York, 1993.
This book explains why rituals are important to people.

Starhawk. *The Spiral Dance: A Rebirth of the Ancient Religion of the Great Goddess*. Harper Collins Publishers: New York, 1979, revised and updated 1989 and 1999.
The best description and introduction to Feminist Wicca.

_____, *The Pagan Book of Living and Dying*. Harper: San Francisco, 1997.
An excellent guide to death, dying, and all that surrounds it in a Pagan context.

Stevens, Jose, Ph.D. and Lena S. Stevens. *Secrets of Shamanism: Tapping the Spirit Power Within You*. Avon Books: New York, 1988.
This book illustrates the techniques of Shamanism, which is not necessarily a specific religion, but a way of practicing religion. Good exercises for visualization and other things.

Sui, Choa Kok. *Pranic Healing*. Samuel Weiser, Inc.: York Beach, ME, 1990.
One of the better books that introduces Bio-Energy or Chi.

Summer Rain, Mary and Alex Greystone. *Mary Summer Rain on Dreams*. Hampton Roads Publishing: Charlottesvilla, VA, 1996.
This is Estelle's favorite dream dictionary. It is amazingly complete, not Christian in orientation, and not based upon a lot of the old Victorian interpretations that aren't valid in today's world.

Teish, Luisah. *Jambalaya: The Natural Woman's Book of Personal Charms and Practical Rituals*. Harper: San Francisco, CA, 1985.

Tuitéan, Paul and Estelle Daniels. *Pocket Guide to Wicca*. The Crossing Press: Freedom, CA, 1998.

This is a very basic introduction to the Wiccan religion and practices for both the novice and the people they know. It is one the best single descriptions of what Wicca is and is not. If you want to give the relatives a book explaining what you are into, this is good and inexpensive.

Valiente, Doreen. *The Rebirth of Witchcraft*. Robert Hale: London, 1989.
A description of the history of the "first generation" of modern Wicca. Almost anything by Doreen Valiente is excellent. She is British, so her perspective will be from that culture and country.

Walker, Barbara G. *The Women's Encyclopedia of Myths & Secrets*. Harper & Row: New York, 1983.
An excellent resource on Goddesses and other magickal information.

Weinstein, Marion. *Positive Magic: Occult Self-Help*. Phoenix Publishing, Inc.: Custer, WA, 1980.
Another look at Wiccan magick.

SCIENCE FICTION AND FANTASY BOOKS

The fiction books are chosen for their illustration of magick, paradigm shifts, and all-around good reads. This list is not exhaustive, but are ones we like and recommend to others. Some are strictly fantastic, some depict alternate worlds, some are more realistic. Most are written for adults. There are some children's books. Sometimes some of the best magickal fiction is written for children, like the *Harry Potter* books.

Abbey, Lynn. *The Guardians*.

Alexander, Lloyd. *The Prydain Series*.

Anderson, Poul. *Operation Chaos*.

_____, *Operation Luna*.

Barrett, Frances. *The Magus.* (1801). A classic but still applicable. See if you can spot where the author deliberately misleads the readers, so as not to spill any secrets—a common practice in older occult literature.

Baum, L. Frank. *The Oz Series.*

Blackwood, Algernon. *Best Supernatural Tales.*

Blish, James. *Black Easter.*

_____, *The Devil's Day.*

Bradley, Marion Zimmer. *The Darkover Series* (especially *The Forbidden Tower*).

_____, *The Mists of Avalon.*

Bryant, Dorothy. *The Kin of Ata Are Waiting for You.*

Bull, Emma. *The War of the Oaks.*

Card, Orson Scott. *The Alvin Maker Series.*

Cooper, Susan. *The Dark Is Rising Sequence.*

Craven, Margaret. *I Heard The Owl Call My Name.*

Crowley, Aleister. *Diary of a Drug Fiend.*

_____, *Moonchild.*
Both these books are considered controversial, and contain adult material, but are classics of magickal literature by a master of magick.

Dalkey, Kara. *Eurale.*

De Camp, L. Sprague and Fletcher Pratt. *The Complete Enchanter Series.*

DeLint, Charles. *Moonheart* (and many others).

_____, *The Jackie of Kinrowan Series.*

Duane, Diane. *The Tale of The Five Series.*

_____, *The Wizardry Series.*

Dunsany, Lord. *The King of Elfland's Daughter.*

Eddings, David. *The Belgariad Series* and *The Malorian Series.*

Edgehill. Rosemary. *The Bast Mystery Series.* The main character in these books is Wiccan, and they provide useful insight into Wiccan life in the modern world. The magick is quite genuine and real, with no fantastic exaggeration. They also spotlight the Wiccan Community, warts and all, so be prepared to have a few illusions shattered.

Farrar, Stewart. *Omega.*

Fortune, Dion. *Moon Magick.*

_____, *The Sea Priestess* (and many other titles).

Foster, Alan Dean. *Into The Out Of.*

Fowles, John. *The Magus.*
    This is not the occult classic (see Frances Barrett), but a modern novel. Be careful not to be confused. We neither endorse it nor warn you off.

Furlong, Monica. *The Wise Child Series.*

Gardner, Gerald (sometimes published under his pseudonym Scire). *High Magic's Aid.*
    The fiction book that brought this whole religion to the public's attention.

Garner, Alan. *The Weirdstone of Brisengamen Series.*

Garret, Randal. *The Lord Darcy Series.*

Graves, Robert. *The White Goddess.*
> This is a Craft classic, and has been the basis for several Traditions. Though difficult to read and outdated, it is still a valid resource. Also his books *I Claudius* and *Claudius the God* are excellent historical novels and depict life in a Pagan culture.

_____, *Watch The Northwind Rise.*

Hambly, Barbara. *The Darwath Trilogy.*

Hamilton, Laurell, K. *The Anita Blake Vampire Hunter Series.*

_____, *The Sun-Cross Duology.*

Heinlein, Robert A. *Stranger in a Strange Land.*
> This book is the basis for The Church of All Worlds (CAW), which was founded with the knowledge and blessing of Heinlein.

_____, *Waldo & Magic, Inc.*

Henderson, Zenna. *The Chronicle of the People Series.*

Jackson, Nigel. *The Call of the Horned Piper.*

Jordan, Robert. *The Wheel of Time Series.*

Kay, Guy Gavriel. *The Fionavar Tapestry Trilogy.*

Kaye, Marvin and Parke Godwin. *The Masters of Solitude.*

Kerr, Katherine. *The Deverry Series.*

Kurtz, Katherine. *The Deryni Series.*

_____, *Lammas Night.*
> A book of fiction about a coven which magickally protects Britain during

WWII. Supposedly based upon actual events as experienced by Gerald Gardner and his covenmates.

Kurtz, Katherine and Deborah Turner Harris. *The Adept Series.*
More High Magick than Wicca, they still illustrate the role of psychic abilities and life in the modern world.

Lackey, Mercedes. *The Diana Tregarde Trilogy.*

_____, *The Many Valdemar Series* (especially *Arrows Flight* and several more).

Leiber, Fritz. *Conjure Wife.*

_____, *Our Lady of Darkness.*

Leguin, Ursula K. *The Earthsea Series.*

_____, *The Left Hand of Darkness.*

Leland, Charles Godfrey. *Aradia: Gospel of the Witches.*

Lisle, Holly. *Fire in the Mist* (and several other titles).

MacDonald, George. *Lilith.*

_____, *Phantasies,*

Machen, Arthur. *The Hill of Dreams.*

Mason, David. *Kavin's World.*

_____, *The Return of Kavin.*

McCaffrey, Anne. *The Dragon Singer Series.*

_____, *The Crystal Singer Series.*

McIntyre, Vonda N. *Dreamsnake.*

McKillip, Patricia A. *The Quest of the Riddle-Master of Hed Trilogy.* Ballantine Books.

Merritt, A. *Burn, Witch, Burn!/Creep, Shadow, Creep!*

————, *The Ship of Ishtar* (and several other titles).

Moon, Sheila. *Knee Deep in Thunder.*

————, *Hunt Down the Prize.*

Norton, Andre. *The Witch World Series.*
    This is a classic series which depicts a world which is quite compatible with Wicca. Many of the techniques translate to actual magickal techniques in Circles.

————, *Storm Over Warlock* (and many other titles).

Paxson, Diana L. *Brisingamen* (and many others).

————, *The Odin's Children Trilogy.*

Prachette, Terry. *The Diskworld Series* (especially *Wyrd Sisters*).

Renault, Mary. *The King Must Die.*

Robbins, Tom. *Another Roadside Attraction.*

García y Robertson, Rodrigo. *The Spiral Dance.*

Robinson, Spider. *The Callahan's Series.*

Roessner, Michaela. *Walkabout Woman.*

Rowling, J. K. *The Harry Potter Series.*
   Extremely popular and widely available. These books do not depict Wicca, but are wonderful as they create a magickal world that is coherent, logical, and holds together. They illustrate the time, patience, and study it takes to learn magick, and are ripping good yarns. Fun for the whole family.

Salmon, Jessica Amanda. *The Tomoe Gozen Saga Trilogy.*

Scarborough, Elizabeth Ann. *The Godmother Series.*

Schmidt, Dennis. *The Wayfarer Trilogy.*

Shwartz, Susan M. (ed.) *The Heirs to Byzantium Trilogy.*

_____, *Hecate's Cauldron.*

Sky, Kathleen. *Witchdame.*

Starhawk. *The Fifth Sacred Thing.*

Sutclif, Rosemary. *Sword at Sunset.*

_____, *Warrior Scarlet.*

Tolkien, J. R. R. *The Hobbit.*

_____, *The Lord of the Rings Trilogy.*

Travers, P. L. *Mary Poppins.*
   Classic children's books with a magickal theme.

Vidal, Gore. *Julian.*

Walton, Evangeline. *The Maginogion Series.*

Wilson, Robert Anton & Robert Shea. *The Illuminatus! Trilogy.*

Windling, Terri. *The Wood Wife.*

Wrede, Patricia, *Caught in Crystal.*

_____, *Daughter of Witches* (and many other titles).

Wrightson, Patricia. *The Saga of Wirrun the Hero Trilogy.*

Zelazny, Roger. *The Chronicles of Amber* (first & second series).

_____, *Lord of Light* (and many other titles).

REFERENCE BOOKS FOR EXERCISES AND MEDITATIONS

Chia, Mantak and Maneewan Chia. *Fusion of the Five Elements I.* Healing Tao
Books: Huntington, New York, 1989.
Comes from a series of Chinese alternative medicine/healing books, involv-
ing various meditative Chi and physical acupressure manipulative techniques.

Dong, Y. P. *Still as a Mountain, Powerful as Thunder.* Shambhala Publications,
Inc.: Boston, Massachusetts, 1993.
Contains a regime of meditative and physical exercises used as an additional
supplement to regular Tai Chi practice by some schools.

Echanis, Michael D. *Stick Fighting for Combat.* Ohara Publications, Inc.:
Burbank, California, 1978.
Is one book in a series of hard combat techniques based on the Korean mar-
tial art, Hwarangdo.

Harner, Michael. *The Way of the Shaman.* Harper Collins Publishers: San
Francisco, 1980.
Introduced the concept of Shamanism to modern popular culture.

Houston, Jean. *Manual for the Peacemaker.* The Theosophical Publishing House:
Wheaton, Illinois, 1995.
Uses American Indian concepts and stories to base a regime of guided

meditative exercises that are intended to develop both personal and community conflict resolution skills.

Jwing-Ming, Dr. Yang. *The Root of Chinese Chi Kung*. YMAA Publication Center: Jamaica Plain, Massachusetts, 1989.
One of a series of books that teach both healing and martial arts concepts of Chinese Kung Fu.

King, Serge Kahili. *Kahuna Healing*. The Theosophical Publishing House: Wheaton, Illinois, 1983.
Serge King's books on Hawaiian-style Shamanism, known as Huna, are some of the best at teaching modern Americans about Shaman/Spiritual techniques. This one focuses on healing.

Masters, Robert and Jean Houston. *Mind Games*. Dorset Press: New York, 1972.
One of the original books available to the general public concerning the concepts of improving an individual's personal mental skills and awareness.

Starhawk. *The Spiral Dance*. Harper & Row: San Francisco, CA, 1979.
One of the original, and still one of the best standard texts on Wicca and Goddess Religions. What else can one say?

Witney, Thomas and Vishnu Karmakar. *Advanced Archer, 12 Easy Lessons*. Center Vision, Inc.: Littleton, Colorado, 1992.
Uses "typical" breathing and relaxation, grounding and centering and guided meditation exercises to teach archers to better hit their targets. Integrates some of the Japanese Kyudo ("art of the bow")-style techniques with modern western-style archery.

BIBLIOGRAPHY

Adler, Margot. *Drawing Down the Moon*. Beacon Press: Boston, 1979.

Apuleius, Lucius, translated by Robert Graves. *The Golden Ass*. Penguin Books: Middlesex, UK, 1950.

Bidart, Gay-Darlene. *The Naked Witch*. Pinnacle Books: New York, 1975.

Buckland, Raymond. *The Tree: The Complete Book of Saxon Witchcraft*. Samuel Weiser Inc.: New York, 1974.

Chambers, Howard V. (compiled by). *An Occult Dictionary For the Millions*. Sherbourne Press: Los Angeles, CA, 1966.

Chuhlain, Kerr. *A Law Enforcement Guide to Wicca*/3rd Edition. Horned Owl Publishing: Victoria, B.C., 1997.

Farrar, Janet and Stewart and Gavin Bone. *The Pagan Path*. Phoenix Publishing: Custer, WA, 1995.

Fitch, Ed. *Grimoire of Shadows, Witchcraft, Paganism and Magick*. Llewellyn Publications: St. Paul, MN, 1996.

Gardner, Gerald R. *High Magic's Aid*. Houghton Mifflin Co.: London, 1949.

_____,*Witchcraft Today*. Rider: London, 1954.

Geddes and Grosset. *Guide to The Occult and Mysticism.* Geddes and Grosset, Ltd.: New Lanark, England.

Gibson, Walter B. and Litzka R. *The Complete Illustrated Book of Divination and Prophecy.* Signet: New York, NY, 1973.

Leek, Sybil. *The Complete Art of Witchcraft: Penetrating the Secrets of White Witchcraft.* Harper & Row: New York, 1971.

Leland, Charles G. *Aradia: Or the Gospel of the Witches.* (originally published in 1899) Phoenix Publishing, Inc.: Custer, WA, 1990.

Simms, Maria Kay, *Circle of the Cosmic Muse, A Wiccan Book of Shadows.* Llewellyn Publications: St. Paul, MN, 1994.

Webster's Seventh New Collegiate Dictionary. G.C. Merriam Company: Springfield, MA, 1965.

Wedek, Harry E. *Dictionary of Magic.* Philosophical Library: New York, NY, 1956.

Winter, Mick. *How to Talk New Age.* 1996 (and earlier).

Zell, Otter and Morning Glory. *Witchcraft, Paganism and the Occult: A Basic Glossary of Common Terms and Symbols.* Green Egg Magazine: Ukiah, CA, 1988.

Zolar. *The Encyclopedia of Ancient and Forbidden Knowledge.* Popular Library: New York, NY, 1970.

INDEX

BOOKS BY THE CROSSING PRESS

Advanced Celtic Shamanism

by D.J. Conway

D.J. Conway uses the four paths of shamanism (healer, bard, warrior, and mystic) to translate Celtic spirituality into a usable form for today's seekers. Unlike beginners' guides now on the market, this book is an advanced study of the practice and expands on the author's previous books about Celtic spirituality.

Paper • ISBN 1-58091-073-4

All Women Are Healers: A Comprehensive Guide to Natural Healing

by Diane Stein

Stein's bestselling book on natural healing for women teaches women to take control of their bodies and lives and offers a wealth of information on various healing methods including Reiki, Reflexology, Polarity Balancing, and Homeopathy.

Paper • ISBN 0-89594-409-X

All Women Are Psychics

by Diane Stein

Women's intuition is no myth; women really are psychic. But your inborn psychic sense was probably suppressed when you were very young. This inspiring book will help you rediscover and reclaim your dormant psychic aptitude.

Paper • ISBN 0-89594-979-2

Apprentice to Power: A Wiccan Odyssey to Spiritual Awakening

by Timothy Roderick

Sharing enchanting tales, meditations, rituals, and magical techniques, neopagan Timothy Roderick weaves a colorful introduction to Wicca, Old Europe's earth-centered mystical tradition. Demonstrating how to build a relationship with the divine in all things and access the power of spirit in everyday life, *Apprentice to Power* offers an accessible path toward greater fulfillment, profound change, and mystical insight.

Paper • ISBN 1-58091-077-7

Ariadne's Thread: A Workbook of Goddess Magic

by Shekhinah Mountainwater

One of the finest books on women's spirituality available.—Sagewoman
Shekhinah Mountainwater's organized and well-written book encourages women to find their own spiritual path. This is a very good, practical book...recommended. —Library Journal

Paper • ISBN 0-89594-475-8

Casting the Circle: A Women's Book of Ritual

by Diane Stein

A comprehensive guide including 23 full ritual outlines for the waxing, full and waning moons, the eight Sabbats, and rites of passage.

Paper • ISBN 0-89594-411-1

BOOKS BY THE CROSSING PRESS

A Complete Guide to Magic and Ritual:
Using the Energy of Nature to Heal Your Life

by Cassandra Eason

Cassandra Eason, a world-renowned psychic, explains how magic can change your life, from attracting love and improving family relationships to encouraging good health and prosperity. Learn how to tap in to the magic of plants, flowers, and essential oils and harness the energy of the sun, moon, and seasons to reverse bad luck, rekindle hope and passion, and trust instinct and inspiration—the most important magic of all.

Paper • ISBN 1-58091-101-3

Diane Stein's Guide to Goddess Craft

by Diane Stein

Originally published as *The Women's Spirituality Book*, this guide describes the beliefs and practices of the goddess craft as it relates to the daily lives of women. Designed to be useful to both men and women, it emphasizes achieving power and control through healing, visualization, Tarot, and the women's I Ching.

Paper • ISBN 1-58091-091-2

Fundamentals of Jewish Mysticism and Kabbalah

by Ron Feldman

This concise introductory book explains what Kabbalah is and how study of its text and practices enhance the life of the soul and the holiness of the body.

Paper • ISBN 1-58091-049-1

A Little Book of Altar Magic

by D.J. Conway

This third addition to the successful "A Little Book" series shows us how we, sometimes unknowingly, create altars in our daily surroundings. D.J. Conway offers information on the power and use of colors, and the historic and symbolic meaning of the elements, animals, and objects to help us create magical altars in our personal surroundings.

Paper • ISBN 1-58091-052-1

Pocket Guide to Celtic Spirituality

by Sirona Knight

The Earth-centered philosophy and rituals of ancient Celtic spirituality have special relevance today as we strive to balance our relationship with the planet. This guide offers a comprehensive introduction to the rich religious tradition of the Celts.

Paper • ISBN 0-89594-907-5

BOOKS BY THE CROSSING PRESS

Shaman in a 9 to 5 World

by Patricia Telesco

A complete guide to maintaining a powerful connection with nature, even when sacred groves and wild rivers are far away. Patricia Telesco adapts an array of ancient shamanic traditions to city life, including fasting, drumming, praying, creating sacred spaces, interpreting omens, and divination.

Paper • ISBN 0-89594-982-2

Shamanism as a Spiritual Practice for Daily Life

by Tom Cowan

This inspirational book blends elements of shamanism with inherited traditions and contemporary religious commitments. An inspiring spiritual call. —Booklist

Paper • ISBN 0-89594-838-9

Spinning Spells, Weaving Wonders: Modern Magic for Everyday Life

by Patricia Telesco

This essential book of over 300 spells tells how to work with simple, easy-to-find components and focus creative energy to meet daily challenges with awareness, confidence, and humor.

Paper • ISBN 0-89594-803-6

Wicca: The Complete Craft

by D.J. Conway

What is Wicca? D.J. Conway is the voice of reason who states clearly what the religion of Wicca is as well as what it is not. Whether already in the craft or just beginning, this book is the definitive resource for all those gentle souls looking for a guide to Wicca.

Paper • ISBN 1-58091-092-0

The Wiccan Path: A Guide for the Solitary Practitioner

by Rae Beth

This is a guide to the ancient path of the village wisewoman. Writing in the form of letters to two apprentices, Rae Beth provides rituals for the key festivals of the wiccan calendar. She also describes the therapeutic powers of trancework and herbalism, and outlines the Pagan approach to finding a partner.

Paper • ISBN 0-89594-744-7

A Wisewoman's Guide to Spells, Rituals and Goddess Lore

by Elizabeth Brooke

A remarkable compendium of magical lore, psychic skills, and women's mysteries.

Paper • ISBN 0-89594-779-X

Visit our website at **www.crossingpress.com**